Victorian Literature

Victorian Literature: Criticism and Debates offers a comprehensive and critically engaging introduction to the study of Victorian literature and addresses the most popular and vibrant topics in the field today.

Separated into twelve sections, this anthology investigates issues as diverse as sensation fiction, religion and literature, colonialism, psychology, economics, and print culture. Each section contains at least three classic essays from leading scholars offering a variety of theoretical and historical approaches from the liveliest areas of current criticism and debate in the field. Each section concludes with a newly written essay from a subject expert that reflects on this work and looks forward to new directions. A sign-posted introduction to the key critical contributions in Victorian studies from the past twenty-five years sets the reader on their path.

Providing both the essential criticism along with clear introductions and analysis, this book is the perfect guide for students and scholars of Victorian literature.

Lee Behlman is Assistant Professor of English at Montclair State University, USA.

Anne Longmuir is Associate Professor of English at Kansas State University, USA.

Routledge Criticism and Debates in Literature

The *Routledge Criticism and Debates in Literature* series offers new perspectives on traditional and core subjects from Medieval Literature to Postmodernism. Exploring different approaches and critical directions, essays range from 'classic' and newer criticism to brand new papers. Sections give an essential overview of key topics and inspire lively debate, enhancing subjects through modern takes, angles or arguments against classic debates.

Ideal for students approaching a topic for the first time, the volumes are also useful for those looking for important critical background. Each contains section introductions that usefully situate the topic within wider debates, and glossaries of key terms, people and places. Challenging and provocative, the *Routledge Criticism and Debates in Literature* series shows how subjects and their criticism have travelled into the twenty-first century in an intelligent and accessible way.

Available in this series:

Medieval Literature
Holly Crocker and D. Vance Smith

British Romanticism
Mark Canuel

Victorian Literature
Lee Behlman and Anne Longmuir

Nineteenth Century Poetry
Jonathan Herapath and Emma Mason

Victorian Literature

Criticism and Debates

**Edited by Lee Behlman and
Anne Longmuir**

Routledge
Taylor & Francis Group

LONDON AND NEW YORK

First published 2016
by Routledge
2 Park Square, Milton Park, Abingdon, Oxon OX14 4RN

and by Routledge
711 Third Avenue, New York, NY 10017

Routledge is an imprint of the Taylor & Francis Group, an informa business

British Library Cataloguing-in-Publication Data
A catalogue record for this book is available from the British Library

Library of Congress Cataloging-in-Publication Data
Victorian literature : criticism and debates / [edited by] Lee Behlman and Anne Longmuir.
pages cm. — (The Routledge criticism and debates in literature)
Includes bibliographical references and index.
1. English literature—19th century—History and criticism. 2. Literature and society—Great Britain—History—19th century. I. Behlman, Lee, editor. II. Longmuir, Anne, editor.
PR463.V536 2015
820.9′008—dc23
2015009248

ISBN: 978-0-415-83097-3 (hbk)
ISBN: 978-0-415-83098-0 (pbk)

Typeset in Times New Roman
by Swales & Willis Ltd, Exeter, Devon, UK

MIX
Paper from
responsible sources
FSC® C013604

Printed and bound by CPI Group (UK) Ltd, Croydon, CR0 4YY

Contents

Figures

Contributors

Amanda Anderson is Caroline Donovan Professor of English Literature at Johns Hopkins University. She is the author of *Tainted Souls and Painted Faces: The Rhetoric of Fallenness in Victorian Culture* (1993), *The Powers of Distance: Cosmopolitanism and the Cultivation of Detachment* (2001), and *The Way We Argue Now: A Study in the Cultures of Theory* (2006).

Isobel Armstrong is a fellow of the British Academy, Emeritus Professor of English (Geoffrey Tillotson Chair) at Birkbeck, University of London, and Hon Foreign Scholar of the American Academy of Arts and Sciences. She has published widely on nineteenth-century literature and culture and feminist thought. She has lectured and taught in many contexts, including Harvard and Johns Hopkins University. Among her works are a critical history of Victorian poetry (1993), currently being revised for a new edition, a co-edited anthology of nineteenth-century women's poetry (1996), and *The Radical Aesthetic* (2000). Her most recent book, *Victorian Glassworlds: Glass Culture and the Imagination 1830–1880*, won the Modern Language Association's James Russell Lowell Prize in 2008. She is working on several projects, including a book on the nineteenth-century novel and the democratic imagination, and a reading diary of a group of Victorian poems. Poems by her appeared in Shearsman's anthology of poetry by women, edited by Carrie Etter, *Infinite Difference: Other Poetries by UK Women Poets* (2010).

Nancy Armstrong is Gilbert, Louis, and Edward Lehrman Professor of English at Duke University and editor of the journal *Novel: A Forum on Fiction*. Her books include *Desire and Domestic Fiction: A Political History of the Novel* (Oxford University Press, 1986), *The Imaginary Puritan: Literature, Intellectual Labor, and the Origins of Personal Life* (University of California Press, 1992) (with Leonard Tennenhouse), *Fiction in the Age of Photography: The Legacy of British Realism* (1999), and *How Novels Think: The Limits of Individualism, 1719–1900* (2005). She is currently finishing another book co-authored with Tennenhouse, *The Conversion Effect: Early American Aspects of the Novel* (University of Pennsylvania Press, forthcoming 2016).

Gillian Beer is King Edward VII Professor Emeritus at the University of Cambridge and former President of Clare Hall College. Among her books are *Darwin's Plots* (1983; 2000), *Open Fields: Science in Cultural Encounter* (1996), and *Virginia Woolf: The Common Ground* (1996).

Lee Behlman is Assistant Professor of English at Montclair State University. He has published essays on Augusta Webster, Alice Meynell, Walter Pater, and Matthew Arnold, and on the subjects of Victorian motherhood and nineteenth-century classicism.

Laurel Brake is Professor Emerita at Birkbeck, University of London. Her recent work includes *Nineteenth-Century Serials Edition* (ncse), a digital edition of seven nineteenth-century periodicals (www.ncse.ac.uk); *DNCF: Dictionary of Nineteenth-Century Journalism* (2009), and *W. T. Stead: Newspaper Revolutionary* (2012), both co-edited. She is currently co-editing a book on the *News of the World*, writing *Ink Work* (a biography of Walter and Clara Pater), and editing Pater's journalism for his *Collected Works*.

Patrick Brantlinger is James Rudy Professor of English (Emeritus) at Indiana University and a former editor of *Victorian Studies*. His most recent book is *States of Emergency: Essays on Culture and Politics* (2013).

Deborah Cohen is the Peter B. Ritzma Professor of the Humanities and Professor of History at Northwestern University. She is the author of three books: *Family Secrets* (2013), *Household Gods: The British and their Possessions* (2006), and *The War Come Home: Disabled Veterans in Britain and Germany* (2001).

Ann Cvetkovich is Ellen Clayton Garwood Centennial Professor of English and Professor of Women's and Gender Studies at the University of Texas at Austin. She is the author of *Mixed Feelings: Feminism, Mass Culture, and Victorian Sensationalism* (Rutgers, 1992), *An Archive of Feelings: Trauma, Sexuality, and Lesbian Public Cultures* (Duke, 2003), and *Depression: A Public Feeling* (Duke, 2012). For additional information, see www.anncvetkovich.com.

Michael Davis is Lecturer in English at The University of the West of England, Bristol, UK. He is author of *George Eliot and Nineteenth-Century Psychology: Exploring the Unmapped Country* (2006) and has published essays on Stevenson, Hardy, and Wilde.

Gowan Dawson is Professor of Victorian Literature and Culture at the University of Leicester, UK. His recent books include *Show Me the Bone: Reconstructing Prehistoric Monsters in Nineteenth-Century Britain and America* (University of Chicago Press, 2016), *Victorian Scientific Naturalism: Community, Identity, Continuity* (University of Chicago Press, 2014), and *Victorian Science and Literature*, 8 vols. (Pickering and Chatto, 2011–12).

Catherine Gallagher is the Eggers Professor of English Literature, Emeritus, at the University of California at Berkeley. Her books include *The Industrial Reformation of English Fiction: 1832–67* (1985), *Nobody's Story: The Vanishing Acts of Women Writers in the Literary Marketplace* (1994), and *The Body Economic: Life, Death, and Sensation in Political Economy and the Victorian Novel* (2006). She is currently writing a history of counterfactual history.

Pamela K. Gilbert is the Albert Brick Professor of English at the University of Florida. She has published widely in the areas of Victorian literature, gender, and the history of medicine. She is currently working on a book on Victorian skin.

Lauren M. E. Goodlad is Kathryn Paul Professor Scholar, Provost Fellow, and Professor of English at the University of Illinois, Urbana, where she directed the Unit for Criticism & Interpretive Theory from 2008 to 2014. Her publications include *Victorian Literature and the Victorian State: Character and Governance in a Liberal Society* (2003), *The Victorian Geopolitical Aesthetic: Realism, Sovereignty, and Transnational Experience* (2015), and the *The Ends of History* (2013), a co-edited special issue of *Victorian Studies*.

Jennifer Green-Lewis teaches courses in Victorian and Modernist literature and visual culture at the George Washington University in Washington, DC, and at the Bread Loaf School of English in Middlebury, Vermont. She has published extensively in the field of photo-literary studies.

Melissa Valiska Gregory is an associate professor of English at the University of Toledo. She has published articles on both Victorian poetry and the novel and is working on a book that explores how nineteenth-century women writers use the subject of motherhood as an occasion for generic experimentation.

Elaine Hadley is Professor of English at the University of Chicago. Her publications include *Living Liberalism: Practical Citizenship in Victorian Britain* (2011) and *Melodramatic Tactics: Theatricalized Dissent in the English Marketplace, 1800–1885* (1995).

Catherine Hall is Professor of Modern British Social and Cultural History at University College London. Her work has focused on the relation between Britain and its empire. *Civilising Subjects: Metropole and Colony in the English Imagination* was published in 2002 and *Macaulay and Son: Architects of Imperial Britain* in 2012. Her most recent work is the collectively authored *Legacies of British Slave-Ownership: Colonial Slavery and the Formation of Victorian Britain* (2014).

Linda K. Hughes, Addie Levy Professor of Literature at TCU in Fort Worth, Texas, is author of *The Cambridge Introduction to Victorian Poetry* (2010) and co-editor with Sharon M. Harris of *A Feminist Reader: Feminist Thought from Sappho to Satrapi* (Cambridge University Press, 2013).

Kelly Hurley is Associate Professor of English at the University of Colorado, Boulder, where she teaches Victorian studies, popular genres, and literary theory. She is the author of *The Gothic Body: Sexuality, Materialism, and Degeneration at the Fin de Siécle* (1996) and is currently completing a monograph on contemporary horror film and literature.

Anna Maria Jones is Associate Professor of English at the University of Central Florida. Her recent articles appear in *Neo-Victorian Studies, Criticism, Victorian Literature and Culture*, and *European Romantic Review*. She is also co-editor of an essay collection on Victorian and neo-Victorian graphic texts (Ohio University, forthcoming).

Mark Knight is Associate Professor in the Department of English at the University of Toronto. His publications include *Chesterton and Evil* (2004), *Nineteenth-Century Religion and Literature: An Introduction* (with Emma Mason, 2006), and *An Introduction to Religion and Literature* (2009).

John Kucich is Professor of English at Rutgers University. He is the author of *Excess and Restraint in the Novels of Charles Dickens* (1981), *Repression in Victorian Fiction* (1987), *The Power of Lies: Transgression in Victorian Fiction* (1984), and *Imperial Masochism: British Fiction, Fantasy, and Social Class* (2007), as well as numerous essays on Victorian literature and culture.

Charles LaPorte is an associate professor of English at the University of Washington in Seattle. His 2011 book *Victorian Poets and the Changing Bible* (University of Virginia Press) was awarded the Sonya Rudikoff Prize for a best first book in Victorian studies.

George Levine is Professor Emeritus of English at Rutgers University. Among his many publications on nineteenth-century literature and culture are *The Realistic Imagination* (1981), *Darwin and the Novelists* (1988), and *The Cambridge Companion to George Eliot* (ed.) (2001).

Anne Longmuir is Associate Professor of English at Kansas State University. Specializing in Victorian Literature and contemporary American fiction, she has published articles and book chapters on Charlotte Brontë, Wilkie Collins, Don DeLillo, and Elizabeth Gaskell.

Tricia Lootens is Josiah Meigs Distinguished Teaching Professor at the University of Georgia. Author of *Lost Saints: Silence, Gender, and Victorian Literary Canonization* (Virginia, 1996), she is also co-editor, with Paula M. Krebs, of the Longman Cultural Edition of Rudyard Kipling's *Kim* (2011).

Daniel S. Malachuk is Associate Professor of English at Western Illinois University. He is the author of *Perfection, the State, and Victorian Liberalism* (Palgrave Macmillan, 2005) and co-editor (with Alan M. Levine) of *A Political Companion to Ralph Waldo Emerson* (Kentucky, 2011).

Sharon Marcus is the author of *Apartment Stories: City and Home in Nineteenth-Century Paris and London* (1999) and *Between Women: Friendship, Desire and Marriage in Victorian England* (2007). With Stephen Best, she co-edited a special issue of *Representations* in 2009 and guest edited a special issue of *Public Culture* on "Celebrities and Publics in the Internet Era" in 2015. She is currently completing a book on theatrical celebrity in the nineteenth century.

Emma Mason is Professor of English and Comparative Literary Studies at the University of Warwick. Publications include *Reading the Abrahamic Faiths: Re-thinking Religion and Literature* (Bloomsbury, 2014), *Elizabeth Jennings: The Collected Poems* (Carcanet, 2012), and *The Cambridge Introduction to Wordsworth* (Cambridge University Press, 2010).

Jill Matus is a professor of English and Vice Provost, Students at the University of Toronto. Her research focuses on Victorian fiction and its relationship to theories of body and mind in psychological and medical writing of the period. She has published widely on George Eliot, Gaskell, Dickens, and the Brontës. In 2010 she was elected a member of the Royal Society of Canada.

William R. McKelvy, Associate Professor of English at Washington University in St. Louis, is the author of *The English Cult of Literature: Devoted Readers 1774–1880* (2007). More recent publications include "New Histories of English Literature and the Rise of the Novel, 1835–1859" in *The Oxford Handbook of the Victorian Novel* (2013) and "Children of the Sixties: Post-Secular Victorian Studies and Victorian Secularization Theory" in *Nineteenth-Century Prose* (2012).

Richard Menke, Associate Professor of English at the University of Georgia, is the author of *Telegraphic Realism: Victorian Fiction and Other Information Systems* (2007). His essays on literature, science, and media history have appeared in journals such as *Modern Fiction Studies*, *ELH*, *PMLA*, *Critical Inquiry*, and *Victorian Studies*.

Daniel Novak is Associate Professor of English at Louisiana State University. He is the author of *Realism, Photography, and Nineteenth-Century Fiction* (Cambridge University Press, 2008), and co-editor with James Catano of *Masculinity Lessons: Rethinking Men's and Women's Studies* (Johns Hopkins University Press, 2011).

Jeff Nunokawa is Professor of English at Princeton University. His published works include *Tame Passions of Wilde: Styles of Manageable Desire* (2007), "Eros and Isolation: The Anti-Social George Eliot," and "Speechless in Austen." He is the author of *Note Book* (May 2015), a miscellany of brief literary essays he writes every day on Facebook.

Muireann O'Cinneide is a lecturer in English at the National University of Ireland, Galway. She has published *Aristocratic Women and the Literary Nation, 1832–1867* (Palgrave Macmillan, 2008), and has edited two volumes in the Pickering & Chatto *Collected Works of Margaret Oliphant*. She is working on nineteenth-century travel writing and imperial conflict narratives.

Linda H. Peterson was Niel Gray Professor of English, Jr., at Yale University. A notable authority on life-writing and women's writing in particular, Peterson's books include *Victorian Autobiography* (1986), *Traditions of Victorian Women's Autobiography* (1999), and *Becoming a Woman of Letters: Myths of Authorship and Facts of the Victorian Market* (2009). Peterson died shortly before this volume's publication in 2015.

Jennifer Phegley is Professor of English at the University of Missouri-Kansas City, where she teaches nineteenth-century literature. She has written numerous books and articles, including *Educating the Proper Woman Reader: Victorian Family Literary Magazines and the Cultural Health of the Nation* (2004) and *Courtship and Marriage in Victorian England* (2011). She is currently working on a book about the development of Victorian niche-market periodicals.

Mary Poovey is the Samuel Rudin University Professor of Humanities and Professor of English at New York University. She also holds an honorary doctorate in economic history from Uppsala University in Sweden. She is the author of five monographs on eighteenth- and nineteenth-century British culture and has just completed a co-authored history of financial modeling in the United States.

Leah Price is Francis Lee Higginson Professor of English at Harvard University. Her books include *How to Do Things with Books in Victorian Britain* (2012) and *The Anthology and the Rise of the Novel* (2000); she also edited *Unpacking my Library: Writers and their Books* (2011). She writes on new and old media for the *New York Times Book Review*, *London Review of Books*, *Times Literary Supplement*, *San Francisco Chronicle*, and *Boston Globe*.

Jill Rappoport is Associate Professor of English at the University of Kentucky, author of *Giving Women: Alliance and Exchange in Victorian Culture* (Oxford University Press, 2012), and co-editor of *Economic Women: Essays on Desire and Dispossession in Nineteenth-Century British Culture* (The Ohio State University Press, 2013).

Matthew Rubery is a Reader in the English Department at Queen Mary University of London. He is the author of *The Novelty of Newspapers: Victorian Fiction after the Invention of the News* (Oxford University Press, 2009), editor of *Audiobooks, Literature, and Sound Studies* (Routledge, 2011), and co-editor of *Secret Commissions: An Anthology of Victorian Investigative Journalism* (Broadview, 2012).

Jason R. Rudy is an associate professor of English at the University of Maryland, College Park. Author of *Electric Meters: Victorian Physiological Poetics* (2009), he is currently finishing a monograph on poetry written in the context of nineteenth-century British colonialism.

Rick Rylance is Chief Executive of the Arts and Humanities Research Council (AHRC) in the UK and Executive Chair of Research Councils UK (RCUK). He is Honorary Professor of English at the University of Exeter. His latest book is *Literature and the Public Good* (Oxford University Press, forthcoming).

Edward Said was University Professor of English and Comparative Literature at Columbia University and the author of more than twenty books, including *Orientalism* (1978) and *Culture and Imperialism* (1993). A leading literary critic, public intellectual, and passionate advocate for the Palestinian cause, he was born in Jerusalem in 1935 and died in New York in 2003.

Hilary M. Schor is Professor of English at the University of Southern California. She is the author of *Scheherezade in the Marketplace: Elizabeth Gaskell and the Victorian Novel* (1992), *Dickens and the Daughter of the House* (1999), and *Curious Subjects: Women and Trials of Realism* (2013), as well as articles on Victorian literature and culture.

Jan-Melissa Schramm is a lecturer in nineteenth-century literature at the University of Cambridge, and a Fellow of Trinity Hall. She is the author of two monographs, *Testimony and Advocacy in Victorian Law, Literature, and Theology* (2000) and *Atonement and Self-Sacrifice in Nineteenth-Century Narrative* (2012), and is also the co-editor of *Fictions of Knowledge: Fact, Evidence, Doubt* (2011).

James Secord is Professor of History and Philosophy of Science at the University of Cambridge, Director of the Darwin Correspondence Project, and a Fellow of Christ's College, Cambridge. His most recent book is *Visions of Science: Books and Readers at the Dawn of the Victorian Age* (2014).

Sally Shuttleworth is Professor of English Literature at the University of Oxford. She has published widely on the interrelations of literature and science in the nineteenth century, most recently *The Mind of the Child: Child Development in Literature, Science and Medicine, 1840–1900* (Oxford University Press, 2010).

Jonathan Smith is William E. Stirton Professor of English at the University of Michigan-Dearborn. He is the author of *Charles Darwin and Victorian Visual Culture* (2006) and *Fact and Feeling: Baconian Science and the Nineteenth-Century Literary Imagination* (1999), and the co-editor, with Piers Hale, of *Negotiating Boundaries* (2011), Volume 1 of *Victorian Science and Literature*.

Herbert F. Tucker teaches at the University of Virginia, where he serves as Victorian series editor for the University Press and associate editor for *New Literary History*. He is most recently author of *Epic* (pbk 2013) and editor of *A New Companion to Victorian Literature and Culture* (2014).

Acknowledgements

We're grateful to a number of individuals and institutions for providing invaluable assistance during the creation of this volume. Our contributors' critical acumen, diligence, and collegiality made our work on this project a pleasure, while our editors at Routledge—Emma Joyes, Polly Dodson, Elizabeth Levine, and Ruth Hilsdon—have been unfailing in their patience, support, and advice. The anonymous reviewers at Routledge provided excellent advice that helped us shape this book at a key point in its development, while Kansas State University and Montclair State University provided much-needed and much-appreciated sabbatical leave.

Thanks to Getty's Open Content program for allowing us to reproduce the "The Open Door" (1844) by William Henry Fox Talbot and to Royal Holloway College, University of London for allowing us to reproduce "The Railway Station" (1862) by William Powell Frith.

From A. L.

I'd like to thank Lee Behlman for inviting me to become part of this project: I've benefitted throughout from his extraordinary breadth of reading and razor-sharp editing. Thanks also to Philip Nel, Erica Hateley, and Naomi Wood for sharing their expertise with me at crucial points in the development of this project. My work on this volume is dedicated to my parents for their unflagging support over the years; to my son James for the joy and happiness he brings me (most days); and to Phillip, who continues to be a model of untiring patience and wry good humour. Thank you.

From L. B.

Anne Longmuir made this book happen. I'm grateful for her superb editorial stewardship, her kindness, and the gift of her friendship. My thanks also to Emily Harrington, Meilee Bridges, Heather Varnadore, Jonathan Greenberg, and Jessica Restaino for their comments, advice, and support along the way. Thanks, too, to my research assistant, Kyle Kovacs, for his fine work on this volume, and to Montclair State University for providing the assistantship. My daughter, Elinor, was a joyful, entertaining distraction whenever she popped her head into our editorial Skype sessions (which was often). My wife, Carolyn, never lost faith and has every bit of my love and admiration. My work on this volume is dedicated in loving memory to my sweet mother, Diane Simon Behlman.

Permissions

Part I: Victorian poetry and form

1 Armstrong, Isobel. (1993) *Victorian Poetry: Poetry, Poetics, and Politics*, London and New York: Routledge.
2 Tucker, Herbert F. (1999) "The Fix of Form: An Open Letter," *Victorian Literature and Culture* 27(2), pp. 531–35.
3 Rudy, Jason R. (2009) *Electric Meters: Victorian Physiological Poetics*, Athens, OH: Ohio University Press. This material is used by permission of Ohio University Press, www.ohioswallow.com.

Part II: Women poets and the poetess tradition

5 Lootens, Tricia. (1996) *Lost Saints: Silence, Gender, and Victorian Literary Canonization*, Charlottesville and London: University Press of Virginia © 1996 by the Rector and Visitors of the University of Virginia. Reprinted with permission of the University of Virginia Press.
6 Peterson, Linda H. (1999) "Rewriting *A History of the Lyre*: Letitia Landon, Elizabeth Barrett Browning and the (Re)Construction of the Nineteenth-Century Woman Poet," from Isobel Armstrong and Laurel Brake, eds., *Women's Poetry, Late Romantic to Late Victorian: Gender and Genre, 1830–1900*, New York: St. Martin's Press: 115–32.
7 LaPorte, Charles. (2006) "Atheist Prophecy: Mathilde Blinde, Constance Naden, and the Victorian Poetess," from *Victorian Literature and Culture* 34(2), pp. 427–41.

Part III: Realism and photography

9 Armstrong, Nancy. (1999) *Fiction in the Age of Photography: The Legacy of British Realism*, Cambridge, MA: Harvard University Press.
10 Menke, Richard. (2008) *Telegraphic Realism: Victorian Fiction and Other Information Systems*, Stanford: Stanford University Press. All rights reserved. Used with the permission of Stanford University Press, www.sup.org.
11 Novak, Daniel A. (2008) *Realism, Photography, and Nineteenth-Century Fiction*, Cambridge: Cambridge University Press.

Part IV: Genre fiction and the sensational

13 Cvetkovich, Ann. (1992) *Mixed Feelings: Feminism, Mass Culture, and Victorian Sensationalism*, New Brunswick, NJ: Rutgers University Press.
14 Hurley, Kelly. (1996) *The Gothic Body: Sexuality, Materialism, and Degeneration at the Fin de Siècle*, Cambridge: Cambridge University Press.
15 Jones, Anna Maria. (2007) *Problem Novels: Victorian Fiction Theorizes the Sensational Self*, Columbus, OH: The Ohio University Press. This material is used by permission of Ohio University Press, www.ohioswallow.com.

Part V: Religion and literature

17 Mason, Emma. (2002) "Christina Rossetti and the Doctrine of Reserve," *Journal of Victorian Culture* 7(2), pp. 196–219.

18   McKelvy, William R. (2006) *The English Cult of Literature: Devoted Readers, 1774–1880*, Charlottesville, VA: University Press of Virginia. © 2006 by the Rector and Visitors of the University of Virginia. Reprinted with permission of the University of Virginia Press.

19   Schramm, Jan-Melissa. (2012) *Atonement and Self-Sacrifice in Nineteenth-Century Narrative*, Cambridge: Cambridge University Press.

Part VI: Darwin and victorian culture

21   Beer, Gillian. (2000) *Darwin's Plots*, 2nd edn, Cambridge: Cambridge University Press.

22   Levine, George. (1988 rpt. 1991) *Darwin and the Novelists*, Chicago: University of Chicago Press.

23   Secord, James. (2003) *Victorian Sensation: The Extraordinary Publication, Reception, and Secret Authorship of "Vestiges of the Natural History of Creation"*, Chicago: University of Chicago Press.

24   Dawson, Gowan. (2007) *Darwin, Literature and Victorian Respectability*, Cambridge: Cambridge University Press.

Part VII: Psychology and literature

26   Shuttleworth, Sally. (1996) *Charlotte Brontë and Victorian Psychology*, Cambridge: Cambridge University Press.

27   Rylance, Rick. (2000) *Victorian Psychology and British Culture, 1850–1880*, Oxford: Oxford University Press. By permission of Oxford University Press.

28   Matus, Jill L. (2009) *Shock, Memory, and the Unconscious in Victorian Fiction*, Cambridge: Cambridge University Press.

Part VIII: Gender, sexuality, domesticity

30   Marcus, Sharon. *Between Women: Friendship, Desire, and Marriage in Victorian England*. © 2007 Princeton University Press. Reprinted by permission of Princeton University Press.

31   Schor, Hilary M. (2013) *Curious Subjects: Women and the Trials of Realism*, Oxford: Oxford University Press. By permission of Oxford University Press, USA.

32   Cohen, Deborah. (2013) *Family Secrets: Shame and Privacy in Modern Britain*, Oxford: Oxford University Press. By permission of Oxford University Press, USA.

Part IX: Disinterestedness and liberalism

34   Anderson, Amanda. *The Powers of Distance: Cosmopolitanism and the Cultivation of Detachment*. © 2001 Princeton University Press. Reprinted by permission of Princeton University Press.

35   Goodlad, Lauren M. E. (2003) *Victorian Literature and the Victorian State: Character and Governance in a Liberal Society*, Baltimore, MD: Johns Hopkins University Press.

36   Hadley, Elaine. (2010) *Living Liberalism: Practicing Citizenship in Mid-Victorian Britain*, Chicago: University of Chicago Press.

Part X: Imperialism and literature in the age of colonialism

38   Said, Edward. (1987) "Introduction," *Kim*, London: Penguin Classics; reprinted in Kipling, Rudyard. (2011) *Kim*, London: Penguin Classics, 291–331. Reproduced by permission of Penguin Books Ltd.

39   Brantlinger, Patrick. (1988) *Rule of Darkness: British Literature and Imperialism, 1830–1914*, Ithaca, NY: Cornell University Press. © 1988 by Cornell University. Used by permission of the publisher, Cornell University Press.

40   Hall, Catherine. (2002) *Civilising Subjects: Metropole and Colony in the English Imagination 1830–1867*, Chicago: University of Chicago Press.

41   Kucich, John. (2007) *Imperial Masochism: British Fiction, Fantasy, and Social Class*, Princeton: Princeton University Press.

Part XI: Economics, the market, and Victorian culture

43   Nunokawa, Jeff. *The Afterlife of Property: Domestic Security and the Victorian Novel.* © 1994 Princeton University Press. Reprinted by permission of Princeton University Press.

44   Gallagher, Catherine. *The Body Economic: Life, Death, and Sensation in Political Economy and the Victorian Novel* © 2006 Princeton University Press. Reprinted by permission of Princeton University Press.

45   Poovey, Mary. (2008) *Genres of the Credit Economy: Mediating Value in Eighteenth- and Nineteenth-Century Britain*, Chicago: University of Chicago Press.

Part XII: Print culture

47   Brake, Laurel. (2011) "The Advantage of Fiction: The Novel and the 'Success' of the Victorian Periodical," in Beth Palmer and Adelene Buckland, eds., *A Return to the Common Reader: Print Culture and the Novel, 1850–1900*, London: Ashgate, pp. 9–21.

48   Rubery, Matthew. (2009) *The Novelty of Newspapers: Victorian Fiction after the Invention of the News*, Oxford: Oxford University Press.

49   Price, Leah. *How to Do Things With Books in Victorian Britain.* © 2012 Princeton University Press. Reprinted by permission of Princeton University Press.

Introduction

Anne Longmuir and Lee Behlman

In the opening sentence of *Eminent Victorians* (1918), Lytton Strachey's iconoclastic assault on nineteenth-century mores, Strachey wrote that "[t]he history of the Victorian Age will never be written; we know too much about it" (Strachey 2003: 5). Strachey's famous epigram may these days hold true not just for the historian of the Victorian age but also for the historian of scholarship produced *about* that time. Victorian studies has become a vast field, one that is increasingly interdisciplinary and is currently in the throes of grappling with an explosion of readily available primary texts, thanks to digitization projects initiated in both the private and the public sector. A diversity of methodological approaches, combined with this remarkable mass of content (over 50,000 novels and around the same number of periodical titles (Phegley [Chapter 50: 428])), can make this area of study appear overwhelming to the scholars who work in it—and nearly impregnable to students new to the field.

It's with these challenges in mind that this volume has been created. We offer a sign-posted introduction to many of the key critical contributions in Victorian studies from the past twenty-five years. Even as Strachey recommends that the cautious historian drop "here and there, a little bucket, which will bring up to the light of day some characteristic specimen, from those far depths [of the Victorian past]" (Strachey 2003: 5), recently scholars have been able to draw from a wider and deeper sea of sources, often reaching strikingly contrasting conclusions from their surveys. This collection lays out this critical territory for the intrepid investigator, whether they be a novice or an experienced hand.

We have organized our survey into twelve prominent subjects of debate. Our choice of topics is not intended to be fully comprehensive—it is not *the* map but rather *a* map that we hope students of the period will find helpful. Following the titles of all volumes in this new series, our selections represent what we judge to be the strongest and most lively areas of criticism and debate in the field. The sections vary deliberately from the broadly conceived and widely influential ("Imperialism and Literature in the Age of Colonialism," "Gender, Domesticity, and Sexuality") to the narrowly focused ("Women Poets and the Poetess Tradition," "Realism and Photography") in order to give readers a taste of the different kinds of conversations taking place. These include issues which have become unavoidable for almost all working in Victorian studies as well as emerging topics chosen as much for their ongoing potential as for their present currency. In selecting these topics, we've tried to reflect several recent developments, among them the resurgence of interest in aesthetics and form; the increasingly interdisciplinary nature of contemporary scholarship; the expansion of interest in nineteenth-century psychology and embodiment; the changing fortunes of broader theoretical movements, including feminism and Foucauldian theory, and the impact of technological change on the field (more of which later). Although some subject areas in this collection are the nexus of direct, highly charged debates, we have sought to reflect the fact that with several of them, scholars have instead offered a variety of distinct, nonconflictive critical approaches. Our goals—and those of our new contributors—have been to capture the full diversity of these approaches and to compare them without exaggerating their oppositional qualities.

Each section assembles three or four excerpts from some of the best critical work published in Victorian studies in the past two-and-a-half decades, with a bias towards the last ten or fifteen years, and with priority given to material which has not yet been discussed or excerpted in other surveys of criticism. We have favored more recent work in order to maximize readers' understanding of the current state of the field; however, where an earlier work has been so influential that omitting it would impoverish our understanding of current scholarship (e.g., Isobel Armstrong on Victorian poetry or Gillian Beer on Darwinism), we've included it in the volume. We've also taken seriously the first part of this collection's title, *Victorian Literature*, so while we include excerpts from cultural studies and historical scholarship, we've tended to favor criticism that is oriented around literary work—though much of it also makes use of nonliterary documents, such as legal and medical texts. Our selections vary in character but are generally of two kinds: introductory chapters to books that set up the argumentative terrain and critical readings of well-known literary texts. Most of the twelve sections include both kinds of selections. Nearly all of our selections have been edited for length and clarity; interested readers are encouraged to turn to the original sources.

Inevitably, of course, our attempt to represent the last few decades of Victorian studies scholarship must be defined as much by what it leaves out as by what it includes. We're acutely conscious of the absence not just of work on certain Victorian authors, such as Emily Brontë, Thomas Hardy, Harriet Martineau, and Oscar Wilde, but also of important recent scholarship in other areas that we would have liked to cover, including *fin-de-siècle* aestheticism, children's literature, cities and crowds, masculinity, objects and thing theory, transatlanticism, and Victorian drama (to name a few). An entire other volume, indeed, could be written dealing with these and other subject areas, drawing on the many outstanding scholars whose work we were not able to include. Despite the generous number of subjects and authors included here, incompleteness is an unavoidable characteristic of any collection like this; we hope readers will forgive us our omissions.

With this in mind, we believe that what most distinguishes our volume from other Victorian studies readers is the presence of a newly commissioned capstone essay in each category. Freed from the task of situating its topic within a wider literary historical context by the short explanatory notes that open each section, these essays, written by experts in the field, are evaluative and judgmental rather than detached introductions to the subject area. We've encouraged our contributors to foreground their own polemical positions as they discuss the excerpts, the broader debates that they articulate, and potential future directions in the scholarship. Not only do these new essays constitute important scholarly contributions in their own right, but they also model what teachers often want their students to do: to frame arguments within the context of existing critical conversations. The volume thus encourages undergraduate and graduate students to recognize and respond to literary studies as a dynamic, argument-driven conversation and to refine their own critical positions through active engagement with such arguments.

We have sought in this book to meet the needs of the contemporary college classroom in other ways, as well. The volume covers traditionally taught topics in courses on Victorian literature and culture while introducing emergent topics in contemporary pedagogy, such as print culture. What's more, our selections deliberately coalesce around some of the most frequently taught authors: Charlotte Brontë, Elizabeth Barrett Browning, Charles Dickens, George Eliot, Elizabeth Gaskell, and Alfred Lord Tennyson. This decision, we hope, will allow students and teachers the flexibility to approach recent scholarship through both topics of debate and individual authors. And while we do largely focus on dominant literary figures—both to reflect common pedagogical practice and to ensure that excerpts can talk to each other across sections—we've also tried to broaden this range of texts wherever possible by reference to writers historically on the second tier of the traditional canon such as Wilkie Collins and H. G. Wells, and also through discussion of now-obscure authors such as Charlotte Brame ("Genre Fiction and Sensation").

Beyond its twelve defined areas of Victorianist debate, the essays and extracts included in this book also point repeatedly to several underlying concerns in Victorian studies right now, including the place of history in literary scholarship, the impact of digitization, the ongoing processes of canon revision—and the legacy of Michel Foucault. Although French historian and philosopher Michel Foucault died more than thirty years ago, his theories—and later reworkings of them—continue to be highly influential. The appeal of his work to Victorianists is perhaps unsurprising: several of his books do, after all, directly address the nineteenth century and in particular Victorian Britain, most notably *Discipline and Punish* (1975) and *The History of Sexuality*, Volume 1 (1976). But although Foucault's specific work on madness, sexuality, and governmentality has inevitably attracted scholars working in these particular areas, perhaps his most persistent and pervasive influence in Victorian studies has lain, as James Eli Adams suggested in a 2001 review essay, in reframing the "fundamental questions about human identity and agency in relation to various forms of authority and power" (Adams 2001: 828). In the late 1980s and early 1990s, critics began to examine Victorian literature, along with other nineteenth-century cultural productions, through his work. Prompted by Foucault's influential understanding of discourses not simply as "groups of signs" but instead as "practices that systematically form the objects of which they speak" (Foucault 1989: 54), scholars such as Nancy Armstrong, D. A. Miller, and Ann Cvetkovich began to recognize one vehicle for discourse, the novel, as a crucial mechanism of power. Rejecting the notion that literature operates in opposition to society, these critics suggested instead that one of the primary effects of the nineteenth-century novel was the "systematic formation" of the objects of which it spoke, most particularly, individual subjectivity. Rather than affirming the autonomy of the individual, such Foucauldian readings countered essentialist understandings of the self by suggesting that subjectivity is a product of the interplay of power and knowledge. To quote Armstrong's succinct formulation, "written representations of the self allowed the modern individual to become an economic and psychological reality" (Armstrong 1987: 8). For such critics, then, even ostensibly subversive genres such as sensation fiction (routinely seen as threatening social norms by the Victorians themselves) could "work in a conservative way as a means of naturalizing ideology" (Cvetkovich 1992: 24–25 [Chapter 13: 123]).

While Foucault's theorization of the relationship between power and knowledge and his later work on sexuality each generated an enormous amount of scholarship in the 1980s and 1990s, the essays collected in this volume reveal how in recent years scholars have become more alert to limitations in Foucauldian rhetoric and analysis. As Anna Maria Jones notes, Armstrong, Miller, and Cvetkovich have been accused of "erasing difference, reading all texts and context into a giant uniform power/knowledge edifice" (Jones 2007: 7). Still other critics have identified crucial historical gaps in Foucauldian approaches: Sharon Marcus argues, for example, that Foucault's historical sources are simply insufficient for scholars considering female sexuality, while Lauren Goodlad urges caution in applying his "Franco-oriented and presentist" theories to "Britain's self-consciously liberal society" (Goodlad 2003: x [Chapter 35: 305]). Even those scholars who seek to defend Foucault himself from these critical reassessments fault earlier applications of his theories as oversimplified. No longer seen as being devoid of agency, the neo-Foucauldian subject must be situated as "always a subject, or agent within a network of power," as Pamela Gilbert remarks in this volume (Chapter 16: 143).

What we see in contemporary Victorian studies is not a full rejection of Foucault but a continued engagement with Foucauldian vocabulary and his analysis of power, tempered with an acute consciousness of the limitations of his arguments in the context of nineteenth-century Britain. Gender and sexuality studies no longer rely so heavily on readings of *The History of Sexuality*, for example, while scholars increasingly recognize Foucault's "genealogical works on discipline" as "less useful to the Victorianist than are his later essays on governmentality, pastorship, and liberalism" (Goodlad 2003: xi). But perhaps most significant, when critics draw on Foucault in the early twenty-first century, they do so, as Michael Davis notes here, with a "more concentrated attention to the specific historical contexts of texts and ideas than is to be found in some earlier Foucauldian studies" (Chapter 29: 252). Increasingly wary of applying his ideas anachronistically or ahistorically, in the last decade or so critics have drawn on ever more meticulous historical understandings of Victorian culture.

Beyond the legacy of Foucault, a second underlying concern shaping Victorian studies has been the role of history itself in literary analysis. The last twenty-five years have seen a thorough absorption of New Historicist approaches to literature, which were themselves influenced by Foucauldian models of history, and a partial turn away from high theory. Encouraged to cast a wider critical net that includes nonliterary texts as well as literary ones by New Historicism, literary scholars have increasingly moved "towards historicist, interdisciplinary readings of texts and cultures" (Davis [Chapter 29: 250]). As a result, it's more than a shift of gender focus that separates Eve Kosofsky Sedgwick's *Between Men* (1985) and Sharon Marcus's *Between Women* (2009), for example: there is a quantitative difference in each work's employment of history, with "Marcus's use of historical evidence far exceed[ing] Sedgwick's as she supports her thesis through an exceptionally wide variety of sources" (Gregory [Chapter 33: 288]). Indeed, such is the trend towards detailed historical analysis that the "broader cultural brushstrokes" of even classic studies of the 1980s such as George Levine's *Darwin and the Novelists* (1988) and Gillian Beer's *Darwin's Plots* (1983) can, as Jonathan Smith points out, "begin to appear too imprecise" when read against current scholarship (Chapter 25: 225).

But the rise of historicist approaches to literature has not been without its detractors, with a number of commentators fearing that, to put it crudely, attention to context comes at the expense of attention to the text. Just as Herbert Tucker warned back in 1999 that "the quantitative shift in focus" associated with historicist readings could result in "a qualitative change in attentiveness" (Tucker 1999: 533 [Chapter 2: 23]), so in a newly written essay for this volume, Muireann O'Cinneide cautions that we "cannot allow attention to form, genre, and rhetoric to become swamped by a wealth of historical contextualisation" (Chapter 42: 367). Rather than abandoning what Marjorie Garber has called "literary questions" (Garber 2003: 13), both Tucker and O'Cinneide argue instead that literary studies must continue to engage with issues of form and genre—even as it asks historical questions—or risk becoming a "perpetual subordinate, or at best complement, to history, politics, and associated disciplines" (O'Cinneide [Chapter 42: 367]). It is this combination of literary and historical sensitivity that Mark Knight addresses when he suggests that the best recent critical work on religion "is shaped by . . . attention to form and a willingness to pursue close readings that draw fluently on history and theory to develop their lines of theological interpretation" (Chapter 20: 181).

So central do we see the debates surrounding the relationship of text and context in contemporary Victorian studies that we open the collection with a section that addresses it explicitly, "Victorian Poetry and Form." While scholars historically subjected Victorian poetry to formalist critique, the introduction to Isobel Armstrong's highly influential *Victorian Poetry* (1993), which opens this section, initiated a critical approach that sought to broaden such readings by exploring the relationship between poetic form and historical context. Known variously as "neoformalism," "strategic formalism," and "cultural neoformalism," this "new formalism," as Charles LaPorte argues in this volume, "has recently invigorated literary scholarship by blending genre study and questions of aesthetics with a rigorous historicization of social and material contexts" (Chapter 4: 37). Though the rise of historicist approaches in the past three decades has turned scholarly attention towards the novel, a genre often regarded as more thoroughly embedded in its social and cultural context than poetry, neoformalism demonstrates both the historical situatedness of Victorian poetry and, perhaps more importantly, the inseparability of text and context.

But the recent dominance of historicist readings in Victorian studies speaks to more than the ebb and flow of critical fashions within literary studies; it also points to a wholly new phenomenon, the impact digitization has had upon the field. Scholars' access to the majority of the material published in the Victorian period was once restricted by their physical proximity to archives and the availability of travel funding and research leave, but since the turn of the twenty-first century, digital repositories have made an enormous range of texts instantly (and often freely) available to anyone with an internet connection. If the "broader cultural brushstrokes" of earlier critical work on Darwin "begin to appear imprecise" in comparison to contemporary scholarship, this is partly because today's scholars have far more historical resources at their fingertips (quite literally). The archival material that used to require Darwin scholars to make a trip to Cambridge, for example, can now, as Jonathan Smith reminds us, "be accessed online in searchable form," giving researchers immediate access to Darwin's complete publications, a number of his manuscripts, and other papers (*Darwin Online*) as well as around 7,500 letters (*Darwin Correspondence Project*) (Chapter 25: 224).

Despite the mouthwatering scholarly opportunities presented by this smorgasbord of searchable collections of nineteenth-century texts, digitization is not without its problems. *Darwin Online* and the *Darwin Correspondence Project* may make their texts freely available, but, as Jennifer Phegley notes, other databases come with hefty price tags that only select institutions have the means or inclination to purchase. As a result, institutional funds remain a factor in determining scholars' and students' access to archival resources. Furthermore, digitization itself is by no means neutral: if our twentieth-century view of Victorian publishing was unavoidably influenced by the dominance of those texts that remained in print, then our twenty-first-century view of the Victorians will inevitably be shaped by what educational and corporate institutions decide to digitize. As Phegley puts it pithily, "What is digitized will, to a large degree, determine how we study the history of nineteenth-century print" (Chapter 50: 428–9). But perhaps most significantly, the very possibility of instant access to nearly a century's worth of text brings problems of its own, prompting feelings of unease that mirror the Victorians' (and Lytton Strachey's) own response to their mushrooming print culture. Close reading, that cornerstone of literary studies, excels with individual texts, but it's inadequate dealing with decades of accumulated print, a concern that prompted Laurel Brake to suggest in 2011 that "we are in the last moments before changes in access and searchability affect our methodology in this field profoundly" (Brake 2011: 10 [Chapter 47: 406]). One available—and controversial—option is to shift from close reading to what Franco Moretti calls "distant reading" (Moretti 2005: 1), drawing on computational and quantitative approaches to literary analysis to ask data-driven questions of larger corpuses of texts than ever before.

The increased access to Victorian texts permitted by digitization is likely to affect more than just our methodology. As Linda Hughes, Pamela Gilbert, and Jennifer Phegley observe, making once-marginalized material readily available, is likely to perpetuate another recurrent theme in this volume: canon revision. While feminist critics such as Ellen Moers, Elaine Showalter, Sandra Gilbert, and Susan Gubar began to expand the nineteenth-century literary canon in the 1970s, over the last twenty-five years, we've seen the study of women writers (poets in particular), along with previously denigrated genres (such as sensation fiction) and literary forms (including all manner of periodical writing) continue to move from the margins of scholarship to the front and center of Victorian studies. This trend can only accelerate with the increasing online availability of previously difficult-to-access material, with digitization enabling not just distant reading but also more targeted close reading, by drawing our attention to texts we might otherwise have missed. Already there have been a number of major shifts: scholars have turned back to once-popular but long-neglected women writers, such as Augusta Webster and Alice Meynell; made mass-market novelists such as Mary Elizabeth Braddon and Ellen Wood the subject of expanded critical and pedagogical attention; and significantly expanded the number of critical monographs focusing on individual nineteenth-century publications.

Yet perhaps more important than critics' increasing willingness to work with literature traditionally excluded from the canon is the recent reconceptualization of the qualities that make a text worthy of academic study. During the last few decades of the twentieth century, critics interested in gender, race, sexuality, and class sought to build a more representative canon by recovering previously marginalized writers. Recognizing the canon as inescapably political, critics no longer assumed that texts had been omitted in the past because they lacked literary merit; instead, the relationship of a literary work to the traditional canon was understood to be ideologically determined. As Ann Cvetkovich writes of Victorian responses to sensation fiction, "these judgments of aesthetic value were often the covert means by which high culture was distinguished from an increasingly visible mass culture" (Cvetkovich 1992: 19 [Chapter 13: 119–20]). In striving to expand the canon, then, critics justified their selections via recourse to textual politics rather than increasingly challenged standards of aesthetic value, with the result that literature was often assessed, in Bruce Robbins's words, through the "unstable currency of subversion and transgression" (Robbins 1994: 366). Politically driven critiques of aesthetic values have not receded in the last decade or so, but scholars have become less concerned with identifying texts that seem to anticipate our own political positions and more interested in Victorian literature's articulation of nineteenth-century political, social, and cultural mores. Thus, contemporary feminist scholars are, as Melissa Gregory notes, "more preoccupied with the subtle variations within domestic ideology than in identifying the ways in which female subjects disavowed or rejected it" (Chapter 33: 287). As Pamela Gilbert suggests, scholars working with noncanonical literature once commonly sought to validate their work by emphasizing their ideological resistance to dominant power structures, but such gestures are now less common (along with their mirror image, the Foucauldian commonplace that resistance is futile). This recent work constitutes, at its best, not a departure from ideological critique but its refinement alongside a mode of self-conscious critical detachment—a neo-Victorian practice recommended by Amanda Anderson in her influential book (Anderson 2001: 9 [Chapter 34: 300]).

Indeed, if contemporary critics increasingly "resist the temptation to read" Victorian literature "through the lens of twentieth-century ideologies," as Daniel Malachuk suggests ([Chapter 37: 327]), then we've perhaps reached the point at which we should reconsider the ways in which we group these works. As Linda Hughes notes in her essay, although the 1980s and 1990s saw the publication of a number of anthologies of women's writing—creating, arguably, a separate canon—it has become increasingly unclear "whether there is value in studying women's poetry as such, especially when the category marks off women's verse as somehow 'other' than men's" ([Chapter 8: 81]). Instead, as her closing analysis of L.E.L.'s poetry in the context of *Friendship's Offering* reveals, there is much to be gained from considering once-marginalized women writers not in isolation but alongside their male colleagues if we are to apprehend what Hughes calls "women's complex position in literature and culture" ([Chapter 8: 82]). In a similar fashion, critics interested in empire have recently challenged the geographic and national borders that have traditionally bounded our notion of the Victorian. By incorporating anglophone literature produced by colonial subjects, like the fiction of Bankim Chandra Chatterjee, author of the first English novel by an Indian, *Rajmohan's Wife* (1864), or the poetry of Toru Dutt, Victorian studies moves from what Mary Ellis Gibson calls "a dyadic model of metropole and colony" towards a fuller understanding of the "imperial circuits and transperipheral exchanges" that characterized empire in the nineteenth century (Gibson 2014: 325). In recognizing the multiple interchanges that took place not just between Britain and its colonies, but also between the different regions of the empire, we not only gesture towards the intricacies and ironies within Britain's own imperial history, but—more importantly, given the decentering impulse of this shift in scholarly focus—also gain a clearer sense of the "complex position in literature and culture" of the colonies themselves.

This collection's opening extract—one of its earliest, from Isobel Armstrong's *Victorian Poetry*—exhibits a clear defensiveness about the study of Victorian culture. Countering the denigration of the Victorian period by modernists like Lytton Strachey, as well as what she sees as more recent charges of political naivety from Marxist and feminist critics, Armstrong argues that Victorian poetry is "bolder and more self-conscious than most poetry subsequent to it" (Armstrong 1993: 16 [Chapter 1: 18]). Although such pugnaciousness about the period has largely evaporated in Victorian studies over the course of the past two decades, Armstrong's sense of the Victorians as more knowing than earlier critics had given them credit for pervades this volume. Thus, Jill Rappoport argues we must "grant to nineteenth-century fiction some of the interest in gender and class that we take up ourselves" (Chapter 46: 399), while Jennifer Green-Lewis suggests that the Victorians were quite as aware that they were "creatures of an image culture" as we are today (Chapter 12: 108). As we look to the future of Victorian studies, it's this increasingly nuanced awareness of the Victorians' own intellectual sophistication and the complexities of their history that seem to predominate. Whereas linear-development narratives once shaped our understanding of the Victorians (the secularization thesis, the repressive hypothesis, the Darwinian Revolution, the displacement of Orientalist approaches by Anglicist ones in India, the narrative of press decline), by the second decade of the twenty-first century, our conception of this culture is more akin to Darwin's image of the "entangled bank": we increasingly imagine Victorian culture as populated by "elaborately constructed forms, so different from each other, and dependent on each other in so complex a manner" (Darwin 1985: 459). But this rejection of linear or teleological models doesn't just characterize contemporary conceptions of Victorian literature and culture. Victorian studies itself is currently distinguished not by "a clearly discernible progression of theoretical or methodological models" (Gregory [Chapter 33: 286]) but rather by its own diversity of approaches, resembling—like the digital network that is transforming both the content and the methodology of the field—a matrix or web. And because no self-respecting Victorianist can think of webs without thinking of *Middlemarch* (1871–72), let us conclude by stating that while this collection can't promise Casaubon's "key to all mythologies," we do hope it offers a thread, Ariadne-like, to guide readers through the complexities of contemporary scholarship in Victorian studies.

Bibliography

Adams, J. E. (2001) "Recent Studies in the Nineteenth Century," *SEL: Studies in English Literature*, 41: 827–79.

Anderson, A. (2001) *The Powers of Distance: Cosmopolitanism and the Culture of Detachment*, Princeton: Princeton University Press.

Armstrong, I. (1993) *Victorian Poetry: Poetry, Poets and Politics*, London: Routledge.

Armstrong, N. (1987) *Desire and Domestic Fiction: A Political History of the Novel*, Oxford: Oxford University Press.

Brake, L. (2011) "The Advantage of Fiction: The Novel and the 'Success' of the Victorian Periodical," in B. Palmer and A. Buckland (eds.) *A Return to the Common Reader: Print Culture and the Novel, 1850–1900*, London: Ashgate, 9–21.

Cvetkovich, A. (1992) *Mixed Feelings: Feminism, Mass Culture, and Victorian Sensationalism*, New Brunswick: Rutgers University Press.

Darwin, C. (1985) *On the Origin of Species*, London: Penguin.

Foucault, M. (1989) *The Archaeology of Knowledge*, London: Routledge.

Garber, M. (2003) *A Manifesto for Literary Studies*, Seattle: University of Washington Press.

Gibson, M.E. (2014) "Introduction: English in India, India in England," *Victorian Literature and Culture*, 42: 325–33.

Goodlad, L.M.E. (2003) *Victorian Literature and the Victorian State*, Baltimore: The Johns Hopkins University Press.

Jones, A.M. (2007) *Problem Novels: Victorian Fiction Theorizes the Sensation Self*, Columbus: The Ohio State University Press.

Moretti, F. (2005) *Graphs, Maps, Trees: Abstract Models for Literary History*, London: Verso.

Robbins, B. (1994) "'Real Politics' and the Canon Debate," *Contemporary Literature*, 35: 365–76.

Strachey, L. (2003) *Eminent Victorians*, ed. J. Sutherland, Oxford: Oxford University Press.

Tucker, H. (1999) "The Fix of Form: An Open Letter," *Victorian Literature and Culture*, 27: 531–35.

Part I

Victorian poetry and form

Introduction

In recent decades, studies of Victorian poetic form have often begun by invoking Coventry Patmore's 1856 *Essay on English Metrical Law*, one of the first manifestos on a subject that attracted poets, grammarians, linguists, and not a few cranks during a flurry of activity that lasted into the early twentieth century. This impulse to lay down the law on nineteenth-century prosody is also characteristic of the past two decades of scholarship on Victorian poetic form, for one of the bracing pleasures of this remarkably fertile field has been its own polemicism. Despite the diversity of terms that have sprouted up to define this new scholarly work (including new formalism, neoformalism, historical poetics, and cultural neoformalism), scholars of Victorian poetic form have not been arguing with each other so much as with two broader tendencies at work within literary scholarship itself: the long-lasting effects of the Modernists' turn against Victorian poetry and the more recent shift against critical formalism in literary studies.

As Charles LaPorte mentions in his capstone essay, Isobel Armstrong first took a shot across the bow against Victorian poetry's detractors in her 1993 book *Victorian Poetry: Poetry, Poetics, and Politics*. Armstrong's introduction maintains that since the early twentieth century, Victorian poetry has been misread as formally unadventurous and constrained, containing only tick-tock rhythms and predictable, fixed rhyme schemes that match its ideological conservatism. This was in contrast to the revolutionary poetics and theoretical sophistication of not only High Modernism but also Romanticism, reflected in the twentieth-century theoretical apparatuses (including deManian deconstruction) that developed around them. Armstrong counters this critical tendency on multiple fronts, making both historical and theoretical claims. For Armstrong, not only were poetics in the Victorian period the first to be "modern," and Victorian poets more formally inventive than the Modernists that followed them, but this modernity was also specifically reflected in the exquisite Hegelian structure of what she calls the Victorian "double poem" (Armstrong 1993: 13 [Chapter 1: 15]).[1]

While the prejudice Armstrong tarried with was a by-product of literary periodization, other critics have dealt with an even more vexed issue from more recent critical history: the shifting positions of formalism and historicism. While the explicitly formalist New Criticism that dominated at U.S. universities in the middle decades of the twentieth century was a turn against an older historicism, it was in turn displaced (outside the classroom, at least) in later decades by a return to historical inquiry in literary studies in the form of New Historicism. In the wake of these changes, Herbert Tucker and Jason Rudy (both excerpted here) and other figures such as Meredith Martin and Yopie Prins have each posed a crucial question for poetry studies: how can we deal with inescapable matters of form in an adequate way yet without returning to the naïvely ahistorical aestheticism of an earlier era?

These critics have taken a variety of approaches to this question, including Prins's recent use of deconstruction to place the stability of metrical "law" in question. More representative of recent critical trends, however, has been Rudy's and Martin's practice of historicizing prosody itself in—respectively—the contexts of Victorian science and of national culture. Their work has also redirected Victorian poetry scholarship towards new archival resources, including scientific writing, elocution manuals, and grammar books.

Herbert Tucker shares Rudy's and others' interest in opening up Victorian poetry scholarship to New Historicist and cultural studies approaches, but unlike that of some of his contemporaries, his work returns insistently from these approaches to aesthetically informed readings of individual poems. Tucker's self-consciously polemical effort to reconcile two such historically divergent modes of English studies scholarship—formalism and historicism—is indicative of the ways in which recent work on Victorian poetry and form pushes against the boundaries of current critical shibboleths.

See also: *Women poets and the poetess tradition*; *Psychology and literature*

Notes

1 After Armstrong's 1993 manifesto, theoretical work on Victorian poetry and poetics expanded in new directions with Matthew Rowlinson's neo-psychoanalytic *Tennyson's Fixations* (1994) and the broadly deconstructive approach of Yopie Prins's brilliant *Victorian Sappho* (1999).

1 Rereading Victorian poetry

Isobel Armstrong

What kind of history?

Critical history generally divides literature into blocks, corresponding with literary periods. I begin with the difficulty of thinking about history in this way.

The habit of thinking of literary periods as segments creates the same kind of history that produces it. The Victorian period has always been regarded as isolated between two periods, Romanticism and modernism. Thus Victorian poetry is seen in terms of transition. It is on the way somewhere. It is either on the way from Romantic poetry, or on the way to modernism. It is situated between two kinds of excitement, in which it appears not to participate. What has been called the 'genetic' history of continuous development through phases and periods, a form of history which the Victorians themselves both helped to create and to question, sees Victorian poetry as a gap in that development.[1] Modernism, in spite of its desire to see itself in terms of a break with history, actually endorses that continuity, for a radical break must break with something. And correspondingly it endorses the gap which Victorian poetry is seen to inhabit. The anxieties of modernism, trying to do without history, repress whatever relations the Victorians may seem to bear to twentieth-century writing. Thus Joyce's frivolous 'Lawn Tennyson, gentleman poet' appears dressed for tennis in *Ulysses*. Virginia Woolf dissociates herself from the Victorians in her unscrupulously brilliant impressionistic account of them in *Orlando*.[2] There ivy covers buildings and large families come into being with almost equally magical suddenness. She intuitively registers the drive to produce in Victorian society, whether it is children or industrial goods, and the need to muffle. The eroticisms and the euphemisms of bourgeois capitalism and its ideology, its inordinate excesses and concealments, are embodied in the voluptuous taxidermy of the stuffed sofa.

So the major critical and theoretical movements of the twentieth century have been virtually silent about Victorian poetry. As the stranded remnants of high bourgeois liberalism, the poets have been consigned to sepia. New criticism, encouraged by T. S. Eliot, who said that Tennyson and Browning merely 'ruminated', considered Victorian poetry to lie outside its categories.[3] When Raymond Williams began to theorise the cultural criticism which has been so fruitful in *Culture and Society*, he concentrated on the nineteenth-century novel.[4] Feminism likewise made its claims through a critique primarily of the novel.[5] Deconstruction concentrated on Romantic poetry, blatantly periodising in a way which goes against its theoretical preconceptions.[6] No major European critic has seen Victorian poetry as relevant to his or her purpose. It is symbolism and imagism which have proved attractive when the novel was displaced as a centre of interest. Walter Benjamin wrote wonderfully on Baudelaire,[7] but Lukács or Bakhtin on Tennyson would be unthinkable. Oddly, biography in this area *has* flourished. The worse the poets seem to be, the more avidly their lives are recuperated. We 'covet' biography, as Browning once brilliantly said.[8] And biographers have dominated in literary scholarship of the Victorian period, even though Browning turns out to be a brash opportunist and Tennyson a surly and duplicitous snob.[9] An honourably uncovetous study is Lionel Trilling's classic biography of Matthew Arnold.[10]

What, then, can be the motive for writing about Victorian poetry? Is it worth it? The enterprise cannot be justified in terms of the genetic history which would simply fill in the gap, re-create continuity and restore the forgotten. Some principles must govern this reclaiming process beyond the notion of even continuity and positivist accounts of development. For if continuity exists at all, we create it ourselves. There is no unbroken continuity independent of us with its own external process. Foucault's suspicion of positivist history is based on a belief that it is precisely asymmetry, discontinuity and difference, which we also create ourselves, that are important.[11] Nor can this poetry simply be 'revalued', for since value is a function of the unstable movement of current adjustments of aesthetic worth, the likelihood is that a body of literature will be unquestioningly translated into the terms of whatever theory is deemed to be important at the moment. Unless some principles secure revaluation, it becomes simply a means of appropriating new literary territory. However transcendent it may seem, the notion of value is as relativistic and incoherent as positivist history. Too often to 'revalue' the Victorian poets is to claim that they were like us, but inadvertently.

A way of beginning to rediscover the importance of Victorian poetry is to consider the heavy silence surrounding it in the twentieth century as a striking cultural phenomenon in itself. We have to see that silence historically. T. S. Eliot's dismissive account of Tennyson deflects attention from the Tennysonian echoes in *The Waste Land* and *Four Quartets*. Yeats, virtually quoting Shelley in 'The Second Coming', silently appropriates Tennyson's 'The Kraken' as the governing motive of his poem.[12] We have learned to understand that to constitute something as a gap is a strategy for concealing anxiety. What kind of anxieties could the Victorians have created for the twentieth century and why are they still culturally significant? To clarify these anxieties it is necessary to see what the Victorian poets themselves were worried about.

They thought of themselves as modern. 'Modern', in spite of its long history, has a resurgence as a Victorian term – the 'modern' element in literature (Arnold), 'modern' love (Meredith), a 'modern' landlord (William Allingham).[13] To see yourself as modern is actually to define the contemporary self-consciously and this is simultaneously an act which historicises the modern. Victorian modernism sees itself as new but it does not, like twentieth-century modernism, conceive itself in terms of a radical break with a past. Victorian modernism, as it emerges in its poetics, describes itself as belonging to a condition of crisis which has emerged directly from economic and cultural change. In fact, Victorian poetics begins to conceptualise the idea of culture as a category and includes itself within the definition. To be modern was to be overwhelmingly secondary. Harold Bloom's term, 'belatedness', would be useful to describe this perception, except that his belatedness is far too restricted. It is narrowed to an essentially personalised oedipal struggle with the precursor poet – Browning and Shelley, Tennyson and Keats, Arnold and Wordsworth. If his term is adopted it must be used to designate a far wider and more consciously searching understanding of what it is to be secondary.[14] The Victorian poets *were* post-Romantic but to understand the political and aesthetic consequences of this it is necessary to see what being post-Romantic entailed. For to be 'new', or 'modern' or 'post-Romantic' was to confront and self-consciously to conceptualise *as* new elements that are still perceived as the constitutive forms of our own condition. Whether a poet was a subversive reactionary, as Tennyson was, or attempting to write a radical poetry, as Browning was, such a poet was 'modern' or secondary in a number of ways, all of which involved the reformation of the categories of knowledge. A belated poet was post-revolutionary, existing with the constant possibility of mass political upheaval and fundamental change in the structure of society, which meant that the nature of society had to be redefined. Belatedness was post-industrial and post-technological, existing with and theorising the changed relationships and new forms of alienated labour which capitalism was consolidating, and conscious of the predatory search for new areas of exploitation which was creating a new colonial 'outside' to British society. It was post-teleological and scientific, conceiving beliefs, including those of Christianity, anthropologically in terms of belief *systems* and representations through myth. Simply because of its awareness of teleological insecurity, Victorian poetry is arguably the last theological poetry to be written.

Lastly, the supreme condition of posthumousness, it was post-Kantian. This meant, in the first place, that the category of art (and for the Victorians this was almost always poetry) was becoming 'pure'. Art occupied its own area, a self-sufficing aesthetic realm over and against practical experience. It was *outside* the economy of instrumental energies (for in Kant art and technology spring into being simultaneously as necessary opposites). And yet it was at once apart and central, for it had a mediating function, representing and interpreting life. These contradictions were compounded by post-Kantian accounts of representation, which adapted Kant to make both the status and the mode of art problematical by seeing representations as the constructs of consciousness which is always at a remove from what it represents. Thus the possibility of a process of endless redefinition and an ungrounded, unstable series of representations was opened out. So the Victorian poets were the first group of writers to feel that what they were doing was simply unnecessary and redundant. For the very category of art itself created redundancy.

[. . .]

It is possible now to return to the modernists' silence about Victorian poetry. It is clear that the nature of the experiencing subject, the problems of representation, fiction and language, are just as much the heart of Victorian problems as they are the preoccupations of modernism. The difference is that the Victorians see them as problems, the modernists do not. Where the Victorians strive to give a content to these problems, political, sexual, epistemological, and to formulate a cultural critique, the moderns celebrate the elimination of content. Victorian problems become abstracted, formalised and aestheticised. The difference is ideological, as the stuffing of the Victorian sofa disappears and art becomes self-reflexive and self-referential. Eliot shores up the ruins of a culture with the fragments of art, Yeats strives to make the golden bird of aesthetics sing out of the frenzied images of creation. The modernist repression of the Victorians comes surely from an understanding that the Victorians had anticipated the self-reflexive condition and rejected it. The modernists are haunted by the Victorians because they are haunted by the plenitude of content which eludes them. For them the Victorians are lumpenly ethical or theological.[15] The task of a history of Victorian poetry is to restore the questions of politics, not least sexual politics, and the epistemology and language which belong to it. I have left the generalisations about modernism here flagrantly unsupported in the belief that a study of Victorian poetry will bear them out. It is interesting, though beyond the scope of this study, that postmodernist writers often attribute a teleology to modernism in just the same way that modernists denigrated the teleological Victorians.

[. . .]

The link between cultural complexities and the complexities of language is indirect but can be perceived. We might start with the nature of language in Victorian poetry. For to read a Victorian poem is to be made acutely aware of the fact that it is made of language. Whether it is the strange, arcane artifice of Tennyson's early poems or the splutter of speech in Browning, the limpid economy of Christina Rossetti, Swinburne's swamping rhythms, Hopkins's muscle-bound syntax, the sheer verbalness of poetry is foregrounded. It is as if the poet's secondariness takes a stand on the self-conscious assertion of the unique discourse of poetry. This is connected with the overdetermination of ambiguity. The open nerve of exposed feeling in Tennyson is registered in a language fraught with ambiguity. Christina Rossetti's distilled exactitude analyses into an equally precise ambiguity. Signification in Browning shifts and lurches almost vertiginously. The structural ambiguities of Romantic syntax have intensified to an extent that coalescing syntax and semantic openness is the norm. In an age of 'movable type' and mechanical reproduction in which signification moves beyond the immediate control of the writer it is as if the writer can only resort to an openness in advance of the reader, testing out the possibilities of systematic misprision. Such language draws attention to the nature of words as a medium of representation. In the same way poets resort to songs and speech, as if to foreground the act of reading a secondary text, for the song is not sung but read, and the speech is not spoken but written.

Hopkins saw the openness of his contemporaries as anarchy and flux and desperately tried to arrest it, reintroducing an agonised, sundered language of ambiguity in spite of himself.[16] Arnold saw it as the product of disorganised subjectivity, and in a brilliant phrase, summed up nineteenth-century poetry as 'the dialogue of the mind with itself', and attempted to freeze poetry back into classical form.[17] Neither, however, saw that this was a systematic and organised ambiguity. The doubleness of language is not local but structural. It must be read closely, not loosely. It is not the disorganised expression of subjectivity but a way of exploring and interrogating the grounds of its representation. What the Victorian poet achieved was often quite literally two concurrent poems in the same words.

Schopenhauer wrote of the lyric poet as uttering between two poles of feeling, between the pure undivided condition of unified selfhood and the needy, fracturing self-awareness of the interrogating consciousness.[18] The Victorian poet does not swing between these two forms of utterance but dramatises and objectifies their simultaneous existence. There is a kind of duplicity involved here, for the poet often invites the simple reading by presenting a poem as lyric expression as the perceiving subject speaks. Mariana's lament or Fra Lippo Lippi's apologetics are expressions, indeed, composed in an expressive form. But in a feat of recomposition and externalisation the poem turns its expressive utterance around so that it becomes the opposite of itself, not only the *subject's* utterance but the *object* of analysis and critique. It is, as it were, reclassified as drama in the act of being literal lyric expression. To re-order lyric expression as drama is to give it a new content and to introduce the possibility of interrogation and critique. Mariana's torture in isolation, for instance, is the utterance of a subjective psychological condition, but that psychological expression is reversed into being the object of analysis and restructured as a symptomatic form by the act of narration, which draws attention to the reiterated refrain of the poem as Mariana's speech, speech which attempts to arrest temporality while time moves on in the narrator's commentary. The poignant expression of exclusion to which Mariana's state gives rise, and which is reiterated in the marking of barriers – the moat itself, the gate with clinking latch, the curtained casement, the hinged doors – is simultaneously an analysis of the hypersensitive hysteria induced by the coercion of sexual taboo. These are hymenal taboos, which Mariana is induced, by a cultural consensus which is hidden from her, to experience as her own condition. Hidden from her, but not from the poem, the barriers are man-made, cunningly constructed through the material fabric of the house she inhabits, the enclosed spaces in which she is confined. It is the narrative voice which describes these spaces, not Mariana as speaker.

The dramatic nature of Victorian poetry was understood by its earliest critics, by W. J. Fox and Arthur Hallam in particular, but seems to have been lost to later readers.[19] Twentieth-century readers have been right to see the dramatic monologue as the primary Victorian genre, even though they have too often codified it in terms of technical features. Other devices, such as the framed narrative or the dream, dialogue or parody, are related to it. All enable double forms to emerge. Rather than to elicit its technical features, it is preferable to see what this dramatic form enabled the poet to explore. By seeing utterance both as subject and as object, it was possible for the poet to explore expressive psychological forms simultaneously as psychological conditions *and* as constructs, the phenomenology of a culture, projections which indicate the structure of relationships. I have called this objectification of consciousness a phenomenological form because phenomenology seeks to describe and analyse the manifestations of consciousness rather than its internal condition. Thus such a reading relates consciousness to the external forms of the culture in which it exists. The gap between subjective and objective readings often initiates a debate between a subject-centred or expressive and a phenomenological or analytical reading, but above all it draws attention to the act of representation, the act of relationship and the mediations of language, different in a psychological and in a phenomenological world.

The double poem is a deeply sceptical form. It draws attention to the epistemology which governs the construction of the self and its relationships and to the cultural conditions in which those relationships are made. It is an expressive model and an epistemological model simultaneously. Epistemological and hermeneutic problems are built into its very form, for interpretation, and what the act of interpretation involves, are questioned in the very existence of the double model. It must expose relationships of power, for the epistemological reading will explore things of which the expressive reading is unaware and go beyond the experience of the lyric speaker. It is inveterately political not only because it opens up an exploration of the unstable entities of self and world and the simultaneous problems of representation and interpretation, but because it is founded on debate and contest. It has to give the entities of self and world a provisional content in order to dramatise the debate. The Victorian dramatic poem is not the dialogue of the mind with itself so much as the dialogue of the poem with itself, using the dialogue of the mind, the labour of the self on the world, as its lyric entry into the phenomenological world which is a labour on that labour. If the poet knows that the act of representation is fraught with problems, and if it is not clear to what misprisions the poem might be appropriated, then a structure which analyses precisely that uncertainty and which makes that uncertainty belong to struggle and debate, a structure which fills that uncertainty with content, is the surest way to establish poetic form. The surest way to answer uncertainty is creative agnosticism.

The dialogue created by the debates between expressive and phenomenological modes might seem to lead to a kind of poetry which can be described as 'dialogic' in Bakhtin's terms. Bakhtin denied poetry the dialogic form on the ground that it was irreducibly monologic, the product of a single, unified and non-conflictual poetic voice. It would be easy to educe examples of poetry, and particularly Victorian poems, which suggest otherwise, but there are difficulties in assimilating Victorian poetry to a dialogic model, although this is a step in the right direction.[20] The struggle between two kinds of reading is highly complex. It is not a question of a simple dialogue or dialectic form in which the opposition between two terms is fixed and settled. Such an opposition too often is what the dialogic has come to mean. But we have only to look at 'Mariana' to see that the cultural or phenomenologi-cal reading which changes the status of Mariana's utterance as lyric expression is subject to unsettling pressures in its turn. In the phenomenological reading, Mariana's anguish becomes no longer something for which she is psychologically responsible. When under the scrutiny of phenomenological critique the terrible privacy of her obsessional condition, her inability to gaze on the external world except at night, becomes the function of a death wish to which she has been induced without fully realising that she has been driven to it. On the other hand, this suicidal condition asks questions of the cultural reading. Is not the phenomenological reading too ready to concede that this is a situation 'without hope of change', too ready to metaphorise Mariana's emotions in terms of projection onto the external world ('blackest moss', 'blacken'd water'), which becomes an extension of her condition even though the landscape operates quite independently of her? The external world becomes both her psychic environment and an existence from which she is irretrievably estranged. The phenomenologi-cal reading seems uncertain of these relations. Is it not too ready to narrow the grounds of feminine sexuality as the passive object of experience (notice the 'wooing wind')? Thus it arrives at a self-fulfilling reading of estrangement in which Mariana *must* be alienated. And so the status of the phenomenological reading is changed. It cannot be metacommentary with clean hands entirely in charge of the grounds of debate. And this reflects back onto Mariana as subject. Her loathing of the day and the derangement of her perception is a rebellious act in this context, and questions have to be asked about her autonomy and the extent of her passiv-ity. It might well be that the fragmented self she becomes is both cause and effect of a particu-lar way of conceiving of feminine subjectivity. And it is difficult to say whether Mariana's condition is a violent protest or a passive response to such conceptions of the feminine. What is here is nothing so straightforward as a simple opposition but a dynamic text in which lyric description and analysis are repeatedly redefining the terms of a question and contending for its ground. To probe the status of one form of utterance is to call forth an analysis of the status of *that* interpretation, and so on. If this is a dialogue or a dialectical form it is so in all the antagonistic complexity of the Hegelian master–slave dialectic in which the mediations between different positions are so rapid and subtle, so continually changing places in the rela-tionship of authority, that the play of difference can hardly be resolved. Bakhtin's dialogism is clearly derived from this, indeed, just as Volosinov's (preferable to me) linguistic model is, but it is worth going back to Hegel to restate the complexity of the case. For the status of the hermeneutic act is continually reinvestigated in the double poem at the same time as the terms of the struggle are invested with a new content.

To see the text as struggle continually investing terms with a new content is to see it as a responsive rather than as a symptomatic discourse. Both the Marxist and feminist readings to which I have referred consider the Victorian poem in different ways as a symptom of the political unconscious and thus irrevocably blind to its own meaning. No text can account for the way it is read in future cultures but it can establish the grounds of the struggle for meaning. There is a difference between what is blindfold and what is unpredictable. What I would call a new Hegelian reading avoids symptomatic interpretations, just as it avoids the endless ludic contradictions which sometimes emerge from deconstruction. A text which struggles with the logic of its own contradictions is in any case arguably nearer, though not identical with, Derridean principles, in which a text is threatened by collapse from internal oppositions, than to the systematic incoherence which deconstruction sometimes elicits.

True to its status as a transitional form Victorian poetry has either been used to confirm a general critical theory, as in the readings of Bloom, or been seen simply as an instance of a particular historical case, for which a particular critical reading is necessary, as in the readings of Johnson or Langbaum. What I have done is to develop the political implications of Johnson's work and the epistemological implications of Langbaum. Langbaum is also concerned with the double reading, though his way of seeing the judgemental reading as a *control* on the empathetic reading seems to me to state the problem too rigidly in moral rather than analytical terms. It is without that sense of a new content which evolves when the subjective reading reverses into critique and so back and forth between critique and expressive form. 'Mariana' is an exemplary case of this process.

When the full importance of Victorian poetry is recognised, however, it becomes apparent that it need not be discussed either as illustrative material for theory or as a particular case. It surely marks an extraordinarily self-conscious moment of awareness in history. A poetic form and a language were evolved which not only make possible a sophisticated exploration of new categories of knowledge in modern culture but also the philosophical criticism adequate to it. The sense of secondariness with which Victorian poetry comes into being produces the double poem, two poems in one. The double poem, with its systematically ambiguous language, out of which expressive and phenomenological readings emerge, is a structure commensurate with the 'movable type' which Carlyle saw as both the repercussion and the cause of shifts in nineteenth-century culture. The double poem belongs to a post-teleological, post-revolutionary, post-industrial and post-Kantian world and its interrelated manifestations. The double poem signifies a godless, non-teleological world because as soon as two readings become possible and necessary, the permanent and universal categories of the 'type' dissolve. For the 'type' is of course an ancient theological word, meaning those fixed categories of thought and language ordained by God which governed relationships, well before it becomes associated with print. The double reading inevitably dissolves such fixity, just as it means a shift from ontology to epistemology, a shift from investigating the grounds of being to a sceptical interrogation of the grounds of knowledge, which becomes phenomenology, not belief. In a post-revolutionary world in which power is supposedly vested in many rather than a privileged class, the double poem dramatises relationships of power. In the twofold reading, struggle is structurally necessary and becomes the organising principle, as critique successively challenges and redefines critique. Movable type, where technology mobilises the logos, makes the process of signification a political matter as it opens up a struggle for the meaning of words which is part of the relations of power explored through the structures of the poem. Hence the poet's systematic exploration of ambiguity. This reveals not only the confounding complexities of language and the anxieties this generates but boldly establishes that play of possibility in which meaning can be decided. It draws attention to the fact that meaning *is* decided by cultural consensus even while its ambiguity offers the possibility of challenging that consensus through the double reading. The poem of the post-industrial world recognises the displacement of relationships in its structure as well as in its language. The formal ploy in which the uttering subject becomes object and the poem reverses relationships not once but many times indicates that epistemological uneasiness in which subject and object, self and world, are no longer in lucid relation with one another but have to be perpetually redefined. The structure of the double poem emerges from the condition in which self-creation in the world is no longer straightforward but indirect and problematical and in which, as Carlyle said, 'nothing is done directly'. Finally, the double structure inevitably draws attention to the act of interpretation, since one reading encounters another and moves to a new content in the process. Hermeneutic self-consciousness leads in its turn to concentration on the nature of representation, for if interpretation is in question as a construct, so also are the categories of thought it deals with. In a post-Kantian world the double poem becomes a representation of representation, not only secondary historically but a second-order activity in itself. Mariana's poignant utterance is framed as the solipsistic constructions of her world and this reflects back on the complexity of the framing process which presents that self-enclosed utterance. It too cannot be exempted from the second-order status. If one utterance is a representation, so is the other. Both are ideological and both confront one another.

It would not be too much to claim that the genesis of modern form and its *problems* arise in the double poem, just as the possibilities for a criticism which interrogates the nature of the speaking subject and deconstructs the contradictory assumptions of the text are generated out of the double reading. The philosophical premises for a criticism commensurate with this complexity arise in the twentieth century and not in the nineteenth century but they follow from nineteenth-century poetic experiment which, I suggest, is bolder and more self-conscious than most poetry subsequent to it. This is not to argue neatly that Victorian poetry should be studied because it 'produces' and confirms the deconstructive moment and that here we have the 'original' deconstructive form. Rather it should be recognised that the deconstructive moment *is* a historical moment, and that Victorian poetry anticipates its strategies and moves beyond it. For, committed to going through the process of 'movable type', the double poem confronts the scepticism of the deconstructive moment and challenges it. Victorian poems are sceptical and affirmative simultaneously for they compel a strenuous reading and assume an active reader who will participate in the struggle of the lyric voice, a reader with choices to make, choices which are created by the terms of the poem itself. The active reader is compelled to be internal to the poem's contradictions and recomposes the poem's processes in the act of comprehending them as ideological struggle. There is no end to struggle because there is no end to the creative constructs and the renewal of content which its energy brings forth.

Rereading Victorian poetry, then, involves a reconsideration of the way we conceptualise history and culture, and the way we see the politics of poetry. It also involves rethinking some of the major criticism of this century, Marxist and feminist criticism and deconstruction, and considering how the language and form of Victorian poetry question the theories they have developed. Putting the stuffing back into the Victorian sofa then becomes a process of reconstruction which asks living questions.

[. . .]

Notes

1 Michel Foucault makes a critique of continuous 'genetic' history in his foreword to the English edition of *The Order of Things: An Archaeology of the Human Sciences* (1966), London and New York, 1974. 'It was not my intention, on the basis of a particular type of knowledge or body of ideas, to draw up a picture of a period, or to reconstitute the spirit of a century' (x). Such a history ignores 'the implicit philosophies . . . the unformulated thematics . . . the rules of formation' of knowledge which were not always consciously understood by those who were living at the time (xi). 'Archaeology' abandons the notion of 'genesis' and 'progress' and adopts instead a procedure for looking at 'unformulated thematics' which considers 'widely different theories and objects of study' (xi).
2 The Tennyson joke is given to Stephen Daedelus in the 'Proteus' section of *Ulysses* (1922) and Tennyson reappears in 'Circe'. Virginia Woolf's *Orlando: A Biography* (1933) describes the onset of Victorianism as a morbid condition in chapter 5.
3 T. S. Eliot, 'The Metaphysical poets', *Selected Essays*, 3rd edn, London, 1951, 288.
4 Raymond Williams, *Culture and Society, 1780–1950*, London, 1958.

5 The new wave of influential feminist writing on the nineteenth-century novel in the late 1970s is represented by Elaine Showalter, *A Literature of Their Own: British Women Novelists from Bronte to Lessing*, Princeton, N.J., 1977.

6 Illustrative of the preoccupation with Romantic poetry among deconstructionist critics is the collection of essays by Harold Bloom, Paul De Man, Jacques Derrida, Geoffrey Hartman and J. Hillis Miller, *Deconstruction and Criticism*, London, 1979.

7 See 'On some motifs in Baudelaire', *Illuminations* (1955), London, 1973, 157–67.

8 Essay on Shelley (1852), *Robert Browning: The Poems*, John Pettigrew, Thomas J. Collins, eds, 2 vols, New Haven and London, 1981, I, 999–1013: 1001.

9 Substantial biographical work has appeared on Tennyson and Browning. In particular see, for instance, Robert Bernard Martin, *Tennyson, The Unquiet Heart*, London, 1980; William Irvine and Park Honan, *The Book, the Ring, and the Poet,* London, Sydney and Toronto, 1974. John Maynard, *Browning's Youth*, Cambridge, Mass., 1977.

10 Lionel Trilling, *Matthew Arnold*, London, 1939.

11 Foucault, *The Order of Things*, xx. 'Order is, at one and the same time, that which is given in things as their inner law, the hidden network which determines the way they confront one another, and also that which has no existence except by the grid created by a glance, an examination, a language.'

12 Fifteen years after his disparaging comments on Tennyson, T. S. Eliot came to consider *In Memoriam* as a great poem. He described it as a spiritual diary, a description which is also appropriate to *Four Quartets* and its preoccupation with time. *Selected Essays*, 334. Tennysonian echoes in both *The Waste Land* and *Four Quartets* are numerous but it is the poems of nightmare and madness which seem to press closely on Eliot's work. See, for instance, *The Waste Land*, 377–84, and section LXX of *In Memoriam*; and *Four Quartets*, 'Burnt Norton', II. 1–15, and *Maud*, 102–7, 571–98. The allusion to Shelley's *Prometheus Unbound* in Yeats's 'The Second Coming' is familiar. See *Prometheus Unbound*, I. ii. 625–8. Less frequently remarked is the inversion of the ending of Tennyson's 'The Kraken' in 'The Second Coming'. Tennyson's barely sentient monster dies a violent death on the surface of the sea in apocalyptic upheaval. Yeats's 'rough beast' stumbles towards a violent, apocalyptic birth at the end of his poem.

13 Matthew Arnold's inaugural lecture as Professor of Poetry at Oxford was entitled 'On the modern element in literature' and published in *Macmillan's Magazine*, 1869. George Meredith's *Modern Love* was published in 1862, two years before William Allingham's *Laurence Bloomfield in Ireland, A Modern Poem*, 1864, reissued in 1869 and subtitled *Or, the New Landlord*.

14 Harold Bloom's work on the Victorians and their predecessor poets is mainly collected in *Poetry and Repression*, New Haven and London, 1976.

15 Lytton Strachey, *Eminent Victorians*, London, 1918, is the notorious spokesman of this view.

16 G. M. Hopkins believed that the looseness of the language of nineteenth-century poetry reflected the lax relativism of the age, which he describes in some of his earliest writings. 'The probable future of metaphysics', *The Journals and Papers of Gerard Manley Hopkins*, Humphrey House, Graham Strong, eds, London, 1959, 118–21.

17 Arnold's brilliant but limited diagnosis of modernity and its problems appears in the Preface to his *Poems* of 1853, in which he explained his reasons for withdrawing that modern poem, *Empedocles on Etna* (1852), from his volume: 'the dialogue of the mind with itself has commenced; modern problems have presented themselves'. *The Poems of Matthew Arnold* (Longman Annotated English Poets), Kenneth Allott, ed., London, 1965, 591.

18 Nietzsche quotes Schopenhauer's account of lyric critically in *The Birth of Tragedy*: 'It is the subject of the will, i.e. his own volition, which fills the consciousness of the singer, often as a released and satisfied desire (joy), but still oftener as an inhibited desire (grief), always as an affect, a passion, a moved state of mind . . . the stress of desire, which is always restricted and always needy'. *The Birth of Tragedy* (1872), trans. Walter Kaufmann, New York, 1967, 51.

19 Both W. J. Fox and A. H. Hallam conducted sophisticated analyses of Tennyson's early poems in terms of drama. See *Victorian Scrutinies: Reviews of Poetry 1830–70*, Isobel Armstrong, ed., London, 1972, 75–9, 99–101.

20 Mikhail Bakhtin, *The Dialogic Imagination: Four Essays*, ed. Michael Holquist, trans. Caryl Emerson and Michael Holquist, Austin, Texas, 1981. Bakhtin's dialogic form is not quite the same thing as Volosinov's struggle for the sign and I prefer to keep the two names separate rather than viewing them as two names for the same person. Bakhtin writes of the literary text, whereas

Volosinov's interest is in challenging post-Sausserean linguistics. Bakhtin's dialogic form is oppositional and depends on the reversal of fixed positions, whereas Volosinov's struggle for the sign is a dynamic on-going process in which contending ideologies constantly redefine the content of the sign. Neither believed that poetry could generate dialogic structures or that poetic texts could participate in struggle. Manifestly, however, the Victorian double poem generates the drama of contending principles. I prefer the model of linguistic struggle rather than dialogism because the nature of language is crucial to Volosinov's thought (whereas it is not to Bakhtin's) and his model seems particularly appropriate to *poetic* forms, where the complexity of language is foregrounded. Moreover, the model of struggle leads to perpetual redefinition in a way which the dialogic form does not. Volosinov's ideas, however, require far more rigorous development than they can be given in a book of this kind. That is why I have placed this discussion of Victorian poetry in a general post-Hegelian tradition, to which, of course, both Marx and Volosinov belong.

2 The fix of form

An open letter

Herbert F. Tucker

Charlottesville
Fin de siècle XX

O thou that after toil and storm
  Mayst seem to have reached a purer air,
  Whose faith has centre everywhere,
Nor cares to fix itself to form,
  or—as the undersigned trusts to find you still—

Dear Reader,

There was a time when the New Criticism taught you to pay attention to literary form as the embodied elaboration of meaning. You knew that authors had a design on you, but you learned to bracket questions of intention and affect so as to concentrate on the design itself, where creative purpose got built out in verbal deed. You dealt, by and large, with the concrete particular, anatomizing complexities for the sake of an analytically earned appreciation of distinct instances of formal unity. While every instance was unique, what you found to say about the unity of this poem or that novel did evince a family resemblance among literary works, and among critical interpretations, that linked them to each other and, presumably, to a family of wholesome universals. Or did it just seem to? If you couldn't be sure then, and can't be sure now either, that's because these larger issues were somehow off in the background and beside the point, which was to practice criticism as a cognition of integral form.

Then the background swam up and swallowed the point, or nearly: a New Theory called all in doubt. The presuppositions that grounded the interpretation of literary texts suddenly demanded a scrutiny no less intense than you had lately bestowed on the texts themselves. For that matter, you learned to wonder whether "texts themselves" had any ontological status not conferred on them by arbitrary means of framing the aesthetic object, and whether those very means were not just as "textual"—did not need analytic interpretation—as much as the object they framed. Your critical formalism now looked liked small fry next to the big game of theory, arresting and interrogating the forces that produced forms for inspection in the first place. Intervening in the hitherto little theorized practices of literary-critical appreciation, philosophical aesthetics did to your customary close reading what philosophy has always done to custom: it charged custom to account for itself on better grounds than mere disciplinary habit or self-justifying result. You found it heady work complying with the new regime: high stakes and windswept exposures—with great views—but by the same token a little dry. If you noticed *en passant* some sameness in the readings theory tended to produce, that was because the general pursuit of signs as constitutive semiotic forces had a way of postponing, perhaps indefinitely, the diversifying effects that might come with scrutiny of actually constituted forms and contents. When you did attend to these, in off hours, you tasted a pleasure that wasn't guilty exactly but was no longer innocent either.

Is that why you jumped at the New Historicism and the chance it offered to replenish literary interpretation with grain and heft? The historicist movement struck you at the time, to be sure, as progress rather than return. The reclamation of historical reference seemed to be not so much lifting theory's embargo on the signified as fulfilling and vindicating it; the always implicit politics of theory were emerging at last, and at the most prestigious levels of interpretation too, from contemplative debate to something more like practical activism. For if literary theory had pushed critical inquiry back from form to force, then New Historicism showed you how to supply that force with a local habitation and a name, and moreover how to do things with it like break or shape a canon, reward neglected merit, promote an urgent cause. The world rushed back into the text that theory had lately evacuated; or, as you started more ambitiously to put it, the "text" under analysis proved to *be* the world, through an inside-outing of literature and its determinants that showed you how the elements of what an old historicism had called "context" were forces that had always already dwelt or circulated within textual forms. Dense with event and astir with motive, the world-historical scene became the object of your interpretation, which took the shape of as thick a description as you could manage.

How you managed was chiefly by cultivating an eye or ear—was it a sixth sense?—for isomorphic correspondences among the materials you studied. You assembled your world-historical scenery out of structural configurations (phrasal or rhetorical, perspectival or hierarchical) that yoked together artifacts spanning a range of venues: a play, a map, and a census; a catalogue, a statute, and a novel. The work felt politically significant, but it also felt like fun; and one source of the fun, you realized, was that you got to rehearse in a brand-new way the old skills you had honed as a textual formalist. Nobody was about to confuse your New-Historicist analysis of hegemonically interlocked ideologemes with your New-Critical appreciation of verbal iconicity; and yet, viewed from the structural point of view that both forms of analysis shared, the two had a lot in common. You were discerning patterns of formal unity all over again, only now the materials you operated with arose from a vaster historical pageantry than you had formerly dreamed of, and they resonated with nothing less than the immense complex of culture itself. To analyze that great system—tense to the point of paradox with the forces that braced it up and the stresses that wrought forth its changes—was a challenge you could no more decline than be equal to. Interdisciplinary practically by definition, the mission of culture analysis led you well out of your depth and far afield from your literary training; but you beat back vertigo and nostalgia with the theory-borne conviction that disciplinary fences were, if not down, then renegotiable to the point of flimsiness. Accordingly, you seasoned your interdisciplinary arguments with reminders about the vexed and contingent cultural history of the disciplines whereby normative "cultural history" had been produced. One day it occurred to you how slender a margin distinguished the kind of historical pattern-recognition you were now learning to practice from the kind of speculative guide to contemporary life that you found academicians of today and prophets of tomorrow publishing on every hand. If their Cultural Studies was in essence a New History of the present, what did you have to lose by saying that you did Cultural Studies too?

Well, something maybe. Wondering about that something, you went back to the structural likeness you had remarked between cultural historicism and critical formalism as fundamentally holistic modes of interpretation. Each mode in its day trained on its object the skills of what you called the Higher Matching: correspondences among specific data, and then among increasingly aggregated systems of data, were made to manifest with as full a suggestiveness as possible the shape and tendency of the inexhaustible whole to which the data belonged and referred. (There you were at your Higher Matching again, noting correspondences between schools of correspondence-notation.) The difference in modes was an affair of scale, nay entire orders of magnitude, as interpretation zoomed out from the consideration of a whole poem to that of a whole culture. And there lay the trouble: where the quantitative shift in focus was so enormous, you had to worry lest it entail a qualitative change in attentiveness. You welcomed, on the whole, the radical enlargement of vista that came with Cultural Studies to quicken the novice, rejuvenate the old hand, and make scholarship matter to the world. Great, yes, *on the whole.* But what about the *part*? Wasn't substantial signifier-inflation going to be virtually inevitable, the very bigness of the cultural signified obliging you to base inter-pretation on proportionately big themes and historical categories of the kind that textbooks scooped up from research subcontractors at discount and printed in large boldface type? The ambiguous trope, the ingredient *mot juste*, the play of ironic tone and curve of prosodic form, the constituent verbal body of sense: would these even count as quarry, under the *de facto* rules of the new big game? The panoramic scope of Cultural Studies might well make such detailed textual signifiers, no matter how much respect they garnered in principle, compara-tively invisible, and therefore functionally *insignificant.* Maybe you did have something to lose, then: the endangered constituency of literary forms as exceptionally nuanced cultural artifacts. And who was to represent that constituency, if not you who remembered how to notice such things?

Could this, Dear Reader, mean you? Is this tale of toil and storm any concern of yours? Let Tennyson have another try:

> O thou that after toil and storm
> > Mayst seem to have reached a purer air,
> > Whose faith has centre everywhere,
> Nor cares to fix itself to form. . . .

Feeling interpellated? Probably not. Section 33 of *In Memoriam*, which this passage opens, is a scold of a lyric easy to despise on numerous accounts: patronizing sexism, self-righteous-ness, and a bad blend of unction with complacency, all epitomized in the contrast it goes on to draw between the adventurous *thou* hailed here and his good little sister: "Her faith thro' form is pure as thine." Poor prospects, admittedly, for the calling of an evangelizing neoformalist. Still, if there is any new fetch at all in the old stanza, it's likely to lurk in the repeated concern with "faith," "form," and the unstable relation between them.

What would it take for Tennyson's outmoded summons to make a claim on you now? It might take, first, your conceding that it did make such claims once: an ample paper-trail of Victorian testimony establishes that *In Memoriam* spoke directly to thousands for years. But this by itself would be a tourist's concession rather than a pilgrim's. In order to become an engaged critic of the passage, and not just its disinterested scholar, you would have to observe that in its substance Tennyson's apostrophe to the reader is all about what interpel-lation in modern society is all about: namely, how the liberal subject learns to dispense its budget of attention across a diffuse and relativized field of competing options. Come to think of it, Tennyson's "faith," here as across the entire poem, denotes something not much like dogma but a lot like what you would call *ideology*: a belief system definitively decentered (or, same difference, centered "everywhere") and indeterminate (unfixed "to form"). Wouldn't the stanza exert some pull on you if it proved to describe, not commitment, but rather an orientation toward commitment, halfway between affirmative open-mindedness and allergic negativity? The stanza hails a free spirit, a quintessentially liberal soul not unfamiliar in our time but whose cultural coordinates you could go back and plot on the reformist and consumerist axes of Victorian political economy—one part spiritual refugee jealous of a hard-won freedom, one part shopper having a good look around. The disposition *not* to fix on a form of faith was shaping up in the early Victorian decades as an ideology unto itself, a free-form cultural formation already recognizable in Tennyson's day. Suppose the stanza turned out to appeal to the choice that modern subjects make to safeguard choice, to remain cool customers in the faith market. Would it then appeal to you? Would you have the ears to hear?

If you literally did—if having found a personal ideological stake in the content of the stanza you repaid its interest by *listening*—then you might surprise yourself into a neoformalism that, despite long odds, Cultural Studies could yet put to use. Much of what you heard in the stanza would serve to reinforce what the analysis of content had previously given you; and this supportive redundancy would be as welcome to Cultural Studies as to any hermeneutic practice. For example: a convalescent care to avoid overstimulation "after toil and storm" emerges through the bland assonance of stressed syllables within the last two lines—staid short *e* in the main ("center," "everywhere," "cares," "itself"), with a nod toward neighbors on either side of the vocalic spectrum (long *a* in "faith," short *i* in "fix"). Furthermore, in metrical terms the regulation iambics of these lines spell out, with rhythmic prudence, much the same homogeneity of affect that dwells in the homophony of the vowels. Valetudinarian strokes for latitudinarian folks, the lines render the sandblasted affect of a Broad Church communicant who neither feels very much faith nor, all told, "cares to." The physical soundings of the verse thus remind you that apathy is feeling, and indeed a kind of feeling to which modern ideology has more than once since Tennyson's time assiduously beamed its blandishments.

The stanza can produce this culturally coded numbness so effectively only because it has done something else first, something which is inaccessible to merely thematic analysis but which neoformalism is ideally suited to open up. For the vocal-rhythmical humdrum of lines 3 and 4 is an effect that lines 1 and 2 have set off. Having established his iambic norm in the first line, Tennyson proceeds to vary it in the second with fine ironic finesse: "Mayst seem to have reached a purer air." The second metrical foot, "to have reached," is the strategic stumbling block here, and once you trip on it you fall into some fancy footwork that is ultimately ideological in nature. To begin with, it takes you longer than it should to reach "reached": in a sense your late arrival ratifies that toilsome and stormy struggle from line 1, but in another sense the vowel chime that "reached" makes with "seem" makes you suspect that agnostic poise may be a less stable position than it seems. After all, the poet could have written "Hast reached at last," or even "Mayst seem to reach"; the slightly needling metrical imperfection of what he did write unbalances the stance of the man who, if he believes nothing else, believes that he has come through into the perfect tense.

One extra syllable is the problem, which you can resolve by scanning the second foot as either an anapest or a rather heavy-breathing elided iambic. The choice is free between these two scansions, but each has strings attached. For, whichever scansional form you fix yourself to, the choice involves a crux of pronunciation, of accent and arguably of class-bound dialect, that resumes at the level of phonology something rather like what the whole stanza is about. Would you aspirate the aitch in "have" (to mark the anapest) or not (to oil the elision)? Would Tennyson? Would his Lincolnshire neighbor the Northern Farmer? Would his dead friend from Cambridge, the subject of *In Memoriam A. H. H.*, the man Sam Weller and his Cockney cronies would presumably have called Harthur Allam? Get a set of Victorians to say line 2, and by their aspirations you will know them. To audition these possible speakers and their diverse subcultural allegiances is to hear the spirit of the age in a puff of breath, ventilating for a prosodically amplified moment questions of class and region that articulated nineteenth-century Britain's changing conception of itself.

One more invisible detail and then farewell. You know how the primary objects of Victorian liberal reform were to secularize the state and extend the franchise, and how each step in these reforms was at once the result and the further instrument of a national identity in the making. This identity had a linguistic analogue in the standardization of the Queen's English: a hyperglot, ostensibly transregional medium of denomination and exchange for which, were you an aspiring Poet Laureate circa 1850, you would cherish special regard—and for which, were you an aspiring Cultural Neoformalist circa 2000, you might find a trope right here in this stanza: "purer air." The phrase looks nice on the page but, coming on the heels of that shibboleth second foot, proves delicately embarrassing to say aloud. The risk lies in running all those *rs* together: if you don't want to stutter your way through them in Northern burr, or stammer along in Western brogue or transatlantic twang, then you must insert a glottal stop between "purer" and "air." But what a perverse place for it! Could anything be more mischievous than a glottal stop in the very flow of breath that utters "purer air"? Tennyson invites you to choke on your own tongue, your own proper Queen's English—or whatever its contemporary equivalent may be in metropolitan cultural capital—and thereby puts into all but subliminally intimate question the secular state and liberal society for which *In Memoriam* made such suave apology that you now take it for granted. If the words stick in your throat, that's because the values they stood for stuck in Tennyson's at a time when, in order to publish his national testament of a poem, he had to stifle a tempest of private doubt. A Poet Laureate's gag if ever there was one.

So are we doing Cultural Studies yet? Let's fix ourselves to form and try again.

Yours in vocative case,

Herbert F. Tucker
University of Virginia

3   Physiological poetics; Patmore, Hopkins, and the uncertain body of Victorian poetry

Jason R. Rudy

O for a Life of Sensations rather than of Thoughts!
—John Keats, letter to Benjamin Bailey (1817)

Man acts by electricity.
—Alfred Smee, *Instinct and Reason: Deduced from Electro-biology* (1850)

Nearly five hundred years separate the Florentine poet Angelo Poliziano from the American Charles Olsen [*sic*], but the two agree in their understanding of poetry as a dynamic, charged mode of communication. Echoing Plato, Poliziano describes poetry as working like a magnetic stone, exerting its "hidden force" on readers; for Olsen, poetry "is energy transferred from where the poet got it . . . by way of the poem itself to, all the way over to, the reader" ([. . .] Poliziano, 125; Olsen, 240).[1] The discerning reader confronts in both Poliziano and Olsen two possible—and somewhat contradictory—directives for poetic experience. The first treats literature figuratively and understands poetry to be *like* a magnet, *like* the transfer of energy. The experience of reading poetry in this model remains primarily an intellectual endeavor; the individual who picks up Tennyson's *In Memoriam*, for example, feels the tug of strong emotion because she has thought strongly about Tennyson's words and the ideas and feelings they represent. The energy transferred from poem to reader occurs here through the medium of the thinking brain. Not so for the second model of poetic experience, which erases the distance between the poem and the reader and understands poetry quite literally *as* magnetic, a direct transfer of energy. In this instance, the reader of *In Memoriam* feels Tennyson's charge of thought/feeling as it moves—magnetically, electrically—from page to body. The reader remains mostly unconscious of the transference of energy; she experiences the poem viscerally, intimately, bodily. This second model of poetic experience, which locates the body as central to the individual's encounter with a poem, rests at the heart of *Electric Meters*. This book tells the history of physiological poetics in the British nineteenth century, focusing on the period between 1832 and 1872 as the height of Britain's poetic engagement with bodily modes of experience.

Indeed, the history of Victorian poetry is in no small part a history of the human body. Whether we look to Alfred Tennyson's "poetics of sensation," the midcentury "Spasmodic" phenomenon, or the so-called fleshly school of the 1870s, Victorian poetry demands to be read as physiologically inspired: rhythms that pulse in the body, a rhetoric of sensation that readers might feel compelled to experience. Like Poliziano and Olsen, Victorian poets turned to various manifestations of electricity—lightning strikes, electric shocks, nerve impulses, telegraph signals—to articulate the work of physiological poetics. The electrical sciences and bodily poetics, I argue, cannot be separated, and they came together with especial force in the years between the 1830s, which witnessed the invention of the electric telegraph, and the 1870s, when James Clerk Maxwell's electric field theory transformed the study of electrodynamics. Because much of nineteenth-century electrical theory had to do with human bodies, and specifically with the ways that individual human bodies might be connected to one another, electricity offered Victorian poets a figure for thinking through the effects of poetry on communities of readers. Electricity, in other words, serves in the nineteenth century as a tool for exploring poetry's political consequences. Scholars have long identified the political work of Victorian poetry, just as they have recognized the astonishing physicality of Victorian poetics.[2] *Electric Meters* insists that these phenomena be understood as two sides of the same coin, and it uses electricity as a model for reading that aesthetic and physiological conjunction.

More specifically, I argue that Victorian readers understood the connections between bodily and poetic experience in ways that took more seriously the unself-conscious effects of poetic form. "Physiological poetics" thus refers to the metrical, rhythmic, and sonic effects that, along with other formal poetic features, were increasingly imagined as carrying physiological truths. Whereas the predominant eighteenth-century model of poetic transmission privileged the mind's interpretive role (the brain acting as mediator between the poem and the individual), nineteenth-century readers gave credit to the body as an arbiter of poetic truths. Whether one ought to read Poliziano and Olsen figuratively or literally, then, depends on the period in which one encounters their texts. Readers prior to the physiological trends of the Victorian period were more likely to opt for figuration, to understand a poem's semantic presence but not its mimetic facility. In contrast, the Victorian poets and critics at the center of this study err on the side of the literal: the poem is itself a magnetic force, "a high energy-construct" (Olsen, 240).

Poetry and electricity

[. . .]

Electricity has long been a privileged figure for those describing the ineffable qualities that make poetry *poetic*. Percy Shelley tells us that poetry "startle[s]" with "the electric life which burns within . . . words," and this electric life is precisely what enables poetry, in Shelley's view, to rejuvenate language and thought (Shelley, 7:140). This figurative yoking of electricity and poetry articulates some of the most pressing concerns of nineteenth-century poetic theory. Newly harnessed as a tool of industry, science, and communication (the electric telegraph being the most important of electricity's new uses), electricity serves as a touchstone for nineteenth-century poets reflecting on the complex interactions of thought, emotion, and physiological experience. From the earliest electrical experiments, electricity has been depicted as having physiological and noncognitive effects on those who encounter it (the shock of an electric current, say), and poets throughout history have turned to the same language of bodily shock in describing "lyrical" experience. "[L]ike a lightning flash," writes Longinus, "[the sublime] reveals, at a stroke and in its entirety, the power of the orator"; Longinus's primary example of such sublime power is the poetry of Sappho, which "gather[s] soul and body into one, hearing and tongue, eyes and complexion; all dispersed and strangers before" (Longinus, 23–24). Through the "shock" of a felicitously placed word, a compelling linguistic friction, or a moving rhythmic pressure, poetry transmits, lightning-like, new truths to its readers.

[. . . I]n different ways, Mary Robinson, Felicia Hemans, Alfred Tennyson, Elizabeth Barrett Browning, Gerard Manley Hopkins, Algernon Swinburne, and Mathilde Blind look to electricity to make sense of poetry's effects on the human body, distinguishing themselves from their predecessors in their overriding concern with physicality, with the material human body through which we experience poetry. Yet this physicality must be read within a larger political framework for nineteenth-century poetry and poetic theory. Whitman's "body electric" is only the most familiar of nineteenth-century poetic elisions between physiology and electricity, elisions that ask us to think about affinities between bodily affect and poetic communication, between physiological shock and intellectual absorption, and between individual experience and communal consciousness.

[. . .]

The following chapters foreground [. . .] intersections of poetry, physiology, and the electrical sciences, suggesting how "physiological poetics" both depend on and enhance the phenomenon I call "electric meters," the complex interplay of poetic form and electrical epistemologies (ideas or structures of thought inspired by the work of electricity).

In focusing on the interplay of physiology and electricity, I remain true to scientific history. The human body is very much at the heart of the earliest electrical experiments, and it was often by means of their own bodies that scientists, from roughly the 1740s on, came to understand the nature of electric charges (Delbourgo, 25–30). I want to emphasize from the outset the distance in these experimental moments between bodily feeling (experiencing the electric shock) and thoughtful engagement with scientific ideas (thinking through electrical theories, hypotheses, and physical laws). Electricity becomes a compelling literary figure in part due to the gap between physiological experience and mental cognition. Consider, for example, the language Benjamin Franklin uses to describe an electrical shock, an accident that occurred during an experiment in 1750: "It seem'd an universal Blow from head to foot throughout the Body, and followed by a violent quick Trembling in the Trunk, which went gradually off in a few seconds. It was some Minutes before I could collect my Thoughts so as to know what was the Matter. . . . My Arms and Back of my Neck felt somewhat numb the remainder of the Evening, and my Breast-bone was sore for a Week after, as if it had been bruised" (letter to William Watson, 4 February 1750; quoted in Cohen, 94). Franklin does not lose consciousness from the shock, but at the moment of electrification his physical body takes center stage, fully pushing his active mind to the wings. Only after "some Minutes" can Franklin "collect [his] Thoughts" as he gradually awakens from his stupor, the point at which he becomes conscious of what happened. Franklin's physiological experience makes apparent the truth of electricity's vast power, yet only subsequently is Franklin's brain able to perceive the truth of his experience; the electric shock imposes a temporal gap between experience and cognition.

Franklin's mishap was accidental, but attempts to make sense of electrical shocks and their noncognitive effects on the human body were surprisingly common in the mid-1700s. Perhaps the most infamous of these experiments transpired in 1746, when Jean-Antoine Nollet, a French scientist who was soon to become the foremost European expert on electricity, amassed a circle of nearly two hundred Carthusian monks, each linked to his neighbors by a twenty-five-foot line of iron wire. When Nollet connected the ends of the wires to a rudimentary electric battery, a great communal spasm among the monks offered spectators one of the most important scenes in eighteenth-century science. "It is singular," wrote Nollet after the experiment, "to see the multitude of different gestures, and to hear the instantaneous exclamation of those surprised by the shock" (quoted in Heilbron, 312).[3] Like the temporal lapse between Franklin's physiological experience of the electric shock and his conscious realization of what had happened, Nollet here achieves knowledge only subsequent to and at a distance from the violent, noncognitive physiological experiences of the Carthusian monks. Nollet's experiment both demonstrates the communicative potential in electricity (the circuit of electrified monks might be thought of as leading ultimately to the development of the electric telegraph in the 1830s) and suggests the necessarily physiological nature of such communication.

Nollet's and Franklin's experiments also resonate with a mounting interest in the physiology of poetic experience. Writing in 1757, Edmund Burke frames his discussion of *Paradise Lost* with language that echoes, and seems to make use of, contemporary electrical science: "The mind" of Milton's reader "is hurried out of itself, by a cro[w]d of great and confused images" (Burke 1968, 62). Poetry communicates not by conscious thought but "by the contagion of our passions" (175). Those genuinely affected by poetry experience emotional shocks that, in their disjunction from conscious thought, seem not unlike the electric pulses enjoyed by Nollet's monks. "If the affection be well conveyed," Burke concludes, "it will work its effect without any clear idea; often without any idea at all of the thing which has originally given rise to it" (176). Burke's language looks forward to the poetics of sensibility that soon would dominate eighteenth-century aesthetics, imagining poetry as affective experience transmitted, via spoken language, from composing poet to reading individual. My point here is not to suggest that eighteenth-century science makes the physiology of poetic experience suddenly visible. Poetry has always, in various ways, been associated with bodily experience, from Longinus's exhortations on Sappho's sublimity, to Poliziano's magnetic attachments, to the "heavenly harmony" celebrated in Dryden's 1687 "Song for St. Cecilia's Day." But there can be little doubt that the poetics of sensibility push physiology to the foreground of poetic theory in new and increasingly demonstrative ways, setting the scene for the Victorians' all-out engagement with a poetics of the body. We witness this attention to physiology in reading John Stuart Mill's 1833 assertion that poetry represents "thoughts and words in which emotion spontaneously embodies itself"; poets, he concludes, are "[t]hose who are so constituted, that emotions are links of association by which their ideas, both sensuous and spiritual, are connected together" (Mill, 1:356). Across the nineteenth century, poets and literary critics grappled with this notion of embodied lyricism, from Arthur Hallam's poetics of sensation in 1831 to Robert Buchanan's 1871 critique of the "fleshly" school of poetry. In the many permutations of these thoughts, poetry remains a bodily experience, felt like an electric shock through and through.

It is as physiological experience that poetry facilitates the "association"—in Mill's words, which intentionally reference the associationist tradition of Locke, Hume, Hartley, and others—of "ideas . . . sensuous and spiritual." The very qualities of associationist philosophy that made Coleridge wince—that is, its privileging of the "primary sensations" and its skepticism of "an infinite spirit . . . an intelligent and holy will" (Coleridge, 75)—were for Mill and many of his Victorian peers fundamental to poetic practice in its ideal form.[4] This ideal remains in circulation today: for example, with Barbara Hardy's suggestion that lyric poetry "does not provide an explanation, judgment or narrative; what it does provide is feeling, alone and without histories or characters" (Hardy 1977, 1), and Susan Stewart's description of lyric creation as "the transformation of sense experience into words" (Stewart, 26). The continuity among these writers rests in their understanding of poetry as physiological and essentially noncognitive. Within this mode of poetic interpretation, a mode that came to dominate poetic practice in the nineteenth century, electricity most powerfully stands as a figure for poetic experience. But electricity is not simply a trope used to describe or to elaborate a poetic function. In the nineteenth century, electricity was the most prominent figure for a more widespread and pervasive interest in communication, from William Cooke and Charles Wheatstone's invention of the electric telegraph to Alexander Bain's analysis of nerve impulses in the human body. The nineteenth century, as John Durham Peters has argued, "saw unprecedented transformations in the conditions of human contact," which played out through new technologies for transmitting and recording information (Peters, 138).

[. . .]

Like nerve impulses that seem universal in their experience, the rhythmic pulsing of electric meters inspired poets to consider how, or whether, language might be reconfigured to vibrate in tune with all human individuals. Nineteenth-century poets looked to electricity in anticipation of a language that might render indistinct the boundaries between sound and sense, between emotion and thought, and—perhaps—between individuals isolated in the modern world. Keats's early call for "a Life of Sensations rather than of Thoughts!" echoes throughout the century as a fantasy of interpersonal connection and communication. *Electric Meters* examines the enthusiasms and, ultimately, the frustrations inspired by this utopian project.

[. . .]

Patmore, Hopkins, and the uncertain body

[. . .]

I wish to suggest that electricity was an especially helpful figure for [Gerard Manley] Hopkins in negotiating what he saw to be an uneasy relationship between the material and the spiritual worlds. In a series of notes taken in 1868, for example, he writes of words expressing mental ideas by means of a "physical" and "refined energy accenting the nerves" (Hopkins 1959, 125). Words in Hopkins's view are physical things, and they effect change by "accenting the nerves" with their "energy." Rhythm facilitates this connection, with the "accenting" of stress ideally embodying the nature of the word's referent (M. Campbell, 191); Hopkins's terms *inscape* and *instress*, among others, work in different ways to describe this phenomenon. That said, Hopkins remained wary of a simple one-to-one or deterministic relationship between a word and its physiological experience. As he writes in an undergraduate essay, "The Probable Future of Metaphysics" (1867), "it is all to no purpose to show an organ for each faculty and a nerve vibrating for each idea, because this only shows in the last detail what broadly no one doubted, to wit that the activities of the spirit are conveyed in those of the body" (Hopkins 1959, 118). Electricity appeals to Hopkins insofar as he views it as both concrete physical communication—words "accenting the nerves"—and as a sign of "the spirit" as it moves through the body. The challenge as Hopkins sees it is to develop a poetics that reflects this double nature, avoiding a deterministic model for an individual's encounter with language and instead opening poetry to experiences both earthly and transcendent. As Armstrong puts it, a poem for Hopkins "must fuse thinking and feeling or, if possible, thought and sensation in an irreducibly concrete configuration of particulars seized as epiphany and oneness" (Armstrong 982, 15). Electricity is Hopkins's figurative vehicle for this fusion, the work of poetic embodiment.

Let us then consider the opening stanza of Hopkins's "Wreck of the Deutschland" (1875–76), the poet's first full-out experiment with sprung rhythm:

> Thou mastering me
>   God! giver of breath and bread;
> Wórld's stránd, swáy of the séa;
>   Lord of living and dead;
> Thou hast bóund bónes and véins in me, fástened me flésh,
> And áfter it álmost únmade, what with dréad,
>   Thy doing: and dost thou touch me afresh?
> Óver agáin I féel thy fínger and find thée.
> (GMH, 119, lines 1–8)[5]

In terms of its substance, the passage depicts the speaker's questioning engagement with the Christian deity. Ostensibly an elegy on the death of five nuns aboard a foundered ship, Hopkins's poem is more significantly an inquiry into the pain of existence on the one hand and the sensuousness of bodily life on the other. The poem "seeks to clarify," as Julia Saville puts it, "in terms of a long-standing Catholic hermeneutic tradition, the meaning of intense suffering" (Saville, 63), while at the same time acknowledging what Norman White calls the "sensuous pleasure about martyrdom" (White, 252).[6] That it is also an explicit challenge to Victorian prosody almost goes without saying. Consider first the distance between Hopkins's depiction of touch and the hesitant, largely figurative touching of Felicia Hemans's poetry. [. . .] Hemans imagines a kind of physiological touching in "The Lyre's Lament"—and many other poems—but the lyric ultimately fails to make that touch a literal act. Elizabeth Barrett Browning makes a similar gesture toward physicality in *Aurora Leigh* when she celebrates poetry's "divine first finger-touch" (EBB, 4, book I, line 851), but this too remains almost exclusively a figurative endeavor. Aurora experiences feeling and transmits that feeling to her readers; she "touches" us emotionally. Her poetry, though identified as Spasmodic by Aytoun (Aytoun 1857, 40), avoids the sheer physicality that would allow readers literally to feel her touch. Hopkins gives us no choice: "I féel thy fínger and find thée" instructs us precisely how to feel, both through its alliteration and the accompanying stress marks. If the speaker is touched "afresh," so too is the reader of the stanza; Hopkins's intent is to bring together these different modes of touching (rhythmic, physiological, spiritual), such that the speaker's experience of touch becomes the reader's experience of the poem.[7]

"The Wreck of the Deutschland" ultimately proposes two kinds of poetic touching—one destructive, the other healing—and it imagines electricity as a figure for each. The more violent form of electricity emerges in the second stanza, when the "fire of stress" (GMH, 119, line 16) comes to the speaker through "líghtning and láshed ród":

>   I did say yes
>   O at líghtning and láshed ród;
> Thou heardst me, truer than tongue, confess
>   Thy terror, O Christ, O God
>
>   (lines 9–12)

Though in real life it was a snowstorm that caused the *Deutschland* to run aground, stranding the passengers near the mouth of the Thames, Hopkins returns throughout the poem to the image of lightning, violent and frightful. Hopkins "confess[es]" here to his "terror" at what he takes to be the manifest power of the Christian deity, a terror that coincides with the strong stresses of "líghtning and láshed ród": lightning, stress, and sublime terror synthesized in poetic form.[8] Hopkins turns again to lightning to account for a shipwreck in "The Loss of the Eurydice," a poem dated April 1878 in which a sudden storm strikes "deadly-electric" (GMH, 150, line 24).[9] Lightning breaches, in Hopkins's view, the gap separating the spiritual from the physical; it is literally a moment of connection between the heavens and the earth, much as sprung rhythm is meant to connect the physical and the metaphysical. But it is a terrifying form of synthesis, suggesting an Old Testament view of religion—a vengeful deity, a suffering humankind—that Hopkins, as the rest of "The Wreck of the Deutschland" shows, was eager to reject.

Brilliant as it appears at the poem's opening, then, lightning ultimately plays a dubious role in the theological argument of Hopkins's poem. As editor Norman H. Mackenzie shows, the end of the poem posits "a new era in which Christ . . . will blaze resplendent on the world," in a notably peaceful—not turbulent and lightning-wielding—manner (GMH, 348). This is especially apparent in the penultimate stanza 34:

> Not a dóomsday dázzle in his cóming nor dárk as he cáme;
>   Kínd, but róyally recláiming his ówn;
> A released shówer, let flásh to the shíre, not a líghtning of fíre
>   hard húrled.
>   (GMH, 128, lines 270–72)

The "lightning and láshed ród" of stanza 2 are here replaced by a more gentle shower, as in the Christian Bible: "He shall come down like rain upon the fleece; and as showers falling gently upon the earth" (Psalm 72:6). Not "electrical-horror" (GMH, 126, line 213), then, but a different kind of fire; a dispersed electrical "flásh" takes the place of a more pointed and violent bolt of electricity. This is the gentle, "[k]índ" deity of the New Testament, a soothing and paternal figure of light. Hopkins seems torn between the sublimity of the lightning strike—the power of the all-encompassing experience—and the comforting beauty of the electrical shower; he desires the strength of the former but settles, ultimately, on the promise of the latter. Sprung rhythm, ideally, is not like a lightning bolt that destroys, but rather a rain of fire that encompasses, or resonates with, all it touches; stress, as Hopkins puts it, "is the bringing out of . . . nature," not the destruction of it.

This ideal persists throughout Hopkins's work. "The world is charged wíth the grándeur of God," declares a sonnet of 1877; "It will flame out, like shining from shook foil" ("God's Grandeur"; GMH, 139). Hopkins at one point revised "shining" to "lightning," but at the urging of his friend Robert Bridges, he decided to keep the original (GMH, 361). According to Nixon, Hopkins imagines the "electromagnetic energy" of "God's Grandeur" as a form of divine "seminal fluid," energy that "flows from God" (Nixon, 144). Electricity, vitality, and poetic stress thus merge as one. "All things," Hopkins writes in his sermon 195, "are charged with God and if [but only if?] we know how to touch them give off sparks and take fire, yield drops and flow" (quoted in GMH, 362). In his letters to Patmore, Hopkins writes of his belief in a "moulding force" present in all life, a vital and internal energy that manifests—in poetry, but also in the natural world—as "outward beauty" and "proportion" (Hopkins 1956, 306–7). [. . .] The "charge" that Hopkins believes integral to the best poetry is ultimately expressed through rhythm—a physical force that "fuse[s]" experience with language. "Like a charge of electricity," Isobel Armstrong notes, stress for Hopkins "brings together and fuses the material and the non-material, spirit and sense, form and matter" (Armstrong 1993, 422). In this, Hopkins sympathizes more with Sydney Dobell than with Patmore. There are important connections, for example, between Hopkins's notion of instress and Dobell's suggestion that poetry "is actually in tune with our material flesh and blood," that it embodies "certain modes of verbal *motion* . . . certain *rhythms* and measures [that] are metaphors of ideas and feelings" (Dobell 1876, 22, 25). Hopkins also follows Dobell in believing poetry and religious affect to be similar in nature. As Emma Mason has shown, Dobell finds poetry to be "religious" because "it reconciles the 'spirit' with 'Matter,' securing our physical reality in a world we only come to know through the immaterial feelings that give rise to language"; rhythm thereby acts as a "numinous" force of communication between the earthly and the spiritual (Mason 2004, 544, 546). Patmore's insistence on metrical immateriality, his celebration of duration over stress [. . .] places him at odds with Hopkins's model of electric poetics, the "fire of stress" that for Hopkins epitomizes what poetry does best.

   Only through the lens of culture might one make sense of Hopkins's attention to Patmore and the New Prosody, with which he disagreed so forcefully, and his concurrent avoidance of the Spasmodics (specifically, Dobell's theory of rhythm). Hopkins's implicit rejection of Dobell's poetics might best be understood alongside his outright dismissal of Whitman, another poet with whom Hopkins shares obvious formal sympathies. In 1881 Hopkins writes, famously, "I always knew in my heart Walt Whitman's mind to be more like my own than any other man's living. As he is a very great scoundrel this is not a pleasant confession. And this also makes me the more desirous to read him and the more determined that I will not" (Hopkins 1955, 155). Hopkins acknowledges the similarities between his style and Whitman's but insists on important distinctions as well. As Saville has noted, Whitman is Hopkins's "repudiated double," in terms of both style and sexual expression (Saville, 173). Hopkins continues, "Of course I saw that there was to the eye something in my long lines like his, that the one would remind people of the other. And both are in irregular rhythms. There the likeness ends. The pieces of his I read were mostly in an irregular rhythmic prose: that is what they are thought to be meant for and what they seemed to me to be. . . . [I]n short what he means to write—and writes—is rhythmic prose and that only" (Hopkins 1955, 155–56). Aside from calling him a "great scoundrel," then, Hopkins resists engaging with the content of Whitman's poetry, concentrating instead on formal concerns. In his criticism of Swinburne, too, Hopkins glances over the subject matter to dwell at length on issues of style: the poems show "passion but not feeling" and "genius without truth"; Swinburne "has no real understanding of rhythm" (Hopkins 1955, 79, 303). In all these examples, poetic form stands in as illustrative of poetic content. Swinburne is one of the "plagues of mankind" (Hopkins 1955, 39), but judging from Hopkins's letters this is so because of his poetic style, not his penchant for writing about necrophilia, for example, or sadomasochism. Hopkins thus formulates his distance from Whitman and Swinburne in terms of style and form, not character and cultural values.

   In the end, Hopkins sympathizes most with those who urge a retreat from physiological poetics, including Edmund Gosse's 1877 call [. . .] to "dismiss the purely spontaneous and untutored expression" of poetry (Gosse 1877, 53).[10] Gosse closes his essay with a rhetorical flourish, hoping that he "may be dead before the English poets take Walt Whitman for their model in style" (71). Hopkins hews to the conservative line because he cannot stomach identifying with those who, like Whitman and Swinburne, use poetic innovation to challenge contemporary culture in addition to aesthetic taste. In this way, Patmore's attention to meter offers an antidote to the physiological poetics to which Hopkins was by nature drawn. Hopkins insists on the metrical regularity of "The Wreck of the Deutschland"; even "the long, e.g. seven-syllables, feet of the *Deutschland*," he writes to Bridges, "are strictly metrical"

(Hopkins 1855, 45). Following the rule of sprung rhythm, Hopkins determines regularity by the number of stresses in each line, not the number of syllables.[11] [. . . I]t is in this way that Hopkins's sprung rhythm sympathizes with Patmore's isochronous method, another metrical system that disregards almost entirely syllable-counting. Sprung rhythm and isochrony open poetic form to a kind of limited freedom, resisting the complete liberty of spasmody or Whitmanian "rhythmic prose" while also avoiding the strict meters advocated by Gosse and other post-Spasmodic critics. There was much in Patmore that Hopkins found distasteful or simply in bad aesthetic taste (the feeling was entirely mutual), but the two were more alike than different in their attempts to locate a poetic middle ground.

In 1932, F. R. Leavis claimed that the "Wreck" shows clearly "that Hopkins has no relation to . . . any nineteenth-century poet." For Leavis this is a compliment, writing as he does at a time that largely anathematized the Victorians, and he justifies the point by noting Hopkins's "association of inner, spiritual, emotional stress with physical reverberations, nervous and muscular tensions" (Leavis, 26). However, it is exactly because of this association of the "inner, spiritual, emotion" with the "physical" and physiological that Hopkins emerges as a representative poet of his day. Hopkins's developments in physiological poetics take place within a literary culture struggling to reconcile a range of new scientific data—on the human body, on the physical sciences—with shifting aesthetic values and tastes.

[. . .]

Notes

All quotations are cited parenthetically by author and page number, with the year of publication added to distinguish multiple works from one author. Longer poems include line references and, when appropriate, section divisions.

1 My thanks to Gerard Passannante for directing me to Poliziano's work. In Plato's *Ion*, Socrates explains the work of poetic experience—"an inspiration . . . divinity moving you"—to be "like . . . a magnet"; just as a magnetic force can pull through a chain of iron rings, so too the strength of "the Muse" works through the poet, by way of the poem, to the reader (Plato, 1:107).
2 On the politics of Victorian poetry, the most important recent studies include Armstrong 1993; Kuduk Weiner 2005; and Reynolds 2001. On the physiology of Victorian poetry, see Blair 2006; M. Campbell 1999; and Prins 2000.
3 Tom Standage reviews Nollet's experiment and its aftermath in *The Victorian Internet* (1–2). On Nollet's relation to eighteenth-century science, especially his rivalry with Franklin, see Riskin 2002, 69–103; and Delbourgo 2006, 39–40.
4 For more on Coleridge's ambivalent relation to materialism, associationist philosophy, and the sciences, see A. Richardson 2001, 39–65; and Roe 2001.
5 All quotations from Hopkins's poetry are cited by page and line number.
6 On "the relationship between Christianity and desire" in Hopkins's "Wreck," especially with respect to same-sex desire, see Roden 2002, 109–19; Armstrong writes that the "project of the poem is the attempt to justify the 'lash' of language by restoring and giving meaning to 'unshapeable' sound, just as it attempts to give meaning to the flux of the sea" (Armstrong 1993, 434).
7 The finger returns in stanza 31: "lovely-felicitous Providence / Fínger of a ténder of, O of a féathery délicacy" (GMH, 127, lines 245–46).
8 Daniel Brown suggests that for Hopkins, "God's presence [is] a huge charge of energy that can be actualized at any moment" (Brown 2000, 154–55).
9 The ship was actually capsized by a "blinding snow" that hit the ship unexpectedly (GMH, 391). My thanks to Meredith Martin for pointing me to this poem.
10 Patmore refers to Gosse's essay in a letter to Bridges, 8 August 1877 (Hopkins 1955, 42).

11 MacKenzie notes that, for the most part, the lines of "The Wreck of the Deutschland" follow a pattern of 2–3–4–3–5–5–4–6 stresses per line; the first line takes three stresses in the second part of the poem (GMH, 318).

References

Armstrong, Isobel. 1993. *Victorian Poetry: Poetry, Poetics, and Politics*. New York: Routledge.

Aytoun, William Edmondstoune. 1857. "Mrs. Barrett Browning—Aurora Leigh." *Blackwood's* 81 (January): 23–41.

Blair, Kirstie. 2006. *Victorian Poetry and the Culture of the Heart*. Oxford, UK: Clarendon.

Brown, Daniel. 2000. "Victorian Poetry and Science." In *Cambridge Companion to Victorian Poetry*, edited by Joseph Bristow, 137–58. Cambridge: Cambridge University Press.

Burke, Edmund. 1968. *A Philosophical Enquiry into the Origin of Our Ideas of the Sublime and Beautiful*. [1757]. Edited by James T. Boulton. Notre Dame: University of Notre Dame Press.

Campbell, Matthew. 1999. *Rhythm and Will in Victorian Poetry*. Cambridge: Cambridge University Press.

Cohen, Bernard. 1941. *Benjamin Franklin's Experiments*. Cambridge, MA: Harvard University Press.

Coleridge, Samuel Taylor. 1997. *Biographia Literaria* [1817]. London: J. M. Dent.

Delbourgo, James. 2006. *A Most Amazing Scene of Wonders: Electricity and Enlightenment in Early America*. Cambridge, MA: Harvard University Press.

Dobell, Sydney. 1876. *Thoughts on Art, Philosophy, and Religion: Selected from the Unpublished Papers of Sydney Dobell*. London: Smith, Elder and Co.

Gosse, Edmund. 1877. "A Plea for Certain Exotic Forms of Verse." *Cornhill Magazine* 36: 53–71.

Hardy, Barbara Nathan. 1977. *The Advantage of Lyric: Essays on Feeling in Poetry*. Bloomington: Indiana University Press.

Heilbron, J. L. 1979. *Electricity in the 17th and 18th Centuries: A Study of Early Modern Physics*. Berkeley: University of California Press.

Hopkins, Gerard Manley. 1955. *The Correspondence* [sic] *of Gerard Manley Hopkins to Robert Bridges*. London, New York, Oxford University Press.

——. 1956. *Further Letters of Gerard Manley Hopkins, Including his Correspondence with Coventry Patmore*. London: Oxford University Press.

——. 1959. *The Journals and Papers of Gerard Manley Hopkins*. London: Oxford University Press.

——. 1990. *The Poetical Works of Gerard Manley Hopkins*. Edited by Norman H. Mackenzie. Oxford, UK: Clarendon.

Kuduk Weiner, Stephanie. 2005. *Republican Politics and English Poetry, 1789–1874*. New York: Palgrave Macmillan.

Leavis, F. R. 1966. "Gerard Manley Hopkins" [1932]. In *Hopkins: A Collection of Critical Essays*, edited by Geoffrey H. Hartman, 17–36. Englewood Cliffs, NJ: Prentice Hall.

Longinus. 1906. *On the Sublime*. Translated by A. O. Prickard. Oxford, UK: Clarendon.

Mason, Emma. 2004. "Rhythmic Numinousness: Sydney Dobell and 'The Church.'" *Victorian Poetry* 42 (Winter): 537–51.

Mill, John Stuart. 1981. *Collected Works*. Edited by John M. Robson and Jack Stillinger. 19 vols. Toronto: Univ. of Toronto Press.

Olsen [sic], Charles. 1997. *Collected Prose*. Berkeley: University of California Press.

Peters, John Durham. 1999. *Speaking into the Air: A History of the Idea of Communication*. Chicago: University of Chicago Press.

Plato. 1953. *The Dialogues of Plato*. 4th ed. 4 vols. Translated by Benjamin Jowett. Oxford, UK: Clarendon.

Poliziano, Angelo. 2004. *Silvae*. Translated by Charles Fantazzi. Cambridge, MA: Harvard University Press.

Prins, Yopie. 2000. "Victorian Meters." In *Cambridge Companion to Victorian Poetry*, edited by Joseph Bristow, 89–113. Cambridge: Cambridge University Press.

Reynolds, Matthew. 2001. *The Realms of Verse, 1830–1870: English Poetry in a Time of Nation-Building*. Oxford: Oxford University Press.

Richardson, Alan. 2001. *British Romanticism and the Science of the Mind*. Cambridge: Cambridge University Press.

Riskin, Jessica. 2002. *Science in the Age of Sensibility: The Sentimental Empiricists of the French Enlightenment*. Chicago: University of Chicago Press.

Roden, Frederick S. 2002. *Same-Sex Desire in Victorian Religious Culture*. New York: Palgrave.

Roe, Nicholas. 2001. "Introduction: Samuel Taylor Coleridge and the Sciences of Life." In *Samuel Taylor Coleridge and the Sciences of Life*, edited by Nicholas Roe, 1–21. Oxford: Oxford University Press.

Saville, Julia F. 2000. *A Queer Chivalry: The Homoerotic Asceticism of Gerard Manley Hopkins*. Charlottesville: University Press of Virginia.

Shelley, Percy Bysshe. 1965. *The Complete Works*. Edited by Roger Ingpen and Walter E. Peck. 10 vols. New York: Gordian Press.

Standage, Tom. 1998. *The Victorian Internet: The Remarkable Story of the Telegraph and the Nineteenth Century's On-Line Pioneers*. New York: Walker and Co.

Stewart, Susan. 2002. *Poetry and the Fate of the Senses*. Chicago: University of Chicago Press.

White, Norman. 1992. *Hopkins: A Literary Biography*. Oxford, UK: Clarendon Press.

4   Victorian poetry and form

Charles LaPorte

The three excerpts included in this section present field-defining examples of the revival of interest in form, the so-called "New Formalism," that has recently invigorated literary scholarship by blending genre study and questions of aesthetics with a rigorous historicization of social and material contexts.[1] Sometimes scholars call this critical approach "strategic formalism," following the example of Caroline Levine; others adopt "cultural neoformalism," a term first offered by Herbert Tucker (Tucker 1999: 535 [Chapter 2: 25]). Whatever we elect to call it, such scholarship stands out for its close attention to the shape and scope of literary works as they emerge from a given cultural climate, political situation, educational system, and material environment and, frequently, as they are consumed by a given culture or cultures. Possibly Isobel Armstrong, Herbert F. Tucker, and Jason R. Rudy do not conceive of themselves as New Formalists, but these days they often find themselves invoked in this context. And for good reason: these particular passages provide a context for the origins of the movement within the field of Victorian studies, and evidence (to which much recent work must be added) of its ongoing promise. We see in the first excerpt how in the early 1990s, Armstrong constructs a crucial frame for its emergence in Victorian studies.[2] Later, at the cusp of the twenty-first century, Tucker sets the new formalism into a fuller theoretical context, and Rudy at the cusp of the 2010s shows how the more mature field continues to incorporate previously overlooked historical contexts. All three readings, as will be apparent, exemplify our general turn toward historical poetics, a thorough engagement with the literature's material and political situation coupled with an ongoing appreciation for what makes it artistically distinctive.

Armstrong's epoch-marking introduction to *Victorian Poetry: Poetry, Poetics and Politics* (1993) has never previously appeared without the book's 500 pages of densely argued literary criticism looming behind it (if I may say so) like a scholarly Mont Blanc. Still, even an uninitiated reader of the present volume will gain some sense of its monumental status in the field from the ambition here on display, as Armstrong explores the crisis of modernity in poetry that much of the twentieth century had dismissed as unadventurous, stilted, sentimental, and twee. She asks that we look again at the post-Romantic self-consciousness of this art form and its struggle with what she calls the modern "conditions of being post-revolutionary, post-industrial, post-teleological and post-Kantian" (Armstrong 1993: 4 [Chapter 1: 17]). In a most convincing and theoretically canny way, she brings us back to an art form shot through with political and emotional investments that had remained invisible to the overwhelming majority of twentieth-century readers, from Modernism onward, and she asks what could be more enlivening than its continued study.

Armstrong's introduction has served as a kind of recuperative project, then, but it does not merely place Victorian poetry on a par with the Romantic and Modernist poetics that have historically been granted more widespread scholarly respect. Rather, Armstrong strives to show how Victorian poetry's peculiar historical situation gives it a special urgency and purchase. For instance, a poem like Alfred Tennyson's "Mariana," taken here as paradigmatic, struggles with the ideals and failures of Romanticism even as it refuses the Modernist axiom that a radical break with literary history is desirable or even truly possible. "Victorian modernism," writes Armstrong, "sees itself as new but it does not, like twentieth-century modernism, conceive itself in terms of a radical break with a past" (Armstrong 1993: 3 [Chapter 1: 12]). Far from exhorting one another to make things "new" *à la* Ezra Pound, Victorian poets found themselves preoccupied by the too-obvious newness of their "problems of representation, fiction and language" (Armstrong 1993: 7 [Chapter 1: 13]) while working within traditional verse forms. It is their fraught self-awareness and their creative responses to it, she avers, that combine to make Victorian poetry "the most sophisticated poetic form, and the most politically complex, to arise in the past two hundred years" (Armstrong 1993: 21). Such audacious claims have roused to life more recent scholarship in Victorian poetics and made it less complacent, made its scholars less tolerant of it being "consigned to sepia" (Armstrong 1993: 1 [Chapter 1: 11]) or otherwise lost.

The chapter has also been prized for its depiction of what Armstrong calls the Victorian "double poem," in which a "poet's secondariness takes a stand on the self-conscious assertion of the unique discourse of poetry" (Armstrong 1993: 11–12 [Chapter 1: 14]). Such doubling occurs whenever the poetic work invites us to consider its expressive lyric utterance as itself "the *object* of analysis and critique" (Armstrong 1993: 12, italics original [Chapter 1: 14]). "Mariana," for instance, both gives voice to the title character's famous plaint and also pulls it inside out "so that it becomes the opposite of itself," a genuine expression of pain, yet "simultaneously an analysis of the hypersensitive hysteria induced by the coercion of sexual taboo" (Armstrong 1993: 12–13 [Chapter 1: 14]). "Mariana" can sound poignantly naive, and yet Armstrong shows how it cannot be merely so in the political situation from which it emerges. In Armstrong's reading (and her book offers an all-but-endless succession of further examples), early nineteenth-century gender politics get neatly folded into the epistemological crisis that follows Romanticism. Indeed, poetry like this interrogates its own conditions as an expression so thoroughly that "[w]hat the Victorian poet achieved was often quite literally two concurrent poems in the same words" (Armstrong 1993: 12 [Chapter 1: 14]). Verse traditions matter, we see, and they matter most where poets cannot take full command of meaning, where they "can only resort to an openness in advance of the reader, testing out the possibilities of semantic misprision" (Armstrong 1993: 12 [Chapter 1: 14]). The expressive lyric voice of the double poem asserts a relationship to others and to the world; it actively contemplates those relationships, and at the same time it offers grounds for a serious cultural and linguistic critique of any such representation. And it may be added that poetry presents this critique more readily than the novel because it does not chiefly aspire to pull readers into what David Lodge calls a "rapt immersion in an imagined reality" (as the Victorian novel aspires to do) (Lodge 1992: x). Poetry keeps artistic craft itself more conspicuously in the reader's ear and eye.

One sees the double poem quite clearly in the dramatic monologue, the Victorian era's most distinctive poetic genre. Anyone who has read Robert Browning's "My Last Duchess" can appreciate to some extent how the Victorian poet sees "utterance both as subject and as object" (Armstrong 1993: 13 [Chapter 1: 15]) and explores "expressive psychological forms simultaneously as psychological conditions *and* as constructs, the phenomenology of a culture, projections which indicate the structure of relationships" (Armstrong 1993: 13, italics original [Chapter 1: 15]). But while the innovation of the dramatic monologue may have been granted by the most disdainful of the Modernists, Victorian poetry's generally ferocious critique of modernity was not. In truth, this critique provides the real drama of the poetry, as Armstrong insists of very different forms of lyric.

> It is possible now to return to the modernists' silence about Victorian poetry. It is clear that the nature of the experiencing subject, the problems of representation, fiction and language, are just as much the heart of Victorian problems as they are the preoccupations of modernism . . . The modernist repression of the Victorians comes surely from an understanding that the Victorians had anticipated their self-reflexive condition and rejected it. (Armstrong 1993: 7 [Chapter 1: 13])

What Armstrong here says of the Victorians' early twentieth-century heirs, she also attributes to their later ones. Poetry enables cultural work that cannot be reduced to the play of meaning, she insists, or the *mise-en-abyme* of reference so often traced by deconstructionist critics in whose immediate wake she writes. The generosity that animates Armstrong's text admittedly falters when she turns to the Modernists, for she all but accuses them of the bad faith and false consciousness from which she so successfully redeems the Victorians. Nonetheless, such a passage as this deserves revisiting because it so shrewdly drives at how the Victorians strove to do things with their poetry, to realize their Romantic ideals, to give them legs to run with—or to kick. It took a long time for scholars to unearth the Victorians from beneath Modernist contumely, and much longer to feel the full urgency of their poetics. Armstrong continues to make it felt.

Herbert Tucker's "The Fix of Form: An Open Letter" nicely follows Armstrong's introduction, then, especially for the deftness with which it brings together certain of her claims about how we ought to approach Victorian poetics. In the above, Tucker makes a case for a future return to form among scholars of Victorian literature, or rather (to speak from a position of hindsight), for our present return. In his retelling, the literary criticism of the previous forty years had increasingly lost touch with the best parts of a New Critical legacy that was central (in North America, at least) to the establishment of English Studies as a significant discipline; for Tucker, this imperiled legacy includes an appreciation of imaginative literature as a repository of "exceptionally nuanced cultural artifacts" (Tucker 1999: 533 [Chapter 2: 23]) and a concomitant attention to fine detail: "[t]he ambiguous trope, the ingredient *mot juste*, the play of ironic tone and curve of prosodic form, the constituent verbal body of sense" (Tucker 1999: 533 [Chapter 2: 23]). Tucker's essay anticipates later, perhaps better-known calls for a return to the art of close reading—Levine's, for instance—but also essays like Jane Gallop's recent *cri de cœur* in *Profession*, which describes the eclipse of close reading in English as a form of "disciplinary suicide" (Gallop 2007: 184). For his part, Tucker remains sanguine about formalist criticism, guessing (or, as it were, prophesying) that literary scholars would continue to take artistic forms seriously as both products and producers of culture, and offering a remarkable little reading of a passage from Tennyson as a model for how to include prosody within the ambit of a politically informed cultural study.

"The Fix of Form" begins with a crash course in academic literary scholarship from the New Criticism of the 1950s and early 1960s, through 1970s deconstruction and the age of theory to the New Historicism of the 1980s and 1990s. Only from this vantage does Tucker come to champion a twenty-first-century revival of interest in form among literary critics. Few present-day scholars of Victorian literature may remember firsthand the moment when theory first upended the complacencies of the New Criticism, and yet most of us will be broadly familiar with the various ages of literary scholarship as he draws them up, including the turn to theory, its subsequent purported death, and the ensuing questions about what kinds of historical criticism we all now seem to be doing. "You" in this essay means both "you" and "I"; Tucker writes from a position of close acquaintance with the first great turn to theory, having graduated from the Amherst College of William H. Pritchard in the early 1970s and, in what may have been a head-snapping theoretical re-orientation, commenced his graduate training at the Yale of Paul de Man. Tucker's depiction of the field remains thus both personal and (nonetheless) broadly representative. And his account of the manner in which we grew restless with each theoretical mode, in particular, provides both inside humor for the initiated (who will remember the New Historicist one about "a play, a map, and a census" (Tucker 1999: 532 [Chapter 2: 22]) from many a mid-nineties conference) and a crib sheet for advanced undergraduates and graduate students, who can feel confusion about what legacy each passing critical vogue has left behind.

Tucker urges a "both/and" (not an "either/or") approach to theory and history *en route* to a fuller understanding of form, enlisting both in the service of the particular features of the given work of art. Like Armstrong, whose scholarly approaches visibly arise from late twentieth-century Marxist and feminist as well as deconstructive theories, Tucker embraces the chief lessons of the theoretical modes that he delineates while repudiating their wearier (or at least more routine) deployments. Like Armstrong, he holds the best scholarship to engage in a strenuous exploration of the individual features of a given work of art as well as its cultural context. As we have seen, Armstrong insists upon an agonistic understanding of a poetic text so as to forestall predictable and unproductive habits of reading: "The active reader is compelled to be internal to the poem's contradictions and recomposes the poem's processes in the act of comprehending them as ideological struggle" (Armstrong 1993: 17 [Chapter 1: 18]). His miniature history of the field, too, reminds us of what the field still does extremely well, which is (A) *explication de texte*, and (B) the art of identifying correspondences among fields of cultural artifacts, though he is careful to point out the pitfalls of shallow correspondences. For the rip-tides created by each theoretical movement of the late twentieth century have been navigated by a common set of techniques:

> Nobody was about to confuse your New-Historicist analysis of hegemonically interlocked ideologemes with your New-Critical appreciation of verbal iconicity; and yet, viewed from the structural point of view that both forms of analysis shared, the two had a lot in common. You were discerning patterns of formal unity all over again. (Tucker 1999: 532 [Chapter 2: 22])

To this extent (and in a way that younger critics have taken up), Tucker points out that literary scholars have never entirely lost hold of form as a guiding principle.[3] Neither is this legacy unique to the twentieth century. When Tucker names his observations about the isomorphic correspondences between critical methodologies, his sort of emergent theory of theories, he calls it "the Higher Matching" (Tucker 1999: 533 [Chapter 2: 23]), a characteristically broad-minded nod to Victorian scholars, whose encounter with the Higher Criticism had similarly unsettled and enlivened their textual world.[4]

Attentive readers moving from the first excerpt to the second will note that Tucker feels no compulsion to defend Victorian poetry as a field of study in the way that Armstrong had, perhaps because her prior work had helped to relieve that burden. Instead, his essay focuses our attention on literary form more generally, on the kinds of literary details that only a skilled close reader of texts can begin to notice—details like *meter*, which many fiction-oriented Victorianists still shy away from as an esoteric science but which were central to Victorian ideas about what literature is and does. Section 33 of Tennyson's *In Memoriam* provides a powerful example both because the Victorians took the poem to heart ("an ample paper-trail of Victorian testimony establishes that *In Memoriam* spoke directly to thousands for years" (Tucker 1999: 534 [Chapter 2: 23])) and because their widespread embrace of the poem itself creates a number of different Section 33s:

> Would you aspirate the aitch in "have" (to mark the anapest) or not (to oil the elision)? Would Tennyson? Would his Lincolnshire neighbor the Northern Farmer? Would his dead friend from Cambridge, the subject of In Memoriam AHH, the man Sam Weller and his Cockney cronies would presumably have called Harthur Allam? Get a set of Victorians to say line 2, and by their aspirations you will know them. (Tucker 1999: 535 [Chapter 2: 24–25])

This is the heart of G. B. Shaw's *Pygmalion* (1912) reduced to the scansion of a single tetrameter line. And even such a glance in the direction of dialectology ("Would you aspirate the aitch . . . ?") has real political implications, as Tucker, like Shaw, reminds us. But to read the meter as closely as Tucker is to realize that one *must* glance in that direction: "The choice is free between two scansions, but each has strings attached" (Tucker 1999: 535 [Chapter 2: 24]). The poem thus literally breathes out its crux between "faith" and "form" in a manner that Armstrong would call agonistic and Tucker "unstable" (Tucker 1999: 533 [Chapter 2: 23]). Prosody, indeed, features so largely in recent New Formalist work, as Tucker mentions, because it encodes ideological attitudes that were felt strongly by contemporary practitioners and readers, though these attitudes frequently remain invisible to posterity. Tucker himself, as it happens, had gently chided Armstrong for neglecting meter in his otherwise laudatory review of *Victorian Poetry: Poetry, Poetics and Politics* when it first appeared, and she has since given it more extensive consideration (Tucker 1995). (His other objection was that she was slow to credit scholars doing related work (Tucker 1995: 185), though it feels funny to say so in a reprise of "The Fix of Form," which has no scholarly citation at all. Apparently he came around to her approach, as well, and saw how singling out individual works of scholarship could awkwardly skew his sketch of the field.)

Finally, in light of the renewed focus on form and prosody brought to bear in the second excerpt, we can see Jason Rudy's *Electric Meters: Victorian Physiological Poetics* (2009) as representative of the kind of exciting work enabled by both Armstrong's and Tucker's ground-clearing scholarship. Rudy (very rightly) takes for granted that the finer points of Victorian meter have cultural repercussions, and his work here sets Victorian poetics into a fuller and more dynamic history of prosodic form. In particular, Rudy calls to our attention the ways that Victorian poetics took a distinctly physiological turn when new developments in the electrical sciences suggested the possibility that human responses to poetic rhythms were not so much an intellectual experience as a somatic one: "Whereas the predominant eighteenth-century model of poetic transmission privileged the mind's interpretative role . . . , nineteenth-century readers gave credit to the body as an arbiter of poetic truths" (Rudy 2009: 3 [Chapter 3: 27]). Armstrong and Tucker remind us how attention to the idiosyncrasies of a given body of poetry remains a necessary condition of the best poetic criticism, and Rudy ingeniously extends this lesson to the idiosyncrasies of Victorian metrical theory. Historical changes in scientific culture here generate a whole new poetics—or, rather, competing types of poetics. Whereas Armstrong brings us to see how Victorian poets wrestled with a post-Kantian philosophical legacy, a "supreme condition of posthumousness" (Armstrong 1993: 3 [Chapter 1: 13]) that posed art against, or held it in contradistinction to, technology, Rudy shows us how they aspired to harness the lessons of technology and to make consciousness (or at least sensation) and representation one. Arch-Romantic images of poetry and the poet as an aeolian harp stirred by the breezes of nature, so famously depicted in poems like S. T. Coleridge's famous 1796 work of that name, here give way to a vision of electric communication between people via the newly invented telegraph. What changes is not the introduction of technology *per se* (the aeolian harp must count as a technology, after all) but the promise of concrete, explicit, instantaneous ways to transfer meaning. In this new climate, Victorian poets tried to integrate with their technological modernity Romantic ideas of inspiration such as are to be found in Coleridge, with his grand sense of the divine that infuses the world and the poet. But the progress of Victorian technologies also drove Victorian poets to an alternative fantasy that the material aspects of language might be better developed into a musical science, one that "might be reconfigured to vibrate in tune with all human individuals" (Rudy 2009: 16 [Chapter 3: 30]), as Rudy puts it.

Whereas in the second excerpt Tucker takes for a case study a poem universally beloved by the Victorians, Rudy shows the fruitfulness of historical poetics for two poems that were unknown in their era: Gerard Manley Hopkins's "The Wreck of the Deutschland" (1918, composed 1875–76) and "God's Grandeur" (1918, composed 1877). In doing so, he demonstrates how emergent Victorian poetic forms that have often been described as atypical—such as those of the Spasmodic poets, of Walt Whitman, and of Hopkins—actually participate in and arise from this historical confluence between bodily poetics and the emergence of the electrical sciences. On the one hand, Hopkins sees modern theories of the interrelationship between mind and body as expressive of what poets have always known; the undergraduate Hopkins complains that physiological science "only shows in the last detail what broadly no one doubted, to wit that the activities of the spirit are conveyed in those of the body" (Rudy 2009: 130 [Chapter 3: 30]). Yet, on the other hand, Rudy shows how Hopkins's poetry repeatedly invokes differing types of electrical charge as he attempts to trace experience on the body itself. So does Hopkins's prose ("[a]ll things . . . are charged with God and if . . . we know how to touch them give off sparks and take fire" (Rudy 2009: 133 [Chapter 3: 32])), but the distinctiveness of the verse lies in its efforts to galvanize its readers with an analogous kind of physical charge.

Theology meets technology in the poems here selected by Rudy. Hopkins relentlessly seeks to take hold of his readers in ways that suggest a divine rapture ("Thou mastering me / God! giver of breath and bread . . ."). But the ancient tradition of the divine afflatus, the poetic breath that moves the strings of that aeolian harp, here is replaced with the instantaneous electric charge. Rudy juxtaposes Hopkins's strong-stress meter both with Coventry Patmore's *The Unknown Eros* (1877), a work that asks a reader to mark time in isochronous (or equal) intervals, and with the accentual-syllabic meter of Elizabeth Barrett Browning's *Aurora Leigh* (1856), which was felt to be excessive by many contemporary critics because of its emphasis on the somatic:

> Her poetry, though identified as Spasmodic by Aytoun . . . , avoids the sheer physicality that would allow readers literally to feel her touch. Hopkins gives us no choice: "I féel thy finger and find thée" instructs us precisely how to feel, both through its alliteration and the accompanying stress marks. (Rudy 2009: 131 [Chapter 3: 31])

Rudy's formulation about Hopkins giving us "no choice," in fact, forcibly reminds us of the choice that Tucker finds lurking in the prosody of Tennyson. In such passages of "The Wreck of the Deutchland," our choice is emphatically *not* "free between two scansions" (and this despite Hopkins's reassurances to Robert Bridges in a letter of 1877 that his sprung rhythm was "the least forced, the most rhetorical and emphatic of all possible rhythms" (Pick 1966: 144)). Rudy shows Hopkins to be both intrigued and repulsed by the physiological project of midcentury poetry like *Aurora Leigh*, with its attempt to achieve a closer correspondence between charge and meaning. Still, a reader must wonder to what we are here tied ("láshed," as it were) by this rhythmical compulsion, by the "strings attached" to Hopkins's meter—not to a uniquely Catholic form of somatic response, it seems, though perhaps to a non-denominational sense of wonder at the passion of the lines themselves.

In Rudy we also see the ongoing fruits of the historically nuanced work on Victorian prosody that has appeared since Tucker's "The Fix of Form"; here we might link *Electric Meters* to such studies as Yopie Prins's ground-breaking work on Victorian classical forms (2000, 2005, 2006), the collected essays of Jason Hall's *Meter Matters* (2011) and Meredith Martin's remarkable *The Rise and Fall of Meter* (2012), to name only a few. Traditionally, pedagogy in English poetics (as in classical poetics before that) has stressed a single correct scansion of a given poetic line, instead of several possible scansions that elicit different meanings. But Rudy describes the nineteenth-century ideal of a single poetic rhythm imposing a single meaning as a "utopian" project (Rudy 2009: 16 [Chapter 3: 30]), remarking that "the play of rhythm on individual human bodies remains in the end too variable for consistent objective analysis" (Rudy 2009: 98). Meanwhile, Tucker's linguistic lesson in "The Fix of Form" seems to be even more widely applicable than he himself always grants. Take Tucker's interactive online tutorial at the University of Virginia, *For Better for Verse* (http://prosody.lib.virginia.edu/), which rewards readers for good scansion with a green ✓ (misreadings receive a red ✖).[5] *For Better for Verse* scans thus the famous opening to "God's Grandeur," placed so nicely by Rudy into the framework of Victorian science:

⏑   /   ⏑ /   ⏑   ⏑   /   / ⏑/
The world is charged with the grandeur of God.

Such a rendering of Hopkins's stresses makes sense, to be sure, and merits our assent. But other legitimate renderings of this line also leap to mind, such as the following:

⏑   /   ⏑ /   ⏑   ⏑   /   ⏑ ⏑/
The world is charged with the grandeur of God.

For Better for Verse rejects this second reading as incorrect (✖) in favor of the first (✓). And then it nonetheless grants in a footnote that most readers will incline to the second reading:

> Note on line 1: Most readers will hear this line as a tetrameter, 2 iambs plus 2 anapests. But the rest of the sonnet is so manifestly written in pentameter that a prosodic pedant will return to line 1 and suppose that Hopkins, wanting to make his title word "grandeur" as spacious and dignified as he could, brought out its French-import quality and flourished it as a spondee.

"[P]rosodic pedant[ry]" here jars in fascinating ways with what Tucker openly grants to be the majority practice of reading this sonnet. He urges that Hopkins "want[s]" a "French-import quality" to his vowels, but takes for granted that grán•déur is grander than grán•deur, a linguistic association that might be as culturally relative as the transposed aspirates of "Harthur Allam" in "The Fix of Form." Tucker the sociolinguist might raise an eyebrow at Tucker the digital humanist pedagogue. Native English speakers adopt French vowels no more frequently than we nasalize "r"s and "d"s, yet *For Better for Verse* seems almost to question our ability to pronounce this poem's title.[6] To a reader like Rudy, Prins, or Martin, the manner in which the site provides a correct scansion for such ambiguous cases will seem like perverseness. No one demonstrates more regular sensitivity to the aural qualities of Victorian poetry than Tucker, but this acknowledgement of a gap between an ideal reader and general readerly praxis introduces a real philosophical problem, and perhaps a more widespread one than a pedagogical site can easily accommodate.[7] And it is Rudy's virtue to point out how the crazy blue chalk marks with which Hopkins embellished "The Wreck of the Deutschland" owed to his very despair at bringing readers (or possibly even himself) into a proper inflection without them: we "féel" and "find" Hopkins in complete unison only where the poet, having been unnerved and dissatisfied by the examples of his contemporaries, marks his accents in ways impossible to miss.[8]

It is good, in fact, to end this review essay with Hopkins's genius, his rigor, even his fruitful despair, since I have hoped to use this space to emphasize how fruitful this kind of close formal study remains when joined, as in these examples, with a vibrant cultural criticism. The recent revival of formal criticism in twenty-first-century Victorian studies enlivens and steadies us not only because it brings to life the invisible details of nineteenth-century art, as it unquestionably does, but because it also brings together large parts of the invisible whole: that world of nineteenth-century anglophone literature of which the most learned scholar can command only a fraction. Understanding nineteenth-century poetry in particular requires our entertaining that kind of minute attention to form that its creators gave it ("I cannot think of altering anything," writes Hopkins to Bridges (Pick 1966: 144)) and our attention to the fact that poems were then part of public culture in ways that are hard to reimagine today. Shifts of scale between newly visible details and an invisible whole require critical balance, of course. Writing recently with B. Venkat Mani about today's scholars' attention to such crucial issues of translation, circulation, and distribution within the context of world literature, Levine (again, a leading light of New Formalism) goes so far as to grant that "[a]n interest in world literature might even require us to abandon close reading, with its stress on the subtlest linguistic nuances, in favor of world-systems theory and patterns of global circulation" (Levine and Mani 2013: 142). No doubt our formal attention will continue to be altered and shaped by such new trends in the field as the global turn, cognitive studies, and digital humanities, to suggest only a few. But I hold with Tucker on the "the constituent verbal body of sense," as does everyone else I have cited here (including Levine in her other writings), and the poets above all. Hopkins continues to extend to us the advice that he offers to Bridges: "I think if you will study what I have said here you will be much more pleased with it and may I say? converted to it" (Pick 1966: 144).

When *Victorian Poetry: Poetry, Poetics and Politics* first appeared in the early 1990s, Tucker rightly hailed it as "*the* work that scholars new to the field [will] turn to, and turn against, for the clearly foreseeable future" (Tucker 1995: 174, italics original). I myself write as that scholar, then new to the field, and I can heartily affirm Tucker's prophecy from the ensuing two decades of personal experience. But I continue to turn to Tucker and to Rudy as well, both for the ways that their scholarship dovetails with Armstrong's and for their distinctive strengths. The two decades following *Victorian Poetry: Poetry, Poetics and Politics* have brought a raft of tremendous scholarship on Victorian poetics, far more than I could ever begin to do justice to in this essay, and nothing has been more exciting to witness than the continued strength and insight of our debates about form. I have thought a lot about this way of approaching nineteenth-century literature, and I am, may I say? converted to it.

Notes

1 The New Formalism does not derive exclusively from (neither is it restricted to) nineteenth-century studies, but Marjorie Levinson's recent "state-of-the-field" piece for *PMLA* rightly puts much emphasis there.
2 Levinson identifies Armstrong's *The Radical Aesthetic* (2000) as an especially key text in the New Formalism, but here we see the earlier versions of those arguments.
3 Levine puts it more bluntly: "Cultural Studies is, we might say, *formalist despite itself*" (635, italics original).
4 In his earliest book, as well, Tucker had described the Victorian Higher Criticism as "the Continental deconstruction of its day" (Tucker 1980: 8).
5 Site launched 2010. Here accessed July 2013.
6 Granting the anglicization of the word and the evolutionary varieties of global nineteenth-century English, in fact, syllabic variants such as gránd•eur might merit consideration. Tucker notes that *For Better or Verse* gives away syllabification like "the dictionary," but the *OED* eschews pronouncing on this syllabic break (Tucker 2011).
7 In a related *Victorian Poetry* article, Tucker acknowledges the dilemmas inherent to his goal of providing a normative scansion, going so far as to say that in many ambiguous cases he has had to impose a "uniformity [that] gave the student something to depend upon—perhaps eventually to rebel against" (Tucker 2011: 275).
8 The chalk marks are described in a letter to R. W. Dixon in October of 1878. "However I had to mark the stresses in blue chalk, and this and my rhymes carried on from one line into another . . . and a great many more oddnesses could not but dismay an editor's eye" (Pick 1966: 147).

Bibliography

Armstrong, Isobel (1993) *Victorian Poetry: Poetry, Poetics, and Politics*, London and New York: Routledge.
—— (2000) *The Radical Aesthetic*, Oxford: Blackwell.
Blair, K. (2006) *Victorian Poetry and the Culture of the Heart*, Oxford: Clarendon Press.
—— (2012) *Form and Faith in Victorian Poetry and Religion*, Oxford: Oxford University Press.
Gallop, J. (2007) "The Historicization of Literary Studies and the Fate of Close Reading," *Profession*, 1: 181–86.
Hall, J. (ed.) (2011) *Meter Matters: Verse Cultures of the Long Nineteenth Century*, Athens, OH: University of Ohio Press.
Levine, C. (2006) "Strategic Formalism: Toward a New Method in Cultural Studies," *Victorian Studies*, 48.4: 625–57
Levine C. and Mani, B. V. (2013) "What Counts as World Literature?," *MLQ*, 74. 2:142.
Levinson, M. (2007) "What Is New Formalism?," *PMLA*, 122. 2: 558–69.
Lodge, D. (1992) *The Art of Fiction*, New York: Penguin.
Martin, M. (2012) *The Rise and Fall of Meter: Poetry and English National Culture, 1860–1930*, Princeton: Princeton University Press.
Pick, J. (ed.) (1966) *A Hopkins Reader: Selections from the Writings of Gerard Manley Hopkins*, New York: Image Books.
Prins, Y. (2000) "Victorian Meters," in J. Bristow (ed.), *The Cambridge Companion to Victorian Poetry*, Cambridge: Cambridge University Press.
—— (2005) "Metrical Translation: Nineteenth-Century Homers and the Hexameter Mania," in S. Bermann and M. Wood (eds.), *Nation, Language and the Ethics of Translation*, Princeton: Princeton University Press.

—— (2006) "Ladies' Greek (with the Accents)," *Victorian Literature and Culture*, 34.2: 591–618;

Rudy, Jason R. (2009) *Electric Meters: Victorian Physiological Poetics*, Athens, OH: Ohio University Press.

Tucker, H. F. (1980) *Browning's Beginnings: The Art of Disclosure*, Minneapolis, MN: University of Minnesota Press.

—— (1995) "Victorian Poetry: Poetry, Poetics and Politics, by Isobel Armstrong," *Victorian Poetry*, 33. 1: 174–87.

—— (1999) "The Fix of Form: An Open Letter," *Victorian Literature and Culture*, 27.2: 531–35.

—— (2011) "Poetic Data and the News from Poems: *A For Better or Verse* Memoir," *Victorian Poetry*, 49. 2: 267–81.

Part II

Women poets and the poetess tradition

Introduction

By our own non-scientific reckoning, no area of Victorian scholarship during the past twenty-five years has had a greater impact on course syllabuses than the study of Victorian women poets. Nineteenth-century and Victorian poetry courses now regularly cover poets who were taught infrequently in the past, such as Augusta Webster, Michael Field (Katherine Bradley and Edith Cooper), Mathilde Blind, Constance Naden, and Alice Meynell.[1] These courses also now typically include a wider range of works by the most well-established women poets from the late Romantic period (Felicia Hemans and Letitia Elizabeth Landon) and the Victorian period (Elizabeth Barrett Browning and Christina Rossetti). As Linda Hughes's capstone essay notes, such expansions to the teaching canon were the result of an intrepid collective scholarly enterprise in recovery and reconsideration that was inspired by the feminist scholarship of the 1970s and 1980s and that found its own footing in the early 1990s.[2] Critics drew our attention to poets who in their own time typically enjoyed popular or critical success but later fell out of favor—and out of the cultural memory—with the advent of Modernist aesthetics and its resistance to domestic, sentimental verse. An early high point of this scholarly enterprise was reached with two mid-1990s anthologies that reoriented the field, Angela Leighton and Margaret Reynolds's *Victorian Women Poets: An Anthology* (Oxford: Blackwell, 1995) and Isobel Armstrong and Joseph Bristow's *Nineteenth-Century Women Poets: An Oxford Anthology* (Oxford: Oxford University Press, 1996).[3]

Just as significant as this archival work has been a critical reconceptualization of the figure of the poetess by both Romanticists and Victorianists. The contemporary Irish poet Eavan Boland has described poetess writing of the early- to mid-nineteenth century as the result of a set of cultural "expectations" for women poets to produce "an obedient music"—that is, "the lyric of religious yearning, of disappointed love, and sacred surrender"; one might well add to this restrictive list the subjects of motherhood and domesticity (Boland 2008: xiii). As scholars have consistently shown, though, the figure of the poetess was not just a limiting expectation but a persona that professional women writers could adapt in order to address otherwise unfeminine political concerns such as slavery, the class system, and the Napoleonic wars, and which they could draw on to make connections to ancient traditions of Sapphic lyric authority and biblical prophetic power. Yet despite the relative malleability of the poetess tradition, its strictures were real, and by the 1850s it was already in decline. The readings below each address the repercussions of that tradition on mid- to late-Victorian women writers.

In the first excerpt, Tricia Lootens surveys the posthumous canonization of Elizabeth Barrett Browning as the author of the *Sonnets from the Portuguese* and an icon of happy wedded love. Lootens describes how the lingering aftereffects of the poetess model, even into the 1970s, narrowed the reception of not only Barrett Browning's *Sonnets* themselves but the whole of her multifaceted, vastly ambitious body of work into a hackneyed biographical anecdote—an episode that recalls the way in which Ovid reduced Sappho's robust and far-ranging poetry to a simple tale of love gone wrong in his *Heroides*. The second excerpt, by Linda Peterson, is also concerned with Barrett Browning and the issue of literary reception, but Peterson focuses on Barrett Browning's own reception of an earlier woman poet, Letitia Elizabeth Landon. In *Aurora Leigh*, Barrett Browning pushes back against the generic and ideological limitations observed by her forebear in making a case for epic ambition in women's poetry. In the third excerpt, Charles LaPorte treats a more positive aspect of the poetess tradition—how it allowed women poets like George Eliot to claim prophetic authority in religious verse. LaPorte demonstrates how a later poet, Mathilde Blind, secularizes Eliot's female prophetic voice while redeploying its characteristic language. All of these complex transactions in literary influence and reputation, as well as the broader landscape of women's poetry studies for the past twenty-five years, are put into context by Linda Hughes in her capstone essay.

See also: *Victorian poetry and form*; *Gender, sexuality, domesticity*

Notes

1 The deeper and wider range of women's poetry taught in current courses is no doubt partially due to the relatively limited course time that lyric poetry demands (especially when compared to triple-decker Victorian novels).

2 For a stimulating critique of the theoretical limitations of literary recovery, see Yopie Prins and Virginia Jackson's "Lyrical Studies," in *Victorian Literature and Culture*, 27.2 (1999): 521–30. Prins and Jackson assert that "lyric's historical function" lies in "displacing" those fixed identities—both characters and authors—that scholars seek to restore (529).

3 Both of these anthologies are, alas, now out of print, but two recent ones remain in print: Virginia Blain's *Victorian Women Poets: An Annotated Anthology* (London: Longman, 2000; revised edition published in 2009); and Florence S. Boos's *Working-Class Women Poets in Victorian Britain* (Peterborough, Ont.: Broadview, 2008). A briefer collection, Catherine Reilly's *Winged Words: Victorian Women's Poetry and Verse* (London: Enitharmon, 1994), remains in print, as well. The leading Victorian literature anthologies, published by Longman, W. W. Norton, and Broadview, all now include representative selections from several of these 'recovered' poets.

For a critical take on the "distort[ing]" effects of several of the above anthologies, see Isobel Armstrong, "The Long Nineteenth Century: Where Have All the Women Poets Gone?," posted on *The Victorian Poetry Network*, 1/17/2011 (http://web.uvic.ca/~vicpoet/2011/01/the-long-nine-teenth-century-where-have-the-women-poets-gone/); accessed 12/9/2014.

Bibliography

Boland, E. (2008) "Introduction," *Charlotte Mew: Selected Poems*, Manchester: Carcanet.

5   Canonization through dispossession

Elizabeth Barrett Browning and the "Pythian shriek"

Tricia Lootens

"How do I love thee? Let me count the ways." Surely no line of Victorian poetry is quoted so frequently, or in such dichotomous contexts, as the opening of Poem 43 in Elizabeth Barrett Browning's *Sonnets from the Portuguese*.[1] Under most circumstances, the line raises a smile. "How do I love this job?" snarls a puffy Boynton cartoon cat, printed on reminder notes; "Let us count the ways," reads a slogan for Arby's fast food. Occasionally, the parody is more pointed. In a *New Yorker* cartoon, for example, an exhausted, beringletted Miss Barrett accepts an abacus— and a reminder to carry the fives—from a bearded Browning. In certain cases, however—in wedding ceremonies, for example, and in Valentine's Day readings—"How do I love thee . . ." evokes a reverent, if edgy, hush. Moved, perhaps in spite of themselves, audiences participate in the ritual invocation of Barrett Browning's verse as a pure and absolute expression of romantic love. Sentimental the *Sonnets* may be, popular culture acknowledges, but they are also sacred.

Are the *Sonnets* sacred as literature, however, or as something else? Moreover, what does their dual canonization as standing jokes and ritual readings have to do with the canonization of Barrett Browning or of her other works? The two questions are interconnected: although the *Sonnets* have long defined E. B. B.'s fame, they themselves have not been defined as suitable objects for critical attention. Most of us think we know the *Sonnets*, but how many of us, even students and teachers of English literature, have actually studied them? Like their author, they have come close to being simultaneously canonized and lost.[2]

For a sense of the shape of this paradox, one need only turn to a self-described "living monument in the field of American Letters": Houghton Mifflin's 1974 Cambridge edition of Barrett Browning's *Poetical Works*, which has served many students in the United States as an affordable standard resource. The dustjacket of this volume promises to "meet all the needs of the general reader and student." Its introductory essay, by Ruth M. Adams, clearly numbers canonical revision and editing among those needs: "Who reads Elizabeth Barrett Browning? More people, but not a vast number. Historians . . . will read selectively in *Casa Guidi Windows* and *Poems before Congress*. *Aurora Leigh* has been rediscovered by those who appreciate its vignettes of society, high and low, its concentration on women, their aspirations to independence and self-sufficiency, and its rejection of mid-Victorian taboos on subject matter. But the audience that is most assured and most numerous consists of those in love or in love with love, who find the *Sonnets from the Portuguese* a full and satisfying expression of their emotions. Certainly some of these sonnets are destined for a modest immortality, but immortality nonetheless" (xiii).

True to the dustjacket's promises, Adams thus "identifies the [relatively few] poems of Mrs. Browning that have proved of lasting value or interest," assigning to each an authorized audience.[3] With *Casa Guidi Windows*, *Poems before Congress*, and a few other verses relegated to the historians, lovers of literature are left only *Aurora Leigh* and the *Sonnets*—that is, insofar as they seek only a first reading. For after that, "it is not to *Aurora Leigh*, effective as parts may be, that the reader will return. It is too discursive, too tedious, too platitudinous in most of its sentiments, too much on the level of melodrama in its basic narrative to command respect or liking" (xxii). Thus, this standard edition of Barrett Browning firmly admonishes against any temptation to reread *Aurora Leigh:* the "living monument" is inscribed with a keep-off sign. Only the *Sonnets* remain, to "give Elizabeth Barrett Browning her modest but secure place as a true lyric poet" (xxii).

The *Sonnets*, that is—and something else. Having reduced Barrett Browning's canonical claims to a single work, Adams proceeds to locate the cultural value of that work not only in its capacity to offer a "full and satisfying expression" of the "emotions" of "those in love or in love with love" but in its service as clear documentation for the poet's love story: "Directness of communication, plus the legend of her own life, assures that [Barrett Browning] will be read both for the pleasure the poems give and from curiosity about her own romantic love affair with Robert Browning" (Introduction, xiv). The *Sonnets'* glory is that of the legend.

Adams's introduction first appeared in 1974. By 1977, William S. Peterson was writing that "the chief obstacle to an intelligent understanding of Mrs. Browning's poetry is the mythological fog which envelops her life" (Introduction, vii). That cloying fog, which was thickest in the vicinity of the *Sonnets*, was already beginning to lift. In the slow-moving world of standard pedagogy, as represented by the Cambridge edition, however, it has yet to dissipate. Conservative at its first printing, the Adams introduction still stands—and with it a long-standing tradition that both limits E. B. B.'s claim to literary recognition to the *Sonnets* and sets up obstacles even to the *Sonnets'* critical study.

In such a context, Peterson's description of the *Sonnets* as a "dark, allusive work irradiated with occasional visionary glimpses" might come as a surprise (xvi). So, too, might the *Sonnets* themselves, however. Indeed, so natural has it become to value—and devalue—the Portuguese sonnets as a simple, transparent, and thus "full and satisfying expression" of the emotions of those who are "in love or in love with love," that it is worth pausing here to reconsider the sequence that Robert Browning termed his "strange, heavy crown" (*Robert Browning and Julia Wedgwood*, 99). For recognition of the *Sonnets'* strangeness, heaviness, and eccentric richness is an indispensable prerequisite for understanding their virtual loss as works of art.

To gain a sense of what is at stake, one need only focus on the first action in the sequence. To quote the sonnet in full:

> I thought once how Theocritus had sung
> Of the sweet years, the dear and wished-for years,
> Who each one in a gracious hand appears
> To bear a gift for mortals, old or young:
> And, as I mused it in his antique tongue,
> I saw, in gradual vision through my tears,
> The sweet, sad years, the melancholy years,
> Those of my own life, who by turns had flung
> A shadow across me. Straightway I was 'ware,
> So weeping, how a mystic Shape did move
> Behind me, and drew me backward by the hair;
> And a voice said in mastery, while I strove,—
> "Guess now who holds thee?"—"Death," I said.
>   But, there,
> The silver answer rang,—"not Death, but Love."

In a sense, this sonnet offers what Adams's introduction and conventional literary tradition promise: a moving evocation of the power of love and a verse record of the Brownings' courtship. The speaker here is no Everywoman, however. Not only does she believe herself to be near death, but she seeks consolation by quoting Theocritus in the "antique tongue." One has to revise and edit a great deal to render such a lover generic. Even then, if one expects the speaker to offer a "full and satisfactory expression" of one's own emotion, one may tend not only to read her peril of death as overblown but to flatten the poem's eroticism.[4] The image of Love drawing back the speaker's hair is one whose passionate precision arises from historical specificity. Love's mystic shape is of the speaker's time, not ours. His gesture not only refutes a genuine expectation of death but establishes an intimate claim whose erotic power is deeply, thoroughly Victorian.[5]

Victorian, that is, in the sense of arising from a specific moment in time—but not necessarily Victorian in the sense generally associated with the *Sonnets*. For if the *Sonnets*' speaker is too individual, too historically determined to sing the praises of generic love, her speech itself is surely too abstract, too inwardly focused, and too transgressive or ambivalent to suit readers in search of a representatively quaint historical romantic love affair. Here, too, the drawing back of the hair suggests how such expectations not only overlook the *Sonnets*' very sources of power but block their recognition. For though the *Sonnets* have become justifiably renowned for reversing the courtly tradition of love poetry by speaking romantic desire in a woman's voice, they radically rewrite another famous encounter as well: the courtship of Death and the Maiden.

Much as the lovely, doomed Maiden awaits her lover, only to be overwhelmed by the sinister gallantry of another guest, the *Sonnets*' faded, weeping speaker sits in apparent expectation of Death's "mystic Shape." When Love arrives in his place, the erotic, gothic struggle that ensues is both new and uncannily familiar. As the medieval maiden insists upon life, Barrett's speaker struggles for death. Love has made a mistake, she insists, or is offering one final test of faith. For God has laid the "curse" of "Nay" on her eyelids, like pennies on the eyes of a corpse (ii, 4–9). If God offers her a saving "baptism" through the sweetness of Love, he must be presenting it in a self-sacrificial "cup of dole" (vii, 7–8). Death's dew has anointed her forehead, the speaker implies: she is doomed and shriven, promised elsewhere (iii, 13). No (mere) earthly lover should attempt to intervene in the performance of such a promise. Brandishing that equivalent of a "sepulchral urn," her smoldering heart, she warns her would-be lover to back off, lest fire "scorch and shred" him (v, 2, 9–14). Her very breath, she assures him, is poison fit to shatter his "Venice-glass" (ix, 12).

Like her predecessor, the *Sonnets*' speaker ultimately accepts the substitution of suitors. In place of the heavenly reward she had believed promised by her own "ministering life-angel," whose eyes were fixed "upcast" to the "white throne of God" (xlii, 3–5), she accepts an earthly lover, "not unallied / To angels" (xlii, 6–7)—a lover who is a worker of lifegiving miracles as well as a poet: "budding, at thy sight, my pilgrim's staff / Gave out green leaves" (9–10). Now ranked among "God's gifts" (xxvi, 14), her lover proves that "Love, as strong as Death, retrieves as well" (xxvii, 14). The speaker's eventual submission to the "mastery" of this "new angel" is paradoxical, however (i, 12; xlii, 14): she has been crushed low as if by "sword," and yet her conqueror has lifted her up from "abasement" (xvi, 8–9, 13). Saved and vanquished at once, she abandons not the conventional modesty of maidenhood but the heroic discipline of divinely ordained asceticism:

> *my soul, instead*
> *Of dreams of death, resumes life's lower range.*
> *Then, love me, Love! look on me—breathe on me!*
> (xxiii, 11–14)   *As brighter ladies do not count it strange,*
> *For love, to give up acres and degree,*
> *I yield the grave for thy sake, and exchange*
> *My near sweet view of Heaven, for earth with thee.*

Perhaps one form of sainthood has been replaced by another. Once "a poor, tired, wandering singer . . . leaning up a cyprus tree," she had told her lover, "The chrism is on thine head,— on mine, the dew,— / And Death must dig the level where these agree" (iii, 11–14). Now, anointed by a kiss, "the chrism of love, which love's own crown, / With sanctifying sweet- ness, did precede" (xxxviii, 10–11), she no longer "sings" while weeping. She longs, toward the poem's close, to shoot "My soul's full meaning into future years, / That *they* should lend it utterance, and salute / Love that endures, from Life that disappears!" (xli, 12–14). The patient ascetic has become a noisy prophetess; the deathly ash of her "heavy heart" has been transformed into the fertile (if weedy) "heart's ground" from which the *Sonnets* themselves have been drawn (v, i; xliv, 5–14).

"Romantic" this may be—and expressive, no doubt, at least at points, of the emotions of those in love (or in love with love). One cannot help wondering, however, how often close reading may have thwarted readers' recourse to the *Sonnets* for "a full and satisfying expres- sion" of their own emotions. To a reader such as Christina Rossetti, the *Sonnets'* ambivalence about restoration to life and to earthly love may well have been deeply resonant, for example, but what of other readers? As Dorothy Mermin points out, there is a long history of "embar- rassment" over the *Sonnets* ("Female Poet," 351–52). Although such embarrassment no doubt has many origins, one may well be the text's capacity to transform would-be condescension into confusion. Expecting a Victorian valentine, one finds instead the "strange, heavy crown" of a difficult, ambitious, and deeply personal art—not to mention the passionate idiosyncra- sies of a speaker whose angelic lover, in one version of the *Sonnets*, makes her feel "as safe as witches" (Barrett Browning, *Sonnets*, ed. Peterson, 25). If the *Sonnets* are embarrassing, it may be because the experience of reading them reveals the extent to which we, and not they, rely upon dreams of simple, innocently sentimental Victorian love. We must question our faith in that love—in that safe form of secular sanctity—if we are to come to terms with the *Sonnets'* strangeness and power.

Styles of sanctity: Barrett Browning's early canonic crises

Though Elizabeth Barrett Browning came closer to achieving full literary canonicity than any of Victorian England's other female poets, hers was always an unstable cultural presence. Decades of criticism agreed with the *Eclectic Review* that Barrett Browning's existence had done something "in a very emphatic way" to "settle the question" of the "intellectual relation of the sexes" ("Elizabeth Barrett Browning," 189). The question was, what? Metaphoric monu- ments to Barrett Browning's glory tended to teeter between extremes—between evocations of a Comtean honorary "Great Manhood" and of the "eternal," generic category of femininity, for example; or between emphasis on poetic wonder and feminine virtue. Although such instabili- ties were inherent in any attempt to canonize a woman poet, in Barrett Browning's case they were exacerbated both by the poet's own active role in shaping feminine canonicity and by the complex and at points paradoxical relations between her public and private personae.

Surely few women poets can have been more deeply and explicitly concerned with issues of feminine canonicity than Elizabeth Barrett Browning—or more challenging, during their lifetimes, as subjects for critical attempts at stabilizing the poet-heroine's role. E. B. B. worked actively to enter and shape that role; but first for biographical and then for political reasons, she rendered her position as a would-be poet-heroine an extraordinarily difficult one.

By fourteen, the "Poet Laureate of Hope End" had already composed an *autobiographia literaria*, "Glimpses into My Own Life and Literary Character." By twenty, she had written the "Fragment of an 'Essay on Woman,'" a work that not only rejected conventional praise for preceding generations of women poets but enrolled its author in a sacred feminine literary canon of her own naming (12). Indeed, although Deirdre David surely goes too far in implying that responsibility for the Barrett Browning legend lies primarily with the poet herself (98–99), E. B. B.'s career could be read as one long succession of attempts to accommodate—and to alter—the shape of feminine literary canonicity. Though only highlights can be sketched here, her career provides an indispensable context for understanding the canonization/decanonization process that started as soon as Barrett Browning died.

In her second signed volume of verse, the 1844 *Poems*, Elizabeth Barrett entered Victorian literary historiography as not only a strikingly ambitious and intellectual poet but an explicit candidate for feminine literary sanctity. It was an auspicious debut. Throughout much of the nineteenth century, long after her elopement had rendered its inclusion deeply ironic, editions of her complete works still opened with E. B. B.'s dedication of that volume to her father: "Somewhat more faint-hearted than I used to be, it is my fancy thus to seem to return to a visible personal dependence on you, as if indeed I were a child again; to conjure your beloved image between myself and the public, so as to be sure of one smile,—and to satisfy my heart while I sanctify my ambition, by associating with the great pursuit of my life its tenderest and holiest affection" (*Complete Works*, 2:142–43).[6]

Sanctifying literary ambition was already a central project for the poet, as the remainder of the volume reveals. In her preface, Barrett speaks as a poet-heroine whose domestic devotion converges with self-abnegating Christian devotion—and blends, almost imperceptibly, with the "patience angélique du génie." Aligning herself with holy visionary predecessors, she celebrates her own multifaceted suffering as the source of glorious "knowledge" and "song" (147–48). She also insists that she has been "hurried into speech" by "adoration" for divinity, driven to attempt a sacred subject that "fastened on" her "rather . . . than was chosen" (146, 143). "Life," she writes, is a "continual sacrament," and "poetry has been as serious a thing to me as life itself" (146, 148).

Such prose opens the way for "A Vision of Poets," a poetic work in which Barrett not only explicitly addresses "the necessary relations of genius to suffering and self-sacrifice" (147) but evokes an eerie architectural canon whose monuments simultaneously celebrate Romantic genius, Pythian inspiration, and the agonies of Christian sanctity (lines 220–50). Instructed by a female figure who comes "forth / To crown all poets to their worth," the masculine poet of the "Vision" imbibes first "starry water" that separates him from humanity, leaving him "holy and cold," and then the vile bitterness of "world's use," "world's love," and "world's cruelty" (lines 56–57, 140–41, 149, 158, 183). He awakens within a "great church" in which, "Pale and bound / With bay above the eyes profound," he finds a "strange company" of poet-saints (lines 221, 271–73): "Deathful their faces were, and yet / The power of life was in them set— / Never forgot nor to forget" (lines 274–76). "Glorified," their faces remain "still as a vision, yet exprest / Full as an action—look and geste / Of buried saint in risen rest" (lines 282–85).

Only one woman is named among the "poets true, / Who died for Beauty as martyrs do / For Truth—the ends being scarcely two" (lines 289–91). She is, of course, Sappho; and she is crowned not only with bay but "with that gloriole / Of ebon hair on calmèd brows—" (lines 318–19). To her as to no other poet, Barrett Browning's narrator speaks directly and in a tone of reassurance: "O poet-woman! none forgoes / The leap, attaining the repose" (lines 320–21).

Poetic, Christian, and perhaps Marian monuments, the figures in this cathedral of art stand

> *All, still as stone and yet intense;*
> *As if by spirit's vehemence*
> *That stone were carved and not by sense.*

> *But where the heart of each should beat,*
> *There seemed a wound instead of it,*   (lines 424–32)
> *From whence the blood dropped to their feet*

> *Drop after drop—dropped heavily*
> *As century follows century*
> *Into the deep eternity.*

Soon, however, they sing a harmony that makes them "burn in all their aureoles"—until (in another line that resonates with Browning's "Childe Roland"), "the blood which fell / Again, alone grew audible, / Tolling the silence as a bell" (lines 504, 508–10).

An angel breaks the silence. In his challenging question, the agonies of the female Pythia, the passion of saints, and the "angelic patience of genius" meet:

> *"If to speak nobly, comprehends*
> *To feel profoundly,—if the ends*
> *Of power and suffering, Nature blends,—*

> *"If poets on the tripod must*
> *Writhe like the Pythian to make just*
> *Their oracles and merit trust,—*

> *"If every vatic word that sweeps*
> *To change the world must pale their lips*
> *And leave their own souls in eclipse,—*

>   . . . .

> *"If ONE who did redeem you back,*
> *By His own loss, from final wrack,*
> *Did consecrate by touch and track*

> *"Those temporal sorrows till the taste*
> *Of brackish waters of the waste*   (lines 523–58)
> *Is salt with tears He dropt too fast,—*

> *"If all the crowns of earth must wound*
> *With prickings of the thorns He found,—*
> *If saddest sighs swell sweetest sound,—*

> *"What say ye unto this?—refuse*
> *This baptism in salt water?—choose*
> *Calm breasts, mute lips, and labour loose?*

"Or, O ye gifted givers! ye
Who give your liberal hearts to me
To make the world this harmony,

"Are ye resigned that they be spent
To such world's help?"

The Spirits bent
Their awful brows and said "Content."

Content to writhe like the female Pythia and to drink in suffering and bitterness as if they were the tears of Christ, Barrett Browning's "strange company" accepts not only suffering but suffering in potentially feminine form.

Not incidentally, the strange company also implicitly accepts E. B. B., who stands metaphorically ready for any number of crowns of thorns. Such associations were not lost upon several of the volume's initial reviewers, in whose pages the poet appeared not only as a sacred model whose "pain-perfected" voice offers "Revelations," but as a "Margarita or Perpetua of the Christian mythology" (Wicksteed 445; Grant 322; "Poems of Elizabeth Barrett Barrett," 132).[7] E. B. B. was already beginning to succeed as a sacred poet-heroine of resignation and suffering.

Around a month after the 1844 volume appeared, however, Barrett received her first letter from Robert Browning. She responded; and by so doing, the woman who had publicly aired her "fancy . . . to seem to return to a visible personal dependence" on her father set into motion a series of events that would drive her to an act of filial disobedience of the first order (*Complete Works*, 2:142). Barrett had cast herself as seeking to embody the highest traditional values both of feminine submission and of poetic ambition, without openly redefining either in the process. The task would have been impossible to fulfill; her life made it impossible to undertake.

A woman who chooses to take a lover and marry can no longer draw upon the symbolic power of ascetic sanctity. With Barrett Browning's marriage, one kind of saint was lost, though another might be found.

[. . .]

Notes

1 Unless otherwise noted, all references to Barrett Browning's work are to *Complete Works.*
2 This situation has been changing for some time, of course. Early indications of reviving interest in the *Sonnets* include Mermin, "The Female Poet"; Leighton, "Stirring a Dust"; and Sullivan. Stephenson's and Dow's works also represent critical landmarks.
3 Further reading will benefit a "sympathetic" reader, Adams writes, though "the reward is rather in separate coins than in a golden shower" (xiii–xiv). E. B. B. is, among other things, "too feverishly intense for twentieth-century taste" (xiii).
4 Such a reading seems to underlie Alethea Hayter's disparagement of the *Sonnets* as "personal, even idiosyncratic . . . not enough removed from personal relationship" (105). See Cooper, *Elizabeth Barrett Browning*, 101; Leighton, *Elizabeth Barrett Browning*, 98; Stephenson 69–73.
5 The gesture may also be Greek. It derives, editors Porter and Clarke suggest, from the *Iliad*, where Athena seizes Achilles' hair (Barrett Browning, *Complete Works*, 3:393).
6 See, for example, the 1883 Thomas Y. Crowell edition of Barrett Browning's *Complete Poetical Works.* Close to sixty years later, *The Best Known Poems of Elizabeth and Robert Browning* still opens with the 1844 dedication.
7 Barrett was also compared to other figures, of course, including Prometheus and Milton (Grant 324). Sandra Donaldson's *Elizabeth Barrett Browning* has been an invaluable resource in identifying authors of periodical literature on Barrett Browning.

Works cited

Browning, Elizabeth Barrett. *Complete Works*. Ed. Charlotte Porter and Helen A. Clarke. 6 vols. New York: AMS, 1973.

——. "Fragment of an 'Essay on Woman.'" *Studies in Browning and His Circle* 12 (1984): 10–12.

——. *The Poetical Works of Elizabeth Barrett Browning*. Cambridge Edition. Boston: Houghton Mifflin, 1974.

——. *Sonnets from the Portuguese*. Ed. William S. Peterson. Barre, Mass.: Imprint Society, 1977.

Browning, Robert. *Robert Browning and Julia Wedgwood*. Ed. Richard Curle. New York: Frederick A. Stokes, 1937.

Cooper, Helen. *Elizabeth Barrett Browning: Woman and Artist*. Chapel Hill: Univ. of North Carolina Press, 1988.

David, Deirdre. *Intellectual Women and Victorian Patriarchy: Harriet Martineau, Elizabeth Barrett Browning, George Eliot*. Ithaca: Cornell Univ. Press, 1987.

Donaldson, Sandra. *Elizabeth Barrett Browning: An Annotated Bibliography of the Commentary and Criticism 1826–1990*. New York: G. K. Hall, 1993.

"Elizabeth Barrett Browning." *Eclectic Review* 115 (1862): 189–212.

[Grant, Charles.] "Miss Barrett's Poems." *Metropolitan Magazine* (1845): 322–34.

Hayter, Alethea. *Mrs. Browning: A Poet's Work and Its Setting*. New York: Barnes and Noble, 1963.

Leighton, Angela. *Elizabeth Barrett Browning*. Bloomington: Indiana Univ. Press, 1986.

——. "Stirring a Dust of Figures: Elizabeth Barrett Browning and Love." *Browning Society Notes* 17 (1987–88): 11–24.

Mermin, Dorothy. "The Female Poet and the Embarrassed Reader: Elizabeth Barrett Browning's *Sonnets from the Portuguese*." *ELH* 48 (1981): 351–67.

Peterson, William S. Introduction to *Sonnets from the Portuguese, by Elizabeth Barrett Browning*. Barre, Mass.: Imprint Society, 1977.

Stephenson, Glennis. *Elizabeth Barrett Browning and the Poetry of Love*. UMI Research Press, 1989.

Sullivan, Mary-Rose. "'Some Interchange of Grace': 'Saul' and *Sonnets From the Portuguese*." *Browning Institute Studies* 15 (1987): 55–68.

[Wicksteed, Charles.] "Poems by Elizabeth Barrett Browning." *Prospective Review* I (1845): 445–64.

6 Rewriting *A History of the Lyre*

Letitia Landon, Elizabeth Barrett Browning and the (re)construction of the nineteenth-century woman poet

Linda H. Peterson

At the beginning of Letitia Landon's *A History of the Lyre*, a male speaker looks at the portrait of a female poet and meditates on the function of memory and autobiographical self-construction:

> 'Tis strange how much is mark'd on memory,
> In which we may have interest, but no part;
> How circumstances will bring together links
> In destinies the most dissimilar.
> This face, whose rudely-pencill'd sketch you hold,
> Recalls to me a host of pleasant thoughts,
> And some more serious. – This is EULALIE.[1]

At the beginning of Elizabeth Barrett Browning's *Aurora Leigh*, a speaker, now a female poet, meditates on the function of memory and autobiographical self-construction in a simile alluding, I think, to Landon's poem but revising its plot and intention:

> Of writing many books there is no end;
> And I who have written much in prose and verse
> For others' uses, will write now for mine –
> As when you paint your portrait for a friend,
> Who keeps it in a drawer and looks at it
> Long after he has ceased to love you, just
> To hold together what he was and is.[2]

Like Landon, Barrett Browning remarks on the importance of memory, which 'hold[s] together' the subject, 'what he was and is'. Like Landon, too, Barrett Browning analogizes portrait painting and autobiographical writing – with L.E.L.'s 'rudely-pencill'd sketch' and its capacity for linking past and present becoming the portrait Aurora Leigh will create in verse to construct a coherent poetic self and a new vision of the woman poet.

Yet these opening passages are significantly different. In *A History of the Lyre*, it is the male lover who holds the poetess's sketch and contemplates it for 'a host of pleasant thoughts' and the construction of his *own* history and identity, whereas in *Aurora Leigh* it is Aurora who writes of herself for her 'better self'. Landon's analogy between autobiography and portrait painting gets subordinated to a simile ('As when') as if Barrett Browning means to subordinate the traditional function of women's memoirs to the more pressing need of the woman poet. There is a shift, in short, from a male viewer to the female poet, from art produced to satisfy masculine desire to art for the sake of the female poet, from a literary tradition of biographical memoirs *about* women poets to a new tradition of autobiography *by* women writers (hinted at in the next allusion of *Aurora Leigh* – the one in lines 9–13 to Wordsworth's *Immortality Ode* and *Prelude*, the latter published just six years before Barrett Browning's poem). Barrett Browning, I shall argue, corrects Landon's opening passage – and, more broadly, the preface to and plot of *A History of the Lyre* – by taking (auto)biographical forms identified with the Romantic *poetess* and reconfiguring them to serve the development of the Victorian woman *poet.* In these corrections she revises the constructions of the poetess as they appeared in Landon's works and in a spate of biographies about Landon published in the two decades before *Aurora Leigh.*

I

Like many of Landon's poems, these biographies reproduce – indeed, they help to construct – the myth of the Romantic poetess. As Glennis Stephenson has pointed out, biographies of the poetess invariably associate her work with her body and depict it 'as the intuitive and confessional outpouring of emotion':

> Words like 'gushing' and 'over-flowing' abound in [the works of Landon and Hemans]. . . . These women are . . . fountains, not pumps. The flow is from nature, not art. Usually the creative woman in these poems is betrayed and abandoned, and finds that with the loss of love the flow dries up.

Thus a poetess like Landon came to exemplify a debased or inferior form of Romanticism – 'Wordworth's "spontaneous overflow of powerful feelings" which, rather than being recollected in tranquility, [were] immediately spewed out on the page'.[3] Angela Leighton has further pointed out that 'although L.E.L. insists on art as an overflow of the female body, she also frequently freezes the woman into a picture, a statue, an art object' – something that occurs at the beginning and end of *A History of the Lyre.* 'Such frozen postures', Leighton notes, have 'a way of turning the woman into a form of sexual or artistic property for the man'.[4]

[. . .]

Such depictions of Landon began as early as 1839 with Emma Roberts's 'Memoir of L.E.L.', included in the posthumously published *The Zenana and Minor Poems.* According to Roberts,

> While still a mere child, L.E.L. began to publish, and her poetry immediately attracted attention. . . . [S]he rushed fearlessly into print, not dreaming for a moment, that verses which were poured forth like the waters from a fountain, gushing, as she has beautifully expressed it, of their own sweet will, could ever provoke stern or harsh criticism.[5]

Laman Blanchard, who brought out *The Life and Literary Remains of L.E.L.* in 1841, similarly treats her poetry as natural productions: 'Just as the grass grows that sows itself'.[6] Like other biographers who would follow, Blanchard associates Landon herself with the title character of *The Improvisatrice*, noting that the heroine of that poem was 'youthful, impassioned, and gifted with glorious powers of song; and, although introduced as a daughter of Florence . . . she might be even L.E.L. herself; for what were the multitude of songs she had been pouring out for three years past, but "improvisings"?' (vol. I, p. 40). When William

Howitt published his biographical *Homes and Haunts of the Most Eminent British Poets* in 1847, he, too, associated Landon with her *Improvisatrice*, noting that 'the very words of her first heroine might have literally been uttered as her own: –

> "Sad were my shades; methinks they had
> Almost a tone of prophecy –
> I ever had, from earliest youth,
> A feeling what my fate would be."'[7]

Such associations had, of course, been encouraged by Landon herself who, after translating the poetical odes in Madame de Staël's *Corinne*, took to appearing publicly in the Sappho–Corinne mode, dressed in Grecian costume with her hair done à la Sappho, and who continued writing and rewriting the Sappho–Corinne myth, including the archetypal version in *A History of the Lyre*.

The myth of the poetess as *improvisatrice* had certain advantages: it linked her to the cult of genius and her work to inspired rather than mechanical or pedantic production. But it also had disadvantages: in its emphasis on the poetess's natural genius and her youthful, sometimes even infantile poetic effusions, it tended to restrict the poetess to a youthful, immature stage of development and to mitigate against more mature, serious writing. All of the major nineteenth-century women poets – Robinson, Hemans, Landon, Barrett Browning, Rossetti – were infant prodigies, young geniuses who could recite hundreds of lines of verse as children (Hemans), or who composed poems and stories almost before they learned to hold a pen (Landon), or who published volumes of ambitious verses in early adolescence (Robinson, Hemans, Barrett Browning, Rossetti). This myth of youthful genius, as Norma Clarke has pointed out, tended to work against the development of the woman poet's career – and serious treatment of her poetry – once she moved beyond youth into maturity or middle age.[8]

[. . .]

[D]isclaimers of Sapphic tragedy, most written after Landon's mysterious death by an overdose of prussic acid and intended to offset rumours of suicide, have the strange effect of reinforcing the third feature of the myth of the Romantic poetess – that of model or statue, of the poetess as a performer who strikes a pose for the pleasure of her audience but to her own detriment. The plot of *A History of the Lyre* reinforces this notion. Like many of Landon's works, it reproduces the Sappho–Corinne myth: it tells the tale of an inspired poetess, half-Italian, half-English, who spends her daytime hours in solitude, awaiting inspiration, and her nights in company, performing for her audience and winning great fame. She meets a man who listens and gazes raptly but who, in the end, abandons her for a more conventional, domestic Englishwoman. In *A History of the Lyre* the Englishman tells the tale of his encounters with Eulalie and of his eventual marriage to Emily. Landon adds the touch of having the poetess Eulalie create her own statue – 'a sculptured form' that becomes a funeral monument:

> 'You see', she said, 'my cemetery here: –
> Here, only here, shall be my quiet grave.
> Yon statue is my emblem: see, its grasp
> Is rais'd to Heaven, forgetful that the while
> Its step has crush'd the fairest of earth's flowers
> With its neglect'.

(p. 231)

This conclusion recognizes that the poetess sacrifices herself in performance for men: for their erotic pleasure, obviously, but also for their corporate benefit in that she does not interfere with (or intervene in) the patriarchal structures that allow Eulalie to die solitary and Emily, her passive, domestic counterpart, to marry and reproduce English culture. In *A History of the Lyre*, far more than in earlier poems, the poetess becomes complicit in her own death.

Of the early biographers, only Howitt seems to have noticed the element of self-sacrifice and self-destruction in Landon's life and work. Although he presents it only as a possibility, he speculates that L.E.L. must have seen her fate 'from earliest youth' and understood the destructiveness of the poetic myths she was creating:

> Whether this melancholy belief in the tendency of the great theme of her writings, both in prose and poetry; this irresistible annunciation, like another Cassandra, of woe and destruction; this evolution of scenes and characters in her last work, bearing such dark resemblance to those of her own after experience; this tendency, in all her plots, to a tragic catastrophe, and this final tragedy itself, – whether these be all mere coincidences or not, they are still but parts of an unsolved mystery.[9]

Despite the tentative phrasing, Howitt was not a believer in 'mere coincidences'. His treatment of Landon's death makes it clear that he found foreshadowings in her poetical and fictional work, of her tragic end. He recognized, as I believe Elizabeth Barrett did also, that Landon's self-construction as a Sapphic poetess destined her for an early death, that she more or less wrote herself into that fatal plot.

II

Elizabeth Barrett was a careful reader (and admirer) of Landon's poetry, and she read carefully as well Blanchard's 1841 biography of the poetess. In a letter to Mary Russell Mitford, she compared Landon with Hemans, concluding that 'if I had those two powers to choose from – Mrs Hemans's and Miss Landon's – I mean the *raw* bare powers – I would choose Miss Landon's'. Yet Barrett also believed that Landon had not fully realized her promise or power. To Mitford she further commented, 'I fancy it would have worked out better – had it *been* worked out – with the right moral and intellectual influences in application'.[10]

Barrett Browning's most sustained commentary on Landon's work comes, as I shall argue here, in the opening books of *Aurora Leigh*, where she acknowledges, yet rejects, the self-construction of the poetess who preceded her.[11] In these books she gives to Aurora those 'right moral and intellectual influences' and shows, in the later books of the poem, how the life of the woman poet might 'work out better' with them.

I have already suggested that, in allusions to *A History of the Lyre* and *The Prelude*, Aurora determines to write an autobiography for her own poetic development, as Wordsworth had done and Landon had not. Her allusion to Wordsworth's poetry –

> I, writing thus, am still what men call young;
> I have not so far left the coasts of life
> To travel inland, that I cannot hear
> That murmur of the outer Infinite
> Which unweaned babies smile at in their sleep . . .

(lines 9–13)

– claims partnership with an undebased Romantic tradition and a masculine form of auto-biography.[12] Aurora Leigh is still young enough that she recollects Wordsworthian joy and, more importantly, that her autobiography may usefully trace 'the growth of a poet's mind' and provide evidence, to adapt Wordsworth's phrase, that 'May spur me on, in [wo]manhood now mature, / To honorable toil' (*The Prelude*, lines 624–5). This turn to a Wordsworthian form of autobiography swerves away from Landon's view of the poetess as erotic object or as performer for the pleasure and benefit of men.

In the opening books of *Aurora Leigh*, Barrett Browning also abandons the model of the female poet as improvisatrice. In Book I Aurora admits that young poets often write spontane-ously and effusively:

> Many tender souls
> Have strung their losses on rhyming thread,
> As children, cowslips.
> (Book I, lines 945–7)

Although she figures such rhyming as natural, she is not content to remain in this immature artistic state:

> Alas, near all the birds
> Will sing at dawn – and yet we do not take
> The chaffering swallow for the holy lark.
> (Book I, lines 951–3)

In Books II and III, often taking the lark as her counterpart,[13] Aurora traces her develop-ment beyond the stage of natural effusions toward that mature poetic production of which Wordsworth wrote in *The Prelude*. At the end of this sequence she notes:

> So life, in deepening with me, deepened all
> The course I took, the work I did.
> (Book III, lines 334–5)

As she traces Aurora's career, Barrett Browning includes many details of plot that specifically recall Landon's life, thus suggesting that she means to treat the life of the Romantic poet-ess as a stage in the development of the Victorian woman poet – as ontogeny recapitulating phylogeny. This treatment allows Barrett Browning to acknowledge the achievement of the Romantic poetess but with the implication that she, representative of the next generation, will progress further. For example, in Book III Aurora moves to an attic room in London, to 'a certain house in Kensington' and 'a chamber up three flights of stairs' (Book III, lines 160, 158).[14] Barrett Browning never lived in a writer's garret, but Landon certainly did – at 22 Hans Place in an attic space invariably described in the biographies as a 'homely-looking, almost uncomfortable room, fronting the street, and barely furnished'.[15]

So, too, Barrett Browning makes Aurora a hack writer of prose as well as an aspir-ing poet. It was Landon, not Barrett Browning, who churned out reviews for the *Literary Gazette* and whose biographers mention, usually as evidence of her wide reading, her enor-mous prose production.[16] Like Landon, Aurora works 'with one hand for the booksell-ers / While working with the other for myself / And art' (Book III, lines 303–5). Even

Aurora's popularity with her readers suggests Landon's early career. The fanmail 'with pretty maiden seals' from girls with names like 'Emily' (Book III, lines 212–13) or the 'tokens from young bachelors, / Who wrote from college' (Book III, lines 215–16) recall both the sweet, domestic bride of *A History of the Lyre* (also named Emily) and the anecdote related by Edward Bulwer Lytton and repeated in virtually all of L.E.L.'s biographies about admiring young male readers:

> We were young, and at college, lavishing our golden years, not so much on the Greek verse and mystic character to which we ought, perhaps, to have been rigidly devoted, as 'Our heart in passion, and our head in rhyme'. At that time poetry was not yet out of fashion, at least with us of the cloister; and there was always in the reading-room of the Union a rush every Saturday afternoon for the 'Literary Gazette'; and an impatient anxiety to hasten at once to that corner of the sheet which contained the three magical letters 'L.E.L.' All of us praised the verse, and all of us guessed at the author. We soon learned it was a female, and our admiration was doubled, and our conjectures tripled. Was she young? Was she pretty? And – for there were some embryo fortune-hunters among us – was she rich?[17]

Such details in Book III not only allude to Landon's life but signal more generally, I think, the determination of Aurora, like other Victorian women writers, to pursue a professional career. In the 1820s, 1830s, and 1840s many women writers, like Landon and Roberts at 22 Hans Place, Harriet Martineau in Fludyer Street, and George Eliot at 142 The Strand, moved to lodgings in London to signal their professional aspirations, and they were not above writing reviews, translating foreign literature, or doing other hack work to provide the financial means needed to support their literary careers. Aurora's life as a 'city poet' represents this new, if not quite glorious stage in the nineteenth-century woman writer's professionalization.

The differences from Landon's life are also significant, however – most notably Aurora's unsullied reputation and her unwavering commitment, despite early fame, to produce high art. Landon's reputation had come to ruin (or close to it) with rumours of illicit liaisons with William Jerdan, editor of the *Literary Gazette*; William Maginn, the heavy-drinking Irish journalist associated with *Blackwood's* and *Fraser's*; and Daniel Maclise, the painter. Although they name no names, the early biographers acknowledge these 'atrocious calumnies', in Howitt's phrase, invariably to refute them. None the less, the biographers admit that Landon's public persona, 'the very unguardedness of her innocence' and her lack of concern 'about the interpretation that was likely to be put upon her words',[18] contributed to the problem, as did the life histories of her fictional poetesses. Eulalie in *A History of the Lyre* confesses that she is more like the 'Eastern tulip' with its 'radiant' yet short-lived colours than the pure 'lily of the valley' with its 'snowy blossoms'. In contrast, Aurora can say unequivocally,

> I am a woman of repute;
> No fly-blow gossip ever specked my life;
> My name is clean and open as this hand,
> Whose glove there's not a man dares blab about
> As if he had touched it freely.
> (Book IX, lines 264–8)

As she begins her career, she self-consciously resolves to live 'holding up my name / To keep it from the mud' (Book III, lines 311–12).

More important to artistic development, Barrett Browning revises Aurora's attitude toward fame and sustained poetic achievement. Eulalie, like Erinna before her, laments that she has lost the desire (or perhaps that she lacks the ability) to sustain her work:

> I am as one who sought at early dawn
> To climb with fiery speed some lofty hill:
> His feet are strong in eagerness and youth
> His limbs are braced by the fresh morning air,
> And all seems possible: – this cannot last.
> The way grows steeper, obstacles arise,
> And unkind thwartings from companions near.[19]
>
> (p. 226)

But whereas Eulalie laments that early fame has proved a fatal opium –

> I am vain, – praise is opium, and the lip
> Cannot resist the fascinating draught,
> Though knowing its excitement is a fraud, –

that she can 'no longer work miracles for thee [fame],' and that now 'Disappointment tracks / The steps of Hope,' Aurora determines that she will progress beyond simple 'ballads', the form identified with female poetesses, and work her way up through the generic ranks that have long challenged English male poets: from pastoral through epic. Indeed, one can read the opening monologue of Book V as Aurora's challenge to Eulalie's tragic lament in *A History of the Lyre*. It presents a counter-argument that women poets can indeed 'last' as 'The way grows steeper, obstacles arise, / And unkind thwartings from companions near.' It imagines women poets treating 'The human heart's large seasons', from 'that strain of sexual passion' to 'the great escapings of ecstatic souls' (Book V, lines 13–20), not just Landon's more simple romantic and domestic love. Significantly, too, Barrett Browning turns Eulalie's admission of inadequacy into Romney's assertions of the female poet's limitations (in Book II, lines 180–225, and Book IV, lines 1115–24, 1159–68, 1202–11).[20] In *Aurora Leigh* it is the male critic who denigrates the woman poet's abilities and achievements, not the woman poet who initiates her own destruction.

What Barrett Browning does not alter or avoid is Landon's psychological insight that the female poet longs for, perhaps even needs, the approval of her male reader. In *A History of the Lyre* Eulalie performs for large audiences but in particular for the pleasure of the Englishman who follows her about for a year; when he leaves Italy without offering marriage, she more or less 'hang[s] [her] lute on some lone tree, and die[s]'.[21] L.E.L.'s arrangement of these details is significant: Eulalie, in a long monologue reproduced by the male speaker, laments the ill effects of fame, and praises the virtues of 'the loveliness of home' and 'support and shelter from man's heart' (p. 226). When the monologue ends, he abruptly states, 'I soon left Italy; it is well worth / A year of wandering, were it but to feel / How much our England does outweigh the world' (p. 230). We might read this hiatus simply as an acknowledgement that poetic genius is unsuited to domestic life. Landon seems to have intended, however, a stronger link between the continuing work of the female poetess and the continuing approval – including love – of her male audience.

Aurora confronts the issue of male approval in Book V, where she lays out her plan for progress up through the generic ranks and then identifies the primary obstacle to that progress:

– I must fail
Who fail at the beginning to hold and move
One man – and he my cousin, and he my friend.

(Book V, lines 30–2)

Aurora fears 'this vile woman's way / Of trailing garments', yet determines, unlike Landon's poetess, that it 'shall not trip me up' (Book V, lines 59–60). If Landon framed the issue in erotic and romantic terms, Barrett Browning re-frames it in poetic and aesthetic terms. Aurora admits her loneliness as a woman writer and her envy of male artists who are rewarded with love, whether the love of a mother or of a wife. But the need for love, we should note, is not peculiar to the *woman* artist; it affects male artists like Graham, Belmore, and Mark Gage, all of whom rely on domestic affection (Book V, lines 502–39). Aurora expresses her desire for Romney's approval in rather different terms from those of L.E.L. – that is, in terms of the poet's vocation and specifically the female poet's terrain: Is her work, contrary to what Romney believes, equal to that of the social activist? Shall the woman poet be confined, as in Romney's view at the end of Book IV, to 'the mythic turf where danced the nymphs' (Book IV, line 1161), or shall she treat the whole range of human experience and passion that Aurora details at the beginning of Book V? In Barrett Browning's poem it is Aurora's view, not Romney's opinion or Landon's precedent as a poet of lyric love, that finally determines the career of the woman poet – and the plot of the remainder of the poem.

After Book V, very little of Landon's life and work informs *Aurora Leigh* – except, of course, that Barrett Browning revises the conclusion to *A History of the Lyre* (a conclusion some biographers thought Landon had enacted in her life). Eulalie, Sappho-like, dies an abandoned woman; Aurora lives to marry Romney. Eulalie's history is told only after her death, by her male admirer; Aurora Leigh's is written at the peak of her power by the poet herself. If the marriage ending of *Aurora Leigh* has been controversial among contemporary feminist critics, primarily for seeming to succumb to the conventions of the marriage plot,[22] it looks different in its historical and generic contexts. In the context of women's autobiography, it represents a determination to write one's own life and not let others construct one's life history. In the context of biographies of the nineteenth-century woman poet, it represents a writing against a prior tradition, a rejection of Landon's dying for (male) pleasure, and a progression from the poetess to the woman poet.

Barrett Browning is famous for having written, 'I look everywhere for grandmothers and see none'.[23] Perhaps Landon, born in 1802 only four years before her, was too close in age to be considered a literary 'grandmother'. Perhaps Dorothy Mermin is right that, in making such a comment, Barrett Browning was ignoring 'the popular "poetesses" who adorned the literary scene', as they did not represent 'the noble lineage with which she wished to claim affiliation'.[24] Perhaps between the statement to Robert Browning in 1845 and the writing of *Aurora Leigh* a decade later, she owned up to the existence of women writers who had influenced her, if only (or primarily) as negative examples. Whatever the case, when Barrett Browning came to write her autobiography of the new woman poet, she framed its plot and some of its features in terms of the female literary figures of the preceding generation. If in revising *A History of the Lyre*, she lets Eulalie's lyre stay hanging on a tree and gives Aurora instead a Gideon's trumpet, 'a clarion' to press 'on thy woman's lip' (Book IX, line 929), she none the less acknowledges, in the scope and density of her allusions, the importance of Letitia Landon's work in the history of nineteenth-century women's poetry. Like it or not, the Romantic poetess was one progenitor of the Victorian woman poet.

Notes

1 *Poetical Works of Letitia Elizabeth Landon, 'L.E.L.'*, ed. F. J. Sypher (Delmar, NY: Scholars' Facsimiles and Reprints, 1990) p. 223. Unless otherwise indicated, all citations of Landon's work will be to this edition, which is a reprint of the volume edited and illustrated by William B. Scott and published by George Routledge in 1873.

2 Elizabeth Barrett Browning, *Aurora Leigh*, ed. Kerry McSweeney (Oxford: Oxford University Press, 1993) lines 1–8. All citations will be to this edition.

3 Glennis Stephenson, 'Poet Construction: Mrs Hemans, L.E.L., and the Image of the Nineteenth-Century Woman Poet', in *ReImagining Women: Representations of Women in Culture*, ed. Shirley Neuman and Glennis Stephenson (Toronto: University of Toronto Press, 1993) p. 66. See also Landon's *Erinna:* 'It was my other self that had a power; / Mine, but o'er which I had not a control. . . . A song came gushing, like the natural tears, / To check whose current does not rest with us' (*Poetical Works*, p. 216).

4 Angela Leighton, *Victorian Women Poets: Writing Against the Heart* (London: Harvester, Wheatsheaf, 1991) p. 61.

5 E[mma] R[oberts], 'Memoir of L.E.L.', in *The Zenana and Minor Poems* (London, 1839) p. 9. Roberts also refers to Landon's poetry as 'her effusions' (p. 10).

6 Laman Blanchard, *Life and Literary Remains of L.E.L.* (London: Henry Colbum, 1841) vol. I, p. 17.

7 William Howitt, *Homes and Haunts of the Most Eminent British Poets* (London: Richard Bentley, 1847) vol. II, p. 134. Elizabeth Barrett knew of Howitt's project to write biographies of the major poets by focusing on their characteristic locales; Robert Browning wrote disapprovingly of Howitt's method of gathering information on 1 May 1846, and Elizabeth replied the next day, 'How bad of William Howitt! How right you are, always!' See *The Letters of Robert Browning and Elizabeth Barrett Barrett, 1845–1846* (London: Smith, Elder, 1899) vol. II, pp. 118–21.

8 Norma Clarke, 'The Cause of Infant Genius', paper given at the International Conference on Women's Poetry, Birkbeck College, London University, 21 July 1995.

9 Howitt, *Homes and Haunts*, vol. II, p. 137. Following this passage, Howitt repeats an anecdote he heard from Emma Roberts, which she apparently suppressed: that Landon, 'when calumny was dealing very freely with her name', told Roberts that she had a 'remedy' for her 'suffering' and showed her friend 'a vial of prussic acid'. Howitt treats his anecdote as a real-life version of a fictional incident in Landon's novel *Ethel Churchill*, thus suggesting another link between the poetess's life and her work.

10 Letter to Mary Russell Mitford, 16 July 1841, in *Elizabeth Barrett to Miss Mitford: The Unpublished Letters of Elizabeth Barrett Barrett to Mary Russell Mitford*, ed. Betty Miller (London: John Murray, 1954) pp. 77–8.

11 There is, of course, Elizabeth Barrett's implicit commentary in her poem 'L.E.L.'s Last Question', which suggests that, had L.E.L. thought more of Him 'who drew / All life from dust, and for all tasted death', her poetry might have achieved a greater, more long-lasting significance. This sense of the poetess's focus on things domestic and mundane, to the omission of higher, spiritual matters, continues in *Aurora Leigh.*

12 Kathleen Blake traces the parallels to Wordsworth's *The Prelude* in 'Elizabeth Barrett Browning and Wordsworth: The Romantic Poet as Woman', *Victorian Poetry*, 24 (1986) pp. 387–98. My point, a slightly different one from Blake's, is that Barrett Browning uses allusions to Wordsworth to distinguish Aurora from the Romantic female poetess.

13 Aurora takes the lark as her counterpart, e.g., in Book II, lines 744–5: 'The little lark reached higher with his song / Than I with crying,' and in Book III, lines 151–2: 'The music soars within the little lark, / And the lark soars.'

14 See Leighton, *Victorian Women Poets* p. 51, that in this detail Elizabeth Barrett Browning 'may well be remembering the life of LEL.'

15 Blanchard, *Life and Literary Remains*, vol. I, p. 79. This description also appears in Mrs Elwood's *Memoirs of the Literary Ladies of England* (London: Henry Colbum, 1843) vol. II, p. 319, and William Howitt's *Homes and Haunts of the Most Eminent British Poets* vol. II, p. 130. It continues: '– with a simple white bed, at the foot of which was a small, old, oblong-shaped sort of dressing-table, quite covered with a common worn writing-desk heaped with papers, while some strewed the ground, the table being too small for aught besides the desk; a little high-backed cane-chair which gave you any idea rather than that of comfort – a few books scattered about completed the author's paraphernalia'.

16 See, e.g., Emma Roberts's comment ('Memoir of L.E.L.', p. 17) that 'the history and literature of all ages and all countries were familiar to her . . . the extent of her learning, and the depth of her research, manifesting themselves in publications which do not bear her name'.

17 Blanchard, *Life and Literary Remains*, vol. I, pp. 32–3.

18 Howitt, *Homes and Haunts*, vol. II, p. 137; Blanchard, *Life and Literary Remains*, vol. I, p. 52.

19 Cf. Hannah More's use of the myth of Atalanta in *Strictures on the Modern System of Female Education* (in *Works* [New York: Harpers, 1835] vol. I, p. 367) to argue that women writers cannot sustain their careers as men can.

20 On this score, Angela Leighton is incorrect to suggest that Aurora's father is more important than Romney to her poetic development: 'It is not the realization that she has loved and lost Romney, but that she has lost her father, which tests and educates her imagination', Leighton writes in *Elizabeth Barrett Browning* (Brighton, Sussex: Harvester Press, 1986) p. 136. Romney is important because he becomes the patriarchal mouthpiece, arguing the traditional challenges to women's abilities and for Aurora's 'proper' place in the domestic sphere. Her father is not put in this position because Barrett Browning wants Aurora to claim her paternal inheritance – the learning, the intellectual contribution – without complication.

21 *A History of the Lyre*, p. 229.

22 Cora Kaplan, in her ground-breaking study of the sources of *Aurora Leigh*, calls it the 'most vulgar' alteration of the Corinne myth ('Introduction', *Aurora Leigh and Other Poems*, ed. Cora Kaplan [London: Women's Press, 1978] p. 17). Dorothy Mermin writes more ambivalently: 'Perhaps the oddest thing about *Aurora Leigh*, after all, is the triumphantly happy ending – happy for the heroine at any rate, if not for her disempowered and humiliated lover' (see Dorothy Mermin, *Elizabeth Barrett Browning: The Origins of a New Poetry* [Chicago, IL: University of Chicago Press, 1989] p. 217).

23 *The Letters of Elizabeth Barrett Browning* (1898), ed. Frederic G. Kenyon, 2 vols (London: Smith, Elder), vol. 1, p. 232 (letter dated 7 January 1845 addressed to Mr Chorley).

24 Mermin, op. cit., p. 1. Later Mermin suggests that Barrett Browning's 'real rival was L.E.L., not Homer or Byron or even Mrs Hemans, whom she considered too ladylike and deficient in passion to be seriously reckoned with' (p. 32). If Mermin is correct, as I think she is, then the density of allusions to Landon's work in *Aurora Leigh* points to that rivalry.

7   Atheist prophecy

Mathilde Blind, Constance Naden, and the Victorian poetess

Charles LaPorte

Scholars of nineteenth-century women's poetry often recount that the sentimental piety—indeed, the quasi-religiosity—of the Victorian "poetess" disappears from women's poetry in the mordant irony of the *fin de siècle*. Virginia Blain, for instance, has recently identified Mathilde Blind and Constance Naden as representatives of "the new breed of post-Darwinian atheists" that comes to replace an earlier, implicitly Christian feminine tradition associated with Elizabeth Barrett Browning (Blain 332). On a related note, I have recently proposed that George Eliot's *Legend of Jubal* collections (1874, 1878) present a rather late instance of this poetess tradition (LaPorte 159–61). In what follows, I would like to argue that *fin-de-siècle* iconoclasts such as Blind and Naden actually work hard to reclaim and redeem some of the prominent religious elements of the mid-century poetess tradition, and that Eliot's unusual combination of sentimental piety and religious skepticism gives them a particularly useful model for doing so.[1]

Barrett Browning's *Aurora Leigh* (1856) anticipates the emergence of a prophetic line of female poets akin to the one that I will describe here. In an audacious revision of the Biblical Book of Kings, *Aurora Leigh* depicts a female Elisha attending the cloak of the poetess prophet Aurora (3: 53–60). And though Eliot herself might seem an unlikely Elisha to Barrett Browning's Elijah, she was deeply invested in the religious character of the poetess. Eliot's 1865 journal, for instance, pays homage to the late Barrett Browning in its description of Robert Browning's London home:

> In the evening walked home with Browning, went into his house, and saw the objects Mrs. Browning used to have about her, her chair, tables, books etc. An epoch to be remembered. Browning showed us her Hebrew Bible with notes in her handwriting, and several of her copies of the Greek dramatists with her annotations. (*Letters* 4: 205)

This journal entry conveys both Eliot's respect for her predecessor's erudition (the Hebrew notes, the Greek annotations) and reverence for her literary remains. Perhaps it even uses "epoch" in the traditional senses suggested by the *Oxford English Dictionary,* such as 1.1 "The initial point assumed in a system of chronology," or 1.2, "The beginning of a 'new era.'" By these definitions, Eliot's expression "An epoch to be remembered" refers not just to Barrett Browning's mid-century, but to Eliot's 1865 visit, which marked an epoch in her own life. Indeed, it is around this time that Eliot first began pursuing poetry as a serious alternative to her very successful career as a novelist. Eliot's response to Barrett Browning merits particular attention because of her status as her generation's most prominent female intellectual; only after having achieved this extraordinary position in the 1860s and 70s did Eliot too begin publishing feminine verses embodying the figure of the poetess.

Most importantly for "the new breed" of atheists identified by Blain, Eliot embraced the religious dimensions of the poetess despite being a famous skeptic. This is apparent in her personal testimony above, where she depicts Browning's London home as a sort of reliquary, a shrine to Barrett Browning's "chair, tables, books etc." But it is more clearly evidenced in the religious themes of Eliot's poetry. Her unambiguous adoption of Barrett Browning's quasi-religious poetic model provided younger poets with a means of reconciling religious skepticism with the prophetic cultural authority familiar to scholars of the mid-century poetess tradition. Where mid-century poetesses such as Barrett Browning had presented themselves as zealous theists, Eliot presents herself as a zealous agnostic whose verses reproduce the mechanical structures of religious belief. Yet this comparatively irreligious aesthetic nonetheless adheres to Barrett Browning's portrayal of the relationship between poetry and prophecy, for Eliot too conceived of the poetess as she who best propagates the most revolutionary lesson of Romantic-era Biblical criticism, the higher criticism: that is, that imaginative literature is itself a real and valid form of prophecy. It is this conviction that finds revivified expression in the poetry of Blind and Naden. Although Blind's and Naden's provocative, iconoclastic, and ambitious poetic projects invert the standard topoi of nineteenth-century women's poetry (love, loss, religion, domesticity) with a boldness that would have astonished and dismayed Barrett Browning, yet their brand of iconoclasm is not, finally, alien to her tradition.

I should add that I relate Blind's and Naden's literary achievements to those of Eliot in part because so many Victorians did so. In Blind's case, comparison to Eliot is easy because she actively sought it. Even had she not written Eliot's biography in *George Eliot* (1883), still it seems significant that she, too, began her career in *belles lettres* with scholarly articles in the *Westminster Review* before translating a major work of the higher critic David Friedrich Strauss, *The Old Faith and the New* (1873, trans. of *Der alte und der neue Glaube* 1872), and then turning to poetry and to novels. According to the memoir of her friend, Richard Garnett, Blind was actually surprised when *The Old Faith and the New* failed to recreate the uproar of Eliot's Strauss translation, *The Life of Jesus* (1846, trans. of *Das Leben Jesu,* 1835) (Blind, *Poetical Works* 27).[2] But Blind need not have cultivated an Eliotic reputation. Conspicuously intellectual *fin-de-siècle* literary women received comparison to Eliot as a matter of course.

[. . .]

I. Eliot: "A Minor Prophet"

To show how the Victorian poetess and the female prophet remain intimately associated even so late as the *fin-de-siècle* poetry of Blind [. . .] it is helpful to select from Eliot's *Legend of Jubal* collections a brief illustration of her own post-Christian notion of prophecy. One may be found in the lyric "A Minor Prophet," a pastiche of some unusual religious views held by one Elias Baptist Butterworth, an American Quaker whose faith prophesies a progressive Millennium just around the corner (Armstrong and Bristow 381–88).[3] In some ways, Eliot's poem is rather conservative. Radical Americans presented an obvious target for English satire in the first half of the 1860s (when this poem was written) because of international tensions during and after the American Civil War. Anthony Trollope, for instance, created similar caricatures in Jonas Spalding and Wallachia Petrie, the radical Northerners of *He Knew He Was Right* (1868–69). Like Baptist Butterworth, Trollope's Spalding and Petrie emphasize the follies of radical American political theory to show, by contrast, the commonsense sagacity of old-fashioned British ways.

Yet "A Minor Prophet" is only ostensibly about the Millennial hopes of this American zealot. Rather, the bulk of the poem presents the reflections of a skeptical female voice, who doubts her friend's prophecies, and who extends that doubt to all supernatural religious prophecies. So when the narrator's distinctly feminine voice emerges midway through this poem, it also becomes radical, in its way. The narrator instructs that, properly conceived, prophecy is not the product of supernatural insights, but of sentimental ones: images of the future derive from the prophet's fullness of heart. For, as she recounts,

> Full souls are double mirrors, making still
> An endless vista of fair things before
> Repeating things behind: so faith is strong
> Only when we are strong, shrinks when we shrink.
> It comes when music stirs us, and the chords
> Moving on some grand climax shake our souls
> With influx new that makes new energies. (295–301)

These lines express a fundamentally skeptical view of prophecy, it is clear; the "endless vista of fair things" seen before a prophet are merely reflections of her own full-souled past, creating strong faith out of her own strength. And it is important to observe that this is a higher critical skepticism, based upon the Romantic apologetics of Strauss, rather than an iconoclastic one derived from the better-known skeptical traditions of the Enlightenment Deists.

Part of the genius of the higher criticism, after all, was its repudiation of the skeptical Deist argument (seen in the works of Thomas Paine, for instance, or Voltaire) that the authors of the Holy Scriptures were simply frauds. Instead, the higher critics held that the Scriptures were inspired in a thoroughly poetic way, and that it was through and as poetry that those writings were most fully appreciated. Strauss, for instance, maintained that religious myths emerge as truths out of their authors' sympathies with their subject. This is the idea that Eliot's narrator adopts to describe religious faith in general. As Eliot translated from Strauss's *Life of Jesus:*

> [A]n inventor of the *mythus* in the proper sense of the term is inconceivable . . . the idea of a deliberate and intentional fabrication, in which the author clothes that which he knows to be false in the appearance of truth, must be entirely set aside as insufficient to account for the origin of the *mythus*. . . . It is this notion of a certain necessity and unconsciousness in the formation of the ancient *mythi*, on which we insist. (1: 76)

In other words, Strauss claims that the formation of myth derives from a spiritual and affective sympathy that Eliot would come to associate with the poetess tradition, especially as practiced and personified by Barrett Browning. Eliot locates prophecy (as Strauss had before her) in earnest sympathy—the sympathetic soul reflects its desires into its future, as well as into its past. So just as Eliot's narrator voices her gentle reproof of one E. B. B. (Elias Baptist Butterworth), she implicitly affirms the confident prophecies of another (Elizabeth Barrett Browning). And, in the end, the epithet of the poem's title, "a minor prophet," seems best applied to the post-Christian female skeptic, rather than the male religious zealot to whom it initially seems to belong.

II. Blind: the prophecy of St. Oran

Given Blind's and Naden's scholarly inclinations, it should come as no surprise that Eliot's influence on them owes partly to the fact that Eliot incorporated radical intellectual ideas into her poetry more ably than had many earlier poetesses. The influence of Eliot's poetry upon

Blind has been underestimated by scholars because we have taken for granted the assessment that Blind offers in *George Eliot:*

> Here, as in her novels, we find George Eliot's instinctive insight into the primary passions of the human heart, her wide sympathy and piercing keenness of vision; but her thoughts, instead of being naturally winged with melody, seem mechanically welded into song. . . . [Her verses] indubitably prove to the delicately-attuned ear the absence of that subtle intuitive music, that "linked sweetness" of sound and sense which is the birthright of poets. (168–71)

It seems imprudent, however, to accede too quickly to Blind's view that Eliot lacks "that 'linked sweetness' of sound and sense which is the birthright of poets"—or even to take it at face value. Blind recorded this judgment only after an initially divided critical community had decided against Eliot's poetic efforts. In this context, Blind's verdict seems reflexive and peremptory: it appeals to the *je ne sais quoi* that Victorian conservatives invariably found missing in women's art. At the same time, *George Eliot* attests that Blind studied Eliot's poetry despite her disappointment, recommending that it "should be carefully studied by all lovers of her genius, as affording a more intimate insight into the working of her own mind" (169). It therefore seems critical that Blind takes pains to praise Eliot's formal method and subject matter, reserving complaint for her style. She finds fault with Eliot's manner, but not with her method or matter. *George Eliot* depicts Eliot's poetry as a serviceable poetic model which lacks only the advantage of a truly felicitous music, or what Eliot called the "chords / Moving on some grand climax" in the quotation above. And Blind's consideration of this poetic model suggests an ambition to strike those missing chords. *The Prophecy of St. Oran* gives form to that ambition.

Blind first conceived of *The Prophecy of St. Oran* in 1873, while visiting the Isle of Iona in Scotland; she recorded there that the religious austerity of its very landscape appealed to her literary sensibilities: "Here every stone, every mouldering cross speaks of St. Columba and his devoted little band, and whatever of truth and beauty was contained in Christianity forces itself on the imagination in this lonely spot" (*Works* 30). The plot of Blind's poem derives from a set of ancient legends surrounding St. Oran, a follower of the famous sixth-century Irish missionary to the Picts of Scotland, St. Columba. In Blind's account of the Oran legend, the young saint breaks his monastic vow of chastity with a Pictish woman who resides on the Isle of Iona, the site of Columba's first mission. When Oran is discovered, Columba orders him to be buried alive. And when he digs himself out of the grave, Columba orders him buried alive again.

Richard Garnett's memoir affords an account of how Blind's poem was read by her contemporaries:

> Of all her longer poems it is the most powerful, the most original, and the most artistically wrought, without a line too much or too little. The striking theme is derived from an ecclesiastical legend holding a place in hagiographical literature akin to that which, in the opinion of some, the Book of Job occupies in the Hebrew Canon—the resurrection of a saint to intimate that the faith in which he died is *not* true. (Blind, *Works* 27; emphasis Garnett's)

Oran's "resurrection," as Garnett puts it, occurs between his first and second burial, when he seizes the chance to rebuke his fellow monks (understandably, given the circumstances) and to mock the creed to which they subscribe:

"Deluded priests, ye think the world a snare,
Denouncing every tender human tie!
Behold, your heaven is unsubstantial air,
Your future bliss a sick brain's phantasy;
There is no room amid the stars which gem
The firmament for your Jerusalem.

   .   .   .   .

"Cast down the crucifix, take up the plough!
Nor waste your breath which is the life in prayer!
Dare to be men, and break your impious vow,
Nor fly from woman as the devil's snare!
For if within, around, beneath, above
There is a living God, that God is Love." (*Prophecy* 61–64)

The lengthy monologue from which these lines are excerpted is delivered by Oran from the mouth of his own grave. The monologue itself is, presumably, the prophecy promised in Blind's title, and the apostate monk who delivers it has widely been supposed by critics—then as now—to be the mouthpiece of Blind's progressive nineteenth-century views. The poem ends with Oran's second burial, during which the monks chant the Gaelic proverb that Blind uses as an epigraph to her poem: "Earth, earth on the mouth of Oran, that he may blab no more" (1).

In retrospect, however, it seems surprising that Garnett should represent the religious implications of Blind's poem as he does in the above paragraph. Among other things, Garnett encourages the misimpression that *The Prophecy of St. Oran* refurbishes an important minority religious tradition from the history of Ireland and Scotland, one that affords a Joblike challenge of Christian orthodoxy. Yet the highly developed field of nineteenth-century hagiographical scholarship provides little to justify Garnett's notion of Oran's significance. Oran's legends are not only obscure, but they lack the formal coherence that one finds in the Book of Job, to which Garnett compares them. Oran scarcely receives mention in the two great histories of Columba to appear in the nineteenth century, those of William Reeves and of Charles René Forbes, the Count de Montalembert.[4] Rather, Blind's interest in Oran seems to stem from the fact that there are so very few extant legends of the saint, and that those few seem radically dissimilar in tone. Some traditions at Iona testify to Oran's perceived holiness. For instance, Montalembert notes that the burial ground chapel at Iona is "called St. Oran's, from the name of the first of the Irish monks who died after their landing on the island" (464). Reeves records that an otherwise healthy "Odhran" volunteered himself to be buried on the island in order to consecrate the soil of the chapel, and that for this voluntary death he ascended to Heaven (288). Yet these legends, or fragments of legends, represent the sum of nineteenth-century scholarly knowledge of Oran, and both seem curiously at odds with the aforementioned Gaelic proverb: "Earth, earth on the mouth of Oran, that he may blab no more."

Scrupulous scholar that she was, Blind's interest in St. Oran seems to have been fired by the mutually incompatible state of the existing Oran traditions. It is not coincidental that parallels to their narrative fragmentation may be found in Strauss's *Old Faith and the New*, which Blind finished translating the year before she began her poem. Like Reeves's and Montalembert's hagiographical scholarship, Strauss's Biblical scholarship consisted in piecing together and making sense of ancient, incomplete, and often irreconcilable records. Yet unlike these more conventional scholars, who essayed to craft a coherent picture from the historical records of Columba, Strauss was primarily concerned to articulate the implications of his sources' limitations. As he summarized his own career in *The Old Faith and the New*:

> I have only wished to throw out a hint as to the uncertainty of everything on this head, how we cannot make sure of the sayings and teachings of Christ on any one point, whether we really have his own words and thoughts before us, or only such as later times found it convenient to ascribe to him. (66)

For Strauss, the Gospels represent an imperfect binding together of the diverse Christian narratives circulating in the first century, just as Blind's poem presents an imperfect compilation of the fragments of Oran's legends. But the flip side of this hermeneutic is Strauss's insistence on the integrity of the evangelist's—and, by extension, the hagiographer's—impulse, especially from the evangelist's or hagiographer's personal standpoint. Blind understood from Strauss that to be Oran's latest hagiographer, she need not repeat all the inconsistencies and historical puzzles unearthed by Reeves and Montalembert. She might, in good faith, "find it convenient" (as Strauss puts it) to ascribe to her own historical hero, St. Oran, a profound conviction that Christians embrace a false creed—or, at best, that they misunderstand the better part of a true one.

This is not to say that Blind simply has Oran voice her own opinions. There is a difference between suggesting that John the Evangelist put his words into Jesus's mouth and saying that a first-century writer who assumed the allonym "John" found it just and true that the Christ should have expressed certain convictions in certain ways. Strauss repeatedly makes this distinction in *Das Leben Jesu*, and Blind, though she takes many liberties with Oran's history, surely appreciated Strauss's idea.[5] It was all the more natural that she should do so because Eliot had so vividly evoked the same idea in such poems as "A Minor Prophet": a genuinely sacred history always derives from a later author's sympathy towards an historical figure, and never from willful misrepresentation. Instead of suggesting that Blind uses Oran as her mouthpiece, then, as scholars have insinuated from Garnett to the present day, one should say that from the fragments of Christian history, Blind reconstructs a figure befitting the stature of a saint as she conceived of one. Oran's voice is not Blind's: rather, Oran's voice is the voice of the holy prophet, who can see as far into Victorian astronomy as Blind, his hagiographer, and who could announce to Oran's sixth-century contemporaries, "your heaven is unsubstantial air, / Your future bliss a sick brain's phantasy; / There is no room amid the stars which gem / The firmament for your Jerusalem."

Oran's prophecy is simply true when viewed from the cosmogony of nineteenth-century scientist. Oran's fellow monks placed their faith in the Heavenly Jerusalem promised in Revelation, and doubtless located that Jerusalem in the firmament above them. For his part, Oran tells them that this place will never be found there. The New Jerusalem works wonderfully as a Biblical metaphor, but there was no room for it in a cosmos that the Victorians associated with telescopes, solar systems, and Sir John Hershel. As Ralph Waldo Emerson had put it with admirable succinctness, "I regard it as the irresistible effect of the Copernican astronomy to have made the theological *scheme of Redemption* absolutely incredible" (157). Of course, it is not the metaphor of Heaven but the metaphor's fixity as religious dogma that Oran protests: their heaven "is unsubstantial air," as he puts it, but this does not preclude the possibility of more substantial heavens. As Strauss writes of Genesis, "Nor shall we make it a reproach to the old Hebrew prophet that he was ignorant of the system of Copernicus, of the modern discoveries in geology. How unjust to such a biblical narrative, in itself dear and venerable, to thus petrify it into a dogma!" (17, trans. Blind). Doubtless inspired by Strauss, Blind's Oran reclaims the Biblical metaphor to urge his fellows to seek their Heavenly Jerusalem on Earth.

Thus Blind's poetry, like Eliot's, represents scientifically compelling prophecy from a committed unbeliever, and it represents the very idea of prophecy as compatible with *fin-de-siècle* positivism and post-Darwinian atheism. But linked to Oran's anticipation of Victorian science, and eclipsing it in importance, is his anticipation of the moral power that the nineteenth century found so often wanting in Christian theology and so powerfully figured in women's verse—after all, what is at issue in this passage is not the "firmament" of stars, but the "tender human ties" on Earth such as those that bound Oran to his Pictish lover. Oran ends his prophecy with the lines quoted above: "Dare to be men and break your impious vow, / Nor fly from woman as the devil's snare / For if within, around, beneath, above, / There is a living God, that God is Love." Thus, for Oran, the uncertain existence of God is far less important than His substitution by beneficent sentiment.

It is this wedding of higher criticism and the poetess tradition for which Blind found so cunning a model in George Eliot's pious verses. Like Eliot's prophetess, Blind the hagiographer reshapes the Christian past in ways that more clearly resonate within the secular present, and the authorities she has for doing so are none other than the Evangelists themselves as understood by the higher critics. Following the examples of Strauss and Eliot, Blind saw the past as always receptive to such literary reconstruction. And confirmation of this method is found in Garnett's enthusiasm for the "saint" of Blind's poem, an enthusiasm that is meaningful for all its historical carelessness. According to Strauss, recorded history always entails such carelessness, and such enthusiasm. So if Oran is not the Job of the Hebrew scriptures, that did not mean that he could not become, through poetry, the Job of Garnett's *fin de siècle*.

[. . .]

Notes

Warm thanks to Yopie Prins, Marion Thain, Ana Vadillo, and other attendees of the "Women's Poetry and the *Fin de Siècle*" conference for their comments upon earlier drafts of this essay.

1 Scheinberg has recently discussed religious diversity within this poetess tradition; for instance, she traces the influence of Judaism on Amy Levy, another atheist poet identified by Blain as part of "the new breed." My argument dovetails with Scheinberg's, though I address irreligious—rather than religious—diversity (see Scheinberg).
2 Presumably, Blind's translation created so little uproar because Strauss's heterodoxy was taken for granted in the 1870s.
3 I cite the Armstrong and Bristow anthology as the most widely available version of this poem.
4 Montalembert mentions Oran only in appendices—nowhere in the main text of his history. Neither does he mention Oran among the original twelve disciples of Columba. Nor does Oran's legend appear in Reeves, except intermittently, and again only in the appendices. This is particularly striking because these two biographies attempt to be exhaustive with reference to Columba's circle. Accordingly, William Smith's multi-volume *A Dictionary of Christian Biography, Literature, Sects and Doctrines during the first eight centuries* (1877–87), one of the great dictionary projects of Victorian scholarship, makes no mention of Oran and claims that Montalembert and Reeves "leave little to be further done or desired" on Columba (see *A Dictionary of Christian Biography, Literature, Sects and Doctrines* 602; Montalembert, *Précis D'histoire Monastique Des Origines À La Fin Du Xi Siècle*; Reeves, *Life of Saint Columba, Founder of Hy*).
5 Strauss is emphatic on this point because it was so common to Deist accounts of the Gospels. Again, for Strauss, "an inventor of the mythus in the proper sense of the term is inconceivable . . ." (I: 76). True, Blind essays the formerly "inconceivable" role of a knowing hagiographer ("an inventor of the mythos"), but her scholarly vantage is still clearly in Strauss, rather than the skeptical tradition that he criticizes.

Works cited

Armstrong, Isobel, and Joseph Bristow. *Nineteenth-Century Women Poets*. Oxford: Oxford University Press, 1996.

Ashton, Rosemary. *The German Idea: Four English Writers and the Reception of German Thought, 1800–1860*. Cambridge: Cambridge University Press, 1980.

Barrett Browning, Elizabeth. *Aurora Leigh*. Ed. Margaret Reynolds. New York: Norton, 1996.

Blain Virginia, ed. *Victorian Women Poets*. Harlow: Longman, 2001.

Blind, Mathilde. *George Eliot*. London: W. H. Allen, 1883.

———. *Poetical Works of Mathilde Blind, with a Memoir by Richard Garnett, C. B., LL D*. Ed. Arthur Symons. London: T. Fisher Unwin, 1900.

———. *The Prophecy of Saint Oran and Other Poems*. London: Newman, 1881.

Eliot, George. *The George Eliot Letters*. Ed. Gordon Sherman Haight. 9 vols. New Haven: Yale University Press, 1954.

———. trans. *The Life of Jesus, Critically Examined*. By David Friedrich Strauss. 3 vols. Bristol: Thoemmes, 1998 [1846]. 1st.

———. *Selected Critical Writings*. Ed. Rosemary Ashton. Oxford: Oxford University Press, 1992.

Emerson, Ralph Waldo. *The Complete Sermons of Ralph Waldo Emerson*. Ed. Albert J. von Frank. Vol. 4. Columbia: University of Missouri Press, 1989–92.

LaPorte, Charles. "George Eliot, the Poetess as Prophet." *Victorian Literature and Culture* 31.1 (2003): 159–79.

McTaggart, J. M. E. *The Nature of Existence*. 2 vols. Cambridge: Cambridge University Press, 1921–27.

Montalembert, Charles René Forbes. *The Monks of the West, from St. Benedict to St. Bernard*. Trans. unknown. Edinburgh: W. Blackwood, 1861.

———. *Précis D'histoire Monastique Des Origines À La Fin Du Xi Siècle*. Paris: J. Vrin, 1934.

Reeves, William. *Life of Saint Columba, Founder of Hy. The Historians of Scotland*. Vol. 6. Edinburgh: Edmonston and Douglas, 1874.

Scheinberg, Cynthia. *Women's Poetry and Religion in Victorian England: Jewish Identity and Christian Culture*. Cambridge: Cambridge University Press, 2002.

Smith, William, and Henry Wace. *A Dictionary of Christian Biography, Literature, Sects and Doctrines*. Boston: Little, Brown, 1877.

Strauss, David Friedrich. *The Life of Jesus, Critically Examined*. Trans. George Eliot. 3 vols. Bristol: Thoemmes, 1998 [1846].

———. *The Old Faith and the New. A Confession*. Trans. Mathilde Blind. 3d English ed. London: Asher, 1874.

Trollope, Anthony. *He Knew He Was Right*. Ed. John Sutherland. Oxford: Oxford University Press, 1985.

8   Women poets and the poetess tradition

Linda K. Hughes

Linguistically, historically, and critically, "poetess" is most notable for its inscription of difference in the suffix "ess" (aptly called a "derivative" in the *Oxford English Dictionary*). "Woman poet" likewise registers difference, since male poets are generally known as "poets." Any examination of the poetess or the broader category of women poets, then, inevitably involves issues of embodiment, identity, agency, and status; poetic forms, themes, and literary tradition; and changing critical frameworks and historical contexts, including the history of feminism.

Nineteenth-century critics almost always set women apart from men as poets but disagreed about the status of their work. Nor did they use "poetess" consistently. To some, "poetess" was a term of praise, designating a genuine poet of the female sex; others essentialized the poetess and her work as equivalent embodied forms; still others aggressively asserted women's inferiority. The March 1837 *Blackwood's Edinburgh Review*, for example, endorsed women as genuine poets in reviewing a new poem by Caroline Bowles (later Caroline Bowles Southey), though it reserved the greatest poetry for men:

> The magic tones which have added a new existence to the heart—the tremendous thoughts which have impressed a successive stamp on the fluctuation of ages, and which have almost changed the character of nations—these have not proceeded from woman; but her sensibility, her tenderness, her grace, have not been lost nor misemployed: her genius has gradually risen with the opportunities which facilitated its ascent . . . Surely the pure expression of pure thoughts and feelings—the staple of common life—if embued with a certain sweetness of soul-felt sound beyond that of ordinary speech . . . is poetry. (Rev. of *The Birth-Day* 1837: 404)

If a woman's poetry had to be "pure" and "sweet" to succeed, the poetess nonetheless possessed "genius."

A decade later, in *Tait's Edinburgh Magazine*, the Rev. George Gilfillan treated poetesses as reliable guides to domesticity and sentiment but also as mere versifiers who were inferior to men in intellect and shaping power:

> [O]n all questions affecting proprieties, decorums, what we may call the *ethics* of sentimentalism . . . , their verdict may be considered oracular, and without appeal. But we dare not say that we consider them entitled to speak with equal authority on those higher and deeper questions where not instinct nor heart, but severe and tried intellect is required to return the responses. (Gilfillan 1847: 359)

Thus Felicia Hemans's poetry and her womanhood were inseparable: "All the woman in her shines. You could not (unknowing of the author) open a page of her writings without feeling this is written by a lady. Her inspiration always pauses at the feminine point." If she occasionally sought to speak truth in a prophetic voice, "[i]t is emotion only that is audible to the sharpest ear that listens to her song. A bee wreathing round you in the warm summer morn, her singing circle gives you as much new insight into the universe . . . . We are reluctantly compelled, therefore, to deny her, in its highest sense, the name of poet . . . . A *maker* she is not" (Gilfillan 1847: 360).[1]

Such divergent reactions to the poetess's "genius" persisted late into the century. In "English Poetesses" Oscar Wilde calls Elizabeth Barrett Browning (hereafter EBB) the "one great poetess" that England has given to poetic tradition, one fit to stand alongside Sappho, the great lyric poet of classical Greece. If he compares EBB only to other women, not to pre-eminent men, his calling her "great" and insisting on her artistry—"She disliked facile smoothness and artificial polish. In her very rejection of art she was an artist"—confirm her stature as a poet. She, unlike Gilfillan's Hemans, is indeed "a Sibyl delivering a message to the world" (Wilde 1888: 742–43). Only two years later, however, an anonymous reviewer in the *Scots Observer* flatly declared:

> In woman, indeed, the capacity of art—the faculty of selection in union with the sense of style—is rarely if ever completely developed, while a gift of lyric utterance and the lyric sentiment are frequent enough. In Mrs. Browning, for instance, there is fervor—a little tremulous, perhaps—and rapture—a hectic rapture, no doubt—for half-a-dozen ordinary bards; but how much of Mrs. Browning's six volumes is tolerable as art? ("Poetry" 1890: 438)

The implied answer of course is "none." Of women poets generally the reviewer concludes, "They feel, therefore they sing: they are women and therefore lyric poets. Art and style they have none—not to speak of, at any rate . . . Poetry in petticoats is only poetry on sufferance: only woman essaying to do the man's part, and . . . failing relatively if not absolutely" ("Poetry" 1890: 439).

Insofar as the "poetess" signified "pure" femininity, limited range and poetic technique, the inability to stamp an era with a distinctive voice, or outright inferiority, it is unsurprising that the poetess figure was quickly forgotten in the twentieth century. The impersonality, layered allusions, and hard-edged imagery of high Modernism allowed scant space for the domestic themes and sentiment of the nineteenth-century poetess. Nor was the term "poetess" with its derivative suffix immediately welcome in second-wave feminism or feminist criticism of the 1970s. In their landmark book *The Madwoman in the Attic*, Sandra Gilbert and Susan Gubar devote the bulk of their study to seeking out women writers' identities hidden under masks imposed by men. Their representative figure, referenced in their title, is Bertha Mason in Charlotte Brontë's *Jane Eyre* (1847), a desiring woman full of rage and aggression against her controlling male keeper who functions as Jane's subversive complement, expressing the protest that Jane keeps in check. In poetry, Gilbert and Gubar locate Bertha's counterpart in "The Other Side of the Mirror" (1896) by late nineteenth-century poet Mary Elizabeth Coleridge: Coleridge's female speaker sees a wild female imprisoned in the mirror, her mouth a bleeding wound and her "lurid" eyes expressing madness, rage, thwarted desire, and "fierce revenge"; with a shock, the speaker realizes that the mirrored figure is a version of herself (Gilbert and Gubar 1979: 15–16).

The Madwoman in the Attic inspired immense interest in other instances of subversion, resistance, and transgression in women writers. An important example is Angela Leighton's

Victorian Women Poets: Writing Against the Heart (1992). Leighton's subtitle articulates her investment in poetry that subverts the poetess stereotype. She explicitly dismantles Gilfillan's commentary on Hemans, for example, pointing out that for Hemans's principal readers—women—Hemans's "sentimentalism" functioned as a validating enactment of female creativity (Leighton 1992: 29–30). Above all, Leighton draws attention to underexamined figures such as the lesbian aunt and niece who collaboratively wrote lyrics under the name Michael Field, writers whose overt expression of sexual desire and pleasure exploded the constraints imposed on the poetess.

The recovery of women writers' hidden identities and new, complex layers of signification in their works spurred recovery of a wider range of women writers, including women poets. In the mid-1990s, three anthologies of Victorian women poets appeared,[2] raising new questions about women poets' cultural position, their relation to each other, and their aims. If "subversion" remained a frame of reference, scholars also examined the epistemologies, market forces, ideologies, and motives underlying their poems. One of the most influential new studies was Isobel Armstrong's chapter on women poets in *Victorian Poetry: Poetry, Poetics and Politics* (1993). Armstrong's theory and method paralleled those of Gilbert and Gubar insofar as she posited both an overt surface level that was often expressive or conventional in meaning and an oblique, less immediately apparent structure or configuration that called the first into question. Armstrong's theory of the double poem involves struggle and negotiation between a poem's language used expressively and its politics, and her exploration of poetess verse as double poems opened a fascinating new avenue of investigation. She suggests that in assimilating a recognizably feminine mode of poetry (rather than, as in Gilbert and Gubar or Leighton, resisting it), women poets could use this imposed mask as an analytic to think through the construction of the poetess and female subject (Armstrong 1995: 15–16ff). If one poetess strategy was to conform to expectations of sentiment and tears so determinedly that it pathologized lyric (Armstrong 1993: 323–24), another was to set one imposed duty (nurturing the nation at large through solacing affect) against another (representing the rifts and violence occasioned by imperial wars in acts of mourning), which interrogated rather than upheld the national exploitation of feminine sentiment uttered from subordinate social positions (Armstrong 1999: 11–15).[3]

Another key study was *Victorian Sappho* (1999) by Yopie Prins. Prior to Henry Wharton's scholarly edition of Sappho's fragments in 1885, Sappho was best known through Ovid's *Heroides* (written during the reign of Augustus Caesar). Ovid's Sappho speaks after Phaon, the young man with whom she falls desperately in love, abandons her, and she responds by leaping to her death in the sea. If the historical Sappho's poetic renown demonstrated women's capacity to write poetry at the highest level, the Ovidian Sappho modeled the poetess as a woman abandoned, mournful, and tearful, who silenced her poetry from the more powerful imperative of heterosexual love. Prins's study, informed by Greek classical studies as well as poststructuralist theory, probes the implications of a founding poetess figure who expresses herself in the act of extinguishing herself and who predetermines the ephemerality of poetess verse (likewise here, then gone). To Prins, this Sappho also hopelessly complicates the assumption of unmediated, spontaneous, directly expressive poetess verse often assumed by Victorian reviewers, for in Sappho's case there is no extant feminine body from which verses can overflow (Prins 1999: 3–4, 17–18). The founding figure of Sappho was further circulated in nineteenth-century Europe, Prins notes, through the adaptation of Ovid's text (a kind of "afterlife" novel) by French writer Madame de Staël in *Corinne, or Italy* (1807), the story of a brilliantly successful Anglo-Italian improvisatrice (i.e., performer of spontaneously composed lyric verses) who is first loved, then abandoned, by a Scottish peer who chooses a more conventional bride for his wife, leaving Corinne to waste away and die. The novel was almost immediately translated into English and is clearly the inspiration for L.E.L.'s *Improvisatrice* (1824) and *A History of the Lyre* (1827), this last discussed by Linda Peterson.

Three other key developments have been especially formative in studies of the poetess from the 1990s onward. First is the theory of gender and sexuality articulated by philosopher Judith Butler in *Gender Trouble* (1990). By demonstrating (in part through an examination of drag) the degree to which any expression of sex as well as gender is a contingent cultural construction rather than a direct manifestation of biology, Butler's work encourages literary analysis of gender as performance, an approach especially well suited to the performing improvisatrice. In this critical context, the more a poetess assumes an essentially feminine role, the more she can be interpreted as performing rather than registering an identity. The gap between performance and identity in turn allows for more complex readings of the poetry and for the poetess's knowing rhetorical manipulation of her performance. Performativity also introduces issues of commodification, whether an audience consumes the spectacle of female displays of emotion, the feminine poetic body, and artless effusion (as in *A History of the Lyre*), or the poetess engages in self-commodification for profit.

Second, critics have increasingly complicated assumptions about the poetess's domestic sequestration and apolitical passivity by documenting her political agency. As early as 1993 Isobel Armstrong observed that poetesses often projected themselves across national boundaries in their verse (as L.E.L. did with Eulalie in *A History of the Lyre*) (Armstrong 1993: 324–25). Richard Cronin (2002: 180–93) and Alison Chapman (2003: 57–77) have extended this insight by examining how actively and assertively women poets, including EBB and Theodosia Garrow Trollope, advocated for the Italian Risorgimento[4] and called for international support—sometimes critiquing British policy—in their poetry. Since under Austrian occupation no Italian, man or woman, enjoyed citizenship, EBB, according to Cronin, was disadvantaged neither by sex nor by foreignness in her outspoken calls for Italian resistance against oppression. Chapman emphasizes the expatriate poetess's hybrid identities and the license they granted to Garrow Trollope in particular to evade complicity in English national identity and to expand the range of the poetess's political alignments from within the "tradition of sensibility" (Chapman 2003: 77). Third, Cynthia Scheinberg and others have reinstated the significance of religion in studies of women's poetry. Scheinberg reads women poets in relation to Jewish and Christian tradition, including the poetess's empowered self-identification with inspired biblical prophetesses of the Old Testament such as Miriam. In such alignments, the poetess could entirely conform to expectations of feminine piety and reverence while also occupying the culturally powerful position of seer, as in the ending of *Aurora Leigh* (Scheinberg 2002: 89–105).

If we now turn to the critical excerpts about women's poetry and the poetess by Tricia Lootens, Linda Peterson, and Charles LaPorte, we can more clearly see the historical and critical underpinnings of their arguments. All three are notable for critical acuity, deft insights, and admirably clear writing styles. But each adopts a slightly different method and emphasis in approaching the poetess. Tricia Lootens's *Lost Saints* (1996) demonstrates how a writer could be demoted from major to minor status, then dismissed as irrelevant to serious poetry because she was perceived as a poetess. In EBB's own time, John Ruskin, one of Victorian Britain's foremost critics, called *Aurora Leigh* "the greatest poem which the century has produced in any language" (Ruskin 1903–12: 15:227). But after EBB's early death in 1861 and the meteoric rise of Robert Browning's poetry (whose work was embraced by Modernist poets), her overtly political *Casa Guidi Windows* and ambitious novel-epic *Aurora Leigh* fell out of the canon and she became associated most closely with *Sonnets from the Portuguese*, then simply with the expression of romantic love expressed in "How do I love thee? Let me count the ways"—the only line many would know (but not necessarily have read in the complete sonnet). In becoming a shorthand signifier of romantic love, EBB had become a poetess. If the poetess's special province was love, a line suggesting endless expression of it ("Let me count the ways") could be deemed mere effusion.

Having demonstrated the contingency of reputation that besets all poets but is complicated for women by gender ideologies, Lootens counters the eclipsing of EBB's significance by two means: demonstrating the originality and challenging complexity of the *Sonnets* (aesthetic qualities valued in today's canonical authors) and reconstructing EBB's public negotiation of female domestic identity prior to marriage. In her close reading of the *Sonnets*' complicated syntax and erudite allusions, Lootens reveals poetry defined not by sappy sweetness but by "strangeness, heaviness, and eccentric richness" (Lootens 1996: 118 [Chapter 5: 50]), making a convincing case that EBB's poetry as a whole was "difficult, ambitious, and deeply personal art" (Lootens 1996: 120 [Chapter 5: 52]).

In her early career, EBB felt impelled to find a place for women within the canon and to "sanctify" her own high poetic ambition. This she did by dedicating her 1844 volume to her father, enfolding her ambitions within the identity of a loving daughter. As well, in "A Vision of Poets" and other poems EBB repeatedly linked genius to "'suffering and self-sacrifice'" (Lootens 1996: 122 [Chapter 5: 53]), which aligned her with the sacredness and suffering of Christ. Thus in 1844, Lootens concludes, EBB "was already beginning to succeed as a sacred poet-heroine of resignation and suffering" (Lootens 1996: 124 [Chapter 5: 55])—a female, to be sure, but elevated above the level of poetess by Christ-like qualities that made her a "heroine." The thrust of Lootens's argument is to detach EBB from the poetess tradition and to re-establish her as a singular poet in twentieth-century critical terms, especially her textual difficulty and complex intellectual frameworks. Because Lootens's principal concern in the excerpt is how women form, enter, and fall out of the canon, issues of transgression or resistance receive little attention. But in recovering EBB as a heroic figure and strong, complex poet, her analysis emphasizes aspects of female poets also valued by Gilbert and Gubar.

The 1999 Linda Peterson essay likewise explores how EBB fashioned her public identity and locates EBB as poet rather than poetess. But Peterson places EBB on a continuum between the poetess L.E.L. and the canonical William Wordsworth. Peterson relies more on intertextuality than single-author analysis, an approach consistent with mid-nineties anthologies that likewise placed woman poets and their poetic practices alongside each other. Peterson's work explicitly builds upon the historicizing and theorizing of the poetess by Armstrong and others; indeed, her sustained attention to L.E.L. registers the new interest of feminist critics in the poetess. In connecting L.E.L.'s *History of the Lyre* to the "Sappho-Corinne myth" (Peterson 1999: 121 [Chapter 6: 59]), Peterson also notes patterns discussed by Prins.

Peterson's expertise in nineteenth-century life writing informs her examination of EBB's negotiation of the poetess conventions she inherited and her ambition to stand as an equal beside canonical male poets. In *A History of the Lyre* Eulalie directs her inspired performances toward a beloved who leaves her as Phaon did Sappho. L.E.L. also encouraged her own association with the Sappho-Corinne myth through vaguely Greek fashion choices, but the strategy backfired. As Peterson concludes, "Landon's self-construction as a Sapphic poetess destined her for an early death . . . she more or less wrote herself into that fatal plot" (Peterson 1999: 122 [Chapter 6: 60]).

EBB, who knew Landon's poetry well, explicitly revised Eulalie's story to effect a transition for her protagonist Aurora Leigh from Romantic poetess to a Victorian poet imbued, like Wordsworth, with the power of transcendent vision. In the transition Peterson traces, gender explicitly intersects with genre. Whereas the poetess L.E.L. favors ballads or improvised effusion, Aurora begins with the ballad and ephemeral periodical contributions but moves beyond them to write an autobiographical epic, as did Wordsworth in *The Prelude*; whereas L.E.L. was plagued by scandalous rumors of sexual impropriety (confirmed by Lawford 2000: 36–37), Aurora proudly declares her unstained reputation. If in the end Aurora still writes for a male critic's approval, she also replaces the lyre with a prophetic clarion trumpet. The poetess is here indispensable for understanding *Aurora Leigh*, but it is a modality left behind for a role of greater stature.

Charles LaPorte cites Lootens (176n.8) and, like Peterson, investigates the continuum between poetess and poet and the intersection of genres in women's roles as poet, poetess, and prophet. All three scholars, moreover, examine the status (and stature) of the woman poet. But LaPorte additionally incorporates Victorian religion into his analysis. Following Scheinberg, he identifies biblical prophetesses as empowering figures for women poets, but he also maps the role that the higher criticism (studies of the Bible as an historical document) played in Eliot's self-construction as a poetess—an especially relevant consideration because Eliot had translated two exponents of the higher criticism, David Friedrich Strauss (in 1844) and Ludwig Feuerbach (in 1854).

In an anonymous review of *Aurora Leigh* for the *Westminster Review*, Eliot termed EBB a poet who had added to masculine poetics the qualities associated with the poetess. What EBB innovated, LaPorte argues, was thus available as a deliberately adopted strategy for Eliot when, as a highly successful novelist whose literary status was secure, she turned to poetry. Eliot conjoined the tenderness and domesticity of the poetess with intellectually challenging material to craft a prophetic moral voice and "humanistic sentimentality" (162). If she drew upon the frequent lament of poetesses for a dead child in locating the origin of song in "The Legend of Jubal," Eliot also subtly incorporated elements of the higher criticism. In Genesis no cause for Jubal's invention of music is given. In creating one, Eliot implies that the poetess's reworking of Genesis parallels scriptural writers who created mythic accounts of events long past (as the higher criticism argued). Just as Lootens argues that EBB aligned the female poet with Christ's self-sacrifice, so Eliot, according to LaPorte, also aligned herself with Moses, the presumed author of the Pentateuch, in her revisionary midrash "The Death of Moses." This assumption of prophetic voice in turn became an empowering precedent for *fin-de-siècle* poets like Mathilde Blind (like Eliot, an agnostic), who appropriated a prophetic voice to pronounce on secular, post-Christian culture in, for example, *The Ascent of Man*. In LaPorte's essay, the poetess is a chosen rather than imposed mask in service to high cultural aims.

Where, then, do studies of the poetess and women poets stand in the early twenty-first century? The distinction between poetess and woman poet has diminished in importance among critics since there is general agreement that women writers moved fluidly between these roles and that the "poetess" was a construction of ideology and the Victorian literary marketplace (see Ledbetter 2009: 2).[5] The marketability of the poetess was no bad thing for women since, as Armstrong points out, "an account of women's writing as occupying a particular sphere of influence, and as working inside defined moral and religious conventions, helped to make women's poetry and the 'poetess' . . . respected in the nineteenth century as they never have been since" (Armstrong 1993: 321). Women poets' entry into the marketplace has received important attention (see, e.g., Peterson 2009), and digital resources such as *The Poetess Archive* (Mandell 2006) have widened access to materials available for fresh investigations. In an essay on research devoted to Victorian women poets in *Victorian Poetry*, Alison Chapman indicates additional directions suggested by work published in 2011: "the turn to transnational, colonial studies and Atlanticism; prosody, rhyme, and close reading; the politics of canon revision and recovery of writers; and the importance of print culture, especially periodical poetry, illustration, and the mass market" (Chapman 2012: 411).

Left unresolved is the question begged in the title of this section of *Victorian Literature: Criticism and Debates*: whether there is value in studying women's poetry as such, especially when the category marks off women's verse as somehow "other" than men's. To the degree that women inspired other women poets and were subjected to widespread assumptions about decorum, authority, and transgression, there is every reason to study women's poetry. Yet the category is potentially misleading since not all women shared similar orientations or identified as women poets; since numerous male poets adapted features of poetess verse; and since male and female poets wrote and read interactively. The question of women's poetry may also depend on the unit of analysis. Analysis of a single poem or poet, especially canonical figures like EBB or Christina Rossetti, may not always benefit from consideration in the context of women's poetry. For example, more might be gained from relating Christina Rossetti to male religious writers such as John Keble or Gerard Manley Hopkins (see Blair 2012: 210–20) than to Dora Greenwell or EBB. And the pleasure of reading a complex poem closely, teasing out its multiple layers of meaning, may occur in the absence of gender considerations altogether (or, alternatively, depend absolutely on them). Especially in a subfield that dates back little more than three decades, it is crucial that multiple approaches and methods remain open rather than that they be winnowed down.

To test what might be gained from examining women's poetry in a gendered or ungendered context, I close with two brief forays into literary annuals, the genre closely associated with the poetess. In *Fisher's Drawing Room Scrap Book; with Poetical Illustrations by L.E.L.* (1832), L.E.L.'s individual poems do not always fascinate or brim with complex meaning. They are easily read as the output of an improvisatrice who successively rehearses (before a crowd of consumers) different strains inspired by sequential engravings. Glennis Stephenson identifies the principal aim of the volume as educating young middle-class female readers and celebrating English nationality (Stephenson 1995: 147–52). But read in relation to its paratexts the volume acquires added interest for its multiple roles and effects. L.E.L.'s notes, often learned and recherché, may fulfill the educative role identified by Stephenson, but they also align L.E.L. with the canonical poet Sir Walter Scott, whose book-length poems were often accompanied by lengthy antiquarian notes. In devoting lines to the legend of King Arthur in her verses on the celebrated Cornish landmark St. Michael's Mount, L.E.L. appends a note detailing not only the English legend but also Welsh, Portuguese, Swiss, and Danish parallels (L.E.L. [1832] 11–12). In doing so she participates in the medieval revival, as did Scott in appending a note to *Marmion* (1808) that reprinted an excerpt from Malory's *Le Morte d'Arthur*. L.E.L.'s notes to "Lismore Castle" open with a quotation from Edmund Spenser's *Faerie Queene* with, further down, a lengthy note on Spenser's *Colin Clouts* and Spenser's former home near Lismore. The notes complement L.E.L.'s lyric, which closes by asserting that of all the distinguished names associated with Lismore Castle, she is "most proud" of the "bard, of whose fancy I never shall weary . . . Spenser, the titleless minstrel of Faëry" (L.E.L. [1832]: 21–23). Implicitly L.E.L. associates her volume and its legendary material with English literary tradition and positions herself as a critic empowered to adjudicate it.

If L.E.L. thus aligns herself with prominent male poets, she also pays tribute to an important author associated with the poetess in her notes on "Blarney Castle" (45–46), which cite Madame de Staël. In general the volume's juxtaposition of female-authored lyrics and prose notes complicates issues of voice and identity, so that the *Scrap Book* both confirms L.E.L. as an improvisatrice and implies underlying instability rather than feminine essence in her identity.

Friendship's Offering; and Winter's Wreath: A Christmas and New Year's Present (1833) presents prose and poetry by women and men, the more distinguished of whom appear close to the front, where they were more likely to be seen by prospective purchasers. Mary Russell Mitford's tale opens the volume, and poems by Thomas Babington Macaulay and "the Hon. Mrs. Norton" (Caroline Norton) immediately follow. Tennyson contributed the sixth poem, Norton the ninth—her double contribution highlighting her significance. The mixing of sexes gestures toward a literary scene in which women poets participate on equal terms rather than being assigned roles based on physical embodiment. The challenge this poses to later constructions of the canon is also evident in the juxtaposition of Mary Howitt's "The Morning Walk" and a sonnet by John Clare in the volume's middle (*Friendship* 1833: 109–13). Howitt's lyric, paired with an accompanying color illustration, adjures a prosperous young maid innocent of knowledge of the world's ills to read her poetry book—resembling no doubt the annual Howitt's readers hold—under a tree but to recall that she will one day set aside pleasant dreams for greater cares. In identifying herself as formerly a girl who delighted in al fresco reading of poetry before she encountered adult duties and sorrows, the female poet enforces domestic roles yet also suggests that adult womanhood is not incompatible with poetry, especially its creation. John Clare's sonnet opens, "I love to wander at my idle will, / In summer's joyous prime, about the fields" and "To lie and dream a quiet hour away" (113). Here a masculine perspective is no more mature or grand than that of the innocent maid delighting in her morning walk. Nor does any paratext mark off Clare as a poet superior to Howitt. Potential containment of the woman poet within the straightjacket of gender or restricted genres gives way to a demotic mingling consistent with reformist gender ideals. Examining L.E.L. as a poetess, then, reveals what she shares with men, and the mixed-sex contents of *Friendship's Offering* suggest women's complex position in literature and culture.

Notes

1 Gilfillan was supportive of working-class poet Alexander Smith, and "Female Authors" appeared in a progressive magazine. But Gilfillan's reformist sensibility did not cross gender lines in this essay. His judgment was all the sterner in that Hemans was considered one of the best of women poets.
2 For further details on this sudden quickening of interest in Victorian women poets and the scholarship it generated, see Hughes 2006: 290–301.
3 For more on the impact of Armstrong's *Victorian Poetry* on the field, see Charles LaPorte's essay "Victorian Poetry and Form" in this volume and the extract from Armstrong's book that precedes it.
4 Italian efforts to overthrow Austrian rule and achieve independence.
5 Marion Thain suggests that the poetess role itself be considered a genre (2003: 579).

Bibliography

Armstrong, I. (1993) *Victorian Poetry: Poetry, Poetics and Politics*, London: Routledge.
—— (1995) "The Gush of the Feminine," in P.R. Feldman and R.M. Kelley (eds.), *Romantic Women Writers: Voices and Counter-Voices*, Hanover, NH: University Press of New England.
—— (1999) "Misrepresentations," in I. Armstrong and V. Blain (eds.), *Women's Poetry, Late Romantic to Late Victorian: Gender and Genre, 1830–1900*, London: Macmillan.

Blair, K. (2012) *Form and Faith in Victorian Poetry and Religion*, Oxford: Oxford University Press.

Butler, J. (1990) *Gender Trouble: Feminism and the Subversion of Identity*, New York: Routledge.

Chapman, A. (2003) "The Expatriate Poetess: Nationhood, Poetics and Politics," in A. Chapman (ed.) *Victorian Women Poets*, Cambridge, UK: D. S. Brewer.

—— (2012) "Women's Poetry, 2011," *Victorian Poetry*, 50.3: 402–11.

Cronin, R. (2002) *Romantic Victorians: English Literature, 1824–1840*, Houndmills: Palgrave Macmillan.

Friendship's Offering; and Winter's Wreath (1833), London: Smith, Elder & Co.

Gilbert, S. and Gubar, S. (1979) *The Madwoman in the Attic: The Woman Writer and the Nineteenth-Century Literary Imagination*, New Haven: Yale University Press.

Gilfillan, G. (1847) "Female Authors. No. I.—Mrs. Hemans," *Tait's Edinburgh Magazine*, 14: 359–63.

Hughes, L.K. (2006) "Recent Studies in Nineteenth-Century Women Narrative Poets, 1995–2005," *Dickens Studies Annual*, 37: 287–323.

L.E.L. [Landon, Letitia] (1832) *Fisher's Drawing Room Scrap Book*. Online. Available HTTP: <http://archive.org/details/fishersdrawingro00lelluoft> (accessed 19 June 2013).

LaPorte, Charles (2006) "Atheist Prophecy: Mathilde Blinde, Constance Naden, and the Victorian Poetess," *Victorian Literature and Culture*, 34.2: 427–41.

Lawford, C. (2000) "Diary," *London Review of Books*, 21 September: 36–37.

Ledbetter, K. (2009) *British Victorian Women's Periodicals: Beauty, Civilization, and Poetry*, Houndmills: Palgrave Macmillan.

Leighton, A. (1992) *Victorian Women Poets: Writing Against the Heart*, Charlottesville: University Press of Virginia.

Lootens, Tricia. (1996) *Lost Saints: Silence, Gender, and Victorian Literary Canonization*, Charlottesville and London: University Press of Virginia.

Mandell, L. (ed.) (2006) *The Poetess Archive*. Online. Available HTTP: <http://idhmc.tamu.edu/poetess/> (accessed 10 June 2013).

Millett, K. (1970) *Sexual Politics*, New York: Doubleday.

Peterson, L. H. (1999) "Rewriting A History of the Lyre: Letitia Landon, Elizabeth Barrett Browning and the (Re)Construction of the Nineteenth-Century Woman Poet," in Isobel Armstrong and Virginia Blain (eds.), *Women's Poetry, Late Romantic to Late Victorian: Gender and Genre, 1830–1900*, New York: St. Martin's Press: 115–32.

—— (2009) *Becoming a Woman of Letters: Myths of Authorship and Facts of the Victorian Market*, Princeton: Princeton University Press.

"Poetry in Petticoats" (1890) *Scots Observer*, 8 March: 438–39.

Prins, Y. (1999) *Victorian Sappho*, Princeton: Princeton University Press.

Rev. of *The Birth-Day. A Poem*, by Caroline Bowles (1837), *Blackwood's Edinburgh Magazine*, 41: 404–28.

Ruskin, J. (1903–12) *The Works of John Ruskin*, ed. E.T. Cook and A. Wedderburn, 39 vols, New York: Longmans Green.

Scheinberg, C. (2002) *Women's Poetry and Religion in Victorian England: Jewish Identity and Christian Culture*, Cambridge: Cambridge University Press.

Stephenson, G. (1995) *Letitia Landon: The Woman Behind L.E.L.*, Manchester: Manchester University Press.

Thain, M. (2003) "What Kind of a Critical Category is 'Women's Poetry'?," *Victorian Poetry*, 41.4: 575–84.

Wilde, O. (1888) "English Poetesses," *Queen*, 74 (8 December): 742–43.

Part III

Realism and photography

Introduction

Though generally regarded as the dominant mode of Victorian fiction, realism's status in Victorian studies has sometimes been a vexed one. During the poststructuralist theory boom of the late 1970s and 1980s, realism came under intense scrutiny as literary critics became increasingly suspicious of what they saw as realism's attempts to reach beyond language to the world of things. Despite George Levine's warning that no Victorian novelists ever actually believed they were giving their readers direct access to the real, some critics pilloried realism for its philosophical naivete, specifically its confidence in an ordered and knowable reality. By the end of the 1980s, accusations of political conservatism accompanied this charge, as scholars, notably Catherine Belsey and D. A. Miller, argued that the realist novel was implicated in maintaining a dominant ideology of control and repression in the Victorian period.

What might have been a fatal impasse was breached in the 1990s with the rise of New Historicism. Rather than condemning or defending realism's politics or its assumptions about reality, critics began instead to use realism to analyze the Victorians' own historically specific notions of the real. With this move came an emphasis on visual culture, as critics placed increasing importance on the relationship between seeing and knowing in the nineteenth century. This connection between visual culture and literary realism was not new: many earlier critics, notably Elizabeth Deeds Ermarth, had argued that literary realism shared important assumptions about the nature of the real with the visual arts. What was new, however, was a special emphasis on the impact of nineteenth-century technology, including photography, on Victorian understandings of the real. Jonathan Crary's somewhat polarising *Techniques of the Observer: On Vision and Modernity in the Nineteenth Century* (1990) was key to development of this debate. While Ermarth had seen nineteenth-century realism as continuous with Renaissance visual practices, Crary argued that "a reorganization of vision in the first half of the nineteenth century" occurred, producing "a new kind of observer," and as a consequence, a new kind of realism (Crary 1990: 2–3).

Crary's contention that this epistemological shift occurred before photography became widely available to the Victorian population implicitly informs much of the later work produced on Victorian visual culture, especially that of photography. By the 1990s, authors such as Jennifer Green-Lewis, Geoffrey Batchen, and Nancy Armstrong would demonstrate that photography had had a major cultural impact by the 1850s, and that there was a clear relationship between mid-century literary realism and this new mode of visuality. Rather than understanding literary realism as an attempt to depict the world through language, these critics treat literary realism as a formal response to an increasingly image-driven culture. As Armstrong argues, what literary realism's visual descriptions seek to depict are not things but visual (usually photographic) representations of things. The consequences of this shift in critical thought are major, pushing the origins of an image culture, long associated with the twentieth century, back into the nineteenth. Building on the assumption that photography changed both literary realism and its readers, critics such as Richard Menke and Daniel Novak have continued to explore the relationship of literature and photography in the last decade or so. Each complicates this relationship in the nineteenth century, through a focus on—respectively— new methods of photographic dissemination and composite photography, as each argues that the interplay between literary realism and photography was more sophisticated and complex than earlier critics allow.

As Jennifer Green-Lewis concludes, in an age as image-saturated as ours has become, the relationship between literary realism and photography is likely to become the subject of even greater critical attention. Victorian realism may ultimately have much to teach us about our own historical moment.

See also: *Genre fiction and the sensational*; *Disinterestedness and liberalism*; *Print culture*

Bibliography

Crary, J. (1990) *Techniques of the Observer: On Vision and Modernity in the Nineteenth Century*, Cambridge, MA: MIT Press.

9   What is real in realism?

Nancy Armstrong

[. . .]

From time to time, literary scholarship has floated the question of what if anything is real about Victorian realism, but I believe that investigation should be pushed significantly further than scholars have been willing to go. From the importance that visual evidence assumes in Victorian literature of all kinds, the fact that images can serve iconically for whatever they represent, one can infer that Victorians willingly participated in a change of reading practices that eventually turned conventional mimesis on its ear. Beginning in the late 1850s, new literary techniques and new technologies of seeing promised to bring the reader ever closer to the material world. In order to do so, however, these same techniques and technologies reversed the traditional relationship between image and object observed. The so-called material world to which Victorians were apparently so committed was one they knew chiefly through transparent images, images which in turn seemed to bring them conceptual and even physical control over that world. It was to cash in on the giddy expansion of referential possibilities afforded by the reversal of the mimetic priority of original over copy that fiction developed the repertoire of techniques most commonly associated with realism. When a novel such as *Bleak House* refers to the street people and dilapidated tenements of nineteenth-century London, that novel is actually referring to what either was or would become a photographic commonplace. But if this mutually authorizing relationship between fiction and photography was so obvious to Victorian readers as I am suggesting, then why did it not become a commonplace of literary history?

The pictorial turn

In fact, whenever some critic addresses the question of realism and what makes it real or not, we will find the impact of popular images registering in literary criticism, provided we know how to recognize it. In his preface to *Studies in European Realism*, Georg Lukács charges realism with the sacred duty of maintaining "the organic, indissoluble connection between man as a private individual and man as a social being, a member of a community."[1] His study of the historical novel identifies 1848 as the year when the novel abandoned this mission. Lukács blames this failure on a sudden infusion of "ornamental detail," "immobile background," "pictorialism," "picturesque atmosphere," and "photographic authenticity" which fiction slipped in between readers and the social world around them.[2] More recent studies of the novel describe realism much as Lukács did—as exposing the brutal social order sometimes obscured by an increasingly complex and fluctuating economy. Yet, despite this common ground, those who write on the novel today generally assume that realism was just coming into its own in 1848, the very moment when Lukács claimed it had begun its downward spiral. Whether one sees the second half of the nineteenth century as the age in which realism flowered rather than as the period of its decline depends entirely on the literary historian's attitude toward images and whether visual description prevents or provides access to the realities of modern urban existence. Critics from Ian Watt and Harry Levin to George Levine, Elizabeth Ermarth, D. A. Miller, Naomi Schor, and Michael Fried understand the Victorian novel as the culmination of a tradition that was part and parcel of the modernization process itself.[3] Each acknowledges that the novel's use of painterly technique, perspective, detail, spectacle, or simply an abundance of visual description served to create, enlarge, revise, or update the reality shared by Victorian readers. Indeed, today many of us would hold the very kind of description we associate with realism at least partly responsible for changing the terms in which readers imagined their relation to the real.

But what do we make of the fact that the novel's turn to pictorialism coincided with the sudden ubiquity of photographic images in the culture at large? Why did *pictures* begin to speak louder than words? Even our most sophisticated explanations of realism continue to beg this question. In his well-known discussion of reification, Fredric Jameson argues that "the ultimate form of commodity reification in contemporary consumer society is precisely the image itself."[4] In his view, we will never grasp what he calls "an increasing, tendential, all-persuasive visuality as such" so long as we simply rail against mass culture and yearn for the relation to objects we imagine to have existed prior to commodification.[5] Whenever we define the objects worthy of analysis in opposition to reproducible images, we simply enhance the allure of commodity culture. To resist that allure, Jameson urges us to subject "the image" itself to historical analysis. I accept the proposition that to understand the power of visuality and to discover how it emerged and gained authority in modern culture are essentially the same task. But I do not think this can be done in quite the way Jameson proposes, namely, by examining the emergence and development of popular cinema.

As I have already suggested, what might be called the rise of the photograph was under way a good half-century before the motion picture was even on the drawing board. Until that moment, European fiction may actually have stuck to the task that Lukács assigned it and told the story of class struggle out of which both a modern middle class and an imperial nation state were going to emerge. But by the late 1840s, about the time Dickens was becoming England's favorite author, fiction had begun to turn in another direction and was devising a new set of formal procedures for just this purpose. One's family and religion and manner of speaking no longer proved sufficient bases for assigning that individual a place within the new social order. Written in 1852–1853, a novel like *Bleak House* demonstrates the conceptual muddiness of social identities once they had mingled in the streets of London, only to offer a finite number of visual fields in which virtually everyone could be placed. The same demand that encouraged fiction to turn to certain kinds of visual description during the 1850s was also responsible for the rapid production and wide dissemination of photographic images. Victorian fiction was the first English fiction, I am suggesting, to convert a particular kind of visual information—infinitely reproducible and capable of rapid and wide dissemination— into what was both a way of seeing and a picture of the world that a mass readership could share. The following propositions attempt to reconceptualize literary realism in relation to the new medium of photography, whose privileged relationship to the modern city that fiction simultaneously foresaw and emulated:

Proposition I: By the mid-1850s, fiction was already promising to put readers in touch with the world itself by supplying them with certain kinds of visual information.

Proposition 2: In so doing, fiction equated seeing with knowing and made visual information the basis for the intelligibility of a verbal narrative.

Proposition 3: In order to be realistic, literary realism referenced a world of objects that either had been or could be photographed.

Proposition 4: Photography in turn offered up portions of this world to be seen by the same group of people whom novelists imagined as their readership.

I have taken care not to suggest that England was awash with photographs of every important genre during the 1850s, when Lukács pinpoints the onset of an encroaching pictorialism. Indeed, the images distributed during the 1840s and 1850s were mostly daguerreotypes, and these were generally portraits of respectable people rather than denizens of the busy city streets and sordid tenements. Thus the sequence of my propositions is meant to indicate that, when it came to portraying disreputable places and people, fiction often came first and referred to things and people in a way that would only later materialize as a familiar genre of photography.

Fiction could not have taken the pictorial turn to the extent or in the way it did, were its readership not already hungry for certain kinds of visual information. This fact is not in dispute. There are, however, at least two different explanations for evidence of photographic desire before the fact. One traces the origins of photography back from Louis Daguerre and William Henry Fox Talbot to the lithography and line drawings that had become a burgeoning business in the decades before the discovery of modern photographic technology.[6] This account observes the one visual medium ceding naturally to the other as the two existed side by side and interchangeably with each other until the 1870s, when photography became substantially cheaper and more accessible. This explanation is troubled, however, by the fact that various men and women of science, art, and manufacturing were known to have been experimenting with methods of taking images directly from objects well before 1802, when Thomas Wedgwood was reported to have copied images onto glass. Geoffrey Batchen argues compellingly that the discovery of the photographic process was not a cause but an effect of more than a century of extremely ingenious individuals wishing to capture and produce absolutely unmediated images, a wish that could at first perhaps be attributed to a few quirky intellectuals but which quickly became what Batchen calls "a universal imperative" once the technology was available.[7] There are indeed ample indications to suggest that the nineteenth-century readership saw it Batchen's way. That is to say, they understood the advent of mass visuality as something that had been in the works for over a century by the time photographic studios opened up in all the major towns and photographs began to bring the world to readers on pieces of paper the size of playing cards.

An 1867 essay entitled "Photography: Its History and Applications" begins by describing photography as "a fact of the day" whose "origin, growth, and variety of application have had no parallel in the history of the graphic and pictorial arts." This history credits Thomas Wedgwood, "the celebrated potter," and Sir Humphry Davy, who "had assisted in the experiments," with having "discovered but half the spell; the pictures could not be fixed."[8] At the same time, this account sees even Wedgwood and Davy's experiments with visual reproduction as the expression of an attempt to fix the image that begins "as early as the sixteenth century."[9] Another essay from the same period, entitled "A Suppressed Art," represents the prehistory of photography as something of a scandal. The estate of one Matthew Boulton, regular host to the infamous Lunar Society which boasted Thomas Wedgwood among its members, contained "two curious pictures, which bore a strong resemblance to photographs; and two other pictures on copper plated with silver, that were undoubtedly of a class precisely the same as those commonly known as daguerreotypes."[10] Lady Elizabeth Eastlake, something of an expert on the new art of photography, observes that although the images of Daguerre and Talbot have made the English readership feel "the existence of a power, availing itself of the eye of the sun both to discern and to execute," that same readership has yet to acknowledge "the unclaimed and unnamed legacy of our own Sir Humphry Davy."[11] Coming at the history of photography with quite different purposes in mind, these various critics nevertheless assume that history extends back well before Daguerre's and Talbot's discoveries.[12] Such accounts assume, further, that the desire to fix an unmediated image of an object has a purely English origin.

The history of literary realism is no less hypothetical than the history of photography. In describing the production of a new visual order, my argument assumes there is no work of Victorian realism pure and simple about which we now care all that much. The novels of Mrs. Gaskell, Benjamin Disraeli, and Mrs. Humphry Ward are the first that come to mind of a second tier of fiction that more than occasionally strives for a documentary effect. A study of realism might very well read Charles Dickens, George Eliot, and Thomas Hardy in relation to these lesser figures in order to show that they all have a similar purpose in mind. My own study pursues another tack, however, on the assumption that conventional historicism significantly misrepresents what realism actually accomplished. I believe that Lukács is indeed partly right in claiming that realism began to disappear at almost the same moment it came into being. As a result, any novel that sought to offer an accurate representation of social conditions in the manner of Disraeli or Ward holds relatively little interest for all but a handful of specialized scholars today. At the same time, it is also true that such authors as Dickens and Gaskell did usher in a moment in literary history that extended well into the twentieth century. During this period, everyone knew what realism was; authors wrote in relation to it, and readers read with a standard in mind based on the fidelity of language to visual evidence. Indeed, we still recognize this kind of writing as realism today.

This book will consider several genres of fiction, most of which are usually discussed in opposition to realism. My point is to show that it is precisely their violation of the visual standard that prompts us to classify *Wuthering Heights*, *Alice's Adventures in Wonderland*, *The Picture of Dorian Gray*, or *King Solomon's Mines* as romance and fantasy. There is no doubt in my mind that these novels, as emphatically as any scene from Dickens, defined what was real in terms of what could and would eventually be depicted by a photographic image. As I use the term, then, realism does not indicate a genre or mode of writing that strives to document actual social conditions by means of visual description. On the contrary, the documentary effect is only one result of the collaboration between fiction and photography. By "realism," I mean the entire problematic in which a shared set of visual codes operated as an abstract standard by which to measure one verbal representation against another. I believe it is accurate to situate not only works of romance and fantasy within this problematic, but literary modernism as well. No less dependent on a visual definition of the real than Victorian realism, modernism nevertheless located whatever it considered authentic in nature or culture within an invisible domain on the other side of the surfaces one ordinarily sees. Indeed, it was in order to lay claim to this greater realism beyond the conventional that modernism reduced the category of realism to a caricature of its former self—a futile attempt at documentary fidelity to the object world. By thus reducing realism to a genre, modernism did not situate itself historically beyond the limits of realism but squarely within the same problematic with the very writing it deemed superficial.

[. . .]

Notes

1 Georg Lukács, *Studies in European Realism*, trans. Edith Bone (New York: Grosset & Dunlap, 1964), 8.

2 Georg Lukács, "The Crisis of Bourgeois Realism," *The Historical Novel*, trans. Hannah and Stanley Mitchell (Lincoln: University of Nebraska Press, 1983), 171–250.

3 Ian Watt, *The Rise of the Novel: Studies in Defoe, Richardson and Fielding* (Berkeley: University of California Press, 1957); Harry Levin, *The Gates of Horn: A Study of Five French Realists* (New York: Oxford University Press, 1963); George Levine, *The Realistic Imagination: English Fiction From Frankenstein to Lady Chatterley* (Chicago: University of Chicago Press, 1981); Elizabeth Deeds Ermarth, *Realism and Consensus in the English Novel* (Princeton: Princeton University Press, 1983); D. A. Miller, *The Novel and the Police* (Berkeley: University of California Press, 1988); Naomi Schor, *Breaking the Chain: Women, Theory, and French Realist Fiction* (New York: Columbia University Press, 1985); Michael Fried, *Realism, Writing, Disfiguration: On Thomas Eakins and Stephen Crane* (Chicago: University of Chicago Press, 1987).

4 Fredric Jameson, "Reification and Utopia in Mass Culture," *Signatures of the Visible* (New York: Routledge, 1990), 11–12.

5 Ibid., 12.

6 In *The Cult of Images: Baudelaire and the 19th-Century Media Explosion* (Santa Barbara: UCSB Art Museum, 1977), Beatrice Farwell describes an explosion of mass-produced lithographic images that rapidly displaced "the folkloric aspect" of "popular imagery" with "urbanity" and "sophistication" during the period between 1820 and 1860 in France. Although the English were neither so careful nor so consistent in preserving the record of this media event, it is likely that lithography had a similar impact on England as well. "It is clear," Farwell contends, "that in its early years, much photographic work made for commercial sale dealt in the same kind of imagery as lithography." Also see Patricia Anderson, *The Printed Image and the Transformation of Popular Culture 1790–1860* (Oxford: Clarendon Press, 1991), for a compelling description of the pictorial literacy of the working classes up through the decade when photography assumed the role occupied by lithography in this regard.

7 Geoffrey Batchen, *Burning with Desire: The Conception of Photography* (Cambridge: MIT Press, 1997), 53.

8 "Photography: Its History and Applications," *Living Age* 92 (1867): 195.

9 Ibid.

10 "A Suppressed Art," *Once A Week* 19 (1864): 368.

11 Lady Elizabeth Eastlake, "Photography," *The Quarterly Review* 101 (1857): 443.

12 Indeed, as Larry J. Schaaf demonstrates, William Henry Fox Talbot was acutely aware of his predecessors while working on calotype technology. He was narrowly beaten out as the inventor of photography by Louis Daguerre, and during the decade when he held a patent on the process, other intellectuals were developing similar methods on their own. *Out of the Shadows: Herschel, Talbot, and the Invention of Photography* (New Haven: Yale University Press, 1992).

10 Information unveiled

Richard Menke

[. . .]

The accuracy of a sun-picture

In "The Natural History of German Life" (1856), an essay composed shortly before her own entry into fiction-writing, Marian Evans invoked the photograph to measure the promise of aesthetic realism against the achievements of science. The potential of realistic representation is great, she argues, for "Art is the nearest thing to life; it is a mode of amplifying experience and extending our contact with our fellow-men beyond the bounds of our personal lot."[1] After citing Teniers's and Murillo's paintings of the poor as models from the visual arts, Evans affirms that "[w]e have one great novelist who is gifted with the utmost power of rendering the external traits of our town population" (*NH*, 271). But she immediately qualifies that praise, forbearing to name Dickens yet referring to his novel in progress:

> if he could give us their psychological character—their conceptions of life, and their emotions—with the same truth as their idiom and manners, his books would be the greatest contribution Art has ever made to the awakening of social sympathies. But while he can copy Mrs Plornish's colloquial style with the delicate accuracy of a sun-picture . . . he scarcely ever passes from the humorous and external to the emotional and tragic, without becoming as transcendent in his unreality as he was a moment before in his artistic truthfulness. (*NH*, 271)

As a copyist of appearances, Dickens approaches photography—perhaps nowhere more closely than in *Little Dorrit* (1855–57), a novel not only blessed with the comic presence of Mrs. Plornish but also structured by explicit perspectival shifts and sun-and-shadow contrasts. By the 1850s, laudatory comparisons of Dickens to "a taker of daguerreotypes, sun-pictures, [or] photographs" were common in reviews of his work.[2] But here the "sun-picture" image only reinforces the complaint about Dickens's superficiality, his unreal rendering of character, his presentation of exterior appearances without inner life. The "psychology" offered by Dickens is "frequently false," Evans claims (*NH*, 271). While conceding the "delicate accuracy" of the medium, and of Dickens's art, "The Natural History of German Life" treats photography as a figure for precise outward mimicry without deep human resonance, a mode of copying without the power of "awakening . . . sympathies."

Following up on her earlier praise of Teniers and company, Eliot would declare the homely realism of Dutch genre painting a model for her fiction in *Adam Bede* (1859), the humane and conventionally realistic novel she wrote just before "The Lifted Veil." In a famous "pause" in its seventeenth chapter, *Adam Bede* hails "Dutch paintings" for their "rare, precious quality of truthfulness"; such "faithful pictures of a monotonously homely existence" allow the "delicious" experience of "deep human sympathy."[3] Yet as Eliot's comments on Dickens indicate, modern technology offered newer models for imagining how fiction might turn real life into pictures, reality into fictional information. And the traits of photography that encapsulate Dickens's limitations might threaten to unsettle the alliance between accuracy, commonality, and fellow-feeling on which Eliot bases her theory of realism.

Like genre painting, photography promised truthful images of the everyday, but as "light-writing," it did so in a way that seemed to remove human agency—and, for Eliot, human sympathy—from the machinery of representation. More than a decade earlier, the photographic pioneer William Henry Fox Talbot had justified photography's potential for humble realism in precisely the same terms as Eliot in *Adam Bede*.[4] Talbot invented the calotype, which used a two-step negative/positive process to place images on paper, allowing the production of multiple prints, in contrast to the uniqueness of the metal daguerreotype. His *The Pencil of Nature* (1844–46), the first book illustrated by photographs, includes a picture of a rustic broom slanted against the open door of a rural stable, an image that would become perhaps his most famous.[5] Compared to *The Pencil of Nature*'s photographs of classical busts or the cloisters of Talbot's Lacock Abbey, the ordinary scene captured in "The Open Door" might seem unworthy of memorializing, but Talbot defends it as art: "We have sufficient authority in the Dutch school of art, for taking as subjects of representation scenes of daily and familiar occurrence. A painter's eye will often be arrested where ordinary people see nothing remarkable."[6]

An 1845 review approvingly took up Talbot's comparison; "[w]ith this broom the famous broom of [the seventeenth-century Dutch painter] Wouverman must never be compared: it becomes at once a clumsy imitation."[7] But for all such invocations of painting by photographers such as Talbot, photography remained "mysterious" for the Victorians, "a hybrid difficult to situate. It resulted in . . . pictures which resembled those of the Dutch school; yet . . . these pictures came into being 'naturally.'"[8] Despite Talbot's treatment of the camera lens as the artist's eye, Victorians came to see "the photograph . . . as an automatic recording device," largely equivalent to "what the average person would have seen standing in the same spot at the same time."[9] "The relay of truthful information, however insignificant, was central to the larger cultural importance of photography," finds Jennifer Green-Lewis, and "photography's potential for detail, for verisimilitude, and for stasis became a standard in other forms of realism."[10] Against the hallucinatory accuracy of the mid-Victorian photograph, the truthful ordinariness of Dutch painting might seem nostalgic or outmoded—commonplace indeed.

"The Lifted Veil" challenges or inverts so much of Eliot's early theory and practice of fiction that it seems appropriate for it to draw upon an alternative model of visual realism. The tale mixes psychology, science, and sensation fiction to set forth the dark tale of the narrator, a delicate young man cursed with the power of prevision and the ability to read—really, the inability to screen out—the thoughts of those around him. That is, Latimer gets precisely what Eliot had missed in Dickens, the "psychological character" of others, "their conceptions of life, and their emotions," rendered with the immediacy of direct observation. His powers bring him the amplified experience and contact beyond his individual lot that Eliot craved from the highest art—and this development produces not sympathetic understanding but alienation and horror. Recounting the story of his life, Latimer tells us that its happiest period was a time in boyhood when his mother had to tend to him because an illness made him temporarily blind. But in his early adulthood, this experience is reversed and transformed: another illness permanently alters his powers of perception, extending them far beyond ordinary vision into "incessant insight and foresight."[11] Only the mind of the beautiful and haughty Bertha, his brother's fiancée and Latimer's own future wife, initially remains veiled to him, making her an "oasis of mystery in the dreary desert" of certainty (*LV*, 18).

Latimer's first and most elaborately presented prophetic vision arrives "like the new images in a dissolving view" (the fading of one magic-lantern image into another) when he hears the name of a city mentioned as a destination for his future travels (*LV*, 10). "My father was called away before he had finished his sentence, and he left my mind resting on the word *Prague*"; suddenly, as if completing the sentence in another register, Latimer envisions "a new and wondrous scene":

> a city under the broad sunshine, that seemed to me as if it were the summer sunshine of a long-past century arrested in its course—unrefreshed for ages by dews of night, or the rushing rain-cloud; scorching the dusty, weary, time-eaten grandeur of a people doomed to live on in the stale repetition of memories. . . . The city looked so thirsty that the broad river seemed to me a sheet of metal; and the blackened statues, as I passed under their blank gaze, along the unending bridge, . . . seemed to me the real inhabitants and owners of this place, while the busy, trivial men and women, hurrying to and fro, were a swarm of ephemeral visitants infesting it for a day. (*LV*, 9)

Julian Wolfreys recognizes the elaborate "textual-optical machinery" of "The Lifted Veil," a tale that seems to suggest some "ill-defined . . . new means of tele-technological communication."[12] But in fact, as the reference to a magic lantern show hints, we can be much more specific in defining the textual-optical technology involved. Eliot had traveled to Prague with Lewes in the summer of 1858.[13] In contrast, Latimer has never visited the city and has "seen no picture" of it (*LV*, 9). But this image of a Prague in "perpetual midday, without the repose of night or the new birth of morning" precisely mimics a very particular kind of picture indeed (*LV*, 9): the cityscapes of early Victorian photography, that technology with the power to detain the light of the past in a perpetual repetition of memory, to arrest the flow of time in its course.

In nearly every detail, Latimer's vision incorporates the traits of an early photographic view: the sense it conveys of a changeless scene etched by sunlight (in the standard phrase, photography meant "printing pictures by means of the sun");[14] the dead, metallic appearance of a body of water when its flows are petrified in silver nitrate on paper or upon the actual "sheet of metal" that made up a daguerreotype; the impression that a place's "real inhabitants" are its stationary objects, which obligingly hold their poses for even the longest exposure time, while its living, moving populace becomes a "swarm" of hazy, transient ghosts. A Victorian photograph even begins with the act of lifting an opaque veil or cover in order to set a new scene before a sensitized medium. Although Latimer assures us he has never seen an image of Prague, this scene precisely describes the view of the Prague Bridge which was starting to become one of the city's signature photographic images.

Eliot could have viewed one of these pictures—indeed, she could have seen a photograph of Prague produced specifically to mark photography's attainment of the technical reproducibility of print. In late 1858, a few months before Eliot wrote "The Lifted Veil," the London-based *Photographic News* distributed hundreds of copies of "Bridge over the River Moldau, at Prague, Bohemia" as the first in a series of prints created to demonstrate Talbot's new "photoglyphic process" for engraving photographs on metal plates so that they could be "printed off . . . with the usual printer's ink" just like any written text.[15] The predecessor of modern photogravure processes, this "immensely important invention" turned photographs into printable plates.[16] Perhaps the ultimate textual-optical technology of the 1850s, Talbot's photomechanical system "inaugurated a vast new field offering rapid, mass visual communication of graphic information."[17] As one historian of photography gushes, such an ample distribution of photographic images via printed paper was a tribute to "the significance of photoreproduction" and "[q]uite a novelty for the year 1858!"[18]

The art historian Carol Armstrong has recently urged us to rethink the history of photography on paper, treating it not alongside painting but in relation to the original reproducible "paper art," printed writing; moreover, she finds the intersection of photography and the book in mid-Victorian Britain "particularly rich and peculiar."[19] Convinced that the iterability of the paper photograph was the defining advantage of his "English process" over the higher-definition daguerreotype, Talbot promoted his techniques in terms of print as early as the 1840s; one of his patents includes a proposal for composing lines of type to be copied onto paper via photography instead of with a printing press.[20] Talbot's "photoglyphic" process and its successors confirmed photography's importance as a technology not just for recording or representing reality but for disseminating it. The technique greatly reduced the cost of printing from photographs; photoglyphy would soon place photographic reproductions within the reach of "the masses," predicted the inevitable process article in *All the Year Round*.[21] It also brought greater detail and permanence to the reproduced image, a special concern of Talbot, since some of his early attempts at photographic publishing had failed when the images pasted into *The Pencil of Nature* and other books proved chemically unstable.[22]

Talbot's reproduction of "Bridge over the River Moldau," originally half of a stereoscope image by the French photographers Clouzard and Soulier, circulated widely as one of the first testaments to the accuracy and above all the permanence of photoglyphy, a new way to register reality in printer's ink. We might be tempted to speculate that Talbot selected the image as not simply an example but an icon of his techniques. The photoglyphic process lends photography the endurance of print, if not quite of statuary; the bridge between Prague's Old and New Towns becomes an endless connection between the past and the future, between an old textual medium and a modern visual technology. Arresting and reproducing the world's Heraclitean flux, photographic printing gives us the same river any number of times.

Talbot and *The Photographic News* printed hundreds of copies of "Bridge on the River Moldau" and a series of similar images. I know of no evidence that Eliot saw these particular images, but in a real sense, she didn't need to. For all its promise as a photoglyphic icon, the dissemination of this image and its fellows makes it clear that they ultimately offered not aesthetic originality but purposely generic testaments to the accuracy of a new media innovation. As with Latimer's vision, which also functions as both the icon of a visual mode and general proof of concept, the medium of "Bridge on the River Moldau" is extraordinary, but its actual pictorial content is perfectly standard—a detailed, well-composed image entirely typical of contemporary photographic cityscapes: the sense of an arrested midday, the scorched river, the black statues, the bridge disappearing into the horizon, the blurry figures made by real human beings (one of whom is barely visible as a ghost, just to the left of the lamp in the central foreground). If Victorian realism represents the intersection of novelistic representation with modern, standardized forms of mass visuality, as Nancy Armstrong claims, then Talbot's image of Prague, or Latimer's, might betoken a new scene in that conjunction. In terms of nineteenth-century printed writing, the photoglyphic process recalls not handset text so much as stereotype, the casting of an entire plate upon a single piece of metal.

Overwhelmed by the clarity and force of his unexpected vision, Latimer wonders at first whether "illness ha[s] wrought some happy change in my organisation—given a firmer tension to my nerves"; could it be a sudden stirring of his latent poetic genius (*LV*, 10)? "Surely it was in this way that Homer saw the plain of Troy, that Dante saw the abodes of the departed, that Milton saw the earthward flight of the Tempter" (*LV*, 10). The awkward coupling of bardic vision with the language of nervous psychology suggests the implausibility of the theory. As an experiment, Latimer tries to envision Venice, hoping that "the same sort of result would follow," the same sense of a real scene rising before him (*LV*, 10). But no; for his pains, Latimer receives not the "vivid images" he seeks, no lifelike "accident of form or shadow," but only scattered memories of "Canaletto engravings" (*LV*, 10). Compared to the mental sun-picture of Prague, the mass visuality of landscape painting seems a feeble and secondhand experience. Like Latimer's visions, a photograph preempts the work of memory with a stable image taken out of the flux of contingency and time.

Latimer's new power might strike us as nearly godlike. Yet the very force of his visions makes Latimer submissive before them. In an essay on the relationship of Victorian photography to a growing consciousness of forgetting and oblivion, Green-Lewis points out that photography does not change the past but "changes . . . the relationship we have with it."[23] Altering the word *past* to *future* would summarize Latimer's relationship to his photograph-like visions of the static, evacuated landscape of his own destiny. As he begins to suspect that they are no artist's fancies but alienated glimpses of his own coming experience, Latimer becomes as passive as the sensitized surface of a photographic plate, treating them as scenes that have already been photographed or texts that have already been printed. Even a vision of his conjugal misery with Bertha—a vision he fully credits—does not dissuade him from marrying her. This might seem puzzling, but, as Thomas Nagel observes, viewing our own actions from "an objective or external standpoint" can make us seem "helpless" before them.[24]

This passivity too may be a corollary of the uncanny photorealism of the sun-picture in 1859. It is no great leap from the stability hailed by *The Photographic News* and *All the Year Round* to the disturbing sense of stasis expressed in Eliot's passage. Perhaps the possibility of such representational deadness inheres in all descriptive realisms, even Dutch genre painting, but here Latimer's photographic vision makes the rift between teleperception and lived experience inescapable. Only the image of "a patch of rainbow light on the pavement, transmitted through a coloured lamp in the shape of a star" seems to escape the pictorial desiccation of Latimer's visionary Prague (*LV*, 9). The single spot of color dabbed on a monochromatic scene, this feature fuses Old and New Testament signs of hope with the Barthesian impression of random, haphazard detail. But hope and hap both disappear when Latimer arrives in Prague and verifies that the images he saw were indeed his own future perceptions, temporarily disconnected from embodied experience as well as from the normal chronology of his life. The rainbow light becomes the confirmation of his vision's accurate reproduction, a sign of narrative foreclosure. And Barthes's reality effect turns into his *punctum*, the "element which rises from the scene" of a photograph to pierce the beholder with its truth, "that accident which pricks me."[25]

For the Victorians, photographic technology seemed to exemplify the registration of appearances without an intervening subjectivity.[26] Lady Eastlake's "Photography" (1857), the age's best-known essay on the topic, credits the photograph with "the accuracy and the insensibility of a machine"; what could better represent the divorce of experience from perception, embodied knowledge from abstract information?[27] Just as Latimer ruefully discovers that his visions are not poetry, so Eastlake determines that photography is not art. Art requires "whatever appertains to the free-will of the intelligent being, as opposed to the obedience of the machine," but photography's "business is to give evidence of facts, as minutely and as impartially as, to our shame, only an unreasoning machine can give."[28] Devices that impartially and exhaustively disconnect facts from intelligence and reason, with no question of free will: Latimer, and the camera, produce information at the expense of human subjectivity. Both Talbot's and Eliot's images of Prague mark the changelessness of the scene by turning real human passers-by into half-absent ghosts. Eliot herself would soon admit that her experience with a photographic portrait in 1858 had given her "rather a horror of photography."[29]

[. . .]

Notes

1 Eliot, "Natural History of German life," 271. Hereafter cited in the text as *NH*.
2 Collins, Introduction to *Dickens*, 6. Collins's collection includes five pieces published between 1845 and 1857 (including Marian Evans's) which compare Dickens's work to photographic technologies. On photography and *Little Dorrit*, see Marsh, "Inimitable Double Vision," 266–68.
3 Eliot, *Adam Bede*, 223–24.
4 Monika Brown notes that by the time of *Adam Bede*, "'Dutch painting' was already an established code for certain features of realistic novels as well as a tool for explaining 'how to read' new works"—and, I would add, how to read a new medium. "Dutch Painters," 155.
5 The familiarity of "The Open Door" persists. Green-Lewis includes it in her informal "top twenty (or so)" of widely reproduced Victorian photographs. "At Home," 63.
6 Talbot, *Pencil of Nature*, plate 6.
7 Quoted in Newhall, Introduction to *The Pencil of Nature*.
8 Jeffrey, *Photography*, 24.
9 Marien, *Photography*, 74.
10 Green-Lewis, *Framing the Victorians*, 4, 31. Even for Talbot, photography's "over-riding objective" was finally not to create art but "to record information." Ward, "William Henry Fox Talbot," 24.
11 Eliot, "Lifted Veil," 3. Hereafter cited in the text as *LV*.
12 Wolfreys, *Victorian Hauntings*, 92.
13 Susan Reynolds points out that Latimer's narrative of his actual, physical visit to Prague echoes Eliot's enthusiastic diary entries of July 1858 "almost word for word"; with some puzzlement, she can only blame the darkness of his earlier prophetic vision on Eliot's personal difficulties since her visit. "The Most Splendid City," 230.
14 "Photographic Print," 162.
15 "Mr. Fox Talbot's New Discovery," 25; see also "Our Photoglyphic Transparencies."
16 Buckland, *Fox Talbot*, 112.
17 Ostroff, "Photomechanical Process," 125.
18 Buckland, *Fox Talbot*, 116, 115.
19 C. Armstrong, *Scenes in a Library*, 4, 17.
20 Arnold, *William Henry Fox Talbot*, 137 [. . .].
21 "Photographic Print," 163.
22 Buckland, *Fox Talbot*, 89.
23 Green-Lewis, "Not Fading Away," 579.
24 Nagel, *View from Nowhere*, 110.
25 Barthes, *Camera Lucida*, 26, 27.
26 See N. Armstrong, *Fiction in the Age of Photography*, 77; Levinson, *Soft Edge*, 46.
27 Eastlake, "Photography," 454.
28 Ibid., 466.
29 Eliot, *Letters*, 3:307.

Works cited

Armstrong, Carol M. *Scenes in a Library: Reading the Photograph in the Book, 1843–1875*. Cambridge, MA: MIT Press, 1998.
Armstrong, Nancy. *Fiction in the Age of Photography: The Legacy of British Realism*. Cambridge, MA: Harvard Univ. Press, 1999.

Arnold, H. J. P. *William Henry Fox Talbot: Pioneer of Photography and Man of Science*. London: Hutchinson Benham, 1977.

Barthes, Roland. *Camera Lucida: Reflections on Photography*. 1980. Translated by Richard Howard. New York: Noonday Press, 1981.

Brown, Monika. "Dutch Painters and British Novel-Readers: Adam Bede in the Context of Victorian Cultural Literacy." *Victorians Institute Journal* 18 (1990): 113–33.

Buckland, Gail. *Fox Talbot and the Invention of Photography*. Boston: Godine, 1978.

Collins, Philip. Introduction to *Dickens: The Critical Heritage*, edited by Philip Collins, 1–26. New York: Barnes & Noble, 1971.

[Eastlake, Elizabeth]. "Photography." *Quarterly Review* 101 (April 1857): 442–68.

Eliot, George [Marian Evans]. *Adam Bede*. Edited by Stephen Gill. London: Penguin Books, 1985.

——. *Essays of George Eliot*. Edited by Thomas Pinney. New York: Columbia Univ. Press; London: Routledge and Kegan Paul, 1963.

——. *The George Eliot Letters*. Edited by Gordon S. Haight. 9 vols. New Haven, CT: Yale Univ. Press, 1954–78.

——. "The Lifted Veil." 1859. In *The Lifted Veil; Brother Jacob*, edited by Helen Small, 1–43. Oxford: World's Classics/Oxford Univ. Press, 1999.

——. "The Natural History of German Life." *Westminster Review* 66 (1856): 51–79. Reprinted in Eliot, *Essays*, 300–24.

Green-Lewis, Jennifer. "At Home in the Nineteenth Century: Photography, Nostalgia, and the Will to Authenticity." *Nineteenth Century Contexts* 22.1 (2000): 51–75.

——. *Framing the Victorians: Photography and the Culture of Realism*. Ithaca, NY: Cornell University Press, 1996.

——. "Not Fading Away: Photography in the Age of Oblivion." *Nineteenth Century Contexts* 22.4 (2001): 559–85.

Jeffrey, Ian. *Photography: A Concise History*. New York: Oxford Univ. Press, 1981.

Levinson, Paul. *The Soft Edge: A Natural History and Future of Information Revolution*. London: Routledge, 2005.

Marien, Mary Warner. *Photography: A Cultural History*. New York: Abrams, 2002.

Marsh, Joss Lutz. "Inimitable Double Vision: Dickens, *Little Dorrit*, Photography, Film." *Dickens Studies Annual* 22 (1993): 239–82.

"Mr. Fox Talbot's New Discovery: Photoglyphic Engravings." *The Photographic News: A Weekly Record of the Progress of Photography* (24 September 1858), 25–26.

Nagel, Thomas. *The View From Nowhere*. New York: Oxford Univ. Press, 1989.

Newhall, Beaumont. Introduction to Talbot, *Pencil of Nature*, n.pag.

Ostroff, Eugene. "The Photomechanical Process." In *Henry Fox Talbot: Selected Texts and Bibliography*, edited by Mike Weaver, 125–30. Boston: Hall, 1993; Oxford: Clio, 1992.

"Our Photoglyphic Transparencies." *The Photographic News: A Weekly Record of the Progress of Photography* (12 Nov. 1858), 109.

"Photographic Print." *All the Year Round*. 1 (11 June 1859): 162–64.

Reynolds, Susan. "The Most Splendid City in Germany?': George Eliot and Prague." *Contemporary Review* 282 (2003): 228–31.

Talbot, William Henry Fox. *The Pencil of Nature*. 1844–46. Facsimile reprint. New York: Da Capo, 1969.

Ward, John. "William Henry Fox Talbot." In *Printed Light: The Scientific Art of William Henry Fox Talbot and David Octavius Hill with Robert Adamson*. By John Ward and Sara Stevenson, 9–27. Edinburgh: Her Majesty's Stationery Office, 1986.

Wolfreys, Julian. *Victorian Hauntings: Spectrality, Gothic, the Uncanny, and Literature*. New York: Palgrave, 2002.

11 Composing the novel body

Re-membering the body and the text in *Little Dorrit*

Daniel Novak

In the practice, theory, and discourse of Victorian photography, the technology of realism produced its opposite: a body that is at once fragmented and interchangeable, divisible and abstract. Nineteenth-century critics repeatedly complained that the medium of photography had no "design," only offering a loosely connected set of parts. Such a body would at first seem to be less than useful for the purposes of realistic fiction. Yet it was precisely this incoherence of the photograph that induced critics to compare photography and the realist novel. What photography and realism shared was not necessarily their fidelity to detail but rather their inability to present these details in any coherent form. For example, comparing Dickens's style to a daguerreotype, an anonymous reviewer for the *Spectator* (1853) noted "[s]o crowded is the canvas which Mr. Dickens has stretched and so casual the connexion that gives to his composition whatever unity it has, that a daguerreotype of Fleet Street at noon-day would be the aptest symbol to be found for it; though the daguerreotype would have the advantage in accuracy of representation."[1] While the reviewer argues that Dickens's style is photographic despite being *less accurate* than a photograph, his/her complaints about the "casual connexion" of elements that provide only a tenuous "unity" suggest that it is the breakdown of compositional integrity that links writing and photography.

Perhaps the most famous complaint of this kind, as well as the most famous comparison of Dickens's style to photography, is George Eliot's description of Dickens in "The Natural History of German Life" (1859):

> We have one great novelist who is gifted with the utmost power of rendering the external traits of our town population . . . But while he can copy Mrs. Plornish's colloquial style with the delicate accuracy of a sun picture, while there is the same startling inspiration in his description of the gestures and phrases of "Boots," as in the speeches of Shakespeare's mobs or numskulls, he scarcely ever passes from the humorous and external to the emotional and tragic, without becoming as transcendent in his unreality as he was a moment before in his artistic truthfulness.[2]

Eliot's backhanded compliment to Dickens suggests that Dickens's style is photographic not despite, but because of his failure to represent the psychological identity – the "character" of his characters. For Eliot, Dickens is an author who produces *only* photographs or "sun pictures," because he only represents "external traits." She argues that even the photographic author fails to form this excess material into a whole body, because he/she is unable to signify a connection between body and character, "external traits" and internal "emotion." Or rather, she suggests that this failure defines the photographic aesthetic as such, and even locates this failure at the level of structure and grammar. Only a collection of "gestures and phrases," the photograph is grammatically impaired, because no matter how much raw material the photographer or photographic author assembles, these fragments can never add up to a proper whole through the mechanics of the most elementary syntactical arithmetic. Photographic writing only produces ill-fitting and agrammatical details or collections of "phrases" that fragment internally and threaten to disrupt the grammatical coherence of the textual "composition."[3]

In these accounts, then, what photography and literary realism share is the disruption of form – a sense that realist detail disrupts the "grammar" of pictorial and novelistic structure. Yet, seen in another way, it is precisely the fragmentation and abstraction of the body – its transformation into a set of homogeneous, interchangeable pieces – that makes possible the artistic photography of Rejlander and Robinson, the commodities Marx describes in *Capital*, and the artistic body described by Dickens. In other words, both dismemberment and abstraction are the enabling condition for photographic, economic, and artistic wholeness and form. More specifically, this chapter will use Dickens's fragmented artist's model as a *model* both for novelistic representation and for novelistic form. In the "Ghost of Art" it is both the figure of synecdoche and the process of forgetting that enables the viewer to re-imagine and re-member the body-in-pieces as whole.[4] Building on the connections [. . .] among photographic aesthetics, Marx's aesthetics of commodity production, and Dickens's theory of the model, I will argue that Dickens's *Little Dorrit* foregrounds and connects the problems of bodily coherence, economic value, and novelistic form. Moreover, in a novel in which the phrase "Do Not Forget" plays such an important role, it is forgetting that ultimately makes whole its strange and partial bodies and transforms the novel from a fragmented narrative into a coherent novel.

While my reading of the links between photographic fiction and literary realism form the background of this chapter, I do not intend to link Dickens to particular photographers or photographs.[5] I do not explore every reference to photography in Dickens's work, of which there are only a handful.[6] Nor do I offer readings of photographs inspired by Dickens's novels, even though Rejlander is responsible for three of these images: one of Joe [*sic*] from *Bleak House* and two loosely adapted from *Hard Times* [. . .]. *Little Dorrit* even had a kind of photographic accompaniment, with a prominent advertisement for the London Stereoscopic Company on the first page of the monthly numbers.[7] Instead, I explore how Dickensian "realism" produced the same aesthetic and formal problems as photography did for nineteenth-century critics. I focus on the way in which the novel-form in the age of photography offers a similar meditation on parts and wholes, form and forgetting.

[. . .]

In making this connection, however, photography does not merely operate as an analogy for, or another version of literature. Rather, these questions of form are intimately linked both to *the practice and discourse* of Victorian photography.

[. . .]

Composing the novel body

> Imagine me if you please with No.5 [*of Little Dorrit*] on my head and hands, sitting to Scheffer yesterday for four hours! . . . It is a fine spirited head, painted at his very best and with a very easy and natural appearance in it. But it does not look to me at all like, nor does it strike me that if I saw it in a gallery I should suppose myself to be the original. It is always possible that I don't know my own face.
>
> Charles Dickens[8]

People don't know their own faces . . . [D]irectly they see a pair of eyes and a nose, they fancy they are their own.

Photographer in Henry Mayhew, *London Labour and the London Poor*[9]

While Dickens was in Paris working on *Little Dorrit*, during the winter and early spring of 1855 to 1866 [*sic* 1856], he became a model – that is, he sat for a portrait by Ary Scheffer [. . .]. In his description of sitting for his portrait, Dickens's language encourages an unlikely association between the novelist and the model, and between portraiture and fiction.[10] Alienated both from his portrait and his body, Dickens fails to recognize himself as the "original" of the painting. Instead he has become the occasion to produce an "original" and new subject.[11] Dickens, then, neither sees himself nor knows what that self should look like. He too has become a "ghost of art" – a negative image that produces new and fictional subjects.[12]

The connection Dickens makes between his role as a model and the text of *Little Dorrit* is symptomatic of the way in which the construction of the model's body and the construction of the text are entangled. That is, Dickens has "heads" and "hands" on his mind in writing the novel. This anxiety about parts that don't fit together shows up again in Dickens's preface to the first edition of the novel. While insisting that his novel needs no introduction, that he should "leave its merits and demerits . . . to express themselves on its being read as whole," he goes on to explain how the text should be read and literally seen as a whole:

> But, as it is not unreasonable to suppose that I may have held its threads with a more continuous attention than anyone else can have given them during its desultory publication, it is not unreasonable to ask that the weaving may be looked at in its completed state, and with the pattern finished. (*Little Dorrit*, 35)[13]

Dickens's anxiety here is that his reader will be unable to piece together the "desultory" "threads" of the serially produced parts and unable to see the text as a whole – that he or she will be unable to follow the "thread" of the narrative. The reader accustomed to seeing the text in parts may literally be unable to read the text in its completed form. In other words, Dickens fears that the reader of this serial novel will never be able to *remember* the piecemeal text into a memorable novel.

Dickens betrays an equal anxiety that this patchwork fictional text itself contains too many fictions and worries that his own likenesses are more fictional than real. If the process of being painted has turned him into a fictional subject who has no recognizable identity outside the frames of his portrait, he feels called upon to defend the realism of his fictional creations:

> If I might offer any apology for so exaggerated a fiction as the Barnacles and the Circumlocution Office, I would seek it in the common experience of an Englishman, without presuming to mention the unimportant fact of my having done that violence to good manners, in the days of a Russian war, and of a Court of Inquiry at Chelsea. If I might make so bold as to defend that extravagant conception, Mr. Merdle, I would hint that it originated after the Railroad-share epoch, in the times of a certain Irish bank, and of one or two other equally laudable enterprises . . . But, I submit myself to suffer judgment to go by default on all these counts, if need be, and to accept the assurance (on good authority) that nothing like them was ever known in this land. (*Little Dorrit*, 35)

Despite his disingenuous and sarcastic offer to concede the fictionality of his characters – that "nothing like them was ever known in this land" – Dickens's claim of an authority of "likeness" is less convincing because of the "extravagance" of his own defense. Moreover, in arguing for the accuracy of his images, Dickens relies on the same, unstable logic of likeness that fails him with his own portrait. What Dickens's anxiety about both the cohesiveness of his text and the realism of his portraits suggests is that both can be, or rather must be, simulated. Both in the best *and* worst case scenarios, textual wholeness and novelistic realism are at once extravagant and necessary fictions.[14]

If Dickens has models on the brain while writing *Little Dorrit*, the following passage represents one in a series of complaints about models and their disturbing parts:

> In a word, it was represented . . . that many people select their models, much as the painters, just now mentioned, select theirs; and that, whereas in the Royal Academy some evil old ruffian of a Dog-stealer will annually be found embodying the cardinal virtues, on account of his eyelashes, or his chin, or his legs (thereby planting thorns of confusion in the breast of the more observant students of nature), so, in the great social Exhibition, accessories are often accepted in lieu of the internal character. (*Little Dorrit*, 190–91)

Ironically, Dickens echoes Eliot's complaint about his own inability to represent "internal character," and his tendency to merely reproduce "accessories" "with the accuracy of a sun picture." But the passage also reproduces the same anxieties Dickens expressed in earlier essays on the model. Like the "shabby man" of "The Ghost of Art," this "evil old ruffian of a Dog-stealer" can embody any ethical, class, or aesthetic character. That is, by calling attention to the model's markedly low class and "evil" status, Dickens only calls attention to the fact that the model's body bears no marks of any kind. The model frustrates the speaker not because he/she is an "evil old ruffian," but because he/she is nothing at all – because he/she is a ghost. Moreover, like his other models (and like all ghosts), this model returns again and again, "annually embodying" a certain character. And, like the "Ghost of Art," this model has a variety of different parts to sell. Describing all of the model's parts as "accessories," Dickens suggests both that the model is infinitely divisible and marketable, and that he or she is composed only of miscellaneous parts – loose members in the world of commodities. By using "or" to move from the model's "eyelashes" to "his chin" and "his legs," he turns a progression from marginal to vital parts into a list of qualitatively equal and interchangeable pieces.[15] Having become indistinguishable from the "accessories" and props in the painting, the model has no proper body, no vital parts, and no center. All surplus and margin, all "accessories" and no essentials, the model-body is a picture of the impossible. If, then, we understand this passage only as a satire on the "deception" of art or caricature, for lack of a better term, we risk covering over Dickens's disturbing fictional body.[16] Even more important, however, is that in this critique of representation and form in painting, Dickens echoes not only the discourse around photographic realism, but also the very terms used to critique his own literary "realism."

However, this passage also provides a way out of this biological or pictorial impossibility – a way in which Dickens covers and recovers this grotesque body. As Dickens puts it, the model "embod[ies] the cardinal virtues" through a single, though arbitrary part. That is, with the figure of synecdoche, Dickens gives this impossible figure a body that can "embody" something, if not everything and anything. Through a rhetorical sleight of hand, this body that is not *one* becomes representable and possible as a body and as a fictional character in a painting or a novel. In other words, through the implicit assumption that a part refers to whole, synecdoche produces the fiction that such a body can stand, walk, exist, and represent a whole body without falling apart.

More specifically, if Dickens worries about his readers' ability to see and read his novel as something more than a collection of parts, I locate this effort to produce the novel as a cohesive form in the rhetorical figure of synecdoche, and in Dickens's representation of bodies through synecdoche. Rather than scattering the body's parts, synecdoche projects a virtual whole to which these parts refer – a process similar to what Naomi Schor calls the "virtuality of the fragment."[17] In other words, as I put it earlier, synecdoche functions as a defense against the fragmentation that it is usually taken to produce. Both on the level of representing bodies and on the level of the text as a whole, in *Little Dorrit*, Dickens attempts to produce the fiction of a totality through the use of synecdoche. Moreover, attempting to differentiate his aesthetic of fiction from other uses of fiction within the novel, Dickens foregrounds the failure of economic fiction in the character of Merdle. Through Merdle, he associates fragmentation with a failed, dangerous, and excessive fictionality. But just as he uses Merdle's similar techniques in order to legitimate novelistic fiction, Dickens emphasizes the importance of memory – of not forgetting economic secrets – in order to make invisible another kind of forgetting that ensures that the novel can become a totalized text.[18]

My reading of *Little Dorrit* will focus on the ways in which Dickens makes visible this process of re-collection, the process by which these bodies are made fit for novels, and the way in which the novel-form itself depends on the same fiction of a totalized and whole body. I offer a theory of the novel-form and its composition that intersects with both photographic and economic practices: namely that the effort to produce the novel as a totality depends on techniques and protocols of composition analogous to those of composition photography and commodity production.[19] Just as commodity production depends on consumers forgetting how disjoined bodies become marketable products, the novel depends on the reader forgetting how disconnected moments of reading become a text with an organic totality.[20]

[. . .]

Notes

1 *Spectator*, September 26, 1853, 924; qtd in Kate Flint, *Dickens* (Sussex: The Harvester Press, 1986), 28. Flint argues that Dickens is not a "realist" in "the simple sense of the word, which seeks an equation between the written form and a photographically verisimilitudinal representation of the world." She continues, suggesting that if "Dickens holds a mirror up to his society, it is, one might say, a cracked one: one which produces playful distortions and exaggerations for the sake of social, moral, and aesthetic effect . . . [The] unevenness of the reflection reminds us that the society observed can be seen from a multitude of angles and induces us to look beyond it" (28–29).
2 [George] Eliot, *Selected Essays, Poems, and Other Writings*, [ed. A. S. Byatt and Nicholas Warren. (New York: Penguin, 1990),] III. Like Eliot, many critics invoke Dickens's photographic accuracy and ability to record "gestures" and details. See Stephan Zweig's *Three Masters: Balzac, Dickens, Dostoeffsky*, trans. Eden and Cedar Paul (New York: The Viking Press, 1930). Describing Dickens's accurate and detailed vision, he writes: "He has an uncannily sharp eye for the detection of these insignificant externals; he never overlooks anything; his memory and his keenness of perception are like a photographic plate which, in the hundredth part of a second, fixes the least expression, the slightest gesture, and yields a perfectly precise negative" (76). In his famous essay "Dickens, Griffith, and the Film Today," Sergei Eisenstein also invokes Dickens's photographic accuracy and ability to record "gestures" and details: "We can see for ourselves that his descriptions offer not only absolute *accuracy* of detail, but also an absolutely *accurate drawing of the* behavior and actions of his characters. And this is just as true for the most trifling of details of behavior – even gesture, as it is for the basic generalized characteristics of the image" (*Film Form and the Film Sense*, trans. Jay Leyda [New York: Meridian Books, 1960], 211). See also T.A. Jackson, *Charles Dickens: The Progress of a Radical* (New York: International Publishers, 1938). For Jackson, like a camera, Dickens takes in reality at a glance and in a photographically accurate single image. And, see Joss Marsh, "Inimitable Double Vision: Dickens, *Little Dorrit*, Photography, Film," *Dickens*

Studies Annual, 22 (1993), 239–82. "Much of the visual imagery that has attracted commentators on *Little Dorrit* . . . seems to me to demand a specifically photographic frame of reference if we are to appreciate it to the full" (267). The oscillation of sun and shade in the novel suggests "the dual negative-positive quality of the daguerreotype" and early photography (267).

3 See Roman Jakobson, who links Cubism and film to synecdoche: "the manifestly metonymical orientation of cubism, where each object is transformed into a set of synecdoches . . . [T]he art of cinema . . . ranged an unprecedented variety of synecdochic 'close-ups' and metonymic 'set-ups'"; "Two Aspects of Language and Two Types of Aphasiac Disturbances," *Selected Writings* (The Hague: Mouton, 1962), 11: 256.

4 Charles Dickens, "The Ghost of Art," *Household Words*, 1:17 (July 20, 1850), 385–86.

5 For more on Dickens and photography, see Claude Baillargeon, ed., *Dickensian London and the Photographic Imagination* (Rochester, MI: Meadow Brook Art Gallery, 2003), and Melissa Sue Kort's unpublished PhD dissertation, "Facing the Camera: Dickens, Photography, and the Anxiety of Representation," University of Southern California, 2001. See also [Ronald] Thomas, "Making Darkness Visible[: Capturing the Criminal and Observing the Law in Victorian Photography and Detective Fiction." *Victorian Literature and the Victorian Visual Imagination.* Ed. Carol T. Christ and John O. Jordan. Berkeley: University of California Press, 1995. 124–68] and "Double Exposures[, Arresting Images in *Bleak House* and *The House of the Seven Gables*." *Novel: A Forum on Fiction.* 31.1 (Fall 1997): 87–113]; [Emily Walker] Heady, "The Negative's Capability[: Real Images and the Allegory of the Unseen in Dickens's Christmas Books." *Dickens Studies Annual.* 31 (2002): 1–21]; [Regina B.] Oost, "'More Like Than Life'[: Painting, Photography, and Dickens's *Bleak House*." *Dickens Studies Annual* 30 (2001): 41–158]; Armstrong, *Fiction in the Age of Photography*[: The Legacy of British Realism.* Cambridge, MA: Harvard University Press, 1999].

6 In these instances, however, Dickens most often invokes photography in order to describe a mode of fiction, not of "photographic" realism. Perhaps the most memorable reference to photography in Dickens is the opening of *Great Expectations*, in which Pip bases his image of his parents on the shape of the letters in their headstones because "their days were long before the days of photographs" (New York: Penguin, 1965, 35). *Our Mutual Friend* also describes Reginald Wilfer through a strange reference to a "conventional Cherub" who if it could "ever grow up and be clothed, he might be photographed as a portrait of Wilfer" (New York: Penguin 1971, 97). The exception to my claim that Dickens often describes photography in fictional rather than realistic terms is *Oliver Twist*, where Mrs. Bedwin claims that "the man that invented the machine for taking likenesses might have known *that* would never succeed; it is a deal too honest" (New York: Penguin, 1985, 128).

7 Oost points out that the monthly issues of *Bleak House* also contained advertisements for photographers ("'More Like Than Life,'" 143).

8 John Forster, *The Life of Charles Dickens*, ed. J. W. T. Ley (London: C. Palmer, 1928), 619.

9 Mayhew, *London Labour and the London Poor*, [New York: Penguin, 1985,] 341.

10 What Dickens called the "nightmare portrait" was not done until March of 1866 [*sic* 1856]. In an earlier letter, Dickens puts his discomfort at sitting for his portrait in these same terms:

> You may faintly imagine what I have suffered from sitting to Scheffer every day since I came back. He is a most notable fellow . . . but I can scarcely express how uneasy and unsettled it makes me to have to sit, sit, sit, with *Little Dorrit* on my mind, and the Christmas business too . . . On Monday afternoon, *and all day on Wednesday*, I am going to sit again. And the crowning feature is, I do not discern the slightest resemblance, either in his portrait or his brother's! They both peg away at me at the same time. (*The Letters of Charles Dickens*, ed. Madelaine House, Graham Storey, and Kathleen Tillotson, 12 vols. [Oxford: Clarendon Press, 1993], VII: 758 [qtd in [John] Forster, *Life [of Charles Dickens*. Ed. J. W. T. Ley. London: C. Palmer, 1928,] 618])
>
>   For further discussion of Dickens's comments on the Scheffer sittings, see [Ira] Nadel, "'Wonderful Deception': Art and the Artist in 'Little Dorrit,'" [*Criticism: A Quarterly for Literature and the Arts.* 19.1 (Winter 1977): 17–33].

11 Even Scheffer, however, was not entirely pleased with the likeness: "At this moment *mon cher* Dickens, you look more like an energetic Dutch admiral than anything else"; qtd in Frederic G. Kitton, *Charles Dickens: His Life, Writings, and Personality* (New York: D. Appleton and Company, 1908), 446. After the portrait was finished, Dickens repeats this sense of pictorial self-alienation:

"As a work of art I see in it spirit combined with perfect ease, and yet I don't see myself. So I come to the conclusion that I never *do* see myself"; *Letters*, VIII: 66 (qtd in Forster, *Life*, 619).

12 In a letter to Scheffer, Dickens describes the sitting as "our Scéances" (*Letters [of Charles Dickens.* Ed. Madelaine House, Graham Storey, and Kathleen Tillotson. 12 vols. Oxford: Clarendon Press, 1965–2000]*, VII: 752).

13 See also Dickens's postscript to *Our Mutual Friend*, in which he offers the same metaphor to lodge a milder complaint against serial publication:

> [I]t would be unreasonable to expect that many readers, pursuing a story in portions from month to month through nineteen months, will, until they have it before them complete, perceive the relations of its finer threads to the whole pattern which is always before the eyes of the story-weaver at his loom. Yet, that I hold the advantages of the mode of publication to outweigh its disadvantages, may be easily believed of one who revived it in the Pickwick Papers after long disuse, and has pursued it ever since. (893)

> In the postscript to *Our Mutual Friend*, Dickens not only defends serial publication and his role in reviving it, but also expresses a greater faith in the reader's ability to see the "whole pattern" of the novel once it can be read as a single volume. See also Julian Markles, "Toward a Marxian Reentry to the Novel" (*Narrative*, 4:3 [October 1996], 209).

14 [Charles Dickens, *Little Dorrit*, ed. John Holloway. (New York: Penguin, 1985).] See Elaine Showalter, "Guilt, Authority, and the Shadows of *Little Dorrit*," *Nineteenth Century Fiction*, 34:1 (June 1979), 20–40. Showalter points out that not only do characters in the novel "construct protective fictions" (22), but that Dickens constructs his own fiction of narrative benevolence to distance himself from an intrusive and suspect authorial invasion of characters' secrets. She reads the doubling of characters in the novel as a "strategy" that allows Dickens to "exercise narrative authority without surrendering his own fiction of benevolence towards his heroes and heroines" (31).

15 In her well-known essay on *Great Expectations*, in *The English Novel: Form and Function* (New York: Rinehart & Company Inc., 1953), Dorothy Van Ghent briefly discusses the "signatures" of Dickens's characters ("that special exaggerated feature or gesture or mannerism which comes to stand for the whole person") as well as the ways in which people take on "thing-like characteristics" and are associated with the things they use, in the context of industrialism and the fetish (128–31). Yet, as in all discussions of Dickens's caricature or technique, for Van Ghent, synecdochic parts operate not as "lawless fragments" in themselves, but rather as fragments that "stand for the whole person" (130).

16 See Nadel on the "deception" of art in *Little Dorrit* ("'Wonderful Deception': Art and the Artist in 'Little Dorrit,'" 21). Many critics, both Victorian and modern alike, have used the category of caricature to celebrate or denigrate Dickens's art, and have also argued over which pictorial tradition in which to situate Dickens (i.e., whether he is a Hogarthian caricaturist or closer to the contemporary Victorian narrative painting). For example, as in John Ruskin's famous comment on Dickens's use of caricature in *Unto This Last*, critics have wished to see through the bodily "circle of stage fire" to a "truth," which "though often gross is never mistaken"; *Unto This Last*, ed. Clive Wilmer (London: Penguin, 1985), 171. See also, John Dixon Hunt, "Dickens and the Traditions of Graphic Satire," *Encounters: Essays on Literature and the Visual Arts*, ed. John Dixon Hunt (London: Studio Vista Publications, 1971), 124–40; Richard Lettis, "Dickens and Art," *Dickens Studies Annual*, 14 (1985), 93–151; Ormond, "Dickens and Painting: Contemporary Art," 13; Donald H. Ericksen, "*Bleak House* and Victorian Art and Illustration: Charles Dickens's Visual Narrative Style," *Journal of Narrative Technique*, 13:1 (Winter 1983), 31–46; Michael Hollington, "Dickens and Grotesque Art," *Dickens Studies Newsletter*, 13:1 (March 1982), 5–11.

17 Qtd in Naomi Schor, *Reading in Detail: Aesthetics and the Feminine* (New York: Methuen, 1987), 28. As Hegel writes of sculpture and its organic cohesion, "The result is that the whole can be recognized in fragments, and such a separated part affords the contemplation and enjoyment of an unbroken whole" (*ibid.*, 28). Like the whole body of the sculpture virtually projected by the synecdochic fragment, the fiction of a totalized text is achieved through a form of synecdoche. Dickens's use of synecdoche makes visible the way in which synecdoche projects a totality that can only be a fiction. That is, by using synecdoche to describe bodies that seem irrevocably fragmented, he shows how useful synecdoche can be to manufacture the organic and the organically whole.

In her discussion of Hegel and the sublimation of detail into an organic whole, Schor draws a fine distinction between "fragments" and "details." Drawing on the German Romantic tradition of the "noble fragment," the fragment (in Hegel) signifies an organic totality and operates synecdochally, while the detail remains unredeemed.

18 For Eagleton (*Criticism and Ideology*[*: A Study in Marxist Literary Theory.* (New York: Verso, 1978)]), the "anarchic, decentered, and fragmentary forms" of Dickens's early fiction degenerate into the totality of the later fiction. Yet Eagleton specifically differentiates Dickens's aesthetic of totality from an "organicist ideology" (127) best exemplified by George Eliot. This division, however, ignores the ways in which both large social systems and literary systems stage their own totality *as* organic. As Lukács's analysis of the rational totality of capitalist systems shows, such a "decentered totality" (in Eagleton's terms, *Criticism and Ideology*, 130) stages its own organic totality. That is, the totality of capitalist social forms is perhaps the best model for an organicist aesthetic, precisely because it is a *fiction* of organic totality. One can read Dickens's critique of these systems, then, as a way of staging the novel's organic form. Just as Dickens stresses the transparent fictionality and spuriousness of Merdle's forgery, he focuses on the laughable fictionality and fragmentation of systems like the Circumlocution Office in order to distance his own work from forms of totality that fail to cohere.

19 For a parallel but different argument about the relationship between the text and the commodity-form in Dickens, see Matthew Rowlinson, "Reading Capital With Little Nell," *Yale Journal of Criticism*, 9:2 (1996), 347–80.

20 Of course, the connection I draw between the novel and montage has a long critical history. Mikhail Bakhtin's *Dialogic Imagination* explores the heterogeneity of the novel-form at the linguistic level with his theory of the "heteroglossia" of the novel; *The Dialogic Imagination*, ed. Michael Holquist, trans. Caryl Emerson and Michael Holquist (Austin: University of Texas Press, 1981). Eisenstein famously argued that Dickens was the inspiration for D. W. Griffith's technique of filmic montage; *Film Form and The Film Sense*, [Trans. Jay Leyda. (New York: Meridian Books, 1960),] 211. For more on Dickens and Film, see Grahame Smith's "Dickens and the City of Light," *Dickens Quarterly*, 16:3 (1999), 178–90.

12 Realism and photography

Jennifer Green-Lewis

Just how meaningful is it to talk about Victorian literature without also talking about visual culture? In the past couple of decades that question has effectively been put to rest by a variety of studies, many of which make the rich visual experience of the Victorians their primary focus. Indeed, most accounts of nineteenth-century reading now give over at least some space to the subject of images and their influence on the day-to-day lives of readers; and few works are, it seems, more interested in the intimacy of the relationship between words and pictures in Victorian Britain than those engaging with the subject of realism.[1]

Literary realism has been increasingly viewed in recent years as more than just a genre of fiction sensitive to the pictures that surround it; it is now more frequently perceived as part of a cultural response to a world of objects whose relationship to reality was—and arguably remains—predicated on their potential to become images. From the 1840s, those images were no longer necessarily the production of pencil, pen, or water-color, but were potentially, and increasingly, made by cameras. An image in the mind's eye of Victorian fiction was as likely to be a photograph as a painting or a sketch, and in our own time, and especially since the mid-1990s, critical interest in the significance of that image as it relates to literature in general, and to realism in particular, has expanded into a thriving field of study.

Of course, the tricky part of any foray into something that touches on realism is that term's implied relationship to what is *real*. Indeed, we may sometimes try to steer clear of defining realism for the simple reason that the ground from which the word itself springs is shifting, complex, and demanding of more attention than a brief summary of literary history can give it. We may feel that we really *don't* know what it means to be "real," and we fear that "reality" itself can't be easily, or usefully, defined. Nonetheless, the term *realism* has had, since its earliest use, both meaning and utility, initially and most significantly in the discourse inspired by developments in French painting. Art historian Linda Nochlin's crisp definition remains a good place to start: realism is, she writes, "an historical movement in the figurative arts and in literature"—indeed, it was the "dominant movement from about 1840 until 1870–80"—and its aim was "to give a truthful, objective and impartial representation of the real world, based on meticulous observation of contemporary life" (Nochlin 1971: 1). George Becker claims that "[p]robably the first use of the term 'realism' in England occurred in a *Westminster Review* article on Balzac in 1853, although the phrase 'realist school' had been used but not defined in *Fraser's Magazine* two years earlier" (Becker 1963: 7). In what has turned out to be something of an understatement, Becker writes from his vantage point of 1963 that, by mid-century, "The term was launched, though its meaning was still to be defined" (Becker 1963: 7).

It's debatable, in fact, whether consensus has ever been reached on the "meaning" of realism, particularly when it began to be applied to literature. No matter what decade you dip into for critical accounts of it, you'll find dissent regarding its reach, its implications, its value, and its ideology. In 1972, Mary Francis Slattery could maintain without protesting too much that realism is "by its nature referential, and its particular brand of reference seems to be that of correspondence, and the supposed correspondence is with the mundane or at least with accessibilities, familiar to us from our habituation" (Slattery 1972: 56). George Levine, however, found it necessary to begin his influential study of 1981 by noting that "[t]o take the word realism and the idea of representation seriously entails a challenge to the antireferential bias of our criticism and to the method of radical deconstruction that has become a commonplace" (Levine 1981: 3). In other words, Levine found the theoretical climate at that point largely hostile to his understanding of realism's accomplishment and significance, and the popular account of it to be at odds with his actual experience of being a reader.

Levine's account of realism speaks, it should be noted, specifically to the idiosyncrasies of English realism; he might be describing *Middlemarch* itself when he finds that English realism "belongs, almost provincially, to a 'middling' condition and defines itself against the excesses, both stylistic and narrative, of various kinds of romantic, exotic, or sensational literatures" (Levine 1981: 5). But Levine does more than merely refer the reader to other texts against which realism might seek to "define itself"; he suggests that realism has to do with the world as much as the word. "Whatever else it means," he insists, realism "always implies an attempt to use language to get beyond language, to discover some non-verbal truth out there" (Levine 1981: 6). That desire for discovery of "some non-verbal truth" is, he argues, shared across the ages: "Writers and critics return to 'realism,' from generation to generation, because each culture's perception of reality changes and because literature requires ever new means to intimate the reality" (Levine 1981: 7).

Levine's line of thinking provides a useful bridge for addressing how photography has become part of the twenty-first century debates about Victorian realism. Recent critical interest in the relationship between realism and photography stems not only from the growing belief that the nineteenth-century "perception of reality" changed, in ways that related to their use of photographs, but also from the recognition that our own historical moment "intimates" reality in more overtly photographic terms than any before it. I'm referring, of course, to the intensification of the relationship between photography and reality that has come about largely through the digitalization of images and subsequent explosion of their use in online social networking and virtual identity performance. It's hard to imagine a conversation about identity, representation, and reality taking place nowadays that wouldn't call for consideration of photography's role in our understanding of those concepts. It's also worth noting that while we are undeniably creatures of an image culture, that's not to say we don't recognize that fact about ourselves—a point that should be made about the Victorians as well. While we may be tempted to imagine them as uncritically in thrall to the truth-telling function of photographs (a temptation enabled in part through the early rhetoric associated with photography), throughout much of the nineteenth century it was in fact widely understood that photographs could be manipulated in both their pre-and post-production phases, and that they might be altered in the service of a particular narrative or desired version of reality.

The history of creative play in photography is as long as the practice itself. Once aware of such play, the Victorians learned to be skeptical readers and enthusiastic consumers of all kinds of photographs, including the apparently true and the obviously false. Think, for example, of hand-tinting, by which color was lent to the clothes and complexions of the earliest daguerreotype portraits; or the later painting-in of backdrops on paper prints, so that a family might appear to be at the beach, or in the countryside, rather than in a studio. Think of the photographer's benign addition of clouds to an otherwise blank sky, pasted onto a combination print made from multiple negatives, long after the original sunny day had passed; or, less benign, think of the removal of individual portraits from group photographs as certain persons fell politically out of favor and were, thanks to photography, written out of history's visual record.[2]

A recognition of interventionist practices, however, and a growing awareness of the opportunity for creative play on the part of the photographer, do not negate the fact that much of the discourse surrounding Victorian photography also had to do with its realism, by which at mid-century, likely borrowing from a painterly rather than a literary discourse, writers seem to have meant the startling new visual correspondence between a photograph and what it represented. Equally significant for a discussion of literary realism, moreover, a photograph made sense and had meaning in the broader context of *community*. Although we might justifiably think of Dutch realism and thus of a particular school of art when we look at Henry Fox Talbot's early photograph of a broom in a doorway (figure 12.1) (and, as Richard Menke notes in his extract, we may find ourselves encouraged in that regard by Talbot himself), we are in a far larger community of viewers when we merely assent to the implicit proposition that Talbot's photograph of a broom looks like a broom. In other words, while some Victorian viewers might have considered Talbot to be making a reference to the history of art in general or to Dutch genre painting in particular, far more were simply impressed with the image as looking remarkably like the thing it represented. The image denotes a community of viewers

Figure 12.1 William Henry Fox Talbot: "The Open Door" (1844). Reproduced by the permission of the Getty's Open Content Program.

who agree, as we ourselves still might, that for all its beauty, and notwithstanding its symbolic and associative possibilities, this photograph of a broom is what a broom *is*.

That leap from appearance to existence—from what the broom looks like to what it is—is important, but when photography is the subject it often happens without our noticing it. One shared subject of the different studies excerpted in this book is the *naturalization* of that leap, the way in which the Victorians ceased, in some ways, to notice the gap between the photograph and the thing. Image and object, representation and reality, are, these works suggest, not only perceptually related but increasingly interdependent; indeed, Nancy Armstrong argues that throughout much of the nineteenth century not just the photograph itself but also *the ability to be photographed* was proof of existence, fundamental to a commonly held sense of reality. To be real in the Victorian period was, according to this line of thought, to be a potential subject for the camera. Or to put it another way, the proof of the broom was in its photographing, because the photograph of the broom conferred a kind of reality upon its subject that was different in degree to what painting could accomplish. As much as it represented what was real, as an object in its own right the photograph was also a piece of that same reality.

For some novel writers, perhaps especially those interested in the representation of modern human experience, the ekphrastic photograph (that is, the photograph depicted in words) proved a useful symbol of the period, and its associations with a kind of primary reality, a world of empirically knowable objects, gave heft to literary descriptions of that world. A photograph might serve as a sign of middle-class taste or of social aspirations, a detail to evoke a specific historical moment through a taste or a fad. A reference to a photograph on a mantelpiece (Hardy, "An Imaginative Woman," 1894) or the use of a photograph in the machinations of plot (Conan Doyle, "A Scandal in Bohemia," 1891) were not so different in function from the later trains and motor cars of E. M. Forster or D. H. Lawrence. Like the car or the bicycle, the photograph was for many authors a piece and a proof of the real world, a morally ambiguous sign of modernity or simply a marker of the novel's investment in its own moment in time.

Yet a photograph also functions rather differently from a car or a bicycle in a novel, for while, like them, it is an object, a material thing like any other, a photograph is also and always a representation of something else. Because of this small but complicated fact, when it appears in a literary text, no matter how incidentally, the photograph invites our consideration by implicitly aligning itself with all the other ekphrastic paintings and music and sculpture of nineteenth-century fiction and poetry. The effect of such representational self-consciousness is, inevitably, to focus our attention on the relationship between art and life—to bring back into view, as it were, that very process of naturalization whereby photography became a part of life. And the question begged by the use of photography in novels, whether as a plot device, or a detail in home furnishing, or a philosophical consideration of photography's role in shaping our perception of the world, turns out to be the one with which we started: What is the nature of the relationship between realism and what is real?

It's a question that Armstrong confronts head-on in *Fiction in the Age of Photography* (1999), which of the three books extracted here argues most strenuously for an understanding of the real that defers to the visual correspondences of a photographic culture, while calling for a reassessment of those terms by which we identify literary realism. If, Armstrong asks, from mid-century, photography defined reality for the Victorian readers of *all* novels—novels by Brontë, Dickens, Eliot, Thackeray, and so on—then how are we to understand the variousness of such works in terms of *realism*, a term that, she claims, historically has suggested that surface verisimilitude is the measure of a work's worth? In other words, why aren't these novels, all born of the age of photography, both more alike and more "photographic" in style? Moreover, if literary realism is, as some suggest, a matter of the correspondence between word and thing, a measure of the closeness between sign and referent, then, Armstrong argues, it's not clear why we should care much about it any more, given that its purest examples are, according to her, not in fact those written by the authors just mentioned. Indeed, Armstrong proposes that those novels that adhere most strictly to the standard of realism above are "second-tier" works that few read for pleasure nowadays—she includes novels by Gaskell, Disraeli, and Mrs. Humphrey Ward—and she goes on to suggest, less controversially, that the Victorian novels that people do continue to read and value (the headliners, presumably, of canonical nineteenth-century novel courses) do much more than merely reference a world of objects that mark their authors as *au courant*.

From mid-century, the culture of photography permeated society at every level, from the initially privileged pastime of making photographs and writing about that expensive and laborious practice, to the various contexts for reading the images, either privately or in public, in albums or in shop windows, in large frames, tiny lockets, even, before long, in illustrated texts. The more it came into view, however, the less photography was, in a sense, visible. It became part of the ordinary world. It was, arguably, in this indirect, extraordinarily powerful (because largely unnoticed) way, that photography changed the novel, and it did so because it changed the novel's readers. For if Armstrong and Menke and Novak are right concerning the shaping force of photography on Victorian consciousness, then we must surely suppose that, because of photography, people began to read differently. From the mid-century, and through all the subsequent decades of Victoria's reign, novels were read by people who were reading, dreaming, and remembering in a photographic culture. Photography produced ways of seeing, judging, and making sense of the visible world, ways that could not be either turned off or invoked at will, and whether or not they had ever laid eyes on a photograph, Victorian readers nonetheless inhabited a world in which photography existed. For those readers, like us, the world was *photograph-able*, a point that is fundamental to Armstrong's argument. Indeed, and as I myself have argued elsewhere, regardless of whether the subject of photography was present to any specific literary work, Victorians were beginning to read *all* literature differently because of the wider public discourse that the invention of photography had generated and the different creative and memorial practices that it produced.[3] Victorian novels that mention photographs, and that might appear to merit the descriptor of "realist" because of their interest in the shared and visible world, are, as Armstrong suggests, no more or less immersed in the broader photographic culture than novels that show little interest in contemporary technological innovations. If photography came to define the terms on which reality was understood, then Armstrong is surely right that an account of literary realism that speaks to notions of what is real must be incomplete—nonsensical, even—without close consideration of photography.

Unsurprisingly, the authors represented here share some primary material in the metaphors and similes first reached for by photography's earliest critics, and there is frequent if unacknowledged agreement among them concerning the implications of such figurative language. Both Novak (*Realism, Photography, and Nineteenth-century Fiction*, 2008) and Menke (*Telegraphic Realism*, 2008) are alert to the implications of George Eliot's famous statement that the surface details of *Little Dorrit* (1857) have "the delicate accuracy of a sun-picture" (Eliot 1956: 271). For Eliot, it seems, Dickens's skill of depiction was more of a party trick than an indication of literary greatness. Dickens may be able to churn out literary "photographs," but his brand of visual realism does not satisfy her demand for an authentic inner life, a sense of the "emotional and tragic" that is fully real. His charm is merely panoramic, documentary, real only in its attention to surface detail.

This is an important critique, and one that crystallizes both the achievement and the "problematic," as Armstrong puts it, of Victorian realism (Armstrong 1999: 11 [Chapter 9: 90]). As Novak observes, "Eliot's backhanded compliment to Dickens suggests that [his] style is photographic not despite, but because of his failure to represent the psychological identity—the 'character' of his characters" (Novak 2008: 63 [Chapter 11: 99]). It's also worth noting that while Eliot chooses a photographic metaphor, she might equally well have referenced the work of the painter William Powell Frith, whose busy canvases (frequently modeled after photographs) attend to the very kinds of surface detail that Eliot felt revealed a want of depth in Dickens (Figure 12.2, "The Railway Station"). As a metaphor, Eliot's reference to the "sun picture" operates beyond its original context; in this case, it refers not just to the "delicate accuracy" with which the daguerreotype represents the world, but also to Eliot's own assumptions about what novels ought to do.

We seem to be in territory already marked by Charlotte Brontë's well-known (though originally private) observation regarding Jane Austen being "more *real* than true" (Brontë 2000: 14).[4] Brontë's conviction that Austen was capable of producing perfect brushwork, or, in her own metaphor, "a daguerreotype but nothing more,"[5] is akin to Eliot's understanding that to tell the truth about what it is to be human requires more than the intervention of the camera (Brontë 2000: 10). What's missing for Eliot in *Little Dorrit,* and other of Dickens's works, is the "inner life," a life that can be apprehended only through compassion—the active moral imagination that enables an author to inhabit the lives of her characters, and for her characters to transcend their own limited boundaries (as Dorothea learns to do in *Middlemarch*). For Eliot, the source of such human sympathy is human suffering, and its practical application is outward. Sympathy is a response to the world and represents an effort to re-engage with it. What results—"Art" in Eliot's words—"is a mode of amplifying experience" (Eliot 1963: 271).

Figure 12.2 William Powell Frith: "The Railway Station" (1862). Reproduced by permission of Royal Holloway College, University of London.

Note that Eliot says "Art," and not "realism." Her aim was, one assumes, to produce the former, and at the time of writing this essay ("The Natural History of German Life," 1856) she did not, apparently, feel the need to argue that novels might be considered art (indeed, the opening to *Adam Bede* just three years later suggests that she felt confident on that point). Whether photography was art, however, was a question that the nineteenth century had not resolved, and it stemmed in part from the question of agency. Could the photographic "operator" be understood to be the creative agent of his images, or had he merely enabled their coming into being? And there were other questions: what criteria was one to use to judge among such images? Was it visual fidelity (such as the clarity of detail of a daguerreotype) or aesthetic effect (such as the watery focus of an early calotype)? What role might chance, or accident, play in the creation of art? Did the techniques of pictorial photographers such as Henry Peach Robinson or O.G. Rejlander –techniques that left nothing in the final frame to chance—disqualify their pictures from artistic status because their effect was achieved by staged scenes, actors, and finally scissors and glue? Or was it the intervention itself that made art a possibility where photography was concerned? Using Brontë's terms, might a photograph tell something *true*, but not real (like the crafted tableaux of Robinson and Rejlander)? Or *real*, but not true (like a mug-shot, or a formal portrait, that tells us nothing about the inner lives of its subject)?

Photography's ontological slipperiness, the difficulty that many experienced in trying to categorize it, may be understood best as a result of the many varieties of the relationship between realism and what is real. Novak claims that the intellectual incoherence of photography in the Victorian period ultimately aligned it with realism. He considers Dickens's prose, with its attention to detail and its surface verisimilitude, and finds that it "produced the same aesthetic and formal problems as photography did for nineteenth-century critics . . . the novel-form in the age of photography offers a similar meditation on parts and wholes, form and forgetting" (Novak 2008: 65 [Chapter 11: 100]). Novak's study is premised upon the idea that questions of aesthetic form are "intimately linked both to the *practice and discourse* of Victorian photography" (Novak 2008: 66 [Chapter 11: 100]). His focus on composition photography, such as that mentioned above by Robinson and Rejlander—the product of more than one negative, multiple prints, and/or some cutting and pasting—allows for a more subversive take on the idea of the real as it relates to photography. More than mere metaphor, combination printing, with (to a modern eye) its weirdly postmodernist affect, its family resemblance to Victorian scrapbooking, and its anticipation of Modernist temporal simultaneity, provides Novak with an unconventional model for understanding nineteenth-century reading practices, most notably the practice of forgetting that is fundamental to novelistic coherence.[6]

It's worth noting, incidentally, that each of the works extracted here is highly theoretical, and that none finds the study of *individual* photographs to be the necessary linchpin for its argument. While Novak makes the peculiarities of composition photography relevant to a discussion of novel production and consumption, Armstrong's focus is broader. Her book begins with the claim that the notion of realism has been misunderstood, and that this misunderstanding came about largely because of our failure to grasp the primacy of visual culture: "in establishing a relationship between fiction and photography," she writes, "I will insist that the kind of visual description we associate with literary realism refers not to things, but to visual representations of things" (Armstrong 1999: 3). Noting that the visual standard of photography remains valid and fully operational in those novels we are most likely to deem non-realist (such as works of fantasy, supernaturalism and romance), Armstrong claims that such works are as informed by what the real might look like as any traditionally "realist" text.

In this her work overlaps in emphasis with Menke's, notwithstanding the fact that Menke's comments on photography represent only a small part of his book's much broader study of Victorian technological innovation.

Like Armstrong and Novak, Menke believes that photography cannot be extracted for discussion from the culture in which it is fully enmeshed. In his discussion of realism, his choice of Eliot's novella "The Lifted Veil" (1859) is, perhaps, unexpected—critics with a visual interest in Eliot are more likely to choose the previously mentioned opening scene of *Adam Bede*—but Menke's sense of Eliot's realism is informed by the complexities of the relationship between the visual world and the idea of reality rather than a specifically or more traditionally defined sense of Eliot's work as "painterly." Noting that Latimer's first vision appears "like the new images in a dissolving view," Menke draws our attention to Eliot's magic lantern reference. In her choice of simile, Eliot shows us that her apprehension of the relationship between inner and outer worlds has been inflected by a visual technology that belongs to both science and magic.

As Menke suggests, how things are described is far more significant than the things themselves. The technologies with which the making and display of images were associated—the magic lantern, the camera, the stereoscope, the phenakistiscope, the kinetoscope—appear in nineteenth- and early-twentieth-century literary texts as ways of structuring experience, modes of seeing that cast the relationship between their subjects and objects in retrospective, analytic, often profoundly sentimental ways. For Menke, the culture of realism to which such technology belongs shapes Eliot's work by providing her with language forms to accommodate what needs to be said, but it also supplies certain kinds of images that correspond to a world she has seen—a world of images as well as of things. As Menke notes, Latimer's description of Prague in "The Lifted Veil" refers not to his own experience of Prague (he has never been there), and not, indeed, to Eliot's either, but more subtly, in Menke's words, to "the traits of an early photographic view" (Menke 2008: 142 [Chapter 10: 94]). Menke writes that Latimer's vision "precisely describes the view of the Prague Bridge which was starting to become one of the city's signature photographic images" (Menke 2008: 142 [Chapter 10: 94]), but ultimately, he suggests, it really makes no difference whether Eliot has seen such images or not. Latimer's vision speaks instead to the question of how things become "known" in a general way. Menke's argument is an important one: "the dissemination of [the picture of Prague and others like it] makes it clear that they ultimately offered not aesthetic originality but purposely generic testaments to the accuracy of a new media innovation" (Menke 2008: 144 [Chapter 10: 95]). In other words, Eliot's reference may or may not be specific to a particular image or a particular memory. What matters more for Menke, as for Armstrong and Novak, is the manner in which individual photographs, disseminated by the broader workings of Victorian culture, ultimately shaped a shared general consciousness of how things looked, and, over time, of *how they were supposed to look*. And how things were supposed to look, in literature as in life, was how they looked in photographs.

For this reason if for no other, the fields of Victorian photography and literature are likely, in our own time, to become ever more closely connected. Today, in the age of online digital self-representation, the age of lives that are always already photographed, the verbs "to look" and "to be" have come startlingly close. Indeed, the visual documentation of daily life is now a matter of public relations in which one's brand of existence is the product of manipulation. We are arguably more sensitive to the nuances of appearance and reality than any age before us; in our postmodern taste for authenticity we already demonstrate a nostalgia for the real, arguably even for realism itself.[7]

As a result, and despite the fact that Victorian novels may be a hard sell to modern readers—big books seemingly out of place in an age of tweets—future critical interest in photography, literature, and realism is likely to bring the Victorians into sharper focus for us, for the simple reason that their viewing habits and rituals wrote the history of our own. Our modern day practices echo, recall, and reinvent those of a century and a half ago; we are ready to connect in new ways with the Victorians. What is writing on someone's "wall," if it's not leaving a calling card, a marker of presence, a sign of *having been* somewhere? What are the bloodlines between the snapchat and the *carte de visite,* because surely they're related? What does it mean that a sepia cast—once designating antiquity, value, the careful hand-to-hand relay of an image through time—is now available courtesy of an iPhone app at the *beginning* of the life of an image? What are we to make of the fact that our sense of what is real increasingly depends upon its potential to be not merely documented but shared? The road to understanding current working concepts of identity, visual culture, and realism—a scholarly path which seems more interesting than ever before—will surely take us back to the nineteenth century, which may thereby, according to the photographic terms of postmodernity, become ever more real.

Notes

1 See, for example, Byerly 1997, Flint 2008, Thomas 2004. For works focusing specifically on photography, literature, and Victorian culture, in addition to Armstrong and Novak, see Batchen 1999, Green-Lewis 1996, and Groth 2003.
2 See Fineman 2012 for a full account of creative play with photographs from the 1840s. Most striking is chapter 3, "Politics and Persuasion," which includes the various incarnations of a photograph of Stalin and four other party members originally taken in 1926. By 1949, only two of the five men remain. (A similar Stalinist episode involving a 1948 photo is memorably discussed in the opening pages of Milan Kundera's novel *The Book of Laughter and Forgetting* (1980).)
3 "Put simply: our image-making mental processes when we read are deferential to those processes by which we make images when we're not reading. Looking at photographs, which was a popular pastime by the mid [nineteenth]-century, and in a matter of decades part of ordinary daily existence in a commercial culture, dramatically shaped those image-making mental processes" (Green-Lewis 2013: 329).
4 Charlotte Brontë to George Lewes, 18 January 1848.
5 Brontë to Lewes, 12 January 1848.
6 For elaboration of this idea, see Dames 2003.
7 See Green-Lewis 2000.

Bibliography

Armstrong, N. (1999) *Fiction in the Age of Photography: The Legacy of British Realism*, Cambridge, MA: Harvard University Press.
Batchen, G. (1999) *Burning with Desire: The Conception of Photography*, Cambridge, MA: MIT Press.
Becker, G. (ed.) (1963) *Documents of Modern Literary Realism*, Princeton, NJ: Princeton University Press.
Brontë, C. (2000) *The Letters of Charlotte Brontë*, ed. M. Smith, Oxford: Clarendon Press.
Byerly, A. (1997) *Realism, Representation, and the Arts in Nineteenth-century Literature*, Cambridge: Cambridge University Press.
Crary, J. (1992) *Techniques of the Observer: On Vision and Modernity in the Nineteenth Century*, Cambridge, MA: MIT Press.
Dames N. (2003) *Amnesiac Selves: Nostalgia, Forgetting, and British Fiction 1810–1870*, Oxford: Oxford University Press.

Eliot, G. (1856) "The Natural History of German Life," *Westminster Review*, 66: 51–79; reprinted in T. Pinney (ed.) (1963) *Essays of George Eliot*, New York: Columbia University Press.

Ermarth, E. D. (1983) *Realism and Consensus in the English Novel*, Princeton: Princeton University Press.

Fineman, M. (2012) *Faking it: Manipulated Photography before Photoshop*, New York: Metropolitan Museum of Art.

Flint, K. (2008) *The Victorians and the Visual Imagination*, Cambridge: Cambridge University Press.

Green-Lewis, J. (1996) *Framing the Victorians: Photography and the Culture of Realism*, Ithaca, NY: Cornell University Press.

—— (2000) "At Home in the Nineteenth Century: Photography, Nostalgia, and the Will to Authenticity," in J. Kucich and D. Sadoff (eds.), *Victorian Afterlife: Contemporary Culture Rewrites the Nineteenth Century*, Minneapolis: University of Minnesota Press, 29–48. Reprinted in *Nineteenth-century Contexts*, 22 (2000): 51–75.

—— (2013) "Victorian Photography and the Novel," in L. Rodensky (ed.) *The Oxford Handbook of the Victorian Novel*, Oxford: Oxford University Press: 313–34.

Groth, H. (2003) *Victorian Photography and Literary Nostalgia*, Oxford: Oxford University Press.

Levine, G. (1981) *The Realistic Imagination: English Fiction from Frankenstein to Lady Chatterley*, Chicago, IL: University of Chicago Press.

Menke, R. (2008) *Telegraphic Realism: Victorian Fiction and Other Information Systems*, Stanford, CA: Stanford University Press.

Nochlin, L. (1971) *Realism*, London: Penguin.

Novak, D. A. (2008) *Realism, Photography, and Nineteenth-Century Fiction*, Cambridge: Cambridge University Press.

Slattery, M. F. (1972) "What is Literary Realism?," *Journal of Aesthetics and Art Criticism*, 31: 55–62.

Thomas, J. (2004) *Pictorial Victorians: The Inscription of Values in Word and Image*, Columbus, OH: The Ohio University Press.

Part IV

Genre fiction and the sensational

Introduction

Thanks to new printing technologies, a steady reduction of taxes on paper and knowledge through the period, and—most importantly—rising rates of literacy, the nineteenth century saw an unprecedented increase in fiction aimed squarely at a mass audience. With the emergence of this popular reading market came an explosion of genre fiction, a phenomenon greeted with dismay by many Victorian reviewers, as the scare over sensation fiction in the 1860s illustrates. Contemporary critics perceived this loose collection of novels, united by what Ann Cvetkovich calls their "capacity to shock, excite, and move audiences" (Cvetkovich 1992: 14), as a fundamentally pernicious genre. Understood to act as much on readers' bodies as on their minds, Sensation novels' depictions of sensational events (murder, bigamy, suicide, adultery) were believed to produce physical sensations in those who read them that could—potentially—disrupt Victorian Britain's social equilibrium. That these novels often were themselves popular "sensations" proved another source of anxiety, as their massive sales seemed also to threaten the boundary between literature as art and literature as commodity. In response, late Victorian reviewers increasingly assumed a division between high-culture and low-culture fiction, as they attempted to contain what they saw as the corrupting influence of the popular novel.

This late nineteenth-century division of fiction into high and low forms was so successful that for much of the twentieth century Victorian genre fiction received little scholarly attention compared to its canonical sibling. A turning point was reached with the rise of feminist criticism in the 1970s. As critics sought to expand (or explode) a male-dominated canon, sensation fiction was rediscovered as an object of critical study. Long associated with women, as both producers and consumers, the Sensation novel also offered critics such as Elaine Showalter, Winifred Hughes, and Sally Mitchell rebellious and sometimes criminal heroines who were ripe for resurrection as proto-feminist icons. As Pamela Gilbert notes in her capstone essay, however, such relatively uncomplicated readings of genre fiction as subversive were short-lived. By the 1980s, with the rise of Marxist-inflected cultural studies and Foucauldian readings of Victorian culture (notably, D. A. Miller's *The Novel and the Police* (1988)), popular fiction like the Sensation novel was just as likely to be read as enforcing dominant cultural norms as challenging them.

The period following the publication of Miller's book saw a flourishing of scholarship on Victorian popular fiction that has continued to the present. Important work by the likes of Jenny Bourne Taylor, Tamar Heller, Lyn Pykett, Ann Cvetkovich, Lillian Nayder, Pamela Gilbert, Marlene Tromp, and Anna Maria Jones has deepened our understanding of the social, cultural, and legal contexts surrounding the Sensation novel, while also offering much more nuanced readings of the politics of this particular form. Increased interest in sensation fiction has also seen scholarship produced on other related varieties of Victorian popular fiction, such as Kelly Hurley's work on the *fin-de-siècle* gothic novel and Ronald R. Thomas's and Caroline Reitz's on detective fiction, while the very notion of genre itself has been significantly complicated. Not only have critics such as Andrew Maunder considerably widened the parameters of the Sensation novel, but the relationship of genre fiction to the mainstream realist novel is also now understood as far more complex than late nineteenth-century critics suggest. But perhaps the most important shift in recent scholarship is the one in reading practices. While once twentieth- and twenty-first-century critics read genre fiction in book form, scholars—led by the likes of Graham Law and Deborah Wynne—have begun to read nineteenth-century popular fiction as many Victorians themselves did: in serial form. As Pamela Gilbert's essay below indicates, the consequences of this are manifold. Increasingly working with once-popular genres, like Sentimental fiction, that have been long ignored by modern scholarship, contemporary scholars have begun to explore the full multigeneric landscape of Victorian fiction and its connections to new print forms, technologies, and reading practices.

See also: *Psychology and literature*; *Gender, sexuality, domesticity*; *Print culture*

13 Marketing affect

The nineteenth-century sensation novel

Ann Cvetkovich

The appearance of the Victorian sensation novel in the 1860s marks the moment at which sensations became sensational. Whereas the use of the term "sensation" to refer to perceptions originates in the 1600s as part of the ideology of empiricism, the sensation novel prompted a less neutral use of the term to refer to literature whose aim was to produce "an excited or violent feeling" (OED). The "sensational" became an aesthetically, morally, and politically loaded term used to dismiss both particular kinds of representations and the affective responses they produce.

In exploring the politics of sensationalism and affect, I presume that the process of naming and assigning social and cultural meanings to bodily responses, such as "sensations," has a history. My project is thus part of the larger enterprise of producing a history of the body and of physiological experiences such as affect and sexuality. Recent scholarship in this area has been profoundly revisionist because it has provided histories of phenomena that had previously been considered natural or outside the work of culture. The importance of Foucault's work on the history of sexuality, for example, resides not just in its specific details, but in its claim that sexuality *has* a history and is not a natural or prediscursive entity.[1] Tracing the cultural construction of the body or sexuality has revealed how ideologies are naturalized by the often invisible work of attaching meanings to physical processes. I have studied the sensation novel and the politics of sensation in order to participate in this broader project of exploring the political consequences of constructing the body, sexuality, and affect as "natural." Thus, I am less interested in offering a descriptive history of the sensation novel than in considering how a discourse about the "sensational" or affective serves as a vehicle for the promulgation of ideologies of gender and mass culture. And I have found in Victorian criticism of the sensation novel an opportunity to examine how and why "sensationalism" acquired its new meaning and a bad reputation. What I have uncovered points to a more general theory of the politics of sensationalism.

[. . .]

Victorian critics and the discourse of affect

Prominent in the Victorian critics' attempts to explain the appeal of the sensation novel were their fears about the dangerous affects that such literature produces. Explaining why sensational fiction sold so well, one critic claimed: "Excitement, and excitement alone, seems to be the great end at which they [sensation novels] aim—an end which must be accomplished at any cost."[2] Not only was a discourse about affect crucial to Victorian constructions of the differences between good and bad literature, but these judgments of aesthetic value were often the covert means by which high culture was distinguished from an increasingly visible mass culture. The critics repeatedly emphasized the emotional state produced by the sensation novel, the form that "preaches to the nerves," rather than the content of the novels themselves.[3] Sensational content was simply the vehicle for sensational affect: "Sensational stories were tales aimed at this effect simply—of exciting in the mind some deep feeling of overwrought interest by the means of some terrible passion or crime."[4] Even when critics emphasized the immorality of the events, such as murder or adultery, that moved sensation novel readers, they seemed especially concerned about the immorality of feeling itself, taking it as a sign of an absence of control or rationality. As the term "sensation" novel itself suggests, the critics feared the prospect of a reader reduced to a body reacting instinctively to a text. The attraction to sensation was constantly referred to as an "appetite" or "craving," and the critics were concerned that cultural experience had descended to the level of base natural functions: "There is something unspeakably disgusting in this ravenous appetite for carrion, this vulture-like instinct which smells out the newest mass of social corruption, and hurries to devour the loathsome dainty before the scent has evaporated."[5] According to this discourse, the sensation novel is deplorable because it reduces its readers to the condition of animals who are driven by instincts. The publishing industry stimulates demand by creating a need that resembles an "appetite," but the inappropriateness of the model of eating to describe cultural consumption means that satisfying that appetite is a form of addiction or perversion.

The Victorian critics explained the attractions of reading sensation fiction in terms that resemble those of twentieth-century explanations of mass culture's appeal. H. L. Mansel, for example, suggested the functional relation between life in an industrial and urbanized society and leisure reading: "The exigencies of railway travelling do not allow much time for examining the merits of a book before purchasing it; and keepers of bookstalls, as well as of refreshment rooms, find an advantage in offering their customers something hot and strong, something that may catch the eye of the hurried passenger, and promise temporary excitement to relieve the dullness of a journey."[6] Here we are given what amounts to a materialist analysis of the role of culture; in an era of rapid travel, quick-fix amusements are necessary, and the "hot and strong" content of the novels acts as an advertising come-on to "catch the eye" of the consumer. In a similar account, the sensation novel was likened to a drug that soothed the mind, an argument reminiscent of more recent theories about mass culture's capacity to relieve anxieties: "They are recommended, moreover, as good stimulants in these days of toil and worry, and as well fitted for relieving overtaxed brains by diverting our thoughts from the absorbing occupations of daily life."[7] Capitalism and the body are connected in so far as stimulating the nerves is a way of stimulating exchange. The reader's body becomes a machine hooked into the circuit of production and consumption, rather than a disinterested entity floating above economic exigencies in search of aesthetic or moral truth. In the following passage, the word "stimulant" is also used to describe the process of production rather than the action on the body: "The violent stimulant of serial publication—of *weekly* publication, with its necessity for frequent and rapid recurrence of piquant situation and startling incident—is the thing of all others most likely to develop the germ, and bring it to fuller and darker bearing."[8] The reader's body reproduces the logic of capital, responding obligingly to the "frequent and rapid recurrence" of sensational episodes in order to keep the wheels of production rolling. As George Henry Lewes says of the "exciting" situations and "breathless rapidity of movement" that mark the sensation novel: "Whether the movement be absurd or not matters little, the essential thing is to keep moving."[9] There is a slippage here between what is in the novels and what they produce; the content has the effect of "exciting" the reader, and what keeps moving is as much the reader's nerves as the novel's plot. Thus, a similar slippage is possible between bodily and economic activity, as indicated by how the term "sensation" was used to describe the content of the novels, the affects they produced, *and* the sales they achieved.

The plots of sensation novels were declared to be merely vehicles to sustain the reader's interest so that constant and rapid consumption would be guaranteed. Grappling with the problem of describing the fascination of the "page-turner," the critics assumed that there is something cheap about a novel whose content is subsumed to the task of producing a constant level of interest, and vulgar about an audience that values the emotional state reading produces, rather than the object that produces it. The reader becomes passive in the face of the violent mechanics of the novel, "compelled to go on to the end, whether he likes it or not."[10] Although the reviews contain moralizing objections to the fact that sex and crime seem most easily to arouse attention, the real target of criticism seemed to be an experience of reading that is purely affective. "Violent and illegitimate means," in the opinions of the critics, were used to create "arbitrary sensations"; realism was invoked as a value in order to decry the incidents that create sensation as false. Characters such as Lady Audley or Isabel Vane were declared untrue to life; authors were accused of making bigamy, adultery, murder, and vice seem rampant.

The critics' discourse also demonstrates the connections between sensation and gender that lead twentieth-century feminist critics, such as Elaine Showalter and Nina Auerbach, to emphasize the importance of the genre as a forum for women authors to depict the condition of women. Lurking behind the descriptions of the biological nature of the response to sensational fiction is the suggestion that this form of arousal is closely akin to sexual excitement. As D. A. Miller has pointed out, descriptions of the body's reaction to sensation fiction resemble descriptions of the hysterical woman;[11] one way to disavow or scapegoat sensation is to deem it the province of the feminine. For the critics, one of the most distressing aspects of the sensation novel's focus on sexuality was its depiction of women who transgress social conventions. Lady Audley, for example, "is at once the heroine and the monstrosity" of *Lady Audley's Secret.* The following critic deplored how the sensation novel represented women as sexual beings:

> What is held up to us as the story of the feminine soul as it really exists underneath its conventional coverings, is a very fleshly and unlovely record. Women driven wild with love . . . in fits of sensual passion . . . who give and receive burning kisses and frantic embraces. . . . She waits now for flesh and muscles, for strong arms that seize her, and warm breath that thrills her through, and a host of other physical attractions. . . . The peculiarity of it in England is that it is oftenest made from the woman's side—that it is women who describe those sensuous raptures—that this intense appreciation of flesh and blood, this eagerness of physical sensation, is represented as the natural sentiment of English girls.[12]

The bodily sensations the critics deplored in the sensation novel received additional censure when they were connected to female sexuality.

Underlying the critics' discourse about sensation fiction are the assumptions that body and emotion are distinct from and inferior to mind and reason and that culture should make its appeal to the "higher" faculties. The construction of mass culture as primarily appealing to feeling rather than reason underwrites the dismissal of it as aesthetically inferior. Affect also figures prominently in the moral panic that pervades such aesthetic pronouncements.

Feelings and emotions, like sexuality, are construed as "natural" and, hence, uncivilized and irrational. Bad art appeals to the emotions, and aroused emotions are dangerous because they prompt people to behave immorally. This ethical discourse also frequently masks a political discourse, enabling the disparagement of cultural forms that appealed to marginalized groups, such as the working-class or women. The subtext of dismissals of the sensation novel as bad art is the fear that it encourages those who enjoy it to rebel against social restrictions.

From the perspective of the twentieth century, the Victorian critics' outraged reactions to the sensation novel might seem to have exaggerated the threat the genre represented and to be at least as emotionally excessive as their target. Still, their discourse established a relation between affective states and their social meanings that remains with us. The language of bodily sensation and addiction that the Victorian critics invoked continues to be prevalent in dismissals of mass culture that construct the desire for mass culture as analogous to a bodily need symptomatic of moral or social corruption. Even the more sympathetic accounts of the sensation novel or of contemporary mass culture endorse its potential subversiveness by means of a discourse about its affective power. Rather than being cause for alarm, the dangerous sentiments produced by mass culture can be celebrated as signs of resistance or transgression. Whether, as the equivalent of a drug, mass culture deadens or stimulates affective responses, the consumer is constructed as a reading body, and affective experience, conceived in physical terms, is assigned moral or political value.

Sensationalism and the construction of affect

In order to understand the politics of affect, then, we must trace how affective experience is made meaningful. How "sensations" become "sensational" is one instance in a larger history of the discourse of affect. The ambiguity of the term "sensation" novel, which can refer either to the sensational events in the texts or to the responses they produce is not accidental. The sensation novel, and sensationalism more generally, makes events emotionally vivid by representing in tangible and specific terms social and historical structures that would otherwise remain abstract. Sensationalism works by virtue of the link that is constructed between the concreteness of the "sensation-al" event and the tangibility of the "sensational" feelings it produces. Emotionally charged representations produce bodily responses that, because they are physically felt, seem to be natural and thus to confirm the naturalness or reality of the event. The tangibility (and hence "realness" or "naturalness") of feeling or nervous response is invested with significance as a sign of the concreteness or reality of the representation.

I also contend that this connection between sensational events and bodily sensation or affect has a political dimension. What are the political consequences, for example, of the frequent dismissal of sensationalism as the product of exaggerated or unrealistic representations and correspondingly false or exaggerated responses? What political or cultural work is performed by this gesture, which often seems to be no more than an aesthetic evaluation? If, as the example of ACT UP suggests, sensationalism can also be endorsed as a useful tactic for goading people into an awareness of social problems, what political possibilities are overlooked when sensationalism is condemned?

Not only do I assume that the link between sensational events and bodily sensations is constructed rather than natural, I also assume that the apparent naturalness of bodily sensation or affect is itself a construction. Like sexuality and other physical processes, affect is not a pre-discursive entity, a fact that is often obscured by the construction of affects or bodily sensations as natural. To study the politics of affect, then, is more broadly to study the politics of cathexis and to explore how meanings are given to the energy attached to particular events and representations.

The link between the "sensational-al" and the "sensational," or between the apparent tangibility of feelings and the apparent reality of events, is often accompanied by a link between affective power and visibility. Sensationalism renders social structures not just tangible or concrete, but visible. Borrowing from the theatrical melodrama, the sensation novel achieved its effects through spectacle. Sensational events often turn on the rendering visible of what remains hidden or mysterious, and their affecting power arises from the satisfaction or thrill of seeing. Sensationalism's use of the visual, of the relation between the hidden and the seen, contributes to its capacity to make the abstract seem concrete. It rests on the assumption that the immediately perceptible, because it can be seen or felt, is real and true and natural because perception itself is natural. The apparent naturalness of these connections between the visible, the real, and the affectively powerful can be called into question at moments when the meaning of a visible event is not as natural or self-evident as the emotions it produces seem to be.

Sensationalism thus produces the *embodiment*, in both the literal and figurative senses, of social structures. It not only renders them concrete, by embodying them in a single and powerful representation, but the responses it produces are bodily or physical experiences that seem immediate and natural. The capacity of sensationalism to make both representations and their meanings seem as natural as bodily responses raises a number of questions about its political consequences. It suggests, for example, why sensationalism might work in a conservative way as a means of naturalizing ideology. Furthermore, if affective responses are not as natural as they seem to be, then the construction of affect as natural might well be part of a discursive apparatus that performs the work of what Foucault has described as the disciplining of the body. Discipline is powerful precisely because it functions as though it were natural rather than imposed. A disciplinary apparatus that functions by means of the individual subject's feelings is quite literally embodied in the self. I will explore how the reading body whose nervous responses are engaged and regulated by popular texts learns to cope with emotional shock and excess.

The Victorian critics' responses to the sensation novel also suggest that the relations between sensation and ideologies of gender and femininity need to be explored. The sensation novel's sensational representations are very often literally bodies, particularly women's bodies, whose erotic appeal is part of their sensational appeal. The apparent naturalness of sensational responses is closely tied to the apparently natural capacity of women's bodies to produce sensations. It also emerges from the apparently natural capacity of women's bodies to *experience* sensation. The association of femininity with emotional excess underwrites, for example, the nineteenth-century production of ideologies of domesticity, which depended on the construction of the middle-class woman as responsible for and ideally suited to the affective labors to be performed in the home.

Because recent feminist theory has challenged the naturalness of ideologies of gender, it is possible to question Victorian constructions of the relation between femininity and affect. If femininity is falsely naturalized, then affect has also been falsely naturalized. The point, however, is not to correct the "error" of assuming that affect is natural, but to examine the effects of constructing it as such. Central to examining the politics of affect is the exploration of how ideologies of gender and ideologies of affect are mutually dependent. Furthermore, the construction of a non-essentialist feminist agenda would have to include the project of constructing a politics of affect that does not rest on an essentialist conception of affect. This book seeks to contribute to that project by tracing how the nineteenth-century sensation novel and its Victorian critics constructed affect and constructed the connection between affect and gender.

Notes

1 See Michel Foucault, *The History of Sexuality, Volume 1: An Introduction*, trans. Robert Hurley (New York: Vintage, 1980).
2 [[H. L.] Mansel], "Sensation Novels," [*Quarterly Review* 113 (April 1863):] 482.
3 Ibid.
4 "Sensation Novelists: Miss Braddon," [*North British Review* 43 (September 1865):] 203.
5 [Mansel], "Sensation Novels," 502.
6 Ibid., 485.
7 "Sensation Novelists: Miss Braddon," 202.
8 [(Margaret) Oliphant], "Sensation Novels," [*Blackwood's* 91 (May 1862):] 568.
9 George Henry Lewes, "Farewell Causerie," *Fortnightly Review* 6 (1 December, 1866): 894.
10 "The Popular Novels of the Year," [*Fraser's* 68 (August 1863):] 257.
11 D. A. Miller, "*Cage aux folles:* Sensation and Gender in Wilkie Collins's *The Woman in White*," *Representations* 14 (Spring 1986): 110.
12 [Oliphant], "Novels," *Blackwood's* 102, 259.

14 The abhuman; Chaotic bodies

Kelly Hurley

A naked man was lying on the floor, his arms and legs stretched wide apart, and bound to pegs that had been hammered into the boards. The body was torn and mutilated in the most hideous fashion, scarred with the marks of red-hot irons, a shameful ruin of the human shape. But upon the middle of the body a fire of coals was smouldering; the flesh had been burnt through. The man was dead, but the smoke of his torment mounted still, a black vapour.

"The young man with spectacles," said Mr. Dyson.

Arthur Machen, *The Three Imposters* (p. 353)[1]

As the archaeology of our thought easily shows, man is an invention of recent date. And one perhaps nearing its end.

Michel Foucault, *The Order of Things* (p. 387)

The topic of this book is the ruination of the human subject. Such a ruination, figured in the most violent, absolute, and often repulsive terms, is practiced insistently, almost obsessively, in the pages of British Gothic fiction at the end of the nineteenth century and the beginning of the twentieth. Or perhaps it would be more precise to say that the topic of this book is the ruination of traditional constructs of human identity that accompanied the modeling of new ones at the turn of the century. In place of a human body stable and integral (at least, liable to no worse than the ravages of time and disease), the *fin-de-siècle* Gothic offers the spectacle of a body metamorphic and undifferentiated; in place of the possibility of human transcendence, the prospect of an existence circumscribed within the realities of gross corporeality; in place of a unitary and securely bounded human subjectivity, one that is both fragmented and permeable. Within this genre one may witness the relentless destruction of "the human" and the unfolding in its stead of what I will call, to borrow an evocative term from supernaturalist author William Hope Hodgson, the "abhuman."[2] The abhuman subject is a not-quite-human subject, characterized by its morphic variability, continually in danger of becoming not-itself, becoming other. The prefix "ab-" signals a movement away from a site or condition, and thus a loss. But a movement away from is also a movement towards – towards a site or condition as yet unspecified – and thus entails both a threat and a promise.

The word "abhuman" may be seen as resonating with the psychoanalytic philosopher Julia Kristeva's formulation of "abjection" in *Powers of Horror: An Essay on Abjection.* Literally meaning "cast away" or "cast under, abased," "abjection" is shaded by Kristeva to describe the ambivalent status of a human subject who, on the one hand, labors to maintain (the illusion of) an autonomous and discrete self-identity, responding to any threat to that self-conception with emphatic, sometimes violent, denial, and who on the other hand welcomes the event or confrontation that breaches the boundaries of the ego and casts the self down into the vertiginous pleasures of indifferentiation. To be thus "outcast" is to suffer an anxiety often nauseating in its intensity, but to embrace abjection is to experience *jouissance*.³ The *fin-de-siècle* Gothic is positioned within precisely such an ambivalence: convulsed by nostalgia for the "fully human" subject whose undoing it accomplishes so resolutely, and yet aroused by the prospect of a monstrous becoming. One may read its obsessive staging and restaging of the spectacle of abhumanness as a paralysis, a species of trauma, but one must also note the variety and sheer exuberance of the spectacle, as the human body collapses and is reshapen across an astonishing range of morphic possibilities: into slug-men, snake-women, ape-men, beast-people, octopus-seal-men, beetle-women, dog-men, fungus-people.

The last decades of the nineteenth century witnessed the reemergence of the Gothic as a significant literary form in Great Britain, after its virtual disappearance in the middle of the century. While certain broad narrative and thematic continuities link this form to the late eighteenth-century and Romantic Gothic novel, the *fin-de-siècle* Gothic rematerializes as a genre in many ways unrecognizable, transfigured, bespeaking an altered sensibility that resonates more closely with contemporary horrific representations than those generated at the far edge of the Enlightenment. More graphic than before, soliciting a more visceral readerly response than before, the *fin-de-siècle* Gothic manifests a new set of generic strategies, discussed below, which function maximally to enact the defamiliarization and violent reconstitution of the human subject.

In *Marxism and Literary Criticism*, Terry Eagleton argues that a new artistic mode, or a "significant development in literary form," may evolve out of a "collective psychological demand" having its roots in some massive social or ideological shift within a culture (pp. 20–7). Such an approach seems especially appropriate to the analysis of popular genres, of like-minded and -structured texts produced in quantity and consumed by a wide-ranging audience, since the very popularity of a genre speaks for its efficacy in interpreting and refiguring unmanageable realities for its audience. Gothic in particular has been theorized as an instrumental genre, reemerging cyclically, at periods of cultural stress, to negotiate the anxieties that accompany social and epistemological transformations and crises.

In the pages that follow I will situate the *fin-de-siècle* revival of the Gothic, in its new avatar as a genre centrally concerned with the horrific re-making of the human subject, within a general anxiety about the nature of human identity permeating late-Victorian and Edwardian culture, an anxiety generated by scientific discourses, biological and sociomedical, which served to dismantle conventional notions of "the human" as radically as did the Gothic which arose in response to them. Evolutionism, criminal anthropology, degeneration theory, sexology, pre-Freudian psychology – all articulated new models of the human as abhuman, as bodily ambiguated or otherwise discontinuous in identity. The end-of-century Gothic is a genre thoroughly imbricated with biology and social medicine: sometimes borrowing conceptual remodelings of human physical identity, as it did from criminal anthropology; sometimes borrowing narrative remodelings of human heredity and culture, as it did from the interrelated discourses of evolutionism, degeneration, and entropy; sometimes borrowing spatial remodelings of the human subject, as it did from the psychologies of the unconscious.⁴

As I have formulated my argument thus far, the *fin-de-siècle* Gothic might appear as purely reactive, emerging within late-Victorian culture as a symptom of a general malaise occasioned by the sciences. The relationship between scientific and Gothic literary discourses is, however, far more complex than the formulation of genre-as-symptom would indicate. In the first place, without arguing a direct influence on the sciences by the Gothic, I will be attentive throughout this study to the "gothicity" of a range of scientific discourses, to rhetoric, modes of imaging, and narrative structures which reveal the surprising compatibility of empiricism and supernaturalism at this historical moment. The province of the nineteenth-century human sciences was after all very like that of the earlier Gothic novel: the pre-Victorian Gothic provided a space wherein to explore phenomena at the borders of human identity and culture – insanity, criminality, barbarity, sexual perversion – precisely those phenomena that would come under the purview of social medicine in later decades. A number of critics have pointed out the ways in which the earlier Gothic's invention of a systematic discourse of the irrational was radically to complicate and reshape understandings of human subjectivity and the "realist" narrative forms increasingly concerned with the intricacies of human consciousness.[5] Understanding scientific inquiry as a culturally embedded rather than disengaged activity, one may speculate on its indebtedness, however subtle, to a "Gothic sensibility" newly available in the nineteenth century, despite the relative attenuation of the genre for fifty years.

One must as well emphasize the sheerly disruptive force of such new concepts as natural selection, or the human unconscious. Pre-Freudian modelings of the unconscious, to take one example, increasingly revealed a human subject fractured by discontinuity and profoundly alienated from itself. The implications of Darwinism,[6] to take another, were perceived as disastrous and traumatic – one might say "gothic" – by a majority of the population. Gothic fiction, working in the negative register of horror, brought this sense of trauma to vivid life, supernaturalizing both the specific content of scientific theories and scientific activity in general. In this sense it can be said to manage the anxieties engendered of scientific innovations by reframing these within the non-realistic, and thus more easily distanced, mode of gothicity.

The *fin-de-siècle* Gothic, however, did more than throw into relief and negotiate a crisis in the epistemology of human identity. For the Gothic served not only to manage anxieties about the shifting nature of "the human" but also to aggravate them. I mean this in no pejorative sense. A crucial strand of argument in this study identifies the Gothic as a *productive* genre: a highly speculative art form, one part of whose cultural work is the invention of new representational strategies by which to imagine human (or not-so-human) realities. Here it should be seen as in opportunistic relation to the sciences. To take one example, the Darwinian narrative of the evolution of species was a narrative within which any combination of morphic traits, any transfiguration of bodily form, was possible; species integrity was undone and remade according to the immediate, situational logic of adaptation to environment.[7] Gothic plotting seized upon this logic as a device by which to generate a seemingly infinite procession of admixed embodiments – monstrous embodiments to be sure, but nonetheless appealing in their audacious refusal to acknowledge any limitations to bodily plasticity. Darwinism opened up a space wherein hitherto unthinkable morphic structures could emerge; the *fin-de-siècle* Gothic occupied that space and pried it open further, attempting to give shape to the unthinkable. That the Gothic frequently concluded by checking its own movement towards innovation – its vampires staked, its beetle-women squashed, its anthropophagous trees dynamited – need not, I think, argue against its role as a fundamentally speculative, even theoretical, genre.

[. . .]

"Generalized animalism": Wells' *The Island of Dr. Moreau*

> The gray creature in the corner leant forward. "Not to run on all Fours; that is the Law. Are we not Men?" He put out a strangely distorted talon, and gripped my fingers. The thing was almost like the hoof of a deer produced into claws . . . His face came forward . . . into the light of the opening of the hut, and I saw with a quivering disgust that it was like the face of neither man nor beast, but a mere shock of gray hair, with three shadowy overarchings to mark the eyes and mouth. (*The Island of Dr. Moreau*, p. 60)

The Island of Dr. Moreau sets out, to a remorseless and almost overwhelming degree, the tenuousness of human identity, and the provisional and mutable nature of species identity in general. The greater part of the novel takes place on an unnamed island[8] inhabited by monstrosities. These are "beast people," the abortive results of vivisectionist experiments by which Dr. Moreau attempts to turn animals into humans. The beast people are liminal entities, like the "gray creature" in the quote above, "neither man nor beast" but something in between which, in resembling both, resembles nothing at all.

One may chart a certain physical likeness between the not-quite-evolved beast people and the atavistic "criminal types" elaborated by Lombroso.[9] Their deformities include some of the stigmata Lombroso identified as prevalent among atavists: "prognathous" face, "malformed" ears and noses, sloping forehead, shifty eyes and "furtive manner," twisted and dispropor-tionate limbs and torso, hunched posture, clumsy, misshapen hands and fingers, and lack of "tactile sensibility" (*Moreau*, pp. 25, 83–4). What interests me more, however, is a broader similarity between Lombroso's and Wells' works: each theorizes a human body both chaotic and entropic, both hybridized and prone to reversion.

Moreau constructs his abhumans[10] from an indiscriminate range of animal materials – the island population includes a Leopard Man, Dog Man, Ape Man, Puma Woman, Sloth Man, Monkey Man, Wolf Woman, and Swine Men and Women. The human body, in other words, reveals its morphic compatibility with, and thus lack of distinction from, the whole world of animal life, including those species occupying different lines of descent. Humanness in gen-eral is fractured across many boundaries separating the human from the not-human, and indi-vidual beast-people bodies may violate multiple species categories as well. M'Ling, whom Prendick finds so disgusting, is "a complex trophy of Moreau's horrible skill," a human con-structed of bear, dog, and ox (p. 85). "Moreau had blended this animal with that" in his experiments, "so that a kind of generalized animalism appeared through the specific disposi-tions" (p. 129). Like Hodgson's octopus-seal-men, these multiple hybrids – a Hyena-Swine Man, Vixen-Bear Woman, Bear-Bull and Mare-Rhinoceros Person – are chaotic bodies. They are "complex" bodies, as Prendick notes, but complexity here denotes indifferentiation and abomination rather than integrity and perfection.

Moreau's "horrible skill" is insufficient: his creatures approach humanness but inevitably revert, returning to the more compelling animal histories inscribed within their bodies. But "true" humans, as well, are prone to reversion; human identity in *Moreau* is an insubstantial thing, continually in danger of dissolution. Like other entropic narratives, *Moreau* can imag-ine only one narrative line, which moves inexorably "backwards" into loss of specificity. But the prospect one finds there is not barren and silent. It is teeming with abominations, whose changeful and chaotic forms include the "dwindling shreds" of human identity (p. 129).

[. . .]

Notes

1 Written 1890–4; first published in its entirety 1895.
2 Hodgson uses the term "Ab-Human" in *The Night Land* (1912; see Hodgson, *"The House on the Borderland" and Other Novels*) and *Carnacki the Ghost-Finder* (1913; the individual *Carnacki* stories were published in various magazines 1910–1912). While Hodgson's "Ab-Human" at times denotes a condition of being in pure opposition to that of "me human," the opposition is continually in a state of collapse within his fiction.
3 Kristeva, *Powers of Horror*, especially pp. 1–31.
4 I have deliberately excluded consideration of Gothic literatures outside of Great Britain in order to focus on the relations of Gothic discourse to a specifically British *fin de siècle*. A secondary

but significant goal of this study is to demonstrate the extraordinary density and range of British Gothic literature at the turn of the century. In discussing such discourses as criminal anthropology and degenerationism, however, it has been impossible to consider these as other than fundamentally international, albeit differently inflected within different national contexts. Whenever possible, when drawing on the work of Continental scientists, I have worked from articles translated and published by mainstream British journals.

5 For instance, George E. Haggerty argues that what essentially distinguishes the genre is its high degree of formal innovation, as the earlier Gothic, struggling to articulate a cultural sensibility at odds with that allowed within both empiricist philosophy and the more conventional novel, experimented with narrative devices whereby private or subjective experience could be figured as "external and objective reality" (*Gothic Fiction/Gothic Form*, p. 7). Haggerty's analysis credits the Gothic with being slightly in advance of the cultural mainstream, not simply responding to shifts in social realities, but also producing new modes for the perception, interpretation, and experience of social realities. Here the Gothic accomplishes not just an intensification of more mainstream discourses, as Tzvetan Todorov argues (*The Fantastic: A Structural Approach to a Literary Genre*, p. 93), but an alteration of these discourses, by transfiguring the terms of discursivity itself.

6 I use "Darwinism" to refer to the specific theory of species evolution through natural selection. The label is more convenient than accurate; many historians of science have pointed out the fallacy of identifying natural selection as Charles Darwin's sole invention. My use of "evolutionism" includes Darwinism, and refers more generally to a range of modes of theorizing the transformations of species and human society and culture (Lamarckianism, Spencerian social evolution, degeneration theory, etc.).

7 My argument here is indebted to Margot Norris' chapter on Darwin in *Beasts of the Modern Imagination: Darwin, Nietzsche, Kafka, Ernst, and Lawrence*. What Darwin imagines, according to Norris, is a scenario in which randomness is productive, creative, capable of manufacturing highly specialized and beautifully intricate forms (pp. 26–52, especially p. 29).

8 Robert M. Philmus notes that Wells changed the location of the island, originally somewhere in the South Seas, from his earlier draft. "Wells now puts it in the vicinity of the Galapagos, the principal scene of Darwin's researches and hence a site at which 'biology invades history'" (*The Island of Dr. Moreau: A Variorum Text*, p. xxvi).

9 Though none of Wells' articles treat Lombroso's work at any length, they show a familiarity with criminal anthropology. For example, "Human Evolution, An Artificial Process" discusses atavism (p. 214), and Wells briefly considers Lombroso's theory of the female offender in his 1894 "The Province of Pain" (Wells, *Early Writings*, p. 196).

I am less concerned to prove Lombroso's influence on Wells than to note similar modelings for abhumanness in both Gothic fiction and "gothic" science.

10 His quest is to construct a "true" human, but he always fails.

Works cited

Eagleton, Terry. *Marxism and Literary Criticism*. Berkeley and Los Angeles: University of California Press, 1976.

Foucault, Michel. *The Order of Things: An Archaeology of the Human Sciences*. New York: Vintage, 1973.

Haggerty, George E. *Gothic Fiction/Gothic Form*. University Park: Pennsylvania State University Press, 1989.

Hodgson, William Hope. *Carnacki, the Ghost-Finder*. Sauk City, WI: Mycroft and Moran, 1947.

——. *"The House on the Borderland": And Other Novels*. Sauk City, WI: Arkham House, 1946.

Kristeva, Julia. *Powers of Horror: An Essay on Abjection*. Trans. Leon S. Roudiez. New York: Columbia University Press, 1982.

Machen, Arthur. *The Three Imposters*. Ed. Martin Secker. *The Eighteen-Nineties: A Period Anthology in Prose and Verse*. London: Richards, 1948.

Norris, Margot. *Beasts of the Modern Imagination: Darwin, Nietzsche, Kafka, Ernst and Lawrence*. Baltimore: Johns Hopkins University Press, 1985.

Philmus, Robert M. ed., *H. G. Wells, The Island of Doctor Moreau: A Variorum Text* Athens: University of Georgia Press, 1993.

Todorov, Tzvetan. *The Fantastic: A Structural Approach to a Literary Genre*. Ithaca: Cornell University Press, 1975.

Wells, H. G. *Early Writings in Science and Science Fiction*. Ed. Robert Philmus and David Y. Hughes. Berkeley: University of California Press, 1975.

——. *The Island of Dr. Moreau*. New York: Signet, 1988.

15 Toward a sensational theory of criticism; Sensation fiction theorizes masochism

Anna Maria Jones

[. . .]

[S]ensational scholarship posits a triple-layered readership: the susceptible, malleable Victorian reader who was "produced" through the discourses of his or her age; the sensational (and therefore imperfectly critical) Victorianist reader who apprehended some but not all of the mystery from the available clues; and the critically savvy "realist" reader of today who, with the benefit of hindsight, can see what was hidden from the Victorians themselves and from past generations of Victorianists. Thus, for example, Lauren Goodlad claims in *Victorian Literature and the Victorian State* to offer her readers the anachronistically privileged perspective to "view the New Poor Law from within the culture that produced it" (35). One can certainly see how this pattern replicates itself with each new study staking a claim based in some part on the insufficiency of previous work and thereby contracting with readers to provide ever newer and bigger revelations. But, in making this kind of gesture toward "truth," critics belie their sensationalism, or rather, paradoxically, they exhibit "detective feats" and offer "high-impact narrative[s]" based on a newer, more-comprehensive, and more-accurate experience of Victorian literature and culture. As James Eli Adams maintains, the new Victorian studies "offer a more complex, more plausible, and ultimately far more engrossing account" than the familiar "Foucauldian melodrama" (859).[1]

What is interesting about this commitment to faithful representation is that it adopts the same language that the Victorians themselves used to privilege realism over sensationalism. Compare, for example, an 1872 review of Anthony Trollope—in which the reviewer claims that the public, "who eagerly swallowed the sensation poison for a time . . . [now] knows where to turn for the faithful portraiture of the present which alone it loves to study" (Hoey 400)—with Jonah Siegel's review of David Wayne Thomas's *Cultivating Victorians*, which Siegel claims, "may be recommended as a soft-spoken yet effective corrective to influential ideas of liberal values that have been more often assumed than clearly established" (309). According to Siegel, Thomas's "gentility of expression" and "commendable tact" are coupled with "extremely responsible and archivally informed case studies of Victorian culture" (310). By adopting this "realist vs. sensational" rhetoric, critics answer the crisis of faith that Andrew Miller articulates when he questions the "intriguing persistence" of Foucault. The answer is this: having learned to see through the sensational appeal of panoptical power, the critical world now knows where to turn for the "faithful portraiture" of realist criticism.

This privileging of realism is illustrated in Peter Garrett's 2005 review of Caroline Levine's *The Serious Pleasures of Suspense*. If, for Siegel, David Wayne Thomas is the Trollope of Victorian studies, then Levine is Garrett's Mary Braddon. Garrett makes the now-familiar gesture "beyond" Foucault. He begins by remarking that recent works in Victorian studies have "loosened the hold of notions like Barthes's 'classic realist text' or Foucault's panoptic discipline, enabling us to set aside condescending or suspicious assumptions that nineteenth-century realism was hopelessly naïve or enthralled to bourgeois ideology" (490). He argues, however, that while Levine "presents her study as a contribution to this reappraisal," her "curious" version of realism ultimately undermines the validity of her argument. Garrett concludes, "If Levine had recognized the implausible results of her own critical experiment, and abandoned the effort to link realism with suspense, there would still remain much of interest . . . But as an account of the relation between 'Victorian realism and narrative doubt,' her book is as implausible as the most sensational fiction" (490–91).

Garrett's invocation of sensation fiction as an uncomplimentary comparison designates Levine's book as sensational because it reveals realism's "secret" attachment to suspense, a secret that he finds far-fetched. Garrett points to the implausibility of sensation criticism much in the way that Wilkie Collins, perhaps disingenuously, rebuked sensation novelists for the "publication of books that pander to morbid delight in scenes of crime and guilt, which seem to have a special attraction to uneducated and debased minds" and which are "written to gratify a craving after excitement" ("Art of Novel Writing" 392). According to Collins, and Garrett seemingly, the sensational author resorts to far-fetched plot devices in order to pander to his or her audience. Although one would hesitate to suggest that Garrett accuses fellow scholars of possessing "uneducated and debased minds," I don't think we should overlook the sensational appeal of precisely the implausibility that he rebukes, even in the most "responsible and archivally informed" of scholarship.

Indeed, the merits of Levine's book or the accuracy of Garrett's description of it aside, the review itself would seem to occasion at least two widely divergent responses from readers unfamiliar with Levine's work. On the one hand, one might say, "Thank goodness I have been warned away from the implausibilities that this study would inflict on me," and look for a less sensational study of realism. But on the other, one might say, "'Implausible as the most sensational fiction?' You say that like it's a bad thing!" and run over to the campus library first thing to investigate.[2] I would suggest that despite current disavowals of sensationalism, the "implausible" argument is precisely what is prized in Victorian studies, and with good reason. After all, as every reader of sensation novels knows, the most obvious explanation is never the right answer. The pleasure of uncovering the hidden significance of a seemingly inconsequential clue is much the same, I would argue, whether one is reading about Walter Hartright discovering the importance of a railway timetable to Laura Fairlie's "death," or about Nancy Armstrong unearthing the pivotal role of conduct literature in the formation of bourgeois ideology, or about Caroline Reitz revealing the English detective at the outskirts of the Empire.

[. . .]

How masochism works (and how it doesn't)

Masochism offers a tantalizing framework for critics to theorize subversive agency; as a perverse enactment of the subject's relationship to power, deconstructing the pleasure/pain binary, masochism seems cunningly seditious. Yet it has proven elusive as a tool of the revolution. Two problems have plagued theoretical annexing of masochism as subversion: the problem of gender and the problem of the "real" vs. the parodic. As we will see, these two are intertwined. John Noyes, in his insightful *The Mastery of Submission* (1997), situates contemporary critical discussions of masochism in the nineteenth-century "invention" of two kinds of masochistic body. As he writes:

The masochist's body was invented in the late nineteenth century as a machine that could do one of two things, depending on how it was regarded, how it was used, or where it was positioned. It could reduce socially nonproductive aggressivity to an individual pathology, or it could transform social control into sexual pleasure. The one use of the masochist's body supports the project of socially sanctioned aggression and the various stereotypes society has developed in order to invest cultural identity with aggressivity. The other use of the masochist's body subverts this project, initiating an unsettling process whereby cultural identity is parodied, masqueraded, and appropriated in the name of pleasure. These two uses initiate all the conflicts surrounding masochism as we understand it today. (9–10)

It is not, I think, too much of an overstatement to say that these two uses of masochism have been gendered for critics and proponents of masochism: the normative, socially sanctioned kind attached to feminine interpellation, the "unsettling" parodic kind attached to masculine perversion.[3] Partially this paradox arises as far back as Freud's "The Economic Problem of Masochism" (1924), in which he describes the masochistic fantasy as placing "the subject in a characteristically female situation . . . that is, being castrated, or copulated with, or giving birth to a baby" (277). In other words, normative, heterosexual, female experience constitutes the perverse fantasies of the male masochist. Within this structure, there is no room to imagine a female perversion that might be called masochistic; women are by definition masochists.

Following this logic, feminist literary critics have tended to elide the terms *femininity passivity*, and *masochism*, thereby reading scenes of female suffering as inevitably satisfying some sinister, masculine-identified "gaze." For example, in *Schools of Sympathy* (1997) Nancy Roberts describes the role of suffering protagonists such as Clarissa and Tess thus:

The "heroism" or "greatness" of the heroine is measured by means other than her actions. For she can *do*, can *move*, very little. (After all, as victim she is less an actor than one who is acted upon.) Her heroism is measured instead by the pity and sympathy she elicits from others, by the extent to which she *moves* them (us) . . . [She] is placed as an icon, the purpose of which is to draw and invite our response. Often she is represented as having little life or character of her own. (6)

Similarly, in *In the Name of Love* (1992) Michelle Massé describes masochism as one of the primary facts of women's acculturation:

Masochism is the end result of a long and varyingly successful cultural training. This training leaves its trace upon individual characters and upon the Gothic itself, which broods upon its originating trauma, the denial of autonomy or separation for women, throughout the centuries . . . Girls who, seeking recognition and love, learn to forget or deny that they also want independence and agency, grow up to become women who are Gothic heroines. (3)

Even more nuanced arguments about female suffering, like Ann Cvetkovich's chapter on *East Lynne* in *Mixed Feelings*, tend to erase the agency of victimized heroines. In this way, masochism becomes the big blank of passivity, of status quo, of the lack of radical potential for women.[4]

Yet even the "good" kind of masochism—parodic, perverse, and subversive—runs into trouble, for the pleasurable pain of the masochistic fantasy, it turns out, is really real pain, and thus, as Noyes says, "Masochism is a continuation of social violence" (14). This is a problem that Slavoj Žižek poses in his 2003 essay "The Masochistic Social Link," in which he uses the film *Fight Club* to consider masochism as revolutionary social praxis:

> Is then the very idea of the "fight club," the evening encounters of men who play the game of beating up each other, not the very model of such a false transgression/excitation, of the impotent *passage à l'acte* that bears witness to the failure to intervene effectively in the social body? Does *Fight Club* not stage an exemplary case of the *inherent transgression*: far from effectively undermining the capitalist system, does it not enact the obscene underside of the "normal" capitalist subject? (120)

If masochism perpetuates the forms and the outcomes of social regulation and subjection, how can it also instigate a revolutionary break with oppressive social formations?

In several recent articles, John Kucich has suggested that the way around this impasse is to conceive of masochism outside of a Freudian-Lacanian "oedipal" tradition, which, he says, "severely limits cultural and political interpretation" ("Melancholy Magic" 365). He argues instead that relational psychology's model of a preoedipal and nonsexualized masochism offers a way to explain, in particular, "the central role that masochism played in shaping the ideological structures of Victorian middle-class culture" (365). Kucich's application of relational psychology offers its most direct challenge to psychoanalytic discussions of masochism, but his work can also be read as part of the current attempts in Victorian scholarship to move beyond Foucault. He calls to account cultural critics who "regard [masochism] as general trope for power relations," declaring that even these "tend to preserve the oedipal oppositions of dominance and submission—along with the thematics of punishment, forbidden desire, and potentially subversive abjection—that characterize the oedipal narrative" ("Olive Schreiner" 83). As an antidote to these totalizing models, Kucich claims, relational psychology "reimagines many sites of conceptual ordering besides binary hierarchies of power, and it addresses a wide variety of intersubjective conflicts" (83).

Although it is not quite clear how "intersubjective conflicts" might be separated from "hierarchies of power," Kucich offers a salutary warning to critics of masochism not to fall into the trap of universalizing oedipal logic as either a psychological fact or as a metaphor for social power, but instead to see masochism as participating in and enabling an array of social interactions. However, in considering Victorian masochistic logic, we should not be too quick to throw the Daddy out with the bathwater, as it were. By dismissing the oedipal component of masochism, we are not just freeing analysis from the "leftover" of a Freudian master narrative, but rather eliding the very real political and social component of the "law of the father" that structured so many Victorian relationships. What I mean is that the mid-nineteenth-century culture, in which the masochist-as-subject position was so widely articulated, was a culture that understood itself as standing in an increasingly vexed relationship to the code of primogeniture and the structuring principles of patrilineal inheritance and as moving toward a social system in which individual agency was mobilized through economic and juridical invocations of the contract.[5]

This is why Gilles Deleuze's now-classic essay "Coldness and Cruelty" is still important for theorists who wish to account for masochism's complexities. Deleuze emphatically separates masochism from sadism, aligning masochism with contracts and sadism with institutions. He describes the masochist in this manner:

We are no longer in the presence of a torturer seizing upon a victim and enjoying her all the more because she is unconsenting and unpersuaded. We are dealing instead with a victim in search of a torturer and who needs to educate, persuade and conclude an alliance with the torturer in order to realize the strangest of schemes. This is why . . . the masochist draws up contracts while the sadist abominates them and destroys them. The sadist is in need of institutions, the masochist of contractual relations. (20)

The masochistic contract requires punishment, suffering, and sacrifice, but most important, it demands agency. Passive suffering alone is not enough—one must consent to, *contract* to suffer.
   [. . .]

No Name: "You don't know what I can suffer"

"You planned this marriage of your own free will," pursued the captain, with the furtive look and faltering voice of a man ill at ease. "It was your own idea—not mine. I won't have the responsibility laid on my shoulders—no! . . ."

"Look at these," pursued Captain Wragge, holding up the envelopes. "If I turn these to the use for which they have been written, Mrs. Lecount's master will never receive Mrs. Lecount's letter. If I tear them up, he will know by tomorrow's post that you are the woman who visited him in Vauxhall Walk. Say the word! Shall I tear the envelopes up, or shall I put them back in my pocket?" . . .

She raised her head; she lifted her hand and pointed steadily to the envelopes.

"Put them back," she said.

"Do you mean it?" he asked.

"I mean it."

—Wilkie Collins, *No Name* (1862)

No Name *possesses a simpler and more intense interest than* The Woman in White, *but it is a horrible and unnatural interest; the book enchains you, but you detest it while it enchains. The incidents . . . are cleverly told, but the repulsiveness of the matter disturbs the pleasure of the reader.*

—Alexander Smith, Review of *No Name* (1863)

In this passage from Wilkie Collins's *No Name*, the swindler, Captain Wragge, questions the heroine Magdalen's resolve to go through with her marriage to her cousin (and foresworn enemy) Noel Vanstone. The letters that the captain holds out protect her false identity. They also stand as the visible symbol of Magdalen's conflicted desires. To order Captain Wragge to destroy the letters would be to release herself from the miserable prospect of using a disguise she hates to marry a man she hates. Yet the marriage to despicable, degenerate Noel Vanstone is the culmination of all of Magdalen's plotting and efforts; to marry him is to realize her desires. This conversation, like many others in the novel, underscores the fact that it is Magdalen's power to choose that determines the course of the plot (in both senses of the word). The question-and-answer format of the conversation enacts a verbal contract through which Magdalen reasserts her commitment to masochistic suffering.

This passage highlights precisely the reasons that *No Name* has been (and still is) problematic for sensation novel readers and critics.[6] First, the novel makes the reader privy to all the secret plotting and machinations, so that the tension of the plot cannot hinge on unrevealed secrets or hidden motives and actions. It demands, instead, that the reader's suspenseful pleasure come from experiencing, in minute detail, the execution of a clandestine plot. Second, the protagonist, Magdalen, is neither a heroically noble and pure suffering heroine nor a demonically conniving and evil villainess. Instead, the novel tries to present her as somewhere in between—a transgressive, guilty heroine, in constant and painful conflict with herself. *No Name* paradoxically demands a reader who is well disciplined and deviant—one who understands and accepts literary and social conventions, even as he or she is driven by the affective power of the novel to *feel* at odds with those conventions. Through its manipulation of the tropes of heroine (and villainess), plot, and sympathy, the novel forces the reader to examine individual agency in relation to the mechanisms of disciplinary power.

No Name presents a heroine who is an odd mixture of virtuous feminine ideal and "monstrous" perversion. In the beginning of the novel, for example, Magdalen is used as a foil to highlight the virtues of her elder and more-passive sister, Norah. When the parents' misdeeds and the daughters' plight are revealed, the narrator muses, through the governess, Miss Garth:

> Was the promise of the future shining with prophetic light through the surface-shadow of Norah's reserve; and darkening with prophetic gloom, under the surface-glitter of Magdalen's bright spirits? If the life of the elder sister was destined henceforth to be the ripening ground of the undeveloped Good that was in her—was the life of the younger doomed to be the battle-field of mortal conflict with the roused forces of Evil in herself? (147)

The answer, reiterated repeatedly throughout the novel, is a resounding yes. It is not just that Magdalen's actions are misinterpreted by others in the novel as bad;[7] she really does think and do evil things. Magdalen is punished for her parents' wrongs, one might say, but her subsequent plotting earns the punishment she has already unjustly received.[8]

But if Magdalen is not the ideal heroine—the helpless, virtuous victim of a Gothic plot, like Laura Fairlie in *The Woman in White*—neither is she a spectacularly demonized villainess like Lucy Audley in *Lady Audley's Secret*. Rather, she is an active agent in her own suffering. She conspires against her enemies, *and* she suffers acute moral pangs as a result. She transgresses, even as her "natural delicacy" revolts. She writes to her sister: "Try to forgive me. I have struggled against myself, till I am worn out in the effort. I am the wretch-est of living creatures . . . If you knew what my thoughts are; if you knew how hard I have fought against them, and how horribly they have gone on haunting me in the lonely quiet of the house, you would pity and forgive me" (181). Magdalen's distress in contemplating her transgression and its attendant punishments is tempered with the imagined payoff for those transgressions. Her pleasure in transgressing comes from imagining having her actions judged by Norah. Notice, Magdalen imagines that Norah's knowledge of her (evil) thoughts would place Norah in a position to sympathize with rather than despise Magdalen. Likewise, the novel itself imagines a relationship with its reader in which intimate descriptions of the heroine's transgressions and suffering will place the reader in a similarly sympathetic position, despite the reader's knowledge/belief that Magdalen's behavior is wrong, that she is not "good."

In the preface to the 1862 edition of *No Name*, Collins describes his narrative strategy this way:

It will be seen that the narrative related in these pages has been constructed on a plan, which differs from the plan followed in my last novel . . . The only Secret contained in this book, is revealed midway! in the first volume. From that point, all the main events of the story are purposely foreshadowed, before they take place—my present design being to rouse the reader's interest in following the train of circumstances by which these foreseen events are brought about. In trying this new ground, I am not turning my back in doubt on the ground which I have passed over already. My one object in following a new course, is to enlarge the range of my studies in the art of writing fiction, and to vary the form in which I make my appeal to the reader, as attractively as I can. (5–6)

It is clear here that Collins understands the problem with the "new ground" of *No Name*: the reversal of reader identification depends on making the transgression "attractive."

It is equally clear that critics both understood and rejected the project of reversing readers' sympathies. Margaret Oliphant, for instance, remarks in a review of *No Name* in *Blackwood's Magazine*:

Mr. Wilkie Collins, after the skilful and startling complications of *The Woman in White* . . . has chosen, by way of making his heroine piquant and interesting in his next attempt, to throw her into a career of vulgar and aimless trickery and wickedness, with which it is impossible to have a shadow of sympathy, but from all the pollutions of which he intends us to believe that she emerges, at the cheap cost of a fever, as pure, as high-minded, and as spotless as the most dazzling white of heroines . . . This is a great mistake in art, as well as a falsehood to nature. ("Novels" 170)

Similarly, a reviewer for the *Reader* comments: "If Magdalen Vanstone could have sacrificed her character without sacrificing the sympathy of an ordinary English reader, it is impossible to say to what heights of sensational grandeur *No Name* might not have risen" (135). These reviews highlight the readers' difficulty with the novel: Magdalen is constructed by the text as a sympathetic heroine, but one cannot sympathize with her without also sympathizing with or condoning her "vulgar and aimless trickery and wickedness." If she were not sympathetic, then that trickery and wickedness would not create such a moral stumbling block; Magdalen would merely be a spectacular villainess. However, even if one were to view Magdalen antagonistically (a position not at all encouraged by the text), one's expectations would *still* be thwarted because Magdalen doesn't get punished for her wickedness. There is no comfortable reassertion of law and order at the end of the novel that leaves the villains properly contained (imprisoned in a mental institution, or executed by an agent of a secret Italian society, say) and "the good people all happy and at peace" (Braddon, *Lady Audley* 447).[9]

Despite the critics' insistence on the heroine's perversity, however, *No Name* shows that Magdalen's masochism is deeply imbedded in the rhetoric of ideal femininity.

[. . .]

Notes

1 Adams is referring here to Karen Chase and Michael Levenson's *The Spectacle of Intimacy*.
2 In fact, having read Garrett's review before discovering Levine's book, I am describing my own experience.
3 See, for example Leo Bersani's account of the "shattering" of the self through masochism in *The Freudian Body*, or Carol Siegel's *Male Masochism*.

4 For a good critique of the problems in feminist theory with masochism, see Lynda Hart's analysis in *Between the Body and the Flesh*. See also Marianne Noble's *The Masochistic Pleasures of Sentimental Literature*. Noble's analysis of the eroticism of language in sentimental literature does an excellent job of addressing how, precisely, these texts participate in the production and proliferation of masochistic fantasies. However, she also tends to focus on female masochism as submission (albeit willing or at least complicit) to a specifically heterosexual, masculine, dominant regime.

5 F. Scott Scribner, in his article "Masochism and the Modern Ethical Ideal (1788–1887)," makes an interesting argument about what the masochistic contract does by turning away from the moral absolutism of Kantian ethics: "The masochistic contract offers an ethics insofar as it is an reenactment of the social contract, that refuses the totalizing gesture of the universal, while nevertheless offering a sensual ideal, grounded in the uniqueness of the situation and secured through the freely chosen law of the contract. Masoch's fiction is an intervention that affirms the particularity of an individual incarnation of an ideal as a model of social interaction, rather than the universality of the 'law' or the 'Good'" (79).

6 Neither *No Name* nor *Armadale* have received the critical attention of *The Woman in White* or *The Moonstone*, but critics who do address them describe them in superlative terms (most convoluted, most perverse, most radical, etc.). Deirdre David, for example, contends in "Rewriting the Male Plot in Wilkie Collins's *No Name* (1862)" that "no [other] Collins novel . . . so interestingly conflates resistance to dominant aesthetic and sexual ideologies as *No Name*" (34), although she also claims, rather inexplicably, that this resistance means that the novel "rattles no nerves with sensational excitement" (35). Jenny Bourne Taylor, who reads the novel within discourses of evolution and psychology, does acknowledge the novel's sensationalism, remarking that as "Collins's most explicit treatment of the formation of social identity and of the cultural construction of femininity outside and inside the family," *No Name* "is a story of 'perversity.' . . . It is also a perverse story" (132).

7 Think, for example, of the suspicious reticence of *The Moonstone*'s heroine, Rachel Verinder, in regard to the disappearance of the diamond.

8 Magdalen's parents have pretended to be married while Mr. Vanstone is still married to a terrible, degenerate woman in Canada, so both Magdalen and her sister, Norah, are illegitimate. But when the first wife dies, while the daughters are in their teens, the parents marry immediately, unfortunately without realizing that this demands they make new wills so that the illegitimate daughters will not be disinherited. They both die before they can rectify their mistake.

9 Critics have tended to argue that the heroines of sensation novels are morally suspect, citing as the primary example Lady Audley. It seems to me, however, that at no time in the novel is she the heroine or protagonist. Rather, the amateur sleuth Robert Audley is the *hero*, and Lady Audley is the fascinating villainess. This may seem like a minor distinction, but it is crucial to understanding Collins's experimentation with the form of the sensation novel in his portrayal of Magdalen.

Bibliography

Adams, James Eli. "Recent Studies in the Nineteenth Century." *SEL: Studies in English Literature* 41, no. 4 (Autumn 2001): 827–79.

Bersani, Leo. *The Freudian Body*. New York: Columbia University Press, 1986.

Braddon, Mary Elizabeth. *Lady Audley's Secret*. 1862. New York: Oxford University Press, 1987.

Collins, Wilkie. *No Name*. 1862. New York: Oxford University Press, 1986.

——. "The Art of Novel Writing." *The Gentleman's Magazine* (1872): 384–93. In Nadel, Victorian Fiction.

Cvetkovich, Ann. *Mixed Feelings: Feminism, Mass Culture, and Victorian Sensationalism*. New Brunswick: Rutgers University Press, 1992.

David, Deirdre. "Rewriting the Male Plot in Wilkie Collins's *No Name* (1862): Captain Wragge Orders an Omelette and Mrs. Wragge Goes into Custody." In *The New Nineteenth Century: Feminist Readings of Underread Victorian Fiction*, edited by Barbara Leah Harman and Susan Meyer, 33–44. New York: Garland, 1996.

Deleuze, Gilles. "Coldness and Cruelty." In *Masochism*. Translated by Jean McNeil. New York: Zone (1991): 9–18.

Garrett, Peter. Review of *The Serious Pleasures of Suspense: Victorian Realism and Narrative Doubt*, by Caroline Levine. *The Modern Language Review* 100, no. 2 (April 1, 2005): 490–91.

Goodlad, Lauren M. E. *Victorian Literature and the Victorian State: Character and Governance in a Liberal Society*. Baltimore: Johns Hopkins University Press, 2003.

Hart, Lynda. *Between the Body and the Flesh: Performing Sadomasochism*. New York: Columbia University Press, 1998.

Hoey, Frances Cashel. "The Novels of Mr. Anthony Trollope." *Dublin Review* n.s. 19, o.s. 71 (October 1872): 393–430.

Kucich, John. "Melancholy Magic: Masochism, Stevenson, Anti-Imperialism." *Nineteenth-Century Literature* 56, no. 3 (December 2001): 364–400.

——. "Olive Schreiner, Masochism, and Omnipotence: Strategies of a Preoedipal Politics." *Novel: A Forum on Fiction*. 36, no. 1 (Fall 2002). 79–109.

Massé, Michelle A. *In the Name of Love: Women, Masochism, and the Gothic*. Ithaca, NY: Cornell University Press, 1992.

Miller, Andrew H. "Recent Studies in the Nineteenth Century." *SEL: Studies in English Literature 1500–1900* 43, no. 4 (2003): 959–97.

Nadel, Ira Bruce. *Victorian Fiction: A Collection of Essays from the Period*. New York: Garland, 1986.

Review of *No Name*, by Wilkie Collins. *The Reader* (January 3, 1863): 14–15. In Page, *Wilkie Collins: The Critical Heritage*, 134–36.

Noble, Marianne. *The Masochistic Pleasures of Sentimental Literature*. Princeton, NJ: Princeton University Press, 2000.

Noyes, John K. *The Mastery of Submission: Inventions of Masochism*. Ithaca, NY: Cornell University Press, 1997.

Oliphant, Margaret. "Novels." *Blackwood's Edinburgh Magazine* 94 (August 1863): 168–83.

Page, Norman, ed. *Wilkie Collins: The Critical Heritage*. London: Routledge, 1974.

Roberts, Nancy. *Schools of Sympathy: Gender and Identification through the Novel*. Montreal: McGill-Queen's University Press, 1997.

Scribner, F. Scott. "Masochism and the Modern Ethical Ideal (1788–1887): Between Literary and Scientific Visibility." *Literature And Psychology* 48, nos.1 & 2 (2002): 65–88.

Siegel, Carol. *Male Masochism: Modern Revisions of the Story of Love*. Bloomington: Indiana University Press, 1995.

Siegel, Jonah. Review of *The Culture of Property: The Crisis of Liberalism in Modern Britain*, by Joanna Bailkin and *Cultivating Victorians: Liberal Culture and the Aesthetic*, by David Wayne Thomas. *Victorian Studies* 47, no. 2 (Winter 2005): 309–11.

Smith, Alexander. Review of *No Name*, by Wilkie Collins. *North British Review* (February 1863): 183–85. In Page, *Wilkie Collins: The Critical Heritage*, 140–42.

Taylor, Jenny Bourne. *In the Secret Theatre of Home: Wilkie Collins, Sensation Narrative, and Nineteenth-Century Psychology*. New York: Routledge, 1988.

Žižek, Slavoj. "The Masochist Social Link." In *Perversion and the Social Relation*, edited by Molly Anne Rothenberg, Dennis Foster, and Slavoj Žižek, 112–25. Durham, NC: Duke University Press, 2003.

16   Genre fiction and the sensational

Pamela K. Gilbert

Had she not resolved, in her first bitter repentance, *to take up her cross* daily, and bear it? No, her own feelings, let them be wrung as they would, should not prove the obstacle.
—Ellen Wood, *East Lynne* (1861)

Critics interested in popular literature as a vehicle for ideological critique are often baffled by this material's apparently conservative messages about gender and power. Why do readers of popular fiction so often consume stories filled with suffering and punishment for transgression? Here I will trace a lineage of critical approaches to this question of the appeal of painful affect since the early 1990s, when popular Victorian fiction, especially the sensation novel, came to prominence as a topic of scholarship. I will then point to two new directions in the research that may offer fruitful ways of exploring the question above. Periodicals research exposes a previously submerged body of popular fiction, including the understudied genre of late-century sentimental fiction, which foregrounds painful affect. New technologies in neuroscience enable us to engage with questions that the Victorians themselves asked about art and affect with new information.

Late twentieth-century feminist scholars of Victorian literature working to recover women's voices often were inclined to see any example of women's writing as potentially liberatory, and sensation was a feminine genre, widely identified in the Victorian period with female authors and readers (despite the fact that men produced and consumed this fiction as well). However, popular culture scholars, informed by Marxist approaches, were traditionally suspicious of the ideological content of commercially successful popular narratives. It was in this critical environment that Ann Cvetkovich published her study of sensation fiction in 1992. Cvetkovich understands these texts as both transgressive and ideologically conservative in different ways and moments with different audiences, though she sees the conservative messages winning out. Cvetkovich's work draws together three key themes that we will explore further here: affect, the body, and politics. ("Affect" refers here to feelings that may have physiological or cognitive origins.) Cvetkovich uses Foucault's insight that the aspects of human life that seem the most "natural" and thus least open to either ideological critique or historicization have cultural histories. This was the founding insight for his *History of Sexuality* (1976 original, English translation 1978), and Cvetkovich applies the same principle to the seemingly natural category of affect. Her principal interest is in the history and politics of affect—the way in which affective energy is mobilized for political purposes. Influenced by theories of *écriture feminine* by such thinkers as Hélène Cixous and Julia Kristeva, many scholars argued that the narration of women's bodily experience was itself transgressive of hegemonic norms.[1] But Cvetkovich showed that the creation and expression of affect could also be a way of distracting from political action. We cry with the suffering heroine, and at the end, feel redeemed by the exercise of our sympathy. Suffering is transformed into pleasure. But does political change result? If not, then perhaps the form was more conservative than many feminists had thought.

Sensation fiction, a genre of British popular fiction popular in the 1860s, was, as Cvetkovich notes, believed to "preach to the nerves." It was also a feminized genre, and anxiety about it focused disproportionately on its female producers and consumers. One of the main criticisms of sensation as a psychological phenomenon was that it bypassed rationality and appealed directly to the lowest bodily appetite for stimulation at the expense of reflection and moral improvement. Not only did the stories represent women's bodies, but the "sensations" evoked also reminded women readers that they themselves were embodied. Were these bodily sensations—of fear, sympathy, excitement—frightening to Victorian critics because they were believed to mobilize women's discontentment? Cvetkovich finds that the affect mobilized by descriptions of female suffering in these novels was in fact not typically used for feminist ends, but was commonly redirected to reinforce repressive ideological values; in contrast, she evaluates how works of "high-culture" fiction such as Eliot's *Daniel Deronda* or of nonfiction such as Marx's *Capital* use sensational strategies for more innovative ends.

Cvetkovich's work thus demonstrates a few of the trends of feminist Victorian criticism of the early 1990s. First, she uses Foucault to unearth a history of naturalized culture. Second, despite pioneering work on popular fiction, the book displays the period's defensiveness about popular culture, a tendency to treat it as less appropriate for literary analysis and less capable of ideological critique than more canonical works such as Eliot's. My own book on sensation and genre in 1997 was marked by its moment in the same way. It also participated in unveiling a cultural history of the natural (the body), and it read the construction of the sensation genre in the context of both the culture wars of the late twentieth century and their precursor in the mid-nineteenth. The book argued that we should address the work of popular writers with the same seriousness that one would bring to canonical authors, and insisted on this fiction's continuity and dialogue with both Victorian critical writing and canonical fiction. It thus differed with Cvetkovich's work in making more optimistic claims for the potential of popular fiction to resist dominant values. Finally, however, in both cases, our arguments for the importance of popular literature were made precisely through comparison of that literature to canonical works. This was partly a response to the critical climate at the time, in which one still had to defend reading less-known works seriously to a readership often disinclined to read about texts not already part of the existing scholarly frame of reference, and tending to regard any claims for their value as special pleading on the basis of gender. Part of the task of feminist critics in the 1990s, then, was to interrogate the history of genre with the same attention to the ideological charge of the literature's original reception as to the late twentieth-century history of scholarship, and to treat both as artificial and value-laden constructions that had been naturalized, just as gender, affect, and the body had been.

Gothic is the other popular genre that has been the subject of intense critical attention in popular British nineteenth-century fiction. Unlike sensation, a genre that was identified by critics in the 1860s, gothic fiction had been a recognized phenomenon when the century was young, and continued long after it had passed. Gothic was related to sensation, but its use of the supernatural and exotic settings became more pronounced as the century went on, whereas sensation famously focused on the mysteries of apparently ordinary life. Like sensation, gothic literature also became increasingly reflective of Victorians' interest in physiology.

Kelly Hurley's 1996 work is concerned not with body or mind to the exclusion of either, but with their interrelation in the formation (or ruination) of subjectivity. Her interest is in the "abhuman," the abject construction of human subjectivity that challenges the very idea of a definable humanity that could be defended once the insights of Victorian psychology and of Darwin undermined any clear sense of a unified, dignified human awareness. Hurley's book details at length the 1890s fascination with materialism run amok, a humanity that could no longer be clearly distinguished from animality, and bodies forever threatening to disintegrate either into their component parts or into nothing recognizable at all. Worse, these abhuman bodies reflect the status of the subjects who inhabit them, prone at any time to lose coherence and exercise aberrant forms of agency. Her reading of Wells's *Island of Dr Moreau* (1896) (a meld of gothic and what would later be termed science fiction characteristic of the period) shows the continuity of the beastly "Men" on the island, created by Moreau, and the beastliness of the remorseless Moreau and even Prendick the narrator himself, who "reverts" to a pre-human savagery under the influence of the horror of his environment.

Unlike the 1990s scholarship on sensation, Hurley does not engage the critical or "reception" history of the texts, perhaps because the gothic does not, as sensation persistently does, thematize the act of reading. Moreover, gothic was not primarily identified with women authors and readers (though women certainly did author and read it as well as men), so the scholarship tends to focus on the literature's representations of gender rather than the gendering of the genre itself. Furthermore, like sensation, gothic was often considered rather trashy, marketed as distraction rather than serious art. Hurley also engages the subversive potential of popular genres, but her conclusions to some extent oppose that of Cvetkovich: in her argument that gothic is "an instrumental genre, reemerging cyclically, at periods of cultural stress" (Hurley 1996: 5 [Chapter 14: 126]), she sees popular fiction offering innovation and a way forward rather than ideological reinforcement. Both scholars, then, see genre as a way to express and manage anxiety, as well as a structure that mobilizes affect, but Hurley is more optimistic about a popular form's possibilities for social transformation and critique. Her view is closer to my own position in seeing the representation of the transgressive body as challenging more than reinforcing dominant ideologies.

By the time Anna Maria Jones's *Problem Novels* came out in 2007, the genre of sensation fiction had been fairly fully defined, and in turn critics had more insistently questioned what was at stake in earlier scholars' assumption of a clear separation between genres. Jones argues that by this time scholars had begun to tire of Foucauldian (and Marxist) views that many came to see as trapped in a never-varying story of power pre-empting resistance, and had begun to seek a more hopeful model. However, Jones argues against the critical impatience with Foucauldian readings and what she sees as a related and continuing critical championship of realism over sensation. Like detectives, she asserts, sensation scholars advance the non-obvious, more "sensational" explanation of what is happening in texts, but when we do, we are sometimes criticized for our lack of restraint or tact or what amounts to "gentility." Specifically, she cites the critical reaction to Caroline Levine's *The Serious Pleasures of Suspense* (2003), citing reviewers' distaste for Levine's "low" reading of a "high" genre. She argues that the power relation seen in the original reception of Victorian genres—wherein critics derided what they saw as the feminized, unselfconsciously hysterical sensational novel in opposition to the deliberate and dignified rationality of "high" realism—is replicated in the scholarship today. Jones argues that sensational strategies were in fact very consciously used by Victorian authors both inside and outside of the sensation genre as a method to stage the conflict between being "culturally embedded" and "sensationally susceptible" (Jones 2007: 6), that is, between ideology and sensational critique, "theorizing a critically empowered subject" as a reader.

In her reading of female masochism, long considered a particularly vexed subject by feminists—if a woman chooses to suffer, then is her suffering to be considered oppressive or a badge of her own agency?—Jones faults Cvetkovich for falling into what by 2007 seemed an oversimplified reading of Foucault. Yes, one is always subjected to power, but one is also always a subject, or agent, within a network of power, with shifting access to power within that structure. Female characters' suffering, and female readers' enjoyment of it, did not always have to equate to a reinforcement of female powerlessness. For example, Jones reads Collins's *No Name* (1862)—a novel difficult for both Victorian and present-day readers because the female protagonist violates norms of proper behavior and so may lose reader sympathy—as a novel that thematizes the active nature of female masochism. The heroine exercises her power to suffer as part of an active campaign to wrest control of her life and inheritance away from the man she feels has unfairly been given that authority. She wallows in her pain in order to nerve herself to accomplish the "unnatural" deeds she undertakes. In so doing she is portrayed as self-aware, not unconscious or helpless, and the book encourages the reader, too, to be aware of the paradoxical mechanism of active indulgence in passivity, of suffering as a form of pleasure.

Jones's reading of the complex stagings of power in sensation novels is astute, and by 2007, she was no longer burdened with the necessity of defending the simple act of paying attention to sensation novels. Her insight that sensation fiction is a genre that is marked by its theorization of "'problematic' versions of subjectivity" and that these problematic subjectivities still make some readers—especially those committed to what they perceive as the "gentility" and "tact" of Victorian realism—uncomfortable, is a good one. It also seems to suggest that there is something more enduringly and endearingly subversive about these novels than some popular culture critics might have thought.

All three excerpts herein included address these popular genres' representation and manipulation of affect, including sympathy, sadness, fear, and anger. All emphasize the importance and appeal of suffering in their chosen genre, whether in the characters' choices to engage in self-sacrifice or the reader's to sympathize or be horrified by that sacrifice. In each case, suffering and abjection are both themes of the text and sympathetic experiences offered to the reader, as we feel Magdalen steel herself for sacrifice and revenge, or Prendick slowly lose his humanity. The period and its literature, both realist and gothic or sensational, reflect the Victorians' intense interest in psychology, one well grounded in the period's developments in physiology.[2] The mind–body split of the early Enlightenment was fading by the 1860s, as the Victorians were deeply interested in the embodied mind and the effects of physiology upon mental and emotional states. It was this in part that drove the Victorian distrust of sensation fiction that now seems so comically overblown; reading was thought to excite the mind and simultaneously stimulate the body, and could damage readers' health, especially the health of young women, who were thought particularly vulnerable to mental excitement. These studies focused not only on the body, but also on bodily sensations categorized as "affect." Though traditionally scholarship on affect fell under the category of aesthetics, treating it as a product (or by-product) of the aesthetic response, more recent scholarship on affect has privileged affect as a primary mechanism of meaning-production.

In the last several years, intensified interest in affect in humanities scholarship has been driven in part by new discoveries in neuroscience and brain imaging such as fMRI (functional Magnetic Resonance Imaging), which has allowed researchers to track some physiological manifestations of affect in real time. Much of the related work on the embodied reading subject is historically focused, and seeks to situate the discussion of Victorian reading within Victorian understandings of physiology. It continues the 1990s work on Victorian views of reading and situates it in a rigorous reading of the physiological and literary work of the day. Little of this work, however, has addressed popular forms. I would like to show how it might relate specifically to questions of affect in popular fiction. In particular, I want to take up the understudied form of sentimental fiction, one particularly concerned with affect, to challenge some of our critical commonplaces about sensation fiction and the gothic.

Late twentieth-century popular fiction scholarship focused on novels that widely circulated in three-volume form. But this gives a partial picture of popular fiction in the period. By the late 1870s, a number of penny "story paper" serials had appeared, providing for a readership understood to be mostly comprised of servants, and working- and lower-middle-class women. This literature often did not circulate in the bound volumes generally preserved in libraries, and so until recently was more difficult for scholars to access. Complicating the problem of access, however, is perhaps a disinclination to engage this corpus, which appeals less to present-day literary tastes while offering little to scholars seeking heroic agency in female protagonists. Scholarly readers today still tend to value what modernists valued in texts: realism, continuity, complexity, and contemplative interiority, rather than what many Victorians did. Victorian penny-weekly periodical stories, designed for an episodic and interrupted reading experience, valorized melodramatic oppositions, set pieces, stark contrasts, and emotional responsiveness over the complexity offered by most realist or sensational novels. Writers like Charles Dickens, Mary Elizabeth Braddon, and Mrs Henry Wood balanced the demands of periodical publication with the eventual bound volumes in mind, and their work appeals to us today in part because it is fairly continuous in form with "high-culture" fiction. But in penny weeklies, while sensational fiction certainly dominated over the kind of slow-paced reflective writing that we associate with, say, George Eliot, it did not reign alone. In these venues, sentimental fiction, which has received comparatively little attention on the British side of nineteenth-century scholarship, was often dominant. Many writers, often women, wrote exclusively for this public. If we wish to understand fiction as a mechanism for the production of affect and also as a vehicle of ideology, this material is indispensable.[3]

Realism and sensation focus on suspense and resolution. Both are structured along a developmental arc—an agent, a complex, reflective individual, grows through encountering and (usually) overcoming obstacles. But often, sentimental texts describe not an arc but a wave pattern, intensifying emotion through the repetition of a single theme. Difficulties are not overcome but endured. Sentimentalism is often used as a technique within realist narratives, enhancing domestic realism's valorization of sympathy. But it can also be outward looking, emphasizing communal affective ties over individual ones. Glenn Hendler has argued that in nineteenth-century America, sentimental fiction conveyed an implicitly ethical "sentimental politics of affect" (Hendler 2001: 12, 22). But characters in these works often do not have much agency, and thus there may not be a moral at the level of plot. Good people may suffer and that may be the whole story. The moral resolution then is turned outward, as readers are to emotionally "do justice" to the underappreciated sufferer. This brings us back to the question of Cvetkovich's and Jones's suffering subjects, but suggests that the solution to the text's politics lies not in the characters' exercise of agency, but the reader's.

I have chosen two works first printed in the *Family Reader*, a penny weekly fiction miscellany that was cheaper than the great monthly magazines that had long dominated the scene, or the shilling monthlies that challenged their dominance in the 1860s, run by bestselling novelists such as Braddon (*Belgravia*) or Wood (*The Argosy*). Many authors wrote exclusively for the weekly market, specializing in the readers who found their bliss in periodicals such as *Bow Bells* and the *Family Reader*. One such author was the English Charlotte Brame, who wrote over two hundred novels. She was well known in America, where pirated full-length editions sold under several names, including Bertha M. Clay. Clay was a hugely successful brand: her tales were so popular in the US that when Brame died, several other authors, male and female, were contracted to continue to write under this *nom de plume*.[4]

Reading from the vast oeuvre attributed to Brame/Clay in the 1880s, one can gather a sense of what readers expected from these sentimental stories. The narrative generally began with the female protagonist's happy love story, often resulting in a marriage. The marriage is then threatened, then destroyed. Men, though sincere in their promises, are dogs. Their feelings change or they succumb to social pressure. The protagonist suffers. Good protagonists suffer and die under this pressure. More enterprising bad subjects (usually brunettes) rebuild their lives and may even seek revenge, but ultimately they too suffer and die, sometimes in the interest of protecting a good (blonde) woman character from the pain they have already endured. (This converts the brunette into a good protagonist.) Reader interest stays with the suffering character and she is morally vindicated by her correct actions. Suffering is the spectacle and the point of the narrative, even when the protagonist displays more agency and drives some plot events.

For example, in *My Mother's Rival* (marketed under the Clay name, though likely not authored by Brame),[5] the narrator begins the story by describing her parents' ideal marriage, marred when her mother almost dies in childbirth and is left an invalid. She helplessly watches as her father loses interest in her mother and becomes increasingly intimate with her own governess. Unwillingly, she dissembles to protect her mother from knowing what is going on in the house, but finally her father runs off with the governess, and her mother, broken-hearted, dies. In *A Mad Love* (actually by Brame), a heroine's idyllic marriage to an underage upper-class man is destroyed when his parents have the marriage annulled and then persuade him to court another, more appropriate woman. Although she suffers horribly, the beautiful and talented protagonist Leone determines to make a life for herself. She reappears in the text a few pages and some years later as a successful opera singer, and, although swearing revenge on his parents, she does not do anything in particular to carry it out. However, the two meet again and their passion returns. Leone cannot bear, however, to sully herself and betray her lover's saintly (blonde) wife, who reveals to Leone that she is pregnant, so she commits suicide.

A Mad Love is a much longer novel than *Rival*, and more fully plotted, but both narratives begin with happy early scenes, and then take the reader through several episodes wherein the pain of the protagonist is the chief interest. Plot resolution provides neither a revelation of secret knowledge, nor moral resolution, nor does it even solve the problems of the protagonists. So, what do we make of the affective aesthetics of this genre in the *Family Reader*? The pleasure here is not in the suspense, but in the prolonged indulgence in suffering foretold. This invites the question: why did many readers with little time for leisure reading employ it in reading sad sentimental stories? Why did penny readers want to cry? And, indeed, why does anyone "enjoy" experiencing painful emotions through art?

The Victorians also wanted to know the answer to this old question, and sought to answer it in physiological terms, often in relation to the new evolutionary sciences. Tragedy, which had long been thought a noble form exercising the sympathies, is instead seen by Victorian psychologist Alexander Bain as a chance for us to atavistically exercise our "malevolence." He hypothesized that our pleasure in the violence of tragedy is related to our pleasure in war: we enjoy exerting power and hurting enemies. Revenge can be enjoyed, provided moral justification is provided to quiet the conscience. The imagination stimulates our malevolence safely. However, this does not explain our pleasure in sadness without violence, and Bain also suggests that we may enjoy the exercise of our own capacity for benevolent emotion in response to the pain of another: "As a spur to humane and virtuous conduct, Sympathy is the counteractive of our Egotism . . . One of the aims of poetry is to body forth characters and incidents that recall the choicest phases of our own personality" (Bain 1887: 7). Bain agrees with philosopher and evolutionary theorist Herbert Spencer that pity gives us pleasure in our own strength and the ability to relieve another's pain; sympathy, then, gives us pleasure in discovering our best self. However, he cautions that "[r]epeated indulgence in pity as a sentiment, without corresponding action" to relieve suffering becomes a habit of sentimentality, and may actually diminish benevolence, by associating the pleasure with the emotion rather than the action to which it should give rise (Bain 1888: 459). Here we see the same concern as Cvetkovich later voices: that affect or its expression becomes a substitute for ameliorative action.

But is sentiment the same as sympathy? Both Bain and Cvetkovich suggest that it may not be, and may actively subvert the actions (politics) to which sympathy is supposed to move us. Much current work on affect and the Victorian novel focuses on realism and sensation. But as we have seen, sentimental fiction often operates differently, emphasizing suspense and the unknown far less than familiar patterns. The form of sympathy on which it relies focuses less on judgment and analysis than the realist or sensation novel and more on simple emotion. Using the insights of recent work on physiology, I would like to speculate that sentimentality may operate more like music or memorized verse.

In a useful book, neurologist and music-lover Michael Trimble addresses the question of *Why Humans Like to Cry* (2012). He observes that humans are alone among all animals in crying emotional tears; other animals secrete tears in response to pain, but sobbing with the secretion of tears is apparently all ours (Trimble 2012: 2–3 and passim). Aesthetic crying (being moved by music or stage tragedy, for example) is even more mysterious. Trimble argues that tragic joy—the pleasurable "qualm" that many people experience in watching classic tragedy—allows us to engage fear and rage and then resolve it in a shared experience that affirms the community and extends the significance of emotion into the transpersonal future and past (Trimble 2012: 129–30). Trimble concludes that being moved by music (getting chills, for example) is associated with some of these same limbic structures, especially the amygdala.

Trimble's discussion gets at literary scholars' idea that affect can be used to shape and affirm shared values and community. Sentiment may offer another such experience, though without the grand scale and decided resolution that brings "tragic joy." Unlike traditional tragedy, sentimental fiction offers more common, frequent griefs that readers might experience in their own lives. What Trimble does not discuss, perhaps because he is addressing forms of high art such as Greek Tragedy and classical music, is that these forms are not associated with experiential novelty. To be sure, everyone who sees *Eurydice* or hears Beethoven's *Fifth* must have a first experience of it. But Trimble is focused on those who have seen and heard these artworks many times.

I would like to combine his insights with those of another recent work focused on physiology and music. Valerie Salimpoor, et al. have found that there are at least two distinct processes in musical pleasure. The experience of the favorite moments in the music—the ones that give listeners chills—engages one area of the brain. But these musical moments are also preceded by a prolonged increase of dopamine activity in the caudate nucleus. In anticipating a favorite sound sequence, the listener's expectation heightens the pleasure of the reward, a pleasure associated with dopamine activity. We also have a separate pleasure in having them violated, but only in ways that ultimately promise fulfilment—the way a jazz enthusiast enjoys hearing a familiar tune changed and partially "deconstructed" but never quite destroyed.

Like Trimble's work, Salimpoor et al. focus on art that is already well-known, though the particular iteration of a musical work might be new. Aesthetic pleasure that is also affective can be associated with the anticipation of a known outcome, confirmation of that outcome, and (perhaps) pleasure at the novelty of the particular form or timing of the outcome. So, one's pleasure in correctly predicting what is coming is different in kind from the pleasure of perceiving the thing itself, though both pleasures make up part of the experience. I wonder, then, if the pleasures of sentimental fiction, or indeed, any genre fiction that relies on adherence to formal norms and clichés is related to the pleasure we take in a new performance of a well-loved musical piece, or the repetition of a favorite poem. Our expectations are familiar, and we enjoy having them met, but we also enjoy the small variations and surprises of minor differences between versions. Many Victorians copied well-loved poems into commonplace books, memorized them, and performed them; the repetition intensified rather than weakened their emotional force. Sentimental fiction's emphasis might be less on the musicality of the words and rhythm of the prosody, and certainly less on exact repetition. Yet the experience of reading in serial form, intensified by illustration, a story whose plot is in most important ways known in advance, may engage similar affective structures.

So what is the appeal of readers' "sacred tears" over the sentimental story? First, perhaps, the luxury to be suspended in the moment, have a good cry, in a workaday world which allowed little time to indulge in such things. The story could be easily taken up at any time, precisely because the plot was not complex. Like a piece of recorded music, or a familiar poem, the outcome was known, and part of the pleasure of reading was the anticipation of the sadness to befall the heroine. Yet, like a piece of live music, each story also provided variations that provide the thrill of deferral or difference, while still promising the accustomed outcome. The communal appeal of emotion might be that of self-recognition in the potentially universal affective plight of womanhood, (and perhaps self-congratulation on escaping its worst depredations). Is there a political potential in such affect? That is a hard question to answer. But the general evolution of women's rights may indeed have had something to do with a large audience "feeling right" about the suffering of women who were powerless either in marriage or against men who exploited their affections, even though no solution is proposed in these texts. Contrarily, the lack of solution may provide affirmation for a central experiential human truth that is occluded in the realist novel's celebration of individual agency—that many calamities are beyond human control, that suffering and death are common to all. The question of the affective appeal of reading sentimental texts gives us another way to think about what counts as the popular, what counts as the novel, and what counts as women's writing (or writing for women). It offers a way to approach a mode of narration—sentimentalism—that has been largely ignored in favor of more familiar forms, such as realism, the gothic and sensation. It gives us a fresh approach to the still urgent question that Cvetkovich so thoughtfully explored: what are the stakes, political and affective, of popular forms?

Notes

1 See for example Cixous 1976 and Kristeva 1980.
2 See also "Psychology and Literature" in this volume.
3 Laurel Brake, Graham Law, Deborah Wynne, and Andrew King have each contributed greatly to our understanding of periodical publication in the Victorian era. See also "Print Culture" in this volume. See Brake, *et al.* 2000 and Ellegård 1971.
4 See Law *et al.* 2011.
5 Per private communication with Graham Law.

Bibliography

Anon. *My Mother's Rival* by Charlotte Brame [*sic*], Project Gutenberg. Available at www.gutenberg. org/ebooks/15181

Bain A. (1865; 3rd edn. 1888) *The Emotions and the Will*, London: Longmans, Green and Co.

Bain A. (1887) *English Composition and Rhetoric*, Vol. II, London: Longmans, Green and Co.

Brake, L. *et al.* (2000) "Introduction," in L. Brake, B. Bell, and D. Finkelstein (eds.), *Nineteenth-Century Media and the Construction of Identity*, London: Palgrave Macmillan, 1–7.

Brame, C. *A Mad Love* by Charlotte Brame, Project Gutenberg. Available at www.gutenberg.org/ ebooks/31489

Cixous, H. (1976) "The Laugh of the Medusa," trans. K. Cohen and P. Cohen, *Signs*, 1.4: 875–93.

Cvetkovich, A. (1992) *Mixed Feelings: Feminism, Mass Culture, and Victorian Sensationalism*, New Brunswick, NJ: Rutgers University Press.

Ellegård, A. (1971) "The Readership of the Periodical Press in Mid-Victorian Britain: I," *Victorian Periodicals Newsletter*, 4.3: 3–22.

Foucault, M. (1976) *The History of Sexuality Volume 1: An Introduction*, London: Allen Lane.

Gilbert, P. K. (1997) *Disease, Desire and the Body in Women's Popular Novels*, Cambridge: Cambridge University Press.

Heller, T. (1992) *Dead Secrets: Wilkie Collins and the Female Gothic*, New Haven, CT: Yale University Press.

Hendler, G. (2001) *Public Sentiments: Structures of Feeling in Nineteenth-Century American Literature*, Chapel Hill: UNC Press.

Hughes, W. (1980) *The Maniac in the Cellar*, Princeton: Princeton University Press.

Hurley, K. (1996) *The Gothic Body: Sexuality, Materialism, and Degeneration at the Fin de Siècle*, Cambridge: Cambridge University Press.

Jones, A. M. (2007) *Problem Novels: Victorian Fiction Theorizes the Sensational Self*, Columbus, OH: The Ohio State University Press.

Kristeva, J. (1980) *Desire in Language: A Semiotic Approach to Literature and Art*, New York: Columbia University Press.

Law, G. (2000) *Serializing Fiction in the Victorian Press*, London: Palgrave Macmillan.

Law, G. *et al.* (2011) *Charlotte N. Brame (1836–1884): Towards a Primary Bibliography*. Online. Available at www.victoriansecrets.co.uk/wordpress/wp-content/uploads/2012/05/36-Charlotte-May-Brame.pdf

Levine, C. (2003) *The Serious Pleasures of Suspense: Victorian Realism and Narrative Doubt*, Charlottesville: University of Virginia Press.

Maunder, A. (ed.) (2004) *Varieties of Women's Sensation Fiction, 1855–1890*, London: Pickering and Chatto.

Miller, D. A. (1988) *The Novel and the Police*, Berkeley: University of California Press.

Mitchell, S. (1981) *The Fallen Angel: Chastity, Class, and Women's Reading, 1835–1880*, Bowling Green, OH: Bowling Green University Popular Press.

Pykett, L. (1992) *The "Improper" Feminine: The Women's Sensation Novel and the New Woman Writing*, London: Routledge.

Reitz, C. (2004) *Detecting the Nation: Fictions of Detection and the Imperial Venture*, Columbus, OH: The Ohio State University Press.

Salimpoor, V. *et al.* (2011) "Anatomically Distinct Dopamine Release During Anticipation and Experience of Peak Emotion to Music," *Nature Neuroscience*, 14: 257–62.

Showalter, E. (1977) *A Literature of their Own*, Princeton: Princeton University Press.

Taylor, J. B. (1988) *In the Secret Theatre of the Home*, London: Routledge.

Thomas, R. R. (2004) *Detective Fiction and the Rise of Forensic Science*, Cambridge: Cambridge University Press.

Trimble, M. (2012) *Why Humans Like to Cry*, Oxford: Oxford University Press.

Tromp, M. (2000) *Marital Violence, Sensation, and the Law in Victorian Britain*, Charlottesville, VA: University of Virginia Press.

Wynne, D. (2001) *The Sensation Novel and the Victorian Family Magazine*, London: Palgrave Macmillan.

Part V

Religion and literature

Introduction

For the uninitiated, the landscape of Victorian religious history can be intimidatingly complex, but certain dominant features are immediately present: in England and Wales, the state-affiliated Anglican Church establishment remained in place from the sixteenth century, with a beneficed clergy mostly educated at Oxford and Cambridge; in Scotland, the Presbyterian Church was the state-affiliated body, though it underwent a major fracture in 1843 with the Free Church of Scotland emerging as a new, rival sect; while in Ireland, a Catholic-majority populace was dominated by a Protestant Established Church until disestablishment in 1871. Evangelicalism, which had its origins in the mid-eighteenth century, remained a powerful social and cultural force both within and without the Anglican Church. Dissenting Protestants held a wide range of theological positions, from anti-trinitarianism to the strictest Calvinism, and while many attended independent churches, others joined popular non-Anglican bodies such as the Unitarians, Congregationalists, Methodists, Baptists, and Quakers. All of these dissenting groups gained new freedoms with the repeal of the Test and Corporations Acts in 1828 (which allowed dissenters to hold public office) and the passage of the Universities Tests Act in 1871 (which fully opened Oxford and Cambridge to non-Anglicans). While much of the Protestant public remained suspicious of "papist" influences, Catholics were granted voting privileges with the Catholic Relief Act of 1829, and in 1850 an English Catholic Church hierarchy was restored for the first time since the reign of Queen Mary, partly to serve a growing Irish Catholic immigrant population. Finally, along with the Catholics, beginning in the 1880s the metropolitan Jewish population also expanded markedly due to an influx of Eastern European immigrants, many of them fleeing tsarist persecution.

Alongside these legal and demographic changes in Victorian religious history were a set of ideological developments that, as scholars have long demonstrated, were both reflected in and shaped by the work of important Victorian writers; among these developments were the Tractarian movement within Anglicanism (Christina Rossetti and John Henry Newman), liberal Broad Church reform (Charles Kingsley), the introduction of the German higher criticism of the Bible (George Eliot and Matthew Arnold), and even such matters as the controversy over the observance of the Sabbath (Anthony Trollope). Religious controversies large and small also generated a vast number of polemical novels and sermons by lesser-known evangelicals, Catholics, and others.

Despite the pervasive complexity and richness of this social and literary landscape, as Mark Knight's capstone essay makes clear, for too long a single developmental narrative has tended to dominate: that of a gradual and inevitable falling away from religiosity over the long nineteenth century, a phenomenon often extrapolated from the ostensibly representative secularizing career arcs of figures such as George Eliot and Matthew Arnold. This triumphalist, quasi-Hegelian narrative of a modern European turn away from faith has been increasingly questioned by theorists and scholars in the past two decades. The excerpt by William McKelvy directly challenges a key part of this account, specifically the often-made claim that the expansion of print culture was driven by a turn away from religion, when the contrary was the case. While church attendance figures did wane in the late nineteenth and early twentieth centuries, and with it the connection between the state and organized religion, scholars have recently made what David Nash has called a "crucial shift" in recognizing that religious belief—and with it religious discourse—is "capable of a sustained existence beyond the institutions that dispense it in its purest forms" (Nash 2011: 66). This new approach is exemplified in Jan-Melissa Schramm's excerpt, where she reads Dickens's rhetoric of atonement alongside an ongoing theological controversy within English Protestantism. Dickens's religious or secular affiliation is not at issue for Schramm, but instead the more interesting matter of how Dickens uses an available Christian rhetoric in his mid-career fiction.

With the recent turn against the secularization thesis and its associated notion of religious expression as self-evidently retrograde, the past decade's work on Victorian religious poetry—and Tractarian poetry in particular—has been vibrant. Emma Mason's excerpted essay on the "emotional ethos" of reserve in Christina Rossetti's poetry is one of the strongest examples of this new scholarship on Tractarian poetics. A valuable result of this new work promises to be an expansion of the Victorian poetic canon in the classroom. Scholars have increasingly directed our attention toward the work of under-examined religious poets such as Dora Greenwell, Adelaide Ann Procter, and John Keble, as well as the less-explored corners of Christina Rossetti's devotional poetry. Where scholars go, syllabuses are sure to follow.

See also: *Women poets and the poetess tradition*; *Darwin and Victorian culture*; *Psychology and literature*; *Disinterestedness and liberalism*; *Print culture*

Bibliography

Nash, D. (2011) "Reassessing the 'Crisis of Faith' in the Victorian Age: Eclecticism and the Spirit of Moral Inquiry," *Journal of Victorian Culture*, 16.1: 65–82.

17 Christina Rossetti and the doctrine of reserve

Emma Mason

Recent work on Christina Rossetti has increasingly taken into account her theological position within nineteenth-century debates about religion and faith. Where Rossetti's fervent Christian beliefs were once understood as those of a repressed and tormented writer seeking spiritual guidance in a bleak Victorian world, critics now appreciate the more positive role such faith plays in her work. Her religious verse has been rescued from critical accusations which rendered it simplistic, trivial, pious and naïve, and is instead located within the theology and poetics of Tractarianism, or the Oxford Movement.[1] While religious historian John Shelton Reed argues that 'in Christina Rossetti the movement nurtured a remarkable poet', G.B. Tennyson and Raymond Chapman render her 'directly and fully a product of the Oxford Movement', while Diane D'Amico relates Rossetti to the founder of Tractarianism, John Keble.[2] What follows contributes to the 'religious turn' in Rossetti studies by focusing on the poet's Tractarian theology and how this belief-system is commented upon and reinforced in Rossetti's writing. I focus specifically on the doctrine of reserve, a Tractarian principle forwarded by Isaac Williams and others as part of the Oxford Movement's *Tracts for the Times* series, as an idea paramount within Rossetti's poetry. According to this doctrine, God's word, as evinced through the scriptures and related exegesis, should be available only to the faithful, and not to either unbelievers ill prepared to understand religious knowledge, or to Evangelicals who were considered too familiar with the mysteries of faith. Critics have, in passing, recognised Rossetti's connection to reserve: Isobel Armstrong, for example, has noted that the concept endorsed a repression of feeling in Victorian poetics accentuated for female writers, already expected to withdraw into a private and silent sphere.[3] The following essay elaborates on this work and explores Rossetti's interest in reserve, analysing the doctrine itself and discussing the necessarily secretive manner by which the poet invokes reserve in her poetry. I argue that it was a religious doctrine, then, rather than a broken heart or abused selfhood, that provoked Rossetti's reticent diction, reflecting her commitment to the Tractarian belief-system.

[. . .]

I

The doctrine of reserve indicated that God's scriptural laws should remain hidden to all but the faithful, urging commentators on theology to encode or restrict their presentation of religious knowledge. Devotional poetry and biblical exegesis alike were thus meant to render religious truth through metaphor, figure and allegory in a manner only the initiated believer could understand. Preventing an increasingly literate secular audience from accessing scriptural law, reserve also indicated that some of God's tenets were simply beyond all human comprehension, only to be revealed to the faithful in heaven. Reserve allowed a writer like Rossetti to adopt reticently the role of theological commentator in her writing while exempting her from accusations of vainly flaunting religious learning unsuitable for a middle-class woman. Employing reserve also enabled Rossetti to stress her contemplative nature as a Tractarian believer and poet and thus claim a clerical role almost equivalent to that of a priest. Reserve even required the believer to adopt a restrained, submissive and therefore 'feminine' relation to religious investigation, and many male Tractarian priests and theologians were labelled effeminate and delicate because of their adherence to the concept.[4] Moreover, the manner in which reserve was communicated, obliquely and subtly, was understood as a gentle route to God opposed to the manly directness of Evangelical writing. The Movement strongly denounced Evangelicalism, not least for vainly flaunting the mysteries of the Atonement before a common and unprepared audience, but also for its enthusiastic spilling of religious mysteries.[5]

It was the mystery of God that reserve sought to protect, an idea rooted both within scripture and notably the commentaries of the Alexandrian Fathers, Clement and Origen. The message underscoring Isaiah's proclamation, 'Verily thou art a God that hidest thyself' (45.15) had immediate implications for the Christian Fathers, who both feared to divulge Christian truth to those who might condemn it and also considered such truth overwhelmingly complex. The struggle to express the concept of divine being did not mean that God could not be known; scripture, Christ, the Church, the sacraments, the creation and the natural world all indicated God's reality to Christians.[6] Yet the notion of reserve set aside such revelation to emphasise the danger of attempting to understand what is incomprehensible, God, as Clement argued, 'ever receding and withdrawing from him who pursues'.[7] For Clement, God keeps out of sight 'since we are on trial in our present state, and must not have things made too easy for us': religious truth must be brought instead before the believer in a way suited to his or her faculties.[8] Even when the truth is adapted to human comprehension, the disclosure is necessarily guarded, scripture cloaking its meanings behind enigmas, parables and proverbs and the Fathers too often coding their commentaries to bar readers from knowledge for which they were unprepared. As Origen suggested in *Contra Celsum*, revelation ought to be gradual, 'just as some words are suitable for use with children and are appropriate for their tender age'.[9] The Syrian commentator Pseudo-Dionysius concurred, writing three centuries later that 'it is most fitting to the mysterious passages of scripture that the sacred and hidden truth' be 'concealed through the inexpressible and the sacred and be inaccessible to the *hoi polloi*. Not everyone is sacred, and, as scripture says, knowledge is not for everyone'.[10]

While a genealogy of hiding God can be traced before the nineteenth century, it was only with the development of Tractarianism that reserve came to be constructed as a doctrine. Oxford-Movement theology was founded on the theology of the Church Fathers, especially that of Clement and Origen, and two of their most prolific readers, Keble and Newman, were firm advocates of reserve. Reserve became a principle of sensitivity and religious economy for the Tractarians, who sought to guard religious truth from the increasing numbers of believers involved with low-church religions such as Evangelicalism. Keble's assurance that his party did not wish to prohibit 'open speech' concerning religious matters, however, seems void in the context of his call for Tractarians to write, read, worship and sermonise in Latin.[11] The reserve which Keble and his supporters pushed towards was as marked by elitism as it was by modesty. As I will argue, Rossetti's poetical defence of reserve acknowledges its anti-democratic element, betraying her discomfort with a doctrine which invites the believer to embrace a set of truths from which he or she was barred.[12] Rossetti expresses such ambivalence specifically through poetry, a genre the Tractarians assumed clouded its subject through the devices of irony, metre, paraphrase, allusion, metaphor, symbol, rhythm and rhyme.[13] Following Romanticism's effort to see in nature a secretive shadowing forth of some kind of divine indwelling, be it Christian or otherwise, the Tractarians prized poetry as a magical yet always oblique mode of communication. As Sheridan Gilley argues, the Movement's 'aesthetic doctrine of poetry' signified 'an undisguised theological High Church conviction: the principle of reserve': poetry and prayer alike intensifying experience by subduing it.[14] The epigram *lex orandi lex poeticae* (the law of poetry is the law of prayer) serves to condense neatly the Tractarian theological aesthetic itself: one which sought to affirm the sacramental representation of Christ that the universe offered in a suitably reserved manner.[15]

Keble's *De Poeticae Vi Medica*, delivered in his capacity as Oxford Professor of Poetry between 1832 and 1841, underlines the importance of poetical reserve, the 'very practice and cultivation' of which guides 'the mind to worship and prayer'.[16] Dedicated to Wordsworth, whose Romantic sense of sacramentalism Keble considered close to his own Catholic theology, the lectures stress that God compensates the believer for remaining 'vague and undecided' with 'the gift of Poetry' (*De Poeticae*, I:21). Poetry becomes 'a kind of medicine divinely bestowed upon man' for Keble, one 'which gives healing relief to secret mental emotion, yet without detriment to modest reserve' (I:22). Moreover, the 'chief effect of this modesty, as we may call it, of poets' is 'that they hint at very many things rather than are at pains to describe and define them', using such 'hints as suggestions that they may neither conceal their secrets from worthy readers nor cast their pearls before the unworthy' (I:77, 84–5). Poetry, then, represents God's truths indirectly like a parable, allowing only those armed with faith and knowledge to recognise what Keble elsewhere called 'parabolical lessons of conduct' within its 'symbolical language in which God speaks to us of a world out of sight'.[17] As religion struggles to 'express the emotions of the soul', poetry is able to 'express many things more touchingly, many things more seriously and weightily, all things more truly', guiding us 'to the very utterances of Nature, or we may more truly say, of the Author of Nature'. Only 'Poetry lends Religion her wealth of symbols and similes: Religion restores these again to Poetry, clothed with so splendid a radiance that they appear to be no longer merely symbols, but to partake (I might almost say) of the nature of sacraments' (*De Poeticae*, II:181). For Keble, then, poetic language best conveys religious ideas and sentiments, a favour which religion returns by reconstituting the poem as a work of God – a meek, gentle and compassionate genre urging the reader into a position of devotional reverence akin to reserve.

The reserved poet is not passive or weak, however, but upholds a steadfast faith which is constant rather than excessive, engaging with poetry as a genre 'which always shrinks from pouring forth everything' (*De Poeticae*, I:257). The poet, as Keble argued in his essay 'Sacred Poetry', must beware of the pitfalls of indulgent 'variety and imagery' in his or her compositions, avoiding 'intellectual pride' in such work in order to remain spiritually focused.[18] Poetry should follow the 'grave, simple, sustained melodies' of religious plain chant, 'fervent, yet sober; awful, but engaging; neither wild and passionate, nor light and airy' but marked with a 'noble simplicity and confidence' in God's truth.[19] Shaped in accordance with 'this branch of [. . .] art', poetry produces stunning effects 'upon the human mind and heart', comforting the sinful and penitent reader as it absolves the sinful and penitent poet.[20] While Keble admitted that few achieve such devotional poetry, Rossetti notably does, masking her profound intellectual grasp of theology, controlling her expression of devotional passion, and tormented by her unworthiness in the eyes of God. She repents as she writes and is unwilling to swerve her style into anything more than what Keble called 'noble simplicity'. Rossetti's tendency to use simple language in her devotional verse, then, adheres strictly to a Tractarian dislike of intellectual pride and does not reveal a poet curbed by religious phraseology as some critics have suggested. Her versical reliance on the scriptures, and notably the psalms, accords with both Williams's emphasis upon psalmody and Keble's condemnation of poets who allow the imagination to run 'riot without any reserve'.[21] Rossetti seems even to reserve her awareness of reserve, itself a religious idea which had to be protected behind a poetical form derived from Tractarian poetics: liturgically directed, stanzaically imaginative, but taut and concentrated in its Christian message.[22]

Rossetti probably encountered the doctrine of reserve at Christ Church, Albany Street in London, which she attended from 1843 under the priestly guidance of William Dodsworth.[23] In a register of London clergy compiled for *The Times*, Dodsworth is reported to be a 'Decided Tractarian' and Christ Church described as theologically and aesthetically Anglo-Catholic.[24] Dodsworth's successor, Henry William Burrows, declared that Christ Church was a 'leading church' in the Oxford Movement and it became associated with many major Tractarian figures such as Edward Bouverie Pusey, Henry Edward Manning, John Henry Newman and Richard Frederick Littledale.[25] Albany Street's large congregation was predominantly middle-class and educated, the Rossettis joined by Sara Coleridge and Margaret Oliphant, and most worshippers expecting and receiving a high level of scholarly preaching focused around the *Tracts for The Times* and other Oxford-Movement literature. Reserve was most prominently featured in Williams's 'On Reserve in Communicating Religious Knowledge', a title chosen by Newman and which proved deeply controversial when published in 1838 and 1840. Williams was even forced to revoke his application to succeed Keble as Oxford Professor of Poetry in 1842 because of 'On Reserve', attacked as secretive, devious and papist.[26] Yet Williams's commentaries deserve attention for two reasons: first, they represent a kind of collective Tractarian response to reserve, emerging from discussions on the subject at the new Oxford theological society that met at Pusey's house; and second, because Rossetti's writing exposes her familiarity with Williams's *Tracts* and other work.[27]

Williams declared from the outset of the pamphlets that his goal was 'to ascertain, whether there is not in GOD'S dealings with mankind, a very remarkable holding back of sacred and important truths, as if the knowledge of them were injurious to persons unworthy of them' ('On Reserve' I:1, 3). The objective was addressed through five main thoughts regarding reserve: it was an established Christian doctrine; an insurance against unworthy believers accessing religious knowledge; an indication that the intellect grounds faith; an enhancer, rather than opposer of revelation; and a guard against popular forms of religion which were assumed to be crude. The first of these ideas suggests that the doctrine of reserve is supported by the Christian tradition as outlined by the Church Fathers, especially in their emphasis upon the *Disciplina Arcani*, or 'teaching of the secret'. Designed to hold back religious truths from ill-prepared believers and neophytes, the *Disciplina*, Williams writes, 'kept back in reserve the higher doctrines of our Faith until persons were rendered fit to receive them by a long previous preparation' ('On Reserve' IV:2, 6).

[. . .]

II

For Rossetti at least, reserve was less an invitation for the Church to exclude believers from its educated elite than a signal that men *and* women should be trained in order to qualify as worthy Christians. The Oxford Movement was a haven, not only for 'feminine' and unmanly clerics, but also for women unable to voice their beliefs and opinions regarding theology in any kind of dominant manner.[28] Not only did Tractarianism promote women's education through, for example, pamphlets such as Littledale's *The Religious Education of Women*, but it also highlighted the intellectual ability of female believers.[29] It could do this precisely because of the doctrine of reserve, which dictated a certain kind of quiet and restrained approach to theological study familiar to women. Already aligned with passivity and sensibility, women were recognised as almost essentially reserved: as Keble noted in the *De Poeticae*, there is a certain 'beautiful trait of reserve' to be found in women (*De Poeticae*, II:84). Gill Gregory also recalls Keble's words in her essay on Adelaide Procter's poetical reserve, a mode which Procter uses to describe locations of 'peaceful retreat' in order to secure a solitary 'space within herself' to think and study.[30] Felicia Skene's theological commentaries, Charlotte Yonge's novels and Cecil Frances Alexander's poetry, for example, also employ a certain reserve derived from Tractarianism, subtly alerting the reader to their religious knowledge and so implicit support for women's education. Rossetti's reserved poetry also encourages her female readers to obtain a religious education in order that they might unlock the theological puzzles within, at the same time as her scripturally-based verse fulfilled a pedagogical role.[31] As she claims in *Letter and Spirit*, women are 'quicker-sighted in matters spiritual' than men, and so must have access to religious information and strive to pass it on (57). Those '"that hath ears to hear"', she adds in *Time Flies*, are obliged to convey the 'message' to society, albeit in a strictly reserved manner: indeed, women's 'duty of the moment is to write', justifying women's religious writing as not only valid, but mandatory (22, 62). Hence, when Rossetti states in *Letter and Spirit* that she feels 'it is a solemn thing to write conjectural sketches of Scripture', hoping 'my mistakes will be forgiven me', she is not apologising for intellectual inadequacy, but instead framing her thought within the boundaries of reserve (158).

In 'Hark! the Alleluias' (1893), for example. Rossetti *employs* reserve to indicate that only those who treat religious matters *with* reserve will be saved on the last day.[32] Adhering to Williams's injunction that the spiritually worthy alone should receive God's word, she quietly intimates that only those who have 'kept the truth' will be kindly judged and granted salvation at the gates of heaven:

> Hark! the Alleluias of the great salvation
> Still beginning, never ending, still begin,
> The thunder of an endless adoration:
> Open ye the gates, that the righteous nation
> Which have kept the truth may enter in (ll. 1–5)

In keeping the truth, Rossetti's 'righteous nation' possess religious knowledge and so close it away and protect it from the unworthy, an idea emphasised by the contrast of the 'open' gates. The poem thus implies that the uniting factor of God's people is a strict adherence to the rules of reserve. The believer ignorant of such rules, Rossetti argues, will find herself subject to a painful and arduous existence, striving to uncover a God incomprehensible to a mortal.

[. . .]

The believer who craves for God, then, must compensate such failed desire by the attainment of religious knowledge, (secured through poetry), an argument which, again in line with Williams, presents the intellect as an important foundation for reserved faith. 'A Castle-Builder's World' (1893), for example, declares that to neutralise ideation in faith reproduces the earth as an 'unprofitable space', where the living are replaced by a spectral herd of believers who disguise thought behind grotesque vizards:

> Living men and women are not found there,
> Only masks in flocks and shoals:
> Flesh-and-bloodless hazy masks surround there.
> Ever wavering orbs and poles;
> Flesh-and-bloodless vapid masks abound there,
> Shades of bodies without souls (ll. 5–10).

The striking mask imagery evokes a group of non-questioning devotees who do not desire even to realise that religious secrets are being hidden from them, never mind the content of the denied knowledge. Their zombie-like acceptance of ignorance eats away their souls, and bodies emerge from this dusky scene as mere silhouettes against a bleak, worldly 'space' (l. 4). For the believer who is intent on grounding his or her faith in knowledge, however, the world is not simply a 'space' and instead becomes an arena of ideas and inspiration, open to women as well as men.

Yet the hazy masks the people of 'A Castle-Builder's World' assume may also be read as devices to allow their inhabitors to secrete themselves away as reserve might imply. The ambiguity of this poem accords with the rule of reserve, directing the writer as it does into verbal indeterminacy in order to veil and obscure religious meaning. After all, is Rossetti suggesting that her subjects ignorantly flee from knowledge or that they have been cajoled into a 'vapid' cloaking of what they know due to reserve's injunctions? A similar paradox is at play within 'Ah Lord, Lord, if my heart were right with Thine' (1893), which appears to suggest that thinking about God eases the process of waiting for revelation:

> then should I rest resigned
> Awaiting knowledge with a quiet mind
> Because of heavenly wisdom's anodyne (ll. 1–4)

As an 'anodyne', wisdom is fashioned as a healing power as well as a reward for patience, knowledge being restorative and healthy, naturally leading to love, trust and hope (ll. 7, 8, 9). The relief from pain heavenly wisdom offers, however, implies that believers who reserve what they know endure immense suffering on earth, an inference that betrays the discomfort Rossetti allows to intrude into her rendering of reserve. Even as the sonnet's concluding two lines locate heaven as an eternal place where knowledge is always granted, they underline the painful waiting process the believer must undergo:

> Heaven shared with us thro' all eternity,
> With us long sought, long loved, and much forgiven (ll. 13–14).

The conflicting meanings at play here suggest either that heaven is an eternal and compassionate space, or that the believer must forgive heaven for keeping him or her back from revelation for so long. As Williams acknowledged, this very revealed 'knowledge' might be 'great and infinite' but it is also, he argues quoting Aristotle, 'the going out of mortality, as it were, into the earnest contemplation of things that are wonderful, eternal and divine. Such is the shadow of that truth which Scripture unfolds to us' (II:3, 38–9). Knowledge reserved on earth is only available in heaven to the deceased believer, Williams warns his reader, death the necessary 'shadow' of reserve as Rossetti's more gloomy verse exposes.[33] While only the believer who directly undertakes some sort of theological education may hope to become divinely acquainted with 'the deeper treasures of divine Wisdom', he or she must be dead to do so, an ostensibly welcomed state but one with which Rossetti is, naturally, never fully comfortable (I:10, 28).

Such ambiguity is further apparent in the earlier and less directly devotional poem, 'Winter: My Secret' (1862), a poem whose 'secret' seems both to test and parody reserve.[34] A reading of the text as compliant with reserve cannot fail to associate the narrator with God himself, taunting the believer with the idea that he may or may not have secrets to be revealed:

> I tell my secret? No indeed, not I:
> Perhaps some day, who knows?
> But not today; it froze, and blows, and snows,
> And you're too curious: fie!
> You want to hear it? well:
> Only, my secret's mine, and I won't tell (ll. 1–5).

Curious believers be warned: revelation is for heaven's province and not for the 'today' of mortal existence. It is as if the narrator has been pushed into veiling his mysteries because of immoderate questionings of religion: 'Suppose there is no secret after all, / But only just my fun' he is forced to announce. The use of winter as the metaphorical representation of the secret here is also important, since winter is a season rendered in much devotional writing as a signifier of death and thus the gate to heaven. For God, this makes winter a busy time, a 'nipping day, a biting day' wherein he cannot possibly 'ope to every one who taps' (ll. 10, 13). He calls for a 'shawl, / A veil, a cloak' to further conceal his being as a divine mystery from those who 'come whistling thro' my hall; / Come bounding and surrounding me, / Come buffeting, astounding me, / Nipping and clipping thro' my wraps and all (ll. 11–12, 14–17). This onslaught of believers, figured as icy 'draughts', forces God to retreat behind a 'mask for warmth', protecting himself against their continual questions. He is 'pecked at by every wind that blows' in line twenty, and while he of course refuses to reject the faithful, his weary command that they show him some 'good will' and just 'Believe, but leave that truth untested still' is a direct representation of the doctrine of reserve. As Rossetti later states in her love poem to Christ, 'Twice' (1866): 'All that I am I give, / Smile Thou and I shall sing, / But shall not question much' (ll. 46–8).

The last two sections of the poem shift from the cold and windy limits of the opening verses and invoke a change in weather, moving from the 'sunless hours' of spring into the 'languid' laziness of summer (ll. 27–8). Rossetti's God dislikes spring here, described as 'an expansive time' wherein he is overrun by heavenly newcomers; and yet summer seems somehow worse, evoked as a 'drowsy' and decadent interval when 'golden fruit' ripens 'to excess' (ll. 23, 29–30). It is in the summer too that the narrator suggests that 'my secret I may say, / Or you may guess', as if the hot weather provokes a loosening of the tongue and a disregard for restraint. That the believer might dangerously conjecture the truths behind God's mysteries at this time is also appropriate: summer is distanced enough from the finalities of winter to encourage speculation and it also represents a midway point in life wherein the believer might dare to question the religious laws that dictate youth and comfort old age. Rossetti may be playing with reserve here but she is also employing it, ending her poem with a sunny scene that only the thoughtful believer may work through. For summer and spring alike are never good seasons for the faithful poet precisely because they halt the wintry entrance to heaven by continuing mortal life and thus promising to reveal, rather than veil, God's glory through the propagation of new life. This, as Williams noted, leads 'to the great injury' of the 'moral character' ('On Reserve' V:8, 78). Terminating the year in a state of glacial inertia to signal the close of mortality and the beginning of life in paradise, winter was Rossetti's favourite season as a section from *The Face of the Deep* reveals: 'Spring or summer might satisfy a light heart, if only they could abide. Autumn is a very parable of passing away and sorrow-fulness. Only winter is cheered by our foresight of its coming to an end; winter the death of each year' (300). Signifying death and closure, winter provides her with the ideal metaphor to communicate the end of mortal life and the beginning of heavenly existence. As the narrator of 'Whitsun Tuesday' (1893) notes, only when God signals to the believer that '"Winter is past and gone"' can he intimate that the time is right for him or her to '"Come hither, sit with Me upon My Throne"' and so enter heaven (ll. 12, 14).

Yet Rossetti was invested in such ideas even before the matured devotional prose and poetry of the 1890s, her 1862 *Goblin Market and Other Poems* yielding several poems on the subject, including 'Winter: My Secret'. 'Spring', for example, focuses on the season's fleet-ing splendour, 'Now newly born, and now / Hastening to die' transitory and erratic unlike the nobler 'Frost-locked' nature of winter (ll. 38–9, 1). More explicit still is 'A Birthday' which also betrays spring's lurid and shabby display of decomposing colour, overwhelm-ing the reader with images of the vernal season, trees hanging heavy with fruit, rainbow coloured shells abounding in an effervescent ocean and various exotic birds glittering in the light. Such lavishness signifies decay, however, fruit, blossoms and other budding growth ultimately withering away in hotter weather to produce what Rossetti would figure elsewhere as the ominous 'Goblin pulp' ('Goblin Market', l. 470). The fruit that rots away to excess in 'Winter: My Secret', then, mars the summer passage of the poem as it reminds the reader that only winter may escort him other into the sparkling realm of heaven where all the muddy blemishes of earth are bleached away.

For Rossetti, the believer may only protect him or herself from the contamination of a decaying and increasingly sinful world through reserve, becoming spiritually immaculate and so suitably pure to enter heaven's gleaming environment.[35] Her later devotional poetry, particularly *Verses* (1893), discusses reserve through the idea of becoming pure, erasing and effacing the self into a state of extreme reticence. '"They shall be as white as snow"' (1893), for example, is typical in its injunction: 'Ah, to be clean again / In mine own sight and God's most holy sight!' struggling desperately to 'reach thro' any flood or fire of pain / Whiteness most white' (ll. 1–4). Importantly, Rossetti remains disinclined towards spring in this poetry, stating in '"Who hath despised the day of small things?"'' (1893) that she prefers the 'sweet-ening wintry air' over spring's 'half-awakened' laziness which 'lags incomplete' (l. 5). Yet her overwhelming love of winter and religious purity leads almost naturally to a heralding of the colour white in this period, a colour that signifies reserve and the believer's adherence to this doctrine in three ways: first, it signals the white light associated with Christ and para-dise; second, it metaphorically figures reserve, cleansing the believer before God; and third, it creates a realm of clarity and meditation in which the believer can think and gain religious knowledge.

[. . .]

Notes

1 Stuart Curran, for example, writes that Rossetti is 'full of self-pity and sentimentality', refusing to 'aim beyond a pretty trifle', in 'The Lyric Voice of Christina Rossetti', *Victorian Poetry*, 9 (1971): 287–99 (287, 289); Hoxie Neale Fairchild argues that Rossetti's verse benefits from anthologisation,

a statement that ignores the context in which she was writing, *Religious Trends in English Poetry: Volume IV 1830–1830, Christianity and Romanticism in the Victorian Era* (New York: Columbia University Press, 1957), 309; and Germaine Greer declares that Rossetti's 'religion is a matter of devout sentiment, rather than an intellectual apprehension of the nature of God' and that as 'a religious poet', Rossetti 'must be listed among incorrigibly minor figures, a bare cut above the horde of pious ladies who penned hymns in the nineteenth century', *Slip-Shod Sibyls: Recognition, Rejection and the Woman Poet* (London: Viking, 1995), 359.

2 John Shelton Reed, *Glorious Battle: The Cultural Politics of Victorian Anglo-Catholicism* (Nashville and London: Vanderbilt University Press, 1996), 14, 138–9; G.B. Tennyson, *Victorian Devotional Poetry: The Tractarian Mode* (Massachusetts: Harvard University Press, 1981), 198; Raymond Chapman, *Faith and Revolt: Studies in the Literary Influence of the Oxford Movement* (London: Weidenfeld and Nicolson, 1970); Diane D'Amico, 'Christina Rossetti's *Christian Year*: Comfort for "the weary heart"'. *The Victorian Newsletter*, Fall (1987): 36–42. *Christina Rossetti: Faith, Gender and Time* (Louisiana: Louisiana University Press, 1999); on Rossetti and the Oxford Movement, see also Antony H. Harrison, *Christina Rossetti in Context* (Chapel Hill: North Carolina University Press, 1988); *The Achievement of Christina Rossetti*, ed. David A. Kent (Ithaca: Cornell University Press, 1987). 'Christina Rossetti's Dying', *The Journal of Pre-Raphaelite Studies*, 5 (1996): 83–97; Jan Marsh, *Christina Rossetti: A Literary Biography* (London: Pimlico, 1995); Jerome J. McGann, 'The Religious Poetry of Christina Rossetti', in *The Beauty of Inflections: Literary Investigations in Historical Method and Theory* (Oxford: Clarendon Press, 1985), 232–52; and Linda E. Marshall, 'What the Dead Are Doing Underground: Hades and Heaven in the Writings of Christina Rossetti', *Victorian Newsletter*, Fall (1987): 55–60.

3 Isobel Armstrong, *Victorian Poetry: Poetry, Poetics and Politics* (London: Routledge, 1993), 341; see also Mary Arseneau, 'Incarnation and Interpretation: Christina Rossetti, the Oxford Movement, and "Goblin Market"', *Victorian Poetry*, 31:1 (1993): 79–93, who notes Williams's Tract in a footnote, 92fn5; and Margaret Johnson, *Gerard Manley Hopkins and Tractarian Poetry* (Aldershot and Vermont: Ashgate, 1997), 106, who contends that Rossetti's poetry presents a veiling of meaning 'so heavy that it can barely be seen through at all', but does not discuss her use of reserve.

4 See, for example, David Hilliard, 'UnEnglish and UnManly: Anglo-Catholicism and Homosexuality', *Victorian Studies*, 25:2 (1982): 181–210, and John Shelton Reed, '"Giddy Young Men"; A Counter-Cultural Aspect of Victorian Anglo-Catholicism'. *Comparative Social Research*, 11 (1989): 209–26.

5 Where the Movement's attitude towards Evangelicalism is clear, their reaction to another developing arena of theological thought, that of negative theology, is more ambiguous. Paul Elman suggests that Isaac William's reading of reserve is linked to negative or apophatic theology, even though he refuses to explicitly discuss the subject, see 'Anglican Reserve: Historical Reflections', *Sewanee Theological Review*, 38:2 (1995): 155–64 (156). Negative theology, like reserve, indicates that God cannot be known in terms of human categories and so urges believers to discuss him using a negative form of language. Suspending any intellectual preconceptions of being, the believer is better able to respond to the mystical experience God offers. Yet the Victorians worried that negative theology's construction of God as something unknowable implied atheism. This concern was expressed by the Anglican preacher Charles Girdlestone in an 1861 sermon. 'Negative Theology: An Argument for Liturgical Revision', in which he wrote, 'negative theology [rules that the] laws of nature, no matter whether or not originally enacted by an almighty, intelligent, benevolent Being, are no longer subject to the active control of any such potentate [and] That the notion of wise and loving Will, competent to suspend the laws of its own enacting, and employed in so administering them as to overrule them for good continually, is absurd' (London: Longman, Green, Longman and Roberts, 1861), 5.

6 See Robin C. Selby, *The Principle of Reserve in the Writings of John Henry Cardinal Newman.* Oxford Theological Monographs (Oxford: Oxford University Press, 1975), 4.

7 Clement of Alexandria, *The Writings of Clement of Alexandria*, trans. Revd W. Wilson, 2 vols (Edinburgh: Clark, 1867, 1869), ii. 4, in Selby, *Principle of Reserve*, 5.

8 Clement of Alexandria, *Writing*, ii. 4, in Selby, *Principle of Reserve*, 4.

9 Origen, *Contra Celsum*, trans. H. Chadwick (Cambridge: Cambridge University Press, 1953), 276, in Selby, *Principle of Reserve*, 8.

10 Pseudo Dionysius, *The Mystical Theology* (c.500), in Grace M. Jantzen, *Power, Gender and Christian Mysticism* (Cambridge: Cambridge University Press, 1995), 97.

11 John Keble, *De Poeticae Vi Medica: Praelectiones Academicae Oxonii Habitae Annis MDCCCXXXII . . . MDCCCXLI*, A Joanne Keble, AM, Poeticae Publico Praelector Collegii Orielensis Nuper

Socio, Tom I/Tom II (Oxonii: J.H. Parker, M.DCCC.XLIV), translated as *Keble's Lectures on Poetry 1832–1841*, trans. Edward Kershaw Francis, 2 vols (Oxford: Clarendon Press, 1912). I:74; further references are given in the text, citing the volume and page number.

12 Rossetti would have been familiar with the debates regarding Victorian socialism due to William Michael's strong interest in the subject.

13 See Sheridan Gilley, 'John Keble and the Victorian Churching of Romanticism', in J.R. Watson. *An Infinite Complexity: Essays in Romanticism* (Edinburgh: Edinburgh University Press for the University of Durham, 1983), 226–39 (232).

14 Gilley, 'John Keble', [*The Quarterly Review*, 32 (1825):] 232–3.

15 See Clark M. Brittain, '"God's Better Beauty": Hopkins, Pusey and Tractarian Aesthetics', *Christianity and Literature*, 40:1 (1990) 7–32 (17).

16 Keble, *De Poeticae*, II:482–3.

17 John Keble, 'Tract 89: On the Mysticism attributed to the Early Fathers of the Chinch', in *Tracts for the Times by members of the University of Oxford*, 6 vols (London: J.G.F. and J. Rivington, 1841), 143.

18 Keble, 'Sacred Poetry', 217, 228.

19 Ibid, 219–20.

20 Ibid, 221–2.

21 Williams appealed to the 'gentle Psalmist' in 'Come to me Angel guests!' to: 'Come again, tranquil spirit, oh, unroll / Thy sweet melodious fulness o'er the tide / Of my wild tossing thoughts', *Cathedral*, 80 (ll. 6–8): Keble. *De Poeticae*, I:68.

22 Tennyson, *Victorian Devotional Poetry*, 202.

23 On Rossetti's relationship with Dodsworth, see John O. Waller, 'Christ's Second Coming: Christina Rossetti and the Premillennialist William Dodsworth'. *Bulletin of the New York Public Library*, 73 (1969): 465–82.

24 Anon., 'The Principal Clergy of London: Classified According to their opinions on the Great Church questions of the day' (1844), Bodleian Library, MS Add. c. 290.

25 See Henry William Burrows, *The Half-Century of Christ Church, Albany Street, St. Pancras* (London: Skeffington and Son, 1887).

26 Williams stated in 'On Reserve': 'If it is the name Reserve only which is objectionable, then let the substance of this article be expressed by any other which may be found equally to serve the purpose, whether it be forbearance, or reverence, or seriousness, or religious caution, as long as the full intention of it is equally presented' (V:2, 45–6).

27 Rossetti writes in the 'Prefatory Note' to *Seek and Find* that 'when I have consulted a Harmony it has been that of the late Rev. Isaac Williams' and she would have encountered Williams's other works within the scholarly environment at Christ Church.

28 See footnote 4.

29 Littledale clearly states the women are 'the intellectual rivals of men' in *The Religious Education of Women* (London: Henry S. King and Co., 1873), 3–4: the pamphlet was first published in the *Contemporary Review*, 20 (1872): 1–26.

30 Gill Gregory, 'Adelaide Procter: A Poetics Reserve and Passion', *Women's Poetry, Late Romantic to Late Victorian: Gender and Genre 1830–1900*, ed. Isobel Armstrong and Virginia Blain (Basingstoke: Macmillian, 1999), 355–72 (362, 370).

31 Her devotional prose too was designed to aid believers in achieving such a clerical identity, instructing them on scripture, prayer, typology, the commandments and the apocalypse and grounding their faith in the traditions of the Christian Church; see Christina Rossetti, *Annus Domini: A Prayer for Each Day of the Year, founded on a Text of Holy Scripture* (Oxford and London; James Parker, and Co., 1874); *Called To Be Saints: The Minor Festivals Devotionally Studied* (London: SPCK, 1881); *The Face of the Deep: A Devotional Commentary on the Apocalypse* [1892] (London: SPCK, 1893); *Letter and Spirit: Notes on the Commandments* (London: SPCK, 1883): *Seek and Find: A Double Series of Short Studies of the Benedicite* (London: SPCK, 1879); *Time Flies: A Reading Diary* (London: SPCK, 1885); references to these editions appear in the text; for a good introduction to Rossetti's prose, see, *Selected Prose of Christina Rossetti*, ed. David A. Kent and P.G. Stanwood (London: Macmillan, 1998).

32 Poems are cited from *Goblin Market and Other Poems* (London: Macmillan, 1862), *Goblin Market, The Princes Progress, and Other Poems* (London: Macmillan, 1875) and *Verses: Reprinted from the 'Called to be Saints', 'Time Flies', 'The Face of the Deep'* (London: SPCK, 1893), signified by the date of the collection in which they appear.

33 See for example, 'Remember' (1862), 'After Death' (1862), 'An End' (1862) and 'A Portrait' (1866).

34 While critics have addressed the 'secret' of Rossetti's title, few have associated it with reserve; Angela Leighton, for example, suggests that the poem implies 'the idea of some inherent, unlockable meaning at the heart of poetry', constructing a 'teasing strategy of "fun"' rather than a vindication of the unbeliever, in *Victorian Woman Poets: Writing Against the Heart* (New York and London: Harvester-Wheatsheaf, 1992), 158; Isobel Armstrong's reading of the poem more insightfully notes its concern with 'secrecy and reserve, prohibition, taboo, revealing and concealing', connecting to my argument that the poem brings up the issue of the believer barred from religious law, Armstrong, *Victorian Poetry*, 257; on Rossetti's 'secrecy' see also Nadean Bishop, 'Sacred Frenzies; Repressed Eroticism in the Poetry of Christina Rossetti', in *Reform and Counter-Reform: Dialectics of the Word in Western Christianity Since Luther*, ed. John C. Hawley (Berlin and New York: Mouton de Gruyter, 1994), 139–52; Diane D'Amico, 'Conclusion: Secrets', in *Christina Rossetti: Faith, Gender and Time* (Louisiana: Louisiana University Press, 1999), 173–7: Constance W. Hassett, 'Christina Rossetti and the Poetry of Reticence', *Philological Quarterly*, 65:1 (1986): 495–514; Angela Leighton, '"When I am Dead, my Dearest": The Secret of Christina Rossetti', *Modern Philology*, 87:4 (1990): 373–89; and W. David Shaw, 'Poet of Mystery: The Art of Christina Rossetti', in *Achievement of Christina Rossetti*, ed. Kent, 23–56.

35 The concept of remaining immaculate is realised in the figure of the Blessed Virgin Mary, whom Rossetti writes about in many of her devotional verses, for example, 'Good Friday' (1866), 'Mary Magdalene and the Other Mary' (1888) and 'The Purification of St Mary the Virgin' (1893). This Marian poetry, however, deserves a study of its own and is not addressed in detail here.

18 Orthodox narratives of literary sacralization

William R. McKelvy

[. . .]

[I]n the mid- to late eighteenth century, the period in which most scholars locate the rise of modern literary authority (or Romanticism), the sphere of literature had an important ecclesiastical character. Any portrait of British literary activity from the death of Pope to the publication of the *Lyrical Ballads* that featured clerical writing alone would be a caricature. But so too is the standard portrait of literary history during this time—one foregrounding the economic struggles of the secularized denizens of Grub Street—a kind of caricature. Despite ready evidence to the contrary, the rise of modern literary authority is regularly tied to the cessation of church history. [. . .] Carlyle is an essential figure for disclosing the extent to which the inception of literature's modern vocation is in fact an argument about the eighteenth-century church, its clerical elite, and their historical relevance. In his 1831 essay on Samuel Johnson, Carlyle invokes a mute inglorious church at the critical moment when our hero of Grub Street must be absolved of his pension, absolved of doing what the modern author must not do: write for patrons. So Carlyle asks readers to compare the value of Johnson's pension to actual Episcopal incomes: "The whole sum that Johnson, during the remaining twenty-two years of his life, drew from the public funds of England, would have supported some Supreme Priest for about half as many weeks . . . but who were the Primates of England, and the Primates of All England, during Johnson's days? No man has remembered" (*CE* 28.119).[1] Carlyle is here rephrasing a central article of the faith whose prophet he preeminently was—that modernity's authentic priesthood officiates in a cult of literature. But more than that, Carlyle is helping to endow a tradition in which modern literary authority is post-ecclesiastical. The modern author is born when the church becomes historically forgettable. This decisive act of literary consecration, which includes the canonization of Johnson, is both bad and good history, a distortion of one portion of the past and a clear picture of another. On the one hand, it averts our eyes from too much actual literary activity. On the other hand, this same aversive behavior is useful evidence of the constitutive repression of the activities of religious professionals in the formulation of an ideology of literary authority. Carlyle's bishops would remain forgotten precisely because they served both declinist and constructionist accounts of the cult of literature. Both for the advocates of a secular culture taking up where religious culture had been argued off and for the advocates of a Romantic literary revival inspiring a religious departure from arid eighteenth-century rationalism, the cessation of a meaningful Hanoverian church history is the primary assumption.

Moving beyond the scheme that pits modern English ecclesiastical and literary culture against one another calls for a confrontation with two powerful historiographic myths, what I call Print Culture's Promethean Dream and the Sleepy Century Before the Dawn. The first is tradition of scholarship that implicitly affirms that an expanding print culture is inherently heterodox in religion and radical in politics. Here the defining post-Gutenberg experience is the French Revolution and its "fetishism of printing," which often claimed for itself an anticlerical mission. According to this revolutionary mythology, the printing press had an unparalleled capacity to "unmask priests and dethrone kings." As one enthusiast said, "The Old Regime was the age of the priest; the new would be the age of the publisher" (qtd. in Eisenstein 22). Thus, when William Hazlitt described the Revolution "as a remote but inevitable result of the invention of the art of printing" (13.38), he was repeating a revolutionary article of faith. In England, and as Hazlitt experienced firsthand, measures to muzzle print from the 1790s to the 1820s were signs of a recognition by certain political elites of its potentially subversive nature, just as were the less aggressive "taxes on knowledge" (not fully repealed until 1861). Even so, a balanced account of the rise of print culture needs to show how the Protestant establishment in the late eighteenth century and after exploited print. In any long-term understanding of the printing press as agent of change, "enlightened," "revolutionary" or "plebeian" appropriations of the technology have to take their place beside this religious appropriation, one that had liberal and conservative manifestations. In the late eighteenth century, this tradition of interpreting moveable type in terms of religious destiny was only growing and would culminate in the Caxton Exhibition of 1877. During the same period, there were irreligious and radical traditions that appealed to a deadly feud between priestcraft and the printing press. But it was an explicitly religious version of the same contest—one featuring the rise and triumph of a bibliocentric Protestantism—that set the general tone for British cultural life.[2]

My second myth, the Sleepy Century Before the Dawn, is a larger caricature of the eighteenth century that was established during the nineteenth: the eighteenth century had no real politics; and it also, not incidentally, had no earnest religion. The church was static, doctrinally apathetic, the parsonic element of the vacuous polity of corruption and patronage. And like the political placeman, like the pluralist rereading cribbed sermons, the eighteenth-century poet was just going through the motions, following rules prescribed by Pope in the 1730s when he brought English poetry to its modern perfection.[3] But then the nineteenth century dawned (somewhat prematurely in 1789), and the rest is called Romanticism. Post-Namierite historians have rejected the political, theological, and social dimensions of this caricature, and from at least two bitterly opposed perspectives (J. Clark; Colley). But too much literary history still relies on some portion of it. An essay, "Religion and Literature," by Elinor Shaffer, from which I quote in full the opening paragraph, is one example of the ways in which Carlyle's history of a religious decline survives in distinguished academic discourse:

> The close relations between religion and literature in most societies testify to the vital role of imagination in the sphere of human values. The secular terms in which this statement is cast are characteristic of the period from the late Enlightenment critiques of religion to the various forms of nineteenth-century apologetics, although the latter may appear draped in traditional language. The secular agenda and terms still dominate current thinking. This period [1780–1830], then, marks a major shift in the relations of religion and literature. It can be expressed by saying that literature becomes the dominant partner; if "religion and literature" would have expressed a clear hierarchy at the beginning of the period, it is of "literature and religion" that we have come to speak. Criticism finds its vocation in negotiating this shift. (2000: 138)

As the extract from Carlyle just cited shows, there is available rhetorical evidence for such a claim about the emergent dominance of literature, one vocationally represented by men of letters usurping ecclesiastical functions no longer being usefully performed. And Shaffer's broader point—made here with a redeeming element of self-consciousness—is illustrated by the career of Carlyle, no less than the career of her central literary hero, a Kant-inspired Coleridge. But, if we bear in mind the best historical reconstructions of the same period's culture of print, the statement that literature at the dawn of the nineteenth century began to dominate religion is, in a word, misleading.

A fatal mistake—one confusing the abstract decay of religion with a political process transforming the state's religious character—is primarily responsible for sustaining the scheme whereby knock-kneed religion, circa 1800, yields the way to hale and hearty literature. Consider the following counterargument (my own) to the one Shaffer just summarized:

> The close relations between religious and literary authority in Hanoverian times testify to the vitality of a theo-political ideology of Anglican hegemony. The long period encompassing the erosion of that hegemony, then, marks a major shift in the authorizing foundations of both religion and literature. It can be expressed by saying that the imagination became the dominant literary value and religion became an expression of private opinion. In our time, literary history is called to narrate the negotiation of this shift by means of, in tandem with, the secularization of the state.

Literature, in other words, rises to a position from which it claimed to rival religion at a time when the religious identity of the state is being transformed. The semantic shift aligning the literary with the imaginative took place just as the religious dimension of political authority was emerging as the age's most productive social question.

Secularization has meant many things to many different people, and in the past two decades there has been a renewed and often critical interest in "the secularization thesis."[4] For the purposes of this study, secularization means something specific. It is a political and legal process that leads to the state relinquishing opinions on theological subjects. This approach to secularization is compatible with the loss of religious faith by individuals and social groups. But it is equally compatible with intense religious enthusiasm. Highlighting secularization's compatibility with various forms of religion and irreligion, however, should not distract us from the moral of an unambiguous story about the fate of one religion during a period of one hundred and twenty years. In the 1760s, conformity with Anglican doctrine (expressed by the Thirty-Nine Articles) was deeply involved with civic rights and access to national institutions ranging from municipal and government offices to the ancient English universities and the primary professions; by the 1880s, (non)conformity with those same doctrines had negligible consequences. But while there is an important story to be told about the declining identity of church and state during the long nineteenth century, we must not confuse this event with a general decay of religion, or even a creeping rot within Anglicanism itself.[5]

Other studies of the modern development of literary sanctity have implicit or explicit rationales for not engaging with this political process of secularization. In David Riede's [. . .] study, for example, which covers the 1790s to the 1870s, there is hardly any attempt to characterize the political history of that eventful period. Names of politicians, policies, legislation, or rulings in legal history are, for the most part, absent. The effect is to focus on a tragic history of critical misreadings as Dante Gabriel Rossetti and Swinburne in the 1860s turn Blake into an ineffectual aesthete, and thus the oracular prophet comes to be venerated within a hierophantic tradition, an orthodox Church of Literature. For Riede and the tradition he ably represents, the lack of reference to religious politics is a silent tribute to the belief that serious intellectual culture had already been secularized. Why discuss the details, stages, and major agents of religious politics when one believes that literary sacralization is a response to unconvincing religion? In another way and for other reasons, Tricia Lootens in *Lost Saints: Silence, Gender, and Victorian Literary Canonization* (1996) disengages the politics of the public sphere, downplaying at the outset any connection between her literary history and a public history of contesting the form and boundaries of religious authority. "Nineteenth-century faith in religious sanctity took its own shapes, and sparked its own controversies," Lootens writes, "but these controversies bore no primary or inevitable relation to the development of reverence toward literary figures" (3). Here religious and literary sanctity are deliberately separated and extracted from any single historical context where they might be related. This tactic is in part a useful alternative to the model which presumes that literary sacralization is primarily a reaction to less-convincing religion. But Lootens's self-referential literary hermeneutic avoids a probable scenario in which developing forms of literary reverence did have something to do with the shifting legal status of the church during the same time. This book issues from the principle that our strategic engagement with either the eighteenth or the nineteenth century is impoverished when we segregate religious and literary history—or forget that they shared the same political context. To put it another way, I focus on moments when religious and literary sanctity appeared interchangeable (or were asserted to be so), and I credit the prevalence of these assertions to the prominence of a political process that culminated in the state's embracing a related disinterest in the boundaries of the sacred and the secular. For it was not an extinction of religious belief that characterized most of what we have come to call secularization; it was, as Mark Canuel puts it, "an altered disposition of government towards belief."[6]

[. . .]

The key to understanding the complicated relation of politics and religion in the long nineteenth century is coming to terms with the counterintuitive fact that mainstream liberalism culminates in a secular state but does so—for the most part—for devoutly religious reasons. The main route to the functionally agnostic state, what came to be called the voluntary system, was graded and paved by religion, most obviously and importantly, as liberal Anglicans and Dissenting. Protestants asserted the principle of religious liberty.[7] The formulation and achievement of this agenda has a precise historical setting beginning in the 1770s and ending in the 1880s. In the 1770s liberal Anglicans, Dissenters, and Roman Catholics agitated separately and in concert for what they considered to be a full extension of the principle of religious toleration only partially enacted by the Glorious Revolution. For reformers within the established church, this program centered on a need to revise the Thirty-Nine Articles or to relax the terms of clerical subscription to them.[8] Reformers outside the church tended to focus on relief from various civil disabilities borne by non-Anglican Christians and the terms by which Dissenting ministers were required to submit in nominal ways to the authority of the church. Despite a good deal of clerical support, the attempt to change the Articles, or the terms of subscription required for those entering the church, failed. But the program for extending the terms of toleration to non-Anglicans had successes in the passage of the Catholic Relief Act of 1778 and the Dissenters Relief Act of 1779. [. . . T]he next seventy years saw the piecemeal but near total achievement of an increasingly ambitious (and mostly devout) liberal agenda on religion.

The same period, one needs to concede, witnessed the strength of religiously motivated opponents to this liberal agenda—particularly church-and-state Tories. As James Sack has shown, starting in the 1760s British conservatism most often discovered its coherence in relation to religious issues, and the platform for religious liberty did not advance smoothly or inevitably. But advance, and triumph, it did. By most accounts, this agenda culminates with the passage of the Dissenters' Burials Bill in 1880, and nothing less than a transformation of the basic context of politics (Wiggins). "From the 1880s onwards," as Jonathan Parry writes, "it was evident that the intense evangelical impulse for moral regeneration which had driven the nonconformist political juggernaut . . . was diminishing" (434). And more than any other cause, the movement's power was sapped by its own success. The cumulative effect of all its reforms was to render the impact of an established church negligible. At that point, the final achievement of a secular state, through disestablishment of the church, became as politically implausible as it was functionally unnecessary, and so it remains today.[9]

The agenda for religious liberty also at times shared reformist goals with a political program calling for a general expansion of the right of adult men to elect representatives in Parliament. But the secular element of the late-eighteenth-century liberal platform was defeated as often as its religious component advanced. Here again, I need to qualify my claims, particularly in sight of the fact that these two movements—one seeking the liberty of devotion, the other the liberty to vote—could overlap. One can emphasize a long nineteenth century dominated by a dynamic of extending religious rights and voting rights. In the 1770s and '80s religious liberals tended to be more disposed toward a larger electorate. And the major religious measures of 1828–29, the Repeal of the Test and Corporation Acts and Roman Catholic Emancipation gave some force to what became the Reform Bill of 1832, whose reconfiguration of representation in turn empowered some urban areas where Dissent was strong. Similarly, the parliamentary reforms of 1867 inspired (or, perhaps, required) the last great steps forward in the liberal religious agenda in the late 1860s and '70s. The more important point however, is that the liberal religious agenda and democratization were at odds. Versions of modernization that rely on the synergy between secularization and democratization too often forget that all franchise reforms in the nineteenth century, including the Third Reform Bill of 1884, were crafted as *alternatives* to democracy. Moreover, the failure of a democratic political agenda was in a large part due to the vitality and success of the religious agenda. British politics remained nondemocratic by practicing religious politics in a complicated process, whereby a noninterventionist state developed an agnostic religious conscience so as to allow religion to flourish freely. For these reasons, and by virtue of the repeated defeat of the Chartist agenda, the program for religious liberty is the primary long-term political event of the period under study.

In deciding to focus on the politics of secularization at the expense of a traditional teleology of democratization measured by voting rights, I am emboldened by two other considerations that have helped to determine my chronological scope. In the first place, an implicit teleology of democratization has done much to sustain the independence of the "Lit Crit" disciplines of Romanticism and Victorian Studies and their agreement to use the early 1830s to partition the century. These disciplines are to a significant degree constituted and maintained by different attitudes toward a nonpresent institution of democracy. Old-style Romanticism begins with the formulation of a democratic political agenda and ends with the failure of that agenda signaled by the passing of the Reform Bill of 1832, an event represented as a political tragedy because merely a bourgeois victory. Most Victorianists take up their subject at the same point, but they see it as the installation of a polity dedicated to the achievement of liberal democracy. In the meantime, the primary political story, one of a mainly religious route to secularization, gets subordinated to either the Romantic story of democracy's defeat or the Victorian story of democracy's evolution. Secondly, as I have already suggested, this study foregrounds a teleology of secularization because its final subject—the general claim that literature had assumed a religious function—legitimately directs attention to the fact that the state from the 1770s to the 1880s experienced a radical realignment with religious authority.

Finally, the period 1774–1880 is a device to acknowledge that the evolution of a reading nation in the nineteenth century found its most important obstacles and opportunities in the agenda for religious liberty. Just as the 1880s saw the achievement of an agenda that transformed any possible relationship between the religious and the political, the 1880s also saw the achievement of an educational agenda that transformed the broader cultural context for reading, the process by which the national literary tradition was to be known on a national scale. Along with the Dissenters' Burial Bill of 1880, the other major legislation of that year was an amending Education Act that theoretically instituted compulsory national primary education After 1880, all children up to age ten were required to attend state-inspected schools; thus literacy, the ability to read, became a kind of right guaranteed by the state. This institution of compulsory literacy was the final step in what is by now a familiar story, the expansion of the reading public. What was exceptional about the reading public after 1880 was its scale. It was the first actual mass reading audience, and entertaining or improving printed matter lay within the economic reach of all but the destitute.[10] The history of the making of this reading audience is often coordinated with the master narrative of democratization extending from the Wilkesite agitations of the 1760s up to the Third Reform Bill. In this respect, Robert Lowe's famous call in 1867 for increased state support for education ("We must educate our masters" [qtd. in Brantlinger, *Reading Lesson* 179]) has been an irresistible tag for those seeing democratization as the nineteenth century's main ideological event. The nineteenth-century politics of becoming a reading nation, however, were more closely determined by movements to secure a liberty of religious devotion. And the notoriously belated institution of a program designed to make reading a national activity required the prior fulfillment of that same political quest.

Here I need to recall that, for most of the nineteenth century, the main obstacles to proposals for systemic state-administered primary education were religious in nature. First, there were fears among Protestant Dissenters that these plans would dedicate state resources to an education biased toward the established church. The increasingly powerful force of political dissent was hardly ready to see national education become a state-funded seminary for the perils of episcopacy. On the other hand, there were Anglican fears that reading the Bible in school without note or comment would raise up a generation of Dissenters—natural sectarians taught early on, and at the state's cost, to cherish unmediated encounters with Scripture. Until the 1880s, Anglicans and Dissenters were locked in debates that were regularly resolved by having the state deal with educational needs in very limited ways.[11] The advocates of what might appear to us an obvious solution—secular education—were few. Most Dissenters and Anglicans (in particular those possessing the property which entitled them to vote) could not imagine elementary instruction without religious instruction and Bible study. It was only with the triumph of the platform for religious liberty, only with the de facto secularization of the state, that Dissenters lost the ability and will to upset plans for universal primary education overseen by the state.[12] Furthermore, it was only when the church recognized itself as one sect among many that Anglican religious functionaries gave up pretensions to being the doctrinally bound educators of the nation's youth. The state was able to require and later ensure that all children become schooled in letters only when the state had developed a secular conscience. Literacy was normalized, and illiteracy pathologized, at the point when the state no longer recognized religious heresies.[13]

By referring to a new pathology of illiteracy, I mean something more specific than its increasing rarity. The 1880 requirement that all children up to the age of ten attend school was part of a new vision of the lives of subjects that demanded that reading would precede work. For while children from ten to fourteen were allowed to work, they could be employed only with certification of achievement in reading, writing, and math (G. Sutherland 125–45). Those who failed to acquire these skills could now be sent to a certified day industrial school, an institution that corrected the defect of illiteracy and directly linked this correction to the normative development of *homo economicus*. This socioeconomic pathologization of illiteracy stands out as a striking event in the history of reading in the British Isles. In 1837, for example, the year of Victoria's coronation, one third of all men and one half of all women couldn't read or write. Hardly considered essential human activities, reading and writing were important indicators of social status. In the space of the next fifty years, however, the literacy rate evens out for men and women and goes beyond 90 percent for the nation as a whole.[14] The conceptual transformation attending this numerical expansion is even more impressive: reading and writing had become, rather suddenly, preconditions for legitimate labor.

A truly national cult of literature, although foretold in the 1770s, did not materialize until the last quarter of the nineteenth century. It was then that the state intervened to make all subjects readers and that English literature became the object of instruction from elementary schools (1876) to the ancient universities. Just as the national reading public envisioned over a hundred years before came of age, the late-eighteenth-century formulation of English literary history became an accredited discipline, a profession, and an inheritance carefully conserved for the nation at large. As Joss Marsh has shown, one index of the rise of literary authority during the 1880s was the refashioning of the theological crime of blasphemy into the literary crime of indecency. At about the same time, and in response to many of the same forces, a newly conceived crime against the word, modern illiteracy, was born in tribute to the disappearance, within the new state's registry, of the old religious crimes of infidelity and heresy. One testament to these momentous changes is the commonplace claim this book aims to recontextualize: the claim that literature had assumed a religious authority.[15] But literature did not assume this authority only after religious experience became less possible. Nor did the cult of literature grow up in a space left vacant by religion. It developed in intimate collusion with religious culture and religious politics. The cult of literature had much business to do with secularization, but not that version of secularization defined as "a growing tendency in mankind to do without religion" (Chadwick 1975:17). The climacteric of the version of secularization endorsed in this study occurs when the state first smiled kindly on a free trade in paper and in divine inspiration—and when illiteracy became a disease of the unemployable. In this new view of a new nineteenth century, secularization names the emergent political context in which the individual reader, and the evolving reading of the nation, had become sacralized.

Notes

1 For a less mythic account of Johnson's earnings as a writer, see Fleeman. D. Griffin (1993) makes [sic] some productive historical challenges to a variety of related print mythologies.
2 In addition to Howsam's book [. . .] see Carpenter's account (2003) of the proliferation of illustrated family Bibles, a form that could simultaneously satisfy ornamental and spiritual desires. Hodson's history features excerpts from sermons on the glory of print from Stanley, Bishop Claughton, and Canon Farrar (138–44).
3 See O'Gorman and Turner on this "Victorian repudiation of the eighteenth century" (2).
4 F. Turner (1993: 3–37) has composed the best general critique of the tendency to frame post-Enlightenment history with "the emergence of a secular world view replacing a religious world view" (4). More recent work (C. Brown, S. J. D. Green, and McLeod) indicates that "secularisation theory" is "a narrative in crisis" (C. Brown 2001: 30). In Brown's view, the theory was an influential "field of discourse"

between 1800 and 1950, even as religiosity remained high. But the long slow decline of religion—one chiefly coordinated with urbanization—is in his eyes a great myth. He argues instead for a rapid period of secularization from the 1950s onward. C. Smith makes a somewhat similar argument with reference to the American experience (1–96), which, nevertheless, deserves to be treated separately. For well documented overviews of past and current historiography on the topic, see McLeod (1–30) and S. J. D. Green (5–16). For a sharply divided version of the debate about the secularization thesis (as conducted by sociologists), see the works of Bruce and Stark. For brief comments about the fluctuating conceptual value of secularization in Victorian Studies, see Kent 110–12.

5 Burns has provided a sweeping account of the way in which "the political and social significance of the rise of Dissent and irreligion" did not change "the fact that during the first half of the nineteenth century the Church of England retained an institutional presence in England and Wales rivalled only by that of secular organs of government" (1999: 1). This attention to the vitality of the church also leads him "to play down the epochal significance so often attached to the post-1832 period" in favor of a gradualist approach commencing in the 1790s (1999: 266). More recently, Burns has highlighted a process of internal church reform commencing in the 1780s (2003: 144). Rosman (2003: 207–32) has described the "vigour of Victorian Christianity" both in the church and in chapel.

6 Canuel's study (2002) is the best book about literature and religious politics within a conventional Romantic period since Ryan's earlier work. I share Canuel's earlier view (1996: 268–72) that there is good reason to think of these topics in ways that disregard the traditional Romantic-Victorian frontier.

7 A version of this irony is at work in Halevy's thesis that "the miracle of modern England" could be explained only by understanding that even its "secular opinion" had religious roots (qtd. in Morris 109). R. Davis (37–52) some time ago described the Repeal of 1828 as the fulfillment of Dissenting petitions from the 1770s, which were in part coordinated with liberalizing tendencies from within the church.

8 For an account of the Subscription controversies, see Young (45–80), whose work draws upon Ditchfield (1988). Ditchfield's other work provides details on the topic of religious toleration in general with respect to Parliament and its petitioners in the late eighteenth century. Gascoigne similarly coordinates theological and political movements across establishment-dissenting borders.

9 Before Parry, Machin's study of late-nineteenth-century politics and the church similarly stressed how the politics of religious liberalism moved from the center to the periphery in the 1880s and after. He mentions a possible growth of religious indifference, but more persuasively recalls how Dissenting political zeal subsided with the erosion of Dissenting penalties (1987: 323). Both Ellens and Larsen, though they don't agree on all details and focus on different periods, also highlight religious routes to the voluntary system.

10 See Heathron and Galbraith on the reading habits of elementary students in 1870 and after.

11 See Altick (1998: 141–87) for an account of elementary and secondary schooling throughout the century. Any broad history of the acquisition of basic reading skills for the period must emphasize two primary sources of popular education before its development into a responsibility of the state: Sunday schooling (by a variety of denominations) and working-class autodidacticism. For the frequent synthesis of both forces, see Laqueur and Rose.

12 For more details on the role of religious politics in obstructing and producing national education, see Machin (1987: 31–40) and Parry (295–332, 376–81). The essential account from the perspective of Protestant Dissent is to be found in Watts (2.535–58). For a complementary account lamenting the church's eclipse as the primary source of elementary enlightenment, see Burgess.

13 This is not to say that in 1880 denominational strife ceased to influence the politics of state-administered education. The issues here described stayed alive for some time, and the Education Bill of 1902, in particular, revived debates from the 1870s and earlier. Nevertheless, it is useful to recognize the 1880s as a time when one political paradigm gave way to a new one. From the 1770s to the 1880s, we can speak of Whig-Liberals and Conservatives superintending a small-scale, noninterventionist state, courting constituencies primarily with religious issues. From the 1880s to the 1950s, Conservatives, "new" Liberals, and Labour preside over an increasingly interventionist, large-scale state and court support on issues of empire and welfare.

14 Regarding literacy rates in 1837, it is important to note that they were much higher in some (mostly urban) areas and lower in many other areas. But they average out by most accounts to the figures cited. Vincent gives a useful, comparative account of the rise of mass literacy in Europe.

15 For a rewarding discussion of theories of contextualization, historicism (as a principle of literary criticism), and literary history, see Hume.

Works cited

Altick, Richard D. *The English Common Reader: A Social History of the Mass Reading Public, 1800–1900*. 2nd edn. Columbus: Ohio University Press, 1998.

Brantlinger, Patrick. *The Reading Lesson: The Threat of Mass Literacy in Nineteenth Century British Fiction*. Bloomington: Indiana University Press, 1998.

Brown, Callum G. *The Death of Christian Britain: Understanding Secularism, 1800–2000*. London: Routledge, 2001.

——. "Mechanism of Religious Growth in Urban Societies: British Cities since the Eighteenth Century." *European Religion in the Age of the Great Cities, 1830–1930*. Ed Hugh McLeod. London: Routledge, 1995. 239–62.

Bruce, Steve. *Choice and Religion: A Critique of Rational Choice Theory*. New York: Oxford University Press, 1999.

—— ed. *Religion and Modernization: Sociologists and Historians Debate the Secularization Thesis*. New York: Oxford University Press, 1992.

—— "The Truth about Religion in Britain." *Journal for the Scientific Study of Religion* 34.4 (Dec. 1995): 417–30.

Burgess, Henry James. *Enterprise in Education: The Story of the Work of the Established Church in the Education of the People Prior to 1870*. London: SPCK, 1958.

Burns, Arthur. *The Diocesan Revival in the Church of England, c. 1800–1870*. New York: Oxford University Press, 1999.

Burns, Arthur, and Joanna Innes. Introduction. *Rethinking the Age of Reform: Britain 1780–1850*. Cambridge: Cambridge University Press, 2003. 1–70.

Canuel, Mark. *Religion, Toleration, and British Writing, 1790–1830*. Cambridge: Cambridge University Press, 2002.

—— "Romantic Emancipation: Religion and the Nation in British Letters, 1790–1830." Diss. Johns Hopkins University, 1996.

Carpenter, Mary Wilson. *Imperial Bibles, Domestic Bodies: Women, Sexuality, and Religion in the Victorian Market*. Athens: Ohio University Press, 2003.

Chadwick, Owen. *The Secularization of the European Mind in the Nineteenth Century*. New York: Cambridge University Press, 1975.

Clark, J. C. D. *English Society, 1688–1832*. 2nd edn. New York: Cambridge University Press, 2000.

Colley, Linda. *Britons: Forging the Nation, 1707–1837*. New Haven: Yale University Press, 1992.

Davis, Richard W. *Dissent in Politics, 1780–1830: The Political Life of William Smith, MP*. London: Epworth, 1971.

Ditchfield, G. M. "The Subscription Issue in British Parliamentary Politics, 1772–79." *Parliamentary History 7.1* (1988): 45–80.

Eisenstein, Elizabeth L. "Gods, Devils, and Gutenberg: The Eighteenth Century Confronts the Printing Press." *Studies in Eighteenth-Century Culture* 27 (1998): 1–24.

Ellens, Jacob P. *Religious Routes to Gladstonian Liberalism*. University Park: Pennsylvania State University Press, 1994.

Fleeman, John David. "The Revenue of a Writer: Samuel Johnson's Literary Earnings." *Studies in the Book Trade in Honour of Graham Pollard*. Ed. R. W. Hunt, I. G. Philip, and R. J. Roberts. Oxford: Oxford Bibliog. Soc., 1975. 211–30.

Galbraith, Gretchen R. *Reading Lives: Reconstructing Childhood, Books, and Schools in Britain, 1870–1920*. New York: St Martin's, 1997.

Green, S. J. D. *Religion in the Age of Decline: Organisation and Experience in Industrial Yorkshire, 1870–1920*. Cambridge: Cambridge University Press, 1996.

Griffin, Dustin. "Fictions of Eighteenth Century Authorship." *Essays in Criticism* 43 (July 1993): 181–94.

Hazlitt, William. *The Complete Works of William Hazlitt*. Ed. P. P. Howe. 21 vols. London: Dent, 1930–34.

Heathorn, Stephen J. *For Home, Country, and Race: Constructing Gender, Class, and Englishness in the Elementary School, 1880–1914*. Toronto: University of Toronto Press, 2000.

Hodson, James Shirley. *A History of the Printing Trade Charities*. London: Allen, 1883.

Howsam, Leslie. *Cheap Bibles: Nineteenth-Century Publishing and the British and Foreign Bible Society*. Cambridge: Cambridge University Press, 1991.

Hume, Robert D. *Reconstructing Contexts: The Aims and Principles of Archaeo-Historicism*. New York: Oxford University Press, 1999.

Kent, John. "Victorian Religion and the Decline of Britain." *Victorian Studies* 41 (Autumn 1997): 107–17.

Larsen, Timothy. *Friends of Religious Equality: Nonconformist Politics in Mid-Victorian England*. Rochester: Boydell, 1999.

Lootens, Tricia. *Lost Saints: Silence, Gender, and Victorian Literary Canonization*. Charlottesville: University of Virginia Press, 1996.

Machin, G. I. T. *Politics and the Churches in Great Britain, 1869 to 1921*. New York; Oxford University Press, 1987.

McLeod, Hugh. *European Religion in the Age of Great Cities: 1830–1930*. London: Routledge, 2005.

Marsh, Joss. *Word Crimes: Blasphemy, Culture, and Literature in Nineteenth-Century England*. Chicago: University of Chicago Press, 1998.

Morris, Marilyn. *The British Monarchy and the French Revolution*. New Haven: Yale University Press, 1998.

O'Gorman, Frank, and Katherine Turner. Introduction. *The Victorians and the Eighteenth Century: Reassessing the Tradition*. Aldershot: Ashgate, 2004. 1–13.

Parry, Jonathan. *Democracy and Religion: Gladstone and the Liberal Party, 1867–1875*. New York: Cambridge University Press, 1986.

Riede, David G. *Oracles and Hierophants: Constructions of Romantic Authority*. Ithaca: Cornell University Press, 1991.

Rose, Jonathan. *The Intellectual Life of the British Working Classes*. New Haven: Yale University Press, 2001.

Rosman, Doreen. *The Evolution of the English Churches, 1500–2000*. Cambridge: Cambridge University Press, 2003.

Sack, James J. *From Jacobite to Conservative: Reaction and Orthodoxy in Britain, c. 1760–1832*. Cambridge: Cambridge University Press, 1993.

Shaffer, E. S. "Religion and Literature." *Romanticism: The Cambridge History of Literary Criticism*. Ed. Marshall Brown. Vol. 5. New York: Cambridge University Press, 2000.

Smith, Christian. *The Secular Revolution: Power, Interests, and Conflict in the Secularization of American Public Life*. Berkeley: University of California Press, 2003.

Stark, Rodney, and Roger Finke. *Acts of Faith: Explaining the Human Side of Religion*. Berkeley: University of California Press, 2000.

Sutherland, Gillian. *Policy-making in Elementary Education, 1870–1895*. London: Oxford University Press, 1973. 125–45

Turner, Frank M. *Contesting Cultural Authority: Essays in Victorian Intellectual Life*. Cambridge: Cambridge University Press, 1993.

Vincent, David. *The Rise of Mass Literacy: Reading and Writing in Modern Europe*. Malden: Blackwell, 2000.

Watts, Michael R. *The Dissenters*. 2 vols. Oxford: Clarendon Press, 1978–95.

Wiggins, Deborah. "The Burial Act of 1880, The Liberation Society and George Osborne Morgan." *Parliamentary History* 15.2 (1996): 173–89.

Young, B. W. *Religion and Enlightenment in Eighteenth-Century England: Theological Debate from Locke to Burke*. New York: Oxford University Press, 1998.

19   Sacrifice and the sufferings of the substitute

Charles Dickens and the Atonement controversy of the 1850s

Jan-Melissa Schramm

[. . .]

Dickens and the religion of sacrifice

Sometime in 1842, whilst he was writing *Martin Chuzzlewit*, Dickens began to attend a Unitarian Chapel in Little Portland Street, a practice he continued for three or four years. At the same time, each of his young children was baptised into the Church of England, and Forster records that Dickens 'reverence[d] the memory of Dr Arnold': 'every sentence' in Arthur Stanley's *Life* (1844) was 'the text-book of [his] faith'.[1] In 1843–4, Dickens composed *The Life of Our Lord* for the benefit of his children; this brief biography stressed Christ's ethical teachings, and minimised both the eruption of the miraculous into the natural order and the sinfulness of man which rendered such divine intervention necessary (consistent with both Unitarian and Broad Church sympathies).[2] On closer inspection, the nature of Dickens's religious convictions seems uneven, his Unitarian leanings evidence of what Valentine Cunningham has called 'his retreat from credal fullness'.[3] By his own admission, he adheres to beliefs in progressive revelation,[4] the value of private judgment,[5] and the importance of '[o]ur Saviour['s] role' as 'the model of all goodness': as he wrote to the Reverend David Macrae, probably in 1861, just after the controversy erupted regarding the publication of *Essays and Reviews* –

> With a deep sense of my great responsibility always upon me when I exercise my art, one of my most constant and most earnest endeavours has been to exhibit in all my good people some faint reflections of the teachings of our great Master, and unostentatiously to lead the reader up to those teachings as the great source of all moral goodness. All my strongest illustrations are derived from the New Testament: all my social abuses are shown as departures from its spirit; all my good people are humble, charitable, faithful, and forgiving. Over and over again, I claim them in express words as disciples of the Founder of our religion; but I must admit that to a man (or woman) they all arise and wash their faces, and do not appear unto men to fast.[6]

Dickens does not seem to subscribe to the Ninth article on the existence of original sin: Mr Hubble's account of children as 'naterally wicious' in *Great Expectations* is clearly comic (*GE*, p. 26), and instead Dickens's novels are full of young children described in the most compelling terms as innocent of both moral and legal guilt (Little Nell, Paul Dombey, Sissy, young Esther, little Arthur Clennam) and he is quick to attribute 'goodness' to various adults in the novels of the 1850s alone (Nemo, Jarndyce, Esther, Stephen, Rachel, Little Dorrit,

Arthur Clennam, Sydney Carton, Charles Darnay, Lucie Manette). By 'goodness' Dickens seems to mean not the imputed wisdom which comes with explicit religious devotion ('the mind of Christ' that we acquire on conversion), but a domesticated virtue, linked inextricably to familial politics and the service of a God understood as the 'Universal Parent' of Unitarianism. The 'goodness' of Dickens's sympathetic characters is encouraged not by private contemplation of Christ's Atonement, but by communal participation in the festivities of the Incarnation – his theology is the sentimentalism of the Christmas Books, in which feasts are usually celebratory rather than Eucharistic (even Pip brings Magwitch his 'wittles' on Christmas Eve)[7] and in which conversion is wrought by encounters with the spirits of domestic rituals yet to come. As Bob Cratchit knows only too well, Christmas is a veritable season of 'goodness': a 'kind, forgiving, charitable, pleasant time: the only time I know of, in the long calendar year, when men and women seem by one consent to open their shut-up hearts freely, and to think of people below them as if they really were fellow-passengers to the grave, and not another race of creatures bound on other journeys'.[8]

Yet Dickens does, almost paradoxically, seem to believe in an essential criminality that is beyond the promise of redemption – a 'sinfulness' or criminal proclivity that drives his novels onwards, that collaborates in the act of narration and implements the protagonist's own fantasies of revenge (found in Tulkinghorn, Hortense, Rigaud, and Madame Defarge, to again restrict ourselves to the novels of the 1850s). Of Rigaud in *Little Dorrit*, Dickens writes

> there are people (men and women both, unfortunately) who have no good in them – none. That there are people whom it is necessary to despise without compromise. That there are people who must be dealt with as enemies of the human race. That there are people who have no human heart, and who must be crushed like savage beasts and cleared out of the way. (*LD*, p. 169)

Once again we are reminded of the ways in which the melodramatic register depends upon the same publicly transparent extremes of character as Evangelicalism: Dickens may be interested in the expiations offered by his protagonists for the various sins of their hearts, but his moral economy is also dependent upon the *actions* of those for whom no redemption is possible. Reviewing the corpus of Dickens's fiction, one suspects the essential stasis of his religious convictions over time: the gentle goodnesses of *The Life of Our Lord* remain consistent, ethically and aesthetically, with the sacrifices of *A Tale of Two Cities* or the deathbed repentances and reconciliations of *Great Expectations*.

It is difficult to gauge the extent to which Dickens followed the Atonement controversies of the 1850s from his extant non-fictional prose and correspondence. Cunningham stresses the vigour of his participation in the 'war' of Victorian Biblical hermeneutics, 'a contest over . . . the performative of Scripture' in which Dickens 'wrestl[es] with rival interpreters and expounders of the Big Book, rival teachers and preachers of righteousness'.[9] And certain events leap forth from his biography to suggest a new and traumatic engagement with death, sacrifice, and suffering on Dickens's part throughout the decade. Dickens's father, whose financial irresponsibility had tainted his son's childhood, died on 31 March 1851; thereafter Dickens spoke of his father with greater forgiveness. Two weeks later, his baby daughter Dora died unexpectedly: plunged into mourning on two counts, Dickens regarded with a mixture of admiration and contempt the ostentatious grandeur of the Great Exhibition which ran from May until October of that same year. *Bleak House* (which appeared monthly from March 1852 until September 1853) rooted its social criticism firmly in the dignity of the single suffering life: within the world of the novel, Evangelicals and coroners alike seek to put bodies to very public uses, and we are called to the deathbeds of Jo, Gridley, Tulkinghorn, Lady Dedlock, and Richard Carstone to extract lessons from their passings. When the final instalment of *Bleak House* appeared, international conflict in the Mediterranean and Caucasus was widely seen as inevitable: the very next month, the Ottoman Empire declared war on Russia, and the formal declaration of British hostilities followed on 28 March 1854. The first instalment of *Hard Times* appeared just three days later, and towards the end of that month the government announced the first of the National Humiliation Days designed to encourage communal acts of reflection and reconciliation.

[. . .]

The final instalment of *Hard Times* appeared in August 1854, and whilst it shares many structural and thematic concerns with *Bleak House* (particularly the incommensurability of first- and third-person ways of knowing, [. . .] it is possible to identify in *Hard Times* a newly explicit attention to the fate of the innocent scapegoat, according to René Girard a particularly telling model of narrative resolution often invoked in times of cultural crisis (see pp. 32–3). If Dickens was attentive to what Girard called the scapegoat 'of the text' in earlier works (Uriah Heep, Carker, Lady Dedlock, for example), in *Hard Times* we see a more telling dramatisation of the rituals of expulsion.

Slackbridge, the professional orator, calls upon the working men of Coketown to assert 'the holy and eternal privileges of Brotherhood', to combine in defiance 'of an iron-handed and a grinding despotism' (*HT*, p. 141), yet their only communal act is to expel the man of perfect integrity and correspondingly artless speech from their midst. In his refusal to join the United Aggregate Tribunal, Stephen understands that he forfeits all relations of neighbourliness: no one will be free to act for him as the Good Samaritan – 'I know weel that if I was a lyin' parisht in th' road, yo'd feel it right to pass me by, as a forrenner and stranger' (*HT*, pp. 145–6). Like Arthur Clennam embracing his imprisonment, and Sydney Carton voluntarily contemplating the scaffold, Stephen submits to his expulsion with calm resignation (*HT*, pp. 147–8). Mizruchi reminds us that acts of sacrifice are inherently theatrical,[10] and Slackbridge presides over this ritual like a levitical priest: as the men part to 'open' for Stephen 'a means of passing out', Slackbridge keeps 'his oratorical arm extended . . . as if he were repressing with infinite solicitude and by a wonderful moral power the vehement passions of the multitude', and the rhetoric he deploys to marshall the men is both Hebraic and classical:

> Had not the Roman Brutus, oh my British countrymen, condemned his son to death; and had not the Spartan mothers, oh my soon to be victorious friends, driven their flying children on the points of their enemies' swords? Then was it not the sacred duty of the men of Coketown, with forefathers before them, an admiring world in company with them, and a posterity to come after them, to hurl out traitors from the tents they had pitched in a sacred and a Godlike cause? (*HT*, p. 147)

The bombastic register is that of the Old Bailey perorations Dickens so despised; the content that of the illegitimate sacrifice of domestic affection on the altar of the civic sphere, which Dickens was to return to again in *A Tale of Two Cities* (when Revolutionary justice was seen to demand the sacrifice of one's children in the service of the new Republic). Louisa diagnoses the reasons for Stephen's expulsion: 'by the prejudices of his own class, and by the prejudices of the other [the employers] he is sacrificed alike' (*HT*, p. 161). Kreilkamp argues that Dickens 'sacrifices Stephen in order to resurrect him as a wounded speaker whose barely audible voice conjures up the spirit of a compassionate preindustrial society': '[t]he repeated murder of a storyteller or a doomed speaker, a figure that Victorian fiction in fact conjured up to authenticate itself, is the curious tropology by which fiction after Dickens lays claim to the authority to forge communities where mechanization had silenced speakers'.[11] This is persuasive, but the tropology of the doomed storyteller is not solely a product of industrialization: on the contrary, Christ's words survive only in the posthumous narratives of his followers and their interpretation has been the work of the church since Calvary.

And if Stephen is undone in part by the speech of Slackbridge, he is finally destroyed by the wrongful accusation that he is responsible for the theft from the Bank: although he departs from Coketown like Holman Hunt's *azazel*, he is recalled to it by the ways in which his reputation is held hostage to Tom's lack of moral accountability. As Rachel asserts, '[h]e shall come back of his own accord to clear himself, and put all those that have injured his good character, and he not here for its defence, to shame' (*HT*, pp. 253–4). The interest here is less in the forensic process – Tom's explanation of the mechanics of the theft is a near-redundant concession to the demands of probability – but on the moral freight of the transactions involved. Stephen's death is a 'dreadful' but unintended 'consequence' of the 'shocking action' for which Tom in turn must 'atone, by repentance and better conduct' (*HT*, p. 285) – but there remains a sense in which Stephen suffers the penalty which should have been inflicted upon Tom. Sissy (the embodiment of love) has used the forum of imaginative expression (the circus) to enable an offender, in whose place the innocent substitute has suffered, to escape the claims of the (Mosaic) Law. Tom, the hardened but representative sinner, is allowed the opportunity to 'die in penitence and love' of his family, and Dickens aligns himself here with a reading of God's redemptive scheme that prioritises mercy above justice – this is again God as the Unitarian Universal Parent, not the Evangelical Governor of the Universal judicial administration. That Dickens was prepared to turn away from his usual preoccupation with the proportional punishment of secular crime (in cases like those of Fagin and Jonas Chuzzlewit) in favour of an emphasis upon the merciful treatment of 'sin' is an argument for locating within the text a particular responsiveness to the doctrinal agitation of the period. Ultimately, Tom's account of his own descent into vice, 'so many people, out of many, will be dishonest . . . How can I help laws?' (*HT*, p. 284), is displaced by the lexis of the substitute's 'Fall' into the Old Hell Shaft in which he dies whilst contemplating the Christmas star.

[. . .]

The first instalment of *Little Dorrit* appeared in December 1855: two months later the Crimean War ended. The impact of the war is registered in the novel in two ways. As Stefanie Markovits has noted, the bureaucratic bungling of the Circumlocution Office mirrors that of the War Department whose incompetence was frequently exposed by Wallace Russell in reports for *The Times* and whose amendment was the goal of the Administrative Reform Society, of which Dickens was a member. So too, Little Dorrit's vocation of sacrificial self-service (although popular in works of fiction that pre-dated the war, such as Gaskell's *Ruth* [1853]) received national validation throughout the war years, as the female equivalent of masculine martial heroism.[12] Dickens represents Amy's work in reverent terms:

> It is enough that she was inspired to be something which was not what the rest were, and to be that something, different and laborious, for the sake of the rest. Inspired? Yes. Shall we speak of the inspiration of a poet or a priest, and not of the heart impelled by love and self-devotion to the lowliest work in the lowliest way of life! (*LD*, p. 111)

This passage appeared in the instalment for January 1856: his rhetoric here follows the contours of public praise for the acts of female self-sacrifice undertaken by nursing staff in the Hospitals of Scutari. As observed in the many Sermons of Thanksgiving preached across the land on the National Day of Celebration (4 May 1856):

> The perfection to which [the nursing sister's] system of attention and kindness so rapidly arrived, producing order out of confusion, consolation and comfort out of misery and deep and heart-sinking murmurings, shewed how well such a duty is adapted to the domestic habits and feminine tenderness of our countrywomen . . . [This] beautiful example of female excellence . . . stands in the midst of suffering and death, an impersonation of that Gospel charity which 'beareth all things, believeth all things, hopeth all things, endureth all things'.[13]

But given that the Crimean conflict renewed and redirected theological attention to notions of substitutionary sacrifice and justification, then the effects of the war on *Little Dorrit* arguably exceed the points of contact that Markovits identifies. For *Little Dorrit* is structured according to a complex economy of moral values which situates rapacious capitalism alongside individual acts of reparation, justice alongside mercy, the wrathful rhetoric of the Old Testament alongside the loving language of the New, and which depends for its resolution upon the affirmation of pity and forgiveness at the expense of the rigours of the Law. In a letter to his friend William de Cerjat on 25 October 1864, commenting on the fratricidal ecclesiastical infighting which followed the publication of Bishop Colenso's study *The Pentateuch and Book of Joshua Critically Examined* (1862), Dickens condemned the Established Church for its obsession with 'as many forms of consignment to eternal damnation, as there are articles' (when it should instead have been remedying the plight of the poor):[14] the House of Clennam in *Little Dorrit* exemplifies this self-serving Calvinist preoccupation with judgment. Arthur was 'the only child of parents who weighed, measured, and priced everything; for whom what could not be weighed, measured and priced, had no existence' – their Christian commitment was as unimaginative and as prudent as their capitalism: '[t]heir very religion was a gloomy sacrifice of tastes and sympathies that were never their own, offered up as part of a bargain for the security of their possessions' (*LD*, p. 59). Mrs Clennam has blasphemously constructed her Deity in her own image:

> Great need had the rigid woman of her mystical religion, veiled in gloom and darkness, with lightnings of cursing, vengeance, and destruction, flashing through the sable clouds. Forgive us our debts as we forgive our debtors, was a prayer too poor in spirit for her. Smite Thou my debtors, Lord, wither them, crush them; do Thou as I would do, and Thou shalt have my worship: this was the impious tower of stone she built up to scale Heaven. (*LD*, p. 86)

Arthur makes the connection between his mother's strict economies of obligation and the ruthless commercial acquisitiveness on which the success of the House has been built: he can only assume that the interests of others have been sacrificed in the process:

> 'For Heaven's sake, let us examine sacredly whether there is any wrong entrusted to us to set right . . .
>
> In grasping at money and in driving hard bargains . . . some one may have been grievously deceived, injured, ruined . . .
>
> If reparation can be made to any one, if restitution can be made to anyone, let us know it and make it.' (*LD*, p. 88)

There are echoes here of the nation compelled to count the cost of war, in terms of lives lost and national interests damaged. Arthur wants to make moral reparation on behalf of his father, to offer vicarious satisfaction even where he has not personally been at fault. This is the sense of interdependence fostered by the war – a son or father or brother has died for the nation: what benevolence shall we extend to their family in return? Mrs Clennam's rigid moral accounting is an attempt to sidestep Clennam's more generous economy – if she inflicts upon herself her own punishment, she hopes to evade the punishment of the Lord (like Bulstrode in *Middlemarch*, whose abstention from pleasure is an attempt to deflect the retribution of God for his much greater sins of the past):

> Thus was she always balancing her bargains with the Majesty of heaven, posting up the entries to her credit, strictly keeping her set-off and claiming her due. She was only remarkable in this for the force and emphasis with which she did it. Thousands upon thousands do it, according to their varying manner, every day.
>
> (*LD*, p. 89)

But it is Clennam's economy which is upheld in the novel, and he is given the chance to make reparation for his investment of his partner's money in Merdle's duplicitous swindles – though his lawyer, Rugg, warns him that reparation is 'too emotive' a term for the types of restitution at work here (*LD*, p. 781). In allowing Clennam to be scapegoated for the failures of Merdle, Dickens deploys his most explicit references to the transactions of atonement:

> He told Mr Rugg that to clear his partner morally, to the fullest extent, and publicly and unreservedly to declare that he, Arthur Clennam, of that Firm, had of his own sole act, and even expressly against his partner's caution, embarked its resources in the swindles that had lately perished, was the only real atonement within his power; was a better atonement to the particular man than it would be to many men; and was therefore the atonement he had first to make. (*LD*, p. 782)

In the absence of Merdle, 'a living somebody' was wanted on the scaffold or in this case, perhaps, the altar of commerce. But Arthur is less Christ than Isaac, the innocent sacrifice by which his birth mother was forced to work out her penitence on earth for her youthful passions (*LD*, p. 783).

In his assumption of personal responsibility for the financial crisis which was the product of systemic failure (and could thus be dismissed ironically as 'Nobody's Fault'), Arthur changes places with Amy's father and is immured in the Marshalsea for debt, becoming in turn the object of her sacrificial attentions. Typologically, we are left with the image of Amy as a Christlike figure of innocence tending now to Isaac as she pours out her 'inexhaustible wealth of goodness upon him' (*LD*, p. 825).

The most theologically nuanced dimensions of the novel, then, are the meanings to be extracted from Amy's and Arthur's variant types of innocent sacrifice. The right reading of Arthur's story hinges on an understanding of Dickens's attitude to original sin – what responsibility the illegitimate child bears for the 'sins' of its parents. Mrs Clennam was brought up to dwell on 'the corruption of our hearts, the evil of our ways, the curse that is upon us, the terrors that surround us': upon her discovery that her husband's pre-marital union had produced a son, she felt 'it was appointed to [her] to lay the hand of punishment upon that creature of perdition' (*LD*, p. 843). The child was to be brought up 'in fear and trembling' and 'in a life of practical contrition for the sins that were heavy on his head before his entrance into this condemned world' (*LD*, p. 844).[15] In seeking to be 'an instrument of severity against sin', Mrs Clennam had located her 'justification' in 'the old days when the innocent perished with the guilty, a thousand to one . . . When the wrath of the hater of the unrighteous was not slaked even in blood, and yet found favour' (*LD*, p. 860). Following Christ's example, just as the dispensation of the Old Testament must give way to the New, Little Dorrit counsels her to reject revenge and

> [b]e guided only by the healer of the sick, the raiser of the dead, the friend of all who were afflicted and forlorn, the patient Master who shed tears of compassion for our infirmities. We cannot but be right if we put all the rest away, and do everything in remembrance of Him. There is no vengeance and no infliction of sufferings in His life, I am sure. There can be no confusion following Him, and seeking for no other footsteps, I am certain. (*LD*, p. 861)

And just as Little Dorrit has resolved to follow Christ's example, so too others are called upon to follow Little Dorrit's, in a circle of ever-expanding acts of imitation. In each case the offer of redemption comes through an appropriation of vicarious experience and example. To dwell for a moment on the novel's other sub-plot of ethical reflection, Tattycoram, the repentant foundling girl adopted by the kind-hearted Meagles family, must decide between the model afforded her by very different biographical templates. On the one hand, Miss Wade offered only an image of the sinful 'self grown ripe' (*LD*, p. 880). What model of lived experience can counter-act this example? Like Mr Carson in *Mary Barton*, [. . .], Tattycoram must be made privy to a staged demonstration of embodied goodness, as Mr Meagles reveals to her from the vantage-point of a spectator the morally instructive impact of Little Dorrit on the world of the Marshalsea Prison:

> 'Tattycoram, come to me a moment, my good girl'.
>   She went up to the window.
>   'You see that young lady who was here just now – that little, quiet, fragile figure passing along there, Tatty? Look. The people stand out of the way to let her go by. The men – see the poor, shabby fellows – pull off their hats to her quite politely, and now she glides in at that doorway. See her, Tattycoram?'
>   'Yes, sir.'
>   'I have heard tell, Tatty, that she was once regularly called the child of this place. She was born here, and lived here many years . . . If she had constantly thought of herself, and settled with herself that everybody visited this place upon her, turned it against her, and cast it at her, she would have led an irritable and probably an useless existence. Yet I have heard tell, Tattycoram, that her young life has been one of active resignation, goodness, and noble service. Shall I tell you what I consider those eyes of hers, that were here just now, to have always looked at, to get that expression?'
>   'Yes, if you please, sir.'
>   'Duty, Tattycoram. Begin it early, and do it well; and there is no antecedent to it, in any origin or station, that will tell against us with the Almighty, or with ourselves.' (*LD*, pp. 880–1)

[. . .]

Notes

1 Dickens to Forster, ?13–14 October 1844, in *The Letters of Charles Dickens*, ed. Graham Storey, Madeline House, et al., 13 vols. (Oxford: Clarendon Press, 1965–81; repr. 1993–2000), vol. IV (1844–6), p. 201. See also discussion in Gary Colledge, *Dickens, Christianity and 'The Life of Our Lord'* (London: Continuum, 2009), pp. 140–1.

2 See, for example, Colledge, *Dickens, Christianity and 'The Life of Our Lord'*, and Valentine Cunningham, 'Dickens and Christianity', in David Paroissien (ed.), *A Companion to Charles Dickens* (Oxford: Blackwell, 2008), pp. 255–6.

3 Cunningham, 'Dickens and Christianity', p. 259.

4 See letter to Esther Nash, 5 March 1861, in *Letters of Charles Dickens*, vol. IX (1859–61), p. 389, and letter to W. W. F. de Cerjat, 28 May 1863, in *Letters of Charles Dickens*, vol. X (1862–4), pp. 252–3.

5 Letter to W. W. F. de Cerjat, 25 October 1864, *Letters of Charles Dickens*, vol. X (1862–4), p. 444.

6 Undated letter to David Macrae [?1861], extracted in *Letters of Charles Dickens*, vol. IX (1859–61), pp. 556–7.

7 See discussion in Cunningham, 'Dickens and Christianity', p. 265.

8 Charles Dickens, *A Christmas Carol, and Other Christmas Writings* (Harmondsworth: Penguin, 2003), p. 36.

9 Cunningham, 'Dickens and Christianity', p. 271.

10 [Susan L.] Mizruchi, *Science of Sacrifice*[: *American Literature and Modern Social Theory* (Princeton University Press, 1998)], p. 13.

11 [Ivan] Kreilkamp, *Voice* [*and the Victorian Storyteller* (Cambridge University Press, 2005)], pp. 25, 28.

12 Stefanie Markovits, *The Crimean War in the British Imagination* (Cambridge University Press, 2009), pp. 63–9.

13 M. Harrison, *A Sermon Adapted for a Day of Thanksgiving on the Restoration of Peace* (London: Longman, Brown, Green & Longmans, ?1856), pp. 18–19. See also James Jeremie, *A Sermon Preached in the Cathedral Church of Lincoln, May 4th, 1856, Being the Day Appointed for a General Thanksgiving for the Restoration of Peace* (London: Bell and Daldy, 1856).

14 Letter to Cerjat, 25 October 1864, cited in footnote 5.

15 The phrase 'fear and trembling' is used in the Bible twice, in Ps. 55: 5 and Phil. 2: 12. On Clennam's inheritance, see also Anny Sadrin, *Parentage and Inheritance in the Novels of Charles Dickens* (Cambridge University Press, 1994), pp. 77–81.

Bibliography

Dickens, Charles, *Great Expectations* [1860–1] (Harmondsworth: Penguin, 1996).

——. *Hard Times* [1854] (Harmondsworth: Penguin, 1985).

——. *Little Dorrit* [1856–7] (Harmondsworth: Penguin, 1985).

Girard, Rene *The Scapegoat*, trans. Yvonne Freccero (Baltimore, MD: John Hopkins University Press, 1986).

20 Religion and literature

Mark Knight

The twenty-first century has seen a major resurgence of interest in religion among scholars of nineteenth-century literature. This resurgence is reflected in a burgeoning number of books, journal articles, and conference papers, and there is plenty of evidence throughout the field of Victorian Studies to support Stanley Fish's dramatic prediction in the *Chronicle of Higher Education* that religion would "succeed high theory and the triumvirate of race, gender, and class as the center of intellectual energy in the academy" (Fish 2005). Yet the need for such a resurgence would surely have puzzled a nineteenth-century commentator able to look into the future, for their period was, to them at least, obviously replete with the language of religion. This is not to say that everyone in the nineteenth century considered himself or herself to be religious, or that we can treat Victorian British culture as if it were uniformly Christian. And there are a host of complicating factors: the dispersal of Christian affiliations among the Church of England, non-conformist churches, and Catholicism; the considerable debates among and within these groups; variations in how regularly the Victorians practiced religion; attitudes adopted towards and within non-Christian religious traditions; and how belief was modified by the intellectual and cultural developments of a society in considerable flux. But in spite of the divergent ways in which the Victorians thought about religion, it was almost impossible for people in the period to miss the centrality of religious vocabulary, practice, institutions, and architecture.

There are various reasons why religion faded from view in the minds of many late twentieth century critics who wrote about Victorian literature. These range from the influence of a Marxist-inflected understanding of critique that saw religion as an ideology needing to be exposed, to the more prosaic fact that the generation of scholars I am referring to were less familiar with religious references than their predecessors and less equipped to incorporate religion into their intellectual frameworks in ways that seemed worthwhile. And there are many reasons, too, why religion returned to scholarly prominence as the twentieth century ended and a new century began: the theoretical turn to religion (including the late work of Jacques Derrida and, more recently, the writings of Richard Kearney, Giorgio Agamben, Slavoj Zizek, and Alain Badiou); the pressing awareness of political-theological issues in the aftermath of 9/11; the questions raised by Charles Taylor and others about received notions of secularization; the influence of conferences, journals and informal scholarly networks interested in religion and literature as an interdisciplinary field; and the appeal of religion as a neglected area that was ripe for new scholarship. Whatever one thinks about the reasons for the fall and rise of scholarship on religion, the latter part of the twentieth century was a barren time for work by literary scholars on Victorian religion. There were exceptions, of course, with valuable contributions from Stephen Prickett (1976), Elisabeth Jay (1979), George Landow (1980), Terry R. Wright (1986), Michael Wheeler (1990), Christine Krueger

(1992), Bryan Cheyette (1993), Donald E. Hall (1994), and Ellis Hanson (1997), to name but a few. But one could easily have attended a large academic conference on Victorian literature in the late twentieth century and heard next to nothing about religion, a marked contrast to the considerable interest in religion at recent conferences.

Restoring religion to our understanding of Victorian literature involves more than spotting biblical allusions or identifying a doctrinal reference, helpful though these activities can be. In the case of Christina Rossetti, an appreciation of her religious commitments opens up her poetry in all sorts of ways. The article from Emma Mason extracted here not only shows how Rossetti's poetry was more invested in theology than many critics from the late twentieth century were ready to acknowledge, but also how a theological idea, in this case the Tractarian doctrine of reserve, informs the distinctive simple-yet-profound style of Rossetti's poetry. By insisting that theology is more than an incidental backdrop to literature and by revealing the relevance of a doctrine that might otherwise seem esoteric, Mason demonstrates the vitality of Rossetti's beliefs and links theology to other matters, such as concepts of the natural world, purity, and democracy. Mason's contribution, here and elsewhere, has played a formative role in the renaissance of intellectually agile work on poetry and religion in the Victorian period. Rossetti's poetry has benefitted enormously from this renaissance, with her best-known poem, "Goblin Market," being the subject of stimulating essays by critics such as Marylu Hill (2005) and Albert Pionke (2012), and her broader oeuvre enjoying insightful readings from Mary Arseneau (2004), Constance Hassett (2005), Dinah Roe (2006), and others. In each case, scholars have deployed a flexible and articulate understanding of theology to help us see how religious ideas, from the parabolic as a mode of teaching to the relevance of the Christian practice of the Eucharist, informed Rossetti's poetry.

Rossetti is far from being the only poet to benefit from new scholarship on Victorian religion, and the last few years have seen excellent books by Charles LaPorte (2011), Kirstie Blair (2012), and Karen Dieleman (2012). The treatment of religion in these books is shaped by the authors' attention to form and a willingness to pursue close readings that draw fluently on history and theory to develop their lines of theological interpretation. Another strength is the willingness to think about religion in conjunction with other discourses. This willingness is essential if we are to appreciate how religion permeated the whole of Victorian life rather than existing as a discrete sphere that began when one went to church on Sunday and finished when one returned home. Although theories of secularization have often sought to narrow the space occupied by religion, the reality is that religion interacts with all areas of thought and practice. To take one example that has been prominent in work on poetry and religion, religious thought was integral to the Victorians' multiple understanding of sexuality and gender, and religion should not simply be seen as the source of sexual repression. The value of thinking more expansively about the relationship between religion and sex is evident in a number of intelligent books on Victorian poetry and religion, including those by Lynda Palazzo (2002), Frederick Roden (2003), and Duc Dau (2012).

The realization that theology can be understood in relation to other spheres of knowledge is important if we are to appreciate the way in which religion functioned in Victorian life. How, for instance, should we understand the business decisions made by individuals who were both pious and thoroughly committed to capitalism? Since the work of Max Weber, critics have tended to view the combination in terms of unacknowledged problems within theology. And there is an earlier tradition of writers who thought that the combination of God with mammon can only be explained by seeing the limitations of religious thought in the face of economic concerns. In the case of Bulstrode, one of the most intriguing characters in *Middlemarch*, religion and money can only exist in a state of tension. Eliot's tale of Bulstrode's hypocrisy and compromise offers one explanation of how the Victorians reconciled their religious beliefs with financial demands and other cultural norms, yet the relationship between God and mammon could also be creative and productive, as evidenced by the dramatic growth in religious publishing during the nineteenth century. One of the best books on the religious dimensions of print culture is William McKelvy's *The English Cult of Literature: Devoted Readers, 1774–1880* (2007), extracted here. Rejecting the assumption that literary studies emerged as religion fell into decline, McKelvy shows how much of the fabric of English literature in the nineteenth century was shaped by sacred forms: reading books, writing literature, and developing print culture all came to be seen as religious vocations. McKelvy's insistence on thinking about print culture and religion alongside one another is shared by other critics, too, including Aileen Fyfe (2004), who has written a seminal study of the publishing activity of the Religious Tract Society, and Joshua King (2012), who writes persuasively about the uses of Keble's *The Christian Year* for private reading and the building of an imagined national religious community.

In the extract included here, McKelvy interrogates many of the assumptions that lie behind the secularization thesis, the belief that the modern world marks the inevitable decline of religious belief. McKelvy insists that religious changes in the period deserve a more complex explanation, and he insists that "while there is an important story to be told about the declining identity of church and state during the long nineteenth century, we must not confuse this event with a general decay of religion, or even a creeping rot within Anglicanism" (McKelvy 2007: 29 [Chapter 18: 164]). Recognizing that religious developments in the period are more complex than the secularization thesis allows for, McKelvy explores the close relationship between religion and literature in the period and argues that the moments "when religious and literary sanctity appeared interchangeable" were caused by changes in the political attitude to belief, not the erosion of faith (McKelvy 2007: 29 [Chapter 18: 164]). The "nineteenth-century politics of becoming a reading nation," McKelvy argues, were encouraged by the structures and practices of belief (McKelvy 2007: 33 [Chapter 18: 167]).

The recognition that religion was tied into all aspects of life is a crucial corrective to the mistaken belief that true religion can only exist in a purified form. Older ideas of secularization tended to see all signs of theological ideas being contaminated by other spheres of life as evidence of the secular, but religion has never operated in complete isolation and it is not the case that a literary interest in themes such as sex or money automatically signals the decline of religious belief. At the same time, there is a potential danger in focusing too heavily on the intermingled nature of religious belief: theology can quickly find itself subsumed into other scholarly discourses, to the extent that discussion about religion proceeds as though the history of theology had never existed. Thus studies of religion and empire, to take one example, risk thinking about religion entirely from the theoretical perspective provided by theories of empire and forgetting that theological writings in the Victorian period could be sources of anti-imperial critique as well as places in which imperial ideas were perpetuated. Thinking about religion and empire in a manner that acknowledges the complicity of religion in the purposes of the empire yet also sees religious writing as a potential alternative to the pervading ideology is challenging. There have been some helpful books on the subject by Mary Carpenter (2003) and Anna Johnston (2003), as well as strong contributions from several historians working on Victorian religion, but the scale of the topic and the need for an adequately nuanced understanding of the relationship between Christianity and culture leaves the subject of religion and empire as an area that needs further attention from literary scholars.

The relationship between religion and empire offers an acute instance of one of the great challenges of writing insightfully about Victorian religion and literature. How can we expand our understanding of religion to acknowledge its integration with other discourses while maintaining an appreciation of the distinctiveness of theological vocabulary and grammar, by which I mean the language spoken by the church and also by the academic discipline of theology? There is no easy answer to this challenge but the best scholarship of recent years does a good job of illustrating at a more local level how such work might proceed. One of the most successful scholars in this respect is Jan-Melissa Schramm, whose work is extracted here. Schramm is the author of two authoritative books on Victorian religion and literature (2000 and 2012), both of which bring additional subjects, specifically law and ethics, into conversation with religion and literature. On Schramm's reading, the presence of religion in literature is inseparable from the legal and ethical questions of the period, so that, as she explains in her first book, the changing attitudes to testimony in the Victorian period were shaped by theology and legal philosophy. Schramm's attention to historical theology ensures that theological discourse remains integral to the discussion of literary criticism in the Victorian era.

In the material from Schramm that appears in this volume, we are invited to understand Charles Dickens's novels of the 1850s and their interest in self-sacrifice against the backdrop of Anglican debates in the 1850s about the meaning of Christian atonement and the question of what was achieved through Christ's death on the Cross. *Hard Times* is preoccupied with the figure of the scapegoat, the person who is blamed for others' wrongdoing, and the presence of debates relating to the Christian atonement are even more pronounced in *Little Dorrit*, with Dickens inviting readers to reflect on the sacrifices of Amy Dorrit and Arthur Clennam and to see them as better models than the embodiments of judgment and revenge that confront us in the characters of Mrs. Clennam and Miss Wade. In the chapter of Schramm's book from which this extract is taken, the discussion of these novels carries forward into a more wide-ranging treatment of self-sacrifice in *A Tale of Two Cities*, and we are presented with an interpretation of Dickens that is more theologically dense than much of the critical tradition has been prepared to admit.

Most of Schramm's work deals with realist novels, and her exploration of the religious dimensions of this form offers a useful corrective to the long-standing notion, most eloquently articulated by George Levine (2008), that realism is inherently secular. Levine sees realism's commitment to science, the economic, and material explanations as eroding the space previously occupied by religion. But his concept of religion is overly reliant on transcendence (the idea that God is located beyond the material universe) rather than immanence (the idea that God is manifest within the material universe), and a different account of realism emerges when transcendence and immanence are brought together, as in the readings of religion offered by J. Russell Perkin (2009), Susan E. Colon (2012), Ilana Blumberg (2013), Emily Walker Heady (2013), and Norman Vance (2013). Andrew Miller also acknowledges that religion continues to be heard in the realist novel in his wonderful book *The Burdens of Perfection: On Ethics and Reading in Nineteenth-Century Literature* (2008). Like Schramm, Colon, and Blumberg, Miller is especially interested in ethical readings of the Victorian novel, and although ethics is not a synonym for religion, as George Eliot's work would sometimes have us think, it does create a useful site for mutual discussions about human agency and the question of what God asks of his followers.

While much of the recent scholarship on religion and the novel has focused on realism, there is also a need to think about other manifestations of Victorian fiction, such as fantasy, ghost stories, and nonsense literature. With the exception of gothic fiction, which has been well served by perceptive criticism from Alison Milbank (2002) and Patrick O'Malley (2006), there is relatively little scholarship on the relationship between religion and non-realist fiction in the Victorian period. One of the most important exceptions is the work of John Schad, most obviously his book *Queer Fish: Christian Unreason from Darwin to Derrida* (2004). Schad's monograph moves across a range of genres and is more theoretically experimental than most of the other books mentioned in this essay. His interest in unreason and the idea that Christianity may be best understood as a subversive tradition offers a valuable starting point to those seeking a way of working through the theological ramifications of fiction by authors such as George MacDonald, the Scottish writer best known for his works of fantasy and children's literature. Although it is obvious that a writer like MacDonald read (and wrote) a great deal of theology, those working in the mainstream of Victorian studies tend to lack the conceptual resources needed to tease out the religious contributions to his and others' ideas of nonsense, play, and fairy stories. The problem is even greater when one turns to authors whose religious commitments are less obvious than MacDonald's, and discussions about ghost stories, for example, can be too quick to appeal solely to ideas of the occult rather than acknowledging the ways in which theological ideas also pervaded Victorian ideas about the psychic realm.

As well as a need to consider the world of Victorian fiction more broadly, there is a need to pay further attention to religious traditions other than Protestant Christianity. The most influential religious alternative to Protestant Christianity in the period was Roman Catholicism, and following the trajectory of the Victorian period, which saw Roman Catholicism become increasingly acceptable and appealing to people with an interest in religion, recent scholarship has begun to show greater concern for the Roman Catholic presence in literature. Much of this work is focused on tensions between Protestantism and Catholicism (see Griffin 2004, Wheeler 2006, Moran 2007, LaMonaca 2008, and Burstein 2014), reflecting the fact that it is difficult to think about Catholic literary identity in nineteenth-century Britain apart from the lens of a Protestant literary culture. Scholarship on the relationship between Catholicism and Protestantism is important, and typically very illuminating, but it is not the same as trying to think about Catholicism on its own terms, and there remains a great deal of work to be done coming to grips with the Catholic literary tradition that gathered pace in the latter part of the nineteenth century and was shaped by authors such as Alice Meynell, Gerard Manley Hopkins, and Oscar Wilde.

Beyond the realm of Christianity, there is increasing interest in Judaism and Victorian literature, evident in important studies by Cynthia Scheinberg (2002) and Nadia Valman (2007), among others, and there is a growing scholarly interest in Anglo-Jewish writers such as Amy Levy and Israel Zangwill that is impressively attentive to the close relationship between religion and national identity and the practices of religious community. When it comes to the other major world religions, such as Hinduism, Sikhism, Islam, and Buddhism, scholarship is much more limited. The main reason is the extremely small numbers of writers and critics in the Victorian period who had any sort of immersion in and/or knowledge of these faiths. As a result, scholarship tends to be stuck with noting the negative depictions of these religious traditions in literature, and/or seeing how the Persian religious sources in a text such as Omar Khayyam's *Rubaiyat* are heavily refracted through the British imperial mindset of the Victorian translator, Edward FitzGerald. Although these problems are difficult to surmount, and made worse by the limited understanding that many contemporary literary critics have of world religions, a book such as Jeffrey Franklin's *The Lotus and the Lion: Buddhism and the British Empire* (2008) is informative and insightful in ways that encourage us to see how non-western religion might be brought helpfully into our discussions about Victorian literature. As I have sought to make clear throughout this essay, the challenge is to do so in a way that maintains the distinctiveness of these very different religious discourses while also refusing to separate the religious out from those aspects of Victorian literature and culture that literary scholars are more familiar with.

Bibliography

Arseneau, M. (2004) *Recovering Christina Rossetti: Female Community and Incarnational Poetics*, Basingstoke: Palgrave.

Blair, K. (2012) *Form and Faith in Victorian Poetry and Religion*, Oxford, Oxford University Press.

Blumberg, I. (2013) *Victorian Sacrifice: Ethics and Economics in Mid-Century Novels*, Columbus: Ohio State University Press.

Burstein, M. E. (2014) *Victorian Reformations: Historical Fiction and Religious Controversy, 1820-1900*, Notre Dame: University of Notre Dame Press.

Carpenter, M. (2003) *Imperial Bibles, Domestic Bodies: Women, Sexuality and Religion in the Victorian Market*, Ohio: Ohio University Press.

Cheyette, B. (1993) *Constructions of "the Jew" in English Literature and Society: Racial Representations, 1875–1945*, Cambridge: Cambridge University Press.

Colon, S. E. (2012) *Victorian Parables*, London: Continuum.

Dau, D. (2012) *Touching God: Hopkins and Love*, London: Anthem Press.

Dieleman, K. (2012) *Religious Imaginaries: The Liturgical and Poetic Practices of Elizabeth Barrett Browning, Christina Rossetti, and Adelaide Procter*, Ohio: Ohio University Press.

Fish, S. (2005) "One University Under God?," *The Chronicle of Higher Education*, 7 January 2005.

Franklin, J. J. (2008) *The Lotus and the Lion: Buddhism and the British Empire*, Ithaca, NY: Cornell University Press.

Fyfe, A. (2004) *Science and Salvation: Evangelicals and Popular Science Publishing in Victorian Britain*, Chicago: University of Chicago Press.

Griffin, S. M. (2004) *Anti-Catholicism and Nineteenth-Century Fiction*, Cambridge: Cambridge University Press.

Hall, D. E. (ed.) (1994) *Muscular Christianity: Embodying the Victorian Age*, Cambridge: Cambridge University Press.

Hanson, E. (1997) *Decadence and Catholicism*, Cambridge, MA: Harvard University Press.

Hassett, C. W. (2005) *Christina Rossetti: The Patience of Style*, Charlottesville: University of Virginia Press.

Heady, E. W. (2013) *Victorian Conversion Narratives and Reading Communities*, Farnham: Ashgate.

Hill, M. (2005) "'Eat Me, Drink Me, Love Me': Eucharist and the Erotic Body in Christina Rossetti's 'Goblin Market,'" *Victorian Poetry*, 43.4: 455–72.

Johnston, A. (2003) *Missionary Writing and Empire, 1800–1860*, Cambridge: Cambridge University Press.

King, J. (2012) "John Keble's Christian Year: Private Reading and Imagined National Religious Community," *Victorian Literature and Culture*, 40.2: 397–420.

Krueger, C. (1992) *The Reader's Repentance: Women Preachers, Women Writers, and Nineteenth-Century Social Discourse*, Chicago: Chicago University Press.

LaMonaca, M. (2008) *Masked Atheism: Catholicism and the Secular Victorian Home*, Columbus: Ohio State University Press.

LaPorte, C. (2011) *Victorian Poets and the Changing Bible*, Virginia: University of Virginia Press.

Landow, G. (1980) *Victorian Types, Victorian Shadows: Biblical Typology in Victorian Literature, Art and Thought*, New York: Routledge.

Levine, G. (2008) *Realism, Ethics and Secularism: Essays on Victorian Literature and Science*, Cambridge: Cambridge University Press.

McKelvy, W. R. (2007) *The English Cult of Literature: Devoted Readers, 1774–1880*, Charlottesville: University of Virginia Press.

Mason, E. (2002) "Christina Rossetti and the Doctrine of Reserve," *Journal of Victorian Culture*, 7.2: 196–219.

—— (2006) *Women Poets of the Nineteenth Century*, London: Northcote House.

Milbank, A. (2002), "The Victorian Gothic in English Novels and Stories, 1830–1880," in J. E. Hogle (ed.) *The Cambridge Companion to Gothic Fiction*, Cambridge: Cambridge University Press.

Miller, A. H. (2008) *The Burdens of Perfection: On Ethics and Reading in Nineteenth-Century British Literature*, Ithaca, NY: Cornell University Press.

Moran, M. (2007) *Catholic Sensationalism and Victorian Literature*, Liverpool: Liverpool University Press.

O'Malley, P. R. (2006), *Catholicism, Sexual Deviance and Victorian Gothic Culture*, Cambridge: Cambridge University Press.

Palazzo, L. (2002) *Christina Rossetti's Feminist Theology*, New York: Palgrave.

Perkin, J. R. (2009) *Theology and the Victorian Novel*, Montreal and Kingston: McGill-Queen's University Press.

Pionke, A. D. (2012), "The Spiritual Economy of 'Goblin Market,'" *Studies in English Literature 1500–1900*, 52.4: 897–915.

Prickett, S. (1976) *Romanticism and Religion: The Tradition of Coleridge and Wordsworth in the Victorian Church*, Cambridge: Cambridge University Press.

Roden, F. S. (2003) *Same-Sex Desire in Victorian Religious Culture*, Basingstoke: Palgrave.

Roe, D. (2006) *Christina Rossetti's Faithful Imagination: The Devotional Poetry and Prose*, Basingstoke: Palgrave.

Schad, J. (2004) *Queer Fish: Christian Unreason from Darwin to Derrida*, Brighton: Sussex Academic Press.

Scheinberg, C. (2002) *Women's Poetry and Religion in Victorian England: Jewish Identity and Christian Culture*, Cambridge: Cambridge University Press.

Schramm, J-M. (2000) *Testimony and Advocacy in Victorian Law, Literature and Theology*, Cambridge: Cambridge University Press.

—— (2012) *Atonement and Self-Sacrifice in Nineteenth-Century Narrative*, Cambridge: Cambridge University Press.

Valman, N. (2007) *The Jewess in Nineteenth-Century British Literary Culture*, Cambridge: Cambridge University Press.

Vance, N. (2013) *Bible and Novel: Narrative Authority and the Death of God*, Oxford: Oxford University Press.

Wheeler, M. (1990) *Death and the Future Life in Victorian Literature and Theology*, Cambridge: Cambridge University Press.

—— (2006) *The Old Enemies: Catholic and Protestant in Nineteenth-Century English Culture*, Cambridge: Cambridge University Press.

Wright, T. R. (1986) *The Religion of Humanity: The Impact of Comtean Positivism on Victorian Britain*, Cambridge: Cambridge University Press.

Part VI

Darwin and Victorian culture

Introduction

In 1859 Charles Darwin published *On the Origin of Species by Means of Natural Selection, or the Preservation of Favoured Races in the Struggle for Life*. While discussion of "development theory" had permeated Victorian culture since at least the 1830s, Darwin's work differed in one key respect from earlier accounts: it identified the mechanism—natural selection—by which evolution happens. In place of natural theology's "presumptions of godhead and of pre-emptive patterning" (Beer 2000: 48 [Chapter 21: 193]), Darwin's theory of evolution proposed that random mutations produce change, and that such change is neither inherently progressive nor degenerate. No wonder, then, that James Eli Adams calls *Origin* "arguably the most daring and unsettling book of the century" (Adams 2009: 215).

During the middle decades of the twentieth century, there were relatively few studies of the interactions of science and literature, a phenomenon which can be attributed to the ascendancy of New Criticism, with its emphasis on understanding literary texts as self-sufficient, autonomous objects. The historicist turn of the 1970s resulted in a burgeoning of interest in Victorian science, and most particularly Darwin's theory of evolution. Older critical studies had assumed that the influence was essentially in one direction, from science to literature and culture, but by the early 1980s critics such as Tess Cosslett increasingly recognized the relationship of science and culture as one of mutual influence. It was in this climate that Gillian Beer and George Levine published their monumental works on Darwin. While both explore the influence of Darwin's theories on Victorian fiction, both also assume that Darwin's own writings were shaped in their turn by Victorian literary culture. As Levine puts it with characteristic succinctness, "science and literature help create the conditions necessary for each other's development" (Levine 1988: 130), a phenomenon perhaps most apparent in Beer's careful analysis of Darwin's own use of language. Levine focuses on novelists less obviously embedded in debates about science, such as Dickens and Trollope, thus complementing Beer's earlier work on Eliot and Hardy. There are few other areas in Victorian studies in which two monographs have so comprehensively dominated discussion for so long.

More recently, however, critics adopting broader contextual and materialist approaches have begun to challenge some of their assumptions, with the result that, as Jonathan Smith notes in this volume, the "broader cultural brushstrokes of *Darwin and the Novelists* and even *Darwin's Plots* begin to appear too imprecise" (Smith [Chapter 25: 225]). This more recent work draws upon a newly expanded range of textual sources that includes popular illustrations, satirical cartoons, sermons, and even gossip—a range so extensive as to make Beer's and Levine's once-exemplary bibliographies seem hazardously narrow in retrospect. The resulting analyses challenge our assumptions about the significance, impact, and mode of dissemination of Darwin's ideas in the nineteenth century. Once regarded as an epochal shift, many critics now suggest that the publication of *Origin of Species* in 1859 belongs instead to a more gradualist narrative, with scholars like James Secord reasserting the importance of earlier work on "development theory" such as Robert Chambers's *Vestiges of the Natural History of Creation* (1844). While Beer assumed that Darwin's work "was widely and thoroughly *read* by his contemporaries" (Beer 2000: 3 [Chapter 21: 189]), research by Bernard Lightman indicates that most Victorians got through their evolutionary theory not directly from Darwin, but through Victorian popularizers of science. Perhaps most important, the relationship of science and literature in the nineteenth century has again come under scrutiny from critics who fear earlier scholarly assessments of the relationship of science and literature were "too sanguine" (Dawson 2007: 7 [Chapter 24: 215]), in danger of ignoring both the generic differences between the two discourses and the ways in which their interactions could be mutually exploitative, rather than advantageous. As Jonathan Smith's capstone essay makes clear below, the resulting analyses force us to reconsider what we know about the significance, cultural impact, application, and dissemination of Darwin's ideas in the nineteenth century.

See also: *Genre fiction and the sensational*; *Psychology and literature*; *Imperialism and literature in the age of colonialism*

Bibliography

Adams, J. E. (2009) *A History of Victorian Literature*, Chichester: Wiley-Blackwell.

21 The remnant of the mythical; Fit and misfitting

Anthropomorphism and the natural order

Gillian Beer

[. . .]

In this study I shall explore some of the ways in which evolutionary theory has been assimilated and resisted by novelists who, within the subtle enregisterment of narrative, have assayed its powers. With varying degrees of self awareness they have tested the extent to which it can provide a determining fiction by which to read the world. The book is concerned with Victorian novelists living, in relation to evolutionary theory, in the phase when 'a fact is not quite a scientific fact at all'[1] and when 'the remnant of the mythical'[2] is at its most manifest. I shall analyse works by writers as various in their responses as Kingsley, George Eliot and Hardy. But evolutionary ideas are even more influential when they become assumptions embedded in the culture than while they are the subject of controversy. As Barry Barnes writes in *Scientific Knowledge and Sociological Theory*:

> A successful model in science frequently moves from the status of an 'as if' theory to a 'real description'. From here it may develop into a cosmology, before eventual disintegration into a mass of techniques and procedures, wherein what were key theoretical conceptions become mere operators, the ontological status of which is scarcely given a thought, (c.f. force, temperature, frequency).[3]

That process of naturalisation is the other major topic of my enquiry. We pay Darwin the homage of our assumptions. Precisely because we live in a culture dominated by evolutionary ideas, it is difficult for us to recognise their imaginative power in our daily readings of the world. We need to do so.

In the earlier chapters of this study I shall analyse some of the problems Darwin faced in precipitating his theory as language. He sought to appropriate and to recast inherited mythologies, discourses, and narrative orders. He was telling a new story, against the grain of the language available to tell it in. And as it was told, the story itself proved not to be single or simple. It was, rather, capable of being extended or reclaimed into a number of conflicting systems.[4]

In speaking of evolutionary theory I take as my focus the work of Darwin, though in the course of my argument I shall give some account of other writers such as Lamarck, Lyell, and Robert Chambers whose earlier writings had contributed to the acceptance of evolutionary ideas.[5] I concentrate on Darwin partly because his appreciation of the means through which change, development, and extinction of species took place was to revolutionise our understanding of natural order (though when his book first came out it was not immediately obvious to all that his work did more than substantiate and give authority to ideas already current). A second reason for focusing sharply on *The Origin of Species*[6] is that it was widely and thoroughly *read* by his contemporaries. Reading *The Origin* is an act which involves you in a narrative experience. The experience may seem to diverse readers to be tragic (as postulated by Jacques Barzun) or comic (as Dwight Culler argues) but it is always subjective and literary.[7]

Related to this question of focus is another, of evidence. Perhaps I can best express it by an analogy. We now live in a post-Freudian age: it is impossible, in our culture, to live a life which is not charged with Freudian assumptions, patterns for apprehending experience, ways of perceiving relationships, even if we have not read a word of Freud, even – to take the case to its extreme – if we have no Freudian terms in either our active or passive vocabulary. Freud sufficiently disrupted all possible past patterns for apprehending experience and his ideas have been so far institutionalised that even those who query his views, or distrust them, find themselves unable to create a world cleansed of the Freudian. This was the nature also of Darwin's influence on the generations which succeeded him. Everyone found themselves living in a Darwinian world in which old assumptions had ceased to *be* assumptions, could be at best beliefs, or myths, or, at worst, detritus of the past. So the question of who read Darwin, or whether a writer had read Darwin, becomes only a fraction of the answer. The related question of whether the reader had read Darwin turns out also to have softer edges than might at first appear. Who had read what does not fix limits. On the face of it, then, a very generous use of evidence would have been possible for this study, which would see it as inevitable that all writers were affected by such theory. This would have permitted me to point out analogies of theme and order in almost anyone I chose.[8] But although I do not believe that this would be an improper enterprise, it seems to me to be in one sense an insufficient one, because it does not take account of the *act of reading* and reaction.

Reading creates uncertainty as well as satisfaction. As Richard Ohmann remarks:

> The very act of predication is an emotional act, with rhythms of its own. To state something is first to create imbalance, curiosity, where previously there was nothing, and then to bring about a new balance. So prose builds on the emotional force of coming to know, of pinning down part of what has previously been formless and resolving the tensions which exist between the human organism and unstructured experience.[9]

One's relationship to ideas depends significantly on whether one has read the works which formulate them. Ideas pass more rapidly into the state of assumptions when they are *unread*. Reading is an essentially question-raising procedure. This is one reason why in this study I have limited close discussion to the work of novelists whom we know to have read Darwin, and usually Lyell, Spencer and Huxley as well. I want to track the difficult flux of excitement, rebuttal, disconfirmation, pursuit, forgetfulness, and analogy-making, which together make up something of the process of assimilation.

In the mid-nineteenth century, scientists still shared a common language with other educated readers and writers of their time. There is nothing hermetic or exclusive in the writing of Lyell or Darwin. Together with other scientific writers such as G. H. Lewes, Claude Bernard, John Tyndall, W. K. Clifford, and even so far as his early work is concerned Clerk Maxwell (writers whose works ranged through psychology, physiology, physics and mathematics), they shared a literary, non-mathematical discourse which was readily available to readers without a scientific training. Their texts could be read very much as literary texts. In our own century scientific ideas tend to reach us by a process of extrapolation and translation. Non-scientists do not expect to be able to follow the mathematical condensations of meaning in scientific journals, and major theories are more often presented as theorems than as discourse. We unselfconsciously use the term 'layman' to describe the relationship of a non-scientist to the body of scientific knowledge. The suggestion of a priestly class and of reserved, hermetic knowledge goes mostly unremarked. In the mid-nineteenth century, however, it was possible for a reader to turn to the primary works of scientists as they appeared, and to respond directly to the arguments advanced. Moreover, scientists themselves in their texts drew openly upon literary, historical and philosophical material as part of their arguments: Lyell, for example, uses extensively the fifteenth book of Ovid's *Metamorphoses* in his account of proto-geology, Bernard cites Goethe repeatedly, and – as has often been remarked – Darwin's crucial insight into the mechanism of evolutionary change derived directly from his reading of Malthus's essay *On Population*. What has gone unremarked is that it derived also from his reading of the one book he never left behind during his expeditions from the *Beagle: The Poetical Works of John Milton*. The traffic, then, was two-way. Because of the shared discourse not only *ideas* but metaphors, myths, and narrative patterns could move rapidly and freely to and fro between scientists and non-scientists: though not without frequent creative misprision.

The second premise of my argument is that evolutionary theory had particular implications for narrative and for the composition of fiction. Because of its preoccupation with time and with change evolutionary theory has inherent affinities with the problems and processes of narrative. 'There is not one great question relating to the former changes of the earth and its inhabitants into which considerations of time do not enter,' wrote Lyell in *The Principles of Geology* (1830, I:302).[10] And although Lyell at this time still believed in the fixity of species his exploration of an infinitely extended time-scale for the earth was one of the necessary preconditions of later theory. When Lyell wanted to point out how too short an imagined time-scale had misled geologists into a catastrophist view of the past, he did it by invoking the metaphor of romance time as opposed to historical time:

> How fatal every error as to the quantity of time must prove to the introduction of rational views concerning the state of things in former ages, may be conceived by supposing that the annals of the civil and military transactions of a great nation were perused under the impression that they occurred in a period of one hundred instead of two thousand years. Such a portion of history would immediately assume the air of a romance; the events would seem devoid of credibility, and inconsistent with the present course of human affairs. A crowd of incidents would follow each other in thick succession. Armies and fleets would appear to be assembled only to be destroyed, and cities built merely to fall in ruins. (I:78–9)

As in *Tristram Shandy*, the pace of record and of event are here fatally at odds. Uncle Toby and Trim must build up and knock down their fortifications within the hour to catch up with the events in France. Geologists, too parsimonious of time, are obliged to imagine a world governed by catastrophic events which prepare for present tranquillity.

Evolutionary theory is first a form of imaginative history. It cannot be experimentally demonstrated sufficiently in any present moment. So it is closer to narrative than to drama. Indeed in the then current state of genetic knowledge many of the processes of inheritance were beyond explanation. The rediscovery of Mendel's experiments took place after Darwin's death. It took a century before the discovery of DNA demonstrated the organism as a structural narrative programmed to enact itself through time.[11] Evolutionary ideas proved crucial to the novel during that century not only at the level of theme but at the level of organisation. At first evolutionism tended to offer a new authority to orderings of narrative which emphasised cause and effect, then, descent and kin. Later again, its eschewing of fore-ordained design (its dysteleology) allowed chance to figure as the only sure determinant. On the other side, the organisation of *The Origin of Species* seems to owe a good deal to the example of one of Darwin's most frequently read authors, Charles Dickens, with its apparently unruly superfluity of material gradually and retrospectively revealing itself as order, its superfecundity of instance serving an argument which can reveal itself only *through* instance and relations.

Evolutionary ideas shifted in very diverse ways the patterns through which we apprehend experience and hence the patterns through which we condense experience in the telling of it. Evolutionism has been so imaginatively powerful precisely because all its indications do not point one way. It is rich in contradictory elements which can serve as a metaphorical basis for more than one reading of experience: to give one summary example – the 'ascent' or the 'descent' of man may follow the same route but the terms suggest very diverse evaluations of the experience. The optimistic 'progressive' reading of development can never expunge that other insistence that extinction is more probable than progress, that the individual life span is never a sufficient register for change or for the accomplishment of desire, an insistence which has led one recent critic to characterise Darwinian theory as a myth of death.[12]

Darwinian theory will not resolve to a single significance nor yield a single pattern. It is essentially multivalent. It renounces a Descartian clarity, or univocality. Darwin's methods of argument and the generative metaphors of *The Origin* lead, as I shall demonstrate later, into profusion and extension. The unused, or uncontrolled, elements in metaphors such as 'the struggle for existence' take on a life of their own. They surpass their status in the text and generate further ideas and ideologies. They include 'more than the maker of them at the time knew'. The world Darwin proposes can be felt as either plenitude or muddle. Darwin was much wounded by Herschel's description of his theory as 'the law of higgledy-piggledy',[13] but the phrase exactly expresses the dismay many Victorians felt at the apparently random – and so, according to their lights, trivialised – energy that Darwin perceived in the natural world.

Darwinian theory takes up elements from older orders and particularly from recurrent mythic themes such as transformation and metamorphosis. It retains the idea of *natura naturans*, or the Great Mother, in its figuring of Nature. It rearranges the elements of creation myths, for example substituting the ocean for the garden but retaining the idea of the 'single progenitor' – though now an uncouth progenitor hard to acknowledge as kin. It foregrounds the concept of kin – and aroused many of the same dreads as fairy-tale in its insistence on the obligations of kinship, and the interdependence between beauty and beast. Many Victorian rejections of evolutionary ideas register a physical shudder. In its early readers one of the lurking fears it conjured was miscegeny – the frog in the bed – or what Ruskin called 'the filthy heraldries which record the relation of humanity to the ascidian and the crocodile'.[14] In its insistence on chance as part of a deterministic order it perturbed in the same mode as *The Arabian Nights* – though more profoundly, because claiming the authority of science not exotic fiction. The pip thrown over the shoulder strikes the Grand Genie and vengeance ensues. Such tales – and *The Arabian Nights* was at the height of its imaginative influence at that period so that, for example, we find George Eliot one evening enjoying 'music, *Arabian Nights*, and Darwin' – rouse some of the same elated dread as the idea of minute random mutations with their uncontrollable consequences.[15] But Darwin's theories did not pleasurably assuage the dreads.

One of the persistent impulses in interpreting evolutionary theory has been to domesticate it, to colonise it with human meaning, to bring man back to the centre of its intent. Novelists, with their particular preoccupation with human behaviour in society, have recast Darwin's ideas in a variety of ways to make them seem to single out man. In *The Origin of Species* (1859) man is a determining absence, for reasons that I shall analyse in the succeeding chapters. In *The Descent of Man* (1871) man in all his varieties is the topic. The first is a work primarily of biology, the second of anthropology: together they form the substantial statement of Darwin's published views on evolution. Darwin's is a theory of descent as well as of adaptation: in *The Origin* he concentrated on the mechanism of 'natural' (that is, non-human and unwilled) 'selection' in creating change. In *The Descent*[16] he concentrates on the powers of sexual selection: this concentration brings back into the discussion the ideas of will and culture which are notably and deliberately excluded in *The Origin*. Women and men became his problem.

The power of Darwin's writing in his culture is best understood when it is seen not as a single origin or 'source', but in its shifting relations to other areas of study. As Darwin's notebooks, reading-lists, library, and annotations all show, he was immensely alive to concurrent work in a range of disciplines, including not only other directly scientific work but history, historiography, race-theory, psychology, and literature. The problems raised by his writing often manifest themselves most acutely when they are transferred into another field. Equally, his work was profoundly affected by common concerns. An ecological rather than a patriarchal model is most appropriate, therefore, in studying his work.

Darwinian theory has, then, an extraordinary hermeneutic potential – the power to yield a great number of significant and various meanings. In the course of this study I shall show how differing individual and cultural needs have produced deeply felt, satisfying, but contradictory interpretations of its elements. It is, therefore, important at the outset to emphasise that it cannot be made to mean *everything*. Disraeli's satire on Chambers's *Vestiges of Creation*, in *Tancred* where it is renamed 'The Revelations of Chaos', could not apply to Darwin.[17] Of 'The Revelations of Chaos' it is said: 'It explains everything, and is written in a very agreeable style.' Darwinian theory, on the contrary, excludes or suppresses certain orderings of experience. It has no place for *stasis*. It debars return. It does not countenance absolute replication (cloning is its contrary), pure invariant cycle, or constant equilibrium. Nor – except for the extinction of particular species – does it allow either interruption or conclusion.

[. . .]

Fit and misfitting: anthropomorphism and the natural order

Darwin faced four major problems in precipitating his theory as language. Two of them were intrinsic to all discourse. First, language is anthropocentric. It places man at the centre of signification. Even symbol is defined by its referential value and the Symbolist movement of the later nineteenth century might therefore be seen as the last humanist enterprise. Symbols, despite their appearance of independence, take their point of reference from human interpretative power and depend upon their own functions of reference to human concerns.

Second, language always includes agency, and agency and intention are frequently impossible to distinguish in language. Darwin's *theory* depended on the idea of production. The natural order produces itself, and through reproduction it produces both its own continuance and its diversity. His theory had no place for an initiating or intervening creator. Nor for an initiating or intervening author. Yet terms like 'selection' and 'preservation' raise the question, 'By whom or what selected or preserved?' And in his own writing Darwin was to discover the difficulty of distinguishing between description and invention.

Third, he faced a more particular problem concerned with the natural historical discourse he inherited. Natural history was still imbued with natural theology, and salient terms such as 'contrivance' and 'design' were freighted with presumptions of godhead and of pre-emptive patterning.[18] Darwin was therefore obliged to dramatise his struggle with natural theological assumptions within a language weighted towards natural theology. He must write against the grain of his discourse.

We can see the problem of escaping from creationist language very exactly in the changes Darwin made through several editions to passages in which the question of originating forces is unavoidable. Sometimes he makes small emendations which shift into a more openly metaphoric, even misfitting, language: 'since the first creature . . . was created' becomes 'since the first organic beings appeared on the stage' (Peckham: 757). In the conclusion one sentence in the first edition runs thus: 'Therefore I should infer from analogy that probably all the organic beings which have ever lived on this earth have descended from some one primordial form, into which life was first breathed.' The passive 'was breathed' evades the problem. In the second edition he briefly and somewhat surprisingly reinstates the Creator. The sentence now ends, 'into which life was first breathed by the Creator'. In the third edition he changes the whole sentence considerably:

> Therefore, on the principle of natural selection with divergence of character, it does not seem incredible that, from some such low and intermediate form, both animals and plants may have been developed: and, if we admit this, we must admit that all the organic beings which have ever lived on this earth may have descended from some one primordial form. (Peckham: 753)

The sentence ends without raising the question of the beginning of life itself. It is concerned with descent and it specifies and privileges the explanatory and active powers of 'the principle of natural selection with divergence of character'. As he had earlier written, 'It is so easy to hide our ignorance under such expressions as the "plan of creation", "unity of design", etc, and to think that we have given an explanation when we have only restated a fact' (453). In such examples we see Darwin's persisting struggle to reach explanations which can extend the scope of enquiry, rather than resting within the circle of assumption.

The fourth problem of language that Darwin faced was that of addressing himself towards a general readership as well as to his confraternity of scientists. I have already sketched some of the ways in which such a readership dissolved the limits of words familiar in a natural-historical context.

One of Darwin's own concerns was to demonstrate as far as possible the accord between scientific usage and common speech. His interest in etymology established language-history as a more than metaphorical instance of kinships hidden through descent and dissemination.[19] An aspect of his insistence on congruities, and branchings, was his desire to substantise or substantiate metaphor wherever this could be done. He needs to establish ways in which language may be authenticated by natural order, so that his own discourse and argumentation may be 'naturalised', and so moved beyond dispute: 'Our classifications will come to be, as far as they can be so made, genealogies; and will then truly give what may be called the plan of creation' (456). 'The terms used by naturalists of affinity, relationship, community of type, paternity, morphology, adaptive characters, rudimentary and aborted organs, etc., will cease to be metaphorical, and will have a plain signification' (456). This search for 'plain significa-tion', as for 'one primordial form', is the counter-ideal which leads him into a labyrinth of connection, interrelation, and extension.[20]

The difficulties which Darwin experienced in his writing gave lodgement to interpretation, counter-interpretation, expansion, fracture, and renewals of meaning. His is not a sealed or neutralised text. His language does not close itself off authoritatively nor describe its own cir-cumference. And this is not because Darwin was worsted. He sought to move out beyond the false security of authority or even of the assumption that full knowledge may be reached. The nature of his argument led into expansion, transformation, and redundancy of information. The Darwinian world is *always capable of further description*, and such description generates fresh narratives and fresh metaphors which may supplant the initiating account.

[. . .]

Notes

1 Thomas S. Kuhn, *The Structure of Scientific Revolutions* (Chicago, 1962): 52.
2 *Essays of George Eliot*, ed. Thomas Pinney (London, 1963): 44–5.
3 Barry Barnes, *Scientific Knowledge and Sociological Theory* (London, 1974): 166.
4 Paul Ricoeur discusses in general terms the relationships between theory, language and fiction in *Interpretation Theory: Discourse and the Surplus of Meaning* (Fort Worth, Texas, 1976): 67.

> As Max Black puts it, to describe a domain of reality in terms of an imaginary theoretical model is a way of seeing things differently by changing our language about the subject of our investigation. This change of language proceeds from the construction of a heuristic fiction and through the transposition of the characteristics of this heuristic fiction to reality itself . . . Thanks to this detour through the heuristic fiction we perceive new connections among things.

5 Jean-Baptiste Lamarck, *Philosophie zoologique* (Paris, 1809); J. B. Lamarck, *Histoire naturelle des animaux sans vertèbres* (1815–33); Charles Lyell, *The Principles of Geology* (London, 1830–33); Charles Lyell, *The Antiquity of Man* (London, 1864); Robert Chambers, *Vestiges of the Natural History of Creation* (London, 1844). Darwin's opponents resented the identification of evolutionary theory with Darwinism. St John Mivart, for example, in *Man and Apes* (London, 1873): 2 comments on the injustice of 'popular awards':

> Again, the doctrine of evolution as applied to organic life – the doctrine, that is, which teaches that the various new species of animals and plants have manifested themselves through a purely natural process of hereditary succession – is widely spoken of by the term 'Darwinism'. Yet this doctrine is far older than Mr. Darwin, and is held by many who deem that which is truly 'Darwinism' (namely a belief in the origin of species by natural selection) to be a crude and utterly untenable hypothesis.

6 Quotations from *The Origin* in this study are from the first edition except where specified (*On the Origin of Species By Means of Natural Selection, or the Presentation of Favoured Races In the Struggle for Life*, by Charles Darwin, M. A., Fellow of the Royal, Geological, Linaean, etc., Societies; author of 'Journal of Researches During H.M.S. *Beagle*'s Voyage Round the World', London, 1859). Darwin revised the work extensively between 1859 and 1878. These changes are recorded in Morse Peckham's invaluable variorum text (Philadelphia, 1959) and I wish to express my gratitude to him for this work. All subsequent references to his work run (Peckham: page reference). Page references in my text are to the Pelican Classics volume edited with an introduction by John Burrow (Harmondsworth, 1968). This volume prints the text of the first edition.
7 Jacques Barzun, *Darwin, Marx and Wagner* (New York, 1958); Stanley E. Hyman, *The Tangled Bank: Darwin, Marx, Frazer and Freud as Imaginative Writers* (New York, 1962); A. Dwight Culler, 'The Darwinian Revolution and Literary Form', in *The Art of Victorian Prose*, ed. George Levine (London, 1968): 224–6.
8 'There are men who may never have heard of the books or even the name of Darwin, but despite themselves live within the atmosphere created by him and feel its influences.' Francesco De Sanctis, 'Darwinism in Art', 1883, in F. De Sanctis, *Saggi Critici* (Bari, 1953): 3:355–67.
9 Richard Ohmann, 'Prolegomena to the Analysis of Prose Style', in *Style in Prose Fiction*, English Institute Essays, ed. H. Martin (New York, 1959): 23. See also Wolfgang Iser, *The Act of Reading: a Theory of Aesthetic Response* (London, 1978).
10 All volume and page references to Lyell are to the first edition of *The Principles of Geology* (London, 1830–3).
11 In 1970 Francis Crick specified the problems remaining in molecular biology as:

> a detailed understanding of the replication of DNA and of the unwinding process; the structure of chromosomes, the meaning of the nucleic acid sequences which are not merely the expression of the genetic code but are used for stopping or starting or control mechanisms of one sort or another; the significance of repetitive sequences in DNA; and so on . . . (*Nature*, 280: (1970):615).

12 Michel Serres, *Feux et signaux de brume: Zola* (Paris, 1975).
13 Charles Darwin to Charles Lyell, 12 December 1859, in *Life and Letters of Charles Darwin*, ed. Francis Darwin (London, 1887): 2:37.

14   John Ruskin, *Love's Meinie* (Keston, Kent, 1873): 59.

15   *The George Eliot Letters*, ed. Gordon Haight (London, 1956): 2:109–10. In Notebook 119 Darwin records reading 'some Arabian Nights' in 1840.

16   *The Descent of Man, and Selection in Relation to Sex*, 2 vols. (London, 1870–1).

17   Benjamin Disraeli. *Tancred* (London, 1847).

18   See Neil Gillespie, *Charles Darwin and the Problem of Creation* (Chicago, 1979). Gillespie argues tellingly for Darwin's theism by means of an analysis of his creationist language. See also Pierre Macherey, *Pour une théorie de la production littéraire* (Paris, 1966), or *A Theory of Literary Production*, tr. G. Wall (London, 1978). Macherey polemically substitutes production for creation and argues many of the same difficulties as Darwin without apparently recognising the connection with him. The conceptual mediator is Marx.

19   Darwin pointed out that classification in the case of languages was necessarily genealogical. By the 1870s the evolutionist reading of language development was the prevailing view. See the Müller–George Darwin controversy in the *Contemporary Review*, vols. 25, 26, 27 (1875), especially W. D. Whitney, 'Are Languages Institutions?': 'It is the prevailing belief that the world is filled everywhere with families of related dialects, and that a family of languages, as of individuals or of races, arises by the dispersion and differentiation of a unitary stock' (25: 713–14) and A. H. Joyce, 'The Jelly-fish Theory of Language', (27: 713–23). Compare Darwin's cousin Hensleigh Wedgwood, *The Origin of Language* (London, 1866) and his *Dictionary of English Etymology* (London, 1859–67). Wedgwood held that 'the natural origin of language' was imitative and that this 'accounts for these striking coincidences which are occasionally found in the most remote languages, irrespective of the question whether the common forms of speech are the lingering remnants of a common ancestry'. See also Edward Manier, *The Young Darwin and his Cultural Circle* (Dordrecht, 1978). For further discussion of the analogy between language development and Darwinian evolutionism see below pp. 112–114. A work which develops the connections between humanism, language, and science is Jacques Derrida, *Of Grammatology*, tr. G. Spivak (Baltimore, 1974): grammatology 'ought not to be *one of the sciences of man* because it asks first, as its characteristic question, the question of the name of man' (83). See esp. 'The Supplement of (at) the Origin' (313–16).

20   Hayden White, 'The Fictions of Factual Representation' in *The Literature of Fact*, ed. A. Fletcher (New York, 1976): 21–44 takes Darwin to be a bare empiricist unwittingly betrayed into metaphor. This view leads him to misrepresent Darwin's attitude to analogy. White comments: 'Analogy, he says again and again, is always a deceitful guide' (38). Darwin does no such thing. He demurs at dependence on analogy but uses it as an argumentative tool precisely because it is essential to his *theory* of common descent:

> Analogy would lead me one step further, namely, to the belief that all animals and plants have descended from some one prototype. But analogy may be a deceitful guide. Nevertheless all living things have much in common . . . Therefore I should infer from analogy that probably all the organic beings which have ever lived on this earth have descended from some one primordial form. (455)

22 Dickens and Darwin

George Levine

[. . .]

On the issue of teleology Dickens tried not to be Darwinian. In novels so chance-ridden as his, one would expect to find real compatibility with Darwin, whose theory posited a world without design, generated out of chance variations. But since Darwinian variation occurs without reference to need, environment, or end, Darwin's chance is antiteleological. Contrarily, in traditional narrative of the sort Dickens wrote, chance serves the purpose not of disorder, but of meaning—from Oedipus slaying his father to the catastrophic flood at the end of *The Mill on the Floss*. The order "inside" the fiction might be disrupted—Oedipus's reign, or the life of Maggie—but the larger order of the narrative depends on such disruptions.

The difference might best be indicated by the fact that while both Dickens and Darwin describe worlds in which chance encounters among the myriad beings who populate them are characteristic, for Dickens chance is a dramatic expression of the value and ultimate order in nature, and it belongs recognizably to a tradition that goes back to Oedipus. Each coincidence leads characters appropriately to catastrophe or triumph and suggests a designing hand that sets things right in the course of nature. The "contrivances" in Darwin, however, though they tend to move the species toward its current state of adaptation or extinction, appear to be undesigned. Chance in nature drains it of meaning and value. The variations even in domestic animals, carefully bred, are inexplicable. Only close attention of a breeder, who discards variations he doesn't want, leads to the appearance of design. But the breeder is entirely dependent on the accidents of variation. Darwin and Dickens in a way tell the same story, yet the implications are reversed.

Working in a theatrical and literary tradition, Dickens must use apparent chance to create a story with a beginning, a middle, and an end. And it is a story much like that told by natural theologians, which makes "chance" part of a larger moral design, thus effectively denying its chanciness by making it rationally explicable in terms of a larger structure. The feeling of coincidence is merely local. Such manipulation is a condition of storytelling, where "chance" must always contradict the implications of the medium itself. Even in narratives that seem to emphasize the power of chance over human design, narrative makes chance impossible. Design is intrinsic to the language of storytelling, with its use of a narrative past tense. "Once upon a time" already implies design. Moreover, the focus of narrative attention on particular characters makes everything that happens in the narrative relate to them. It may be that the relation is a negative one: the character, like Micawber, waits for something to turn up, and it never does; but in the end, of course, Micawber has been in the right place at the right time, and while the narrator might applaud Micawber's sudden energy, what happened is not because he chose it. At the same time, the narrative certainly did choose it, both because it in fact helps Micawber achieve the condition to which he has always aspired, and because it allows the exposure of Uriah Heep and the righting of all the wrongs with which that part of the story has been concerned. Ultimately, it is all for the sake of David Copperfield as the happy resolutions of *Mansfield Park* are for Fanny.

Chance in narrative has at least two contradictory aspects. When Eliot's narrator condemns "Favourable Chance" in *Silas Marner*, she is among other things suggesting (what Darwin would have agreed to) that the world is not designed for any individual's interest. What Godfrey or Dunstan wants has no more to do with the way the world operates than what the giraffe wants. The giraffe's long neck does not develop because he wants it, but because longer-necked giraffes had on the whole survived better than shorter-necked ones. Nothing is going to shorten the trees for any given giraffe; nothing, presumably, will put gold in Dunstan's hands or rid Godfrey of his wife. Dickens, I believe, would subscribe to this way of seeing, although his attacks on chance are less obvious and direct. Yet in *Silas Marner* all the major events are the result of "chance."[1] The narrative does not make credible a necessary connection between the events and the behavior of the characters, nor does it try. The fabular structure of the story is outside the realistic mode that the expressed sentiments of the narrator affirm. In being much more self-consciously a "tale," and less a "realistic" representation of the world in all its complexity, *Silas Marner* exposes boldly what is usually more disguised in realistic fiction, where the necessary "coincidences" are normally made to appear natural and causally related.

The "chance" events in *Silas Marner* self-consciously work out a parable (complex as it becomes), in which they all reflect moral conditions and shadow forth a world in which the principle of nemesis, works, in which we bear moral responsibility for what we do; and that moral responsibility is worked out in nature and society. The effect of the narrative is to convey the sense that the "chance" events were determined by a designing power, intrinsic to nature itself, that used to be called God.

Narrative, it is assumed, is different from life, however, and presumably "real" coincidences would not imply the design of some "author." But any language used to describe events will turn into narrative and import design once more. Sudden catastrophes invariably evoke the question, "Why?" "Why did he have to die?" The question implies that there are "reasons" beyond the physiological and that the explanation, he was hit by a car, or his heart stopped, is not satisfactory or complete. What moral end was served? Where is the justice in the death? Or, if catastrophe is avoided, the language is full of "luck," the remarkable luck that we canceled off the plane that crashed, and the accompanying sense that we weren't "meant" to die yet. Often, others' catastrophes inspire guilt, as though the survivors are responsible, or could have managed to swap positions had they the courage. Even in trivial affairs, this tendency of ordinary language is powerful. We talk about bad weather as though it were designed to ruin our one day off, or we carry umbrellas and half believe that this will trick the rain away.

Such anthropocentric language is characteristic of natural theology, and Dickens does not resist it. But Dickens still uses chance to project a world governed by a great designer, even if he often has difficulty doing so. Putting aside the random abundance of the earlier works, we find that the self-consciously less episodic and more thematically coherent later novels use mysterious and apparently inexplicable details for the sake of human significance. Inevitably, Dickens does produce a Darwinian excess, which he needs to ignore or compress into order to achieve the comfort of significance; but his plotting is determined by the illumination and intelligible explanation of *apparently* random detail. The collapse of Mrs. Clennam's house is both literal and figurative, of course. Oliver's innocence is preserved and triumphant. Carker is crushed by the new railway, which we earlier learned opens for all to see the ugliness and misery of London. Dickensian narrative derives much of its energy from the gradual revelation of the design that incorporates all accidents, just as Herschelian science derives its energy from the attempt to explain all of the minutest natural phenomena in terms of general law. Characters struggle to discover its existence, and to work out its particular meaning, while the reader is always several steps ahead of the characters and several behind the author. We know that there is meant to be nothing chancy about Dickensian chance.[2]

Whereas Dickens, then, could exploit the metaphorical implications of language with confidence in its power to reveal design, Darwin had to resist language's intentionality and implications of design in order to describe a world merely there—without design or meaning. We have seen how in the very act of developing his theory and rejecting arguments from design he fell into the metaphorical and storytelling structures of the language to talk about "Natural Selection" as a "being." But the development of genetic variations, as Waddington points out, is not causally connected with the selective process that will determine whether the variations survive. In narrative terms this suggests that there can be no moral explanation, no superphysical "justification" of the development. The gene and its phenotype develop regardless of their narrative context. Such a separation drains nature of its moral significance and links Darwinism with the realist project that Dickens resisted even as he more than half participated in it. The matter of chance and teleology constituted the core of Dickens's defense, his attempt to keep nature from being merely neutral.

But Dickens did not reject science in order to resist that cold neutrality. It was Darwin, most effectively, who split scientific from theological discourse on this issue: science would not allow any "explanation" that depended on unknown principles that might be invoked, erratically, whenever empirical investigation failed. Scientific faith in law need not extend to scientific belief in the good intentions of the natural world. Dickens, like Darwin, would exclude mere caprice from the universe, but Darwinian "law" might well be regarded as capricious from the human point of view.

Yet another essay in *All the Year Round* provides a typical Victorian affirmation of the value of science, which grows from "Patience," while "Magic," its ancient forebear in the quest for meaning and control, is based on "Credulity." For science to emerge, the essay argues, "the phenomena of Nature, at least all the most ordinary phenomena, must have been disengaged from this conception of an arbitrary and *capricious* power, similar to human will, and must have been recognized as *constant*, always succeeding each other with fatal regularity."[3] These are certainly principles to which Darwin, like Lyell and Herschel before him, would have subscribed. The writer here, in eagerness to dispel "caprice," is not considering the full human implications of this apparently unimpeachable, modern, scientific position. In narrative, ironically, the ultimate effect of the "scientific" view of order and regularity is that the world begins to feel humanly erratic. That is, it becomes a fatalistic or deterministic world, like Hardy's, in which events do indeed develop inexorably from the slow accumulation of causes; yet they are, from the human perspective, entirely a matter of chance, because they are not subject to the control either of will or consciousness. Such a world is not, strictly, disordered, but it is, as Mayr has argued, probabilistic: "No one will ever understand natural selection until he realizes, that it is a statistical phenomenon."[4] Not only does it work regardless of the interests of individual members of the population, but its working can only be described statistically, without explanation of why in any case or in the majority of cases, things develop as they do. Natural selection is humanly meaningless. Narrative forces what abstract discourse can avoid, a recognition of the difficulty and potential self-contradictoriness of the very ideas of chance and order.

The radical difference between Darwin and Dickens, despite Dickens's predisposition both to science and to the overall Darwinian vision, is simply in that Darwin's "laws" have no moral significance. Although they can be adapted for moral purposes (and were, immediately and continuingly), they do not answer questions like "Why?" except in physical or probabilistic terms. Birds can carry seeds in their talons, or deposit them thousands of miles away in their excrement. But what design is there in these particular seeds, these particular species making the trip? Why did the bird eat this plant rather than that, travel to this island rather than that? Survival in Darwin's nature is not *morally* significant. Adaptiveness is not designed, being the mere adjustment of the organism to its particular environment, and it has no direction. There is no perfection in Darwin's world, no intelligent design, no purpose. Fact may not be converted to meaning.[5]

This is a very tough sort of "chance," and its toughness evoked resistance from scientists as well as writers and theologians. In Dickens, while Darwinian chance threatens almost instinctively to overwhelm order, chance largely derives from another tradition, the one, in fact, that Darwin was self-consciously combatting. His novels tend to act out the arbitrariness of the connections they want to suggest are natural (and in that unintended sense, even here they are Darwinian). Dickens tries to tie event to meaning in a way that removes from chance its edge of inhumanity. This is the very tradition that Darwin identifies when, in *The Descent of Man*, he explains why he had perhaps overestimated the power of natural selection in the early editions of the *Origin*: "I was not able to annul the influence of my former belief, then widely prevalent, that each species had been purposely created; and this led to my tacitly assuming that every detail of structure, excepting rudiments, was of some special, though unrecognised, service" (I, 15[3]).[6] Every detail, on that earlier model, means something. Insofar as Dickens's later novels begin to suggest a chasm between event and meaning (delicately intimated in the "usual uproar" that concludes *Little Dorrit*), Dickens moves, like the later Darwin, away from the natural-theological tradition that had dominated his imaginative vision.

It is perhaps a measure of how far Dickens has traveled from Austen's way of seeing, however, that even where he persists in the contrivances of coincidence, their discontinuity with the worlds he is creating is disturbing. Such discontinuity is particularly striking in *Little Dorrit* and *Our Mutual Friend*. In most cases, while there are no naturalistic laws by which to account for the "chances" in Dickens's novels, coincidence feels too often like a matter of the conventions of narrative. Of course, Lady Dedlock *must* die at the gate of the wretched source of all plagues, where Jo had given off one ray of light in his gratitude to the now dead Nemo. The characters cannot perceive the design, but it is really there. Still, though there are scientific laws that make the development of organisms intelligible, the comfort of intelligibility does not lead to the comfort of meaning and purpose: in Darwin's world, it is random.

Darwin could get nowhere with his theory as long as language was taken to imply an essential reality it merely named. As Gillian Beer points out, in this respect, as with the question of chance, Darwin was forced to use a language that resisted the implications of his argument. Language, she says, "always includes agency, and agency and intention are frequently impossible to distinguish in language."[7] Yet more generally, to borrow a page from Derrida, language implies "presence." It assumes an originary reality ultimately accessible. Here as elsewhere, Darwin avoided epistemology to stick to his biological business, and here again he was forced to resist the implications of the language with which he made his arguments.

I have shown how at the center of his theory is a redefinition of the word "species," by which he almost undefined it. Species can have no Platonic essence, and Darwin was content to use the word as others used it, while demonstrating that species could be nothing but time-bound and perpetually transforming aggregations of organisms, all of which are individually different. For the most part, Darwin tried to do without a definition of species at all, for a definition would have got him into the kinds of serious difficulties already discussed, leading to the view that his book, as Louis Agassiz claimed, was about nothing: if "species" is merely an arbitrary term not corresponding to anything in nature, then *The Origin of Species* is about nothing.

Definition would have implied an essentialist view of the world, one entirely compatible with natural theology, and incompatible with evolution by natural selection. Essentialism, as Mayr has noted, implies a "belief in discontinuous, immutable essences,"[8] and this belief is reenforced by the reifying nouns characteristic of our language. John Beatty, in a revision of his argument that Darwin in fact was denying the existence of species, points out that Darwin could "use the term 'species' in a way that agreed with the use of the term by his contemporaries, but not in a way that agreed with his contemporaries' *definitions* of the term."[9] Darwin was not a poststructuralist and would not have argued that there is nothing out there to correspond to his language. But he knew he would have been paralyzed by accepting the definitions of "species" current among fellow naturalists. Recall that when Darwin talks of the "something more" naturalists think is implied by the natural system, he is working with their general nonevolutionary understanding of "natural system" and classifications within it; what he does, to follow Beatty's point, is accept their usage but not their definition so that he can replace the essentialist "something more" with the "hidden bond" of "propinquity of descent."

Essentialism was the enemy of evolutionary thinking, creating the greatest obstacle to conceptions of change. Mayr singles out Platonic essentialism, "the belief in constant *eide*, fixed ideas, separate from and independent of the phenomena of appearance," as having had "a particularly deleterious impact on biology through the ensuing two thousand years." Essentialism made it almost impossible to name a *kind* of animal—say, horse—without implying both its permanence and the "real" nature of its identity in all important qualities with all other horses, regardless of its merely accidental, that is, its particular physical and living characteristics. "Genuine change, according to essentialism" notes Mayr, "is possible only through the saltational origin of new essences,"[10] and clearly Darwin, for whom nature made no leaps, found essentialism a large obstruction.[11]

In plotting and characterization, change (as I have earlier said) was Dickens's greatest difficulty. His narratives and his characters seem to belong to a saltational world. For the narratives do make leaps, and when characters change they often do so (particularly in the earlier work) through abrupt conversion, as, for example, Scrooge. As opposed to a realist like Eliot, who writes from within a tradition much more clearly related to Darwinian thought and to the advanced science and psychology of the time, and whose narrator claims that "character is not cut in marble," Dickens writes out of an essentialist tradition. Barbara Hardy has pointed out that his novels rarely escape some tinge of the tradition of the *Bildungsroman*, but Dickens's use of that tradition of character development and change rarely explores the slow processes by which characters in that tradition learn and grow.[12]

Typically, Dickensian characters behave as though they had single, discoverable selves that constitute their essence. Mr. Jarndyce is a good and generous man, all of whose strategies in the world are designed to reaffirm that goodness. To be sure, this also entails a certain deviousness, for if he is to accept congratulations on his goodness, he can no longer regard himself as disinterested. But this ambivalence is built into his essence, and one of his most characteristic self-expressions is his complaint about the wind being in the East, which signals either bad news or the self-division that comes when he is about to receive praise or gratitude. So it is, in other ways, with most of Dickens's characters, who have been criticized through the years by critics seeking more fluid, complex, unstable, and I would say Darwinian, "selves."

The essentialist nature of Dickens's imagination is perhaps most evident in the clarity with which he usually distinguishes goodness and badness. Dickens's tendency is to read character into these categories, even when by virtue of his extraordinary sympathetic imagination he creates sequences like that of Sikes on the run or Fagin in prison, which shift our perspective on the melodramatic narrative. But the moral borders are firmly drawn. As Leo Bersani has observed, "In Dickens, the mental faculties dramatized in allegory are concealed behind behavior which *represents* those faculties. And the critical method appropriate to this literary strategy is one which treats the words and acts of literary characters as signs of the allegorical entities which make up these characters."[13] In this respect Dickens is most distant from Darwin and realism. Eliot's emphasis on mixed conditions, mixed natures, and her virtual incapacity (until Grandcourt in *Daniel Deronda*) to create a figure of unequivocal evil, fairly represents the difference. Dickens, writing within the "metaphysical mode" as Edward Eigner defines it, is heavily dependent on plot and emphasizes the external rather than the internal, but only because he counts on the adequacy of the natural to express meaning. In keeping with the natural-theological tradition, the emphasis on the external itself depends on strong confidence in the legibility of the material world, its expression of spiritual and moral realities comprehensible to those who choose to see. Ironically, when the world is secularized, as in the Darwinian scheme, narrative must turn inward because the material world becomes increasingly unintelligible. In Dickens, whom I have been characterizing as essentialist, there is visible a growing inability to be satisfied with the essentialist imagination.

The process of making narrative more literal by turning from allegorical representation to psychological mimesis under the pressures of secularization parallels the strategies Darwin uses in breaking with essentialism. One of the great Christian metaphors, and one of the central concerns of Victorian writers, becomes in Darwin a literal fact: we are all one family. Not the idea, but physical inheritance connects all living organisms. The move severed event from meaning (in a way contrary to Dickens's largely allegorical use of event) and destabilized all apparently permanent values by thrusting them into nature and time. Essentialism and nominalism were, therefore, no merely abstract metaphysical problems. On the whole, common sense and tradition required a world in which the ultimate realities remained outside time, and in which an ideal essence (as opposed to biological inheritance) defined the self. The concept of "character" itself implies such an essence.

The implications of this distinction extend into every aspect of narrative art. The essentialist mode is, for the most part, metaphorical. On the one hand, it depends on the likeness between physical and moral states, and the Dickensian emphasis on the physical peculiarities belongs to such a metaphorical tradition. On the other hand, the nominalist position, like Darwin's, severs the physical from the moral, and Darwin begins to make the connection metonymically. That is, in *The Expression of the Emotions in Man and Animals*, Darwin tries to read feeling from expression. But his reading is predominantly physiological. For example:

> Although . . . we must look at weeping as an incidental result, as purposely as the secretion of tears from a blow outside the eye, or as a sneeze from the retina being affected by a bright light, yet this does not present any difficulty in our understanding how the secretion of tears serves as a relief of suffering. And by as much as the weeping is more violent or hysterical, by so much will the relief be greater—on the same principle that the writhing of the whole body, the grinding of the teeth, and the uttering of piercing shrieks, all give relief under an agony of pain.[14]

Just as, for Darwin, organisms are connected by physical inheritance, so moral and emotional states are expressed by physiological activity directed at physical defense and relief. All those aspects of human identity and experience that are traditionally regarded as uniquely human, connected with spiritual states unavailable to lower organisms, are in fact physical conditions shared by other organisms. Darwin had observed monkeys in zoos, for example, to discover whether "the contraction of the orbicular muscles" was similarly connected with "violent expiration and the secretion of tears." He notes that elephants sometimes weep and contract their orbicular muscles! Of course, novelists in the realist tradition did not need to accept Darwin's extension of the "uniquely" human to the rest of the natural world, but their emphasis on close analysis of character, increasingly from the inside, corresponded to a decreasing (but never extinguished) reliance on the conformity of physical and moral states, of the sort so characteristic of Dickens.

Nevertheless, Dickens's fiction does participate in the move toward a Darwinian imagination of the world, a growing uncertainty about the notion of an "essential" self or about the possibility of detecting the moral through the physical (a quest that is increasingly professionalized, requiring a Bucket to do the work); and he is thematically urgent about the need for change. Abruptness remains characteristic, yet his preoccupation with the slow but inevitable movements in nature toward change, and with the consequences of refusing it is something more than a throwback to old comic literary traditions. It is as though he accepts uniformitarianism but rejects the gradualism that Lyell imposed upon it; like Darwin he seems to be reconciling the progressivism of catastrophism with the naturalism of uniformitarianism. Several of his most wonderful narratives focus on this problem: Mrs. Skewton in *Dombey and Son*, Miss Havisham in *Great Expectations*, and Mrs. Clennam all succumb to the forces of change their whole lives would have denied. And yet the very figures Dickens uses to thematize change are static (essentialist in conception) and require extravagances of plot to force them into time. They dwell in worlds not where change evolves slowly through time, but where it comes catastrophically, through melodrama, revelation, conversion. In a world of Bagstock and Barnacle, Captain Cuttle and Flora Finching, Mr. Toots and Mr. Merdle, it is hard to imagine that each of us does not have some essential, inescapable selfhood. But Clennam, Sidney Carton, and John Harmon, not to speak of Pip and Eugene Wrayburn, all flirt with doubts about the self so profound that they verge on self-annihilation. Each of them either literally or metaphorically dies, almost as though it were suicide. The question of change, even of the reality of the self, moves from the periphery to the center of Dickens's art and brings him to the edge of the Darwinian world, which feels like a threat, but can also, as for Clennam, be a liberation.

[. . .]

Notes

1 Two recent essays discuss this contradiction in the novel. The form of the novel itself seems to run counter to expressed narrative intent. This problem deserves yet fuller treatment. See Susan R. Cohen, "A History and a Metamorphosis: Continuity and Discontinuity in *Silas Marner*," *Texas Studies in Literature and Language*, 25 (Fall 1983): 410–446; Donald Hawes, "Chance in *Silas Marner*," *English*, 31 (1982): 213–218.

2 "The effect of Dickens's characteristic method," says Harland Nelson, "is an impression of an all-pervading design in human affairs, unexpectedly encompassing and harmonizing the profusely various elements of the story; not (as in a novel by Collins) an impression of an unbroken chain of events, unobtrusively laid down and given a final shake to bring the whole linked series at once into view" ("Dickens's Plots: 'The Ways of Providence' or the Influence of Collins?" *Victorian Newsletter*, 19,

1961: 11). But the strain to make the harmony is evident in the great novels, and the ways of providence or of natural theology are often challenged by the methods designed to affirm them.

3 Charles Dickens, "Magic and Science," *All the Year Round* (March 23, 1861): 562.

4 [Ernst] Mayr, [*Evolution and t*]*he Diversity of Life*[*: Selected Essays* (Cambridge, Mass.: Harvard University Press, 1976)], p. 37.

5 [Edward] Manier's summary of Darwin's views on the wars of nature that help further natural selection demonstrates how inappropriate moral and generalizing application of Darwinian theory was:

> Success in these wars of organic being could *not* be traced to variations which were *favorable* in some *absolute* sense; on the contrary, a variation must be understood to be *successful in relation* to some particular segment of the range of alternative variations, and in the context of the chances of life which happened to be available in the given physical circumstances or conditions. Such expression as "chance offspring" or "round of chances" alluded to the complexity of the predictions used in Darwin's hypothesis, and implied that this complexity could not be reduced in the way that Newton had reduced the complexity of planetary motion by formulating a few generally applicable laws. (*The Young Darwin* [*and his Cultural Circle* (Dordrecht: Reidel, 1978)], pp. 121–122)

6 Charles Darwin, *The Descent of Man and Selection in Relation to Sex* (Princeton: Princeton University Press, 1981).

7 [Gillian] Beer, *Darwin's Plots*[*:Evolutionary Narrative in Darwin, George Eliot, and Nineteenth-Century Fiction* (London: Routledge and Kegan Paul, 1983)], p. 53.

8 Mayr, *The Diversity of Life*, p. 283.

9 [John] Beatty, "Speaking of Species," [*Darwinian Heritage*, ed. David Kohn (Princeton: Princeton University Press, 1986)], 265.

10 [Ernst] Mayr, *The Growth of Biological Thought*[*:Diversity, Evolution, and Inheritance* (Cambridge, Mass.: Harvard University Press, 1982)], pp. 304–305, 38.

11 Darwin was not totally consistent in his rejection of essentialism. Not only is such consistency impossible given the nature of our language, but Darwin could himself employ arguments that imply an essentialist reality. This is particularly so when, under the pressure of antievolutionary arguments, he revises the *Origin* in later editions and makes many more concessions on the inheritance of acquired characteristics. Daniel Simberloff emphasizes the importance of the rejection of essentialist typology in the Darwinian revolution and points to various Darwinian ideas that nevertheless revert to essentialism. See "A Succession of Paradigms in Ecology: Essentialism to Materialism and Probabilism," *Synthese*, 43 (1980): 3–29, where he cites Richard Lewontin in arguing that Darwin's belief in the blending (not particularistic) theory of inheritance is "readily traced to [his] attachment to essentialist, typological thought." Darwin was hampered by his lack of knowledge of genetics and of Mendelian theory, which made evident that inheritance was not a blending but a 1:2:1 distribution of genetic materials, some of which would not be visible in the parent. Simberloff also notes Lewontin's description of Darwin's "retreat to idealism or essentialism" in his theory of "pangenesis," for the hypothetical "gemmules" are "egregiously ideal essence-conferring entities" (pp. 6–7). See also R. D. Lewontin, "Darwin and Mendel—the Materialist Revolution," in *The Heritage of Copernicus: Theories "More Pleasing to the Mind,"* ed. J. Neyman (Cambridge, Mass.: MIT Press, 1974), pp. 166–183.

12 Barbara Hardy, "*Martin Chuzzlewit*," in *Dickens and the Twentieth Century*, ed. John Gross and Gabriel Pearson (Toronto: University of Toronto Press, 1962), pp. 107–120. Hardy points out that the abruptness of Martin's conversion is typical of Dickens: "There is no point in comparing Dickens's conversions here with the slow and often eddying movement traced in George Eliot or Henry James. But I think this change is even more abrupt in exposition, relying heavily on compressed rhetoric, than the fairly abrupt conversions of David Copperfield or Bella Wilfer, though the important difference lies in the context of dramatized moral action. Dombey, Steerforth, Gradgrind, Pip, and other major and minor examples of flawed character—not necessarily changing—are demonstrated in appropriate action, large and small" (p. 114). Hardy is criticizing not the abruptness but the way the abrupt change is dramatized and contextualized. The Dickensian mode of change, belonging to a very different tradition, has its own constraints.

13 [Leo] Bersani, *A Future for Astyanax*[*:Character and Desire in Literature* (New York: Columbia University Press, 1982)], p. 18.

14 Charles Darwin, *The Expression of the Emotions in Man and Animals* (1872; repr., Chicago: University of Chicago Press, 1965), p. 175.

23 Conversations on creation

James Secord

[. . .]

Early in January 1845, Lady Amelia Murray—artist, philanthropist, and maid of honor to Queen Victoria—was invited to a party given by her old friend, Lady Noel Byron. The scene at such a gathering is familiar to us from countless film and television adaptations of contemporary novels—for our culture has inherited the Victorians' fascination with high Society.[1] Gentlemen are wearing fitted black tailcoats, ladies are corseted in dresses of exquisite embroidered silk, taffeta, and ribbons. The colors in fashion are light—delicate shades of rose, sky blues, and pale golds—and the candlelit rooms airy and uncluttered, with guests conversing in animated groups. Music and the mingled scents of wax, punch, and perfume fill the air. The conversation, however, is a surprise. Lady Murray and the other guests are talking about science—about cosmic evolution. Throughout fashionable London, from Buckingham Palace to intimate parties like those at Lady Byron's, the most powerful men and women in the country would be discussing *Vestiges*.

The early editions appeared to target this select readership, not the lower middle classes with which the book later became associated. Copies were presented to leading gentlemen's clubs and to progressive-minded politicians and genteel men of science. The first reviews appeared just as the literary season was getting under way in the late autumn, and during the next four months celebrity was secured. Yet until mid-February 1845 only 1,750 copies were in existence, which makes it possible to infer the broad outlines of the readership and its use of the book. Observers of the London scene had parties like this one very much in mind when they reported that *Vestiges* was "much talked of at present."[2]

Because historians so often view London as the national stage, a local perspective is applied only to events that happened elsewhere. Yet its streets were just as idiosyncratic, with their own sights and smells, as those of any other town. The *Vestiges* controversy affords a prime opportunity for exploring the geographies of reading, both in London itself and throughout the British Isles. Victorian towns and cities were defined through the character of their literary life, which was in turn shaped by industrial structure, class, population size, and tradition. Metropolis differed from province, north from south, York from Leeds, Manchester from Liverpool. Some cities were celebrated for scientific institutions and the eminence of their savants. Others failed to develop any continuous intellectual tradition, worshipping instead what the art critic John Ruskin called "the great Goddess of 'getting on.'"[3]

Reading and the culture of print occupied a key place in civic definition. Most towns of any size had at least one newspaper, often more, together with bookshops, circulating libraries, and literary societies where new publications could be debated and discussed. What happened after parcels of *Vestiges* arrived at the rail stations that were springing up across the country? What role did the book have in the ferocious religious disputes of Edinburgh or Liverpool, or in polite conversation at London soirées? How could it be vilified at Cambridge, but read as supporting a new kind of science at Oxford? Even perceptions of what it might mean to participate in a national controversy differed from place to place. "One ought to try and see the local districts," the traveler Hippolyte Taine wrote, "for it is not possible to understand the social fabric properly until one has studied three or four of its component threads in detail."[4]

To address these issues, the history of reading can best begin as local history. We start in the West End of London [. . .], celebrated for its role in initiating fashion.

[. . .]

Books, like everything from clothes to political news, were part of a culture based on fashion. Tastes in reading changed as quickly as the latest Paris hats, and it became as unthinkable to talk about last year's books as to wear last year's cravat or cut of sleeve [. . .]. At lavish soirées in Mayfair and Belgravia, new books were laid out on tables to serve as conversation pieces. Besides *Vestiges*, the major titles in 1844–45 included the anonymous *Eöthen, or Traces of Travel Brought Home from the East*, a subtle account of a refined sensibility in a region of diplomatic and religious importance; Charles Lyell's *Travels in North America*, which mixed scientific discussions with impressions of society, manners, and education; and Arthur Penrhyn Stanley's biography of the educator Thomas Arnold. Poetry readers welcomed Richard Monckton Milnes's *Palm Leaves*, like *Eöthen* appealing to the rising tide of orientalism, and Elizabeth Barrett's *Poems*. It was a poor season for novels, with *Martin Chuzzlewit* by general agreement having been a less powerful performance than Dickens's earlier works. The same author's *Chimes*, however, was the big Christmas book. The most discussed novel was Disraeli's political *Sybil, or the Two Nations*, which went through three editions in the year. Many of these works were concerned with defining the bonds that might (or might not) hold industrial society together. By the 1840s, reading was typically a silent, solitary act, but the object of reading was social—to maintain relations through civil conversation.

Within weeks of publication, *Vestiges* had become a major talking point. As one diplomat wrote from the Foreign Office in November 1844, "We have a topic here that brings up many lively discussions."[5] Taking just those who borrowed the book from the London Library, which was conveniently located in the West End, the registers show the names of Sir Herbert Compton, Lord De l'Isle, Sir Edmund Head, Major General Sir Charles Pasley, Sir Harry Verney, and dozens of others from the upper strata of metropolitan Society. The duke of Somerset and Lord Morpeth marveled at the "noise" the book had made; Sir John Cam Hobhouse noted that "the book is very remarkable & has produced & must produce a great sensation."[6]

Just how effectively *Vestiges* could serve as a counter in fashionable conversation was shown at a dinner party at Sir William Heathcote's country residence in February 1845. This was a glittering affair, with fancy plate, many courses, and a servant for each guest. The dinner introduced the family of William Edward Nightingale to Alexander Baring, the first Lord Ashburton, and his wife. Baron Ashburton was a leading Tory diplomat; his American wife, Anne Louisa, was from a prominent Philadelphia family. She sat next to the twenty-four-year-old daughter of the Nightingales, Florence, and despite differences in age and status, the two found much to talk about. Nightingale reported the conversation in a self-consciously "clever" letter to one of her regular correspondents, probably her sister.

Nightingale and Lady Ashburton began by talking about Boston, upon which they "swore eternal friendship." Since Nightingale had never crossed the Atlantic, this implied a one-sided conversation: "I having, you know, much curious information to give *her* on that city and its inhabitants." She pretended to be fascinated instead by "a raspberry-tart of diamonds" (raspberries being a slangy reference to the aristocracy) on Lady Ashburton's forehead. Their talk then turned to mesmerism, a topic in the newspapers since the celebrated invalid Harriet Martineau announced that she had been cured in a trance. Mesmerism opened up possibilities for discussing the boundaries of consciousness and knowledge; it also placed women in unprecedented positions of authority, an issue that became central to Nightingale's campaign to create new feminine roles through the manipulation of domestic stereotypes.[7]

Mesmerism led to *Vestiges*. The powers of mind revealed by mesmerism might be one indication that what the book had said was true—that the present race might be succeeded, by "a nobler type of humanity."[8] As Nightingale wrote in her letter, "when we parted, we had got up so high into *Vestiges* that I could not get down again, and was obliged to go off as an angel."[9] In keeping with her ironic tone, Nightingale implied that such lofty matters sat oddly in the opulent context of "such a dinner and such plate as has seldom blessed my housekeeping eyes."[10] Angelic transport was the only escape. This again was a reference to *Vestiges*, which suggested that angels would follow humans in the evolutionary sequence. Nightingale was drawing out the increasingly dominant stereotype of the ideal wife as an "angel in the home," while implying that such lavish dinners were wasteful.[11] As she wrote in another letter, "Is all that china, linen, glass necessary to make man a Progressive animal?"[12]

The formality of such a dinner meant that nothing beyond an acquaintanceship could be formed; Nightingale's reference to "eternal friendship" is (like everything else in her letter) ironic. Talk about God's providential laws could smooth over these kinds of potentially awkward social situations. Natural theology offered a way to express shared religious sentiments while avoiding quarrels over doctrine. It has long been recognized that arguments "from Nature to Nature's God" could be used to sidestep political and religious controversy; but natural theology's mediating role was most critical in conversation. Reflective works of science had achieved their status partly as cornucopias of polite party talk—as a kind of sublime version of discussing the weather.[13] *Vestiges* could be read as the latest in a long tradition of natural-theological conversation books.

General advice manuals often recommended reading science. "Books, balls, bonnets and metaphysics" were suitable topics for talk, according to Captain Orlando Sabertash's semicomic *Art of Conversation* (1842). More seriously, the evangelical Sarah Ellis's *Daughters of England* (1842) proposed God's role in sustaining the universe as an appropriate subject for women:

> 'Science!—what have we to do with science?' exclaim half a dozen soft voices at once. Certainly not to give public lectures, nor always to attend them. . . . Neither is it necessary that you should sacrifice any portion of your feminine delicacy by diving too deep, or approaching too near the professor's chair. A slight knowledge of science in general is all which is here recommended, so far as it may serve to obviate some of those groundless and irrational fears, which arise out of mistaken apprehensions of the phenomena of nature and art; but, above all, to enlarge our views of the great and glorious Creator, as exhibited in the most sublime, as well as the most insignificant, works of his creation.[14]

Science offered a route to moral regeneration. A knowledge of nature made women better Christians and conversationalists, able to listen intelligently when men expatiated on the laws of providence.

Men might have other aims. Captain Sabertash (actually a pseudonym for Society habitué Major General John Mitchell) suggested astronomy as a surefire way to attract the opposite sex. The ideal setting was a warm summer's evening at a country-house party, and the first step was to escape the distracting bustle of the crowd. Alone in the garden, the couple could admire the calm sublimity of the heavens. Women were especially open to the romance of astronomy:

> The stars,—their lustre, number, incalculable distance,—the immensity of space required for their mighty orbits . . . produce strange thoughts in female hearts. Women have more feeling than we have,—their minds are more easily moved by whatever is great, glorious and sublime; and when so elevated they are more open to the impressions of *la belle passion;* which, with them, is always—in its origin, at least—of a pure and ennobling nature.[15]

A discourse on the stars—rehearsed from books, spoken as if on impulse—was thought to have direct physiological effects on the female body. "I have generally observed," Sabertash noted, "that during such astronomical lectures the pretty dears drew closer to me, and leaned more perceptibly upon my arm."[16]

Vestiges offered enticing opportunities. Take, for example, the opening paragraph ("The mind fails to form an exact notion of a portion of space so immense"), and the last sentence before the conclusion ("Thinking of all the contingencies of this world as to be in time melted into or lost in the greater system"). Or take the purple passage at the end of the astronomy chapter ("'Man pauses breathless at the contemplation of a subject so much above his finite faculties, and can only wonder and adore'"). Such passages struck just the right note of tasteful sublimity.[17]

Fashionable readers, both women and men, scanned the reviews for such passages, and more generally for hints about what to say about the latest books. Even printing brief excerpts tended to disaggregate their contents, juxtaposing them in ways appropriate for polite discourse. Reviews broke down unilateral arguments, pointed out fine passages, and gave clues about how the flood of publications might be assessed. In this sense, periodical reviews served as highly specific literary advisors, targeted adjuncts to the literature of conduct. Representing a vast array of diverse opinions, they became crucial aids in opening up possibilities for talk. The reviews were widely valued for this purpose, not least in aristocratic and genteel circles. As one editor of a metropolitan weekly noted (with tongue firmly in cheek), the aim was "to enable people who cannot read all the books published, to talk about them as if they had read them."[18]

Didactic manuals about behavior in general, on the other hand, were dismissed as relevant only to readers whose parents might not be familiar with approved manners. In the real world of Society, the first rule was to avoid being a bore.[19] Talk was an art: quick, witty, cutting, clever. Contemporary diaries and letters show that rules were never static or fixed. Here *Vestiges* had the advantage of making an orthodox subject into something just dangerous enough to be attractive. The book could be read as elaborating the conventional belief that God sustained creation through law; but it drew on naughty new ideas about reproductive physiology and the status of the soul. This gave divine creation a topical frisson for the first time in years.

Conversations verging on the risqué required managing intimacy and bodily deportment. There was much "quizzing" about tails and monkeys. The mathematician Augustus De Morgan, who loved puzzles and conundrums, joined in conversations about the book by putting forward an alternative theory, in which new physical characteristics emerged through mental exercise. He recalled an accomplished guitar player who never practiced, but who mentally rehearsed the motions until his fingers learned their habits. Parodying the *Vestiges* style, De Morgan wondered "if this should be a minor segment of a higher law? What if, by constantly thinking of ourselves as descended from primaeval monkeys, we should—if this be true—actually *get our tails again?*" De Morgan did not attribute this kind of psychic evolution to *Vestiges*, but he did use it to search for the unknown author, who in thinking habitually about human origins would "naturally get the start of his species" and grow a tail. On hearing any man of eminence discourse knowledgeably about *Vestiges*, De Morgan would take "a curious glance at his proportions" to check for the hidden sign of authorship.[20] Such violations of etiquette, suitable only in an all-male setting like the Athenaeum Club, acknowledged fears raised by the prospect of bestial origins, while mocking them into insignificance.

Badly managed talk on such subjects in mixed company could be ridiculed as ungenteel and unfashionable. *Vestiges* figured large in party jokes and puns. As part of a series in *Punch* parodying "The Rising Generation," a slovenly young aristocrat declares at a private party that "Woman is decidedly—aw—an inferiaw—aw—animal"[21] [. . .]. The women he addresses are of all types, from the young musician at the piano to the formidably intellectual matron; their skeptical glances and obvious accomplishments make this particular Vestigian doctrine look crude and improbable. If anyone was "inferiaw," it was the ill-mannered male, with his low forehead and unprepossessing chin. The correlation between intelligence and brain size assumed in such a cartoon was almost universal, although phrenology had become deeply unfashionable in some Society circles. The phrenological character of the later chapters of *Vestiges* could have become the book's most significant hostage to conversational fortune, for single-minded advocacy of what Sabertash called "this exploded old subject" had become the sure mark of a bore. However, the book was generally thought to have handled phrenology with discretion—reference being made only to "the system of mind" of Franz Joseph Gall, and not to bumps on the head or other soft targets for satire.[22] All in all, *Vestiges* offered wonderful opportunities for displaying conversational skill.

[. . .]

Notes

1 Following Davidoff (1973, 103 n. 5), I use the uppercase to distinguish high Society from the more general society.
2 C. Bunbury, diary entry for 19 Feb. 1845, in Bunbury 1890, 1:37. For Lady Murray, see *DNB*; for the party, Carpenter 1888, 34.
3 Quoted in Morrell 1985, 2.
4 Quoted in Briggs 1959, 1.
5 G. W. Featherstonhaugh to A. Sedgwick, 16 Nov. 1844, CUL Add. mss. 7652.I.E.105.
6 John Cam Hobhouse, diary entry for 18 May 1845, BL Add. mss. 43747, f. 112v; issue books 5 and 8, London Library; duke of Somerset to E. Seymour, 20 Jan. 1845, in Mallock and Ramsden 1893, 268; Lord Morpeth, journal entry for 26 Mar. 1845, Castle Howard Archives, J19/8/6.
7 F. Nightingale to [?P. Nightingale], [Feb. 1845], in Cook 1913, 1:37; see also Goldie 1983, fiche 1, G2, 216. On stereotypes, see Poovey 1988, 164–98. On mesmerism, see Winter 1998a.
8 *V[estiges of the Natural History of Creation]*1, 276.
9 F. Nightingale to [?P. Nightingale], [Feb. 1845], in Cook 1913, 1:37.
10 Ibid.
11 For the stereotypical aspects of this image, see Peterson 1984.
12 F. Nightingale to Madame Mohl, July 1847, in Cook 1913, 1:42.
13 The classic analysis of the mediating role of natural theology is Brooke 1991b, 192–225, although this does not discuss how readers used the works in question.
14 Ellis 1842, 68–69.
15 Sabertash 1842, 135–36. Curtin 1987, St. George 1993, Morgan 1994, and Barnes 1995 provide helpful discussions of conduct manuals as a genre.
16 Sabertash 1842, 136.
17 *V*1, 1, 386, 26.
18 *Critic*, 3 May 1845, 1–2, at 2.
19 There is no good general history of boredom, although its literary manifestations are sketched in Spacks 1995.

20 De Morgan 1872, 211.
21 [John Leech] "The Rising Generation," *Punch* 27 Mar. 1847, 128.
22 *V*1, 322, 341.

References

Barnes, Emm[a]. 1995. "Fashioning a natural self-guides to self-presentation in Victorian England." Ph.D. Diss., University of Cambridge.

Briggs, Asa, ed. 1959. *Chartist Studies*. London, Macmillan.

Brooke, John Hedley. 1991. *Science and Religion: Some Historical Perspectives*. Cambridge: Cambridge University Press.

Bunbury, Frances, ed. 1890–91. *Memorials of Sir C J F Bunbury*, Bart. 9 vols. Mildenhall: privately printed.

Carpenter, William B. 1888. *Nature and Man: Essays Scientific and Philosophical*. London: Kegan Paul, Trench & Co.

Chambers, Robert. 1844. *Vestiges of the Natural History of Creation*. London: John Churchill.

Cook, Edward. 1913. *The Life of Florence Nightingale*. 2 vols. London, Macmillan.

Curtin, M. 1987. *Propriety and Position: A Study of Victorian Manners*. New York: Garland.

Davidoff, Leonore. 1973. *The Best Circles: Society, Etiquette and the Season*. London: Croon Helm.

De Morgan, Augustus. 1872. *A Budget of Paradoxes*. London: Longmans.

Ellis, Sarah. 1842. *The Daughters of England: Their Position in Society, Character & Responsibility*. London: Fisher.

Goldie, Sue. 1983. *A Calendar of the Letters of Florence Nightingale*. Oxford: Oxford Microform Publications.

Mallock, W. H., and Gwendden Ramsden, eds. 1893. *Letters, Remains, and Memoirs of Edward Adolphus Seymour Twelfth Duke of Somerset K. G.* London: Richard Bentley.

Morgan, Marjorie. 1994. *Manners, Morals, and Class in England, 1774–1858*. New York: St. Martin's Press.

Morrell, J. B. 1985. "Wissenschaft in Worstedopolis: Public Science in Bradford, 1800–1850." *BJHS* 18: 1–23.

Peterson, M. Jeanne. 1984. "No Angels in the House: The Victorian Myth and the Paget Women." *American Historical Review* 89: 677–798.

Poovey, Mary. 1988. *Uneven Developments: The Ideological Work of Gender in Mid-Victorian England*. Chicago: University of Chicago Press.

Sabertash, Orlando. [John Mitchell]. 1842. *The Art of Conversation, with Remarks on Fashion and Address*. London, G.W. Nickisson.

St. George, Andrew. 1993. *The Descent of Manners: Etiquette, Rules & the Victorians*. London: Chatto & Windus.

Spacks, Patricia Meyer. 1995. *Boredom: The Literary History of a State of Mind*. Chicago: University of Chicago Press.

Winter, Alison. 1998. *Mesmerized: Powers of Mind in Victorian Britain*. Chicago: University of Chicago Press.

24 Darwinian science and Victorian respectability

Gowan Dawson

At a meeting of the Geological Society of London in November 1856, Richard Owen, the foremost comparative anatomist and perhaps the most eminent man of science in mid-Victorian Britain, reached the conclusion of an address on the newly discovered jawbone of an early prehistoric mammal. Turning aside from the structural specifics of the *Stereognathus ooliticus*, he took the opportunity to issue an urgent warning against the irreligious scientific doctrines that had been promulgated in Paris earlier in the century and were now being adopted by a 'small and unfruitful minority' of naturalists in London. Despite their vaunted modernity, these heretical views, Owen insisted, derived originally from the demeaning 'tenets of the Democritic and Lucretian schools' that were formulated in ancient Greece and Rome. Owen was particularly concerned with the potential consequences of such antiquated axioms for nineteenth-century scientific education, and while averring that those 'concerned in the right conception and successful modes of studying organized structures by the Young have little to fear', he nevertheless admonished his audience that the 'insinuation and masked advocacy of the doctrine subversive to a recognition of the Higher Mind . . . call for constant watchfulness and prompt exposure'. Recent exponents of such specious doctrines were, Owen proclaimed, not 'healthy' or 'normal', and, afflicted with 'some, perhaps congenital, defect of mind', they might corrupt the otherwise wholesome minds of others, and the impressionable and conspicuously capitalized 'Young' especially.[1]

The principal aim of Owen's address was to condemn the use of empirical deduction rather than functional correlation – which pointed to the existence of an intelligent creator – in palaeontological reconstructions, and he delivered it, as Joseph Dalton Hooker remarked, with 'cool deliberation & emphasis & pointed tone'. Throughout, Owen's glowering gaze was fixed on one particular member of the elite audience at the Geological Society: the headstrong tyro and advocate of deduction Thomas Henry Huxley. In the ensuing debate, Huxley appeared discomfited and, unable to muster his usual acerbic wit, 'did not defend himself well (though with temper)' against Owen's refutation of his views on palaeontological method.[2] In the following month, moreover, he went on to express an uncharacteristic desire to foster a 'nobler tone to science' without such 'petty personal controversies'.[3] Huxley usually relished his bitter feuds with rival naturalists, and even Owen's strident and authoritative attack on his understanding of palaeontology, in which Huxley actually had little practical experience, seems unlikely to have prompted such a muted response.[4]

What perhaps put Huxley on the back foot in this particular confrontation was the peculiarly moralistic tone of the warning which Owen issued in the peroration to his highly technical palaeontological discourse. After all, he deliberately identified modern scientific approaches like Huxley's which repudiated the role of a higher designing intelligence with the ancient atomistic philosophies of Democritus and Lucretius, who for centuries had been denounced as dangerous pagan sensualists. Owen himself was certainly aware of the strategic potential of such insidious associations with the moral corruption of the ancient world, having earlier condemned his anatomical opponents, in *On the Nature of Limbs* (1849), for sinking into an 'Epicurean slough of despond' from which 'every healthy mind naturally recoils'.[5] Still worse, in his imperative demands for a 'constant watchfulness and prompt exposure' on behalf of vulnerable youngsters, Owen also invoked a distinctive rhetoric of moral anxiety and furtive surveillance which closely resembled the language of numerous contemporary treatises on the dangers of juvenile masturbation. In the nineteenth century, as Thomas W. Laqueur has noted, 'parents were urged by many a guidebook to exercise the utmost vigilance' in order to 'stop the depredations of the supposedly secret vice'.[6] Even Owen's characterization of the supporters of Lucretian scientific views as 'unfruitful', and with unhealthy and defective minds, accorded with prevalent nineteenth-century medical assumptions that the unproductive emission of semen would leave those who indulged in masturbation dangerously depleted and potentially infertile. The 'masked advocacy' of subversive and originally pagan scientific doctrines, Owen's strategic rhetoric implied, was the intellectual equivalent of onanism and required a similarly scrupulous vigilance from society's ethical guardians to prevent its iniquitous effects from spreading.

Owen, of course, drew upon a long, well-worn tradition connecting materialism and unbelief with moral corruption and debauchery, including the entwinement of pornography and materialist philosophies in the Enlightenment.[7] In any case, his particular insinuations at the Geological Society were carefully calculated to remain sufficiently oblique to avoid contravening the gentlemanly standards of the mid-nineteenth-century scientific community, and they seem only to have temporarily discomfited his most persistent and ferocious adversary.[8] Significantly, though, the bitter and protracted palaeontological dispute between Owen and Huxley during the mid-1850s is generally regarded as a precursor to the larger controversy prompted by the publication of *On the Origin of Species* at the end of the decade, which Owen savaged in an anonymous notice for the *Edinburgh Review*.[9] Similarly malevolent and disreputable accusations would become one of the most persistent – if hitherto least acknowledged – aspects of the long-running debates over Charles Darwin's evolutionary theories.

Darwin's particular conception of organic evolution, as many historians have observed, quickly became part of a wider political campaign, which Frank Miller Turner has famously termed 'scientific naturalism', to wrest the last vestiges of intellectual and cultural authority away from the monopolistic Anglican Church establishment, as well as the gentlemanly amateurs who represented its interests in the scientific world.[10] Scientific naturalism instead sought to establish a new secular understanding of both nature and society that could be interpreted correctly only by an emergent cadre of scientific professionals. The metropolitan leaders of this nascent intellectual order, who from 1864 met regularly at meetings of the exclusive and politically influential X-Club, adopted Darwin's competitive, evolutionary view of the natural world, along with the similarly naturalistic principles of the conservation of energy and the uniformity of nature, as a valuable weapon in the wider struggle between Nonconformist Dissenters, with their meritocratic and reformist aspirations, and the established Church, which, through its control of pulpits, schools and universities, remained the chief systematizer of national culture.[11]

In a society already fissured by the shift from a hierarchical clerical culture to a more socially amorphous urban industrialism, it was essential for scientific naturalism to provide a new secular theodicy which might reconcile the expectations of a growing population with the changed realities of the nascent social order. Rather than being simply discarded, traditional religious values were instead naturalized, with law and uniformity supplanting theology as the guarantors of order in both the natural world and human society.[12] Darwin's theories, as part of this wider agenda of scientific naturalism, had to be urgently sequestered from any hostile associations that might tarnish them in the eyes of the various audiences for science in Victorian Britain and consequently undermine the political aspirations of dissident secular intellectuals, who, as Adrian Desmond and James Moore have put it, were busy 'selling themselves to the public as . . . a respectable white-collar body'.[13] The endeavours to dissociate Darwinism from ideologically sensitive epithets such as 'materialism' or 'atheism', and to purge transmutationism of its earlier connotations of scurrilous political radicalism, have, in recent years, received a great deal of historiographic consideration.[14] But, as this book will argue, from the late 1860s attention shifted increasingly from general concerns with political propriety to specific anxieties over sexual respectability, and it was actually Darwin's surprisingly recurrent connection with sexual immorality, in various sectors of the period's burgeoning print culture, which emerged as perhaps the most significant impediment to establishing a naturalistic worldview as a morally acceptable alternative to earlier theological outlooks. These iniquitous associations, moreover, would prove remarkably difficult to shake off.

This aspect of the reception of Darwin's evolutionary theories also reflected wider cultural changes in Britain during the 1860s and 1870s which did much to switch attention from the relatively quiescent political scene to new concerns with sexual and moral transgression. The authority of middle-class norms of respectability, which, shaped by early nineteenth-century evangelicism, had long sought to regulate behaviour in relation to drinking, gambling and sex, was widely perceived to have become markedly weaker in this period, and with regard to the latter in particular.[15] There is, as Michael Mason has argued, 'evidence that the 1860s saw a considerable relaxing of [sexual] codes, especially among young middle class people' which helped establish a 'new environment for sexual reform'.[16] But such changing attitudes towards sex were inevitably accompanied by various anxieties regarding their potentially invidious effects on wider areas of Victorian society and culture. Most notably, the introduction of new legislation on obscenity in the mid-1850s, and the largely adverse critical response to the emergence, during the following decade, of the aesthetic or art for art's sake movement, made the regulation of licentious mass urban culture as well as of studiedly amoral avant-garde art and literature matters of urgent public solicitude. In both cases, it was specific concerns with the regulation of representations of sexuality that, more than ever before, were the central issue. As Martin Myrone has recently contended: 'Lord Campbell's [Obscene Publications] Act of 1857 did not simply represent a tightening of the laws regarding obscenity, but a crucial turning-point in which sexuality is isolated as a cause of social disorder, rather than as something to be treated as part of a wider public order issue.'[17] This separation of sexuality from other forms of disorder inevitably increased its visibility as a social problem, and, as in Michel Foucault's famous thesis of regulation as a mode of production, actually prompted exaggerated fears that polite society was being overwhelmed by an inexorable proliferation of obscene images and other forms of sexual depravity.[18]

In the early 1870s the Scottish critic and poet Robert Buchanan certainly expressed an almost hysterical revulsion upon returning from his native Highlands to the 'great Sodom or Gomorrah' of London and finding 'photographs of nude, indecent, and hideous harlots, in every possible attitude that vice can devise, flaunt[ed] from the shop-windows'. The 'female Leg' in particular was unavoidable in the depraved popular culture of the metropolis; 'Walk along the streets,' Buchanan warned, the 'shop-windows teem with Leg. Enter a music-hall – Leg again, and (O tempora! O mores!) the Can-Can.' While those responsible for such 'matter or prints suggestive of indecency' were, according to Buchanan, 'at last being taken in hand' by recent legislation on obscenity and the prosecutions launched by the Society for the Suppression of Vice, even these were not sufficient to cope adequately with the deluge of material of an 'obscene and vulgar nature' with which the 'streets are full'.[19] Nor, significantly, was the high art and literature produced by members of the aesthetic movement immune from similar imputations, for Buchanan explicitly identified the 'Sensualism' expressed in recent avant-garde poetry by Algernon Charles Swinburne and Dante Gabriel Rossetti as the moral 'cancer of all society', and he insisted that 'all the gross and vulgar conceptions of life . . . emanate from this Bohemian class' with its amoral 'critical theory that art is simply the method of getting most sweets out of one's living sensations'.[20] It is notable that, according to the *Oxford English Dictionary*, the cultural categories 'aestheticism' and 'pornography' were coined within two years of each other during the mid-1850s, and while Buchanan's derisive comments were characteristically hyperbolic, their sentiments were evidently far from uncommon. Instead, they articulate widespread concerns with the increasing prominence of sex in various aspects of modern culture.

What Peter Bailey has termed the 'sexualisation of everyday life' in the final decades of the nineteenth century can be seen to have had some extremely important consequences for the Victorian disputes over evolution.[21] Indeed, as this book will show, it was regularly avowed that the growing licentiousness of modern culture, and the alleged excesses of aestheticism especially, actually gave warning of the repulsive direction in which society was being taken by the increasingly influential doctrines of Darwinism. Such lurid accusations were prompted in part by *The Descent of Man*, published at the beginning of 1871, in which Darwin himself identified sexual desire and reproduction as the driving forces of the whole evolutionary process. In the same book, Darwin also contended that man's moral feelings of right and duty were not innate but had been evolved over time by the natural selection of sympathetic social instincts. It was claimed by his critics that by negating the metaphysical criterion for morality – which, according to many, was the very basis of the civic order – the overtly naturalistic science of Darwin and his inner circle of friends and colleagues threatened to unleash a torrent of immorality and corruption that would surpass the scandalous vices of even the pagan world. These allegations, as will be seen, were generally much more explicit than Owen's rather furtive insinuations concerning paganism in his Geological Society address at the end of 1856.

Several historians have recently challenged stereotypical notions of Victorian prudery and respectability, demonstrating that sexual moralism was not expressed consistently across the nineteenth century nor uniformly adhered to amongst all social groups.[22] The many charges made against Darwinian science were nevertheless potentially extremely damaging in the light of the indubitable emphasis on respectability and sexual restraint maintained in specific sectors of society in this period. In particular, the 'primacy of morality', according to Stefan Collini, remained a defining feature of Victorian intellectual life.[23] In order to neutralize the charges of encouraging sexual immorality, the proponents of evolutionary theory, attempting to forge their own naturalistic social theodicy, had to shield Darwinism equally vigorously from any such invidious connections, in part by distinguishing a self-proclaimed 'pure' science – drawing on all senses of that overdetermined adjective – from the less reputable aspects of nineteenth-century general culture.

Like stereotypes of Victorian prudery, the familiar concept of the 'Darwinian Revolution' in the mid-nineteenth century has also increasingly been questioned in recent historical scholarship, which has instead proposed that the simplistic notion of a triumphant epochal shift instigated by a single individual be replaced by a more nuanced emphasis on what James A. Secord has recently termed 'the debates that took place after the publication of a series of printed books'.[24] This book explores precisely these debates over works such as *The Descent of Man* and Huxley's *Evidence as to Man's Place in Nature* (1863), but, for the very first time, it examines them in relation to the murky underworlds of Victorian pornography, sexual innuendo, unrespectable freethought and artistic sensualism. In so doing, it sheds important new light even on those evolutionary controversies which have already been the subject of extensive scholarship, and contends that such disreputable and generally overlooked aspects of nineteenth-century culture were actually remarkably central to many of these debates. The book integrates contextualist approaches to the history of science with recent work in nineteenth-century literary and cultural history, situating the Victorian disputes over Darwin's scientific theories in a wider set of contexts and material cultures, and those emerging from aestheticism and new legal definitions of obscenity in particular. Such an approach extends dramatically the range of participants actively involved in debates over evolution, from pornographic engravers and clandestine authors of freethinking treatises on sexuality to conservative literary critics and the ostensibly demure wives of prominent men of science, as well as the spaces and formats in which such issues were discussed and contested.[25] Notably, the book provides extensive new evidence of how even Darwin himself became implicated in the attempts of radical freethinkers to challenge both the legitimacy of the recently passed Obscene Publications Act and conventional taboos over issues like birth control and prostitution.

It also offers, amongst other things, a new way of understanding the relations between science and literature in an intellectual milieu of perpetually disputed boundaries. The frequently problematic interconnection of Darwinian science and aesthetic literature considered in this book suggests that the prevalent 'One Culture' model of literature and science scholarship, which implicitly celebrates discursive interchanges between scientific and literary modes of writing as invariably creative and mutually advantageous, has been much too sanguine in its approach to the interrelations of science and literature in the Victorian period.[26] Rather than examining how scientific concepts have informed various aspects of works of literature, or even how science has borrowed different rhetorical structures and tropes from literary forms of writing, the book instead focuses on how the actual interconnection of the two was itself, between the late 1860s and mid-1890s, regularly exploited and manipulated for a variety of strategic reasons. Those seeking to discredit the cultural authority of evolutionary science identified it with the alleged sensual indulgence of aestheticism, while those attempting to establish it as a respectable secular theodicy denied such a connection and instead emphasized links with more reputable literary writers.

Drawing on a broad range of sources including journalism, scientific books and lectures, sermons, radical pamphlets, aesthetic and comic verse, novels, law reports, illustrations and satirical cartoons, as well as less traditional formats such as the gossip and hearsay recorded in private letters, the book reveals the unscrupulous and often extremely effective strategies employed by a variety of different critics, both scientific and otherwise, to undermine Darwinism. While focusing principally on Darwin himself, it also examines how many of his leading allies and followers, including Huxley, John Tyndall, William Benjamin Carpenter and William Kingdon Clifford, were similarly implicated in disputes over their apparent espousal of immorality, although even long after his death in April 1882 it was Darwin who remained the dominant figure in various controversies concerning science and sexual respectability. Significantly, the book shows that the opposition to various aspects of evolutionary science was often much stronger and more potent than has generally been recognized in accounts that adhere to the model of the so-called 'Darwinian Revolution' rather than emphasize the more complex and considerably less one-sided debates of the period. Darwinian men of science, to take only one example, were constrained significantly by the allegations made by antagonists such as Owen, and often had no choice but to fashion their model of professional scientific authority, as well as their public personas, in accordance with the standards of respectability laid down by their most bitter adversaries. While much recent scholarship has been alert to what James E. Strick has termed the 'intense desire to be "respectable"' of figures like Darwin and Huxley, this book makes clear that the fashioning of such respectability was by no means a straightforward or unproblematic endeavour.[27] Maintaining an unsullied personal reputation, vitally important in an age when much of the intellectual credibility of science relied upon the virtuous character of its leading individual exponents, was often an extremely precarious process, even for such an apparent model of scientific propriety as Darwin himself.

[. . .]

Notes

1 Richard Owen, 'On the Affinities of the *Stereognathus Oolitcus* (Charlesworth), a Mammal from the Oolitic Slate of Stonesfield', *Quarterly Journal of the Geological Society of London* 13 (1856), 1–11 (8).

2 Frederick H. Burkhardt *et al.* (eds.), *The Correspondence of Charles Darwin*, 13 vols. (Cambridge: Cambridge University Press, 1983–), 6:260; see also Adrian Desmond, *Huxley: The Devil's Disciple* (London: Michael Joseph, 1994), 229–30.

3 Leonard Huxley, *Life and Letters of Thomas Henry Huxley*, 2 vols. (London: Macmillan, 1900), 1:151.

4 See Adrian Desmond, *Archetypes and Ancestors: Palaeontology in Victorian London 1850–1875* (Chicago: University of Chicago Press, 1982), 57–8.

5 Quoted in Adrian Desmond, *The Politics of Evolution: Morphology, Medicine, and Reform in Radical London* (Chicago: University of Chicago Press, 1989), 366.

6 Thomas W. Laqueur, *Solitary Sex: A Cultural History of Masturbation* (New York: Zone Books, 2003), 46.

7 See Margaret C. Jacob, 'The Materialist World of Pornography', in *The Invention of Pornography: Obscenity and the Origins of Modernity, 1500–1800*, ed. by Lynn Hunt (New York: Zone Books, 1993), 157–202.

8 See Jack Morrell and Arnold Thackray, *Gentlemen of Science: Early Years of the British Association for the Advancement of Science* (Oxford: Clarendon Press, 1981), 17–29 and passim.

9 See, for instance, Desmond, *Archetypes and Ancestors*, 19–55; and Paul White, *Thomas Huxley: Making the 'Man of Science'* (Cambridge: Cambridge University Press, 2003), 32–66.

10 See, amongst others, Frank Miller Turner, *Between Science and Religion: The Reaction to Scientific Naturalism in Late Victorian England* (New Haven and London: Yale University Press, 1974); Frank M. Turner, 'The Victorian Conflict between Science and Religion: A Professional Dimension', in *Contesting Cultural Authority: Essays in Victorian Intellectual Life* (Cambridge: Cambridge University Press, 1993), 171–200; and Adrian Desmond, 'Redefining the X Axis: "Professionals", "Amateurs" and the Making of Mid-Victorian Biology – A Progress Report', *Journal of the History of Biology* 34 (2001), 3–50.

11 See Ruth Barton, 'Evolution: The Whitworth Gun in Huxley's War for the Liberation of Science from Theology', in *The Wider Domain of Evolutionary Thought*, ed. by David Oldroyd and Ian Langham (Dordrecht: Reidel, 1983), 261–87; and Adrian Desmond, *Huxley: Evolution's High Priest* (London: Michael Joseph, 1997), 235–61.

12 See James R. Moore, 'Theodicy and Society: The Crisis of the Intelligentsia', in *Victorian Faith in Crisis: Essays on Continuity and Change in Nineteenth-Century Religious Belief*, ed. by Richard J. Helmstadter and Bernard Lightman (London: Macmillan, 1990), 153–86.

13 Adrian Desmond and James Moore, *Darwin* (London: Michael Joseph, 1991), 432.

14 See, for instance, Desmond, *Politics of Evolution*, 398–414; and James Moore, 'Deconstructing Darwinism: The Politics of Evolution in the 1860s', *Journal of the History of Biology* 24 (1991), 353–408.

15 See Mike J. Huggins, 'More Sinful Pleasures?: Leisure, Respectability and the Male Middle Classes in Victorian England', *Journal of Social History* 33 (2000), 585–600 (586–87).

16 Michael Mason, *The Making of Victorian Sexual Attitudes* (Oxford: Oxford University Press, 1994), 174.

17 Martin Myrone, 'Prudery, Pornography and the Victorian Nude', in *Exposed: The Victorian Nude*, ed. by Alison Smith (London: Tate Publishing, 2001), 23–35 (31).

18 See Lynda Nead, *Victorian Babylon: People, Streets and Images in Nineteenth-Century London* (New Haven and London: Yale University Press, 2000), 149–61.

19 Robert Buchanan, *The Fleshly School of Poetry and Other Phenomena of the Day* (London: Strahan, 1872), 2, 3 and 4.

20 Ibid., 1 and 6–7.

21 Peter Bailey, 'Parasexuality and Glamour: The Victorian Barmaid as Cultural Prototype', *Gender and History* 2 (1990), 148–72 (167).

22 See Huggins, 'More Sinful Pleasures?', 585–6; Myrone, 'Victorian Nude', 23–8; and Michael Mason, *The Making of Victorian Sexuality* (Oxford: Oxford University Press, 1994), 1–35.

23 Stefan Collini, *Public Moralists: Political Thought and Intellectual Life in Britain 1850–1930* (Oxford: Clarendon Press, 1991), 63.

24 James A. Secord, 'Knowledge in Transit', *Isis* 95 (2004), 654–72 (661).

25 On the need for historians to be 'responsive to a greater plurality of the sites for the making and reproduction of scientific knowledge', and especially to 'popular prose and non-scientific texts', see Roger Cooter and Stephen Pumfrey, 'Separate Spheres and Public Places: Reflections on the History of Science Popularization and Science in Popular Culture', *History of Science* 32 (1994), 237–67 (255).

26 See George Levine, 'One Culture: Science and Literature', in *One Culture: Essays in Science and Literature*, ed. by George Levine (Madison: University of Wisconsin Press, 1987), 3–32.

27 James E. Strick, *Sparks of Life: Darwinism and the Victorian Debates over Spontaneous Generation* (Cambridge, MA: Harvard University Press, 2000), 93.

25 Darwin and Victorian culture

Jonathan Smith

In his review of *Middlemarch* (1871–72), Henry James complained that George Eliot's great novel was "too often an echo of Messrs. Darwin and Huxley" (James 1873: 428). Later in that same decade, the critic Edward Dowden, writing in the *Contemporary Review*, declared that the "chief inspiring ideas for literature" in the recent scientific revelations of geology and natural history were the idea of the relative as opposed to the absolute, the idea of heredity, and the idea of human progress, "itself subordinate to the more comprehensive doctrine of evolution" (Dowden 1877: 570).[1] Darwin's influence on Victorian literature and culture was visible to many contemporaries, but it would take more than half a century for literary scholars to explore that impact in a sustained way, and another fifty years still before James's particular insight about Eliot's response to Darwin would become the basis of an extended and detailed study.

Gillian Beer's *Darwin Plots* (1983) and George Levine's *Darwin and the Novelists* (1988) have been so influential for our understanding of Darwinism's relationship to Victorian literature and culture that the critics who came before them have been largely eclipsed, and Beer's and Levine's innovations have actually been under-appreciated, surprising as that is to say. Prior to the appearance of *Darwin's Plots*, studies of Darwin by literary critics tended to take one of two forms: catalogs of appearances of Darwinian ideas in Victorian literary works, or considerations of Darwinism's literary form.[2] Beer and Levine, however, were primarily interested in the question of Darwin's relationship to Victorian literature rather than Darwinism's relationship to literary form. What works of literature had Darwin himself read, and how had these shaped the narratives of origins, of historical change, of individual and species-level development, and of mating and inheritance that he constructed in *The Origin of Species* and *The Descent of Man*? How did Victorian literary writers in turn absorb and respond to these Darwinian narratives? While neither Beer nor Levine contended that Darwin's narratives were strictly realist ones—indeed, both stressed that Darwin deployed and inspired a variety of plots—their attention was mainly directed to realist writers such as Eliot, Hardy, Trollope, and Conrad.[3] It has been impossible ever since not to see the clear similarity between Darwin's science, with its attention to the cumulative effect over time of small changes in a dense, interrelated natural world, and the complex, detailed narrative worlds of Victorian realism.

The work of Beer and Levine was also made possible by changes in the study of Darwin and in the history of science more broadly. The 1959 centennial of the *Origin*'s appearance spurred intense scholarly interest in Darwin and led to the publication of the trove of archival material—correspondence, notebooks, diaries, and marginalia—in the Darwin Papers at the University of Cambridge. Starting in the 1960s, historians and sociologists of science increasingly adopted "externalist" or "contextualist" approaches, focusing on the social, cultural, and political factors shaping the practice and reception of science. Even more strongly, some scholars argued that scientific facts were in fact social constructions—not disembodied, independent "truths of nature" waiting to be discovered, but contested manipulations and interpretations of natural phenomena whose status as "facts" could only be established through a process of debate and consensus-building that depended on such factors as institutional and personal relationships and prestige as well as objective data.[4] Nor did "facts" speak for themselves: scientific writing was an exercise in persuasion, and scientists necessarily deployed the same language tools, such as metaphor and analogy, that poets and novelists did. How else to describe the new but through reference to the known? Darwin, given his importance, the cultural impact of his work, and the sheer mass of archival material on him, quickly became an important object of study for scholars deploying these new approaches. Beer, situated at Cambridge, one of the centers of that work in the UK, was particularly well positioned to combine the literary and historical study of Darwin.

Beer's achievement in *Darwin's Plots* has two main elements, the first of which is highlighted in the excerpt. Most of the book's first two parts is devoted to a careful reading of Darwin's language, his deployment of literary devices like metaphor, and his (unavoidable) use of narrative models for discussing natural phenomena like development, transformation, and extinction. Drawing on the social nature of facts, Beer argues that Darwin and his readers were still part of a common intellectual and literary culture, and thus that Darwin's ideas and assumptions about nature, and his language for describing it, were shaped to a significant degree by the same texts that shaped the ideas and assumptions and language of his contemporaries—in particular, by the Bible and John Milton's *Paradise Lost*, a volume of Milton's poetry being one of Darwin's almost-constant companions during the *Beagle* voyage. In the excerpt, Beer contends that because evolutionary theory was concerned with time and change—because it is itself a form of "imaginative history"—it is inextricably linked with other narratives of imaginative history like myths and novels. If we are to fully understand Darwin's theory, then, we must appreciate those literary narratives that shape—unconsciously as well as consciously, and through counterpoint as well as reinforcement—his account of natural selection, and his audience's reception of it. Even more fundamentally, Beer explains that the challenges and struggles Darwin faced in describing his theory lay in language itself, for language is inherently about agency and design—a subject acting for a purpose—yet natural selection denied agency and design, replacing an omnipotent and beneficent God with an undirected process driven by random variations in the traits of individuals, the shifting fortunes of species, and the fluctuations in what we would call environment or habitat. Beer's analysis of Darwin's language, moreover, is ultimately historical: she offers an explanation for the curious fact that Darwin's theory was appropriated by so many different thinkers to such radically different ends—by socialists and social Darwinists, by Christians and agnostics, by both advocates and opponents of women's education.

Beer's second major achievement was her work in the remainder of *Darwin's Plots*—the close readings of "some of the ways in which evolutionary theory has been assimilated and resisted by novelists who . . . have assayed its powers" and "tested the extent to which it can provide a determining fiction by which to read the world" (Beer 1983: 2 [Chapter 21: 189]). The "plots" inspired by Darwin, like those within Darwin's own work, were multiple and various. That Beer devoted the final part of her book to an examination of the evolutionary narratives of George Eliot and Thomas Hardy, however, is what made the connection between Darwin's science and the Victorian realist novel so firmly established—even without her insisting on the connection.

Although Beer focused on novelists who read and responded to Darwin in their work, she noted that such writers reflected only a small fraction of the response to Darwin. In

Darwin and the Novelists, George Levine took the logical step of focusing on writers who did not share Eliot's deep and up-to-the-moment awareness of contemporary science. "I am more interested here," Levine wrote, ". . . in writers who probably did not know any science first hand, who could have been 'influenced' by Darwin only indirectly" (Levine 1988: 3). Hence Levine devoted much of his attention to Charles Dickens and, more audaciously, Anthony Trollope. In the excerpt we can see Levine frequently referencing and building on the insights of Beer. Indeed, Beer's passing comment that the *Origin*'s vision of nature and its mode of argument seem to owe much to the example of Dickens's fiction, in which "unruly superfluity of material gradually and retrospectively reveal[s] itself as order" (Levine 1988: 6), is precisely one of the issues that Levine elaborates upon in his expansive discussion of Darwin and Dickens. Like Beer, Levine examines a set of thematic elements in Darwin's work: change and history, the blurring of boundaries, connections (ecological and genealogical), abundance, rejection of design and teleology, mystery and order, and chance. Like Beer, he parses the contours of writers' responses to these Darwinian themata, sensitive to complexity and nuance, necessarily drawing the bulk of his evidence not from the writers' pronouncements about Darwin but from their handling of these issues in their novels. In the excerpt, Levine assesses Dickens's own handling of many of these themes. He, too, finds similarities between Dickens's and Darwin's visions of their respective worlds as overflowing, abundant, and interconnected. Whereas Darwin emphasized the power of gradual change and saw species as fluid rather than fixed, however, Dickens's plots depended famously on sudden turns and coincidences, and his characters tended to be fixed personalities, changing only—when they changed at all—through abrupt conversions. Dickens accepted the necessity and value of change, Levine argues, but his view of it differed from Darwin's. And while both men revealed order in the universe beneath its dynamic, teeming surface, for Levine the radical difference between them lay in their understanding of that order. In Darwin's eyes, natural selection had no moral significance; it operated without a plan and certainly not for humanity's benefit. For Dickens, on the other hand, the natural and human worlds ultimately reflect a design and a moral order.

The excerpts from *Darwin's Plots* and *Darwin and the Novelists* exemplify the kind of detailed, erudite, and sensitive readings that Beer and Levine both provided of Darwin and of Victorian novelists. So thorough and compelling were these books, though, that they did not inspire other major literary studies of Darwin (although they did prompt many shorter ones). It was as if, between them, Beer and Levine were felt to have covered all the ground worth covering. It would take nearly a full generation for literary scholars to realize that Beer and Levine had not had the last word.

Beer and Levine had been careful to differentiate their books from traditional studies of "influence." Theirs were cultural arguments—writers didn't have to read and understand Darwin's work to absorb and respond to it, because Darwin's ideas, and the debates surrounding them, immediately became part of a broader cultural discourse about evolution. Indeed, for Beer and Levine, to focus on influence in the traditional sense often reflected mid-twentieth-century cultural assumptions about the oppositional relationship of science and literature: literary scholars who regarded science and literature as opposites tended to assume that writers of the past did as well, and thus that Dickens, say, could not have been influenced by Darwin. In Victorian Britain, by contrast, Beer and Levine stressed, literature and science were not so regarded, certainly not in any simplistic or monolithic way; rather, they were seen as parts of a single intellectual culture, albeit one in which examples of tension or opposition could occur alongside examples of accommodation and harmony. Science and literature, they argued, were better conceptualized as parts of a single, broader, shared culture than as separate, divided, mutually-incomprehensible areas of knowledge, as most famously articulated (and lamented) in C. P. Snow's 1959 "two cultures" thesis.[5] Yet the approaches of Beer and Levine were in another sense quite traditional: they were rooted in the history of ideas at a time when the history of science was heading in a more materialist direction. The cultural turn among historians of science studying Darwin was brought to wide public attention with the publication of Adrian Desmond and James Moore's biography, *Darwin*, in 1991. Desmond and Moore positioned Darwin's theories and writings less in relation to the intellectual history of evolution than in relation to the political, social, and religious controversies of mid-Victorian England. At the same time, historians of science increasingly turned their attention to the material contexts of science—to instruments, machines, laboratories. Interest in reading as a physical practice, writing and publishing as businesses, and books as physical objects became a focus of historical inquiry generally, and found a prominent place among both historians of science and literary historians.

James Secord's *Victorian Sensation* (2000) exemplified this growing interest in the history of reading and publishing. Widely hailed as a major work of scholarship not just in the history of Victorian science but in the history of science generally, Secord's book was devoted not to Darwin but to the Edinburgh writer and publisher Robert Chambers's anonymous bestseller, *Vestiges of the Natural History of Creation* (1844). Chambers's book presented an evolutionary account of the development of the cosmos and of life itself, drawing heavily on evolutionary ideas popular in France and Germany and among the radical medical community of London. *Vestiges* created quite a stir, its popularization of current and controversial science spiced by the guessing game over its author's identity. Many members of the scientific elite were appalled by its errors and its presentation of contested theories as established fact, some seeing in its embrace of evolutionary theory a threat to the social and moral order. Darwin, having just completed an essay outlining his own evolutionary theory, read *Vestiges* with concern; the book's reception contributed to the long delay in publishing his own theory but also clarified what he would have to do to satisfy his scientific peers and to differentiate his work from Chambers's. Secord's interest, however, lay not with Darwin but with *Vestiges* itself, and with its myriad other readers. He thus carefully charted the book's development, publication, reception, and revision. Although Secord of course analyzed the published reviews of *Vestiges*, he went further, often examining their production by particular individuals. And he traced the unpublished responses to the book by individual readers of different social classes, occupations, ages, and gender who read the work in different contexts and locations. By examining these "geographies of reading" (Secord 2000: 156 [Chapter 23: 205]), Secord was able to paint a rich and fine-grained portrait of the ways *Vestiges* was received.

The excerpt from *Victorian Sensation* includes one of these "geographies," that of London's high society. Here we see *Vestiges* being discussed in conversations and letters among the fashionable set. While reading by this point was a solitary activity for the middle and upper classes, talk about the latest books was very much a social practice and even played an important role in individual relationships. Whereas *Vestiges* has traditionally been seen as a scandalous, even dangerous, book, Secord shows that it was taken both seriously and frivolously by this eminently respectable slice of society, fodder for discussion and exchange. Its evolutionary narrative was dressed in a language of Christianity and the romantic sublime that, if not exactly orthodox, was nonetheless familiar to this cultured audience, which liked nothing better than to entertain the latest intellectual trends. For these educated early Victorians, a book like *Vestiges* was definitely part of a single, unified culture, as much a source of conversation and gossip as Dickens's *Martin Chuzzlewit*, Benjamin Disraeli's *Sybil*, or Elizabeth Barrett's *Poems*, all of which appeared in the same year.

Secord describes *Victorian Sensation* as "an experiment in a different kind of history," an effort "to see what happens when a major historical episode is approached from the perspective of reading" (Secord 2000: 518). Rather than mapping evolutionary views onto political or religious ideologies, Secord teases out the cultural controversies sparked by *Vestiges* from the comments by, and exchanges between, individual readers. Paradoxically, a focus on reading generates "a study of cultural formation in action" (Secord 2000: 3). It is, so far, an experiment that literary scholars, and literary readers of Darwin and even of Victorian science, have not really attempted to emulate, at least not on a comparable scale. Perhaps that is because, as Secord himself stresses, *Vestiges* was unusual, even unique, in the number of identifiable traces—the distinctive concepts, terminology, and narrative arc—it left behind in both published and unpublished sources. *Victorian Sensation* is a salutary reminder, however, of the gap that can exist between a modern critic's reading, or even published contemporary reviews, and the responses of actual readers.

With regard to his specific contribution to our understanding of Darwin, Secord reads the *Origin* as a response to *Vestiges*, highlighting not only Darwin's explicit characterization of *Vestiges* as a merely "popular" work but also the many ways in which the *Origin* was shaped with Chambers's book in mind. Secord's attention to Darwin, though, is deliberately restricted, for he argues that *Vestiges* has too often been read solely in relation to the *Origin*, mainly as a "failed" precursor, its significance overlooked or distorted. Indeed, for Secord, the appearance of the *Origin* is better seen as marking the end of a period of cultural crisis over evolutionary theory initiated by *Vestiges* rather than as itself launching such a period of crisis. For Beer and Levine, it is the language and assumptions of the various forms of natural theology that Darwin most prominently seeks to overturn in the *Origin*, but for Secord, *Vestiges* is at least as important as a presence and an adversary.

Gowan Dawson's *Darwin, Literature and Victorian Respectability* (2007), while not attempting as comprehensive and detailed a synthesis as Secord's, nonetheless contains important elements of Secord's approach. Dawson's book was one of the first book-length studies of Darwin by literary scholars since Beer and Levine to move in new directions.[6] Like Secord, Dawson is focused on the worlds of print and material culture. While drawing on "contextualist approaches to the history of science" (Dawson 2007: 7 [Chapter 24: 215]), Dawson is, like Secord, not simply tracing Darwinism's impact on political or religious ideologies, but extending the range of issues and participants involved in the debates over evolution. Indeed, one of Dawson's achievements is to demonstrate that from the late 1860s the debates over Darwinism began to shift from general concerns about the implications of evolution for political and religious propriety to specific anxieties over sexual propriety and social respectability. Particularly after the 1871 publication of Darwin's *Descent of Man*, with its frank and far-reaching discussions of sexuality, morality, and beauty, Darwinism's detractors increasingly associated his work with pornography and obscenity, a brush also used to tar avant-garde literary and artistic movements like aestheticism and decadence, as personified in the work of figures like Algernon Swinburne, Dante Gabriel Rossetti, and Walter Pater. In response, Darwin and his fellow scientific naturalists worked anxiously but diligently to distance themselves and their ideas from these writers and artists as well as from the advocates of free thought and the challengers of repressive sexual mores. Nonetheless, the innuendos about the improper sexual implications of Darwinism, Dawson argues, were more persistent than charges about its associations with political radicalism and more difficult to shake off.

In reflecting some of the new approaches in both literary studies and the history of science since *Darwin's Plots* and *Darwin and the Novelists*, Dawson's book marks a turn from the work of Beer and Levine in several important ways. Perhaps most basically, it embodies an interest in different aspects of Darwin's work. Although Beer's attention to the representation of women in *The Descent of Man* led to a great deal of work on gender and courtship in Victorian literature in relation to Darwin's theory of sexual selection, Dawson's focus on the *Descent*'s own representation of sexuality was new. As such, it joined a slowly growing interest in the cultural and literary significance of Darwin's other works, particularly *The Expression of the Emotions in Man and Animals* (1872) but also *The Variation of Animals and Plants under Domestication* (1868), his various books on plants, and his final book on earthworms. By focusing on poetry and non-fiction prose, Dawson also helped move the literary study of Darwin back to a more capacious arena of literature. Prior to Beer and Levine, the literary critics who wrote about Darwin touched on a wide range of writers—aesthetes, satirists, nonsense versifiers, scientific romancers. Dawson's work reminds us that the novel, and especially the realist novel, was neither the only nor the most obvious place to look for responses to Darwin. Most significantly, perhaps, Dawson's book has helped move the literary study of Darwin firmly from intellectual history to a more thoroughly cultural and material one. Dawson draws on revisionist historical studies of Victorian sexuality, a range of textual and visual sources that includes radical pamphlets, satirical cartoons, and law reports as well as books, essays, and lectures published by respectable writers and publishers. Darwin and his ideas are thus shown to be part of what Elizabeth Barrett Browning in *Aurora Leigh* called "this live, throbbing age, / That brawls, cheats, maddens, calculates, aspires, / And spends more passion, more heroic heat, / Betwixt the mirrors of its drawing-rooms, / Than Roland with his knights at Roncesvalles" (5.203–7).

Despite its debts to Beer and Levine, Dawson's book also constitutes an explicit challenge to the "one culture" thesis of the relationship between literature and science employed by Beer and Levine, and largely adopted by those who have followed in their footsteps. Dawson argues that this model "implicitly celebrates discursive interchanges between scientific and literary modes of writing as invariably creative and mutually advantageous" (Dawson 2007: 7 [Chapter 24: 215]). This, he says, is "much too sanguine," especially in light of his own study, which shows opponents of evolution attempting to link it to aestheticism for the purpose of discrediting it, while Darwin and his allies aligned themselves instead with more respectable literary writers such as Tennyson. We might well quarrel with Dawson's characterization of the "one culture" model as implying an *invariably* creative and mutually advantageous relationship between literature and science—Beer was interested in resistance to Darwin as well as appropriations of him, and Levine draws attention to the limits of Dickensian sympathies with Darwin's vision—but Dawson's concern is a valid one. To assume a symbiotic relationship between scientific and literary writing in the Victorian period would be as erroneous as to assume a hostile relationship. We should not slide from one monolithic, over-simplified conceptualization of this relationship to its opposite.

The recent study of Darwin by literary and cultural scholars has, then, not moved in a single direction so much as—to use a Darwinian word—branched. While novelists working in the realist vein have continued to receive attention, scholars have also returned to works and writers—such as Tennyson, Ruskin, Swinburne, Stevenson, and Wells—who had been a focus of study prior to Beer and Levine, this time armed not only with the insights of Beer and Levine but with the recent work of historians of Darwin and Victorian science. Other scholars, though, have taken up figures and movements whose relationships to Darwinism have been overlooked or only hinted at, such as Wilde, New Woman fiction, and sensation fiction. The once-tight focus on the *Origin* and the *Descent* has gradually expanded to include a number of Darwin's other works, although the impact of the *Variation* and the botanical works in particular remains under-studied. With the exception of attention from some scholars in animal studies, the almost total neglect of the *Variation*—a book whose concerns with heredity, breeding, and domestication echo across the Victorian cultural landscape—leaves a major gap in the literary and cultural study of Darwin. The recent approaches to Darwin have also varied widely in thematic focus, although the best work so far has tended, like Dawson's, to consider Darwin and his work in relation to cultural and material studies, and to pursue Darwinism's connections to gender and sexuality. As Darwin, his ideas, and his books become more firmly grounded in the ferment of Victorian science and Victorian culture, our view of all three has altered significantly. A case in point is Bernard Lightman's *Victorian Popularizers of Science* (2007), which has shown that most Victorians got their Darwin not from Darwin or his allies but from popularizers who packaged natural selection within the very natural theological framework that Darwin was trying to overturn. The popularization of Darwin's theories, it turns out, was the antithesis of the traditional "diffusionist" model, in which scientific elites spread new knowledge to a general audience; rather, the popularizers of Darwinism shaped how Darwinism was understood and interpreted, and some of the most influential described Darwin's theories in ways deeply uncongenial to Darwin and his fellow scientific naturalists.

Scholars entering what has come to be called "the Darwin industry" thus have a tougher task than Beer and Levine did a generation ago, but they also have far greater historical resources at their disposal. Much of what used to require a trip to Cambridge can now be accessed online in searchable form. A scholarly edition of Darwin's massive correspondence commenced publication in 1985 and is now in the final decade of his life; that project's website (*Darwin Correspondence Project*) at present includes the full text of some 7,500 letters. Another website, *Darwin Online* (van Wyhe 2002–), contains a complete collection of Darwin's published writings as well as numerous manuscripts, private papers, and supplementary works. Janet Browne's magisterial, two-volume biography of Darwin (1995, 2002) had the misfortune to appear after Desmond and Moore's *Darwin*, but it is by far the fullest, most nuanced account of Darwin's life and work that we have. Outstanding secondary studies of Darwin and Darwinism have proliferated.[7] In addition to Secord's work on *Vestiges*, major biographies and critical studies have appeared on Darwin's precursors, allies, and rivals.[8] Literary and cultural scholars of Darwin have even less excuse for failing to differentiate Darwinian concepts from those of other evolutionary thinkers than they did more than a half-century ago, when Morse Peckham (1959) labeled such confusions "Darwinisticism."

Into the wealth of recent contextualist work on Darwin has also come a new book from Levine: *Darwin the Writer* (2011). Although it reads in many ways like a coda to *Darwin and the Novelists*, it departs simultaneously from that work's interest in intellectual history and from more recent cultural readings of Darwin. While generous to those who have come after him, Levine insists, *pace* Secord, that it is the *Origin*, not *Vestiges*, that changed the world, and that the success of Darwin's book had as much to do with its artistry—"the form of his argument and the nature of his language" (Levine 2011: 5)—as with the power of his ideas. And the form of that argument, Levine contends, in a return to an issue that had so concerned critics prior to the appearance of *Darwin's Plots*, is comic, a celebration of the wonder of life. Levine in *Darwin the Writer* wants to upend—as he did in his earlier *Darwin Loves You* (2006)—the common contemporary cultural perception of Darwinism (by friend and foe alike) as offering a bleak, mechanistic, and nihilistic view of nature and of human nature. In the process, he shows that careful examination of Darwin's language can still yield insights and surprises about both Darwin and Darwinism. But *Darwin the Writer* is unlikely to herald a turn away from the study of Darwin in his Victorian cultural context. Its chapter on Darwin and Wildean paradox is suggestive, while that on the Darwinian grotesque in Hardy's *The Woodlanders* merely seems plausible, underscoring the fact that the historical particularity and density of Secord and Dawson have now made the broader cultural brushstrokes of *Darwin and the Novelists* and even *Darwin's Plots* begin to appear too imprecise. The intellectual sweep of Beer and Levine has given way to the detailed case studies of Secord and Dawson, much as the "long argument" of the *Origin* required the painstaking collation of evidence and careful experimentation represented by the *Variation* and the botanical studies.

Notes

1 With his reference to evolution and progress, Dowden could also have had in mind Darwin's immediate predecessors in formulating sweeping evolutionary theories, Herbert Spencer and the anonymous author of *Vestiges of the Natural History of Creation*.
2 The most prominent works include Barzun 1942 (2nd edn 1958), Culler 1968, Henkin 1940, Hyman 1962, Stevenson 1932.
3 It is worth noting that both Beer and Levine came to Darwin through an interest in George Eliot; that Beer's first book was a study of another realist fascinated by evolutionary theory, George Meredith; and that Levine's study of nineteenth-century realism, *The Realistic Imagination* (1981), immediately preceded his work on Darwin.
4 Some classic studies include Barnes 1974, Bloor 1976, Latour and Woolgar 1979, and Shapin and Schafer 1985.
5 Snow, an English scientist, novelist, and civil servant, delivered his controversial Rede lecture on "The Two Cultures" at the University of Cambridge in 1959 and published it in book form later that year. The term was quickly taken up in Britain and America to denote the separation between scientists and engineers on the one hand, humanists on the other. For an excellent account, see Collini 1993.
6 Others include Amigoni 2007, Schmitt 2009, and Smith 2006.
7 Among the most important are Bowler 1988, Desmond 1989, Desmond and Moore 2009, Moore 1979, Numbers 1998, and Richards 1987 and 1992.
8 See, for example, Desmond 1994 and 1997, Endersby 2008, Fichman 2004, and Rupke 2009.

Bibliography

Amigoni, D. (2007) *Colonies, Cults, and Evolution: Literature, Science and Culture in Nineteenth-Century Writing*, Cambridge: Cambridge University Press.

Barnes, B. (1974) *Scientific Knowledge and Sociological Theory*, London: Routledge & Kegan Paul.

Barzun, J. (1942) *Darwin, Marx, Wagner: Critique of a Heritage*, London: Secker and Warburg.

Beer, G. (1983) *Darwin's Plots: Evolutionary Narrative in Darwin, George Eliot and Nineteenth-Century Fiction*, London: Routledge.

Bloor, D. (1976) *Knowledge and Social Imagery*, London: Routledge & Kegan Paul.

Bowler, P. J. (1988) *The Non-Darwinian Revolution: Reinterpretation of a Historical Myth*, Baltimore: Johns Hopkins University Press.

Browne, J. (1995) *Charles Darwin: Voyaging*, New York: Knopf.

—— (2002) *Charles Darwin: The Power of Place*, New York: Knopf.

Collini, S. (1993) "Introduction," in C. P. Snow, *The Two Cultures*, Cambridge: Cambridge University Press, pp. vii–lxxi.

Culler, A.D. (1968) "The Darwinian revolution and literary form," in G. Levine and W. Madden (eds.), *The Art of Victorian Prose*, New York: Oxford University Press, pp. 224–46.

Darwin Correspondence Project (2014). Available at www.darwinproject.ac.uk (accessed 20 January 2014).

Dawson, G. (2007) *Darwin, Literature and Victorian Respectability*, Cambridge: Cambridge University Press.

Desmond, A. (1989) *The Politics of Evolution: Morphology, Medicine, and Reform in Radical London*, Chicago: University of Chicago Press.

—— (1994) *Huxley: The Devil's Disciple*, London: Michael Joseph.

—— (1997) *Huxley: Evolution's High Priest*, London: Michael Joseph.

Desmond, A. and Moore, J. (1991) *Darwin*, London: Michael Joseph.

—— (2009) *Darwin's Sacred Cause: How a Hatred of Slavery Shaped Darwin's Views on Human Evolution*, Boston, MA: Houghton Mifflin Harcourt.

Dowden, E. (1877) "The Scientific Movement and Literature," *Contemporary Review*, 30: 558–78.

Endersby, J. (2008) *Imperial Nature: Joseph Hooker and the Practices of Victorian Science*, Chicago: University of Chicago Press.

Fichman, M. (2004) *An Elusive Victorian: The Evolution of Alfred Russel Wallace*, Chicago: University of Chicago Press.

Henkin, L. J. (1940) *Darwinism and the English Novel*, New York: Corporate Press.

Hyman, S. E. (1962) *The Tangled Bank: Darwin, Marx, Frazer and Freud as Imaginative Writers*, New York: Atheneum.

[James, H.] (1873) *Middlemarch* by Eliot, G., reviewed in *The Galaxy*, 15(3): 424–28.

Latour, B. and Woolgar, S. (1979) *Laboratory Life: The Construction of Scientific Facts*, Beverly Hills, CA: Sage Publications.

Levine, G. (1981) *The Realistic Imagination: English Fiction from Frankenstein to Lady Chatterley*, Chicago: University of Chicago Press.

—— (1988) *Darwin and the Novelists: Patterns of Science in Victorian Fiction*, Cambridge, MA: Harvard University Press.

—— (2006) *Darwin Loves You: Natural Selection and the Re-enchantment of the World*, Princeton: Princeton University Press.

—— (2011) *Darwin the Writer*, Oxford: Oxford University Press.

Lightman, B. (2007) *Victorian Popularizers of Science: Designing Nature for New Audiences*, Chicago: University of Chicago Press, 2007.

Moore, J. (1979) *The Post-Darwinian Controversies: A Study of the Protestant Struggles to Come to Terms with Darwin in Great Britain and America, 1870–1900*, Cambridge: Cambridge University Press.

Numbers, R. L. (1998) *Darwinism Comes to America*, Cambridge, MA: Harvard University Press.

Peckham, M. (1959) "Darwinism and Darwinisticism," *Victorian Studies*, 3(1): 19–40.

Richards, R.J. (1987) *Darwin and the Emergence of Evolutionary Theories of Mind and Behavior*, Chicago: University of Chicago Press.

—— (1992) *The Meaning of Evolution: The Morphological Construction and Ideological Reconstruction of Darwin's Theory*, Chicago: University of Chicago Press.

Rupke, N.A. (2009) *Richard Owen: Biology without Darwin*, rev. edn., Chicago: University of Chicago Press.

Schmitt, C. (2009) *Darwin and the Memory of the Human: Evolution, Savages, and South America*, Cambridge: Cambridge University Press.

Secord, J. (2000) *Victorian Sensation: The Extraordinary Publication, Reception, and Secret Authorship of "Vestiges of the Natural History of Creation,"* Chicago: University of Chicago Press.

Shapin, S. and Schafer, S. (1985) *Leviathan and the Air-Pump: Hobbes, Boyle, and the Experimental Life*, Princeton: Princeton University Press.

Smith, J. (2006) *Charles Darwin and Victorian Visual Culture*, Cambridge: Cambridge University Press.

Stevenson, L. (1932) *Darwin Among the Poets*, Chicago: University of Chicago Press.

van Wyhe, J. (ed.) (2002–) *The Complete Work of Charles Darwin Online*. Available HTTP: <http://darwin-online.org.uk> (accessed 20 January 2014).

Part VII

Psychology and literature

Introduction

Study of the mind flourished during the Victorian era, producing new questions about the self and consciousness that remain with us today. At the center of this period of profound rethinking was the emergence in the mid-nineteenth century of "physiological psychology," which drew on physiology, neurology, and, later, evolutionary theory in order to firmly embed the mind within the physical body. While this turn to materialism paved the way for psychology's establishment as an academic and professional discipline in the late nineteenth century, it is important to understand that in the mid-Victorian period the division between professional and amateur approaches to the study of the mind was not yet clear-cut. Psychological questions were regularly debated in the pages of popular journals such as *Household Words* and *The Fortnightly Review*, and some early commentators like G. H. Lewes (partner of George Eliot) and E. S. Dallas became as notable for their contributions to science as to literature. In other words, as Michael Davis reminds us in his capstone essay here, for much of the nineteenth century, literature and psychology belonged firmly to the same discursive sphere.

Such connections between Victorian literature and psychology were largely ignored for much of the twentieth century, thanks in part to the dominance of later Freudian and post-Freudian psychoanalytic theory in literary studies for many years, a phenomenon which resulted—anachronistically, though not always unproductively—in the application of twentieth-century theories of the mind and self to nineteenth-century literature. Such ostensibly transhistorical approaches to the mind were also prevalent in early feminist criticism, notably Sandra Gilbert and Susan Gubar's *Madwoman in the Attic* (1979), which tended to understand fictional representations of mental aberration in post-Freudian symbolic terms, rather than as reflecting an engagement with specifically Victorian theories of the mind.

It is only in the last three decades, with the rise once more of historicist approaches to literature, that scholars have begun to consider fully the interplay of psychology and literature in the nineteenth century. Rejecting earlier accounts of the mind and the self in Victorian literature as ahistorical, in the late-twentieth century scholars such as Jenny Bourne Taylor, Sally Shuttleworth, and Helen Small carefully situated psychological discourse in the Victorian novel in its nineteenth-century context, using a diverse range of sources including medical psychiatry, domestic manuals, newspaper articles, and self-help books. Following the lead of other critics working on the relationship between literature and science, notably Gillian Beer and George Levine, these critics also pushed further to establish that rather than merely serving as a context for the novel, Victorian psychological theory was in fact remade by a fictional form that was dedicated like no other to the elaboration of consciousness.

Rick Rylance's monumental *Victorian Psychology and British Culture 1850–1880* (2000) is in many ways the logical continuation of the work begun in the 1990s. In turning his literary-critical gaze exclusively toward Victorian psychological writings, Rylance supports the earlier critical contention that literature and psychology did indeed operate in the same discursive sphere in the Victorian period. Alongside Shuttleworth's seminal book on Charlotte Brontë, the extraordinary historical detail and nuanced analysis of Rylance's study has grounded much new work on Victorian psychology and literature, which continues to develop in a number of diverse directions. Once largely focused on mental illness and on novelists clearly engaged with psychological theory, scholarship has recently begun to explore Victorian understandings of "ordinary consciousness" and writers rarely associated with Victorian science, as Jill Matus's argument excerpted here illustrates (Matus 2009: 10). Similarly, the novel's stranglehold in this field has been challenged with studies published by Jason Rudy and Gregory Tate that consider the relationship between poetry and Victorian theories of the mind. But perhaps most promising is the increasing interest in the relations between psychology and other branches of medical, scientific, and philosophical thought in the nineteenth century, apparent in William Cohen's and Vanessa Ryan's recent books, which suggests that—as Michael Davis notes below—there's still much left to say about the complex discursive production of Victorian thought about minds, bodies, and selves.

See also: *Genre fiction and the sensational; Darwin and Victorian culture; Disinterestedness and liberalism*

26 *Villette*

'The surveillance of a sleepless eye'

Sally Shuttleworth

[. . .]

[In Charlotte Brontë's *Villette*] Lucy [Snowe]'s resistance to Dr John stems less from the actual content of his medical verdicts, than from his reduction of her to a bundle of symptoms, open to his professional definition and control. Her first preoccupation after her collapse, occasion of her double exposure to the eyes of religious and medical authority, was to re-establish her private domain, subduing feeling so as to be 'better regulated, more equable, quieter on the surface' where the 'common gaze' will fall. The turbulent realm below was to be left to God: 'Man, your equal, weak as you, and not fit to be your judge, may be shut out thence' (p. 255).[1] Dr John, however, attempts just that act of judgment, but in diagnosing her case as one of hypochondria, he is forced to acknowledge limitations in his medical art which 'looks in and sees a chamber of torture, but can neither say nor do much' (p. 261). He is restricted to recommending the cheerful society and exercise listed by Graham as the means by which 'moral management' should attempt to cure hypochondriasis.[2] Even Dr John's more limited claim to an authoritative power of diagnosis is undermined, however, by his failure to remark, as Lucy does, that the King of Labassecour is a sufferer from 'constitutional melancholy' (p. 304). Medical knowledge is matched against experiential understanding and found wanting.

Lucy claims for herself the sole power of deciphering the 'hierogylphics' of the king's countenance which suggest to her that, 'Those eyes had looked on the visits of a certain ghost – had long waited the comings and goings of that strangest spectre, Hypochondria' (p. 303). The conflation of medical and Gothic terminology in this passage echoes Brontë's description of her own experience of hypochondria in a letter written several years earlier. Brontë speaks initially of the suffering of a friend who 'has felt the tyranny of Hypochondria – a most dreadful doom, far worse than that of a man of healthy nerves buried for the same length of time in a subterranean dungeon'. Of her own experience she remarks that she had endured 'preternatural horror which seemed to clothe existence and Nature – and which made life a continual waking Nightmare – Under such circumstances the morbid nerves can know neither peace nor enjoyment – whatever touches – pierces them – sensation for them is all suffering'. Considering her effect upon Margaret Wooler, she concludes she must have been 'no better company for you than a stalking ghost'.[3] The letter, like the novel, suggests a sense of powerlessness in the face of physiological tyranny. The terms of the description offer a similar mixture of metaphorical and physiological language: the idea of being buried alive, literally embodied in *Villette*, is linked to the notion of 'morbid nerves', which are themselves then personified, endowed with the capacity to suffer and experience. The ghostly qualities, attributed to hypochondria in the novel, are here appropriated by Brontë for herself, in a transposition which mirrors the novel's dissolution of the boundaries of the self. Lucy not only dwells in a realm where furniture becomes 'spectral', but also attributes that quality to herself in others' eyes: she feels, at one stage, she must look to Dr John 'like some ghost' (p. 157). Perception, in Lucy's spectral world, is integrally related to the social construction of identity.

Lucy's final discussion of hypochondria returns once more to the question of the relationship between physiology and mental suffering. She contrasts the world's ready acceptance of the idea of physical illness with its reluctant understanding of an equivalent mental disease:

> The world can understand well enough the process of perishing for want of food: perhaps few persons can enter into or follow out that of going mad from solitary confinement. They see the long-buried prisoner disinterred, a maniac or an idiot! – how his sense left him – how his nerves first inflamed, underwent nameless agony, and then sunk to palsy – is a subject too intricate for examination, too abstract for popular comprehension. Speak of it! you might almost as well stand up in an European market-place, and propound dark sayings in that language and mood wherein Nebuchadnezzar, the imperial hypochondriac, communed with his baffled Chaldeans. (p. 392)

The idea of psychological deprivation, dramatized throughout the novel in the motif of live burial, is here grounded in the physiological experience of the nerves which undergo inflammation and then 'nameless agony'. As soon as Lucy moves away from available technical vocabulary she reaches the limits of the expressible: the agony must remain 'nameless'. Unlike her Biblical counterpart, Lucy knows better than to try and describe to others a form of experience that has never received social recognition or articulation. The passage represents an implicit rebuke to the medical establishment who believe that in naming the 'symptoms' of hypochondria, they have somehow mastered the experience. Lucy is both asserting her own belief in the material basis of psychological suffering, and denying Dr John's claim to authoritative knowledge.

Lucy's battle for control over self-definition and interpretation of the processes of her own mind is not conducted solely with Dr John; the fiery M. Paul also enters the lists. On encountering Lucy in the art gallery after her illness, M. Paul berates her for her unfeminine behaviour in not being able to look after the cretin: "'Women who are worthy the name,'" he proclaims, "'ought infinitely to surpass our coarse, fallible, self-indulgent sex, in the power to perform such duties'" (p. 290). The covert subject of this conversation is clearly the model of the female mind which suggested that women are more 'naturally' able than men to suppress their 'evil propensities'. Lucy, in self-defence, resorts to another male model of the female mind, asserting a physical illness: "'I had a nervous fever: my mind was ill'" (p. 290). Diminished responsibility, which figured so largely in mid-Victorian trials of female criminals, becomes the basis of her excuse for 'unwomanly' conduct. Unlike Dr John, M. Paul refuses to accept this model of the mind and so draws attention back again to his own image of the constitution of the feminine. Dismissing the idea of nervous fever, he points instead to Lucy's 'temerity' in gazing at the picture of Cleopatra. The portrait of the fleshy Cleopatra, and the four pictures of 'La vie d'une femme', 'cold and vapid as ghosts', which M. Paul prefers for Lucy's instruction in the arts of femininity, take on iconographic significance in the narrative, representing the two alternative models for womanhood created by men.[4] Lucy's challenge to these models, implicit throughout her narrative, takes decisive form in the Vashti section.

The narrative sequence which culminates in the performance of Vashti actually starts, not in the theatre, but on Lucy's apparent sighting, that evening, of the nun. Dr John, refusing to respect her reticence, invokes once more his professional authority to diagnose the symptoms of her 'raised look', thus provoking Lucy's angry dismissal of his explanation: 'Of course with him, it was held to be another effect of the same cause: it was all optical illusion – nervous malady, and so on. Not one bit did I believe him; but I dared not contradict: doctors are so self-opinionated, so immovable in their dry, materialist views' (p. 368). Lucy rejects the 'doctor's' opinion on principle, although his physiological explanation appears perhaps surprisingly close to views she herself has expressed elsewhere. The grounds of her objection to Dr John's 'dry' materialism are made explicit, however, in her analysis of their mutual responses to the performance of Vashti.

For Lucy, Vashti on stage transcends socially imposed sex-roles; she is neither woman nor man, but a devil, a literal embodiment of inner passion: 'Hate and Murder and Madness incarnate, she stood' (p. 369). Lucy's response is to invoke the male author of a rather different image of womanhood: 'Where was the artist of the Cleopatra? Let him come and sit down and study this different vision. Let him seek here the mighty brawn, the muscle, the abounding blood, the full-fed flesh he worshipped: let all materialists draw nigh and look on' (p. 370). In a significant elision, Lucy has drawn together the materialism of doctors who seek to explain the processes of the mind with reference only to the physiological behaviour of the nerves, and the materialism of men who construct their images of women with reference only to the physical attributes of the flesh. The creation of the feminine in male-executed art is directly allied to the medical construction of women.

Lucy perceives, in Vashti, a force which could re-enact the miracle of the Red Sea, drowning Paul Peter Rubens [*sic*] and 'all the army of his fat women', but Dr John remains unresponsive to her challenge. He replicates, in the 'intense curiosity' with which he watches her performance, the professional gaze he has recently imposed on Lucy. His verdict underscores, for Lucy, his indifference to the inner movements of female experience: 'he judged her as a woman, not an artist: it was a branding judgment' (p. 373). Dr John's response is determined entirely by predefined categories of suitable female behaviour. As in his medical practice, he is insulated from any attempt to understand the causes or experiential detail of the cases he is examining through his possession of a socially validated system of classification which allows him to speak with unreflecting authority. Like his counterparts in the Book of Esther (from where the name Vashti is drawn) he trusts to the codification of male power to protect him from the 'demonic' challenge of female energy. (Queen Vashti's refusal to show her beauty at the king's command had provoked, from a worried male oligarchy, a proclamation 'to every people after their language, that every man should bear rule in his own house'.)[5]

In choosing to equate medical and artistic constructions of the female identity through the notion of 'materialism,' Brontë was drawing on the terms of contemporary debate. As an artistic term, implying the 'tendency to lay stress on the material aspects of the objects represented' the first use of materialism seems to date only from the 1850s (OED). Although the philosophical usage of materialism dates back to the eighteenth century, it had, at the time of Brontë's writing, become the focus of a virulent social and theological debate concerning the development of psychological theories which stressed that the brain was the organ of mind. Phrenology and mesmerism were located, in the popular press, at the centre of this controversy, as evidenced by the 1851 *Blackwood's* article which inveighed against the phreno-mesmerism of authors who believed that 'upon the materialism of life rest the great phenomena of what we were wont to call mind'.[6] Clearly, as Brontë's use of phrenological terms and concepts reveals, she was not stirred into opposition by this controversy. Lucy's objections to materialism are not based on the religious grounds of contemporary debate; nor, as her own use of physiological vocabulary demonstrates, are they founded on an opposition to the use of a physiological explanation of the mind *per se*. Her rejection of medical and artistic materialism stems rather from the rigid and incomplete nature of their conception; she objects less to the idea of an interrelationship between body and mind, than to their rather partial vision of this union. Under the medical and artistic gaze, woman is *reduced* to flesh and the material functioning of nerves.

In describing the impact of Vashti, Lucy herself employs the vocabulary of contemporary physiological psychology; Vashti's acting,

> instead of merely irritating imagination with the thought of what *might* be done, at the same time fevering the nerves because it was *not* done, disclosed power like a deep, swollen, winter river, thundering in cataract, and bearing the soul, like a leaf, on the steep and steely sweep of its descent. (p. 371)

The term 'irritating' here is a technical one as used, for example, in Graham's observation that 'The nervous headache generally occurs in persons with a peculiar irritability of the nervous system.'[7] Coupled with the idea of 'fevering the nerves' it suggests two different levels of response within the nervous system, whilst the concluding imagery of the thundering river draws on physiological ideas of channelled energy within the brain. The power disclosed is both internal and external: it describes the force of Vashti's own inner energy, and the impact on the observer Lucy. What Brontë has done, in this metaphorical usage of contemporary physiological theory, is to dramatize an even closer integration of body and mind than physiology envisaged, while simultaneously breaking down the traditional boundaries of the self. Mind is not reduced to body, it becomes literally 'embodied', as Lucy earlier observed: 'To her, what hurts becomes immediately embodied: she looks on it as a thing that can be attacked, worried down, torn in shreds. Scarcely a substance herself, she grapples to conflict with abstractions. Before calamity she is a tigress; she rends her woes, shivers them in convulsed abhorrence' (p. 370). Whilst the artist reduces woman to a material expanse of flesh, and the doctor to a mere encasement of nerves, Vashti reveals a true union between the worlds of mind and body: abstractions, the experiential details of mental life which physiology cannot describe, are given material form. In her treatment of Vashti, as throughout the novel, Brontë actually employs contemporary physiological theory to break through the narrow definition of the self it proposes.

The description of Vashti tearing hurt into shreds anticipates Lucy's later destruction of the figure of the nun:

> All the movement was mine, so was all the life, the reality, the substance, the force; as my instinct felt. I tore her up – the incubus! I held her on high – the goblin! I shook her loose – the mystery! And down she fell – down all round me – down in shreds and fragments – and I trode upon her. (p. 681)

Like Vashti, Lucy undertakes a material destruction of an inner hurt: the force and *substance* are Lucy's own.[8] The term 'incubus', with its associations of sexuality and mental disturbance, draws together the arenas of physical and mental life. In nineteenth-century psychological usage, incubus had become synonymous with nightmare. In a passage noted by Patrick Brontë, Robert Macnish observed in *The Philosophy of Sleep* that it was possible to suffer nightmare whilst awake and in 'perfect possession of [the] faculties'. Macnish records that he had 'undergone the greatest tortures, being haunted by spectres, hags, and every sort of phantom – having, at the same time, a full consciousness that I was labouring under incubus, and that all the terrifying objects around me were the creations of my own brain'.[9] Brontë takes this idea of waking nightmare or incubus one stage further, giving it a literal embodiment in her fiction which defies attempts to demarcate the boundaries between 'creations of the brain' and external forms.

Brontë offers, in *Villette*, a thorough materialization of the self. The construct 'Lucy' is not a unified mental entity, located within a physiological frame, but rather a continuous process which extends beyond the confines of the flesh. Lucy's entire mode of self-articulation breaks down the hierarchy of outer and inner life upon which definitions of the 'Real' (and sanity) depend. Her description of the death of Hope, for instance, parallels that of the literal burial of the letters: 'In the end I closed the eyes of my dead, covered its face, and composed its limbs with great calm' (p. 421). The burial itself is the wrapping of grief in a 'winding-sheet'. Later, as Lucy pauses beside the grave, she recalls 'the passage of feeling therein buried' (p. 524). Metaphor has become inoperable: it functions, as Lucy's text makes clear, only if the speaker endorses normative social demarcations between different states. Thus the classrooms which initially only 'seem' to Lucy to be like jails quickly become 'filled with spectral and intolerable memories, laid miserable amongst their straw and their manacles' (p. 652). The controlling distance of 'seems' is collapsed, as 'memories', normally restricted to the realm of the mind, take on vivid physical form.

Lucy's intricate dramatizations of her feelings undermine traditional divisions between external social process and inner mental life, revealing their fictional status.[10] Her tale of Jael, Sisera and Heber, for example, simultaneously portrays physiological pain, psychological conflict, and the social drama of repression. Speaking of her desire to be drawn out of her present existence, Lucy observes:

> This longing, and all of a similar kind, it was necessary to knock on the head; which I did, figuratively, after the manner of Jael to Sisera, driving a nail through their temples. Unlike Sisera, they did not die: they were but transiently stunned, and at intervals would turn on the nail with a rebellious wrench; then did the temples bleed, and the brain thrill to its core. (p. 152)

The distinction between figural and literal quickly fades, as the inner psychic drama develops, and the rebellious desires themselves perpetuate their torture, in a description which captures the physiological and psychological experience of socially inflicted repression (the term 'thrill' carried the medically precise meaning, in the mid-nineteenth century, of 'vibratory movement, resonance, or murmur'). The narrative evocation of inner life does not, however, end there. Lucy develops the story, envisaging, with a precision of detail unmatched in the descriptions of the external scenes of her life, the physical landscape of the action under the soothing light of imagination. Jael, the controlling self responsible for maiming the desires to whom she had promised shelter, begins to relent, but such thoughts are soon outweighed by the expectation of her husband, Heber's, commendation of her deed: female self-repression is accorded patriarchal endorsement. This drama of internal pain and division, with its precise enactment of the social processes of control, reveals the falsity of normative divisions between inner and outer experience.

The famous account of Lucy's opiate-induced wanderings into the night landscape of Villette also dissolves the divisions between inner and outer realms, as social experience now takes on the qualities of mental life, defying the normal boundaries of time and space. Amidst the physical forms of Cleopatra's Egypt, Lucy witnesses all the figures of her inner thoughts parade before her eyes (only Ginevra and De Hamal are excluded, but, as Lucy later insists, it was her own excursion which released them into sexual freedom).[11] Even here, however, where she seems most free from external social controls, she is still subject to fears of surveillance: she feels Dr John's gaze 'oppressing' her, seeming ready to grasp 'my identity . . . between his never tyrannous, but always powerful hands' (p. 661). As dominant male, and doctor, empowered by society to diagnose the inner movements of mind, and legislate on mental disease, Dr John threatens Lucy's carefully-nurtured sense of self. Identity, as Brontë has shown throughout *Villette*, is not a given, but rather a tenuous process of negotiation between the subject and surrounding social forces.

The opposition to male materialism, voiced by Lucy in her confrontation with medical authority, gives dramatic expression to the interrogation of male constructions of the female psyche which underpins the narrative form of *Villette*. In seeking to avoid the surveillance of religious, educational and medical figures, trying to render herself illegible, Lucy attempts to assume control over the processes of her own self-definition. Yet her narrative, as I have argued, reveals a clear internalization of the categories and terms of contemporary medical psychology. Lucy employs physiological explanations of mental life and appropriates to herself theories of a female predisposition to neurosis and monomania. In creating the autobiography of her troubled heroine, Brontë explores both the social implications of contemporary psychological theory, and its inner consequences. The form of her account, with its dissolution of divisions between inner psychological life, and the material social world suggests an alternative vision – one that challenges the normative psychological vision implicit in male definitions of the 'Real'.

Notes

1 Charlotte Bronte, *Villette*, ed. H. Rosengarten and M. Smith (Oxford: Oxford University Press, 1984).
2 Thomas John Graham, *Modern Domestic Medicine* (London: Simpkin and Marshall et al., 1826), p. 346.
3 T. J. Wise and J. A. Symington, *The Brontës: their Lives, Friendships and Correspondence*, 4 vols. (Oxford: Basil Blackwell, 1933), II, 116–7 [Cited in future as *Letters*]. To Margaret Wooler, approx. November–December 1846.
4 For an analysis of the functions of these paintings, see [Sandra] Gilbert and [Susan] Gubar, [*The*] *Madwoman* [*in the Attic: The Woman Writer and the Nineteenth-Century Literary Imagination* (New Haven: Yale University Press)], p. 420.
5 *Esther*, I, 22.
6 'What is Mesmerism?' *Blackwood's Edinburgh Magazine*, 70 (1851), p. 84.
7 Graham, *Modern Domestic Medicine*, p. 332.
8 Mary Jacobus, in her excellent article on *Villette*, offers a slightly different reading of this passage: 'The Buried Letter: Feminism and Romanticism in *Villette*', in *Women Writing and Writing about Women*, ed. M. Jacobus (London: Croom Helm, 1979), p. 54.
9 [Robert] Macnish, *Philosophy of Sleep* [Glasgow: W. R. M'Phun, 1830)], p. 136. The Reverend Brontë records under 'nightmare' in his copy of Graham, 'Dr McNish, who has written very ably on the philosophy of sleep – has justly described, the sensations of Night mare, under some modifications – as being amongst the most horrible that oppress human nature – an inability to move, during the paroxysm – dreadful visions of ghosts etc . . . He was, himself – often distressed by this calamity, and justly said, that it was worst, towards the morning. 1838 B.' (Graham, *Modern Domestic Medicine*, pp. 425–6).

10 As Inga-Stina Ewbank has observed in *Their Proper Sphere: A Study of the Brontë Sisters as Early Victorian Female Novelists* (London: Edward Arnold, 1966), the personifications, lengthened into allegories of Lucy's emotional crises 'do not arrest the action of *Villette*, for in a sense they *are* the action: even more than in *Jane Eyre* the imagery of *Villette* tends to act out an inner drama which superimposes itself on, or even substitutes for, external action' (p. 189).

11 The sequence of events is rather unclear since Lucy herself walks easily out of the pensionnat, but in the ensuing debate as to how Ginevra could have escaped, Lucy cannot forget how she, 'to facilitate a certain enterprise' had neither bolted nor secured the door (pp. 684–5).

27   The discourse of physiology in general biology

Rick Rylance

[. . .]

The collision between mechanistic and vitalistic theories troubled psychological debate through most of the [nineteenth] century. For example, June Goodfield-Toulmin has shown how the ideological pressures of the post-Revolutionary period forced William Lawrence to abandon his tentative work on nervous organization under pressure of public attacks that associated it with 'French Materialism'. As she makes clear, the scientific groundwork was in this instance too slender to maintain explanations that were thought to challenge the prevailing vitalism, and Lawrence quickly withdrew his book—*Lectures on Physiology, Zoology and the Natural History of Man* (1819)—and retreated to his (thereafter, highly successful) medical practice.[1] No doubt the political pressures of this period were particularly severe, but the implications of the 'Lawrence affair' rumbled on through the century and became a reference point for quarrels between the new science and old philosophy, innovatory knowledge and reactionary inhibition. Lawrence's book was pirated by the radical press, and Coleridge was still sneering at it in *On the Constitution of Church and State* a decade later as a byword for immature, freethinking speculation.[2] By the mid-century, materialistic physiologists had a more secure standing ground, but one need only mention the evolution debates to recognize a fraught public context for an area of investigation seen to interfere with prevailing conceptions of man. Goodfield-Toulmin notes that, in his preface to *Man's Place in Nature* of 1863, T. H. Huxley (who was a friend of Lawrence) explicitly invoked parallels between his own predicament as a champion of evolution and the hostility visited on Lawrence in 1819.

G. H. Lewes, too, was alert to the ideological force that could be mobilized behind charges of 'materialism', and to the complex mediations between science, philosophy, and politics that the period demanded. In 'The Present Condition of Philosophy', the conclusion to his enlarged *History of Philosophy* in 1867, Lewes lambasts a culture ideologically geared to reject unpalatable scientific findings. Science 'should be refuted as false, not denounced as dangerous. Research is arduous enough without obstructing the path with bugbears.'[3] Like Huxley, he made a parallel with the period after the French Revolution to indicate the difficulties experienced by contemporaries. It is a passage worth quoting at length, because it reveals a physiological psychologist's own sense of the means by which historical pressures deform ideas. Of the post-Revolution period Lewes writes:

> The reaction against the Philosophy of the Eighteenth Century was less a reaction against a doctrine that had proved to be incompetent than against a doctrine believed to be the source of frightful immorality . . . Associated in men's mind with the Saturnalia of the Terror, the philosophical opinions of Condillac, Diderot and Cabanis were held responsible for

the crimes of the Convention; and what might be true in those opinions was flung aside with what was false, without discrimination, without analysis, in fierce impetuous disgust. Every opinion which had what was called 'a taint of materialism', or seemed to point in that direction, was denounced as an opinion necessarily leading to the destruction of all Religion, Morality, and Government. Every opinion which seemed to point in the direction of spiritualism was eagerly welcomed, promulgated, and lauded; not because it was demonstrably true, but because it was supposed capable of preserving social order. And indeed when, looking back on those times, we contemplate the misery and anarchy which disgraced what was an inevitable movement, and dimmed what was really noble in that movement, we can understand how many generous hearts and minds, fluctuating in perplexity, did instinctively revolt not only against the Revolution, but against all the principles which were ever invoked by the revolutionists. Looking at the matter from this distance we can see clearly enough that 'Materialism' had really no more to do with the Revolution than Christianity had to do with the hideous scenes in which the Anabaptists were actors; but we can understand how indelible was the association of Revolution with materialism in the minds of that generation.

Towards the end of the paragraph, the reader is pushed towards a comfortable historical retrospect. However, in his next—in a manner not unlike many moments in George Eliot's fiction—Lewes surprises the reader with a return to the pressing problems of the present:

So profoundly influential has this association been, that a celebrated surgeon of our own day periled his position by advocating the opinion, now almost universally accepted, but then generally shuddered at, that the brain is the 'organ' of the mind. He had to retract that opinion, which the pious Hartley and many others had advanced without offence. He had to retract it, not because it was scientifically untenable, but because it was declared to be morally dangerous.[4]

Lewes presumably had William Lawrence in mind here, but the broad point is central to his thinking and typical of the period.

John Morley, Lewes's successor as editor of the *Fortnightly Review* from the mid-1860s, recollected that advanced physiological research inevitably mixed in political company, at least for the readers of his review:

people justly perceived that there seemed to be a certain undefinable concurrence among writers coming from different schools and handling very different subjects. Perhaps the instinct was right which fancied it discerned some common drift, a certain pervading atmosphere. People scented a subtle connection between speculations on the Physical Basis of Life and the Unseen Universe, and articles on Trades Unions and National Education; and Professor Tyndall's eloquence in impugning the authority of miracles was supposed to work in the same direction as Mr Frederic Harrison's eloquence in demolishing Prince Bismarck and vindicating the Commune as the newest proof of the political genius of France.[5]

The political as well as scientific contention between vitalism and materialism thus persisted. Because vitalistic theories were seen to introduce occult entities into biomedical science, many found them unsatisfactory. But others were often unable to dispense with them entirely, not least because the rival theory was distastefully inhuman. Mary Shelley's *Frankenstein* (1817) [*sic*] provides a neat, if literary, illustration of a continuing theoretical dilemma. Her novel was directly influenced by William Lawrence, and Frankenstein's Creature is mechanistically contrived and animated by galvanic electricity.[6] He appears a 'material' creature through and through. But the theoretical status of the galvanic spark that gives him life is equivocal. Is it a purely mechanical ingredient, or a superadded, vitalizing force? Mechanistic theories in psychology presented similar difficulties. If 'the mechanical engineering of living machines' (in Huxley's words) was like a factory, where did the particularities of human consciousness and culture find their resources? The Frankenstein story in this respect haunts a century of debate, with commentators on both sides abusing opponents for Frankensteinian proclivities.[7] The scientific problem, writes G. J. Goodfield, 'was to find the relation between the two realms—physico-chemical and vital—to find terms that would both allow for the plasticity of organic processes, and at the same time relate them to the familiar regularities of the inorganic world'.[8] But the broader issues appeared even more intractable.

One important aspect of this debate concerned the prospect of human automatism. This controversy was familiar from the 1840s, but it came to a head in the 1870s when post-Darwinian debate amplified anxieties over the direction of psychological theory.[9] The controversy turned on the mechanistic implications immanent in physiological psychology when extended not only to the higher faculties, but to the concept of the whole person. Psycho-physiological humanity increasingly appeared to resemble machines in the writing of energetic and aggressive polemicists such as Huxley, Tyndall, and Clifford. Their pronouncements actively encouraged speculation in this direction, and, if the physiological body could appear mechanistic, so too might the mind. They denied holding such views, and usually stopped short of a full assertion of this position (their agnosticism, avoiding universalist statements on principle, would not allow such generalization, nor would their political tact). But they often left little braking distance between the momentum of their arguments and this conclusion.

John Tyndall's position, in a celebrated address to the British Association for the Advancement of Science at Norwich in 1868, was representative. Tyndall restated the view that, for the scientist, natural processes were 'a purely mechanical problem'. The materialist, he declared, argues that 'the growth of the body is mechanical, and that thought, as exercised by us, has its correlative in the physics of the brain', though it is not legitimate to infer that 'molecular groupings, and motions, explain everything'.[10] Most heard the first part of this statement, found the implication, and set aside the rest. Tyndall's caution was a proper scientific hesitation, as well as prudent intellectual and ideological abstention, but it only checked, and did not halt, the direction of the argument.

Tyndall's views were much cited and discussed by parties on both sides.[11] But the issue was alive in other hands. Huxley, in his consideration of the subject in 1874, scorned the doctrines of dualists, vitalists, and Idealists and proposed a more specific correlation of physiology and consciousness:

> It is quite true that, to the best of my judgement, the argumentation which applies to brutes holds equally good of men; and therefore, that all states of consciousness in us, as in them, are immediately caused by molecular changes of the brain substance. It seems to me that in men, as in brutes, there is no proof that any state of consciousness is the cause of change in the motion of the matter of the organism . . . it follows that our mental conditions are simply the symbols in consciousness of the changes which take place automatically in the organism; and that, to take an extreme illustration, the feeling that we call volition is not

the cause of a voluntary act, but the symbol of that state of the brain which is the immediate cause of the act. We are conscious automata, endowed with free will in the only intelligible sense of that much abused term—in as much as in many respects we are able to do as we like—but none the less we are parts of the great series of causes and effects which, in unbroken continuity, composes that which is, and has been, and shall be—the sum of existence.[12]

Huxley denied fatalism, materialism, and atheism, and hid his swashbuckling message in liturgical rhythms. Ducking and diving with characteristic agility, and looking for convenient allies, he claimed that 'predestinarian' theologians and philosophers authorized his case. Augustine, Calvin, Leibnitz, Hartley, and others, he asserted, all recommended Christian faith on identical premises. But the spectre of automatism was not exorcised. The abstraction of the physiological body, neither fully disappearing nor yet becoming fully corporeal, and haunting the liminal area between machine and animal, troubled scientific speculation and conservative nightmare alike. Its function remained primarily heuristic and schematic, but this quality nourished the fears and, as a result, the physiological automaton clanks into humanistic and traditionalist dreams as one part of a monstrous Siamese twin whose other head is that of a Darwinian beast. This composite monster, half meccano, half brute, plods out of the nineteenth century as a dual-purpose fantasy of the scientific future. For scientific optimists, the physiological body represents a dream goal of rational (and remedial) enquiry, but for others it represents an invasive creature created by the intellectual perversity of the secular mind. Both conclusions are available in the studied neutrality of Huxley's vision: 'as surely as every future grows out of the past and present, so will the physiology of the future gradually extend the realm of matter and law until it is co-extensive with knowledge, with feeling and with action.'[13]

There were, of course, pro-scientific voices who opposed automaticist doctrines. Carpenter, as a Unitarian, criticized Huxley for abolishing the higher faculties, especially the will, in an obsession with mechanism.[14] G. H. Lewes was conscious of extremist arguments on both sides, and his discussion of 'Mechanism and Experience' in *The Study of Psychology* (1879), the fourth volume of *Problems of Life and Mind*, was one of the few genuinely judicious attempts to stand apart from the main lines of battle. This was partly because he situated the debate in the context of comparable European work, and avoided overinflating the tentative and provisional claims of physiological investigation. But it is also because he takes the sensible step—strangely rarely pursued—of insisting that mental development is not just a question of physiological processes. For Lewes [. . .] it was just as much a question of social development.[15] Others, meanwhile, were troubled by the ersatz metaphysics implied in the more extreme of automaticist pronouncements. Huxley may have intended to pre-empt Christian objections by linking his physiological psychology to predestination (though his extreme rationalist determinism led him in that direction anyway), but it also alienated secular-minded supporters. William James, reviewing the debate in 1890, dismissed 'the automaton theory' as 'an *unwarrantable impertinence*' because it mirrored the assertions of its opponents when urged 'on *a priori* and *quasi*-metaphysical grounds'.[16]

Part of the problem lay in the inherent limitations of nineteenth-century psycho-physiological projects, and their sporadic, but massive, theoretical overextension. Relevant physiological research was primarily found in two areas of investigation: that of the sensory-motor arc (which linked brain and mind to the environment through the nervous system), and that of the localization of the cerebral functions in the anatomy of the brain. A linkage between these two, it was thought, would specify physiologically the circuitry of human behaviour. In retrospect, it is easy to see how rudimentary a basis this was for understanding the capacities of human beings. But it is also easy to underestimate the excitement of original discovery. The sensory-motor arc (established in the first decades of the century by Sir Charles Bell in Britain and François Magandie in France, and developed by Marshall Hall in Britain and Johannes Müller in Germany thereafter), and the more elusive hope of localizing the cerebral functions, provided research foundations for general models of considerable (if rather wide and provisional) explanatory power over a long period. What Clifford Geertz, in 1962, described as physiological psychology's 'long enthralment with the wonders of the reflex arc' persisted well into the twentieth century.[17]

It bears repeating at this point that we are not by and large dealing in this book with scientific work that satisfied the theoretical hopes it inspired. Nor with discoveries that, passing all tests of verification, turned the direction of all subsequent work. We are dealing, instead, with a range of arguments, assumptions, opinions, and knowledge which both prepares, and inhibits, the fortunes of disputed theory as it rises and falls. With hindsight, the overinflation of the explanatory power of physiological models based upon the sensory-motor arc and cerebral localization can appear as absurd to us as it appeared alarming to contemporaries. To explain the whole of human activity in terms of the sensory-motor arc is like explaining how a computer works in terms of the flow of power from the electrical grid. Explaining the same thing by cerebral localization is—to follow the metaphor (and without wishing to imply that minds are computers, because they are not)—like pinning one's explanatory hopes on the simple spatial positioning of microchips. Both are crucial, but hardly sufficient. On the other hand, nor is a computer explained by the witnessing of the operations it performs (which might be an analogy for the arguments of the faculty psychologists). Physiological psychology in the nineteenth century was at work somewhere between the extremes of mechanical determinism and airy denial, and it is well to remind ourselves that such denials could go to extraordinary lengths.

John Gordon, an influential anatomist in Edinburgh in the early decades of the century, was an extremist. He denied not only iatromechanical theories but vitalistic ones also. For him, even the notion of a vital spark smacked too much of the materialization of the soul.[18] Gordon reviewed the psycho-physiological debate in an essay on 'Functions of the Nervous System' in the *Edinburgh Review* in 1815. He begins on a note of ill-founded optimism: 'Speculations respecting the nature of Mind seem now universally abandoned as endless and unprofitable. Metaphysicians rest satisfied with the truth that the mental phenomena are ultimately dependent on something essentially distinct from mere Matter; and content themselves with the patient study of the laws, by which these phenomena are regulated.'[19] This is a classic, programmatic statement of the traditional faculty psychology. What is more interesting, however, is the extraordinary and lengthy vehemence of Gordon's denial, based upon purported clinical evidence, not just that the higher faculties might be located in the cerebrum, but that the brain has any role *at all* in the workings of the mind. The bulk of the article is a catalogue of autopsy results from the examinations of brain-damaged individuals, many of them soldiers returning from the war, whose lives had either been little affected by spectacularly gross injury, or who lived a surprisingly long time after it. As well as stories of sword stabs and musket shots, there is a boy of 14 with a three-inch cavity in the left hemisphere full of pus, a man 'whose sensibility remained unaffected till within a few hours of his death; and yet there was found in his brain, an abscess occupying nearly one third of the substance of the right hemisphere, communicating by a large ulcerated opening with the anterior extremity of the right ventricle, and penetrating, by a small orifice, to the inferior surface of the anterior lobe',[20] a man with the whole right hemisphere destroyed by suppuration, a man 'who had not been insensible in any part of the body' whose *corpus striatum* was 'converted into matter like the dregs of wine', a woman whose cerebellum was 'converted into a bag of purulent matter', and a man whose cerebellum was 'without the last vestige of natural structure'.[21] There are abscesses found in the brain weighing half a pound, discharges of brain matter the size of hen's eggs, pigeon's eggs, and nutmegs, accompanied by quarts of liquid; brains have shrunk to two inches diameter, there is a 'brown vascular mass' instead of a brain,[22] and children live without any brain at all, including one whose vital functions were unimpaired for eighteen months. On his sudden, unexpected death, the cranium was opened and 'more than five quarts of very limpid water were found within it; but there was not the smallest trace of membrane, or of brain, except opposite the orbits and *meatus auditorius*, where something like *medulla* still remained'.[23] 'Although we have no doubt', Gordon preposterously concludes, 'that the total destruction of the brain alone . . . will in general be followed by partial or total insensibility, yet we think it has already been shown, that this is not always the consequence.'[24]

Aspirations are as important in scientific as in any other kind of enquiry, and hopes can influence theories. The increasingly confident acceptance that mind was dependent on the architecture of the brain and the nervous system, the inherent, if incautious, fascination aroused by the new neurological discoveries, the enticing possibility of consistent, naturalistic explanations crossing the barriers between mental and physical events, the yearning urgency of linking mind and body like two separated members of an unfortunate family, all of these played a part in the imaginative expectations of physiological psychology in the nineteenth century.[25] Put like this, investigations in physiological psychology present themselves as epic enticements. But hopes are not facts, nor causes necessarily uniform and simple; correlations are not always exact, nor desirable explanations full and thorough. The discovery by Pierre Paul Broca in the 1860s, through the dissection of the brains of recently deceased motor aphasiacs, that a specific part of the left hemisphere of the brain is necessarily implicated in the use of language, validated the hypothesis that the advanced cerebral functions are anatomically localizable.[26] However, the significance of this and other findings is difficult to measure. It is clearly a major physiological breakthrough. But the identification of 'Broca's convolution' in the lowest frontal gyrus of the brain does not explain what conditions and processes govern the acquisition of language in general human development. Nor does it tell us much about its use in individual circumstances. Nor does it explain very much about its role in human cultures. Nor, for that matter, does it specify very thoroughly the role of these localized centres in the whole neurobiological system. The same point can be made about David Ferrier's even more complicated localization of sight. In this case, after Ferrier's results were announced, German work quickly distinguished between 'sensorial blindness' (total insensibility to light) and 'psychic blindness', the 'inability to recognize the *meaning* of optical impressions'. The psychological, let alone the physiological differences between these two conditions—whose discrimination was based on clinical evidence rather than pathological data and animal vivisection, as Ferrier's were—was not resolved even by the time William James came to comment on the matter in 1890.[27]

[. . .]

Notes

1 June Goodfield-Toulmin, 'Some Aspects of English Physiology, 1780–1840', *Journal of the History of Biology*. 2 (1969), 283–320. See also Jacyna, 'Immanence or Transcendence'.
2 S. T. Coleridge, *On the Constitution of Church and State According to the Idea of Each* (1830), ed. John Barrell (London, 1972), 7–8.

3 Lewes, *History of Philosophy*, ii. 745.
4 Lewes, *History of Philosophy*, ii. 743–4.
5 John Morley, 'Valedictory' (1882), in *Nineteenth-Century Essays*, selected and introduced by Peter Stansky (London, 1970), 290–1.
6 Marilyn Butler, 'The First *Frankenstein* and Radical Science', *Times Literary Supplement*, 9 Apr. 1993, 12–14. Robert Chambers, a quarter of a century after *Frankenstein*, had not got much further. He insisted that electricity was the force that powered both mind and body, but, he asserted positively, 'electricity is almost as metaphysical as ever mind is supposed to be' (*Vestiges*, 334).
7 For example, H. L. Mansel describes the monstrosity of materialist 'speculation' in these terms (*Lecture on Kant*, 31–9). More cheekily, W. K. Clifford reversed the argument picturing the vitalistic, Kantian human being as a 'Frankensteinian monster' made by God without free will ('Body and Mind' (1874), in *Lectures and Essays*, ii. 58.) This allegorical possibility is, of course, suggested by Mary Shelley's tale itself. For extended discussion, see Baldick, *In Frankenstein's Shadow*.
8 G. J. Goodfield, *The Growth of Scientific Physiology* (London, 1960), 101. See also Mendelsohn, 'Physical Models and Physiological Concepts'.
9 Roger Smith, 'The Human Significance of Biology', 222. For general discussion, see L. S. Jacyna, 'The Physiology of Mind, the Unity of Nature, and the Moral Order in Victorian Thought', *British Journal for the History of Science*, 14 (1981), 109–32.
10 John Tyndall, *Fragments of a Science: A Series of Detached Essays, Addresses, and Reviews*. 2 vols., 9th edn. (London, 1902), ii. 85–7.
11 See e.g. Calderwood, 'Present Relations', 231, and James, *Principles of Psychology*, i. 147.
12 T. H. Huxley, 'On the Hypothesis that Animals are Automata, and its History' (1874), in *Science and Culture and Other Essays*, 239–40.
13 T. H. Huxley, 'On the Physical Basis of Life', *Fortnightly Review*, NS 5 (1869), 143.
14 William B. Carpenter, 'On the Doctrine of Human Automatism', *Contemporary Review*, 25 (1875). 397–416.
15 Lewes, *Problems*, iv. 29–38.
16 James, *Principles of Psychology*, i. 138.
17 Geertz, 'The Growth of Culture and the Evolution of Mind', in *The Interpretation of Cultures*, 70.
18 [John Gordon], 'Abernathy on Vital Principles', *Edinburgh Review*, 23 (1814), 384–98.
19 [John Gordon], 'Functions of the Nervous System', *Edinburgh Review*, 24 (1815), 439.
20 Ibid. 441.
21 Ibid. 443–4.
22 Ibid. 447.
23 [John Gordon], 'Functions of the Nervous System', *Edinburgh Review*, 24 (1814), 446–7.
24 Ibid. 451.
25 For acknowledgement of this, see G. H. Lewes's own account of the long gestation of *Problems of Life and Mind* in his preface to the first volume dated September 1873. He had first planned 'a treatise on the philosophy of Mind in which the doctrines of Reid, Stewart, and Brown were to be physiologically interpreted' in lectures delivered at Fox's Chapel, Finsbury, in 1837. With its origins in dissenting radicalism, autodidacticism, breathtaking, transdisciplinary ambition, and eventual progress to an unfinished five volumes and 2,000 pages, *Problems of Life and Mind* might stand as a sort of simulacrum of much of the mid-Victorian psycho-physiological project. The physiological interpretation of Common Sense philosophy, incidentally, was abandoned because of lack of progress in physiology and 'growing dissatisfaction with the doctrines of the Scotch school'. That, too, is typical (Lewes, *Problems*, i, p. v).
26 For discussion, see Robert M. Young, *Mind, Brain, and Adaptation*, ch. 4; Jeannerod, *Brain Machine*, 71 ff.
27 James, *Principles of Psychology*, i. 41 ff.

Bibliography

Victorian and pre-Victorian sources

Calderwood, Henry, 'The Present Relationship of Physical Science to Mental Philosophy', *Contemporary Review*, 16 (1871), 225–38.

Chambers, Robert, *Vestiges of the Natural History of Creation and Other Evolutionary Writings*, ed. James A. Secord (London, 1994).

Clifford, W. K., 'Problems of Life and Mind by George Henry Lewes. First Series. The Foundations of a Creed. Vol. 1', *Academy*, 5 (1874), 148–50.

James, William. *The Principles of Psychology* (1890), 2 vols. (New York, 1950).

Lewes, George Henry. *The History of Philosophy from Thales to Comte*, 2 vols., 4th edn. (London, 1871).

——. *Problems of Life and Mind*, 5 vols. (London, 1874–79).

Mansel, H. L., *A Lecture on the Philosophy of Kant* (Oxford, 1856).

Modern commentaries

Baldick, Chris. *In Frankenstein's Shadow: Myth, Monstrosity, and Nineteenth-Century Writing* (Oxford, 1987).

Geertz, Clifford. *The Interpretation of Cultures: Selected Essays* (London, 1973).

Jacyna, Leon S. 'Immanence or Transcendence: Theories of Life and Organization in Britain, 1790–1835'., *Isis* 74 (1983), 311–29.

Jeannerod, Marc, *The Brain Machine: The Development of Neurophysiological Thought*, trans. David Urion (London, 1985).

Mendelsohn, Everett, 'Physical Models and Physiological Concepts: Explanation in Nineteenth-Century Biology', *British Journal for the History of Science*, 2 (1965). 201–19.

Smith, Roger, 'The Human Significance of Biology: Carpeneter, Darwin and the vera causa', in U. C. Knoepflmacher and G. B. Tennyson (eds), *Nature and the Victorian Imagination* (London, 1977).

Young, Robert M. *Mind, Brain, and Adaptation in the Nineteenth Century: Cerebral Localization and Its Biological Context from Gall to Ferrier* (Oxford, 1970).

28   The psyche in pain; Dream and trance

Gaskell's *North and South* as a "condition of consciousness" novel

Jill Matus

[. . .]

It is an increasingly disputed assumption that literature simply follows or reflects what medical science makes available conceptually. As the work of Gillian Beer, George Levine and many others has shown, literature is not just a passive receptor of scientific ideas, but a participatory agent in their formation, able not just "to parallel developments in the sciences, but on occasion to anticipate them by virtue of its willingness to let the imagination, and the language itself, be a guide."[1] Literary texts are not supplemental illustrations but primary cultural documents. They shape culture profoundly and "frequently offer a more complex picture of cultural manifestations than many other written documents."[2] The history of the concept of trauma provides a useful example of this capacity. Far from merely following along and reflecting scientific advancements, literary narratives helped to shape and influence the cultural practices and narratives out of which the concept of trauma developed.[3] A key assumption of this study is that the relation between literary production and medical and psychological writing is a reciprocal one. Victorian fiction, especially, I will argue, participates in the debates of its day about the nature of emotions, unconscious processes and memory, and shapes the way mental physiologists write about the powers and mysteries of the mind.[4] So, for example, William Benjamin Carpenter cites Dickens on the force of the imagination when he writes about latency and memory.[5]

It is often asserted that, during the period under discussion, interiority and individual psychology became the stuff of novelistic material. As D. H. Lawrence remarked, "You see, it was really George Eliot who started it all . . . And how wild they all were with her for doing it. It was she who started putting all the action inside. Before, you know, with Fielding and the others, it had been outside."[6] One may argue with Lawrence about whether George Eliot was indeed the first novelist to put all the action inside, but his point about the shift that Victorian fiction marks is well taken. One of the distinctive characteristics of the Victorian novel with its third-person, often omniscient, narrator is to explore the interior life of characters in an unprecedented way. The narrator, able to move in and out of her characters' minds, has a unique opportunity to provide imaginative access to their subjectivity and to probe questions of consciousness and memory. In a great many Victorian novels, inner life is an object of extreme interest and detailed representation.[7] As Ronald Thomas has astutely pointed out, Freud himself admitted that the "narrative forms of fiction provided the explanatory models that led to his own shift from a physiological to a psychological understanding of hysterical symptoms."[8] Freud remarked that his case histories read like short stories and that he found enabling the works of imaginative writers with their detailed description of mental processes.[9] Although an interest in unconscious processes of the mind meant looking inward at the hidden and mysterious workings of the psyche, this focus was not, however, necessarily a turning away from social representation. Rather, many Victorian writers saw it as quite the opposite. George Henry Lewes, for example, insisted that "to understand the Human Mind we must study it under normal conditions, and these are social conditions."[10]

[. . .]

[In *North and* South, Elizabeth] Gaskell represents intense emotional experience as undoing the equanimity and balance of the self. Indeed, it is often likened to bodily suffering in its threat to wholeness and health: Margaret's mother cries out "*as in some sharp agony*" at the mention of Frederick's name (129).[11] There are several further examples where comparison is abandoned and Gaskell blurs the line between physical and mental anguish. The mutual influence of mind on body and body on mind is also implicitly demonstrated in the way she writes about the effects of emotions. Thus she gives physical form to painful thoughts, feelings, consciousness, and other states of mind that are mental and therefore intangible and invisible. Describing her shock in response to the letter about Frederick's mutiny, Mrs. Hale says, "I could hardly lift myself up to go and meet him – everything seemed to reel about me all at once" (108). In line with the emergent physiological psychology of the 1850s, Gaskell seems to emphasize the correlation between physiological and mental states, and the importance of the former in elucidating the latter. The most cogent example of the representation of agonized consciousness in terms of its physical aftermath is Mr. Thornton's visceral reaction to rejection: he is almost blinded by baffled passion, feels dizzy, and develops a violent headache. Going further, Gaskell shows the destabilizing effects of strong emotion on identity and self-knowledge. Thornton experiences confusion about the apparent incommensurability of the cause of his suffering in relation to the consequences. It is as if such a palpable aftermath ought to have had a more obviously disastrous cause to precipitate it.

> When Mr Thornton had left the house that morning he was almost blinded by his baffled passion. He was as dizzy as if Margaret, instead of looking, and speaking, and moving like a tender graceful woman, had been a sturdy fish-wife, and given him a sound blow with her fists. He had positive bodily pain, – a violent headache, and a throbbing intermittent pulse. He could not bear the noise, the garish light, the continued rumble and movement of the street. He called himself a fool for suffering so, and yet he could not, at the moment, recollect the cause of his suffering, and whether it was adequate to the consequences it had produced. (207)

For a time the overpowering experience dominates consciousness, but then seems to subside: "[i]t seemed as though his deep mortification of yesterday, and the stunned purposeless course of the hours afterwards, had cleared away all the mists from his intellect" (212). Yet, as Gaskell shows, Thornton's self-congratulation at dispelling the effects of the emotion is premature. Powerful feelings return, unbidden, to arrest the mind's focus once more:

> It seemed as though he gave way all at once; he was so languid that he could not control his thoughts; they would wander to her; they would bring back the scene, – not of his repulse and rejection the day before, but the looks, the actions of the day before that. He went along the crowded streets mechanically, winding in and out among the people, but never seeing them, – almost sick with longing for that one half hour. (213)

The narrative focus here on Thornton's wandering attention, and his lack of control over his mind, raises a well-aired question in mid-nineteenth-century physiology – the role of volition or will in controlling psychical states. States in which the will is suspended include wandering attention, reverie, abstraction, absence of mind, and signs of functioning by rote or habit while the mind is otherwise occupied. But as William Carpenter averred, the will

> can determine what shall not be regarded by the Mind, through its power of keeping the Attention fixed in *some other direction*; and thus it can subdue the force of violent impulse, and give to the conflict of opposing motives a result quite different from that which would ensue without its interference. This exercise of the Will, moreover, if habitually exerted in certain directions, will tend to form the Character, by establishing a set of *acquired habitudes*; which no less than those dependent upon original constitution and circumstances, help to determine the working of the "Mechanism of Thought and Feeling."[12]

Throughout Carpenter's discussion of abstracted states of mind, he draws reverential attention to "the Will" as the commander of the ship, in the absence of which it runs without steering or direction. Another frequent analogy to express the relation between the will and the emotions or unconscious mind is that of horse and rider. Thus Carpenter:

> [T]he relation between the Automatic activity of the body, and the Volitional direction by which it is utilized and directed, may be compared to the independent locomotive power of a horse under the guidance and control of a skilful rider . . . Now and then, it is true, some unusual excitement calls forth the essential independence of the equine nature; the horse takes the bit between his teeth and runs away with his master; and it is for the time uncertain whether the independent energy of the one, or the controlling power of the other, will obtain mastery.[13]

While Carpenter's focus on order and control and his advocacy of vigorous mental training has been linked to the Unitarian preoccupation with education and self-regulation,[14] Gaskell herself, also a Unitarian, seems more ready to explore what may emerge in states where self-control is destabilized. She is interested in why the horse takes the bit and runs away, as it were. The text is not quick to dispel those states in which the force of feeling precipitates shifts in ordinary consciousness. Rather more tolerant of such lapses in ordinary consciousness, Gaskell uses states of suspended will in order to explore what lies under the surface – who we are or what we feel when we are not ourselves. The difference between Gaskell and Carpenter is her implicit sense that the undermining of self-control and will can at times be useful and informative – a condition, even, for new growth and change.[15]

Gaskell would of course not dispute the importance of will and rational control. There are several examples in the novel of the dangers of intemperate response: Frederick's mutinous reaction to injustice; the ancestor, "old Sir John" Beresford, who shot his steward for insulting him; and, in an especially stereotypic representation of primitive, working-class mob mentality, the strikers who watch "open-eyed and open-mouthed, the thread of dark-red blood which wakened them up from their trance of passion" (179). While this collective "trance of passion" is a very dangerous thing, the many states of trance or abstraction that Gaskell evokes in the novel are not generally feared as dangerous paths to unreason and not seen as undermining the will in a threatening way. *North and South* undoes the familiar dichotomy of passion and reason, which are less dramatically oppositional in this novel (than say in Brontë's *Jane Eyre*) and more mutually informative. Recognizing the precariousness of the coherent and stable subject, as is evident in her lively epistolary account of her "many me's" [. . .],[16] Gaskell inflects Carpenter's model of selfhood so that it can less threateningly accommodate the displacement of a vigilant, governing consciousness.

Her open-mindedness is here literally that – an attention to the mind opened to its unconscious processes. Significantly, only after the torment of love has opened Thornton up to his capacity to feel strongly is he capable of responding to Higgins. It is not so much Margaret's beneficent womanly and emotional influence that is the cause of this transformation as the almost magical effect of Thornton's own powerful emotions that renders him receptive. That Thornton has always been shown as someone of keen and sensitive perception, highly attuned to his consciousness of those around him, prepares for his responsiveness to powerful emotional states. He notices that the Hales don't like the wall-paper and instructs their landlord to alter it; he is struck by the contrast between Higgins's bent figure and determined way of speaking, which prompts him to find out that the worker had waited five hours to speak to him about employment. Immediately responsive to Margaret on a sensual level, he minutely observes the bracelet tightened about her flesh as she is pouring and serving tea, and the way her father uses her fingers pincer-like in place of sugar tongs; he is highly conscious when they do shake hands that this is the first time they have touched, a fact of which she is quite unaware. And when he brings the fruit to her ailing mother the day after he has declared himself to her, he is hyperconscious of her presence in the room, even though he never looks at her. Often described as unfeeling, he is less unfeeling than controlled.

Thornton's powerful feelings for Margaret destabilize his ability to check or compartmentalize emotional responses. After it strikes Thornton that Higgins must have been waiting five hours to speak to him, he spends two hours of his own time verifying Higgins's account of himself.

> He tried not to be, but was convinced that all that Higgins had said was true. And then the conviction went in, *as if by some spell*, and touched the latent tenderness of his heart; the patience of the man, the simple generosity of the motive (for he learnt about the quarrel between Boucher and Higgins), made him forget entirely the mere reasonings of justice, and overleap them by a diviner instinct. (Emphasis added; 325)

Here Gaskell describes the change in Thornton's attitude to Higgins as the effect of a spell, as if some emotional alchemy has been at work. And though she uses the language of enchantment in describing the process, she is not being evasive or mystifying the nature of his changed attitude. There is some unknown and mysterious way in which feelings unconsciously act upon judgment and in so doing "overleap" justice with mercy and humanity. Thornton, the self-made man, must be slightly unmade by the ministration of tenderness and vulnerability. As Higgins aptly remarks to Mr. Hale, "He's two chaps. One chap I knowed of old as were measter all o'er. T'other chap hasn't an ounce of measter's flesh about him. How them two chaps is bound up in one body, is a craddy for me to find out" (339).

A further instance of Gaskell's interest in abstracted states that suspend will and volition occurs in relation to Thornton's delayed consciousness of Margaret's embrace of him in the mob scene. When Margaret throws her arms around Mr. Thornton to protect him from the strikers, he shakes her off without really thinking about what she has done. Absorbed in his thoughts about the threatening crowd, "he had pushed her aside, and spoken gruffly; he had seen nothing but the unnecessary danger she had placed herself in" (181). But later on, when he is no longer responding to the urgency of the situation with the strikers, he belatedly recalls the feeling of her arms being around him, at which point he cannot stop thinking about it.[17] The idea of delayed or belated recall, along with the concept of latent knowledge, is nicely articulated in this scene. Gaskell seems to be suggesting that an extreme state of emotion can prevent the subject from consciously registering aspects of the experience, but that, once the emotion has passed, the unnoticed elements may intrude upon consciousness to be experienced anew. In this perception are the seeds of what later psychologists will focus on as the belated witnessing or delayed recall of events too overwhelming to process as they are happening.

Gaskell thus looks forward to the examples of latency that begin to accrue in descriptions of survivors of shocking railway accidents, which provided examples of those who walk away from the train accident apparently unharmed, only to manifest psychical and physical symptoms at a later date. She clearly understands the gap between perception and cognition and the belatedness or latency of knowledge to which these examples allude. Recall is available after the fact, but the experience has been unrecognized at the moment of occurrence, suggesting that the violence of powerful feelings (falling in love, in this instance) is about breach and vulnerability.

As we have seen, mental physiologists wrote lengthily about the curious phenomenon of double consciousness in which the subject was able to remember things in an altered state of consciousness that he or she did not know under normal circumstances. Gaskell does not probe the conundrum of how we can know at some level what is beyond recall or conscious knowledge; nor does she enter contemporary debates about whether the mind is just a physical organ like others in the body, and, if so, how one accounts for "spirit" or soul. Nonetheless, her implicit model of a layered self – composed of conscious and unconscious elements – sheds light on her treatment of impulsive action, especially when it works to call into question the subject's governing self-image or undermine her sense of integrity. Several recent critics have written about Gaskell's refusal of absolutes and embracing of complexity and even contradiction in this novel: "We constantly witness the crumbling of absolutes, the clear becoming irresolute, the iron will a vulnerable flesh."[18] Deeply skeptical about solutions and abidingly interrogative, her scrutiny turns also in *North and South* to question the unitary and integrated nature of the self.

[. . .]

Notes

1 See Helen Small, ed., *Literature, Science and psychology, 1830–1970: Essays in Honour of Gillian Beer* (Oxford: Oxford University Press, 2003), 7.

2 Alan Bewell, *Romanticism and Colonial Disease* (Baltimore: Johns Hopkins University Press, 1999), 23.

3 Freud, for example, was a great admirer of George Eliot; he read *Middlemarch and Daniel Deronda*, referred to *Adam Bede* in the *Interpretation of Dreams*, and gave George Eliot's novels as gifts to friends. George Eliot's treatment of questions of consciousness and psychic injury may therefore have been part of a climate of thinking that influenced the way the Freudian concept of trauma developed. On Freud and George Eliot, see Carl T. Rotenberg, "George Eliot – Proto-Psychoanalyst," *The American Journal of Psychoanalysis* 59:3 (1999): 257. See also Nicholas Dames, *Amnesiac Selves: Nostalgia, Forgetting and British Fiction 1810–1870* (Oxford: Oxford University Press, 2001), 167–206, who claims that the sensation fiction of Collins predated the discussion of amnesia in nineteenth-century psychology and physiology.

4 See Helen Small's account of the influence of literary texts on eighteenth-century conceptions of madness in *Love's Madness: Medicine, the Novel, and Female Insanity: 1800–1865* (Oxford: Clarendon Press, 1996).

5 William Benjamin Carpenter, *Principles of Mental Physiology*, 4th edn. (1876; New York: Appleton, 1890), 455.

6 Jessie Chambers, *D. H. Lawrence: A Personal Record*, 2nd edn. (London: Frank Cass and Co., 1965), 105; see also Keith Oatley and Jennifer Jenkins, who discuss George Eliot's "experiments in life" in their text book on the emotions, *Understanding Emotions* (Oxford: Blackwell, 1996), 18–22.

George Levine refers indirectly to Lawrence in his discussion of the inside action in the introduction to *The Cambridge Companion to George Eliot* (Cambridge: Cambridge University Press, 2001), 9.

7 See Lisa Rodensky, *The Crime in Mind: Criminal Responsibility in the Victorian Novel* (Oxford: Oxford University Press, 2003), 6–7, who argues for the special powers of the realist novel's third-person narrator in disclosing a character's interiority but does not discuss other kinds of literature which may creatively represent movements of mind using other modes of narration.

8 Ronald Thomas, *Dreams of Authority: Freud and the Fictions of the Unconscious* (Cornell: Cornell University Press, 1990), 133.

9 I am here paraphrasing Freud's comments in the case of Fraulein Elisabeth von R in *Studies in Hysteria* in the *Standard Edition of the Complete Psychological Works of Sigmund Freud*, ed. and trans. James Strachey (London: Hogarth Press and the Institute for Psychoanalysis, 1955–72), II:160–61, quoted in Thomas, *Dreams of Authority*, 133.

10 George Henry Lewes, *Problems of Life and Mind*, 5 vols. (London: Trübner, 1874–79); first series, *The Foundations of a Creed* (1874), I:127–28. Also quoted in Sally Shuttleworth and Jenny Bourne Taylor, eds., *Embodied Selves: An Anthology of Psychological Texts 1830–1890* (Oxford: Oxford University Press, 1998), 69.

11 Elizabeth Gaskell, *North and South*, ed. Angus Easson, intro. Sally Shuttleworth, Oxford World's Classics (Oxford: Oxford University Press, 1998). Further references are to this edition and will be made parenthetically in the text.

12 See Carpenter, *Principles of Mental Physiology* (New York: Appleton, 1874), 26.

13 Ibid., 24.

14 See Louise Henson, "'The Condition-of-England' Debate and the 'Natural History of Man': An Important Scientific Context for the Social-Problem Fiction of Elizabeth Gaskell," *Gaskell Society Journal 16* (2002): 30–47; Henson finds Gaskell in agreement with the representation of excess of passion in Holland and Carpenter (38–40). While Henson claims that "we can see Gaskell utilizing ethnological and physiological concepts in her social-problem fiction," her brief discussion of *North and South* does not focus on the ways Gaskell departs from Carpenter and the mid-Victorian emphasis on order and control.

15 For a contrasting view, see Louise Henson, "Mesmeric Delusions: Mind and Mental Training in Gaskell's Writings," in *Victorian Literary Mesmerism*, ed. Martin Willis and Catherine Wynne (Amsterdam: Rodopi, 2006), 83–103. Henson sees Gaskell as typically Unitarian in her discomfort with mesmerism as a state of mind that "disabled the judgement and undermined responsibility for moral conduct" (103). She does not, however, discuss *North and South*.

16 Gaskell to Eliza Fox, 1850.

17 I am grateful to Stephanie Lougheed, my student in ENG 458 at the University of Toronto (2005), for making this point in a seminar discussion.

18 [Terence] Wright, *Elizabeth Gaskell*[*: "We are not Angels": Realism, Gender, Values*. Houndsmill: Macmillan Press, 1995], 110.

29 Psychology and literature

Michael Davis

The range of psychological concepts explored in the three extracts included here gives some sense of the sheer richness and variety of Victorian debates about the mind. This is a period in which questions about the self, and especially about the self's relationship with the body, were the focus of unprecedented scrutiny and elicited a diversity of responses. Attempts to understand the connections between mind and physical being were evident, for example, in the proliferation of new, or newly defined, medical concepts such as monomania and hypochondria, which linked psychological experience with the body's emotional, nervous, or sexual energies. Such attempts are instanced, too, in the rise of popular sciences such as physiognomy and phrenology—which offered models for understanding character on the basis, respectively, of facial features and the shape of the skull—and mesmerism, which posited the existence of so-called magnetic fluids in the body which could be manipulated from without. Most importantly in the history of psychology in the period, the mid-century onwards sees the emergence of models of mind which draw on the data of physiology and neuroanatomy, and which thus root their understandings of the self squarely in physical being, rather than in the theological or metaphysical paradigms which had traditionally dominated Western models of mind. Progress in cerebral localization, which demonstrated that certain parts of the brain are associated with particular functions, and the formulation of the Bell-Magendie law, which differentiated between sensory nerves and nerves performing a motor (that is, action-orientated) function, both affirmed the inseparability of mental life from physical being. Such data helped to give the new physiological psychology the authority of experimental science, and were integral to the development of theories of mind which combined attention to subjective experience and to the physical processes which underpin it. Physiological psychology became increasingly influential as the century went on, but, along with other models of the mind/body relationship such as those with which I began, continued to raise fundamental questions in its turn. As is also evident in debates about evolutionary theory, for many Victorians, grounding concepts of the self in the body, and therefore as part of the material world, threatens to dislodge humankind from the privileged position in the universe accorded to it in Christian teaching. For other commentators, from both Christian and agnostic or atheist perspectives, materializing the self raised the issue of whether human beings could still be said to possess free will, or whether, rather, they resembled machines without any real autonomy of action. Other equally crucial questions centered on whether recourse to physiological or neuroanatomical terms risked obscuring the role of social environment in shaping minds, and whether those terms could produce an adequate description of individual subjective experience.

Part of a broader trend in literary studies, over the last three decades, towards historicist, interdisciplinary readings of texts and cultures, Sally Shuttleworth's, Jill Matus's and Rick

Rylance's work exemplifies how exploring Victorian representations of the self can produce new insights both into literary texts in the period and into the history of science, philosophy, and culture more widely. Shuttleworth and Matus offer illuminating and innovative readings of two major Victorian novels, *Villette* (1853) and *North and South* (1854–55), but also help to locate those novels in scientific and cultural history by tracing their active engagement with, rather than merely reflection of, psychological theories. Rylance's study, to which I will turn in more detail later, pays careful attention to the rhetorical strategies employed by theorists of mind—to their writings as texts—and thus illustrates the insights offered by a literary studies approach to the history of science.

This greater emphasis on historicization in scholarly work in the field has brought with it important new developments of, but also challenges to, some previously dominant theoretical approaches to Victorian literature. Matus, for instance, explicitly takes issue with earlier feminist and psychoanalytic readings, arguing that these ignore the historical specificity of texts and obscure the scope and diversity of debates about the mind in the period by anachronistically imposing psychoanalytic concepts on them; Shuttleworth makes a similar point earlier in her book. Both Shuttleworth and Matus nonetheless offer important new insights into the gender politics of Victorian fiction and science. Shuttleworth demonstrates that Victorian psychological and medical theories, though they may claim objectivity and neutrality of approach, are profoundly shaped by historically specific ideologies of gender, economics, and class, and she traces the complex ways in which these are both affirmed and subverted in Brontë's narrative. The contested gender politics of Victorian psychological and medical concepts, articulated in both scientific and literary texts, is evident, too, in the influential anthology of Victorian theories of mind, *Embodied Selves* (1998), which Shuttleworth edited with Jenny Bourne Taylor: there, we find evidence of spirited debate in the period about the gendered assumptions that go with some psychological ideas—a debate in which, as Shuttleworth's book on Brontë shows, fiction engages also.

Matus's work is less explicitly gender-focused than Shuttleworth's, and directs its focus not towards the representations of extreme mental states dealt with by earlier feminist critics, but instead towards fictional and scientific accounts of the workings of "ordinary consciousness" (Matus 2009:10). At the same time, Matus highlights some of the complexities of Gaskell's representations of masculinity and femininity. Thornton's loss of his characteristically masculine and middle-class self-control renders him more aware of his own sexuality and, crucially, a more sympathetic participant in class politics. As Matus discusses later in the chapter from which the excerpt is taken, Margaret's fainting, after having lied to a policeman about her brother Frederick's whereabouts, might seem merely an example of conventionally "Victorian" feminine fragility but in fact manifests the profoundly unsettling psychological effect of the serious moral choice which she makes as a woman heavily engaged with ethical and political questions in the public sphere.

Implicit in these texts, too, is a critique of post-structuralist and Marxian arguments that Victorian fiction treats selves, whether of characters or of readers, as relatively stable and knowable. Instead, Shuttleworth and Matus insist that fiction represents the subject as fundamentally disunited by the competing impulses and energies within and outside it, and all three excerpts included here suggest the complexity of theories of mind in the period. A further implication of these extracts' approaches is to question critical assessments of Victorian fiction, in particular, as epistemologically naive and ideologically conservative.[1]

Nonetheless, as Shuttleworth's writing shows, work in the field in the 1980s and 1990s, as in many other areas of literary studies, was strongly influenced by the theories of Michel

Foucault. Introducing his 1987 edited collection of essays, *One Culture,* for example, George Levine argues that both science and literature should be understood as instances of culturally contingent "discourse"—a concept central to Foucault's work—rather than as the unproblematic expression of apolitical knowledge. The two types of discourse, Levine contends, "are mutually shaped by their participation in the culture at large" (Levine 1987: 5–6). That mutual shaping is clearly in evidence in Shuttleworth's chapter on *Villette,* an earlier version of which is included in Levine's collection. As Shuttleworth shows, Brontë takes up the terminology of sciences of mind but also actively contributes to scientific debate by interrogating the power relations which may go with psychological concepts and by proposing an even more closely integrated model of the mind/body relationship than is adopted by scientific writing. Elsewhere in her discussion, Shuttleworth emphasizes that literary texts' engagement with psychological theory is especially significant because Victorian scientific writing, in comparison with modern-day scientific texts, was non-specialized in its terminology and formed part of the mainstream culture of which fiction is also a facet, so that novelistic representations of mind regularly feature in theoretical discussions of psychology, as well as vice versa.

While these works point to important areas of confluence between literary and scientific discourses about the self, other studies in the field, such as Helen Small's *Love's Madness* (1996) and Jane Wood's *Passion and Pathology in Victorian Fiction* (2001), have instead highlighted the contrasts and tensions between those discourses. Historicizing readings such as these, and indeed Shuttleworth's and Levine's own work, highlight the crucial challenge to researchers who seek to read literary texts through the discourses which these share with scientific writing: to remain alert to the distinctiveness and complexity of literary form, and to the interactions between scientific texts, the histories of scientific disciplines, and culture more broadly. Recent commentators, including Matus and Rylance, have continued to draw on Foucault's theories but have nonetheless prioritized more concentrated attention to the specific historical contexts of texts and ideas than is to be found in some earlier Foucauldian studies. Conversely, Shuttleworth's discussion, which draws on Foucault in its tracing of the interconnections between discourses of psychology, medicine, the law, and the Catholic church in *Villette,* has been supplemented by Janis McClaren Caldwell's more exclusively historicizing approach in her *Literature and Medicine in Nineteenth-Century Britain* (2004). In her chapter on Brontë's novel, Caldwell, herself a medical doctor, argues that we might view Dr. John's medical gaze not as the novel's most prominent expression of male disciplinary power, as Shuttleworth's Foucauldian reading suggests, but instead as part of a close, even intimate, dialogue between doctor and patient. In common with Matus, Caldwell seeks to avoid the danger of possibly ahistorical reading which a theory such as Foucault's might bring with it. Wood's study expresses a similar view, and also takes issue with what she regards as overly prescriptive feminist readings, from the 1970s, of Victorian medical practice.

Elsewhere, historicist readings of the self in Victorian literature have focused on a wide variety of texts and psychological concepts. Nicholas Dames's important study of Victorian fiction's complex representations of memory, *Amnesiac Selves* (2001), argues that Victorian fiction typically endorses a highly selective type of memory, one which strives to preserve a coherent sense of selfhood in characters and readers but in doing so also implies memory's problematic relationship with identity, and shows that this influences later scientific accounts of memory. Jenny Bourne Taylor's influential reading of Wilkie Collins in the context of psychological discourse, *In the Secret Theatre of the Home* (1988), has been added to more recently by Laurie Garrison's *Science, Sexuality and Sensation Novels* (2011), which pays close attention to ways in which Victorian physiology offers insights into characterization in sensation novels themselves but also informed contemporary reviews of sensation fiction. Garrison's interest in physiology is part of a significant recent turn in scholarship in the field of Victorian fiction more widely. This is evident, for instance, in Anne Stiles's *Popular Fiction and Brain Science in the Late Nineteenth Century* (2012), and in recent readings, by Elisha Cohn and myself, of *Dorian Gray* against Victorian physiological and psychological concepts. The potential of such a focus to yield insights not only into literary and scientific texts, but also into Victorians' own reading habits, is suggested in Dames's *The Physiology of the Novel* (2007), which demonstrates that Victorian writing about the novel frequently drew on physiological data to focus on the physical and mental experience of reading rather than on literary form, and that the impact of this emphasis on readerly experience is manifest in diverse ways in fiction of the period. This calls for a revision of how we understand the Victorians as consumers of texts. It suggests that Victorian novelists and reviewers envisaged a range of reading styles in which close attention to the text throughout the process of reading, such as is valorized in the form-centered literary theories of the late-nineteenth and twentieth centuries, is by no means universal or even necessary.

Matus's reading of Gaskell demonstrates the fruitfulness of drawing connections between mental science and novelists who are less explicitly engaged with scientific discourses than, say, Brontë or George Eliot, but who nonetheless powerfully explore subjectivity in its physical and social contexts in ways which share themes, if not specific terminology, with mental science. Athena Vrettos, likewise, has convincingly located Dickens's representations of repetitive behaviors in nineteenth-century debates about the formation of mind, and in doing so suggests scope for further work on how we might understand Dickens's characterizations in relation to psychological science. Recent work by Suzanne Keen and David Sweeney Combes, and my own reading of representations of consciousness in *Tess*, have sought to challenge the dominance of evolutionary themes in discussions hitherto of Hardy's relationship with science, concentrating instead on his engagement with the senses, physiology, and neuroanatomy; these studies suggest that such relatively under-examined contexts for his work might be usefully explored further.

Most strikingly, given Victorian poetry's complex and varied explorations of character, interiority, and embodiment, modern commentaries in this area have paid far less attention to poetry than to fiction. One exception is Ekbert Faas's *The Retreat into the Mind* (1988), which reads poetry in the context of developments in nineteenth-century psychiatry. Recently, Gregory Tate's *The Poet's Mind* (2012) has examined poets' representations of the mind and body as intricately bound up with each other, while Jason Rudy's *Electric Meters* (2010) draws intriguing connections between poetic rhythm and innovations in the technology of electricity and in physiology, the language of which latter science frequently draws on electrical terminology. These studies make important inroads into what may prove as rich an area of critical investigation as Victorian fiction's representations of the self.

As I suggested earlier, Rylance's work demonstrates some of the distinctive strengths that literary scholars are able to bring to the historiography of science. Grounding his discussion in wide and penetrating historical research, which uncovers work by now relatively obscure figures as well as by better-known theorists such as Huxley and Spencer, Rylance also pays a literary critic's close attention to the textual detail of scientific writing. This enables him to demonstrate in fresh ways that scientific debates are shaped by the contingencies of social norms, and sometimes by the cut-and-thrust of political argument, as well as by scientific data itself. Rylance's focus on the history of science, with only brief allusions to contemporary fiction and poetry, permits a detailed engagement with scientific writing that may be difficult to match in critical work primarily centered on literary texts. Nonetheless, his book's deeply researched and nuanced reading both of the internal history of psychology and of that discipline's place in culture, is one which subsequent studies in the field have drawn on and aimed to emulate.

As the Rylance extract demonstrates, his emphasis on the role of cultural, institutional, and political pressures in shaping scientific debate implies no superior twenty-first-century hindsight about now-defunct psychological theories. Instead, his study serves to showcase the variety of Victorian theories of mind and their continued relevance to modern-day debates about the self, as well as exploring the cultural environment that influenced their articulation. The excerpted discussion refers to two seminal discoveries in neuroanatomy—the Bell-Magendie law and Pierre Paul Broca's work on cerebral localization—and shows how these emerged and were utilized in the midst of complex scientific, but also ideological and factional, debate. Yet the excerpted discussion also locates these concepts, together with mechanistic and vitalistic theories of the self, in the much wider context of fundamental, and perhaps transhistorical, questions about the mind/body relationship. Rylance insists that we consider such concepts not merely as matters of historical curiosity, nor yet simply as examples of Foucauldian discourses in action, but also as addressing issues about subjectivity and embodiment with which the twenty-first century continues to grapple. The sophistication with which Victorian theorists of mind were able to address such issues is most clearly demonstrated in the discussion of the work of George Henry Lewes, which is also examined in further depth later in Rylance's book: Lewes points to the crucial importance of physiological and anatomical knowledge to our understanding of the mind, but he also highlights the inherent limitations of such data as the basis for understanding individual subjective experience, and proposes a complex and nuanced account of how the physical and the subjective are related.

Rylance's exploration of the variety of Victorian psychological theories, and of their purchase on questions about the self which remain current for modern readers, is especially suggestive in pointing to areas for ongoing debate, and for possible new investigation, in the field. Future studies might, for instance, examine the question of the self's autonomy, or lack thereof, in the face of the physical, evolutionary, or social pressures which shape it. As Rylance, Matus, and Shuttleworth all show in different ways, this is an issue which is at the core of Victorian fiction and psychological debate. Broadly materialist concepts of the self may undermine notions of human significance, agency, and individual responsibility, yet a range of novelists, and indeed psychologists, are also deeply interested in the possibilities of individual, autonomous thought and action. Questions of agency, of course, have also been central to a wide range of twentieth-century critical theory, which as one aspect of its project has criticized humanist assumptions about individual freedom, focusing instead on the historical and ideological forces that shape individuality. More recently, William Cohen's *Embodied* (2010) has offered an insightful new discussion of Victorian representations of the body which, again, critiques the notion of individual human autonomy. Cohen draws parallels between Victorian literature's explorations of the body in relation to subjectivity and models of the self proposed by late twentieth-century philosophers including Deleuze and Bataille. Both sets of texts, Cohen argues, present the body as in constant flux and interaction with the external, and thus call fundamentally into question the apparent integrity and coherence of the subject, and indeed the validity of subjectivity as a category *per se*. In response, it might be argued that existing critical work in the field, in its emphasis on the self's malleability, has tended to underplay concepts of individual autonomy as they are explored and interrogated in Victorian texts. Some critical work (though not Cohen's), indeed, may have risked reproducing a reductive determinism, fundamentally skeptical of the category of the individual, which resembles that which was so fiercely debated by the Victorians in the wake of mechanistic models of the self. If the difficulties of defining agency are legion, it remains thematically central to Victorian literary and scientific texts, and central to how the readers of those texts, then and now, understand their own selfhoods. Renewed attention to the idea of the discrete, potentially autonomous self, endlessly problematic though it is, may contribute to a fuller and more nuanced sense of how Victorian literary writers and psychologists seek to understand the self's relationship with the social and material world.

One way in which that relationship might be understood more fully is through the connections between Victorian psychological and evolutionary theory. The evolutionary psychologies of Darwin, Spencer, and Huxley, of course, have been discussed by a range of scholars. Elsewhere in their books, Matus and Rylance also examine ways in which other psychologists, such as Lewes, William Carpenter, and James Sully, engage with evolutionary ideas in positive yet also critical ways, as they seek to understand the complexities of the mind in relation to the powerful evolutionary forces which contribute to its formation. Yet Matus's and Rylance's work in this direction points towards what is still a relatively under-explored aspect of Victorian representations of the mind. Further investigation of psychologists' engagement with the evolutionary may offer valuable new insights into the complex impact of evolutionary ideas on Victorian representations of subjectivity.

As well as exploring medical and scientific psychology in the period, Rylance's book demonstrates that philosophical approaches to questions of mind play a crucial part in Victorian psychological debate. One major example is faculty psychology, referred to by Rylance in the excerpted passage and discussed at length elsewhere in the book, which posits the existence of a soul and of innate human mental faculties that are independent of the body. This remains a powerful presence for much of the century, in part because it underpins phrenological reading and its associated theory of moral management, but also, as Rylance argues, because it offers a mode of describing the self which centers on particular mental capabilities which anyone can see in themselves, and is thus more attuned to human subjective experience than is the language of psychology based on physiology and neuroanatomy. The concept of the soul itself, of course, is one which, if it is to some degree displaced by scientific psychology, by no means disappears in the nineteenth century (or indeed in the twenty-first). In its theological connotations, but also as a term in philosophy and popular language, that concept speaks to a shared, if always questionable, sense of subjectivity as in some way special and separate from the world of causation in which it exists. It is worth noting that major figures in psychology, such as Lewes and William James, who accept and develop broadly materialist hypotheses about the mind, by no means entirely dismiss the term. The recent resurgence of interest among scholars in the relations between literature and religious belief in the period suggests scope for further investigation of the connections between scientific, religious, and literary representations of the self: as Edward S. Reed's *From Soul to Mind* (1997) argues, scientific and theological ideas about the mind are by no means necessarily opposed in the period, and in fact are often inseparable.

These still under-explored approaches to understanding Victorian debates about the self suggest multiple new avenues of investigation for scholars. The scope remains wide for future work on literary texts' multifaceted engagements with medical and physiology-based psychology, but studies may range well beyond scientific writing in their choice of contexts. Reading literary representations of the mind in these ways situates them in intellectual and textual culture, but also underlines the peculiar power of literary texts to represent subjectivity in its varied physical, mental, and social facets. In turn, such reading helps in important ways to remind us why we still read Victorian literature.

Note

1 A seminal expression of these attitudes to Victorian "classic realism" and concepts of subjectivity is Catherine Belsey's *Critical Practice* (London: Routledge, 1980). See, for instance, pp. 51 and 73.

Bibliography

Banfield, M. (2011) "Metaphors and Analogies of Mind and Body in Nineteenth-Century Science and Fiction: George Eliot, Henry James and George Meredith," in D. Coleman and H. Fraser (eds.), *Minds, Bodies, Machines, 1770–1930*, Basingstoke: Palgrave: 105–123.

Bourne Taylor, J. (1988) *In the Secret Theatre of the Home: Wilkie Collins, Sensation Narrative, and Nineteenth-Century Psychology*, London: Routledge.

Bourne Taylor, J. and Shuttleworth S. (eds.) (1998) *Embodied Selves: An Anthology of Psychological Texts 1830–1890*, Oxford: Oxford University Press.

Caldwell, J. M. (2004) *Literature and Medicine in Nineteenth-Century Britain*, Cambridge: Cambridge University Press.

Cohen, W. (2009) *Embodied: Victorian Literature and the Senses*, London: University of Minnesota Press.

Cohn, E. (2012) "'One single ivory cell': Oscar Wilde and the Brain," *Journal of Victorian Culture*, 17.2: 183–205.

Dames, N. (2001) *Amnesiac Selves: Nostalgia, Forgetting, and British Fiction, 1810–1870*, Oxford: Oxford University Press.

—— (2007) *The Physiology of the Novel: Reading, Neural Science, and the Form of Victorian Fiction*, Oxford: Oxford University Press.

Davis, M. (2006) *George Eliot and Nineteenth-Century Psychology: Exploring the Unmapped Country*, Aldershot: Ashgate.

—— (2012) "Hardy, *Tess* and Late-Victorian Theories of Consciousness," *The Thomas Hardy Journal*, 27: 46–69.

—— (2013) "Mind and Matter in *The Picture of Dorian Gray*," *Victorian Literature and Culture*, 41.3: 547–60.

Faas, Ekbert. (1988) *Retreat into the Mind: Victorian Poetry and the Rise of Psychiatry*, Princeton: Princeton University Press.

Garrison, L. (2011) *Science, Sexuality and Sensation Novels: Pleasures of the Senses*, Basingstoke: Palgrave.

Keen, S. (2010) "Psychological Approaches to Thomas Hardy," in R. Morgan (ed.), *The Ashgate Research Companion to Thomas Hardy*, Aldershot: Ashgate. 285–300.

—— (2014) *Thomas Hardy's Brains: Psychology, Neurology, and Hardy's Imagination*, Columbus: The Ohio State University Press.

Levine, G. (ed.) (1987) *One Culture: Essays in Science and Literature*, Madison: University of Wisconsin Press.

Matus, J. (2009) *Shock, Memory, and the Unconscious in Victorian Fiction*, Cambridge: Cambridge University Press.

Rudy, J. (2009) *Electric Meters: Victorian Physiological Poetics*, Athens, OH: Ohio University Press.

Ryan, V. L. (2012) *Thinking Without Thinking in the Victorian Novel*, Baltimore: The Johns Hopkins University Press.

Rylance, R. (2000) *Victorian Psychology and British Culture, 1850–1880*, Oxford: Oxford University Press.

Shuttleworth, S. (1984) *George Eliot and Nineteenth-Century Science*: *The Make-Believe of a Beginning*, Cambridge: Cambridge University Press.

—— (1996) *Charlotte Brontë and Victorian Psychology*, Cambridge: Cambridge University Press.

—— (2010) *The Mind of the Child: Child Development in Literature, Science, and Medicine, 1840–1900*, Oxford: Oxford University Press.

Small, H. (1996) *Love's Madness: Medicine, the Novel, and Female Insanity, 1800–1865*, Oxford: Clarendon Press.

Sweeney Coombs, D. (2011) "Reading in the Dark: Sensory Perception and Agency in *The Return of the Native*," *English Literary History*, 78.4: 943–966.

Tate, G. (2012) *The Poet's Mind: The Psychology of Victorian Poetry 1830–1870*, Oxford: Oxford University Press.

Vrettos, A. (2000) "Defining Habits: Dickens and the Psychology of Repetition," *Victorian Studies*, 42.3: 399–426.

Wood, J. (2001) *Passion and Pathology in Victorian Fiction*, Oxford: Oxford University Press.

Young, R. M. (1970) *Mind, Brain and Adaptation in the Nineteenth Century: Cerebral Localization and its Biological Context from Gall to Ferrier*, Oxford: Clarendon Press.

Part VIII

Gender, sexuality, domesticity

Introduction

Gender is the most widely dispersed topic in this book, making appearances in diverse subject areas such as economics, religion, psychology, empire, and Darwinian thought. That it has permeated so much recent scholarship is a testament to the vast intellectual contribution of feminist critics, starting with second-wave academic feminism in the 1970s and continuing through the intersection of feminist criticism with gender studies and queer theory since the 1990s. As Melissa Valiska Gregory's capstone essay demonstrates, the Victorian period has been pivotal for thinking about gender and sexuality more generally, attracting innovative theorists like Michel Foucault and Eve Sedgwick. Regarded as the origin point for modern feminism and the concepts of the homosexual and the heterosexual, the Victorian era witnessed the mingling of new institutionalized discourses of sexuality with those of gender differentiation. Critics' focus on this historical convergence has led to the widespread recognition that gender remains constitutively related to sexuality, and that any discussion of the latter requires a critical model that attends to both. But while Victorian gender studies occupies center stage in this section, it is joined not just by sexuality but also by a third term—domesticity—that has become a focal point in recent scholarship. This period was of course the origin point for the domestic "angel in the house," and the discourses of femininity, masculinity, economics, and science that supported it—a culturally pervasive ideal that, as Gregory notes, "had a powerful influence on the formation of gender and sexual identity for both men and women" (Chapter 42: 285).

In recent work on the intersection of Victorian gender, sexuality, and domesticity, scholars have revisited several critical narratives that have prevailed since at least the 1970s. These include such mainstays as the ideology of separate spheres, in which the middle-class Victorian wife remains nested in the home, where she wields moral, parental, and even limited economic authority while her husband ventures outside each day into the Darwinian competitive environments of masculine labor and public politics; the related phenomenon of the female *bildungsroman*, in which women and girls are trapped in narratives ending with their placement in the home as wives and mothers, a constricted bourgeois path that points to the lack of radical political agency in Victorian fiction; the notion of a lesbian continuum in Victorian women's history that links all forms of female resistance to patriarchy along a chain that culminates in an explicit and self-conscious lesbian identity; and a legislative account that permeates all these critical narratives about the early restrictions on married and other women's rights and their slow progress throughout the century. These critical tales about the Victorians, productive as they still are in the classroom and elsewhere as heuristics, nevertheless have been shown recently to be more fixed for us than they were for the Victorians themselves.[1] The excerpt from Hilary Schor's *Curious Subjects* (2013) addresses one of these accounts, the marriage plot that ostensibly ruled women's lives in realist fiction and in life. Schor notes that in these stories, female characters frequently experience "a moment of hesitation in the imposition of law, a kind of gap that breaches those laws" (Schor 2013: 6 [Chapter 31: 272]) In isolating such moments of "suspension" or "delay," she locates a "space for a curiosity" (Schor 2013: 6 [Chapter 31: 272]) that is also the site of female resistance to the marriage plot. This resistance fuels Schor's own critique of Franco Moretti's commonly cited claim that Victorian realism lacked radical potential.

In another excerpt below, from the book *Family Secrets* (2013), historian Deborah Cohen revises the story of women's gradual political and economic enfranchisement across the century by shifting the focus from marriage and divorce law legislation to the juridical details of how one of those marriage laws was put into practice by judges, lawyers, and the ordinary women and men who acted as plaintiffs and defendants. Cohen's reading of the Matrimonial Causes Act of 1857, which established a permanent Divorce Court in England, demonstrates how unhappily married women and men worked together to manipulate the system and arrange vastly more divorces than the writers of this law and the general public had imagined would occur. Cohen thus turns our attention away from the prevailing historical narrative of slow, Whiggish legislative reform to a much more anarchic and interesting close-up legal story of women colluding with men to change their lives at a relatively early stage in this liberal progress. Cohen merits praise for doing such innovative Victorian scholarship in a book aimed at a general as well as an academic readership (an achievement matched by recent authors such as Judith Flanders, Claire Tomalin, and Ruth Goodman).

Schor and Cohen are both innovative in reframing persistent critical narratives about women's agency in Victorian fiction and history, but in the first excerpt from *Between Women* (2007), Sharon Marcus is less in the business of reframing or refocusing than simply exploding prevailing critical models. Centrally, Marcus takes aim at lesbian continuum theory by asserting its limited value in understanding many Victorian women's erotic and non-erotic attachments to other women, noting that such relationships often supported rather than resisted patriarchy. *Between Women*, like Sedgwick's earlier *Between Men*, is audacious in rewriting the critical map by providing a new story about Victorian gender, sexuality, and domesticity.

See also: *Women poets and the poetess tradition*; *Genre fiction and the sensational*; *Psychology and literature*; *Economics, the market, and Victorian culture*

Note

1 For a recent overview of the mixed critical fortunes of one of these—the separate spheres model—see Boyd Hilton, *A Mad, Bad, & Dangerous People? England 1783–1846* (Oxford: Clarendon Press, 2006), 361–71.

30 The female relations of Victorian England

Sharon Marcus

In 1844 a ten-year-old girl named Emily Pepys, the daughter of the bishop of Worcester, made the following entry in the journal she had begun to keep that year: "I had the oddest dream last night that I ever dreamt; even the remembrance of it is very extraordinary. There was a very nice pretty young lady, who I (a girl) was going *to be married to!* (the very idea!) I loved her and even now love her very much. It was quite a settled thing and we were going to be married very soon. All of a sudden I thought of Teddy [a boy she liked] and asked Mama several times if I might be let off and after a little time I woke. I remember it all perfectly. A very foggy morning."[1] Emily Pepys found the mere idea of a girl marrying a lady extraordinary ("the very idea!"). We may find it even more surprising that she had the dream at all, then recorded it in a journal that was not private but meant to be read by family and friends. As we read her entry more closely, it may also seem puzzling that Emily's attitude toward her dream is more bemused than revolted, not least because her prospective bride is "a very nice pretty young lady," and marrying her has the pleasant aura of security suggested by the almost Austenian phrase, "It was quite a settled thing." Even Emily's desire to be "let off" so that she can return to Teddy must be ratified by a woman, "Mama."

A proper Victorian girl dreaming about marrying a pretty lady challenges our vision of the Victorians, but this book argues that Emily's dream was in fact typical of a world that made relationships between women central to femininity, marriage, and family life. We are now all too familiar with the Victorian beliefs that women and men were essentially opposite sexes, and that marriage to a man was the chief end of a woman's existence.[2] But a narrow focus on women's status as relative creatures, defined by their difference from and subordination to men, has limited our understanding of gender, kinship, and sexuality. Those concepts cannot be fully understood if we define them only in terms of two related oppositions: men versus women, and homosexuality versus heterosexuality. Our preconceptions have led us to doubt the importance of relationships such as marriage between women, which was not only a Victorian dream but also a Victorian reality; many adults found the idea of two women marrying far less preposterous than little Emily Pepys did. When activist and author Frances Power Cobbe published a widely read autobiography in 1894, for example, she included a photograph of the house she lived in with sculptor Mary Lloyd. Throughout the book, references to joint finances and travels, to "our friends," "our garden," and "our beautiful and beloved home" treated Cobbe's conjugal arrangement with Lloyd as a neutral public fact, one Cobbe expressed even more clearly in letters to friends in which she called Lloyd both her "husband" and her "wife."[3]

Female marriage, however, is not the sole subject of this book, which also examines friendship, mother-daughter dynamics, and women's investment in images of femininity, in order to make a fundamental but curiously overlooked point: even within a single class or genera-tion, there were many different kinds of relationships between women. Often when I would tell people I was writing a book about relationships between women, they would assume that was a timid way of saying I was writing about lesbians. There are lesbians in this book, if by that we mean women who had sexual relationships with other women, but this book is not only about lesbians; nor is it about the lesbian potential of all relationships between women. Indeed, if we take "lesbian" to connote deviance, gender inversion, a refusal to objectify women, or a rejection of marriage as an institution, then none of the relationships discussed here was lesbian. Women like Frances Power Cobbe embraced marriage as a model for their sexual partnerships with women even as they sought to reform marriage as a legal institution. Female friendships peaceably coexisted with heterosexual marriages and moreover, helped to promote them. The hyper-feminine activities of looking at fashion plates and playing with dolls encouraged women to desire feminine objects, and mother-daughter relationships were rife with the same eroticized power struggles as those between male and female kin.

[. . .]

Historical and disciplinary borders

Why focus on England from 1830 to 1880? Those decades lie at the core of the Victorian period, which continues to be a touchstone for thinking about gender and sexuality, not least because the Victorian era has the remarkable capacity to seem both starkly different from the present and uncannily similar to it. The general public continues to see Victorians as terribly repressed, while specialists have by and large accepted Foucault's assertion that our own contemporary obsession with sex originates with the Victorians.[4] Having selected Victorian England for its canonical status in the history of sexuality, I stayed within the years from 1830 to 1880 because those years constitute a distinct period, especially with regard to gender, the family, and same-sex bonds between women. During those decades, the belief that men and women were opposite sexes, different in kind rather than degree, took hold in almost every class, and the previous era's concerns about female sexual voracity shifted to a view of women as either inherently domestic, maternal, and self-restrained, or susceptible to train-ing in how to be so.[5] Marriage and family underwent corresponding changes. Historians of kinship argue endlessly about exactly when it first became common to think of marriage as the union of soulmates, but most agree that by 1830 that ideal had become a norm. Before the 1830s, certain classes of people did not valorize companionate marriage: workers often did not legally marry; aristocrats were openly adulterous; and Romantics and revolutionaries challenged the very bases of marriage. By the 1830s, companionate marriage was the stand-ard for measuring alliances in all classes. Finally, the lesbian was not a distinct social type during the years 1830 to 1880, although male sodomy was a public and private obsession.[6] In the eighteenth century, it was possible to name the sapphist or tribade as an explicit object of satire, but by the 1830s new codes of propriety meant that only doctors and pornographers wrote directly about sex between women.[7] The figure of the sapphist came to seem less and less embedded in the social world of domestic conjugality, and therefore less and less related to women who lived in couples and adopted features of legal marriage.

Women, sexuality, and marriage began to change dramatically in the 1880s. Eugenics shifted the meaning of marriage from a spiritual union to a reproductive one that depended on heterosexual fertility and promoted racial purity. New Woman fiction and doctrine criticized men's oppression of women in ways that sexualized marriage, or rather heterosexualized it, by comparing it to prostitution and rape.[8] A new sense of heterosexuality, as a distinct sexual orientation formed in diametrical opposition to homosexuality, made marriage and the family the province of male-female unions.[9] In the 1890s, a discourse of lesbianism began to emerge in Edward Carpenter's homophile writings, Havelock Ellis's sexological studies, and women's responses to them.[10] Awareness of sex between women also increased after two well-publicized trials raised issues of sapphism and female inversion: the Maud Allan trial of 1919 and the Radclyffe Hall trial of 1929.[11] Women in female couples continued to use marriage as a model for their relationships—think of Gertrude Stein and Alice Toklas—but many female couples began to identify either with an ideal of pure, sexless love, or with a bohemian modernism that rejected marriage and monogamy as patriarchal institutions.[12]

[. . .]

How this book engages scholarly debates

Studies of Victorian women have focused on how they both accepted and contested belief systems that defined women in terms of male standards, desires, and power, but have paid relatively little attention to how relationships between women defined normative gender. Scholars have dismissed nineteenth-century dolls and fashion as mere tools for teaching women to become objects for men. Writing on contemporary fashion photography and Barbie dolls has drawn attention to their lesbian dynamics and queer erotics, but no one has used that work to explore how Victorian dolls and fashion iconography encouraged girls and women to desire images of femininity, without marking such desires as queer or lesbian.[13] Studies of nineteenth-century marriage, particularly by literary critics, have explained how it was never only a bond between men and women, but the focus has been on how marriage formed alliances between men, often at the cost of ties between women.[14] Women are at the center of histories of the nineteenth-century family, but primarily in relation to husbands, fathers, and brothers. The links between women within the middle class have thus been remarkably ignored in some of the most important scholarship on gender. Consider *Family Fortunes: Men and Women of the English Middle Class, 1780–1850*, a major work by Leonore Davidoff and Catherine Hall that continues to be a reference point for nineteenth-century studies. Under the category of "femininity," the index lists "brothers' influence," and its "see also" rubric directs the reader to "division of labour by gender," "domesticity," and "motherhood." "Femininity," however, does not include friendship, sisters, or even mother-daughter relationships. The entry for "family" directs us to "see also friendship," but friendship between women takes up only a few sentences in the book. The authors note the "passionate" language used between female friends, then throw up their hands: "There is no way of speculating the exact emotional, much less physical meaning of such relationships." They briefly mention male "homosexuality" on the same page, remarking that it was regarded with "outraged horror," but the concept has no place in their index.[15]

The implicit theory here defines family and marriage as institutions that govern relationships between men, and between men and women, but not between women. The massive increase in scholarship about the history of same-sex relations since the publication of *Family Fortunes* has done little to challenge its view of the family, for much of that research has similarly assumed a basic opposition between lesbians and gay men on one side and marriage and the family on another. Studies of the family and femininity do not consider bonds between women to lie within the purview of their analyses, while work on female bonds situates them either outside the family or in a separate compartment within the family.[16] Female friendship and lesbian love, the two relationships between women that have received the most attention, are conflated as essentially feminist alliances that helped women to subvert gender norms and rebel against the strictures marriage placed on women, or that flourished only because they were sequestered within what Carroll Smith-Rosenberg called "the female world of love and ritual."

In 1975 Smith-Rosenberg contended that before the invention of homosexuality as a pathological form of deviance, sensual and emotional intimacy between women were accepted elements of domestic family life.[17] A few years later, Adrienne Rich proposed the idea of a lesbian continuum in which all forms of female intimacy would be related by their common rejection of "compulsory heterosexuality."[18] In contrast to Smith-Rosenberg, who characterized the female world as secure and serene, Rich underscored that women who placed women at the center of their lives risked stigma, ostracism, and violence. In the late 1980s and early 1990s, Esther Newton, Lisa Duggan, Terry Castle, and others mounted powerful critiques of the continuum theory and the concept of the female world.[19] They cited evidence that some nineteenth-century Americans and Europeans did see women's bonds as deviant or pathological.[20] They showed that both paradigms desexualized lesbianism by equating it with asexual friendships and with mother-daughter bonds purged of the alienation, exploitation, and conflicts inherent in male-female relations. They argued that to define lesbianism as a repudiation of men and masculinity left no room for mannish lesbians and the women attracted to them.

As many readers will recognize, my title alludes to Eve Kosofsky Sedgwick's *Between Men: English Literature and Male Homosocial Desire* (1985), which drew on Rich's notion of a lesbian continuum to speculate briefly that women might not have experienced the panic around boundaries between homo- and heterosexuality that men did (2–3). My response on first reading that suggestive proposition, and on rereading it many times in later years, has always been, "Yes, but . . ." Yes, homophobia was less powerful between women than between men, but was that because all forms of love between women were essentially interchangeable, as the continuum theory suggests? Yes, women's relations were less violently policed than men's, but are they therefore less interesting? Yes, women had more latitude with one another, but aren't we beginning to see that some relationships between Victorian men enjoyed the fluidity Sedgwick considered the monopoly of women? Yes, relationships between women were different, but don't we need at least an entire book to explore that—a book that engages Sedgwick's wise insight that homo- and hetero- are inherently interrelated? Without presuming to have succeeded, I have aimed to provide that book—one that will interest those who answer the last question in the affirmative, and one that takes to heart Sedgwick's powerful precept that to understand any particular aspect of gender and sexuality we must draw equally on feminist and queer theories and histories.

In feminist and lesbian studies, the turn to queer theory inaugurated with the publication of Judith Butler's *Gender Trouble* in 1990 led many to abandon the female world of the lesbian continuum for the project of undoing gender and sexuality categories altogether.[21] But few studies that address Victorian women's bonds have incorporated the insights of queer theory, and most still argue either that women's relationships were asexual or that women in the past anticipated current definitions of lesbians. Those seeking to restore lesbians to history portray their subjects as an outlawed minority defined by their exceptional sexual desire for women, their transgressive identification with masculinity, and their exclusion from the institutions of marriage and family.[22] Ironically, what all of these arguments share is an assumption that the opposition between men and women governs relationships between women, which take shape only as reactions against, retreats from, or appropriations of masculinity. The ongoing dominance of the continuum and minority paradigms is illustrated in the similarities between Lillian Faderman's *Surpassing the Love of Men* (1981) and Martha Vicinus's *Intimate Friends: Women Who Loved Women* (2004), the latter a set of case studies that revisits many of the women Faderman first grouped together. Faderman argued that romantic friendships between women were accepted because they were asexual relationships.[23] Vicinus shows that many of the relationships Faderman studied were in fact sexual, but her decision to use the word "friends" in the title of a book about lesbians indicates her adherence to the continuum theory. Vicinus advances the continuum thesis by using the terms "women's friendships" and "women's erotic friendships" interchangeably and by arguing that both were "consistently marginalized as 'second best' to heterosexual marriage."[24] She defines "intimate friendship" broadly, as "an emotional, erotically charged relationship between two women" (xxiv). But she makes that point in a section whose title, "Defining the Lesbian," evokes the minority thesis, and argues throughout that lesbians posed a "threat to [the] social norms" (59) followed by most women, who are thus implicitly removed from the only nominally inclusive category of "women who loved women." The minority thesis also surfaces in Vicinus's claim that "gender inversion was the most important signifier of same-sex desire" (xxix). Although *Intimate Friends* shows that women in lesbian relationships "created metaphoric versions of the heterosexual nuclear family," she emphasizes that such metaphors "failed when subjected to literal interpretation" (xxvii), thus reasserting a distinction between the lesbian minority and the heterosexual norm.

Because histories of gender, family, and marriage have focused on how women were defined relative to men, bonds between women have been analyzed primarily within lesbian studies. Lesbian studies put relationships between women on the scholarly agenda and produced exponential increases in knowledge, but its premises suggested that bonds between women mattered only to the history of women's resistance to heterosexuality, which to date has been far less common than their participation in it. The use of lesbian theory as a master discourse for understanding all relationships between women has thus made it difficult to conceptualize friendships between women who embodied feminine norms; to see the differences between female friendship, female marriage, and unrequited love between women; and to understand how friendship extended well beyond an isolated "female world." Literary-critical frameworks have also blinded us to the ways in which Victorian marriage plots depended on friendship between women. As my second chapter demonstrates, novels by men and women assigned female friendship so much agency that many narratives represented it as both a cause and effect of marriage between women and men. Idealized versions of the mother-daughter bond, which both Smith-Rosenberg and Rich posit as the origin of all bonds between women, have made it almost taboo to mention the eroticized aggression between mothers and daughters [. . .]. To understand how femininity was objectified and displayed for women as well as for men, [. . .] we need to abandon the persistent assumption that erotic interest in femininity can only be masculine. Finally, in order to see that sexual relationships between women have been part of the history of the family and marriage since at least the nineteenth century, we need to abandon continuum and minority theories that define kinship as exclusively heterosexual and frame female couples in terms of their rejection of marriage or their failed appropriation of it. Many nineteenth-century women in what some Victorians called "female marriages" were not seen as challenging the conventions of kinship. Instead they saw themselves, and their friends, neighbors, and colleagues saw them, as a variation on the married couple. Even a traditionalist like Trollope was able to articulate the ground that female marriage shared with modern forms of marriage between women and men.

In the course of writing this book I have been asked certain questions over and over again. Weren't Victorians too invested in female sexual purity to admit that lesbians existed?[25] Didn't the conviction that women had no sexual desire run so deep that in fact women couldn't have ever had sex with each other? Granted that a handful of women were able to take the plunge—weren't they anomalies, cut off from mainstream society or so privileged they didn't have to worry about what people thought? Didn't most people think of women who had sex with other women as deviants, almost a third sex, who had little in common with women who became wives and mothers? Weren't most women's lives totally governed by heterosexuality—by biological reproduction and by a sense of opposite sexes powerfully drawn to each other but also perpetually in conflict? As is already clear, my answer to these questions is "no"—not because I do not believe that Victorian women were deeply invested in men, nor because I think that secretly all Victorian women were really lesbians, but because I came to see the basic premises of these questions as anachronistic and misguided.

My belief that we should pose different questions comes in part from my engagement with contemporary queer theory. Queer theory led me to ask what social formations swim into focus once we abandon the preconception of strict divisions between men and women, homosexuality and heterosexuality, same-sex bonds and those of family and marriage. That skepticism about the transhistorical truth of gender and sexual categories owes a great deal to Denise Riley, Joan Wallach Scott, Eve Kosofsky Sedgwick, and Judith Butler, who have all argued that woman, desire, sexuality, and kinship are not fixed essences.[26] *Between Women* makes a historical point about the particular indifference of Victorians to a homo/hetero divide for women; this is also a theoretical claim that can reorient gender and sexuality studies in general. Queer theory often accentuates the subversive dimensions of lesbian, gay, and transgender acts and identities. The focus on secrecy, shame, oppression, and transgression in queer studies has led theorists, historians, and literary critics alike to downplay or refuse the equally powerful ways that same-sex bonds have been acknowledged by the bourgeois liberal public sphere.[27] Studies of same-sex practices of kinship and reproduction have undone the idea that the family must be heterosexual, but continue to detect and in some cases advocate for a basic conflict between the heterosexual family and its queer variants.[28] *Between Women* shows, by contrast, that in Victorian England, female marriage, gender mobility, and women's erotic fantasies about women were at the heart of normative institutions and discourses, even for those who made a religion of the family, marriage, and sexual difference.

This book makes new arguments because it brings fresh perspectives to bear on familiar materials, but also because it draws on sources that have been relatively neglected in sexuality studies. The history of sexuality has depended disproportionately on trial records and medical sources that foregrounded pathology and deviance. Women were not included in the legal definition of sodomy and were less likely than men to be arrested for public sex acts, and thus have faded from view in work based on police reports and state records. Studies that adopt Foucault's foundational account of sexuality as the production of desires, bodies, races, and classes through generative prohibitions and the manufacture of sexual identities have defined homosexuality in terms of deviance, secrecy, and subcultures. Women have appeared in those studies only to the extent that they illustrate the reach of medical discourses of difference. In reading over one hundred examples of women's lifewriting, however, I found almost no evidence that women incorporated medical definitions of femininity or sexual inversion into their understanding of their bodies or desires. In lieu of marginal and subversive identities, this book offers an alternative concept that makes it easier to place women in history, and that women themselves used to define their place in the world: the social relationship, which is not reducible to sex, power, or difference. Social relationships are the stuff of everyday life, and of historical documents such as women's letters, diaries, memoirs, and biographies, as well as of novels, fashion magazines, and children's literature. Historians of women and lesbians have studied those sources before, but they have almost always assumed the dominance of a heterosexuality whose evidence stems from the fact that it is all we have been trained to see. A different theory allows us to use these sources to make new distinctions—for example, between how women wrote about friends and lovers. It also establishes new connections—for example, between femininity and homoeroticism, or between female marriages and marriages between men and women.

[. . .]

Notes

1 Emily Pepys, cited in Harriet Blodgett, *"Capacious Hold-All": An Anthology of Englishwomen's Diary Writings* (Charlottesville: University Press of Virginia, 1991), 79. For a fuller edition of the diary, see Gillian Avery, ed., *The Diary of Emily Pepys* (London: Prospect Books, 1984).

2 The foundational texts are Leonore Davidoff and Catherine Hall, *Family Fortunes: Men and Women of the English Middle Class 1780–1850* (Chicago: University of Chicago Press, 1987); Mary Poovey, *Uneven Developments: The Ideological Work of Gender in Mid-Victorian England* (Chicago: University of Chicago Press, 1988); and Thomas W. Laqueur, *Making Sex: Body and Gender from the Greeks to Freud* (Cambridge, Mass.: Harvard University Press, 1990). For a recent synthetic history that cites these views as standard, see Susan Kingsley Kent, *Gender and Power in Britain, 1640–1990* (London: Routledge, 1999), 179–80.

3 Frances Power Cobbe, *Life of Frances Power Cobbe. By Herself*, vol. 2 (Boston: Houghton, Mifflin, 1894), 361, 645. The letters, which Cobbe wrote in 1865 to Mary Somerville, are cited in Sally Mitchell, *Frances Power Cobbe: Victorian Feminist, Journalist, Reformer* (Charlottesville: University of Virginia Press, 2004), 209, 157, 197.

4 For an exception to that rule, see Michael Mason, *The Making of Victorian Sexuality* (Oxford: Oxford University Press, 1994).

5 See Davidoff and Hall, *Family Fortunes*, 155 [. . .]. On the increasingly polarized sense of sexual difference in Victorian scientific and medical models, see Laqueur, *Making Sex*. For the class dimensions of the belief in the domestic, self-regulated woman, see Judith Walkowitz, *Prostitution in Victorian Society: Women, Class, and the State* (Cambridge: Cambridge University Press, 1980), and Nancy Armstrong, *Desire and Domestic Fiction: A Political History of the Novel* (New York: Oxford University Press, 1987). Others have shown that beginning in the late eighteenth century, sex itself began to be increasingly defined as penis-centered and procreative. See Rachel P. Maines, *The Technology of Orgasm: "Hysteria," the Vibrator, and Women's Sexual Satisfaction* (Baltimore: Johns Hopkins University Press, 1999); Henry Abelove's discussion of the history of sexual intercourse in the long eighteenth century, in *Deep Gossip* (Minneapolis: University of Minnesota Press, 2003); and Tim Hitchcock, "Redefining Sex in Eighteenth-Century England," *History Workshop Journal* 41 (1996), 72–90.

6 The most thorough discussion of the Victorian preoccupation with sodomy as a crime is in Harry Cocks, *Nameless Offences: Homosexual Desire in the 19th Century* (I. B. Tauris, 2003).

7 See Randolph Trumbach, "London's Sapphists: From Three Sexes to Four Genders in the Making of Modern Culture," in *Body Guards: The Cultural Politics of Gender Ambiguity*, eds. Julia Epstein and Kristina Straub (New York: Routledge, 1991), 112–41; Elizabeth Wahl, *Invisible Relations: Representations of Female Intimacy in the Age of Enlightenment* (Stanford: Stanford University Press, 1999); and Emma Donoghue, *Passions Between Women: British Lesbian Culture 1688–1801* (New York: HarperCollins, 1993).

8 On the shifts in sexual discourse in the 1880s, see Judith Walkowitz, *City of Dreadful Delight: Narratives of Sexual Danger in Late-Victorian London* (Chicago: University of Chicago Press, 1992), and Elaine Showalter, *Sexual Anarchy: Gender and Culture at the Fin de Siècle* (New York: Viking, 1990). For a vivid illustration of how the increasingly explicit public discourse of sex after the 1880s led to an increasing preoccupation with heterosexuality, see Dora Langlois, *The Child:*

Its Origin and Development: A Manual Enabling Mothers to Initiate Their Daughters Gradually and Modestly into All the Mysteries of Life (London: W. Reeves, 1896), a one-shilling pamphlet that reduced sex and marriage to reproduction and therefore to "the union of the sexes," 11.

9   On the late-nineteenth-century invention of heterosexuality as a distinct concept opposed to homosexuality, see Jonathan Ned Katz, *The Invention of Heterosexuality* (New York: Plume, 1995).

10 For women's responses to Carpenter and Ellis, see Liz Stanley, "Romantic Friendship? Some Issues in Researching Lesbian History and Biography," *Women's History Review* 1.2 (1992), 198–209.

11 On Maud Allan, see Judith Walkowitz, "The 'Vision of Salome': Cosmopolitanism and Erotic Dancing in Central London, 1908–1918," in *American Historical Review* 108.2 (April 2003), 337–76. On the Hall trial and its larger context, see Laura Doan, *Fashioning Sapphism: The Origins of a Modern English Lesbian Culture* (New York: Columbia University Press, 2001).

12 On the overtly asexual ideals of women in the 1890s and after, see Susan Pedersen, *Eleanor Rathbone and the Politics of Conscience* (New Haven: Yale University Press, 2004), 151–75, and Sheila Jeffreys, *The Spinster and Her Enemies: Feminism and Sexuality 1880–1930* (London: Pandora Press, 1985). On lesbians and bohemian sexual modernism, see Terry Castle, *The Apparitional Lesbian* (New York: Columbia University Press, 1993); Martha Vicinus, *Intimate Friends: Women Who Loved Women 1778–1928* (Chicago: University of Chicago Press, 2004); Shari Benstock, *Women of the Left Bank: Paris, 1900–1940* (Austin: University of Texas Press, 1986), and Christine Stansell, *American Moderns: Bohemian New York and the Creation of a New Century* (New York: Henry Holt, 2000).

13 Diana Fuss, "Fashion and the Homospectatorial Look," in *On Fashion*, eds. Shari Benstock and Suzanne Ferris (New Brunswick, NJ: Rutgers University Press, 1994), 211–32; Erica Rand, *Barbie's Queer Accessories* (Durham: Duke University Press, 1995). In *Bound to Please: A History of the Victorian Corset* (Oxford: Berg, 2001), Leigh Summers draws on Fuss's work to speculate about whether women derived erotic pleasure from corset advertisements, but she assumes that Victorian women can be divided into "lesbian and heterosexual" ones who would perceive images "quite differently," with the lesbians providing an "oppositional" reading, 185. This view of lesbians as a distinct minority and the only kind of women experiencing erotic desire for women does not hold for the Victorian period, which is defined precisely by the absence of a lesbian minority role and the diffusion of erotic desire for women among all women.

14 On marriage as a social alliance between men that effaced erotic desire between them, see Eve Kosofsky Sedgwick, *Between Men: English Literature and Homosocial Desire* (New York: Columbia University Press, 1985). On marriage as the cancellation of bonds between women, see Castle, *The Apparitional Lesbian*, 73.

15 Davidoff and Hall, *Family Fortunes*. 569. 568, 402.

16 Some of the most sustained work on female friendship has focused on feminist and cross-class alliances between women. See Seth Koven, *Slumming: Sexual and Social Politics in Victorian London* (Princeton: Princeton University Press, 2004), and Philippa Levine, *Feminist Lives in Victorian England: Private Role and Public Commitment* (Oxford: Basil Blackwell, 1990).

17 Carroll Smith-Rosenberg, "The Female World of Love and Ritual," in *Feminism and the Politics of History*, ed. Joan Wallach Scott (Oxford: Oxford University Press, 1996), 367, 385.

18 Adrienne Rich, "Compulsory Heterosexuality and Lesbian Existence," in *The Signs Reader: Women, Gender, and Scholarship*, eds. Elizabeth Abel and Emily K. Abel (Chicago: University of Chicago Press, 1983), 139–68. For an analysis of the political and theoretical contexts in which Rich developed her argument, see Carolyn Dever, *Skeptical Feminism: Activist Theory, Activist Practice* (Minneapolis: University of Minnesota Press, 2004), 141–61.

19 See Lisa Duggan, "The Trials of Alice Mitchell: Sensationalism, Sexology, and the Lesbian Subject in Turn-of-the-Century America," *Signs: Journal of Women in Culture and Society* 18.4 (1993), 791–814; Castle, *The Apparitional Lesbian;* Esther Newton, *Margaret Mead Made Me Gay: Personal Essays, Public Ideas* (Durham, NC: Duke University Press, 2000); and Amber Hollibaugh, *My Dangerous Desires: A Queer Girl Dreaming Her Way Home* (Durham, NC: Duke University Press, 2000). Gayle Rubin, in "Thinking Sex: Notes for a Radical Theory of the Politics of Sexuality," argued that the continuum theory conflates gender and sexuality, in *Pleasure and Danger: Exploring Female Sexuality*, ed. Carole S. Vance (Boston: Routledge & Kegan Paul, 1984), 267–319.

20 See especially Duggan, "The Trials of Alice Mitchell," and Vicinus, *Intimate Friends.*

21 Judith Butler, *Gender Trouble: Feminism and the Subversion of Identity* (New York: Routledge, 1990). The phrase "undoing gender" is the title of one of Butler's recent books (New York: Routledge,

2004). For work in Victorian studies that addresses the issues raised by feminism and queer theory, such as desire, domesticity, and subjectivity, without relying on oppositional concepts of gender and sexuality, see Amanda Anderson, *The Powers of Distance: Cosmopolitanism and the Cultivation of Detachment* (Princeton: Princeton University Press, 2001), esp. 34–62, and Jeff Nunokawa, *Tame Passions of Wilde: The Styles of Manageable Desire* (Princeton: Princeton University Press, 2003). In *Female Masculinity* (Durham, NC: Duke University Press, 1998), Judith Halberstam makes a related argument that female masculinity past and present cannot be fully explained in terms of lesbianism.

22 See Duggan, "The Trials of Alice Mitchell"; Vicinus, *Intimate Friends*; Lisa L. Moore, *Dangerous Intimacies: Toward a Sapphic History of the British Novel* (Durham, NC: Duke University Press, 1997); and Andrew Elfenbein, who uses the concepts of excess, transgression, and gender crossing to link genius to queerness and same-sex eroticism, in *Romantic Genius: The Prehistory of a Homosexual Role* (New York: Columbia University Press, 1999).

23 Lillian Faderman, *Surpassing the Love of Men: Romantic Friendship and Love between Women from the Renaissance to the Present* (New York: William Morrow, 1981). Though Faderman mistakenly insisted on the asexual nature of nineteenth-century romantic friendship, her exhaustive research on female couples provided an agenda for biographical research that continues to thrive. For a seminal discussion of "minoritizing" and "universalizing" views of homosexuality and the ways they intermingle, see Eve Kosofsky Sedgwick, *Epistemology of the Closet* (Berkeley: University of California Press, 1990).

24 Vicinus, *Intimate Friends*, xv. Further references are to this edition and appear in the text. [. . .]

25 On the persistent tendency to discount even the most explicitly sexual representations as evidence of a broader cultural awareness of lesbian sex, see Sarah Toulalan, "Extraordinary Satisfactions: Lesbian Visibility in Seventeenth-Century Pornography in England," *Gender & History* 15.1 (2003), 50–68.

26 Denise Riley, *"Am I That Name?" Feminism and the Category of "Women" in History* (Minneapolis: University of Minnesota Press, 1988); Joan Wallach Scott, *Gender and the Politics of History* (New York: Columbia University Press, 1988); Scott, *Only Paradoxes to Offer: French Feminists and the Rights of Man* (Cambridge, Mass.: Harvard University Press, 1996); Sedgwick, *Epistemology;* Butler, *Gender Trouble* and *Undoing Gender.* I discuss the connections between feminism and queer theory in "Queer Theory for Everyone: A Review Essay," *Signs: Journal of Women in Culture and Society* 31.1 (2005), 191–218.

27 Foucault has had an enormous influence on the conceptualization of the homosexual as an exile from the family seeking to invent radically new social relations, although he also understood the homosexual as an effect of power and as the creation of bourgeois society. See Michel Foucault, *The History of Sexuality. Volume 1: An Introduction*, trans. Robert Hurley (New York: Vintage Books, 1980), and Didier Eribon's commentary in "Michel Foucault's Histories of Sexuality," trans. Michael Lucey, *GLQ* 7.1 (2001), 39–42, 49, 75. For strong defenses of queerness as subversion, see Michael Warner, *The Trouble with Normal: Sex, Politics, and the Ethics of Queer Life* (New York: Free Press, 1999); Leo Bersani, *Homos* (Cambridge, Mass.; Harvard University Press, 1995); and Lee Edelman, *No Future: Queer Theory and the Death Drive* (Durham, NC: Duke University Press, 2004). Butler and Sedgwick argue for a queerness that subverts the priority and primacy of heterosexuality and thus becomes as original or fundamental as the heterosexuality from which it cannot truly be distinguished. See *Gender Trouble*, *Between Men*, and *Epistemology.*

28 On the relationship between gay people and ideas of family, traditional and alternative, see Kath Weston, *Families We Choose: Lesbians, Gays, Kinship* (New York: Columbia University Press, 1997)

31 The curious princess, the novel, and the law

Hilary M. Schor

[. . .]

Once upon a time there was a princess, who was beautiful, wise and good—or, as she was familiarly known by her subjects, "Handsome, clever and rich." The princess lived in a kingdom crowded with objects. The world was filled with furniture and pianos and clocks, with barometers and weather and clouds, with clothing and jewels and paintings and omnibuses and trains. The princess walked on roads and rode in automobiles and went wherever she pleased and did whatever she liked, and in all the land there was only one law, and it was "Thou shalt not be curious."

The country I am describing is, of course, the landscape of the realist novel, the princess is its heroine, and its law is the subject of this book, for the English novel is full of interdictions, denials, and surreptitious glances at curiosity. "Never wonder," says Thomas Gradgrind to his daughter Louisa. "Without thinking myself a Fatima, or you a Blue Beard, I am a little curious about it," says Esther Summerson, who "wondered all day" and "now I thought it might be for this purpose, and now I thought it might be for that purpose, but I was never, never, never, never near the truth." "I see you would ask why I keep such a woman in my house when we have been married a year and a day, I will tell you, but not now."[1] *Hard Times*, *Bleak House*, *Jane Eyre*: it is only by breaking the interdiction against wonder, repeatedly, obsessively, and each time as if it were for the first time, that the novel gets its plot. The story of the realist heroine and her transgressive curiosity is the story that I shall tell here, and my argument is not only that without curiosity there would never be any such thing as the realist novel, but that it was the novel that brought the modern feminist subject into being.

What is the relationship between the realist novel, the heroine's curiosity, and her emancipation? To tell that story we might look no further than an afternoon in Oxford in the 1860s, when Charles Dodgson took a boat ride with a young girl, as she grew larger and smaller and larger and smaller and (of course) curiouser and curiouser. We could note that at roughly the same moment Matthew Arnold was standing in a lecture hall, also in Oxford, reminding his listeners that it was curiosity, a trait that he described as "the most un-English trait I know," the mind turning on itself, which was the essence of a liberal imagination. Meanwhile, in London, John Stuart Mill was introducing into the debate over the second Reform Bill language that would, for the first time, make women legal "persons"—and Robert Browning was noting the same disappearance of wives into their husband's identity with his fierce and terrifying poem, "A Woman's Last Word":

> What so false as truth is, false to thee?
> Where the serpent's tooth is, shun the tree
> Where the apple reddens, never pry,
> Lest we lose our Edens, Eve and I.

The Victorians understood, that is to say, that there was something powerful, alluring, danger-ous, and lost about female curiosity.[2]

This is not where other histories of the novel begin. Realism in the novel has traditionally been allied not so much with knowledge as with stuff, with the world of material objects, the world that we could similarly have found in Oxford at the Ashmolean Museum, the reposi-tory of Tradescant's rarities, ethnographic, botanical, and artistic curiosities long since moved from their first home in a London tavern.[3]

[. . .]

But if we strip the novel bare of material culture, layettes and epics and the flora of Lapland, we are left instead with the heroine's imagination, testing itself against the world, trying to know something outside itself.

[. . .]

My sense of realism is of something that vibrates between these two possibilities: the novel of steamer trunks and the novel in which a character looks out and says, as Clarissa Dalloway will some seventy years later, "here was one room, there another."[4] This is what Ian Watt referred to as the realism of referentiality, a "full and authentic report of human experience," but one that gets beyond the mere world of stuff, that is, as Elizabeth Ermarth writes, "rela-tively careless of the concrete." In this sense, as Watt, Ermarth, George Levine, and others have made clear, "formal realism is, like the rules of evidence, only a convention," one which connects its readers to a series of (individual) perspectives, gathering consensus as it gathers events.[5] But my definition of realism depends further on a sense of doubleness, one that I connect not only to Watt's classic distinction between the realism of "presentation" and the realism of "assessment" but also to the doubled nature of curiosity that curiosity is both some-thing you have ("I am so curious about Isabel Archer, what will she do?") and something you are ("Isabel Archer is so very curious, what a curious vase that is!"). By curiosity, then, I will throughout this book mean several aesthetically and historically complicated things: a form of inquiry, an innate sense of wonder, a subject unduly interested in looking; an object of true or imagined singularity; and that world of objects cunningly made. That world delights and bewilders us: "Spanish fans, Spezzin straw hats, Moorish slippers, Tuscan hairpins, Carrara sculpture, Trastaverinini scarves, Genoese velvets and filligree, Neapolitan coral, Roman cameos, Geneva jewellery, Arab lanterns, rosaries blest all round by the pope himself, and an infinite variety of lumber," to quote one such novelistic list.[6] But I do not want to lose that other sense of curiosity that realism conjured the subject who, looking out at the world, sees only herself, looking. This book argues that the dialectical relationship between these kinds of curiosity was present at the creation of the novel, that this dynamic sense of curiosity is peculiarly fitting to the formal requirements of the realist novel, and that curiosity is a power-ful engine of plot-making and readerly desire.[7]

Why, then, the curious heroine? We need think no further than Crusoe on his island, meas-uring the weather and counting the goats, to place ourselves in the plot of exploration, a hero like Pip, ambitiously looking around him (in however purblind a fashion), offers a curiosity of his own, of course. In fact, from that perspective, it is a rare heroine who displays any curiosity at all—like the virtuous heroine of Charlotte Lennox's *The Female Quixote*, who has not only no story but also no unseemly curiosity. When the Bennet sisters cluster around the window to see the soldiers passing by, Elizabeth and Jane hold back, when Mr. Rochester asks Jane, "Will you accept my answer?" she does. If, as narrative theory has taught us, "Men have plots of ambition and women have plots of love," it would seem that female curiosity, far from the key to the realist novel's form, is precisely what it must exclude. No man, as

Darcy and Rochester remind us, will marry a woman who not only cannot keep a secret but also yearns to know (let alone to publish) yours.[8]

My point is not that there are no female Crusoes (contemporary narrative experiments such as Jane Gardam's *Crusoe's Daughter* and Marianne Wiggins's *John Dollar* put the lie to that idea), but rather that a very different form of female curiosity not only informs but also shapes the realist novel. That curiosity is one perhaps best summed up by the heroine of the film *The Lady Eve*, when she informs her deluded fiancé that "all women are adventuresses." They have to be, she points out, in the marketplace of female sexuality, to negotiate the high seas of romance, to (as Henry James put it in the preface to *The Portrait of a Lady*) "affront her destiny."[9] "Well, what will she *do*?" is the novelist's as well as the reader's question, the author's question is, "What will she *see*?" The heroine's question is, "What is this world in which I must make my way?" And in her way, the question that lies before her most often is, "whom shall I marry?"

It may be, in fact, that heroines are the keys to readers' curiosity precisely because the high seas are largely denied to them—as are bastions of male authority and male debauchery. Coming to Europe may be a "mild adventure" for Isabel Archer compared to Crusoe's island, but her entry into the clutches of Madame Merle and the sterile, dark rooms of Gilbert Osmond, to whom she all too quickly promises herself, are as terrifying as any cannibal Crusoe confronts. The question for Isabel Archer, for all the "frail vessels" of this tradition, is precisely that of escaping the curio cabinet, of moving freely in the world, of choosing for themselves, in a world that is structured (and here I mean both the novel and Anglo-American society) to allow them one and only one choice: that of a husband.

In short, my view of female curiosity places it securely within two sets of law: the first, the laws of genre that we recognize as the realist novel; the second, the legal constraints of Anglo-American marriage, in which a marriage contract literally "contracts" around the heroine. What the laws of genre and the laws of marriage share is an interest in singular answers, one at war with my sense of doubleness, but what I am arguing for curiosity is precisely a moment of hesitation in the imposition of law, a kind of gap that breaches those laws. The plot of the curious heroine builds into these contracts a suspension, a delay, a space for a curiosity however insufficient to its task, however much always slightly belated in its perspicacity. How is it that the heroine can find out what she needs to know in the time allowed to her to investigate, when what she needs to know awaits her only on the other side of the threshold, the other side of the marriage plot? Or, as Cinderella beautifully puts it in Stephen Sondheim's *Into the Woods*,

> How can you know what you want
> Till you get what you want,
> And you see if you like it?[10]

This is the essential realist question: how can you know? If we take seriously the realist novel's centrality as an interrogative place for characters and readers alike, a place that teaches us not only what but also how to know, then the curious heroine's attempts to gather information, and the risks of these trials, are the novel's central function. What does the curious heroine need to know? Islands, not so much, the marriage bed, all of us, perhaps.

This is the odd relationship of curiosity to desire, even as narratologists such as Peter Brooks have defined it. Is curiosity merely (sexual) desire, displaced always and only into a seduction plot? There is a bluntness overall to the usual solution of the heroine's plot that cuts off interrogation, which in turn blunts the heroine's curiosity. The assumption of many readers of *Emma*, *The Portrait of a Lady*, *Middlemarch*, or *Daniel Deronda* is that there is a single thing the heroine doesn't know, and that is the mystery of sex. No heroine who knew "that" would marry Gilbert Osmond or Edward Casaubon or Henleigh Grandcourt—or, to take the obverse, what the heroine needs is a good fuck, and then she will have all the answers, she will finally know what everyone else knows that she doesn't know; she will have "caught up" to the world. But if that were true, of course, the books could end after the marriage—or more accurately, the heroines would not need to go on learning after their marriages, they would not need an education beyond their husbands' creepy touch in bed, they would not need the law, or its ferocity in interrogating *them* about what kinds of subjects (legal and literary) they want to be.[11]

What holds my two views of curiosity together (the world of objects and roads and omnibuses and the world the heroine sees) is the idea of a subject who can contract, who can *bind* herself through time, who *tries* the world, and finds it lacking; who moves through the world *choosing*—a realm of legal subjectivity unique to the modern world, which goes by the literary shorthand of the marriage plot. The test, the choice, the contract; the world afterward: how are we to live "here—now—in England," as Dorothea Brooke puts it in *Middlemarch.* Realism is where she learns, the uneasy space *between* the asking of a question and the *learning* of an answer, even if that space is one of error, mistake, confusion, and even misery—or, the space more accurately known as marriage. Marriage, curiously, offers in the realist novel exactly what John Stuart Mill imagined for the liberal subject: persistent exposure to that which is most alien. In the novel, a bad marriage is central to the heroine's curiosity, to her movement through realism into full subjectivity—or, as George Eliot again put it, "Doubtless a vigorous error vigorously pursued has kept the embryos of truth a-breathing: the quest of gold being at the same time a questioning of substances, the body of chemistry is prepared for its soul, and Lavoisier is born."[12]

I think this matters because it has stopped seeming obvious to us that realism is a game with knowledge—and even when we did know that, we didn't know it was a game best played by marriageable women. Catherine Gallagher's exploration of women and fictionality reminds us that the heroine who is (in a sense) in pursuit of her own property as well as her own name made the exactly right kind of vessel for fiction: one that is general enough for us to follow her adventures and insert ourselves; one that is named enough to give us a place for our sympathies. But what she is doing is testing the reality of the world against precisely her expectations for the future, a story that will recur in our explorations as the problem of the cruelty of the test in *Clarissa* and *The Golden Bowl*, the problem of probable knowledge and statistical justice in *Hard Times*, of criminal knowledge in *Vanity Fair*, and the deadly doubling of knowledge in *Bleak House*. But it is the heroine's desire to know, and the hints of both cruelty and terrible loss behind it, that runs through all of these texts—the heroine must play the game well; she must learn what she is never to know, she must know without (while) seeking to know too much, and she must do it backward, as Governor Ann Richards said of Ginger Rogers, in heels. When Barbara Stanwyck invokes the pirate heroine, she does so not only as an adventuress of the high seas (for whom the ship's decks are her business office) but as "The Lady Eve," the heroine who, like the first Eve, like Pandora and Psyche, travels beyond the expected realms of knowledge. (The adulteress, as Angela Carter notes, "if she plays her cards right, may evolve into the adventuress, whose status in life . . . has always been that of a free woman.")[13] Only when a curious woman, call her Eve, or Pandora, or Psyche, reaches out her hand, holds up a lamp, and opens a door, can the plot begin; and paradoxically, only by choosing badly does the heroine then get the power to choose well, to enter the law, and to take the law in her own hands. The doubling of the heroine offers the text's meditation on its own status as representation—but it also serves a pedagogical purpose for both the hero and the heroine, one that (in a pattern we will see throughout this book) cannot be overcome through law, but only through the law's higher knowledge. As "Jean" says to Hopsy, now "Eve's" husband, when he warns her he is married—"Why, Hopsy, so am I," and the law has (inadvertently?) performed its work as magical arbiter of romantic destiny.

If that structure reverberates primarily as mythic, Eve dropping apples repeatedly on the hapless, tripping-over-his-own-feet hero's head, it also echoes as a fairy tale, precisely the one Jane Eyre invokes when Rochester asks her *not* to ask her question. Jane has come into Thornfield Hall after standing out on the leads: "Anybody may blame me who likes, that then I longed for a power of vision that might overpass that limit." Instead of finding that vision, Jane returns to the corridors of Thornfield, which stretch before her "narrow, low, and dim, with only one little window at the far end, and looking, with its two rows of small black doors all shut, like a corridor in some Bluebeard's castle." But the presence in Jane Eyre's gritty material world of the Gothic, the romance, the curious, is no accident, reader.[14] It is instead a heightening of the realist "and then . . ." that reminds us that beyond the promise of law lies its threat: the ghosting of the married woman, as she disappears into coverture, all ability to choose, to know, to *contract*, dissolved by her initial promise, the successful completion of the marriage plot. What better story for that than the Bluebeard story, in which the wife, wooed by the very world of materials objects, riches, jewels, all that might tempt the princess from her solitary tower, is trapped in the palace, bound by the very beauty of her clothes and the richness of all that surrounds her, handed a single key, and told, thou must not seek to know. Instead, she goes farther: she walks down the dark corridor, runs down the slippery stairs, opens the doors, and knows the worst—that her body is forfeit; her promise is forever, she herself is contracted away.

What is this knowledge—and what kinds of curiosity does the novel render legitimate and illegitimate? How is the curious heroine ever to be curious enough—and how can the novel create the space for her new knowledge, without blasting open its own most treasured form, the marriage plot? Or, again, as Stephen Sondheim said,

> Now I know.
> Don't be scared
> Granny is right,
> just be prepared.
> Isn't it nice to know a lot?

And a little bit not (p 69)

The heroine's curiosity must walk a similarly fine line: the heroine must have enough curiosity to start a plot, not so much as to overwhelm it (or, put another way, not enough to become herself fallen, beyond the reach of middle-class representation)—but she must also be free to use her knowledge, and that commits the novel not only to the Gothic possibilities Jane Eyre invoked (a surprise that might make us afraid) but to exactly that wider vision that Jane herself longed for from the leads of Thornfield Hall. In the nineteenth century, such knowledge was political, and it linked the curious heroine to a world far beyond her dissatisfied marriage bed, it brought her into the world of choosing that few thought women could enter, the world of legal and political representation. However much the nineteenth-century novel may mock political aspirations, it indulges in them with equal force, particularly when it comes to the romance of women's rights. So when Jane Eyre leaves Rochester because "I respect myself," she sounds less like Eve or Bluebeard's wife than she does like John Stuart Mill, who said, "The question [of what they are to do] rests with women themselves—to be decided by their own experience, and by the use of their own faculties. There are no means of finding what either one person or many can do, but by trying—and no means by which any one else can discover for them what it is for their happiness to do or leave undone." At the moment when Mill is introducing into Parliament a bill for women's right to the franchise, the language of choice, of experience, of *trials*, is rendered political, even where we might least expect it to be, in the heart of the realist novel, when the novelist (and the reader) must ask, "What is she to *do*?"

This intervention of John Stuart Mill's political radicalism into what seemed to be the fairy-tale world of the novelist suggests the way the Anglo-American tradition of the novel has been misread precisely because of the absence of any recognition of feminism as a revolutionary movement. Readers of the novel, following Franco Moretti, have been able to dismiss the marriage plot and fairy tale (and along with them, the realist novel itself) as quietist in the face of the more radical continental novel, arguing, as Moretti does, that "the fairy tale reassures," and hence is the most appropriate narrative genre for "the task of creating a universal culture of law," one which assimilates its subjects into the happy endings of the marriage plot.[15] Of a novel such as *Jane Eyre*, he claims, it offers only the "most irrational escapism," as the heroine on one hand flees sexual pleasure in the name of law, and on the other returns to a quiet happy ending within marital bliss. Moretti here is participating in a much older line of critique of the novel, particularly the Victorian novel of marriage, as Queenie Leavis also scorns Jane Eyre's sexual puritanism, and Virginia Woolf the limitations of being "always a governess, always in love."[16] But this is to miss the central critique of these novels, and what their use of the curious heroine's fairy tale travails makes clear. For what Moretti claims is merely "fairy tale justice" is precisely what these endings trouble, and the disappearance of the wife into the legal structures of marriage (again, what frightens Jane Eyre away from Rochester's domination in the first place) is not the successful completion of but rather the first step in what he rightly declaims as the real plot of the novel: "In the life of the individual, maturity now means one thing only: knowledge" (139). What Moretti does not ask is knowledge of what? And what would it mean if we saw the novel's quest for knowledge, its delay of the marriage plot, its hesitation over the wife's disappearance into her husband's arms and a *new* dispensation of the law, as a quest for a knowledge that goes beyond what every "mature individual" should know, a quest for different knowledge, a new form of curiosity? Then the novel's ambivalent relationship to contract, particularly to the dangerous forms of the bourgeois sexual contract, might have that revolutionary edge that Moretti bemoans in the dispersal of the Chartist revolution and the failure of England to join in wider continental struggles; it has a curious struggle of its own to pursue.

For as Stanley Cavell remarks in discussing the comedy of remarriage, "the achievement of human happiness requires not the perennial and fuller satisfaction of our needs as they stand but the examination and transformation of those needs."[17] This is not a book about sexual prudishness (the heroine just needs to learn about sex) or about individual happiness ("If only he would choose me . . .") or even about certainty of vision. It is instead a book about error, wandering and seeking—about taking seriously *for women* the "examination and transformation" of what it means to be a person capable of choice, however constrained or confused (or even wrong) that choice might be. It is that transformative power that this book claims for female curiosity and the realist novel: a woman reaches out her hand; a woman climbs the tower, a woman walks out into the world and (perhaps) casts a ballot, as did the unexpected heroine Lily Maxwell, who, in defiance of the law, found herself registered as a householder in Manchester and took the opportunity to vote for representation in Parliament.[18] The unhappiness of Gwendolen Harleth, the rape of Clarissa, Jane Eyre out on the leads of Thornfield Hall longing for "a wider power of vision," the misery of Isabel Archer's sterile marriage, Dorothea Brooke's desire to do something heroic "here—now—in England"—these are part of a larger questioning that is at the heart of the realist novel, the novel's curiosity about what *it* is to do. Put the heroine on trial; use the heroine to put the world on trial; "what to do, what to do?" as Angela Carter will ask of the heroine's plot in the twentieth century. "I would like to know . . ." says Offred in *The Handmaid's Tale*. "Know what?" the Commander asks her What's beyond the door, what's beyond the wall, what is it I want, "whatever there is to know," I say; but that's too flippant. "What's going on."[19]

[. . .]

Notes

1 Charles Dickens, *Hard Times* (New York: Norton, 2001), p. 41; Charles Dickens, *Bleak House* (New York: Norton, 1977), p. 749; Charlotte Brontë, *Jane Eyre* (New York: Norton, 2001), p. 243.

2 Charles Dodgson took the boat trip with the Liddell sisters in 1862, finished "Alice's Adventures Underground" in 1864, and published *Alice in Wonderland* in 1865; the Oxford lecture "The Function of Criticism at the Present Time" was delivered in 1864; "A Woman's Last Word" was published in *Men and Women* in 1863.

3 See *Tradescant's Rarities: Essays on the Foundation of the Ashmolean Museum, 1683*, edited by Arthur MacGregor (Oxford: Clarendon Press, 1983), as well as *The Culture of Collecting*, edited by John Eisner and Roger Cardinal (London: Reaktion Books, 1994).

4 Virginia Woolf, *Mrs. Dalloway* (San Diego, CA: Harcourt and Brace, 1925), p. 125.

5 Ian P. Watt, *The Rise of the Novel* (Berkeley: University of California Press, 1959), pp. 10–11; Elizabeth Ermarth, *Realism and Consensus in the English Novel* (Princeton, NJ: Princeton University Press, 1983), p. 78; George Levine, *The Realistic Imagination: English Fiction from Frankenstein to Lady Chatterley* (Chicago: University of Chicago Press, 1981).

6 Charles Dickens, *Little Dorrit* (Oxford: Oxford University Press, 1979), p. 163.

7 See Peter Brooks, *Reading for the Plot: Desire and Intention in Narrative* (Cambridge, MA: Harvard University Press, 1984) and Leo Bersani, "Realism and the Fear of Desire," in *A Future for Astyanax: Character and Desire in Literature* (New York: Columbia University Press, 1984), pp. 51–88. Bersani notes, along lines very much like my own, that in the novels of Henry James and others, "the resistance to potentially disruptive characters itself disrupts the conditions of realistic fiction" (81). I think of this as in part the *text*'s curiosity.

8 See Nancy K. Miller, "Emphasis Added: Plots and Plausibilities in Women's Fiction," *PMLA* 96, no. 1 (January 1981), pp. 36–48 [. . .].

9 "Preface," *The Portrait of a Lady* (Boston: Riverside, Houghton Mifflin, 1963), p. 8.

10 "Into the Woods," quoted from Stephen Sondheim, *Look, I Made a Hat* (New York: Knopf, 2011), p. 70.

11 See Helena Michie's marvelous *Victorian Honeymoons: Journeys to the Conjugal* (Cambridge: Cambridge University Press, 2007) for a similar analysis of why the marriage plot extends far beyond the marriage night and its sexual revelations.

12 *Middlemarch* (Oxford: Oxford University Press, 1996), p. 27; p. 450.

13 Angela Carter, *The Sadeian Woman and the Ideology of Pornography* (New York: Harper Colophon Books, 1980), p. 62.

14 For treatments of the Gothic and realism, see in particular Judith Wilt, *Ghosts of the Gothic* (Princeton, NJ: Princeton, 1980). My sense of the Gothic as the realm of both the psychoanalytic and the pornographic owes much to Terry Castle, *The Female Thermometer: Eighteenth Century Culture and the Invention of the Uncanny* (New York: Oxford University Press, 1995).

15 Franco Moretti, *The Way of the World: The Bilungsroman in European Culture* (London: Verso, 2000), p. 189.

16 See Q. D. Leavis, "Introduction," *Jane Eyre* (Harmondsworth, UK: Penguin Books, 1966), p. 21 and Virginia Woolf, "*Jane Eyre* and *Wuthering Heights*," in *The Common Reader* (New York: Harcourt, Brace and Company, 1925), p. 221.

17 Stanley Cavell, *Pursuits of Happiness: The Hollywood Comedy of Remarriage* (Cambridge, MA: Harvard University Press, 1984), pp. 4–5.

18 Jane Rendall, "Who Was Lily Maxwell? Women's Suffrage and Manchester Politics, 1866–67," in *Votes for Women*, edited by June Purvis and Sandra Stanley Holton (London: Routledge, 2000), pp. 57–83.

19 Margaret Atwood, *The Handmaid's Tale* (New York: Anchor, 1998), p. 188.

32 Revelation in the divorce court

Deborah Cohen

Annie Cheese lived her short life in the shadow of the Divorce Court. The only child of a Herefordshire magistrate, Annie—tall, graceful, with a profusion of golden hair cascading down her back—was the envy of Rotten Row, Hyde Park's fashionable equestrian promenade. Married at the age of nineteen, she was barely twenty-four when her husband sued for divorce. In the newspapers, for all the world to read, were the facts that Annie's heartbroken father could barely bring himself to acknowledge.[1] While her husband, the dissolute Captain Thomas Lloyd, was imprisoned in a debtors' jail, Annie, the mother of a little boy and girl, had eloped to Paris with her lover, and there given birth to an illegitimate child. Worse still was to follow. When the newspapers found Annie Cheese again, two years after her family's dissection in the Divorce Court, she was an exile from polite society, living in Gloucester under an assumed name with another notorious veteran of the Divorce Court, whose own trial had laid bare his cruelty and drunkenness. Barred from remarrying by their failed divorces, the couple passed as Captain and Mrs. Drummond, driving out in a pony basket carriage, for which Annie held the reins.[2]

In 1853, the year that Annie married, divorce was virtually impossible, a prerogative reserved for the very rich.[3] For 300 years, calls to legalize divorce had foundered. The vast majority of English households abominated the "very name of divorce," explained *The Times*, because their own marriages were so content.[4] When the Divorce Court was finally established in 1857, its mandate was to safeguard the sanctity of marriage. The Court would release from the marital bond an innocent yoked to a sinner, provided of course that the victim who brought the charges in fact had no blemishes of his or her own. If these few aberrant unions could be dissolved, the institution of marriage would be strengthened. Because the Court, like every other English tribunal, was to conduct its business openly, the disgrace of publicity would deter all but the most desperate. In the future, too, the threat of a full airing in the papers would have a salutary effect upon family life. Before taking a paramour or beating his wife, a man would think twice about the opprobrium he was courting. Public humiliation would be both the punishment and the cure for marital misconduct.

But by the end of the Divorce Court's second year, when Annie's case was heard, it was clear how disastrously misguided the original conception had been. Far from reducing the numbers of divorces, the Court was immediately besieged by petitioners. In its first two sessions, the Court granted more divorces than had been allowed in the entirety of the previous century. Moreover, publicity did not prove the bar originally intended. Over the course of 1858 and 1859, most of the Seven Deadly Sins made a daily appearance, replete with flamboyantly lurid details, in the British press. Not even the dirtiest French romances, Queen Victoria complained to her Lord Chancellor, were "as bad as what is daily brought and laid upon the breakfast-table of every educated family in England."[5] There were, it turned out, many more unhappy marriages than anyone had imagined—and many more English husbands and wives willing to air their private misery in order to break the marriage bond.

In the uproar that followed the Divorce Court's first two tumultuous years, Annie Cheese's divorce case, *Lloyd v. Lloyd and Chichester*, marked a turning-point. It was the first instance of collusion detected by the Court. In cases of collusion, spouses could agree in advance to confect or sanitize charges and to eliminate counter-charges, finger-pointing and name-calling, thus short-circuiting the exposure that the law intended to inflict. One would play the role of innocent petitioner; the other would accept guilt without even showing up for trial. Such an arrangement struck at the heart of the Court's mission, raising the alarming possibility that unhappy couples could divorce simply because they wanted to. Rather than a punitive exercise in fault-finding, divorce would become effectively consensual. Collusion was the family secret that made possible the end of the family.

What made collusion such an intractable challenge for the new court was that it was difficult, if not impossible, to discover.[6] So long as the family kept its silence, who was to say which party was the malefactor and which the unbesmirched? Even apparently warring spouses would join in a lie in order to be free of each other. What the Court needed, it became clear, was the ability to reach into the bedroom and parlor, to take the roofs off private houses, to make use of all the watching eyes. Enter the Queen's Proctor, a public prosecutor whose sole charge was to ferret out the secrets that petitioners and their families sought to hide.

Given the Victorian investment in domestic privacy, the Divorce Court, bolstered by the prying Queen's Proctor, was a spectacularly invasive innovation. There had always been humiliating Chancery cases that dredged up illegitimate children and insane relatives. And the "criminal conversation" suits that preceded the establishment of the Divorce Court exposed to view the hanky-panky among the well-born. Nosy parkers, too, were nothing new; India men such as Peter Cochrane and Robert Bruce felt all too keenly what Jane Austen termed "a neighbourhood of voluntary spies."[7] But the Divorce Court went a fundamental step further. Now the conduct of marriage was an official public concern.[8] After the Divorce Court's first few startling years, the number of petitions rose only slowly. But like all social experiments, the Divorce Court risked a cascade of unintended consequences. Did the public outing of marital misconduct strengthen or undermine the institution of marriage? Did the threat of investigations into collusive behavior dissuade unhappy spouses from entering the Court or did it just make them into savvier and more determined liars?

* * *

It was always apparent when the Divorce Court was in session. Outside the Gothic buildings of the Royal Courts of Justice was a throng clamoring for admittance. Loafers, so-called "law students," and smartly attired ladies lined up two-deep to witness the proceedings. As soon as the doors opened, they crowded the passage-ways, swarming into boxes reserved for jurors and witnesses.[9] It was the only court in Britain where wooden barriers were required to regulate spectators.[10] The Court itself was small, nearly square, with poor acoustics that required judges continually to admonish emotional witnesses, "Speak out!" Had the ceilings not been so high, though, the room would have been suffocating. The Divorce Court was drenched in perfume—white rose, heliotrope, patchouli; one judge famously complained of a headache brought on by warring scents.[11] Unpolished paneled oak ran halfway up the walls, above which was a stretch of grey stone, punctuated by windows. Facing the witness stand, suspended like a theatre box above the oak paneling, was a cramped public gallery with seating for thirty-three members of the public. For those lucky enough to gain front-row seats, opera glasses allowed scrutiny of the witnesses' countenances.

What most struck observers was the presence of well-dressed ladies. Whether rubbing shoulders with plebes outside in the crowd of spectators, cool and collected, or flushed and trembling on the stand, and everywhere the perfumed cambric handkerchief, the novelty of women made itself felt. Before the Divorce Court opened its doors in 1858, only four women in the history of England had obtained a divorce. Divorce was a rich man's luxury, requiring an arduous tour through the Ecclesiastical Courts, an action in the court of common law to recover damages against a wife's lover, and finally, an Act of Parliament that permitted a man to re-marry. The new Matrimonial Causes Act of 1857 put divorce in the hands of the law courts, bringing it within the pocketbook of drapers and clerks—and most revolutionarily, their wives. For the first time, women could petition for divorce, though they required more stringent grounds than men. Husbands could divorce adulterous wives; wives needed to prove adultery plus one of a number of grievous injuries: incest, bigamy, sodomy, extreme cruelty, or desertion for longer than three years.

Though the Divorce Court ruled her life, Annie Cheese never entered it. Thomas Lloyd's case—as it first appeared—was open-and-shut, an administrative matter so straightforward that neither husband nor wife appeared in court the November day in 1859 that Lloyd's lawyer presented the divorce petition. Like the vast majority of cases that year, *Lloyd v. Lloyd and Chichester* was undefended. The facts were as simple as they were shameful. Three years after his marriage, Captain Lloyd had ended up in prison for his debts. While he was confined in the Queen's Bench, his young wife had formed an attachment with George August Hamilton Chichester, a friend of Lloyd's whom she met when visiting her husband in jail. When Lloyd was imprisoned a second and third time, Annie had eloped with Chichester to Paris. The evidence was all the more compelling, or so it must have seemed, because it came from Annie's own household: Mrs. Morgan, a servant of Annie's father, appeared in court to testify that Annie was living with Chichester in France and that the couple had an illegitimate child. Her evidence was corroborated by Jane Earlam, Annie's own maid.

That evidence should have been the end of it. But just after Jane Earlam's testimony, something unprecedented happened. The presiding judge, Sir Cresswell Cresswell, demanded to question a gentleman in the audience, a Mr. Isaacson, whom neither party had called to testify. Cresswell—tall and slender, supercilious in his manner—was the Divorce Court's first judge ordinary.[12] A curmudgeonly bachelor sixty-five years old, he was, as the wags of the day noted, a curious choice to command the fate of England's five million married women.[13] Cresswell had been disappointed early in love, an experience that left him, or so his critics believed, "soured and cynical."[14] What he lacked in personal experience of marriage he made up for in industry. In the six years he presided over the Court, Cresswell decided more than 1,000 cases, working at a superhuman pace in a term that stretched from November to August. As Cresswell laid down the foundations of England's family law, he just as vigorously rooted out the lies and deceptions that threatened the Court's credibility. The role of autocrat came easily.[15] Cresswell commanded Isaacson to the stand.

Captain Lloyd's divorce case began to unravel as soon as Isaacson told his story. A friend of both Lloyd's and Chichester's, Isaacson had served the divorce papers on Annie in Paris. Though he was ostensibly an agent of Captain Lloyd, it soon transpired that Isaacson was actually bankrolled by Annie Cheese's father. James Cheese had opposed his daughter's marriage to Lloyd, and even refused to receive him after the couple was wed. Now he was working behind the scenes to broker an arrangement by which Lloyd would agree to a divorce. He not only provided family retainers as witnesses, but agreed, after heated negotiation, to pay his ne'er-do-well son-in-law several hundred pounds to file a divorce petition. But James

Cheese's attempt to spare his daughter further disgrace backfired spectacularly when an errant memo found its way into the hands of the Court's clerk, tipping off Judge Cresswell to the plan. A chortling crowd of Divorce Court spectators heard how Isaacson had made merry with Mrs. Lloyd and Chichester over the course of his three weeks in Paris: dining out in restaurants night after night, paying for Chichester's lodgings, even calling on the couple when they were in bed. The bare outlines of Annie's behavior were damning enough. She who should have conducted herself as a penitent, mourning the wreckage she had made of her life, was instead cavorting like a courtesan. Her father, who ought to have cast her off, was instead financing her depravity.[16] The evidence of adultery was undeniable, but so, too, was the fact of collusion, which under the terms of the Divorce Act was an absolute bar to divorce. Captain Lloyd's petition was dismissed.

For the magistrate James Cheese, until this moment a man of standing, his daughter's shame would be compounded by his own dishonor. Excoriated for his part in the "conspiracy," he was assailed in the press: "We cannot conceive a more utterly profligate and disgraceful case."[17] For critics of the Divorce Court, the lesson was obvious. The Court was a "playground of perjurers," upon which Sir Cresswell Cresswell, despite his best intentions, was unable to impose order. Had not Cresswell, in his official Parliamentary report the year before, noted with satisfaction that the Divorce Court had seen no case of collusion? And yet, as Annie's case demonstrated, fraud and collusion were rife, a conclusion reinforced by the fact that over eighty percent of divorce cases were undefended. Without an apparatus to conduct its own investigation into the most intimate realms of family life, the Court was at the mercy of its petitioners.[18]

Before the Divorce Court started work, the notion of a government officer charged with the duty of prying into connubial affairs was almost unthinkable. In the original debates around the new marriage law, the idea was mooted, only to be summarily dismissed as an intolerable intrusion. But after two years scrutiny in the harsh light of the Divorce Court, family life no longer appeared an inviolable bastion of harmony—or morality.[19] The revelations of the Divorce Court stripped away easy notions of conjugal felicity, causing even romantics "to doubt the reality of our eyesight."[20] Nothing was what it seemed. Did the solicitously tender husband of yesterday's dinner party commence to abuse his wife once they entered their carriage? Was the demure young wife a secret drunkard? In 1857, the year that the Divorce Court was written into law, *The Times* had proclaimed the vast majority of English marriages contented, even happy; by 1859, the paper's editors acknowledged the "misery which was silently suffered under the old system."[21] An apparently jovial family party glimpsed through a window would never look the same again.

At stake was nothing less than the middle classes' vaunted reputation for virtue. From the late eighteenth century, Britain's middling orders had insisted that they, of all classes of the land, were uniquely moral; it was on this basis that they had laid claim to the vote in 1832.[22] That aristocrats still fell prey to the old Regency vices of whoring and tippling was to be expected. No one could be surprised that illegitimacy, bigamy, and cruelty were rampant among the lower classes. Entirely unanticipated, however, was the fatal blow that the Divorce Court so quickly dealt to the cherished self-conception of the middle classes. Two weeks after Annie Cheese's debauchery was paraded through the papers, *The Times* declared that Judge Cresswell was "holding up a mirror to the age." Reflected in Cresswell's looking-glass was "a strange revelation of the secret doings of the middle classes in this country."[23]

What the 1859 cases revealed, in fact, was a staggering catalogue of vice, all the more shattering—and enthralling—because of the ordinariness of the lives involved.[24] Samuel

Alexander, son of an Ipswich banker, had been married twenty years when his wife, the mother of four children, committed adultery with a groom in his employ.[25] The confectioner Mr. Wilton's wife ran away with a sailor to Jersey.[26] After seven years of marriage, the engraver Alfred Bacon was cuckolded by his own brother, whom his wife "frequently" concealed in cupboards when he came home unexpectedly.[27] Mr. Allen, a military outfitter with premises in the Strand, sued his wife for adultery with a Captain D'Arcy, only to have it revealed in the course of the trial that he had conspired in his wife's ruin. Critical to what the jury denounced as a "base conspiracy" was the fact that both "Captain" and "D'Arcy" were fictions, concocted by Mr. Allen to turn a crony of his, the unromantically named Mr. Milburn, into an irresistibly dashing hero.[28] According to the *Morning Chronicle*, the demonic home-wrecker Asmodeus, prying the roofs off houses, was "as nothing to Baron Cresswell in the Divorce Court."[29]

Small wonder that many Britons started the day by turning first to the "spicy" pages of the newspaper.[30] In the serious papers like *The Times*, reporting from the Divorce Court was discreetly located on the third or fourth page, but for those less decorous publications, such as the *Pall Mall Gazette*, it was front-page news. Here, in the nexus between the "hideous" Divorce Court and press, fulminated the eminent critic and poet Matthew Arnold, had the "gross unregenerate British Philistine . . . stamped an image of himself."[31] Born at the same moment, the Divorce Court and the mass circulation press were made for each other. The Divorce Court got the publicity to humiliate moral reprobates. The newspapers got the fodder they needed to power a gigantic leap into the mass market. The mid-century explosion of the newspaper industry—fueled by the repeal of the stamp tax in 1855, together with the invention of cheaper printing—soon boosted British circulation figures to the highest in the world. The *Daily Telegraph* printed a staggering 141,700 copies in 1860, an increase of more than 500% over its circulation just four years before.[32] Scandal sold papers at the moment when there were more papers than ever before to sell.

Even the most sanguine of the Divorce Court's original advocates had to acknowledge that its effects had been almost precisely the opposite of what was intended. Lord Campbell, an architect of the original bill, confessed to his journal that he felt like Frankenstein, "afraid of the monster I have called into existence."[33] The tide of filth in the papers, the ever-increasing backlog of cases, the unchecked opportunities for collusion: in the aftermath of the 1859 session, there were few who believed that the Court could continue as originally constituted.[34] Two proposals occupied Parliament. The first was a measure to empower a new public official, the Queen's Proctor, to investigate cases of suspected collusion.[35] The second was to close the court whenever the claims of decency required it.

Creating an office of the Queen's Proctor proved uncontroversial. Collusion was no longer merely a theoretical menace; after Annie's case, it was real and had to be stamped out. Closing the court, however, was another matter. The proposal debated in Parliament was modest: it gave the presiding judge the power to exclude the public and press from those trials either injurious to public morality or likely to cause great pain to the families involved.[36] But the motion ignited a storm of protest. If the Divorce Court could be shut, what would become of the general principle that English justice was conducted openly? Those MPs who defended tradition opposed the measure, but so, too, did liberal champions of working men, who feared that the well-to-do would be shielded while the poor were exposed. Was it right, demanded the radical MP J. A. Roebuck that the middle class "should continue to appear as models of angelic purity when they were as earthly and immoral as any other class?"[37] Against the critics of the Court who despaired of the corrupting influence of publicity were arrayed those who continued to believe in its deterrent power. Secrecy encouraged domestic vice; openness promoted virtue. In a parliamentary vote, virtue triumphed handily. The Court remained open.

What the fate of the two proposals showed was that petitioners to the Divorce Court could not hope to escape the ordeal with their skeletons undisturbed. Even as Parliament refused to shield the most depraved revelations from public scrutiny, it also created in the Queen's Proctor a mechanism for forcing out anything else that might still be hidden. From 1860 onwards, all divorce decrees would be provisional. The Queen's Proctor had three (later six) months to file a motion to intervene in cases of suspected collusion, forcing a second trial before the Court. Proving collusion required the assistance of people with information about the couple's private lives. It was originally envisioned that the Queen's Proctor would gather information by posting notices in the neighborhood where the divorcing couple lived.[38] However, between anonymous letters, nosy tradesmen, and the omnipresent solicitors, the Queen's Proctor soon found that there was enough work to do without advertising for additional leads. Relatives, the Queen's Proctor figured, would be the best informants of all.

[. . .]

Notes

1 *Lloyd v. Lloyd and Chichester*, 164 Eng. Rep. 862 (1859), 1 SW & TR 566–572, 862–65; reports in *The Times*, November 26 and 27, 1859.

2 "London Correspondence," *Belfast News Letter*, October 15, 1861; "Suicide of Lord Forth," *Aberdeen Journal*, October 16, 1861.

3 Especially Roderick Phillips, *Putting Asunder: A History of Divorce in Western Society* (Cambridge, 1988), 95–133, 227–40, 412–22; A. James Hammerton, *Cruelty and Companionship: Conflict in Nineteenth-Century Married Life* (London and New York, 1992); Allen Horstman, *Victorian Divorce* (New York, 1985).

4 "The Law of Divorce," *The Times*, January 27, 1857. As with so much else in law pertaining to the family, Scotland—where divorce had been permitted since the Reformation—was very different from England and Wales. Divorce was available in Scotland equally to men and women on grounds of adultery and later also desertion. See Phillips, *Putting Asunder*, 60–61, 239–40.

5 A.C. Benson and Viscount Esher, eds., *Letters of Queen Victoria* (London, 1907), vol. 3, 482.

6 See, for example, "Working of the Divorce Act," *Saturday Review of Politics, Literature, Science and Art 7*, no. 182 (April 1859): 495.

7 Jane Austen, *Northanger Abbey* (London, 1833), 164.

8 On the interest of the church and state in stamping out clandestine marriages, [John] Gillis, *For Better[, For Worse: British Marriages 1600 to the Present* (Oxford, 1985)], 90–100, 231–59; on the dilemmas that cohabiting couples posed for English courts, [Ginger] Frost, *Living in Sin[: Cohabiting as Husband and Wife in Nineteenth-Century England* (Manchester, 2008)], 9–51.

9 Henry Edwin Fenn, *Thirty-Five Years in the Divorce Court* (London, 1911), 88–89; "London Correspondence," *Belfast News Letter*, June 7, 1860. Before the Royal Courts of Justice opened in 1882, the Divorce Court sat at Westminster.

10 Frederick Payler, "The Divorce Court and the Public," *Macmillan's Magazine* 92, no. 551 (September 1905): 353.

11 Fenn, *Thirty-Five Years*, 35.

12 On Cresswell, Joshua Getzler, "Sir Cresswell Cresswell," *Oxford Dictionary of National Biography*; Edward Foss, *The Judges of England*, vol. 9 (London, 1864), 184–86.

13 "A Lady and a Judge," *Punch*, December 5, 1857, 234; "A Manchester Man," "The Philosophy of Marriage, Studied Under Sir Cresswell Cresswell," *Fraser's Magazine*, November 1860, 555–56.

14 "Sketches of the English Bench and Bar," *London Society*, April 1867, 344.

15 Fenn, *Thirty-Five Years*, 15.

16 "Scenes from the Divorce Court," *Lloyd's Weekly Newspaper*, December 4, 1859.

17 "Scenes from the Divorce Court," *Lloyd's Weekly Newspaper*, December 4, 1859.

18 John George Phillimore, *The Divorce Court: Its Evils and the Remedy* (London, 1859), 14–15, 20.

19 *Morning Chronicle*, November 29, 1859. The evidence for "fastness" that Mason detects in the 1860s may reflect the Divorce Court's influence, both in revealing and in licensing transgressive behaviour. Michael Mason, *The Making of Victorian Sexuality* (Oxford, 2003 [1994]), 119–24.

20 "Manchester Man," "Philosophy," 556–57; Charles Egan, *A Handy Book on the New Law of Divorce & Matrimonial Causes* (London, 1860): "Indeed, until now, no one ever entertained the least idea of the awful depth of matrimonial misery that lulled beneath the silent current of English social existence" (9).

21 Leader, *The Times*, December 26, 1859, 6.

22 Dror Wahrman, *Imagining the Middle Class: The Political Representation of Class in Britain, 1780–1840* (Cambridge, 1995); Leonore Davidoff and Catherine Hall, *Family Fortunes: Men and Women of the English Middle Class, 1780–1850* (Chicago, 1991 [1987][)], 149–92.

23 Leader, *The Times*, December 12, 1859, 8; "Sir Cresswell Cresswell's Knee," *London* Review, July 25, 1863, 89.

24 Mason, *Making of Victorian Sexuality*, 105–33.

25 "Court for Divorce and Matrimonial Causes, Nov. 19," *The Times*, November 21, 1859, 9.

26 "Court for Divorce and Matrimonial Causes, Nov. 22," *The Times*, November 23, 1859, 9.

27 "Court for Divorce and Matrimonial Causes, Nov. 28," *The Times*, November 29, 1859, 11.

28 "Court for Divorce and Matrimonial Causes, Dec. 5," *The Times*, December 6, 1859, 9.

29 *Morning Chronicle*, November 29, 1859.

30 Sir G.H. Lewis, February 28, 1910 in *Minutes of Evidence Taken Before the Royal Commission on Divorce and Matrimonial Causes*, vol. 1 (London, 1912) [Cd. 6479], 75

31 Matthew Arnold, "The Function of Criticism," in *The Complete Prose Works of Matthew Arnold*, vol. 3, ed. R.H. Super (Ann Arbor, MI, 1990 [1962]), 281.

32 G.A. Cranfield, *The Press and Society* (London, 1978), 207.

33 Hon. Mrs. Hardcastle, ed., *Life of John, Lord Campbell* (London, 1881, 2 vols.), II, 361, cited in Gail Savage, "Erotic Stories and Public Decency: Newspaper Reporting of Divorce Proceedings in England," *Historical Journal* 41, no. 2 (June 1998): 513.

34 "A month in the Divorce Court," *Saturday Review of Politics, Literature, Science and Art 7*, no. 167 (January 1859): 36.

35 On the Queen's/King's Proctor, see Gail Savage, "The Divorce Court and the Queen's/King's Proctor: Legal Patriarchy and the Sanctity of Marriage in England, 1861–1937," *Historical Papers: A Selection from the Papers Presented at the Annual Meeting of the Canadian Historical Association*, eds. Dana Johnson and Andrée Désilets (Ottawa, 1989), 210–27; Wendie Ellen Schneider, "Secrets and Lies: The Queen's Proctor and Judicial Investigation of Party-Controlled Narratives," *Law & Social Inquiry* 27 (Summer, 2002): 449–88.

36 [Barbara] Leckie, *Culture and Adultery[: The Novel, the Newspaper and the Law, 1857–1914* [(Philadelphia, 1999)]; Gail Savage, "Erotic Stories," 513–16.

37 Hansard, *Parl. Deb* (Commons), vol. 156, February 7, 1860, 621.

38 Lord Cranworth, Hansard, *Parl. Deb* (Lords), July 21, 1859, 146.

33 Gender, sexuality, domesticity

Melissa Valiska Gregory

The excerpts by historian Deborah Cohen and literary scholars Sharon Marcus and Hilary Schor exemplify some exciting new turns in the study of Victorian gender, sexuality, and domestic life in the last decade. This new work has emerged from a rich tradition of scholarship, now more than three decades old, within the overlapping and mutually stimulating fields of feminist criticism, gender studies, and queer theory. Feminist scholars began to take up nineteenth-century women writers and their modes of representation in the 1970s, and important works such as Ellen Moers's *Literary Women* (1976), Elaine Showalter's *A Literature of Their Own* (1977), and Sandra Gilbert and Susan Gubar's *Madwoman in the Attic* (1979) challenged and forever changed the field of Victorian studies, revising the nineteenth-century literary canon and provoking new modes of critical inquiry. As Marcus remarks, Victorian literature was well-suited for feminist criticism, because while the period "has the remarkable capacity to seem . . . starkly different from the present," it is also "uncannily similar to it" (Marcus 2007: 5 [Chapter 30: 262]). While in the 1830s Victorian women could not sue for divorce, own their own property after marriage, or attend the major degree-granting institutions, and few middle-class women belonged to the workforce, by the 1880s this landscape had changed considerably. Important legislative developments such as the Matrimonial Causes Act of 1857 and the Married Woman's Property Acts of 1870 and 1882, as well as the foundation of Queen's College in 1848 and Girton College at Cambridge in 1869, the social campaigns for suffrage and birth control, and, more generally, the development of first-wave feminism, signaled dramatic changes in the way nineteenth-century women lived their lives. Later feminist historians have found cultural continuities to be as rich a field of study as transformations, as they examine the regulating force of middle-class domestic ideology. Domesticity was a persistent concept in the nineteenth century, and as the Victorian family reorganized around middle-class Christian mores, it was eventually regarded as the main source of stability, security, and virtue in the modern world. This domestic ideal had a powerful influence on the formation of gender and sexual identity for both men and women, and Marcus, Schor, and Cohen address it in a variety of ways.

The second-wave feminist scholarship of the 1970s and 1980s inspired important studies in the 1990s that addressed gender more broadly, taking into account not only women but also constructions of masculinity. At the same time, the evolving field of gender studies often intersected with work in the study of sexuality that had also first appeared in the 1970s and 1980s, and which also tested earlier work on Victorian literature and culture. The first volume of Michel Foucault's *History of Sexuality* (first published in French in 1976 and in English in 1978), for instance, offered a compelling rejection of the long-held assumption that the Victorians repressed sexual expression, instead arguing that sexuality as an object of study was constructed during this period. Less than a decade later, Eve Sedgwick's *Between Men*

(1985) clearly drew inspiration from Foucault's work but also diverged from his historical models to explore what she called male homosocial desire, evident in the homoerotic sub-plots of Victorian novels. Sedgwick claims that same-sex relations between men reside on a continuum, with homosexuality on one end and homosociality on the other, rather than being constructed as a simple binary. Her analysis of the triangulation of same-sex male desire, which redirects a man's desire for another man through a female figure, reinvigorated queer studies and radically revised the understanding of gender and desire in the Victorian period. It continues to be a touchstone in the field, evident—as will be momentarily discussed—in the title of Marcus's *Between Women*, one part homage and one part critique. By the 1990s, Victorian studies scholarship often presented feminist criticism, gender studies, and queer theory bundled together, or, perhaps more accurately, nested within each other. This overlap was particularly evident in the important masculinity studies of the mid-nineties: James Eli Adams's *Dandies and Desert Saints: Victorian Styles of Masculinity* (1995), for instance, engages both feminism and queer theory to challenge monolithic notions of patriarchy that do not accommodate the fluidity and instability of masculine identity, while John Tosh's *A Man's Place: Masculinity and the Middle-Class Home in Victorian England* (1999) explores the impact of domestic ideology on men, who, Tosh argues, increasingly resisted the regu-lating force of the domestic ideal as the century wore on. Marcus, Schor, and Cohen do not engage the question of masculinity as directly as the above works, but they carry on a critical tradition that embraces the productive relations between feminism, gender studies, and queer theory.

At first glance, Marcus, Schor, and Cohen may seem like an idiosyncratic trio, with their differences more apparent than their similarities: interdisciplinary cultural studies and queer theory (Marcus) meet straight-up feminist literary criticism (Schor), which meets the histori-cal archive (Cohen). Furthermore, when grouped together, one writer almost always seems to be the odd one out. Marcus and Schor, as literary scholars, work extensively with the novel, while Cohen, the social historian, shows little interest in literary representation. Marcus and Schor focus on women, while Cohen examines the full range of immediate family relations, including husbands, wives, children, and siblings. Marcus and Cohen depend heavily on life writing, while Schor demonstrates the ways that Victorian realism incorporates the fairy tale, a genre that may seem unexpected within a mode of representation that prioritizes the every-day. Marcus and Schor are overtly theoretical, while Cohen often works through implication, prioritizing the narration of careful and highly engaging stories of past lives over totalizing claims. Marcus limits her historical parameters to between 1830 and 1880, while Schor and Cohen are more chronologically wide-ranging, with Schor referring to Margaret Atwood, Angela Carter, and Joss Wheedon and Cohen concluding with a discussion of psychiatry and privacy in the 1970s. In other words, these three books do not reflect a clearly discernible progression of theoretical or methodological models, nor do they speak to each other directly. Instead, they showcase the diversity of twenty-first-century scholarship on gender, sexuality, and domesticity, revealing the wide range of possibilities available to contemporary scholars.

That said, inviting these excerpts to share the stage dramatizes some fascinating points of connection. They present strikingly similar opening acts, with each one starting off with a heroine. Marcus's Emily Pepys, Schor's beautiful fairy tale princess, and Cohen's Annie Cheese each introduce their respective sections as the authors elaborate their central claims through a single female figure. Beginning an academic analysis with a specific illustration or case study is hardly a new rhetorical strategy, but the prominent placement of these female figures in books by female academics points suggestively to the sometimes shadowy relation between an author's socio-personal context and her scholarship, one that inevitably affects all academic work but which has traditionally been more self-consciously presented within feminist criticism and gender studies. Second-wave feminist scholarship was a response both to a broad political context outside the university and to the concerns of recently minted female PhDs confronting the patriarchy of the academy in which they studied and worked. Though Marcus, Schor, and Cohen all face a transformed cultural landscape for female scholars, their common use of a specific woman as an entry point to their work not only addresses an ongoing need in the academy to adequately address the complexity and importance of individual women's domestic lives but also reveals the fluid boundaries between these private lives and the public act of academic inquiry.

Taken as a group, the heroines that appear at the start of each excerpt also reflect a more specific set of concerns about gender as it relates to agency, choice, and the institution of marriage. In each selection, Marcus, Schor, and Cohen present their initial case studies of women caught in the act of imagining—or, in Schor's case, being forbidden to imagine—alternatives to traditional domesticity as defined by a heterosexual, legally binding marriage contract: thus, we move from Marcus's ten-year-old Emily, who dreams of being married to another woman, to Cohen's defiant Annie, living out of wedlock with another man, to Schor's princess, allowed to live in the beautiful land as long as she doesn't ask questions. This may seem like a familiar extension of second-wave feminism: what else is *Madwoman in the Attic*'s famous chapter on *Jane Eyre* if not an extended meditation on the relationship between feminine agency and the coercive implications of the middle-class domestic ideal? But the way these books treat female agency in relation to dominant ideology distinguishes them from their earlier counterparts in the same critical tradition. Marcus, Cohen, and Schor share an interest in domestic relationships and particularly in marriage, but they are more preoccupied with the subtle variations within domestic ideology than in identifying the ways in which female subjects disavowed or rejected it. Indeed, these authors show the ways in which Victorian domestic structures could produce feminist subjectivity, exploring in particular how feminist identity emerges in relation to the heterosexual, companionate model of marriage. In these works, marriage appears as more nuanced and varied than earlier studies have suggested, either as historical reality or as produced by realist fiction.

Marcus's *Between Women* has advanced the discussion of gender, sexuality, and domesticity in the Victorian period by showing how female friendships helped to stabilize a Victorian domestic institution that previous scholarship had regarded as exclusively heterosexual. As evidenced in her "How This Book Engages Scholarly Debates" section, Marcus attempts both to bring together and to redress a lack within multiple critical fields: the history of domesticity, the history of sexuality, the study of gender, and the study of same-sex relations through queer theory. Responding specifically to Sedgwick's landmark *Between Men* in her title, she offers a strong counterpoint to Sedgwick's analysis, which, as its title suggests, pays little attention to same-sex relations between women. But to explore female same-sex relations, Marcus also suggests that lesbian theory, which she argues has been used "as a master discourse for understanding all relationships between women" (Marcus 2007: 12 [Chapter 30: 265]), must be adapted and revised. She rejects Adrienne Rich's famous continuum model from "Compulsory Heterosexuality and Lesbian Existence" (1980), which she believes "posits female friends and lesbian lovers as united in their opposition to patriarchal marriage" (Marcus 2007: 29), and argues instead that many female lovers adopted the language of heterosexual marriage and thereby received a measure of respectability. For Victorians, in other words, female alliances were often conceptually entangled with rather than separate from companionate, heterosexual relationships. Marcus's analysis breaks new ground because, as she observes, most critical studies of same-sex relations between women in the nineteenth century up to that point tend to define them against traditional family structures, regarding female bonds as secret or subversive. Marcus, by contrast, proposes that female relationships "were at the heart of normative institutions and discourses" (Marcus 2007: 13 [Chapter 30: 266]), and that intimacy between women both laid the groundwork for and sustained hetero-sexual marriage. The idea that same-sex relations between women support or even ground "normative institutions" rather than contesting them may seem like a startling claim in a book so obviously indebted to a feminist tradition of inquiry, but this is precisely why Marcus's thesis is so important. She does not reject the feminist tradition so much as reorient it by exposing the historical complexity of Victorian domestic ideology.

Like Sedgwick, Marcus offers readings of familiar Victorian novels in support of her claims, including extended interpretations of Charles Dickens's *Great Expectations* (1860– 61) and Anthony Trollope's *Can You Forgive Her?* (1864–65). But Marcus's use of historical evidence far exceeds Sedgwick's, as she supports her thesis through an exceptionally wide variety of sources that include life writing ("[t]he letters, biographies, memoirs, and diaries that recorded Victorian women's lives" (Marcus 2007: 32)), visual material such as fashion plates in periodicals and paper dolls, legal writing, and nineteenth-century scientific theory. Marcus's range of evidence is one of *Between Women*'s greatest strengths. One of her goals, she suggests, is to encourage a "skepticism about the transhistorical truth of gender and sexual categories" (Marcus 2007: 13 [Chapter 30: 266]). Marcus's careful analysis of material evi-dence such as the Victorian fashion plate, which she argues teaches Victorian women to enjoy each other as erotic spectacle, goes a long way to show readers how gender and sexuality belong to a particular moment in time.

Martha Vicinus, who is both one of Marcus's critical counterpoints and a touchstone, observes in her review of *Between Women* that one of Marcus's favorite words throughout the book is "matrix" (Vicinus 2007: 83), a term implicit in the introduction when she discusses her own book as embedded within a rich and multilayered critical environment. The idea of the matrix gained traction in the cultural studies work of the 1990s following the publication of Judith Butler's *Gender Trouble* (1990), where Butler uses the phrase "heterosexual matrix" to describe the conditions that compel the performance of heterosexuality. Even when Marcus attempts to move away from Butler's model of heterosexuality, the model of the matrix, a complex structure that supports, encloses, and generates, captures not only the literary and historical relations within her book but also her own methodology. *Between Women* situates itself within a cross-section of disciplinary debates from English studies, History, Philosophy, Anthropology, Art History, History of Science, and other fields.

In order to manage such a complex matrix, Marcus tightly structures her book, alternat-ing between an analysis of nontraditional materials and nimble readings of more traditional literary sources. In a later (non-excerpted) section, for instance, Marcus's interpretation of *Great Expectations* proposes that the novel's most important bond is between mother and daughter—a sly and captivating reversal of Sedgwick well worth the time she gives it. (Any reader who wants to experience the pleasure and excitement of literary critics in direct debate with each other would do well to read Sedgwick and Marcus on Dickens back to back.) For Sedgwick, Dickens's late fiction develops a novelistic tradition of Gothic homophobia, evi-dent in the many erotic triangles that reroute male same-sex desire through women. But if Sedgwick suggests that male homoerotic energy is the animating force of Dickens's novels, a view that explains the intensity of Dickens's depiction of the rivalry between Pip and Orlick in *Great Expectations* or Bradley Headstone and Eugene Wrayburn in *Our Mutual Friend*, Marcus suggests something quite different. In *Great Expectations*, she argues, the presence of desire between *women* is "the form of desire that most distinguishes the novel and that impresses itself most strongly on Pip" (167). Marcus argues that Miss Havisham uses Estella as she would a fashion doll, performing her ownership of Estella to Pip both to show him the appeal of owning an erotic object and to take pleasure in denying him such ownership. Rather than standing at the apex of a Girardian triangle (as women do in Sedgwick's *Between Men*), Pip often finds himself off to the side, adjacent to or excluded from Miss Havisham and Estella's "female dyad" (Marcus 2007: 167). Marcus's reading of female same-sex desire in *Great Expectations* draws upon her preceding chapter on Victorian doll culture and the feminine plaything, since she reads Miss Havisham as an intensification of "the normal dynamics of the Victorian mother–daughter relationship represented in fashion magazines and doll stories" (Marcus 2007: 170). But her decision to place her reading of *Great Expectations* in its own chapter also reveals an investment in upholding certain disciplinary borders. Although Marcus moves fluidly between different theories and critical orientations in the introduction, the rest of the book is not similarly free flowing. There are strong structural divisions within the body of the text between her interpretations of literature and her discussion of other forms of cultural and historical evidence, including the fashion plates discussed at the end of this excerpt. Marcus thus demonstrates the powerful relations between Victorian cultural discourses and literary representation but, at the same time, the internal structure of her book suggests that in order to do justice to both forms of evidence, they also require their own space. The other two books under consideration here, which fall squarely into the camp of either Literary studies or History, also affirm disciplinary boundaries.

   In *Curious Subjects*, Schor is interested less in real historical instances of marriage than she is in the marriage plot of realist fiction and its representation of female choice and agency as that plot progresses. In her survey of largely canonical works of Victorian fiction, Schor argues that the history of the realist novel begins with women seeking knowledge—curious heroines asking questions about themselves and their role in the world. In such works, she argues, women "enter the marriage plot because it was the one place where they had anything that looked like choice. They didn't choose to marry, they married in order to choose" (Schor 2013: 12). In other words, when women are given only the selection of a husband as their main choice in life, the question of whom to marry is an exercise of agency that carries with it the political and possibly radical implications that some scholars feel the Victorian novel lacks. This claim obviously echoes the interest in female agency that appears in earlier feminist scholarship, but it is Schor's focus on the space between knowledge and choice leading up to marriage that tilts the conversation in a new direction. Previous feminist scholarship tended to read the heroine's search for experience as sexual: in this version of the heroine's curiosity, Bluebeard's chamber—a story Schor returns to on multiple occasions—symbolizes the terrors of the marriage bed. But Schor is less interested in what the heroine learns than the process of choosing to know, that moment where the heroine puts herself at risk by collecting bits and pieces of information that may help her to make her choice (even if she often chooses poorly). To describe this dynamic by which the heroine asserts her own agency over the marriage plot, Schor repeatedly uses the language of deferral, remarking that "[t]he plot of the curious heroine builds into these contracts a suspension, a delay, a space for a curiosity however insufficient to the task" (Schor 2013: 6 [Chapter 31: 272]). In this argument, realist fiction depends on the gap that the courtship plot creates between the choice and marriage—that "space of curiosity, between the proposition and the contract" (Schor 2013:

43)—precisely because that deferral exposes the heroine's efforts to use her agency. During this time, the heroine "is testing the reality of the world against precisely her expectations for the future" (Schor 2013: 7), or experiencing trials that bring her self-knowledge. Although this claim may at first appear to be relatively minor, in fact it represents a significant bid for authority within the ongoing tradition of feminist literary criticism because it positions the nineteenth-century heroine's transgressive curiosity not in opposition to realist fiction's marriage plot but as its animating force. Like Marcus, Schor asks her readers to reconsider the role of women within traditional structures that they already think they know, in this case asking her readers to recognize that feminist subjectivity is not antithetical to the marriage plot but central to it. "[M]y argument is not only that without curiosity there would never be any such thing as the realist novel," she asserts, "but that it was the novel that brought the modern feminist subject into being" (Schor 2013: 2 [Chapter 31: 270]).

In order to support her claim that realist fiction grounds the feminist subject, Schor must grapple with an apparently contradictory phenomenon, realism's frequent use of the fairy tale. The figure of the curious woman may seem mythical, the stuff of legend or fairy tale (Eve, Pandora, Bluebeard's wife), and thus at odds with Schor's focus on realism. Indeed, the opening lines of her introduction brilliantly compress and expose the slight sense of discomfort that occurs when traditional fairy tale—"Once upon a time there was a princess"—meets realism—"She lived in a kingdom crowded with objects" (Schor 2013: 1 [Chapter 31: 270]). Even with their congruent rhythm and diction, the two sentences don't quite fit together; the specific objects of the latter distract from the primal quality of the former. As Schor acknowledges in her brief reference to Franco Moretti, she is aware that fairy tale elements within the Victorian realist novel might be viewed as working against its radical potential, and the marriage of the heroine to her prince a species of pure escapism. Schor argues, however, that the fairy tale elements of realist fiction are more radical than they may appear: the presence of the fairy tale, she says, is not an attempt to soothe the reader with romantic fantasy but "a heightening" (Schor 2013: 8 [Chapter 31: 274]) of realism's knowledge of and "ambivalence" (Schor 2013: 10 [Chapter 31: 275]) about the ways in which a marriage contract binds or even erases female identity. Her remarks in the introduction lay the ground for her reading of Lewis Carroll's *Alice's Adventures in Wonderland* (1865) in the third chapter, a novel which arguably features the most curious heroine in all of Victorian fiction yet which is hardly the first that comes to mind as an example of Victorian realism. But Schor claims that the power of *Alice* is that "it is so eerily like our world, so different and yet so immediately recognizable" (Schor 2013: 77–78). Recognizing the relationship between realism and fairy tale reveals the cruelty and terror that heroines may face as they claim their own agency. "To take *Alice in Wonderland* seriously as realism and move from Carroll's world back to Dickens's," says Schor, "is to see the fairy tale at the heart of the novel—and to see that for the curious heroine, as she walks into the haunted chamber, the line between what is matter-of-fact real and what is fantastically dreadful is a very thin line indeed" (Schor 2013: 71). In *Curious Subjects*, Alice and Maggie Verver of *The Golden Bowl* have much more in common than might at first appear.

The blurred line between the real and the fairy tale affects the style of Schor's book, which tends to treat each novel she discusses as a set of multiple, overlapping narratological permutations; just as it is almost impossible to take up only one version of the Cinderella or Snow White story without referring to others, Schor constantly finds repetitions and echoes among James, Carroll, Brontë, Dickens, and all the other novelists she discusses, so much so that her treatment of a single novel often ends up appearing like the middle fold in a series of accordion pleats. In *Curious Subjects*, literature is almost always the ultimate reference point for understanding literature: one story inevitably generates another. "What is the relationship between the realist novel, the heroine's curiosity, and her emancipation?" Schor asks. "To tell that story we might *look no further* than an afternoon in Oxford in the 1860s, when Charles Dodgson took a boat ride with a young girl" (Schor 2013: 2, emphasis added [Chapter 31: 270]). Or: "Why, then, the curious heroine? We need *think no further* than Crusoe on his island . . ." (Schor 2013: 5, emphasis added [Chapter 31: 271]). Schor's ability to highlight the many connections between seemingly unlike works, following the ways in which one leads to the other, can have dizzying effects. But the pattern of stories leading to more stories is also one of the ways in which Schor's book feels like an updated version of earlier feminist work. If that tradition sought to recognize resistance to the marriage plot by individual women writers, then Schor, by contrast, asserts feminist subjectivity at the center of the plot that structures all major realist fiction. Like Marcus, she creates a matrix for gender rather than a single trajectory.

If Schor's book concentrates on the moment between the proposal and the marriage, then Cohen's *Family Secrets* explores what happens when the marriage falls apart. Cohen's book casts its net more widely than the other two excerpts here. First, it is directed toward a general audience. Although her extensive bibliography and endnotes establish Cohen's awareness of previous scholarship on her topic, she does not refer to it as overtly as Marcus or Schor, making her work easier for general readers to navigate. Next, while Marcus and Schor's work focuses on women, Cohen explores whole families, focusing particularly on the kinds of secrets families kept over the course of the nineteenth century, on what they kept secret and why. This topic necessarily involves gender and sexuality, but domesticity is the central issue. Finally, *Family Secrets* is a work of social history, not literary scholarship, and it differs most obviously from the other two books in its use of first-hand archival sources (although Cohen's offhand references to Dickens, Thackeray, Jane Austen, Mary Elizabeth Braddon, and others suggest that she is hardly unfamiliar with nineteenth-century literature). Marcus also examines life writing, particularly letters and diaries, but Cohen's archival research goes deeper and "depend[s] upon exceptional access to confidential files" (Cohen 2013: 6). As Cohen observes in her introduction, although "the records of the Divorce Court . . . are open to anyone who wishes to see them, most of the other twentieth-century archives I consulted are still closed; I was granted permission to read these records on the condition that I anonymize all individuals, changing names and identifying details" (Cohen 2013: 7).

Cohen's description of having to gain permission to study her historical subjects usefully reminds us of the differences between the typical research methods of English studies and of History. In the field of Victorian studies, these two disciplines have a long history of friendly exchange and reciprocal inquiry, and Marcus is a good example of a literary scholar who has benefitted from learning some of the methodological tactics often used by historians. But for all that they share, English and History remain distinct disciplines. Indeed, a primary reason for including Cohen's book in this section is to demonstrate the benefits of juxtaposing History with English studies when it comes to the study of gender, sexuality, and domesticity. More than one Victorian novel aligns with the Divorce Court's view that a ruined marriage can usually be blamed on just one spouse, such as the quintessential abusive husband in Anne Brontë's *The Tenant of Wildfell Hall* (1846)—a literary vision of marriage that acknowledges the failure of individuals within marriage but upholds the ideology of the institution. Cohen's research on and analysis of collusion in Divorce Court proceedings suggest that literary representation could distort the historical reality of Victorian divorce. She thus shares Marcus's and Schor's investment in finding ways in which Victorian domesticity may not have operated as the regulating force it sometimes appeared to be, even as she uses archival sources to uncover the difference between ideology and historical reality. Her book valuably reminds readers of the distinction between Victorian domestic ideology and the actual lives of people who lived under its influence.

Cohen explores a wide range of family secrets in her book, including ones about children born out of wedlock, born with intellectual disabilities, or adopted, as well as ones relating to sexual identity and behavior, including queerness. But the excerpt here focuses on the Divorce Court. As Cohen explains, the Matrimonial Causes Act of 1857 irrevocably altered the legal landscape by moving divorce out of the Ecclesiastical courts and into the common law courts, making it much more accessible to a wider range of social classes and particularly to women, who could now petition for divorce even if they had a greater burden of proof than men. The Matrimonial Causes Act has been the subject of some important feminist scholarship, including Mary Poovey's chapter on Caroline Norton in her landmark book *Uneven Developments* (1988). Cohen's interest, however, lies with the practices of the Divorce Court that were instituted by the Act. She begins by describing the way the Divorce Court changed "the cherished self-conception of the middle classes" (Cohen 2013: 53 [Chapter 32: 281]) by revealing "a staggering catalogue of vice" (Cohen 2013: 54 [Chapter 32: 281]) within ordinary middle-class marriages, challenging the moral high ground the middle class so often claimed over the working classes. In making the claim that the Divorce Court challenged conventions of middle-class domesticity, Cohen builds on the work of scholars such as Lawrence Stone (1993), Lee Holcombe (1982), Mary Lyndon Shanley (1993), Dorothy Stetson (1982), and Kelly Hager (2010), but what is new in Cohen's analysis is her careful examination of the ways in which individual married couples eager to divorce learned to exploit the new Divorce Court rules.

As Cohen demonstrates with the case of Thomas Lloyd and Annie Cheese, the Divorce Court demanded that one member of the married couple be proclaimed to be at fault; if both parties were guilty, they could not obtain a divorce. Spouses or members of their families were prohibited from "colluding" with each other to present a case the court would accept. Married couples, however, quickly learned that they could speed the divorce process along by collaborating with each other. "In cases of collusion," explains Cohen, "spouses could agree in advance to confect or sanitize charges and to eliminate counter-charges, finger-pointing and name-calling, thus short-circuiting the exposure that the law intended to inflict. One would play the role of the innocent petitioner; the other would accept guilt without even showing up for trial" (Cohen 2013: 48 [Chapter 32: 279]). Cohen's observation that real-life men and women may have mutually exploited gender stereotypes in order to work the law to their advantage helps to push past the depiction of divorce in most Victorian literature, which tends to blame only one party. Her research reveals that if only one half of a divorcing couple appeared guilty, it was usually a lie concocted by both parties to game the legal system.

Although other scholars have discussed collusion, Cohen effectively links it to broader changes to conceptions of marriage and family that occurred over the course of the nineteenth century. As the case studies she discusses indicate, collusion subverted the role of the Divorce Court by suggesting that "unhappy couples could divorce simply because they wanted to" (Cohen 2013: 48 [Chapter 32: 279]); thus, by working together to push their divorce through, couples began to see divorce ultimately as a consensual act. Ultimately, Cohen states, "Collusion was the family secret that made possible the end of the family" (Cohen 2013: 48 [Chapter 32: 279]). Cohen's analysis of collusion within the Divorce Court shares Marcus's and Schor's investment in finding ways in which Victorian domesticity may not have operated as the regulating force it sometimes appeared to be; as Cohen remarks, her book "investigates the part that families, so often regarded as the agents of repression, have played in the transformation of social mores from the Victorian era to the present day" (Cohen 2013: 2). In other words, Cohen and the other writers under discussion here discover complexities and in-between spaces that productively revise our idea of gender and sexuality within traditional Victorian domestic structures. As these subjects continue to be resonant for scholars of Victorian studies, this scholarship will surely inspire many new configurations.

Bibliography

Adams, J. E. (1995) *Dandies and Desert Saints: Victorian Styles of Masculinity*, Ithaca: Cornell University Press.

Armstrong, N. (1987) *Desire and Domestic Fiction*, New York: Oxford University Press.

Butler, J. (1990) *Gender Trouble*, London: Routledge.

Cocks, H. G. (2003) *Nameless Offences: Homosexual Desire in the Nineteenth Century*, London: I. B. Tauris and Co.

Cohen, D. (2013) *Family Secrets: Shame and Privacy in Modern Britain*, Oxford: Oxford University Press.

Dellamora, R. (1990) *Masculine Desire: The Sexual Politics of Victorian Aestheticism*, Chapel Hill, NC: University of North Carolina Press.

Foucault, M. (1978) *History of Sexuality, Volume 1: An Introduction*, trans. R. Hurley, New York: Vintage.

Gilbert S. and Gubar S. (1979) *The Madwoman in the Attic: The Woman Writer and the Nineteenth-Century Imagination*, New Haven, CT: Yale University Press.

Hager, Kelly (2010) *Dickens and the Rise of Divorce*, Farnham: Ashgate.

Holcombe, L. (1982) *Wives and Property: Reform of the Married Women's Property Law in Nineteenth-Century England*, Toronto: University of Toronto Press.

Langland, E. (1995) *Nobody's Angels: Middle-Class Women and Domestic Ideology in Victorian Culture*, Ithaca: Cornell University Press.

Marcus, S. (2007) *Between Women: Friendship, Desire, and Marriage in Victorian England*, Princeton, NJ: Princeton University Press.

Mason, M. (1994) *The Making of Victorian Sexuality*, Oxford: Oxford University Press.

Moers, E. (1976) *Literary Women*, London: W. H. Allen.

Nord, D. E. (1995) *Walking the Victorian Streets: Women, Representation, and the City*, Ithaca: Cornell University Press.

Poovey, M. (1988) *Uneven Developments: The Ideological Work of Gender in Mid-Victorian England*, Chicago: University of Chicago Press.

Schor, H. M. (2013) *Curious Subjects: Women and the Trials of Realism*, Oxford: Oxford University Press.

Shanley, M. L. (1993) *Feminism, Marriage, and the Law in Victorian England, 1850–1895*, Princeton: Princeton University Press.

Showalter, E. (1977) *A Literature of Their Own*, Princeton: Princeton University Press.

Stetson, D. M. (1982) *A Woman's Issue: The Politics of Family Law Reform in England*, Westport, CT: Greenwood Press.

Stone, L. (1993) *Broken Lives: Separation and Divorce in England, 1660–1857*, Oxford: Oxford University Press.

Tosh, J. (1999) *A Man's Place: Masculinity and the Middle-Class Home in Victorian England*, New Haven CT: Yale University Press.

Vicinus, M. (2007) Rev. of *Between Women*, by Sharon Marcus, *Victorian Studies*, 50.1: 87–98.

Walkowitz, J. (1992) *City of Dreadful Delight: Narratives of Sexual Danger in Late Victorian London*, Chicago: University of Chicago Press.

Part IX

Disinterestedness and liberalism

Introduction

This book is part of a new series titled "Criticism and Debates in Literature," described by its publisher as providing an introduction to key issues in literary history by "situat[ing] topics within wider debates" and "[e]xploring different approaches and critical directions".[1] Our intellectual model, one widely practiced in the academy, presumes that an informed critical perspective can result only from careful consideration of contrasting arguments and the evidence provided, rather than through monologic appeals to authority. Criticism, in other words, appears both within and as a result of debate. This approach derives originally from Enlightenment rationalism, but its most influential (and controversial) articulation occurred in the nineteenth century with the British liberal ideal of disinterestedness. According to this model, after a process of intellectual *bildung* or growth, a cultivated mind will be prepared to review controversies, and indeed to rearticulate and respond to them in writing, with conviction but without partisanship.

Nineteenth-century liberalism was much more than this, of course: it was a loosely organized set of political, economic, and personal principles that included negative freedom (that is, freedom from interference from others), scientific rationalism, support for gradual social improvement in a capitalist economy through private charity and limited state intervention, and what Amanda Anderson has called "a set of practices of the self, ranging from stoicism to cosmopolitanism to dandyism" (Anderson 2001: 7 [Chapter 34: 299]).[2] Advocates of liberal thought of one kind or another include a gallery of major Victorian writers, including John Stuart Mill, Matthew Arnold, Charles Dickens, and George Eliot, and its influence on Victorian realist and social problem fiction is clear. Yet despite or perhaps because of its dominance in the nineteenth century, for the past 50 years liberal thought in general and the specific notion of disinterestedness have been the subject of intensive critique within the academy.

In his capstone essay, Daniel Malachuk surveys the changing critical fortunes of Victorian liberalism after the Victorians, arguing that twentieth-century ideological schools of the left (and to a lesser extent, the right) have misread and distorted its universalist claims and its goal of an intellectual "view from nowhere." As he notes, in the past 15 years, Victorian liberalism has undergone a resurgence, not just as the object of more refined ideological critique but also as a rehabilitated *vehicle* for critique. The key figure here is Amanda Anderson, author of the first excerpt, who, as Malachuk writes, reveals "the Victorians to be more suspicious about disinterestedness than we knew" while "urg[ing] us to be less so" (Chapter 37: 324). In her introduction to *The Powers of Distance* (2001), Anderson states that she seeks "to consider not only the limits but also the distinctive virtues" of Victorian "conceptions of critical distance" (Anderson 2001: 5 [Chapter 34: 298]).

Anderson, like David Wayne Thomas in his book *Cultivating Victorians* (2003), thus treats Victorian liberalism as a critical disposition involving a universalized (but never fully achievable) goal of intellectual detachment valuable for our current critical moment. The second excerpt included in this section, by Lauren Goodlad, epitomizes a divergent wing of scholarly discourse in treating Victorian liberalism as a historically embedded set of political and economic principles about the individual and the state. Goodlad emphasizes the contradictions in Victorian political liberalism, an ideology which could support a dominant libertarian skepticism about the intrusiveness of the state on individual freedoms as well as a less robust desire for gradualist social improvement through carefully tempered state institutions. Goodlad fleshes out this contradiction through her analysis of the paradoxes within Dickens's idealizations of liberal state power in *Bleak House* (1853): such power will somehow be "rational but unbureaucratic, personal but omnipresent, charismatic but institutionalized, authoritative but liberatory, efficient but English" (Goodlad 2003: 10 [Chapter 35: 308]).

The third excerpt, by Elaine Hadley, shifts the analysis of liberalism to the realm of style. For Hadley, Victorian liberal thought as exemplified in the influential *Fortnightly Review* involved presenting an opponent's perspective in an ostensibly objective and fair-minded manner. The model for the editors of the *Review* was the writings of John Stuart Mill, especially his approach to argument in *On Liberty* (1859) and his system of inductive reasoning in *A System of Logic* (1843). Hadley suggests that "the particular contents under discussion" in any individual article were "of secondary and therefore of more limited interest" than a Millite enactment of fair-mindedness and calm ratiocination (Hadley 2010: 150 [Chapter 36: 317]).

Hadley also notes that the editors of the *Review* regularly juxtaposed multiple essays with contrasting arguments, a practice that in her reading amounts to yet another performance of liberal fair-mindedness. As we've noted above, this practice is exemplified throughout this book and the series of which it is a part. The essays included in this section collectively pose the question: are such gestures a universally valid analytical practice or are they fundamentally an ideological performance?

See also: *Realism and photography*; *Economics, the market, and Victorian culture*

Note

1 Routledge (2015) *Routledge Criticism and Debates in Literature*, London: Routledge. Available HTTP: <http://www.routledge.com/books/series/RCDL/> (accessed 27 February 2015).
2 Both cosmopolitanism and stoicism have, not coincidentally, recently been the subject of renewed interest as critical tools—and not just as critical subjects—by scholars in English studies and philosophy. On cosmopolitanism, see Pheng Cheah and Bruce Robbins, ed., *Cosmopolitics: Thinking and Feeling beyond the Nation* (Minneapolis: University of Minnesota Press, 1998) and Kwame Anthony Appiah, *Cosmopolitanism: Ethics in a World of Strangers* (New York: W. W. Norton, 2007). On applications of stoic thought, see Martha Nussbaum, *The Therapy of Desire: Theory and Practice in Hellenistic Ethics* (Princeton: Princeton University Press, 1996) and Tad Brennan, *The Stoic Life: Emotions, Duties, and Fate* (Oxford: Oxford University Press, 2007). On Victorian dandyism, see James Eli Adams, *Dandies and Desert Saints: Styles of Victorian Masculinity* (Ithaca: Cornell University Press, 1995).

34 Forms of detachment

Amanda Anderson

In an 1856 *Westminster Review* article entitled "The Natural History of German Life," George Eliot considers the ethnographical studies of Wilhelm Riehl, a German scholar committed to the comprehensive analysis of the history and character of social classes and ethnic groups in his home country. Eliot has great admiration for Riehl and uses the occasion to formulate the principles and methodologies that should inform any properly historical social science and any authentic realism in art. In large measure, Eliot pursues this aim indirectly, through a critique of those cultural representations—scholarly, scientific, parliamentary, or aesthetic— that bespeak a detached or distanced relation to social life. For Eliot, such detachment results variously in distortion, idealization, or moral insensitivity. Riehl's ethnography, by contrast, serves as a crucial antidote to abstract or speculative forms of knowledge. Eliot sees in Riehl an ideal participant-observer whose conclusions are appropriately derived from "gradually amassed observations" accrued through "immediate intercourse with the people." Devoted to inductive method, shorn of prejudice, Riehl is, "first of all, a pedestrian, and only in the second place a political author."[1]

Ranging over a wide array of topics and cultural spheres, Eliot's essay serves as an illuminating example of what I argue is a prevalent Victorian preoccupation with distinctly modern practices of detachment, a preoccupation characterized by ambivalence and uncertainty about what the significance and consequences of such practices might be. Indeed, despite its initial strong critique of distance and abstraction, Eliot's essay overall manifests both subtlety and ambiguity when considering the purpose and consequences of cultivated distance, whether it be conceived in scientific, philosophical, or aesthetic terms. Throughout the piece Eliot repeatedly distinguishes among the specific qualities of detachment that attend different modern practices, endorsing some, criticizing others. For example, while Goethe's assiduous antiphilistinism negates all parochial points of view and thereby "helps us to rise to a lofty point of observation, so that we may see things in their relative proportions," distanced viewpoints elsewhere permit only broad outlines that obscure the crucial realities of lived experience (138). This opposition between desirable and undesirable forms of detachment, I contend, exemplifies a more general tendency within Victorian cultural debate. An ideal of critical distance, itself deriving from the project of Enlightenment, lies behind many Victorian aesthetic and intellectual projects, including the emergent human sciences and allied projects of social reform; various ideals of cosmopolitanism and disinterestedness; literary forms such as omniscient realism and dramatic monologue; and the prevalent project of *Bildung*, or the self-reflexive cultivation of character, which animated much of Victorian ethics and aesthetics, from John Stuart Mill to Matthew Arnold and beyond. Yet at the same time many Victorians were wary of certain distancing effects of modernity, including the overvaluing and misapplication of scientific method as well as the forms of alienation and rootlessness that accompanied modern disenchantment, industrialization, and the globalization of commerce. As a result, many writers displayed a complex ambivalence toward the powers of modern distance, one that is legible, for example, in the opposing symbolism attaching to representative figures across the literature of the period. The dandy, the Jew, and the fallen woman, for example, respectively focused anxieties about ironic distance, rootlessness, and heightened exile, while the doctor, the writer, and the professional tended to represent the distinct promises of modernity: progressive knowledge, full comprehension of the social totality, and the possibilities of transformative self-understanding.

The Powers of Distance focuses on a core of writers and texts whose own landscapes of ambivalence reflect some of the culture's most deeply felt concerns about the promises and challenges of modernity. All of the writers that I consider—George Eliot, John Stuart Mill, Charlotte Brontë, Charles Dickens, Matthew Arnold, and Oscar Wilde—explore in a sustained way what it means to cultivate a distanced relation toward one's self, one's community, or those objects that one chooses to study or represent. While each writer manifests unique ways of conceptualizing detachment, and of distinguishing among its different forms, a series of recurrent questions animate Victorian writings about the distanced or impartial view. There are procedural and educational questions about how ideal forms of detachment might best be cultivated; there are philosophical questions about whether such procedures produce reliable forms of knowledge or valuable forms of art; there are psychological and cultural questions about whether individuals are even capable of transcending their interests, their pasts, and their racial heritage; and there are moral and political questions about whether forms of cultivated detachment uniformly promote the well-being or overall progress of individuals, communities, or nations.

In demarcating the cultivation of distance as a distinctive topos within Victorian culture, this study aims to enlarge and reframe current understandings of aesthetic and intellectual practice in nineteenth-century Britain. In large measure it seeks to do so simply by reconstructing the ways in which individual writers actively configured the series of questions I enumerate above. But there is also a polemical thrust to this book. Despite the ostensible neutrality in my repeated references to the self-division or ambivalence that characterizes Victorian thought on detachment, one of the central aims of this study is to take seriously the specific ways in which individual Victorians constructed their ideals, to consider not only the limits but also the distinctive virtues of their conceptions of enabling detachment. This approach goes against the grain of much recent work in literary and cultural studies, which follows the critique of Enlightenment in its insistence that cultural ideals of rationality or critical distance are inevitably erected as the exclusive province of elite groups. It is certainly the case, as my analyses will confirm, that valorized forms of detachment within Victorian culture are often allotted to those empowered by virtue of their gender, their race, their nationality, or their social position. What the philosopher Thomas Nagel memorably dubbed "the view from nowhere" is always actually a view from somewhere, a somewhere determined not only by the social and cultural identity of the author but also by historical and cultural horizons more broadly construed.[2] Yet to call a practice of detachment situated is not quite the same thing as adopting a prevailing attitude of suspicion or dismissal toward it. Thus while I expose hierarchies and exclusions when they occur—and to the extent that they are visible to me—I resist those modes of analysis that too uniformly or precipitously discredit the very attempt to elaborate an ideal of critical distance. The phrase "the powers of distance" is therefore meant to register not only and not even predominantly those forms of domination, control, or management that we associate with specific modern forces such as instrumental reason or institutional surveillance: it is also meant to acknowledge the considerable gains achieved by the denaturalizing attitude toward norms and conventions that marks the project of the Enlightenment and its legacy. While I believe that detachment takes many different forms, and produces many different effects—beneficial, harmful, and indifferent—I defend the progressive potentiality of those modern practices that aim to objectify facets of human existence so as to better understand, criticize, and at times transform them. In defending detachment, however, I do not mean to suggest that absolute objectivity can be achieved, or that one ever fully or finally inhabits any given practice of detachment. When I refer to the cultivation of detachment, I am referring to the *aspiration* to a distanced view. Such aspirations take many different forms and are often envisioned as complex and ongoing self-critical practices. Indeed, many of the writers I examine conceived their ideals in terms of a dialectic between detachment and engagement, between a cultivated distance and a newly informed partiality.

As I have indicated, the promises and dangers of distance were cast not only in terms of their effects on impersonal intellectual, aesthetic, or political goals—they were understood as practices having an intimate and profound bearing on moral character. This may be the facet of Victorian detachment that is most foreign to our current ways of framing questions of identity, critique, and practice. Indeed, insofar as nineteenth-century judgments about distance were suffused with moral rhetoric, it was the result of a recurrent struggle to set characterological dimensions of detachment in some kind of legible relation to more impersonal practices of cultivated distance. This aim is at the heart of the Arnoldian conception of culture, for example, which yokes practices of disinterestedness to the cultivation of character, both drawing on and transforming the tradition of *Bildung*. But it takes negative forms as well, as for example when Dickens worries that the adoption of totalizing views, a practice integral to the project of omniscience, can prompt habits of suspicion that damage character. These characterological cultural formations can be seen as another version of the "moralized objectivities" that historian of science Lorraine Daston demonstrates as inherent to scientific development in the nineteenth century, although the forms of detachment in the realm of aesthetics and the human sciences do not typically subscribe to the ethos of extreme restraint and self-effacement that Daston finds in the natural sciences.[3] A persistent conjoining of ethical and methodological questions, however, marks speculation across the disparate intellectual fields of science, social science, and art. George Levine's recent and forthcoming work on epistemology's dependency on narrative and its "moral urgencies" eloquently speaks to this broader nineteenth-century pattern, a pattern that informs my own analyses.[4]

As a key motif of the study, the issue of moral character lies behind my frequent privileging of the term *detachment* over any other broad rubric that might denote distance, objectivity, and dislocation. *Detachment* is meant to encompass not only science, critical reason, disinterestedness, and realism, but also a set of practices of the self, ranging from stoicism to cosmopolitanism to dandyism. While the choice of a single term to cover such disparate practices inevitably results in some unavoidable moments of compromised precision, I am convinced that the disadvantages are offset by the term's capacity to demonstrate the asserted connection, both within single writers and in the culture at large, between the personal and the impersonal, between character and intellectual practice, between ascesis and aesthetics. Flexibility of reference is also required precisely because the blurring of potentially discrete forms, terms, and concepts characterizes Victorian attempts to assert interrelations between moral and intellectual practices.

Victorian forms of detachment have been underexplored in recent criticism, for reasons very specific to our own current disciplinary conditions. To put the case most generally, and most tendentiously, an incoherence about detachment shadows much of contemporary debate in literary and cultural studies, with discernible effects on the study of historical cultural formations. On the one hand, pointed critiques of detachment have been generated across a broad spectrum of theories that influence current criticism. For example, within much materialist, feminist, poststructuralist, and identity-based criticism, claims to objectivity or reflective reason are seen as illusory, pretentious, hierarchical, and even violent; set against such claims, either implicitly or explicitly, are the opposing ideals of avowed situatedness, embodiedness, particularity, and contingency. On the other hand, within some of these same bodies of criticism, detachment simultaneously and often surreptitiously operates as the negative freedom that permits critique, exposure, irony, or parody. The situation is especially acute within feminist theory, where aestheticist or constructionist tendencies vie with longstanding critiques of those conceptions of disembodied or detached subjectivity that seem to deny or exclude the body, the feminine, and the particular. On the one hand, that is, the feminist project routinely takes a dim and distanced view of cultural representations of femininity, rigorously demystifying their ideological force and exposing them as mere constructs; on the other hand, however, the feminist project often seems to understand women to have a more immediate and authentic relation to experience and the body, and it does so in part by casting aspersions on "masculine" stances of objectivity or detachment.[5]

I take up the conditions of contemporary theory more fully later in the introduction and return to them throughout the study, but the incoherence I identify here has a crucial effect on historical studies that I want to isolate at the outset. Insofar as critiques of detachment have been directed toward Victorian ideals of science, objectivity, or reason, they remain extrinsic approaches fundamentally uninterested in exploring the ways in which Victorians themselves grappled with the issue of detachment.[6] A hermeneutics of suspicion considers investments in critical distance as self-damning, interpreting them as masked forms of power rather than as emergent practices that might themselves be the subject of ongoing critique. [. . .] Even when they incorporate a compensatory insistence on moments of negative freedom or critical subversion, these hermeneutics still do not adequately address the question of how precisely the Victorians conceptualized critique. *The Powers of Distance* tries to present alternatives to such interpretive tendencies, and I explore a particularly salient set of methodological impasses in the following chapter, when I examine feminist approaches to Victorian culture. For the moment I want simply to point out that the prevailing approaches to detachment flatten out the past, ultimately forestalling any real analysis of the ways in which Victorian authors themselves actively and even obsessively engaged questions about critical detachment, questions that lie at the heart of their struggle with the conditions of modernity. Studies that bracket or simplify the question of detachment at the theoretical or methodological levels fail to examine this important dimension of the culture.

Victorian perspectives

The cultivation of distance informed many intellectual and aesthetic practices in the Victorian era, including ethnography, sociology, and novelistic discourse, to name some of the most prominent. By way of introduction, I will explore the approach to detachment in two Victorian polymaths, George Eliot and John Stuart Mill, both of whom were closely involved in debates over the development of various sciences of the human. Eliot is particularly salient here, insofar as her famous essay on Riehl relates the project of the novel to new ethnographic and protosociological methods. Her essay is structured by a series of distinctions that will recur throughout this study, between situated and "objective" knowledge, between science and letters, between false abstraction and the cultivation of self-reflexivity. It begins with a vivid juxtaposition meant to illuminate the limits of those forms of knowledge that are not authorized by direct experience. Remarking that "it is an interesting branch of psychological observation to note the images that are habitually associated with abstract or collective terms," Eliot contrasts the images that the word *railways* might evoke in a person "not highly locomotive" with those of a person who "had successively the experience of a 'navvy', an engineer, a traveller, a railway director and shareholder, and a landed proprietor in treaty with a railway company" (107). While the former would imagine only a series of truncated images deriving from limited experience (a standard train schedule, the station near home, a known stretch of rail), it is probable, according to Eliot, that the range of images presented to the latter "would include all the essential facts in the existence and relations of the *thing*" (107; Eliot's emphasis).

One key distinction that Eliot derives from her example is that between truly comprehensive knowledge and baseless generalities. Multiple forms of experience produce a thorough knowledge based on an aggregate of perspectives and interests, but limited knowledge allows, and even prompts, immodest conclusions and complacent views from nowhere:

> Now it is possible for the first-mentioned personage to entertain very expanded views as to the multiplication of railways in the abstract, and their ultimate function in civilization. He may talk of a vast network of railways stretching over the globe, of future 'lines' in Madagascar, and elegant refreshment-rooms in the Sandwich Islands, with none the less glibness because his distinct conceptions on the subject do not extend beyond his one station and his indefinite length of tram-road. But it is evident that if we want a railway to be made, or its affairs to be managed, this man of wide views and narrow observation will not serve our purpose. (107–8)

The ironic view taken here of sweeping or distant views is reiterated in various ways throughout the essay. Generally, Eliot manifests skepticism about any abstract theory that remains unchecked by lived experience and direct knowledge. Direct acquaintance is most needed in the representation of social life, where abstractions, distortions, and idealizations plague both theory and art. Eliot acerbically faults "the splendid conquests of modern generalization," chief among which is the subsumption of dense social life to "economical science" and "algebraic equations" (111, 112). In a related argument, she asserts that most artistic representations of working people remain in thrall to "the influence of idyllic literature," bearing no relation to a "real knowledge of the People" (109, 112). By way of example, Eliot claims that it is only when haymakers are seen from a distance that they appear jocund, or happy, or that the scene itself appears "smiling" (109). "Approach nearer, and you will certainly find that haymaking time is a time for joking, especially if there are women among the labourers; but the coarse laugh that bursts out every now and then, and expresses the triumphant taunt, is as far as possible from your conception of idyllic merriment" (109).

In contrasting the distortions of distance with a reliable understanding based on situated observation and informed experience, Eliot's critique of social knowledge focuses on inadequacies not simply of method or principle but also, and fundamentally, of stance. Eliot is interested in exposing the falsehoods that issue from acts of distancing, but she is equally interested in examining the psychological and social attitudes that accompany such detached and objectifying relations to the social world. In this, Eliot shares with many of her contemporaries a preoccupation with the distinctly moral dimensions or consequences of modern detachment. From a larger social standpoint, detachment will promote social policies insufficiently attuned to the precise conditions and needs of social groups, insofar as there is a commonality between the "thin" generalizations prompted by narrow experience and the overzealous application of abstract science to human life. But for Eliot acts of distancing produce a more primary effect, which is psychological: the underdevelopment of the moral faculties, particularly the faculty of sympathy. Only the close observation of situated subjects activates the sympathies of the scholar who studies them, and only forms of representation that duplicate that close observation activate the sympathies of the reader. For Eliot, this problem is related to the problem of idealization in realist art, which she likewise construes as a function of distance and deficient experience. Idyllic portrayals of the working class derail the authentic project of art, which is precisely to prompt the development of our moral faculties and the enlargement of our experience: "The greatest benefit we owe to the artist, whether painter, poet, or novelist, is the extension of our sympathies. . . . Art is the nearest thing to life; it is a mode of amplifying experience and extending our contact with our fellow-men beyond the bounds of our personal lot" (110).

[. . .]

Notes

1 George Eliot, "The Natural History of German Life," in *Selected Essays, Poems and Other Writings*, ed. A. S. Byatt and Nicholas Warren (Harmondsworth: Penguin, 1990), 127. Subsequent page number references will be cited parenthetically in the text.
2 Thomas Nagel, *The View from Nowhere* (New York: Oxford University Press, 1986).
3 See Lorraine Daston, "The Moral Economy of Science," *Osiris* 10 (1995): 3–24; Lorraine Daston and Peter Galison, "The Image of Objectivity," *Representations* 40 (1992): 81–128; and Lorraine Daston, "Objectivity and the Escape from Perspective," *Social Studies of Science* 22 (1992): 597–618. For a prominent twentieth-century instance of an approach that calls for the integration of ethos and method in social science, see Max Weber, "Science as a Vocation," in *From Max Weber: Essays in Sociology*, ed. H. H. Gerth and C. Wright Mills (New York: Oxford University Press, 1946), 129–56.
4 George Levine, "The Narrative of Scientific Epistemology," *Narrative* 5 (1997): 227–51; and George Levine, *Dying to Know: Scientific Epistemology and Narrative in Nineteenth-Century England* (Chicago: University of Chicago Press, [2002]).
5 For a symptomatic attempt to finesse this dual relation to detachment through an argument that women hold an "eccentric" position that places them both within and without the culture, see Teresa de Lauretis, *Technologies of Gender: Essays on Theory, Film, and Fiction* (Bloomington: Indiana University Press, 1987).
6 For an example of such an approach applied to Eliot, see Daniel Cottom, *Social Figures: George Eliot, Social History, and Literary Representation* (Minneapolis: University of Minnesota Press, 1987). For an example of such an approach applied to omniscience in Dickens, see D. A. Miller, *The Novel and the Police* (Berkeley: University of California Press, 1988). [. . .] For feminist critiques of scientific objectivity, including specific discussion of the nineteenth century, see Mary Jacobus, Evelyn Fox Keller, and Sally Shuttleworth, eds., *Body/Politics: Women and the Discourses of Science* (New York: Routledge, 1990).

35 Is there a pastor in the *House*?

Sanitary reform and governing agency in Dickens's midcentury fiction

Lauren M. E. Goodlad

The fact is, that a good government, like a good coat, is that which fits the body for which it is designed. A man who, upon abstract principles, pronounces a constitution to be good, without an exact knowledge of the people who are to be governed by it, judges as absurdly as a tailor who should measure the Belvidere Apollo for the clothes of all his customers.

—THOMAS BABINGTON MACAULAY,
"ON MITFORD'S HISTORY OF GREECE"

Why do John Stuart Mill, Harriet Martineau, and Dr. James Phillips Kay, all of whom are cast loosely as "Benthamites," differ so widely both from Jeremy Bentham and often from one another? Why is it that novels written to critique the New Poor Law are more invested in charity than in a kinder, gentler vision of the welfare state? Charles Dickens took an avid interest in a wide variety of philanthropies, and directly oversaw Urania Cottage, a rehabilitative home for fallen women. Why is it, then, that *Bleak House*, his great midcentury novel, is as derisive of charitable ladies as it is of the lawyers, politicians, and policemen who staff Britain's principal public institutions? Why, for that matter, do H. G. Wells's utopian romances tell so strongly against the Fabian socialism he openly supported?

The answers to these and many similar questions are complicated and potentially far-reaching. From one particular point of view, however—that of a scholar engaged in cross-disciplinary Victorian studies, trailing, as it were, on the long coattails of the new historicism[1]—there is a concise answer that I would like to suggest from the start. Victorian Britain was a *liberal* society: "liberal" first and foremost in the sense that, throughout the century, centralized institutions and statist interventions were curbed to preserve the "self-governing" liberties of individuals and local communities.

To be sure, *liberalism* is "a notoriously elusive" term (Bellamy, "Introduction" 1); "a non-systematic and porous doctrine subject to historical change and local variation" (W. Brown 142). Since the nineteenth century it has been variously employed to denote diverse political agendas, a set of capitalist economic ideologies, and a broad cultural investment in promoting freedom. In Victorian Britain, liberalism most persistently asserted itself as antipathy toward statist interference—a discourse that anticipates the ardent neoliberalism or "paleoliberalism" of our own day.[2] But there is another and broader liberal tradition—"a large tendency," as Lionel Trilling once defined it (6)—which is equally important to understanding the Victorian culture described in this book. If the first discourse seems naively to exalt the "free" economic and voluntary activities of discrete individuals, the broader tradition marked by Trilling is more demanding in its conception of citizenship and, at the same time, more likely to view the state as a potential aid to individual and social welfare. Although in hindsight Victorian liberalism is, therefore, best characterized by its pervasive tensions and paradoxes, it is also important to stress the remarkably durable liberal mythology—the ideals, vocabulary, and assumptions—to which contemporaries consciously and unconsciously subscribed. Although many Victorians did not regard themselves as political liberals, most were responsive to the overall projects of liberating individuals from illegitimate authority while simultaneously ensuring their moral and spiritual growth.

Of course, such potentially ambivalent goals could not but engender contradiction and debate. For, in liberal thought, freedom paradoxically signifies "the antonym, the limit *and* the objective" of governance (Barry et al. 2). There was—and remains—a tension within liberal thinking between *negative* liberty (the lodestar of a free society for many radicals, free traders, and eulogists of England's national character) and *positive* liberty (an idea that slowly took hold among social reformers, even those who began by clamoring for laissez faire). Samuel Smiles's best-selling *Self-Help* (1859) opens by affirming a sacred tenet of British liberalism. The "function of Government," he declares, "is negative and restrictive": to protect property rather than to promote virtue among citizens (2). Yet the positive impulse to build character and promote social betterment by collective means of some kind permeates the diverse liberal thought of Thomas Chalmers, John Stuart Mill, Thomas Babington Macaulay, T. H. Green, Octavia Hill, Beatrice Webb, and Winston Churchill—just as it does the later works of Michel Foucault.[3]

It is common in recent critical discourse to define *liberalism* more narrowly, invoking the term to describe bourgeois economic ideologies from John Locke's legacy to the neoliberalism of the present day. Thus, according to John Frow, the liberal social imaginary "draws upon a more or less coherent set of philosophical presuppositions" including negative liberty, methodological individualism, antistatism, and free market capitalism (424–25).[4] Yet to define liberalism in such a constrictive fashion, and to strip it of its internal contradictions, is to forget that "through the nineteenth and twentieth centuries there has grown up a long tradition of attacking" bourgeois self-interest—a humanist tradition that runs deep in liberal culture and extends through Marx and beyond (Pocock, *Virtue* 60; cf. 103–4). My purpose in thus promoting a more rigorous and expansive understanding of liberalism is neither to dissent from a critique of neoliberalism such as Frow's nor to urge a return to a liberal politics such as Trilling's. Rather, I believe that diminished conceptions of Victorian culture impair historicist critique and, in so doing, reduce critics' power to illuminate present-day concerns.

A more complete understanding of Victorian liberalism should include such insistently (if also imperfectly) antibourgeois discourses as the civic republicanism carried over from the seventeenth century, the romantic-influenced "modern" liberalism of the post-French Revolutionary era, and the religious-inflected liberalism of many nineteenth-century Evangelicals and dissenters.[5] In such discourses the recurrent term *character* stands for an antimaterialist concept of the individual which was deeply at odds with *homo economicus*, the hedonistic subject of capitalist ideology. To build "character" in the nineteenth century was, therefore, to resist atomization and embourgeoisement: whether by fortifying the republican's virtuous citizen qualities, by developing the romantic's individuality and diversity, by strengthening the Christian's moral obligations to God and community, or—as often as not—by diverse appeals to all of these ends. Hence, for the purposes of this book, laissez-faire economic theory is understood as an influential (but not uniformly dominant) ideology, the application of which disrupted the antimaterialist underpinnings of liberalism from within. Although politico-economic tenets were often cast as moral prescriptions, their ultimate tendency was to advance the depersonalized and materialistic view of the individual against which the language of character—civic, romantic, and Christian—was persistently pitted. Deep-seated conflicts of this kind expressed themselves in the idiosyncratic development of British governance and, at the same time, Victorian literature repeatedly sought the means by which to transcend this divided legacy: to build character without imposing on Britain's hallowed self-governing ideal.

Exploring these questions has necessarily involved my working with an expanding body of scholarship on nineteenth-century discipline, much of which is indebted to Michel Foucault's seminal analyses of modern power. [. . . C]ritics have long recognized various problems intrinsic to Foucault's genealogical method. Yet Foucault's influence has continued to prompt critics interested in Victorian governance to think more about Bentham than about those who rejected him; more about panopticism than about why it was that nineteenth-century Britons declined to build any Panopticons.[6] Although the last decade has seen a remarkable efflorescence of nuanced post-Foucauldian Victorian studies—a critical legacy to which my own work is indebted—I maintain that we have yet fully to document the differences between the disciplinary subject of Foucault's Franco-oriented and presentist genealogy, and the modes of character idealized by and produced in Britain's self-consciously liberal society over the course of the nineteenth century.

Victorian Literature and the Victorian State does not, of course, single-handedly take on the whole of this potentially vast critical project—for no single volume could. It is neither an exhaustive account of Victorian liberalism, nor of character, nor of governance (a subject I approach through the later-Foucauldian idea of "pastorship"). My humbler aim has been to provide a critical and historiographic account of specific works of Victorian literature as they converged with major developments in the idiosyncratic expansion and modernization of the British state. In so doing, I have sought to mine literature's rich relation to the large-scale rationalizing developments that have long occupied social historians: poor law, sanitary, educational, and civil service reforms, as well as the century-long attempt to substitute organized charity for the state.[7]

If my turn toward social history thus facilitates a distancing from genealogical presentism, my focus on literary texts represents something else still. In the chapters that follow, I read Victorian novels in the company of social scientific treatises, journalistic essays, propagandistic tales, and official reports. As socially embedded writings, nonliterary texts—from Sir James Kay-Shuttleworth's early-Victorian work on public health, to Winston Churchill's turn-of-the-century speeches on national insurance—offer ample critical opportunities to mine ideological contradictions, locate myths, and explore underlying worldviews. Yet the novels of Charles Dickens, Frances Trollope, Anthony Trollope, George Gissing, and H. G. Wells provide something more. Victorian novels, as Andrew Miller has written, provide "the most graphic and enduring images" of the impact of modernization on individual and social experience (7). Such works are extraordinary precisely because they were products of a middle-class engagement with the social world. Their richness is owing to historical conditions that yoked Victorian fiction to the bourgeois process, even as they constituted it as "a major affirmative response"—a protest against capitalist instrumentalization—in the name of human creativity (R. Williams, *Marxism* 50). Novelists were compelled, therefore, "to negotiate between their moral condemnation and their implication in what they opposed" (A. Miller 7).[8]

Hence, for my purposes the most important feature of Victorian novels is their intense grappling with contemporary worldviews, particularly as liberal notions of character and community clashed with the inevitable recourse to modern "pastorship"—that is, to governing innovations inside and out of the expanding state. Here is the duel that, in one form or another, I trace in Frances Trollope's imaginative encounter with the New Poor Law; Dickens's vexed relation to sanitary reform, organized charity, and education; and Anthony Trollope's picture of the model public servant. This kind of historicist enterprise has necessarily involved much emphasis on the synchronic rather than the diachronic: on elaborating deep-seated conflict, variation, and unevenness, rather than on charting unequivocal and hegemonic change. What is offered, therefore, is both a detailed account of the relation between select works of Victorian literature and specific historical debates about character and governance; and, potentially, a useful post-Foucauldian critical frame for studying the Victorian past.[9]

In a late essay on the study of modern society, Foucault asserted that the "word *rationalization* is dangerous. What we have to do is analyze specific rationalities rather than always invoking the progress of rationalization in general" ("Subject" 210). Although the chapters that follow do not conform to any specific Foucauldian method of analysis, they do strive to achieve this level of commitment to critical and historical specificity. In the introductory chapter, "Beyond the Panopticon," I set up a number of theoretical and historiographic premises for the book as a whole, while pursuing one argument to its full: Foucault's genealogical works on discipline are less useful to the Victorianist than are his later essays on governmentality, pastorship, and liberalism. Here, and throughout the book, I emphasize the Victorians' fierce allegiance to a multifarious liberal thought with origins in classical philosophy, Anglo-Saxon mythology, Puritan dissent, Enlightenment theology, Scottish moral philosophy, and German-Romanticism. Although it was the first nation to industrialize, Britain was (as Max Weber repeatedly observed) the last to adopt the centralized bureaucratic structures of the Continent. Throughout the century Britons tenaciously imagined themselves through character, an antimaterialist concept of the individual. Yet character and the moral worldview on which it was predicated were threatened precisely by the materialist underpinnings of a modern state: by depersonalizing bureaucracy, social scientific knowledge, and, more generally, by processes of commodification, embourgeoisement, and the development of a mass culture. Self-consciously progressive authors such as J. S. Mill, Harriet Martineau, Charles Dickens, George Gissing, and H. G. Wells thus faced a terrible quandary. Their paradoxical task was to imagine a modern governing agency that would be rational, all-embracing, and efficient, but also anti-bureaucratic, personalized, and liberatory.

[. . .]

Is there a pastor in the *House*? Sanitary reform and governing agency in Dickens's midcentury fiction

[. . .]

There is [. . . an] important dimension to *Bleak House's* representation of agency: one that, by exemplifying uncompromised pastoral care, works to undermine the novel's "seditious" resistance and to perpetuate the contradictions I have described. Selfless feminine domesticity, especially as personified by Esther, represents a seemingly irreproachable form of guidance—relatively autonomous from the selfish interests served by Bucket and antithetical to the expert will-to-power of Tulkinghorn. In this privileged, gendered form, the ostensibly apolitical pastoral function of the home—including Mrs. Bagnet's suitably working-class variation on the theme—represents Dickens's most optimistic viewpoint on the social order.[10] It is therefore unsurprising to find the novel striving to defend the home along with the gender mythologies on which the home's exceptional qualities are predicated. This defense, I will argue, further involves Dickens in satirizing the professional ambitions of female philanthropists such as Mrs. Jellyby and Mrs. Pardiggle. Ironically, Dickens's conservative domesticity thus pits him against a movement that, in the mid-Victorian era, attempted to realize a halfway house much like that sought by the novelist himself.

To explore this idea further we must first recall that *Bleak House* concludes with a symbolic domestication of the professional. As a private physician of modest means, overseeing the health and welfare of a local community, Woodcourt's medical practice is harmoniously aligned with the feminine domesticity of his wife. Here Dickens deliberately overlooks the extent to which Victorian physicians, including Southwood Smith, aggressively pitted scientific expertise against feminine domestic authority (see Poovey, *Making* 42; 194 n. 51; and S. Shuttleworth). Moreover, by stressing Woodcourt's homeliness, Dickens distances his ideal from the new emphasis on professional gentility. By thus muting the most modern and contentious aspects of the professional ideal, Dickens endows Woodcourt with the cultural capital of Victorian domesticity, creating an unimpeachable mode of pastoral agency.

Yet, for all its ideal qualities, Woodcourt's homely male professionalism has limited practical application to Britain's vast social quandaries. Hence, more significant than this parting gesture is its reactionary underside—Dickens's anti-feminist assault on middle-class women's extradomestic activities. Unsurprisingly, the same imagination that attributes the special aura of female homemakers to male physicians and evokes detectives who enthuse over "domestic bliss" anathematizes the professional ambitions of women (732). In particular, Dickens is at pains to satirize the organized philanthropy of women such as Mrs. Jellyby and Mrs. Pardiggle, emphasizing their derelict domestic duties, and futile public endeavors.[11]

It is therefore absolutely crucial to recognize that the notion of Mrs. Pardiggle as an "inexorable moral policeman" was far less absurd to Dickens's contemporaries than the novel's burlesque treatment implies. Rather, Mrs. Pardiggle's activities illustrated a venerable Christian and civic tradition with origins in Thomas Chalmers's early-nineteenth-century precedent. The practice of home visiting not only expanded throughout the nineteenth century; it also became increasingly rationalized, organized, and ambitious—a process of legitimation which was enhanced by deliberate links to the growing authority of social science. Victorian Britain's multifarious philanthropies performed a substantial, if demonstrably inadequate, pastoral function, employing nearly twice as many paid workers as were employed by the Poor Law (Prochaska 384–85).

[. . .]

[T]he heart of *Bleak House*'s antifeminism is not to shield femininity as such, but to shield feminine domesticity's crucial harborage of the personal. That quality is vitiated once domestic functions take on the cast of administrative machinery. For all their professed femininity the Ladies' National Association, like Mrs. Pardiggle, exemplified a philanthropy that consists in "moving declaratory resolutions . . . at public meetings" (478), rather than in unobtrusive, spontaneous, and sympathetic domestic care. Hence, Dickens's complaint against organized philanthropy was articulated as a normalization of gender, but it was motivated by an anti-materialist impulse very like Thomas Carlyle's. In "Signs of the Times" (1829) Carlyle had excoriated the modern philanthropist's tendency to dismiss society's "mere natural organs" in favor of calling "public meeting[s], appoint[ing] committees," issuing "prospectuses," and eating "public dinner[s]" (467). For Dickens, as for Carlyle, such activities represented a bureaucratization of social life, favoring "machinery" at the expense of the family like relations that charity ought to extend.

Whether reposed in homely doctors, or devoted housekeepers, pristine domesticity was thus, for Dickens, the last preserve of Carlyle's "natural organs." Domesticity's personal relations were a bulwark against the atomization and mechanization of the social body, and a means to preserving individual autonomy. Thus, Dickens commends Esther's motherly care for Charley and sisterly care for Caddy Jellyby while likening Mrs. Pardiggle's wholesale "benevolence" to "a strait waistcoat." Thus, on the very same grounds, he contrasts Woodcourt's compassionate "habit . . . of speaking to the poor" to Bucket's domineering officialism, and to the "patronage" and "condescension" of England's self-appointed philanthropic police (479, 684). Thus, as almoner to the wealthy Miss Coutts, Dickens preferred "personal charity" to "impersonal public relief" (Crowther, *Workhouse* 68).

Yet, lest we underestimate Dickens's extraordinary contradictions, we must also note that the author was positively fascinated by reformatory institutions such as prisons, hospitals, asylums, and schools—praising those establishments that respected the individuality of the inmate.[12] As a public-spirited citizen, Dickens was at the vanguard of mid-Victorian Britain's budding interest in institutional rehabilitation: a positive approach to illness or delinquency, to challenge the negative functions ascribed to the deterrent workhouse and punitive prison (see Crowther, *Workhouse* 63; Walton). In his fiction, however, Dickens refrained from delegating the home's sanctified pastoral functions to the suspect space of the curative institution. Just as *Bleak House* features no model civil servant like Southwood Smith, so it omits the kind of modular establishments supported by Dickens and Miss Courts. Although the novel includes many homes that resemble institutions—Tulkinghorn's Lincoln's Inn chambers, Mrs. Jellyby's home-as-office space—the only benevolent institution it figures is the home. To be sure, the tendency to disclaim institutionalized pastorship is nothing new in Dickens's fiction, which includes a roster of children morally and physically stunted by benevolent establishments.[13] In *Bleak House*, however, it is chiefly through overt hostility to women's organized philanthropy that Dickens expresses profound skepticism toward the curative institutions he privately helped to support.

Dickens's inability to embrace Mrs. Pardiggle, like the absence of a fictional Southwood Smith, is, therefore, symptomatic of the paradoxes that pervade his midcentury novels and, more generally, the self-consciously liberal society these novels represent. Britain's social body manifestly lacked the kind of order, method, and efficiency which makes the Bagnet family thrive. But neither Dickens nor his contemporaries was prepared to vest such comprehensive powers in any but the most homely, personal, and charismatic of agencies. Dickens's ideal of a world that is "pleasantly irregular" requires a catachrestic supervisory power: one that is rational but unbureaucratic, personal but omnipresent, charismatic but institutionalized, authoritative but liberatory, efficient but English. Incapable either of realizing this antithetical ideal, or of recognizing the "seditious" implications of his own critique, Dickens falls back on a conservative mystification of domestic and feminine personality. *Bleak House* thus demonizes Mrs. Pardiggle in order to stave off the protobureaucratic modes of governmentality she portends. Underlying this defensive antifeminism, moreover, is a Millite anxiety about modernity's diminution of individual autonomy.

[. . .]

Notes

1 For all its longevity the *new historicism* remains ambiguous, a term that, as Gallagher and Greenblatt attest, "has been applied to an extraordinary assortment of critical practices" (2).
2 In his conservative critiques of today's right-wing dogmas, Gray uses the term *paleoliberalism* to describe the recent rise of "market fundamentalism" (see *Beyond* and *Enlightenment's*, chap. 7). For a left critique of a related phenomenon, "market populism," see Frank.
3 For a concise (if openly partisan) account of British liberalism, see Bradley, who distinguishes between the negative libertarianism of the first half of the nineteenth century, and the later positive effort to liberate the downtrodden from "poverty, illness, bad housing, and inadequate education"

(26). This shift corresponds to what political theorists typically describe as the distinction between *classical liberalism*, with its focus on emancipating individual self-interest, and *modern liberalism*, with its counter-investment in developing citizenship and community.

4 An exception to the narrowing trend is Warner's trenchant response to Frow, which argues that the critique of neoliberalism would be more powerful were Frow to "lay claim to those [other] parts of liberal thought" which can be seen to motivate Frow's own political goals (431–32).

5 On the continuing importance of the civic republican tradition in the nineteenth century, see Pocock, *Virtue*; and *Machiavellian*; as well as Burrow. Kaufmann's Pocock-influenced account of classical liberalism and the novel in the late eighteenth and early nineteenth centuries focuses on the tensions between propertarian rights and distributive justice. Dowling, by way of explaining the eventual emergence of a homosexual counterdiscourse, concentrates on the Hellenistic liberalism that, through mid-Victorian Oxford, modified what had been a martial civic republican ideal along classical and German-Romantic lines. On the modern liberalism of the post-French Revolutionary era, see also Skorupski, "Introduction"; Kahan; Stafford; and Gibbins; and, on its eventual efflorescence in British Idealism, den Otter. On religion's influence, see Hilton; Burrow; Collini, *Public*; Taylor, *Sources*; and R. K. Webb, "Emergence."

6 Bentham's thought is also artificially simplified by this perspective: for Bentham paradoxically assumed a natural harmony of interests while calling for tutelage to maximize happiness (see, e.g., Conway, esp. 75).

7 In restricting my view of the Victorian state to centralized bureaucratic institutions and the surrounding debates, my approach differs markedly from that of Lloyd and Thomas. In *Culture and the State* (1998) Lloyd and Thomas follow a selective reading of Gramsci, arguing that the allegedly private "institutions of civil society . . . are actually part of" a unified and hegemonic "state formation" (21). At the same time, they insist that Matthew Arnold's philosophy of governance, with its embrace of Continental statism, was dominant throughout the nineteenth century—an assertion that, as my own work on civil service reform especially suggests, is highly debatable [. . .]. Hence, while *Culture and the State* contains many important insights, it tends to ignore what is of central importance to the account of Victorian governance offered in this book: that is, the intense privileging of "self-governing" activities; the reflexive recoil from statist bureaucracy; and, as a result, the "pastoral" dilemmas that faced Victorian Britain and, indeed, continue to face any self-consciously liberal society.

8 See also Nunokawa, who has argued that our historical understanding of the impact of embourgeoisement "may owe its largest debt . . . to the Victorian novel and its narrative heirs; for here, the diffuse, diffusive, subject of commodification comes home" (4). Childers has granted a special "constitutive status" to novels, arguing that novelistic discourse gained primacy over reports and treatises, "subsuming" them and "reshaping" the epistemological and ontological boundaries of, for example, parliamentary politics (*Novel* 4, 47, 40). I have not followed Childers in tracing a competition between literary and nonliterary discourses.

9 Unfortunately, I have been unable to devote space to the interesting question of where and how formal differences between various novelists illuminate the relation between literature and governance.

10 On the domestic woman's perceived apoliticism, see Armstrong, especially 3–27. Nord describes Esther's embodiment of "Right Woman" as "a model for the salvation of society" (*Walking* 85).

11 Because my emphasis is philanthropy within Britain, I focus on Pardiggle rather than Jellyby. For a nuanced reading of the latter, see Robbins "Telescopic."

12 In *Little Dorrit* Dickens detailed the depersonalization of Nandy, an aged pauper, forced to wear workhouse garments "that [were] never made for him, nor for any individual mortal" (354). On Dickens's personal involvement in Urania Cottage, a rehabilitative asylum for prostitutes, see A. Anderson, *Tainted* 73–79.

13 For example, Noah Claypole in *Oliver Twist*, Rob in *Dombey and Son*, and Uriah Heep in *David Copperfield*.

Works cited

Anderson, Amanda. *Tainted Souls and Painted Faces: The Rhetoric of Fallenness in Victorian Culture.* Ithaca: Cornell University Press, 1993.

Armstrong, Nancy. *Desire and Domestic Fiction: A Political History of the Novel.* Oxford: Oxford University Press, 1987.

Barry, Andrew, Thomas Osborne, and Nikolas S. Rose, eds. *Foucault and Political Reason: Liberalism, Neo-Liberalism, and Rationalities of Government*. Chicago: University of Chicago Press, 1996.

Bellamy, Richard, ed. *Victorian Liberalism: Nineteenth-Century Political Thought and Practice*. London: Routledge, 1990.

Bradley, Ian. *The Strange Rebirth of Liberal Britain*. London: Chatto and Windus, 1985.

Brown, Wendy. *States of Injury: Power and Freedom in Late Modernity*. Princeton: Princeton University Press, 1995.

Burrow, J. W. *Whigs and Liberals: Continuity and Change in English Political Thought*. Oxford: Clarendon Press, 1988.

Carlyle, Thomas. "Signs of the Times." 1829. In *Carlyle's Works: Centennial Memorial Edition*. 26 vols. Boston: Dana Estes and Co., n.d.15: 462–87.

Childers, Joseph W. *Novel Possibilities: Fiction and the Formation of Early Victorian Culture*. Philadelphia: University of Pennsylvania Press, 1995.

Collini, Stefan. *Public Moralists: Political Thought and Intellectual Life in Britain, 1850–1930*. Oxford: Clarendon, 1991.

Conway, Stephen. "Bentham and the Nineteenth-Century Revolution in Government." In Bellamy 71–90.

Crowther, M. A. *The Workhouse System, 1834–1929: The History of an English Social Institution*. Athens: University of Georgia Press, 1982.

Den Otter, Sandra. *British Idealism and Social Explanation: A Study in Late-Victorian Thought*. Oxford: Clarendon Press, 1996.

Dickens, Charles. *Bleak House*. 1852–53. Ed. Norman Page. Harmondsworth: Penguin, 1985.

Dowling, Linda. *Hellenism and Homosexuality in Victorian Oxford*. Ithaca: Cornell University Press, 1994.

Foucault, Michel. "The Subject and Power." In *Michel Foucault, Beyond Structuralism and Hermeneutics*. Ed. Herbert L. Dreyfus and Paul Rabinow. Chicago: University of Chicago Press, 1983. 208–26.

Frank, Thomas. *One Market Under God: Extreme Capitalism, Market Populism, and the End of Economic Democracy*. New York: Doubleday, 2000.

Frow, John. "Cultural Studies and the Neoliberal Imagination." *Yale Journal of Criticism* 12.2 (1999): 423–30.

Gallagher, Catherine, and Stephen Greenblatt. *Practicing New Historicism*. Chicago: University of Chicago Press, 2000.

Gibbins, John. "J. S. Mill, Liberalism, and Progress." In Bellamy 91–109.

Gray, John. *Beyond the New Right: Markets, Government and the Common Environment*. London: Routledge, 1993.

——. *Enlightenment's Wake: Politics and Culture at the Close of the Modern Age*. London: Routledge, 1995.

Hilton, Boyd. *The Age of Atonement: The Influence of Evangelicalism on Social and Economic Thought, 1785–1865*. Oxford: Clarendon Press, 1988.

Kahan, Alan S. *Aristocratic Liberalism: The Social and Political Thought of Jacob Burckhardt, John Stuart Mill, and Alexis De Tocqueville*. Oxford: Oxford University Press, 1992.

Kaufmann, David. *The Business of Common Life: Novels and Classical Economics between Revolution and Reform*. Baltimore: Johns Hopkins University Press, 1995.

Lloyd, David, and Paul Thomas. *Culture and the State*. New York: Routledge, 1998.

Miller, Andrew H. *Novels Behind Glass: Commodity Culture and Victorian Narrative*. Cambridge: Cambridge University Press, 1995.

Nord, Deborah Epstein. *Walking the Victorian Streets: Women, Representation, and the City*. Ithaca: Cornell University Press, 1995.

Nunokawa, Jeff. *The Afterlife of Property in Victorian Fiction: Domestic Security in the Victorian Novel*. Princeton: Princeton University Press, 1994.

Pocock, J. G. A. *The Machiavellian Moment: Florentine Political Thought and the Atlantic Republican Tradition*. Princeton, N. J.: Princeton University Press, 1975.

——. *Virtue, Commerce, and History*. Cambridge: Cambridge University Press, 1985.

Poovey, Mary. *Making a Social Body: British Cultural Formation, 1830–1864*. Chicago: University of Chicago Press, 1995.

Prochaska, F. K. "Philanthropy." In *The Cambridge Social History of Britain, 1950–1750*. Ed. F. M. L. Thompson. Cambridge: Cambridge University Press, 1990. 357–93.

Robbins, Bruce. "Telescopic Philanthropy: Professionalism and Responsibility in *Bleak House*." In *Nation and Narration*. Ed. Homi K. Bhabha. London: Routledge, 1990. 213–30.

Shuttleworth, Sally. "Female Circulation: Medical Discourse and Popular Advertising in the Mid-Victorian Era." In *Body/Politics*. Ed. Mary Jacobus, Evelyn Fox Keller, and Sally Shuttleworth. New York: Routledge, 1990. 47–68.

Sigsworth, Eric M., ed. *In Search of Victorian Values*. Manchester: Manchester University Press, 1988.

Skorupski, John. "Introduction: The Fortunes of Liberal Naturalism." In *The Cambridge Companion to Mill*. Ed. John Skorupski. Cambridge: Cambridge University Press, 1998. 1–34.

Smiles, Samuel. *Self-Help: With Illustrations of Character and Conduct*. 1859. Reprint. Boston, 1866.

Stafford, William. "John Stuart Mill: Critic of Victorian Values?" In Sigsworth 88–101.

Taylor, Charles. *Sources of the Self: The Making of the Modern Identity*. Cambridge: Harvard University Press, 1989.

Trilling, Lionel. *The Liberal Imagination: Essays on Literature and Society*. New York: Doubleday, 1949.

Warner, Michael. "Liberalism and the Cultural Studies Imagination: A Comment on John Frow." *Yale Journal of Criticism* 12.2 (1999): 431–33.

Webb, R. K. "The Emergence of Rational Dissent." In *Enlightenment and Religion: Rational Dissent in Eighteenth-Century Britain*. Ed. Knud Haakonssen. Cambridge: Cambridge University Press, 1996. 12–41.

Williams, Raymond. *Marxism and Literature*. Oxford: Oxford University Press, 1977.

36 A frame for mind

Signature liberalism at the *Fortnightly Review*

Elaine Hadley

[. . .]

As Edwin Everett has suggested in his history of the *Fortnightly Review*, the journal seems in many ways an almost perfect exemplification of the brave new world envisioned by J. S. Mill's *On Liberty*. Foregrounding "individual opinion," in contrast to what Mill had unflatteringly called "received opinion" in *On Liberty*, the *Fortnightly* sought to open its pages to a wide range of independent opinion, both familiar and unfamiliar. The *Fortnightly*'s prospectus refers to "questions which have an agitating influence, and admit diversity of aspects" ("Prospectus," 362). The prospectus implicitly evokes *On Liberty* when it suggests that only through eclectic discussion can the truth ever be ascertained. While affording a venue for minority opinion in its many guises and minimizing editorial intrusion on its expression, the journal, however, equally declared its adherence to form—and formality. One ought to note how the aforementioned commentary treats its content as a type of form, emphasizing less the political particularities of the questions published than a standard of complexity ("diversity of aspects") and social, perhaps mental, impact ("agitating influence"), an emphasis on what I would suggest is a peculiarly liberal form that remains consistently apparent throughout the first decades of the *Fortnightly*'s run. Aware that the open-ended editorial policy might result in bad behavior, the founders called as well for a standard of formality—"the tact and sympathy of our contributors, and the candid construction of our readers" ("Prospectus," 362), the sort of good breeding and decency usually presumed to be bred in a drawing room. Such phrasing does not really evoke the rational deliberative standards of Habermas but, rather, behavioral and affective standards of cognitive propriety. In addition to these attitudinal demands, the journal's founders established ground rules of fair play that defined the form of the periodical. Contributors did not choose to append signatures but were required to; writers had to be willing to see their work printed beside articles that might challenge their positions; moreover, authors were expected to have a particular sort of relationship to the opinions they wrote: they needed to believe in them. Unremarkable as that expectation might seem, it points to a central drama of liberalism, the crucial and often highly fraught effort to establish a clear path between the public sphere of politics and opinion and the increasingly privatized brain, but also heart, of the liberalized subject.

Compared to other "sect" publications, the *Fortnightly* in theory gave its writers the freedom to have and express a variety of political, economic, religious, and aesthetic opinions, so that one can read a piece favorable to the Anglican bureaucracy and a critique of that same establishment, or one might read pieces antagonistic toward and admiring of Swinburne. Nonetheless, the journal did have standards, and one might even argue extremely rigorous standards, mostly centering on the ethics of opinion formation. In accord with Mill's passionate plea for minority and individual opinion in *On Liberty*, the *Fortnightly* was willing to publish, for instance, orthodox opinion on the church establishment, even when many of its founders, authors, and readers did not share these views, precisely because there might be some kernel of truth germinating there. The journal, then, adopted what might be called an agnostic editorial approach, expressing humility in the midst of its belief in the appropriate arrogance of truth. However, orthodox opinion had to comply with the *Fortnightly*'s code of opinion formation; that is, an opinion that favored orthodoxy had to emerge from the "disin- terestedness of the critical spirit" that seemed at this time locatable in what was deemed the codifiable logic of the individual mind.[1] One need not think liberally, one need not even think about liberalism, but one certainly had to think *through* liberalism.

On Liberty casts a long shadow over the *Fortnightly*, but Mill's *A System of Logic*, a semi- nal text for many second-generation liberals who read it on their own time while students at Oxford and Cambridge, is an equally apparent influence.[2] Mill's *A System of Logic* had shown to many liberalizing gentlemen at midcentury that there was a describable, comprehensive, and rational methodology of mind: comprehensive even at a time when human thought and invention were felt to be accelerating and dispersing, and rational even when some of these advances (for instance, in historical method and early anthropological practice) seemed to show enormous unevenness among societies in the exercise of thought. Even without a provi- dential order, there was order in the mind. As one writer in the *Fortnightly* asserted, "His book on Logic will remain for a very long time, at all events, the principal organiser and dissemina- tor of positive modes of thought in England, and this, perhaps, will prove the most durable of his contributions."[3] I cannot stress enough the extent to which the *Fortnightly* sought to inject this sort of mindfulness into the public sphere. As Morley reminds his readers: "Let us never forget that the exertion of mental activity upon public transactions, still more upon questions involving some powers of abstract thought is thoroughly exceptional" ("AJ," 291). Certainly writers had thought before the advent of the *Fortnightly*, despite Morley's claim of excep- tionality, but in this journal their mental powers were newly detached from conventional locations, from familiar *bodies* of thought, such that thinking as a particular social practice became itself subject to mental scrutiny.

Not only did the journal applaud a mindfulness toward other points of view, manifest in its mission of editorial eclecticism, but even more insistently it sought to make opinion for- mation, in particular political opinion, more mindful, more logical, more systematic, more consistently guided by principle. In emphasizing "principle," the journal and its contributors were not only complaining that politicians and people more generally were succumbing to expediencies in the accelerating swirl of modern life. Importantly, the *Fortnightly*'s polemic also helped shift the primary ethical milieu for political practice from the civic sphere to the sphere of individual conviction, another way in which it secularized evangelical values. By this I am not quite suggesting that the liberalism of this period espoused a philosophy that privileged thought exclusively over action, though such an argument will find its evidence plentiful. Instead, I am pointing to the way in which thinking itself became not only an ethi- cal practice but a highly privileged political act in liberal discourse, most meaningful in the context of the individual, and often portrayed as a solitary, even heroic "frame of mind." This is the milieu in which Trollope created Septimus Harding.[4]

In attempting to define a finite set of logical propositions that constituted the process of human thinking, Mill labored in an ancient tradition for which he was well-trained by his father's rigorous classical tutelage. *A System of Logic*, however, was most influenced by asso- ciationist models of the human mind that, too simply put, asserted that all thinking, whether basic or advanced, was built on chains of associations that first start out as sense impressions. That Mill aimed, despite his admitted lack of scientific training, to elaborate a logic that still managed to comprehend in its own terms both the more traditional fields of philosophy and art and the myriad nascent procedures of scientific practice at midcentury (natural sciences as well as social sciences) marks his book as very much a product of its time, and in that respect what might seem a quaint remnant of an era prior to professional specialization. The totalizing reach of the book also shows one reason why Mill was so intellectually attracted to Comte's holistic positivism despite their significant temperamental differences concerning the role of religion in the conception of humanism. Both men worked in a period when George Eliot's Casaubon, the prospective author of a "Key to All Mythologies," was a recognizable type for educated middle-class readers, albeit a type of totalist whose classicism and Christianity often became an object of critique for liberals aware of the new criticism.

Reading through Mill's *A System of Logic* as a novice of that philosophical subfield, I am therefore more struck by its implicit narrative drama—to which many Victorians seemed to respond, too—than by its contribution to its field of study or by its influence as a textbook. In his pages, even as they exhaustively elaborate propositions concerning deduction and induction, the abstract and the concrete, Mill seems vitally engaged in codifying the fundamentals of human ratiocination and, in so doing, to afford them a coherence, cogency, and prerogative at a time when human cognition seemed more alone in the universe than ever. A hopefulness is implicit throughout the text: human beings and their cultures may be radically different from one another, even incommensurable, but we all of us have a mind. When that mind reasons as it ought, it operates in recognizable ways, such clear, penetrating, and accurate ways, that we really ought to have faith in it. *Faith* may not be a word one reads in *A System of Logic*, but the total effect of the book, its recognition of but not subsumption into scientific rationality, its concentration of turbulent variety (social, cultural, scientific, etc.) into the mind's orderly exercise of induction, and its drama of Mill's own brain at work, all impressed its readers with what can only be called a religious zeal for the schematizing powers of the individual mind.[5] It was left to the *Fortnightly* over its first few decades of publication to develop the rhetoric of an irreligious religiosity toward the powers of that mind.

To be sure, particularly under the tenure of Morley, the *Fortnightly* solidified its identity in the periodical world by becoming the journal most impatient with religious belief and church establishment. Mostly differentiating itself, as did Mill, from Comte's "Religion of Humanity," the periodical never lost an editorial opportunity to excoriate lazy adherence to the church or to condemn the sort of thought it associated with a flocklike reliance on orthodox thought, as does Morley when writing on anonymity: "As a rule, the writer of leading articles is in the position of an oracle, or a parson in the pulpit. People do not sit down to read what he has written in a critical attitude. They will quite willingly take all he says for gospel."[6] In this passage, one sees the persistent slippage between an anonymous author and the godhead, between abject readers and religious adherents, that is characteristic throughout the first two decades of the *Fortnightly*'s run. As many writers in the journal argued implicitly and explicitly, a society with a state church maintains a systematic orthodoxy that is operative well beyond the confines of that country's religious practices, which becomes, in fact, a habit of thought. The deceit inherent in the use of the anonymous "we" becomes almost symptomatic of the larger deception of organized religion and even the state that authorizes its primacy, both of which by the mid-nineteenth century were seen to animate their god, wizardlike, to assuage an otherwise restive audience. While respecting the virtuous intent of the Tractarians, for instance, John Cotter Morison writes in the *Fortnightly* of that religious movement, "Ritualism is a gorgeous palace, built upon a foundation which is crumbling beneath it every day—a castle in the air, which will vanish like a morning cloud. An iceberg floating in tropical seas is not more certain of dissolving than is Anglo-Catholicism among the critical solvents of the nineteenth century."[7] For a journal so invested in careful categorizing and logical propositions, the *Fortnightly* freely collapsed religious conviction into routinized cognition and narrowed the emotional, bodily, social, and traditional domains of belief into a compact realm of opinion formation.

To many readers of the journal in the 1860s and 1870s, the *Fortnightly's* primary mission seemed to be a rigorous, unstintingly rational engagement with the Anglican establishment, Christianity, and revealed religion in general. The journal regularly published articles aggressively addressing all three categories of religious commitment.[8] And much of the periodical's self-presentation cast its intellectual mission in terms of a liberating demystification of "superstition." All this is true. However, like most people who were then finding themselves detaching from religion and its cultural institutions, who were therefore treating it as an object of critical regard, the editors and writers for the *Fortnightly* found it difficult to sustain a clear division between religion and the state—of mind. So many of the values and practices of cognition that the *Fortnightly* wished to display clearly derived from early-nineteenth-century Evangelicalism, a movement that directly touched many of its writers and from which no one could escape unaffected, as Noel Annan, T. W. Heyck, and Christopher Harvie have noted in various ways. Heyck succinctly notes that "Evangelicalism dramatically heightened the intensity of the individual conscience and of the drive for personal morality."[9] The emphasis in the journal on the individual opinion, the primacy of introspection, and most especially the moral value infusing them both almost certainly owe much to this specifically religious context. It is this genealogy that probably accounts for Morley's acknowledgment that "character is doubtless of far more importance than mere intellectual opinion" (*OC*, 102). As interesting a phrase as it is, "mere intellectual opinion" is indeed an insufficient description of the journal's philosophical position, in part because it does not adequately describe the details of opinion formation that are so crucial to an understanding of the *Fortnightly's* ethic, which presumes that character must be the source of opinion. Even so, it is vital to retain the centrality of intellect in the operation of moral conviction, to show how opinion in the modernizing public sphere of the nineteenth century was somehow to be deeply devised by individual cogitation—its practices of induction, self-reflection, and abstraction.

Despite, then, what seems to be a generalized and at times even careless condescension toward religion, the *Fortnightly* could not abandon belief as thoroughly as it did conventional systems of belief. Morley, for instance, when he writes of a "genuine lover of truth," describes him as "inspired by the divine passion for seeing things as they are" (*OC*, 226). Reading passages such as these, it would be inaccurate to conclude, however, that the *Fortnightly* merely substituted the individual mind for the omniscient godhead and, therefore, simply perpetuated a High Enlightenment apotheosis of reason. Nor is it sufficient to suggest a sort of substitution of psychological cosmologies, as Harvie provocatively does, when he avers convincingly that "the political commonwealth had to occupy in their minds the place that salvation had occupied in their fathers' and grandfathers.'"[10] Rather, I would suggest, the journal's recourse to a secularized religious sentiment centered most forcefully on its attraction to religion's ethic of belief or, more accurately, a Protestant ethic of belief. For example, in his *Fortnightly* essay, "Liberals, Conservatives, and the Church," Viscount Amberley lauds Nonconformists not for the content of their faith but for the form which their adherence to doctrine takes. Unlike Anglicans, Amberley argues, Nonconformists are self-sufficient; they need no "extraneous aid" to sustain their faith.[11] Without financial or sacerdotal intermediaries, they have an unmediated relation to their religious belief.

The liberal individualism of the *Fortnightly* emulates this unimpeded relationship between an individual and his principles, but notably substitutes opinion for belief, opinion being a product of cognition that is necessarily more public, more circulated, and therefore more problematically distanced from the individual than are his religious beliefs, at least as liberalism understands religious belief. Rather than being true to one's god or true to one's class, a liberal individual must be true to his opinions, of especial importance in the free marketplace of ideas that the Victorian public sphere had become. This ethic of devotion to opinion, rather than religious belief, and its accompanying challenges will become most apparent in my subsequent discussion of the *Fortnightly*'s use of the signature.

Although the journal was in the business of publishing opinion in the public sphere, it was always most invested in the *process* of opinion formation, which was, in fact, never intended to take place in its pages. [. . . E]ven in *On Liberty*, one can exaggerate in liberalism the extent to which *public* debate per se is seen to be constitutive or formative of opinion. In the *Fortnightly*, too, the eclectic mix of opinion only *stages* a public debate for sober Philip; Anglican and atheist do not form or change their opinions in his midst. Lewes described his primary editorial criterion as "decided opinion." Likewise, the periodical does not generally publish articles as if engaged in direct hand-to-hand combat in the public sphere, especially once Morley becomes editor. No brawling. There is little response/counterresponse over the course of several issues; even the rare placement of oppositional views in a single issue or contiguous issues lacked the sort of debating rhetoric one might expect and which was evident in other journals.

If "debate" is consistently displayed at all under Morley's editorial direction, it is displayed as rhetorical devil's advocacy what Basil Willey has called the "ventriloquial method," a good-faith summary of another's ideas that nevertheless contains within it or is framed by an oblique critique.[12] A fair accounting of the opposing view is what counts as the "proper form" for a disinterested frame of mind whose ultimate aim, however, is the articulation of its individual opinion. Temperately imbibing these varied but already formed opinions before the fire at home, sober Philip thinks through the diverse viewpoints, ventriloquizes them, that is, mentally voices them, before devising his own.[13] Perhaps a subtle distinction, sober Philip is not unthinkingly reciting the views of others, as do those abject journalists and passive newspaper readers who merely mouth the words of demigods in Morley's description cited earlier. Rather, Willey's description precisely grasps the critical spirit that haunts the locution of a contrary opinion in this sort of liberal discourse. A governing mind as well as a dominant voice enunciate the "other's" opinions. So pervasive is this Millian style in the *Fortnightly* and in the other writings of Morley, Stephen, Bagehot, and Trollope that it is arguably *the* expository style of the mid-century liberal intelligentsia.

[. . .]

The "ventriloquial method" is also at times expressed in the *Fortnightly* through a free and indirect discourse, perhaps giving the impression that the article's author has so purposively comprehended his opponent's position as to be able to think it himself. This is like the omniscient narrator at work in *The Warden*. In J. Godkin's piece on Irish land reform, to cite a chance example taken from the first volume of the *Fortnightly*, he begins by citing an argument in a familiar *Fortnightly* fashion that emphasizes the groupthink of conventional *public* opinion. Using the third-person plural, Godkin writes, "they proceed upon the theory that the owner of land in Ireland is in the position of the owner of any other property." When he finishes his account of this view, he simply voices the position as if it were his own, leaving behind a more reportorial tone ("they proceed upon the theory") and putting in its place a tone of rhetorical individuality—and decisiveness: "It is simply a case of contract between man and man,–nothing more."[14]

In so doing, Godkin demonstrates the brilliant adequacy of Willey's coinage, the "ventriloquial method." In writing about Morley and his liberal associates, Willey coins the phrase out of admiration. Like his subjects, he recognizes the thrust of their historical intervention, the "mindfulness" evinced in their measured attention to opposing opinion in a journalistic marketplace usually engaged in ad hominem attack. However, Willey perhaps misses the full irony at play in their performative rhetoric, which is equally implanted in his term. Like a ventriloquist, the writers for the *Fortnightly* could be accused of treating "the other" as a dummy. In the finale of Godkin's performance of devil's advocacy, the voice who asserts "nothing more" could be construed in a less-Millian spirit. No longer an intelligent opinion worthy of mindfulness, not even a reasonable eccentric, the voice is now one of a blunt reductionist, completely submerging himself in sectarian thought—Mill's "encrustation of creed." In this less-generous interpretation, the opponent is incapable of forming an individual opinion even if a proper liberal mouths it for him. Evident in this oscillating dynamic is the uncertain line between a pedagogical and a patronizing style, and the mere degrees between a persuasive use of devil's advocacy and a coercive pastiche. Of course, in general terms, these mechanisms of argumentation are not exclusively liberal expository techniques. I am simply pointing to both their efficacy and their difficulty for liberalism. The rhetorical interplay between the first-person plural and singular is integral to liberal individualism as it formalizes the diversity of *public* opinion into the private order of thought, but it also captures, as Wendy Brown has argued, the barely veiled impatience, or even disgust, that is often implicit in the liberal conception of tolerance.[15] The extraction of the first-person singular from the first-person plural enacted in the *Fortnightly* is a representative instance of a general trend toward relocating the agential space of the political from the public sphere to the private, from collectivities to individuals. Jacques Rancière, in defining "the political" as those fundamental discussions that negotiate the necessary collocations of "we," seems to me to suggest that the world envisioned in the pages of the *Fortnightly* is a world without *politics* in any meaningfully progressive sense of the term because that particular discussion is over. For Victorian liberals, a fundamental and seemingly mandatory form for discussion—the first-person singular—renders the particular contents under discussion of secondary and therefore of more limited interest.[16]

If Mill's systematic approach exerted an influence on the presentation of opinion in any given article, such that authors were uniformly engaged in the "ventriloquial method" and were careful to define their terms and follow, at least loosely, a propositional logic in their exposition, his influence was even more operative in the journal's editorial presumptions concerning the practices expected of its writers and readers, at the moment when opinion was first formulated through an idea in the author's or the reader's mind. In the case of the reader instantiating the anonymous "we"—whose opinions are said to emerge from an ideology always already there and thus by definition already circulated, "in the air," intrinsically public—he, for instance, simply consumes what he reads as he sips his brandy at the very club whose condition of membership presupposes the same points of view. By contrast, the *Fortnightly*'s first-person singular was presumed to voice opinions that came from the ideas carefully and systematically thought out in an individual's brain, a private space more highly privileged in midcentury liberalism than any club, even than any private drawing room, good manners notwithstanding. Morley spoke often of bringing the teacher out of the tub and thus of bringing intellectual discussion "from the library down to the parlour, and from the serious student down to the first man in the street," but in emphasizing the journal's genuine commitment to a broader-based pedagogical engagement (manifest in its regular calls for universal education) and timely political intervention, scholars have overlooked the vital temporal *progression* in this process.[17] Before public opinion, there is individual opinion, and before individual opinion there are individual ideas: liberal ideas take time.

[. . .]

In his study of Victorian England, Heyck argues that the "idea of the intellectual" first emerged during this period. I think it perhaps more accurate to revise slightly this proposition. As I would like to suggest, with the *Fortnightly* as evidence, this might well have been the period when "the idea" was linked to the individual in such a way (private, systematic, yet affective) as to imagine, or at least prefigure, a subject category called "the intellectual"—a being defined by his ideas—which itself would ultimately become concentrated into specialized professions late in the century. Melding, for this brief moment in the 1860s and 1870s, the generalist propensities of the amateur with the specialist knowledges of the expert, the liberal individual was, it was hoped, a "best self," most capable of distancing himself from if not entirely escaping historical determinations.[18] At the middle of the nineteenth century, the seeming difference only in degree between the liberal subject and the emergent intellectual demonstrates in one direction the rigorous discipline required by liberalism, the assumption that citizens, for instance, ought to become systematic thinkers. In the other direction, the proximity between the intellectual and the liberal subject bespeaks the optimism that was often explicit in liberalism's investment in cognition. At the same time, it expresses the strikingly austere standards—"ungrudging daily trouble," as Morley describes it—for subject formation.

Notes

1 This is the phrase of Basil Willey, when writing about John Morley: "Morley was much influenced, in the early 'seventies, by Matthew Arnold's doctrine about the disinterestedness of the critical spirit and the need for a free play of mind on all stock subjects and notions." Willey, *More Nineteenth Century Studies*, 260.

2 "Scientific truth was the sanction of their criticism; rationalism was their method—rationalism, that is, defined as the application of reason to *religious* belief. This method seemed to stamp a character upon the *Fortnightly Review*. It was a journalistic inheritance, possibly, from the old *Westminster*, and it certainly demonstrated the influence of J. S. Mill. All the characteristic work of the *Fortnightly*— its humanitarianism, its obsession with science, its distrust of theological dogma, its insistence upon human liberties—although it has a distant ancestor in Bentham's Utilitarianism, springs more immediately from Mill, and if from any particular work of his, certainly from his essay *On Liberty*, the book which at Oxford John Morley had known almost by heart." Everett, *Party of Humanity*, 141.

3 Mill, "Critical Notices," 124.

4 That what amounts to a privatization of public opinion could be aligned with the privacies of domestic culture certainly accounts for the pervasive compensatory yoking of battle imagery and tropes of manliness in liberal discourse, in the *Fortnightly* and elsewhere. See Collini. "'Manly Fellows'"; Hilton, "Manliness," 41–59, 60–70. See also Christ: "Sage discourse could become a heroic masculine bulwark set up against a democratized and feminized novel" ("Hero as Man of Letters," 26).

5 In arguing for a certain sort of schematization that emphasizes procedures of thought, and therefore a certain formalism of thought, I am suggesting that Mill's work is indeed pushing up against a Kantian-inflected theory of mind, more in keeping with the work of a psychologist like William Leonard Courtney than Mill's associationism seems to suggest. [Rick] Rylance rightly points out that Mill's thought lacks a biological model that might have helped him "think through the deficiencies in classical sensationalist associationism," but it is nonetheless possible that Mill, who did not appear to know much of Kant, was working toward more formalist conceptions of the mind's operations. Rylance, *Victorian Psychology*, 207.

6 "AJ," 291. It should be noted that Frederic Harrison, for years a close friend of Morley's, wrote often for the *Fortnightly* until an editorial disagreement led to a parting of the ways. Harrison was an acolyte of Auguste Comte and a colleague of Richard Congreve, the strongest public disciple of Comte in England. His presence in the journal and respectful mention of Comte by both Lewes and Morley encouraged many to consider the *Fortnightly* a Comtean organ. This seems an excessive overstatement, given the variety of liberal voices printed in the journal, but Comte's influence on British liberalism and on this variety of liberalism in particular cannot be disputed.

7 Morison, "Significance of Ritualism," 75–76.

8 For a useful overview of the *Fortnightly*'s religious contents and arguments, see Everett, *Party of Humanity*. My own survey of the first twenty issues of the *Fortnightly* indicates that what counted as a "diversity" is mostly a commitment to the scholarly coverage of diverse religions—Anglican, Irish Presbyterian, Catholic, Muslim, Spiritualist, ritualist. These scholarly precepts involve the objective, nonsectarian, and rationalist values of liberalism, which also mostly described the overlapping values—and often practitioners—of the "new criticism" of the Bible, instances of which are also numerous in the early issues of the *Fortnightly* in articles that addressed not just the Bible itself but other central tenets of Christianity. Some instances of the former: "Maori Mahommedanism" in volume 2, "The Irish Presbyterians" in volume 3, and "The Church of England as a Religious Body" in volume 6. Instances of the latter: "The Fourth Commandment" in volume 3, by Anthony Trollope, which queries that commandment's modern pertinence; a review of "Strauss's New Life of Christ" in volume 4; and a critical commentary on miracles' modern acceptance by John Tyndall, "Miracles and Special Providences," in volume 7.

9 Heyck, *Transformation of Intellectual Life*, 83.

10 Harvie, *Lights of Liberalism*, 142.

11 Amberley, "Liberals, Conservatives, and Church," 168.

12 Willey, *More Nineteenth Century Studies*, 263.

13 The only evidence that seems to run counter to my contention comes front the elegiac essay written by Arthur Waugh on the occasion of the periodical's demise in 1929: "Among the judicious the quality and vigour of the new magazine were immediately recognised; it was soon lying on every clubroom table, and its contents were discussed and combated wherever politicians and scientists were congregated" ("Biography of Periodical," 515). I will simply point out that Waugh writes long after the fact, in a celebratory mode, and even so, tellingly emphasizes that the *Fortnightly* was "soon lying on every clubroom table." Suffice it to say, this is a potentially less-influential position than even that "unread periodical" in Mr. Harding's lap.

14 Godkin, "Irish Land Question," 385.

15 See Brown, *Regulating Aversion*, 149–76.

16 Rancière also describes the process in political discourse when individuals posit a third-person plural as a crucial stage of political identification, whereby the first-person singular or plural now concedes the presence of an interlocutor but also thereby identifies himself or themselves as part of a community (*Disagreement*, 47–48). I seek to question mid-Victorian liberalism's commitment to a third-person plural and to emphasize its refusal to see its own individualist commitments as emerging from a community of interests.

17 Everett, *Party of Humanity*, 328–29.

18 Note, for instance, in this passage from Hughes, writing in favor of signature, a kind of language that is just short of describing professionalism: "I believe that letters on important questions, signed by persons who are known to understand their subjects, are far more effective than leaders" ("Anonymous Journalism," 159b). In contrast to expertise, here is the language of a more loosely mobilized public recognition. Valuing those who "understand their subjects," Hughes evokes the well-informed gentleman, cognizant of but by no means cornering the market on his subject (157–68).

Bibliography

Amberley, John Russell. "Liberals, Conservatives, and the Church." *Fortnightly Review* 2 (September 1865): 161–68.

Brown, Wendy. *Regulating Aversion: Tolerance in the Age of Identity and Empire*. Princeton, NJ: Princeton Univ. Press, 2009.

Christ, Carol T. "'The Hero as Man of Letters': Masculinity and Victorian Nonfiction Prose." In *Victorian Sages and Cultural Discourse: Renegotiating Gender and Power*, edited by Thais E. Morgan, 19–45. New Brunswick, NJ: Rutgers Univ. Press, 1990.

Collini, Stefan. "'Manly Fellows'. Fawcett, Stephen and the Liberal Temper." In *The Blind Victorian: Henry Fawcett and British Liberalism*, edited by Lawrence Goldman, 41–59. Cambridge: Cambridge Univ. Press, 1989.

Everett, Edwin Mallard. *The Party of Humanity: The Fortnightly Review and Its Contributors*. Chapel Hill: Univ. of North Carolina Press, 1939.

Godkin, J. "The Irish Land Question." *Fortnightly Review* 1 (July 1865): 385–401.

Harvie, Christopher. *The Lights of Liberalism: University Liberals and the Challenge of Democracy, 1860–86*. London: Allen Lane, 1976.

Heyck, T. W. *The Transformation of Intellectual Life in Victorian England*. Chicago: Lyceum Books, 1982.

Hilton, Boyd. "Manliness, Masculinity and the Mid-Victorian Temperament." Chap. 2 in *The Blind Victorian: Henry Fawcett and British Liberalism*. Cambridge: Cambridge Univ. Press, 1989.

Hughes, Thomas. "Anonymous Journalism." *MacMillan's Magazine* 5 (November 1861–April 1862): 157–68.

Mill, J. S. "Critical Notices: Dissertations and Discussions, Political Philosophical, and Historical." *Fortnightly Review* 2, no. 7 (1867): 123–28.

Morison, J. Cotter. "The Significance of Ritualism." *Fortnightly Review* 1, no. 38 (1867): 68–77.

Morley, John. "Anonymous Journalism." *Fortnightly Review* 2, no.9 (1867): 287–92.

——. *On Compromise; with Swinburne's New Poems*. Edited by John Powell. Edinburgh: Keele Univ. Press, 1997.

"Prospectus of the Fortnightly Review." In *The Party of Humanity: "The Fortnightly Review" and Its Contributors, 1865–1874*, edited by Edward Mallard Everett, 331–32. Chapel Hill: Univ. of North Carolina, 1939.

Rancière, Jacques. *Disagreement*. Translated by Julie Rose. Minneapolis, MN: Univ. of Minnesota Press, 2004.

Rylance, Rick. *Victorian Psychology and British Culture, 1850–1880*. Oxford: Oxford Univ. Press, 2000.

[Waugh, Arthur]. "The Biography of a Periodical." *Fortnightly Review* 126 (October 1929): 512–24.

Willey, Basil. *More Nineteenth Century Studies: A Group of Honest Doubters*. Cambridge: Univ. of Cambridge Press, 1980.

37 Disinterestedness and liberalism

Daniel S. Malachuk

Scholars have long noted that disinterestedness—that is, the quality of being free from self-interest—was one of the virtues most revered by the Victorians. Only in the last decade or so, however, have we begun to fully grasp not only what they meant by it but why it should matter today. This shift in our understanding is the culmination of three key historical debates about disinterestedness. The first debate was the one the Victorians had with themselves, a political debate about how a modern capitalist society of individuals pursuing their interests could still cultivate those disinterested values that hold a society together. Disinterestedness in this way was merely a new way to talk about the old idea of civic virtue, the concept at the heart of the republican tradition that so deeply influenced liberalism from the seventeenth century forward. The republican tradition began with the ancient Greeks, who taught—rather starkly—that disinterestedness was the proper frame of mind for citizens active in the *polis* (or public sphere); indeed, as the philosopher Hannah Arendt once noted, for the Greeks, to dwell upon the interests of the *oikos* (or private sphere) made one an *idiotes* (Arendt 1998: 38). The Victorians were not the first to balk a little at the ancients' austere vision of public service and corresponding disdain for private interests (including commerce); tremendously instructive to them were similar debates of the sixteenth through eighteenth centuries about the feasibility of the ancient model. Those centuries saw the transition, very roughly speaking, from republicanism to liberalism. While the last republican theorists argued for the revival of such selflessness (think of Machiavelli's militias or Rousseau's general will), the first liberals skeptically concluded that interests and "the spirit of faction" (and not disinterestedness) actually define us, and thus, as Alexander Hamilton argued, the best that modern institutions can do is merely check and balance these interests, not enable us (as the ancients prescribed) to overcome them (Publius 1999: 106). Perhaps even more instructive to the Victorians than these strident positions on either side were the moderate recommendations offered by post-Revolutionary French theorists, not least Benjamin Constant, who in "The Liberty of Ancients Compared with that of Moderns" proposed a practical balance of minimal disinterestedness (in the form of modest public duties) with room for the pursuit of private though morally perfecting interests.[1]

The young poet Matthew Arnold initiated his second literary career as a prose author by mulling at some length in the "Preface" to his 1853 *Poems* over just how to check the modern cult of self-interest now that "the calm, the cheerfulness, the disinterested objectivity" of the "early Greek genius" has "disappeared" (Arnold 1960: 1).Throughout his career, the philosopher John Stuart Mill also pondered the best balance of disinterest and interest. Confessing (also in 1853) to admiring "the unostentatious disinterestedness of . . . public virtue" exercised by ancient Greeks like Epaminondas (Mill 1978: 311), Mill nonetheless recognized—like Constant and Arnold, and unlike Machiavelli and Rousseau—that there was no returning to a

Spartan selflessness. In the 1861 *Considerations on Representative Government*, he proposed various liberal institutions that would assume citizens to be both disinterested and interested actors. "Governments," he wrote, "must be made for human beings as they are, or as they are capable of speedily becoming." As they are, human beings indeed think "only of self-interest," but "only a disinterested regard for others, and especially for . . . the idea of posterity" will "ever direct the minds and purposes of classes or bodies of men towards distant or unobvious interests." Mill realistically dismissed "any form of government . . . which required as a condition that these exalted principles of action should be the guiding and master motives in the conduct of average human beings." Rather, only "a certain amount of conscience, and, of disinterested public spirit, may fairly be calculated on in the citizens of any community ripe for representative government" (Mill 1977: 445).

Where the nineteenth century experimented with various political mixtures of disinterest and interest, the twentieth century tended to draw much more extreme conclusions on this subject (as with so many others). This second debate about disinterestedness arguably began with T. S. Eliot's 1919 "Tradition and the Individual Talent," an essay that radicalized Arnold's conclusions in his 1864 "The Functions of Criticism at the Present Time." In his essay, Arnold had famously praised the critic's disinterestedness, by which he meant "keeping aloof from what is called 'the practical view of things'" (i.e., the close-mindedness of the *oikos*) so as to enable "a free play of the mind on all subjects which it touches" (i.e., the open-mindedness of the *polis*) (Arnold 1962: 269–70). That kind of open-mindedness alone can "nourish us"—as a society—"towards perfection" (284). In other words, just as Mill looked to mechanisms like the open ballot and mandatory jury duty as tools for cultivating a more open-and civic-minded *demos*, Arnold looked to what he called "Culture." T. S. Eliot, in contrast, offered "Tradition," a tool (he argued) for delivering "a juster estimation of actual poetry" and of values generally (Eliot 1975: 44). In this project, he was joined by F. R. Leavis and several other critics in the first half of the twentieth century who together developed, in Chris Baldick's summation, "a new kind of critical discourse" that "by its display of careful extrication from controversy" would speak "from a privileged standpoint" (Baldick 1983: 25–26).

Critics in the second half of the twentieth century—Baldick among them—vigorously challenged the kind of disinterestedness championed by Eliot and others in the first half of the century. Politically, Baldick and others argued, Eliot's "Tradition" was not a body of disinterested values at all but a highly interested, partisan weapon to "retard the development and dissemination of new ideas" (31). Unfortunately, Baldick incorrectly traced this aggressively conservative cultural program directly back from Eliot to Arnold (32), a critical move that became entirely habitual by the end of the twentieth century. Most influentially, Terry Eagleton argued in his popular book *Literary Theory: An Introduction* that Eliot's "extreme right-wing authoritarianism" and Leavis's "last ditch stand of liberal humanism" were both the logical fruits of Arnold's original agenda, which was that "men and women must sacrifice their petty 'personalities' and opinions to an impersonal order," be it "Culture" or "Tradition" (Eagleton 1983: 42, 34, 39). Where Victorian readers would have heard in Arnold's *Culture and Anarchy* (1869) echoes of such defenses of civic culture as Samuel Taylor Coleridge's *On the Constitution of Church and State* (1829) or even John Milton's *Areopagitica* (1644), Eagleton was more typical of late twentieth-century readers in hearing in Arnold's pronouncements an Orwellian Minister of Propaganda. By the end of the century, Arnold's supposedly "disinterested" culture was routinely vilified by the academic left as the hegemonic modern state's cudgel, not to cultivate in citizens "a free play of the mind" but (in Gerald Graff's words) to enforce "unreflective custom, tradition, and consensus" (Graff 1994: 188). Within the highly polarized academy of the late twentieth century, academics from the political right only added to the toxicity of this debate by championing Arnold's disinterested culture—as Gertrude Himmelfarb did in *The De-Moralization of Society: From Victorian Virtues to Modern Values* (1995)—as an honored forefather of the *Kulturkampf* launched by Anglo-American conservatives inspired by Ronald Reagan and Margaret Thatcher (Malachuk 2005: 50–55).

Fanning the flames of this already ferocious second debate was a related but more philosophically extreme critique of "culture" that targeted Arnold's disinterestedness particularly. In 1995, the authors of *The Columbia Dictionary of Modern Literary and Cultural Criticism* (themselves dispensing with any semblance of disinterestedness) charged Arnold with wrongly "assum[ing] the possibility of utter selflessness" and thus "us[ing] the word disinterestedness to mean a state of ideal objectivity and neutrality," an impossible goal according to a set of theoretical assumptions known by shorthand as "postmodernism." The *Columbia Dictionary*'s authors described "anti-Arnoldian positions" as now the "orthodoxy in much contemporary criticism," according to which disinterestedness was not only politically authoritarian but philosophically impossible, given "the imbrications of individuals in language, history, and culture" (Childers, Hentzi 1995: 85–86). Instead, critics should strive to expose these imbrications and the partialities and interests to which they give rise. The philosopher Paul Ricoeur traced this hermeneutic process back to "a school of suspicion" led by figures like Marx, Nietzsche, and Freud (Ricoeur 1972: 32). In this way, the anti-Arnoldian orthodoxy combined a fervent commitment to suspecting and exposing authorial interests with a politics that placed any universal moral claims—e.g., "Victorian virtues," "civic virtues," disinterestedness—under suspicion of being authoritarian. Where the nineteenth century, in short, had once debated how best to balance disinterested and interested motives in a liberal, capitalist society, the twentieth century ended with disinterestedness either ardently celebrated by the right as key to (what we can call a) traditionalist libertarianism or ardently reviled by the left as politically and philosophically central to a repressive "disciplinary society."

The third debate about disinterestedness began at the very start of the twenty-first century, 2001 being the year when Suzy Anger opened her collection *Knowing the Past* by essentially encouraging her fellow Victorian scholars to reconsider that anti-Arnoldian orthodoxy. "Certainly there are important problems—epistemological and political—with naïve realism or pure objectivity," she began, for "[r]ecent theory has given us important insights into the often discreditable ways in which appeals to objectivity have operated." But, Anger posited, perhaps "there are strong moral reasons for moving toward an epistemology . . . less skeptical and relativist" (Anger 2001: 10). In his contribution to the volume, too, George Levine made the requisite bow to the axiom that "[d]isinterest and objectivity are always impossible" but then in a sudden shift added that disinterest and objectivity are also "always necessary" (Levine 2001: 53). In support of this striking turn away from the second debate, Levine cited a book still in production that encouraged an admiration of Victorian disinterestedness as an "'aspiration' rather than an achievement."

That book was *The Powers of Distance*, also published in 2001, and the main reason we are debating this subject today.[2] Amanda Anderson's approach to Arnold (from a part of the book not excerpted here) also departs sharply from the polemics of the second debate. Referencing the 1864 "Function," for example, Anderson patiently shows how the second debaters had mistaken "disinterestedness" for "the principle of objective realism." In fact, Arnold's "terminologically and conceptually unsystematic" handling of disinterestedness sought practical more than philosophical expression, specifically as "different forms of detachment" (Anderson

2001: 92). As Anderson notes in the excerpt, along with authors like George Eliot and John Stuart Mill, Arnold developed "practices of detachment" (Anderson 2001: 3 [Chapter 34: 297]) originating in the Enlightenment. Together these Victorians "explore in a sustained way what it means to cultivate a distanced relation toward one's self, one's community, or those objects that one chooses to study or represent" (Anderson 2001: 4 [Chapter 34: 298]).

In Anderson's rendering, then, Arnold *et al.* become the confreres not of T. S. Eliot but of Immanuel Kant, their battle cry not "Tradition" but "*sapere aude*"– "dare to know." And, we, too, are invited into their circle: revealing the Victorians to be more suspicious about disinterestedness than we knew, Anderson (like Anger and Levine) urges us to be less so. She explicitly challenges Ricoeur's "hermeneutics of suspicion," which "considers investments in critical distance as self-damning, interpreting them as masked forms of power"; rather, she contends that we should consider disinterestedness as a set of "emergent practices that might themselves be the subject of ongoing critique" (Anderson 2001: 8 [Chapter 34: 300]).[3] We need a new debate, Anderson suggests, not *over* the Victorians but *with* them, all of us together contemplating "the distinctly moral dimensions or consequences of modern detachment" (Anderson 2001: 10 [Chapter 34: 302]).

In short, Anderson and the others who initiated this third debate in 2001 sought to rescue Victorian disinterestedness from the polemical manipulations of the twentieth century. However, as all three excerpts in this section reveal in different ways, it has proven challenging to leave the second debate entirely behind. In Anderson's case, while she is clearly eager to rectify the twentieth century's philosophical misreading of disinterestedness as objective realism, she seems more hesitant to challenge their political misreading of disinterestedness as aligned with a traditionalist libertarianism: hence her genealogical focus on Kantian epistemology rather than, say, Lockean liberalism. Observing the moralistic tenor of most of the practices of detachment she considers, Anderson confesses that "[t]his may be the facet of Victorian detachment that is most foreign to our current ways of framing questions of identity, critique, and practice" (Anderson 2001: 6 [Chapter 34: 299]). Similarly, her endorsement of the Victorians' plural "practices of the self, ranging from stoicism to cosmopolitanism to dandyism" (Anderson 2001: 7 [Chapter 34: 299]) is generous but also notably reluctant to call these practices what the Victorians did: i.e., "liberal."

In contrast, in the excerpt from her 2003 *Victorian Literature and the Victorian State*, Lauren M. E. Goodlad explicitly aligns Victorian disinterestedness, or "disinterested governance" (Goodlad 2003: xiii), with liberalism. More, she also properly depicts Victorian liberalism as the heir of the civic republican and liberal traditions (Goodlad 2003: 245n5 [Chapter 35: 309]) rather than as the embryo of the very different politics of T. S. Eliot or Gertrude Himmelfarb. In this way, Goodlad's work helps us to understand Victorian liberalism, including disinterestedness, by its own lights rather than through the distorting lens of twentieth-century left and right ideologies.

That said, Goodlad several times in the excerpt relies upon those very ideologies. In her defense, she does so in order to relay just how much more capacious Victorian liberalism was than has been allowed. The Victorian liberal imagination was, after all, broad enough to engage both what we would call right-leaning liberal or (more precisely) libertarian policies (in desiring "that . . . centralized institutions and statist interventions [be] curbed to preserve the 'self-governing' liberties of individuals and local communities" (Goodlad 2003: vii–viii [Chapter 35: 303])) as well as what we would call left-leaning liberal or welfare liberal policies (in seeking "to build character and promote social betterment by collective means" (Goodlad 2003: x [Chapter 35: 304])). As Goodlad summarizes, "[a]lthough many Victorians did not regard themselves as political liberals, most were responsive to the overall projects of liberating individuals from illegitimate authority [i.e., libertarianism] while simultaneously ensuring their moral and spiritual growth [i.e., welfare liberalism]" (Goodlad 2003: viii [Chapter 35: 304]).

Nonetheless, in certain places in this excerpt, Goodlad's reliance upon twentieth-century terminology to identify dawning trends within Victorian liberalism leads to mischaracterizations of Victorian liberalism that are all too familiar from the second debate. For example, Goodlad sometimes characterizes Victorian liberalism as torn between these "duel[ing] poles" (Goodlad 2003: xi [Chapter 35: 306]), one being "classical liberalism" with its "'more or less coherent set of philosophical presuppositions' including negative liberty, methodological individualism, antistatism, and free market capitalism," the other being what I've termed a welfare liberalism mixing "civic, romantic, and Christian" discourses (Goodlad 2003: ix [Chapter 35: 305]). When she then portrays Victorian literature as struggling "to transcend this divided legacy" (Goodlad 2003: x [Chapter 35: 305]), she arguably indulges in the second debate's tendency to impose the twentieth-century's absolutism—i.e., libertarianism versus welfarism—upon the Victorian era.[4] I return to this critique of Goodlad, especially her reading of Dickens's *Bleak House*, to close this essay.

The third excerpt, from Elaine Hadley's *Living Liberalism* (2010), also effectively returns us to the twentieth-century debate, but in yet another way: where Goodlad at times forces upon her Victorian texts alien ideological tensions from the twentieth century, Hadley cannot quite give up the other pronounced obsession of the second debaters: the philosophical suspicion that disinterestedness always masks interestedness. In her introduction (not excerpted here), Hadley presents herself as agnostic about whether Victorian disinterestedness was the beneficent agent of a normatively worthwhile "liberal idealism," as Anderson and Goodlad suggest, or the malignant force that helped to mask the rise of the disciplinary society, as D. A. Miller, a stalwart of the Foucauldian left in the second debate, had vigorously contended in the 1988 *The Novel and the Police* (Hadley 2010: 23–24). But despite her protestations otherwise, Hadley ultimately is not at all neutral; as I have argued elsewhere (Malachuk 2011), the book's allegiance to the older Foucauldian approach is revealed in multiple places, including the excerpt here.

In *Living Liberalism*, a few pages prior to this excerpt, Hadley cites the *Fortnightly Review*'s 1865 prospectus to prove that it "entered the public sphere . . . to transform" that sphere from a space dominated by anonymous partisan journalism into the realm of "free thought," a noble ideal that, as Hadley points out, required "practices that had to be formed and formalized" (Hadley 2010: 126). Looking more closely at those practices, Hadley shows that this attempt to achieve "disinterestedness of the critical spirit" (Hadley 2010: 141 [Chapter 36: 313]) required a writer to emphasize his "principle[s]" and thus "helped shift the primary ethical milieu for political practice from the civic sphere to the sphere of individual conviction." Hadley admits to being suspicious of this move, for in so doing the *Fortnightly* began to "secularize evangelical values" (Hadley 2010: 142 [Chapter 36: 313]) and to transform the liberal thinker into a hero (Hadley 2010: 143 [Chapter 36: 313]) whose mind becomes the object of the journal's worship—its "irreligious religiosity" (Hadley 2010: 144 [Chapter 36: 314]). While the magazine's *ideas* were ostensibly anti-clerical, then, Hadley's exclusive focus on the magazine's stylistic *practices* leads her to suspect that "*Fortnightly* merely substituted the individual mind for the omniscient godhead" (Hadley 2010: 146 [Chapter 36: 315]). In other words, while the magazine mouthed a disinterested tolerance of all religions, it was in practice promulgating a very specific new religion, according to which, "[r]ather than being true to one's god . . . a liberal individual must be true to his opinions" (Hadley 2010: 147 [Chapter 36: 316]). Given this secret but zealous devotion to the sanctity of one's own opinion, the journal's so-called "ventriloquial method" was hardly the disinterested practice that an earlier scholar, Basil Willey, had argued. Willey had coined the phrase in admiration of the *Fortnightly*'s ethic of repeating an opposing point of view as objectively as possible before refuting it (Hadley 2010: 149 [Chapter 36: 316]). But in Hadley's candidly "less-generous interpretation" (Hadley 2010: 150 [Chapter 36: 317]), this "ventriloquial method" is in practice characterized by "barely veiled impatience, or even disgust" with other opinions, which, more generally (Hadley cannot resist adding) "is often implicit in the liberal conception of tolerance" (Hadley 2010: 150 [Chapter 36: 317]). Far from being paragons of liberal disinterestedness, the *Fortnightly* writers (just like other supposedly tolerant liberals) were active and zealous partisans for their own interests.

As performed by Baldick, Eagleton, Miller and other participants in the second debate, these kinds of "less-generous interpretations" certainly helped to debunk the absolute aesthetic objectivity claimed for disinterestedness by T. S. Eliot and others in the first half of the twentieth century. That said, to revive these same old charges against not only twentieth-century conservatives but also Victorian liberals, as Hadley does, seems to thwart the more generous consideration of Victorian disinterestedness promised by the third debate when it was launched in 2001. For example, the promotion by the *Fortnightly* of a kind of religious belief that their hero John Stuart Mill heralded as "weak belief" is certainly vague, but also intriguing, and arguably deserves, today more than ever before, a more generous rather than less generous interpretation. That is, before dismissing the *Fortnightly* journalists for acting in bad faith, perhaps we might consider the value of their religious promotion of liberal opinions for our own post-secular public sphere.[5]

Or, to close, consider an alternative reading of the passage from Dickens's *Bleak House* that Goodlad considers in the second part of her excerpt. For here, Goodlad's reliance on a twentieth-century opposition—traditionalist libertarianism vs. welfare liberalism—closes off rather than opens up our understanding of Victorian disinterestedness. In order to demonstrate that Dickens shared Victorian liberalism's "symptomatic" (Goodlad 2003: 111 [Chapter 35: 308]) tension, Goodlad allows Esther to stand for traditionalist libertarianism ("feminine domesticity's crucial harborage of the personal") and Mrs. Pardiggle and Mrs. Jellyby for welfare liberalism ("organized philanthropy") (Goodlad 2003: 110 [Chapter 35: 307]). Given that in this novel Dickens obviously favors Esther over the philanthropists, that there is any kind of "tension" in Dickens's thought here is not obvious, and so Goodlad points outside of *Bleak House* to Dickens's personal commitment to philanthropies he otherwise reviles in his novels (Goodlad 2003: 111 [Chapter 35: 307]). But if that is the case—if Dickens kept his commitment to welfare liberalism to himself—then this means *Bleak House* itself must merely be a mouthpiece for traditionalist libertarianism. As Goodlad puts it, in the novel Dickens "falls back on a conservative mystification of the domestic and feminine personality" in his portrait of Esther while "demoniz[ing]" Mrs. Pardiggle's "protobureaucratic modes of governmentality" (Goodlad 2003: 111–12 [Chapter 35: 308]).

Consider a more generous reading of this section, specifically of Mrs. Jellyby in Chapters 4 and 5 of *Bleak House*. Clearly, Dickens does indeed take aim at Mrs. Jellyby—but *not* for her attempt to relocate the virtue of disinterestedness from traditional libertarianism to welfare liberalism and its "curative institution[s]." Rather, Dickens objects to Mrs. Jellyby's forsaking disinterestedness entirely. Introduced as someone who "devotes herself entirely to the public" (Dickens 1977: 35), Mrs. Jellyby is instead quickly exposed as pathologically self-interested: her narcissism is such that her husband is "merged" into her (35) ("the union of mind and matter" (41)) along with her daughter Caddy (her "amanuensis" (38)). More, Dickens hints that Mrs. Jellyby's "curious habit of seeming to look a long way off" (37) disguises—to herself as much as to others—the mix of private interests that Dickens insinuates motivate her "charity," i.e., her alliance with Quale in a "project . . . for teaching the coffee colonists to teach the natives to turn piano-forte legs and establish an export trade" (41). In contrast, Dickens seems to admire Esther not for her traditionalist libertarian commitment to the "personal" (as Goodlad writes) but rather for the ways she exemplifies the virtues of the "republican woman," whose disinterestedness (historians have shown) is expressed through civic deeds within the private sphere to members of not just the family but the polity.[6] Whereas Mrs. Jellyby's utter neglect of such duties (46–47) has resulted in her daughter Caddy being "uncivil" (43), Esther helps Caddy to imagine a new civic identity (57). Formally, too, Chapter 4 contrasts Mrs. Jellyby's interestedness and Esther's disinterestedness. While the chapter opens with her husband "merged" into the monstrous Mrs. Jellyby, it closes with Esther's more equitable merging with Caddy in sleep. In this passage, Dickens anticipates by just a few years the conceit of another mid-century civic fantasist, Walt Whitman, whose speaker in the 1855 poem that became "The Sleepers" imagines "dream[ing] in my dream all the dreams of the other dreamers, / And I become the other dreamers" (Whitman 2002: 724). Barred as a woman from floating freely through the public, Esther as she drifts to sleep is otherwise quite like Whitman's speaker in merging not only with friends but strangers; trying "to lose myself," she "began to lose the identity of the sleeper resting on me," until "[l]astly, it was no one, and I was no one" (45). In short, resisting the temptation to read these chapters through the lens of twentieth-century ideologies, we can see that Dickens is imagining a kind of disinterested civic virtue that mixes the private (women in the household) and the public (aid to strangers).

David Wayne Thomas, another important participant in this third debate, has nicely described the "challenge confronting such recuperative efforts" of Victorian liberalism (including disinterestedness) as "how to get past the [ideologically driven] reduction[s]" of the second debate "while still giving ideological critique its due" (Thomas 2004: ix). In 2005, Anderson proposed that we initiate such recuperative efforts by engaging the Victorians through the lens of political theory rather than history (Anderson 2005: 196) so that figures like Mill, Arnold, Eliot, and Dickens are reckoned with as our peers in theorizing liberalism, disinterestedness, and so forth. The risk here, as Thomas subsequently observed in a 2009 article, is that in so doing Anderson perpetuates "an intentionalist paradigm that implies a heroic cognitive agency in her selected authors" (Thomas 2009: 161). But surely we can recognize and even admire the Victorians' intentions as political theorists and independent thinkers generally without surrendering our critical faculties?

If anyone can serve as a model for practicing such engaged criticism, it is Stefan Collini, who has done the most to nudge us out of the second and into a third debate. Readers interested in gauging Collini's influence are encouraged to turn to the footnotes of all the other scholars cited in this essay, but for now note just one of his lessons for obtaining a clearer understanding of what Arnold himself meant by disinterestedness: "Arnold did not intend this as an epistemological claim; an empty victory is secured by [those in the second debate who] demonstrate that, according to the latest findings of philosophy and critical theory, objective knowledge is not so easily come by. Arnold's was a more practical, if also more elusive, point about a frame of mind, a state of intention" (Collini 2008: 7). A fully adequate third debate about disinterestedness will require that we grant to Arnold's and the other Victorians' intentions the respect we hope others grant to our own.

328   *Daniel S. Malachuk*

Notes

1 Pocock 1975 describes the revival of republicanism in the fifteenth through eighteenth centuries. See Malachuk 2013 on ancient and early modern republicanism and Victorian liberalism.
2 Bromwich 1982 offered a contextually nuanced critique of Arnold's disinterestedness, and Jones 1991 defended Arnold's disinterestedness against the hermeneutics of suspicion (95–97); however, neither initiated a third debate. The success of Anderson 2001 was significantly bolstered by Levine 2002, and see also Campbell 2013 for Collini's 2000–02 contributions.
3 Disavowing the hermeneutics of suspicion is a leitmotif in the third debate: see the other 2001 publications (Anger 2001: ix, Levine 2001: 55), Levine 2002 (273), Malachuk 2005 (45), and Miller 2008, which proposes a generous "implicative" hermeneutics as a complement to the "conclusive" critiques of the "hermeneutics of suspicion" (30). Thomas makes a similar observation (2009: 153).
4 On Cold War liberalism distorting our understanding of liberalism before the Cold War and after, see Malachuk 2005: 47–85 and Bird 1999: 1–26.
5 On Mill's "weak belief" and contemporary post-secular liberalism, see Malachuk 2010.
6 On republican womanhood theory, see Rendall and Malachuk 2013; for a consideration of Dickens (though not *Bleak House*) in this context, see Johnston 2001.

Bibliography

Anderson, A. (2001) *The Powers of Distance: Cosmopolitanism and the Cultivation of Detachment*, Princeton: Princeton University Press.
—— (2005) "Victorian Studies and the Two Modernities," *Victorian Studies*, 47.2: 195–203.
Anger, S. (ed.) (2001) *Knowing the Past: Victorian Literature and Culture*, Ithaca: Cornell University Press.
—— (2001) "Introduction: Knowing the Victorians," in S. Anger (ed.) 1–22.
Arendt, H. (1998) *The Human Condition*, 2nd edn., Chicago: University of Chicago Press.
Arnold, M. (1960) *The Complete Prose Works of Matthew Arnold, Volume I: On the Classical Tradition*, ed. R. Super, Ann Arbor: University of Michigan Press.
—— (1962) *The Complete Prose Works of Matthew Arnold, Volume III: Lectures and Essays in Criticism*, ed. R. Super, Ann Arbor: University of Michigan Press.
Baldick, C. (1983) *The Social Mission of English Criticism, 1848–1932*, New York: Oxford University Press.
Bird, C. (1999) *The Myth of Liberal Individualism*, Cambridge: Cambridge University Press.
Bromwich, D. (1982) "The Genealogy of Disinterestedness," *Raritan*, 1 (1982) 62–92.
Campbell, K. (2013) "Culture, Politics, and Arnold Revisited: The Government Inspector, Disinterestedness, and 'The Function of Criticism,'" *Journal of Victorian Culture*, 18.2: 230–245.
Childers, J and G. Hentzi. (1995) *The Columbia Dictionary of Modern Literary and Cultural Criticism*, New York: Columbia University Press.
Collini, S. (1988; reprinted 2008) *Arnold*, New York: Oxford University Press.
Dickens, C. (1977) *Bleak House*, New York: W.W. Norton & Company.
Eagleton, T. (1983) *Literary Theory: An Introduction*, Minneapolis: University of Minnesota Press.
Eliot, T. S. (1975) *Selected Prose of T.S. Eliot*, ed. F. Kermode, Orlando: Harcourt, Inc.
Goodlad, L. (2003) *Victorian Literature and the Victorian State: Character and Governance in a Liberal Society*, Baltimore: The Johns Hopkins University Press.
Graff, G. (1994) "Arnold, Reason, and Common Culture," in M. Arnold, *Culture and Anarchy*, ed. S. Lipman, New Haven: Yale University Press: 186–201.
Hadley, E. (2010) *Living Liberalism: Practical Citizenship in Mid-Victorian Britain*, Chicago: The University of Chicago Press.
Himmelfarb, G. (1995) *The De-Moralization of Society: From Victorian Virtues to Modern Values*, New York: Knopf.
Johnston, S. (2001) *Women and Domestic Experience in Victorian Political Fiction*, Westport: Greenwood Press.

Jones, M. (1991) "Recuperating Arnold: Romanticism and Modern Projects of Disinterestedness," *Boundary 2*, 2:1–2 (Summer), 65–103.

Levine, G. (2001) "*Daniel Deronda*: A New Epistemology," in S. Anger (ed.), 52–73.

—— (2002) *Dying to Know: Scientific Epistemology and Narrative in Victorian England*, Chicago: University of Chicago Press.

Malachuk, D. (2005) *Perfection, the State, and Victorian Liberalism*, New York: Palgrave Macmillan.

—— (2010) "Human Rights and a Post-Secular Religion of Humanity," *Journal of Human Rights*, 9.2 (June): 127–142.

—— (2011) Review of *Living Liberalism*, *Nineteenth Century Contexts*, 33.4: 409–11.

—— (2013) "George Eliot's Liberalism," in A. Anderson and H. Shaw (eds.), *A Companion to George Eliot*, West Sussex: Wiley-Blackwell.

Mill, J. S. (1977) *The Collected Works of John Stuart Mill*, vol. 19, ed. J. Robson, Toronto: University of Toronto Press.

—— (1978) *The Collected Works of John Stuart Mill*, vol. 11, ed. J. Robson, Toronto: University of Toronto Press.

Miller, A. (2008) *The Burdens of Perfection: On Ethics and Reading in Nineteenth-century British Literature*, Ithaca, NY: Cornell University Press.

Pocock, J. G. A. (1975) *The Machiavellian Moment: Florentine Political Thought and the Atlantic Republican Tradition*, Princeton: Princeton University Press.

Publius (1999) *The Federalist Papers*, New York: Signet Classics.

Rendall, J. (1985) *The Origins of Modern Feminism: Women in Britain, France, and the United States, 1780–1860*, Basingstoke: Macmillan.

Ricoeur, P. (1972) *Freud and Philosophy*, trans. D. Savage, New Haven: Yale University Press.

Thomas, D. (2004) *Cultivating Victorians: Liberal Culture and the Aesthetic*, Philadelphia: University of Pennsylvania Press.

—— (2009) "Liberal Legitimation and Communicative Action in British India: Reading Flora Annie Steel's *On the Face of the Waters*," *ELH*, 76.1 (Spring 2009) 153–187.

Whitman, W. (2002) *Leaves of Grass and Other Writings*, ed. M. Moon, New York: Norton Critical Edition.

Part X

Imperialism and literature in the age of colonialism

Introduction

By the end of the nineteenth century, the British Empire was the largest in the world, governing nearly a full quarter of the planet and a fifth of its population. While on Britain's maps and globes its colonies were presented in a uniform color (usually red or pink), as Linda Colley notes in her book *Captives* (2002), the development of this empire was somewhat less homogeneous than its cartographic representation suggested. A product of at least four centuries of irregular military and economic activity overseas, the growth of Britain's empire was largely ad hoc, rather than the result of a systematic program of expansion. Both Britain's territorial regimes of control and the experience of empire within them were shaped by disparate and sometimes contradictory factors, from the domestic demand for raw goods and new markets overseas to a strategic desire to protect trade routes to a self-imposed "civilizing" and religious mission.

Though historians have been studying Britain's imperial activities since the nineteenth century, scholars of literature paid only cursory attention to Britain's empire for much of the twentieth century. Only in the 1970s, in the wake the decolonization of Europe's imperial holdings, did the situation change with the publication of Edward Said's *Orientalism* (1978). Said argued that European writers, artists, and scholars played an integral role in the establishment and perpetuation of imperialism in the nineteenth century. European literature, he claimed, was complicit with the practice of Orientalism, whereby the East was established as the West's exotic—and inferior—other. The significance of Said's insight that literature can and should be read as embedded in the politics of imperialism, which informs and shapes his interpretation of Rudyard Kipling's *Kim* excerpted in this volume, cannot be underestimated; it effectively established one of the late twentieth-century's most influential theoretical schools—post-colonialism—which has become an indispensable area of contemporary literary scholarship.

But despite the obvious applicability of Said's arguments to nineteenth-century British literature, Victorian scholars were slow at first to situate literature from the period within the context of Britain's empire. While imperial themes were obvious in late nineteenth-century adventure fiction, like that written by H. Rider Haggard and Rudyard Kipling, critics tended to view literature of the early and mid-Victorian period as uninterested in empire. Patrick Brantlinger's *Rule of Darkness* (1988), excerpted here, represents an important turning point: not only did he offer new insights into the way adventure fiction focused late Victorian anxieties about empire, but he demonstrated that early and mid-Victorian domestic fiction were substantially implicated in Britain's colonial project. Through the early nineties, scholars continued to build on the insights of Said and Brantlinger, arguing—in the cases of

Suvendrini Perera and Firdous Azim—that the novel's complicity with imperialist ideology existed at the level of form as well as theme, an assertion which renders the novel an inherently "imperial genre" (Azim 1993: 30).

Said's analysis of imperialism was not without its detractors, though. Throughout the 1980s and 1990s, *Orientalism* was criticized for—among other things—homogenizing both metropole and periphery, and for establishing reductive and misleading binaries (a failing Said himself partly acknowledged in *Culture and Imperialism* (1993)). Post-colonial theorists, notably Gayatri Spivak and Homi Bhabha, responded by revising and reformulating understandings of colonial identities and relationships. In emphasizing gender roles and the position of the subaltern, in exploring the phenomenon of cultural hybridity between colonizer and colonized, and in their poststructuralist resistance to totalizing theoretical constructs, Spivak's and Bhabha's work has contributed a new set of analytical tools for the study of imperialism. In the 1990s, critics such as Deirdre David, Susan Meyer, and Anne McClintock scrutinized the role of women and women's writing in empire, with Meyer in particular drawing on the alignment of western women with colonial subjects in the nineteenth century to challenge the notion that the Victorian novel was always unequivocally pro-imperialist. A new school of imperialist historiography also emerged, known as New Imperial History, whose practitioners, including Antoinette Burton and Catherine Hall, embrace post-colonial theoretical models. These historians often do comparative work, describing the British Empire transnationally, while also acknowledging the particularities of empire: as Hall reminds us, British colonial activities in the West Indies cannot be conflated with those in India, for example. Since the turn of the century, scholars David Cannadine and John Kucich have shifted our attention to British social class in the empire, outlining how an internal social hierarchy at home and abroad was reshaped by colonial activities overseas. Kucich argues that, in addition to tales of conquest and victory, Britain's empire generated narratives of self-sacrifice and failure, producing a "pervasive ethos of self-denial" (Kucich 2007: 10 [Chapter 41: 359]) in its middle classes.

As we await the planned withdrawal of most American troops from Afghanistan in 2017, 70 years after the British left India, interest in imperialism in Victorian studies continues to thrive. But while historical scholarship provides more detailed understandings of British imperial activities, we're likely to face questions not just about the relationship between literature and imperialism, but the exigency of literary studies itself. As Muireann O'Cinneide warns in her capstone essay, post-colonial literary critics cannot allow "attention to form, genre and rhetoric to become swamped by a wealth of historical contextualization" (Chapter 42: 367) without losing sight of the literary object itself, let alone its function in nineteenth-century empire. It is, after all, as Said reminds us, *Kim*'s status as a novel—and a great one at that—that makes it such a powerful vehicle of imperial ideology.

See also: *Genre fiction and the sensational*; *Psychology and Victorian literature*; *Gender, sexuality, domesticity*

Bibliography

Azim, F. (1993) *The Colonial Rise of the Novel*, London: Routledge.

38 Introduction to *Kim*

Edward Said

[. . .]

[In Rudyard Kipling's *Kim*, t]here is no resolution to the conflict between Kim's colonial service and loyalty to his Indian companions not because Kipling could not face it, but because for Kipling *there was no conflict* and [. . .] one of the purposes of the novel was, in fact, to show the absence of conflict once Kim is cured of his doubts and the lama of his longing for the River, and India of a couple of upstarts and foreign agents. But that there *might have been a conflict* had Kipling considered India as unhappily subservient to imperialism, of this we can have no doubt. The fact is that he did not: for him it was India's best destiny to be ruled by England. The trouble is that if one reads Kipling not simply as an 'imperialist minstrel' (which he wasn't) but as someone who had read Frantz Fanon, met Gandhi, absorbed their lessons, but had remained stubbornly unconvinced by both, then one seriously distorts the defining context in which Kipling wrote, and which he refines, elaborates, illuminates. There *were* no appreciable deterrents to the imperialist world view held by Kipling. Hence, he remained untroubled, although it is true to say, I think, that his fiction represents both the Empire and conscious legitimizations of it, both of which, as fiction (as opposed to discursive prose), incur ironies and problems, as we shall soon see.

Consider two episodes in *Kim*. Shortly after the lama and his chela leave Umballa they meet the elderly and withered former soldier 'who had served the Government in the days of the Mutiny'. To a contemporary reader 'the Mutiny' meant the single most important, well-known and violent episode of the nineteenth-century Anglo-Indian relationship: the Great Mutiny of 1857, which began in Meerut on 10 May, 1857 and spread immediately to the capture of Delhi by the mutineers. An enormous amount of writing, British and Indian, covers the Mutiny.[1]

What caused the Mutiny directly was the suspicion of Hindu and Muslim soldiers in the Indian Army that their bullets were greased with cow's fat (unclean to Hindus) and pig's fat (unclean to Muslims). In fact the causes of the Mutiny were constitutive to British imperialism itself, to an army largely staffed by natives and officered by sahibs, to the anomalies of rule by the East India Company. In addition, there was a great deal of underlying resentment at the fact of white Christian rule in a country made up of many races and cultures, all of whom most probably regarded their subservience to the British as degrading. It was lost on none of the mutineers that numerically they vastly outnumbered their superior officers.

Without going into the very complex structure of actions, motives, events, moralities debated endlessly since (and even during) the Mutiny, we should acknowledge that it provided a clear demarcation for Indian and for British history. To the British, who finally put the Mutiny down with brutality and severity, all their actions were retaliatory; the mutineers murdered Europeans, they said, and such actions proved, as if proof were necessary, that Indians deserved subjugation by the higher civilization of European Britain. After 1857 the East India Company was replaced by the much more formal Government of India. For the Indians, the Mutiny was a nationalist uprising against British rule, which uncompromisingly re-asserted itself despite abuses, exploitation and seemingly unheeded native complaint. When in 1925 Edward Thompson published his powerful little tract, *The Other Side of the Medal* – an impassioned statement against British rule and for Indian independence – he singled out the Mutiny as the great symbolic event by which the two sides, Indian and British, achieved their full and conscious opposition to each other.[2] Thompson quite dramatically shows that the writing of Indian and British history diverged most emphatically on representations of the Mutiny. The Mutiny, in short, reinforced the difference between colonizer and colonized.

In such a situation of nationalist and self-justifying inflammation, to be an Indian would have meant feeling natural solidarity with the victims of British reprisal. To be British meant feeling repugnance and injury – to say nothing of righteous vindication – given the terrible displays of 'native' cruelty. For an Indian, *not* to have had those feelings would have been to belong to the small minority that did exist to be sure, but which was distinctly unrepresentative of majority Indian sentiment. It is therefore highly significant that Kipling's choice of an Indian to speak about the Mutiny – the major historical event that antecedes the action of *Kim* in the 1880s – is an old loyalist soldier who views his countrymen's revolt as an act of madness. Not surprisingly this man is respected by British 'Deputy Commissioners' who, Kipling tells us, 'turned aside from the main road to visit him'. What Kipling simply eliminates is the likelihood that the soldier's compatriots regard him as (at very least) a traitor to his people. And when, a few pages later, the veteran tells the lama and Kim about the Mutiny, his version of the events is highly charged with the British rationale for what happened:

> A madness ate into all the Army, and they turned against their officers. That was the first evil, but not past remedy if they had then held their hands. But they chose to kill the Sahibs' wives and children. Then came the Sahibs from over the sea and called them to most strict account.

To reduce Indian resentment to 'madness', to characterize Indian resistance (as it might have been called) to British insensitivity as 'madness', to represent Indian actions as mainly the decision to kill British women and children – all these are not merely innocent reductions of the nationalist Indian case against the British, but tendentious ones. Moreover, when Kipling has the old soldier describe the British counter-revolt – with all its horrendous reprisals by white men bent on 'moral' action – as calling the Indian mutineers 'to most strict account', we have left the world of history and entered the world of imperialist polemic, in which the native is naturally a delinquent, the white man a stern but moral parent and judge. The point about this brief episode is not just that it gives us the extreme British view on the Mutiny, but that Kipling puts it in the mouth of an Indian whose much more likely nationalist counterpart is never seen in the novel at all. (Similarly Mahbub Ali, Creighton's faithful adjutant, belongs to the Pathan people who historically speaking were in a state of unpacified insurrection against the British during the nineteenth century. Yet he, too, is represented as happy with British rule, and even a collaborator with it.) So far is Kipling from showing two worlds in conflict [. . .] that he has studiously given us only one, and eliminated any chance of conflict altogether.

The second example confirms the first. Once again it is a small moment in *Kim*, but a significant one just the same. Kim, the lama, and the widow of Kulu are en route to Saharunpore in Chapter 4. Kim has just been exuberantly described as being 'in the middle of it, more awake and more excited than anyone', the 'it' of Kipling's description standing for 'the world in real truth; this was life as he would have it – bustling and shouting, the buckling of belts, and beating of bullocks and creaking of wheels, lighting of fires and cooking of food, and new sights at every turn of the approving eye'. We have already seen a good deal of this side of India, with its colour, excitement and interest exposed in all their variety for the English reader's benefit. Somehow it seems, however, that Kipling also felt the necessity for some authority over India, perhaps because only a few pages earlier he had sensed in the old soldier's minatory account of the Mutiny the need to forestall any further 'madness'. After all it is India itself which is responsible both for the local vitality enjoyed by Kim, and the threat to Britain's Empire. A district superintendent of police trots by, and his appearance occasions this reflection from the old widow:

> These be the sort to oversee justice. They know the land and the customs of the land. The others, all new from Europe, suckled by white women and learning our tongues from books, are worse than the pestilence. They do harm to Kings.

Doubtless some Indians believed that English police officials knew the country better than the natives, and that such officials – rather than Indian rulers – should hold the reins of power. But note that in *Kim* no one is seen who challenges British rule, and no one articulates any of the local Indian challenges that must have been greatly in evidence – even for someone as obdurate as Kipling – in the late nineteenth century. Instead we have one character explicitly saying that a colonial police official ought to rule India and in saying that also adding that she preferred the older style of official who, like Kipling and his family, had lived among the natives and was therefore better than the newer, academically trained bureaucrats. Not only does Kipling reproduce a version of the argument of the so-called Orientalists in India, who believed that Indians should be ruled according to Oriental-Indian modes by India 'hands', but in the process he dismisses as academic all the philosophical or ideological approaches contending with Orientalism. Among those discredited styles of rule were Evangelicalism (the missionaries and reformers, parodied in Dr Bennett), Utilitarianism and Spencerianism (who are parodied in the Babu), *and* of course those unnamed academics lampooned as 'worse than the pestilence'. It is interesting that phrased the way it is, the widow's approval is wide enough to include police officers like the Superintendent, as well as a flexible educator like Father Victor, and Colonel Creighton.

Having the widow express what is in effect a sort of uncontested normative judgement about India and its rulers is Kipling's way of demonstrating that natives accept colonial rule, so long as it is the right kind of rule. Historically this has always been the way European imperialism made itself more palatable to itself, for what could be better for its self-image than native subjects who express assent to the outsider's knowledge and power, while implicitly accepting European judgement on the undeveloped, backward or degenerate nature of native society? If one were to read *Kim* as a boy's adventure story, or as a rich and lovingly detailed panorama of Indian life, one would not be reading the novel that Kipling in fact wrote, so carefully inscribed is the novel with such considered views, suppressions and elisions as these. As Francis G. Hutchins puts it in *The Illusion of Permanence: British Imperialism in India*, by the late nineteenth century, an

> ... India of the imagination was created which contained no elements of either social change or political menace. Orientalization was the result of this effort to conceive of Indian society as devoid of elements hostile to the perpetualization of British rule, for it was on the basis of this presumptive India that Orientalizers sought to build a permanent rule.[3]

Kim is a major contribution to this orientalized India of the imagination, as it is also to what historians have come to call 'the invention of tradition'.

There is still more to be noted. Dotting *Kim*'s fabric is a scattering of editorial asides on the immutable nature of the Oriental world, particularly as it is distinguished from the white world, no less immutable. Thus, for example, 'Kim could lie like an Oriental'; or, a bit later, 'all hours of the twenty-four are alike to Orientals'; or, when Kim pays for train tickets with the lama's money he keeps one anna per rupee for himself which, Kipling says, is 'the immemorial commission of Asia'; later still Kipling refers to 'the huckster instinct of the East'; at a train platform, Mahbub's retainers 'being natives' had not unloaded the trucks which they should have; Kim's ability to sleep as the trains roared is an instance of 'the Oriental's indifference to mere noise'; as the camp breaks up, Kipling says that it is done swiftly 'as Orientals understand speed – with long explanations, with abuse and windy talk, carelessly, amid a hundred checks for little things forgotten'; Sikhs are characterized as having a special 'love of money'; Hurree Babu equates being a Bengali with being fearful; when he hides the packet taken from the foreign agents, the Babu 'stowed the entire trove about his body, as only Orientals can'.

Nothing of this is unique to Kipling. The most cursory survey of late nineteenth-century culture reveals an immense archive of popular wisdom of this sort, a good deal of which, alas, is still very much alive today. Furthermore, as John M. McKenzie has shown in his valuable book *Propaganda and Empire*,[4] a vast array of manipulative devices, from cigarette cards, postcards, sheet music, music-hall entertainments, toy soldiers, to brass band concerts, board games, almanacs and manuals, extolled the late nineteenth-century Empire and often did so by stressing the necessity of Empire to England's strategic, moral and economic well-being, and at the same time characterizing the dark or inferior races as thoroughly unregenerate, in need of suppression, severe rule, indefinite subjugation. The cult of the military personality was prominent in this context, usually because such personalities had managed to bash a few dark heads. Different rationales for holding overseas territories were given during the course of the century; sometimes it was profit, at other times strategy, at still others it was competition with other imperial powers – as in *Kim*. (In *The Strange Ride of Rudyard Kipling*, Angus Wilson mentions that as early as sixteen years of age Kipling proposed at a school debate the motion that 'the advance of Russia in Central Asia is hostile to British Power'.)[5] The one thing that remains constant, however, is the inferiority of the non-white. To this view everyone, from the ordinary lower-middle-class jingoist to the highest of philosophers, seems to have subscribed.

This is a very important point. *Kim* is a work of great aesthetic merit; it cannot be dismissed simply as the racist imagining of one fairly disturbed and ultra-reactionary imperialist. George Orwell was certainly right to comment on Kipling's unique power to have added phrases and concepts to the language – East is East, and West is West; the white man's Burden; somewhere East of Suez – and right, also, to say that Kipling's concerns are both vulgar and permanent, of urgent interest. Now, one reason for Kipling's power is that he was an artist of enormous gifts; what he did in his art was to have elaborated ideas that would have had far less permanence, for all their vulgarity, without the art. But the other reason for his power is that he was also supported by (and therefore could make use of) the authorized monuments of nineteenth-century European culture, for whom the inferiority of non-white races, the necessity for them to be ruled by a superior civilization, and the absolute unchanging essence of Orientals, blacks, primitives, women were more or less undebatable, unquestioned axioms of modern life. The extraordinary status of racial theory, in which it was scientifically proven that the white man stood at the pinnacle of development and civilization, is a case in point.

It would be tedious here to run through the arguments and the names: I have discussed these notions in *Orientalism*.[6] Suffice it to say that Macaulay, Carlyle, Arnold, Ruskin, J. A. Froude, John Robert Seeley, even John Stuart Mill, plus every major novelist, essayist, philosopher, and historian of note accepted as fact the division, the difference and, in Gobineau's phrase, the inequality of the races. Moreover these views were regularly adduced as evidence for the desirability of European rule in less-developed regions of the world. Much the same situation obtains in France, Belgium, Germany, Holland, and the United States. True, there were debates about how the colonies were to be ruled, or whether some of them should be given up. Yet no one with any power to influence public discussion or policy demurred as to the basic superiority of the white European male, who should always retain the upper hand when dealing with natives. Statements like 'the Hindu is inherently untruthful and lacks moral courage' were the expression of wisdom from which very few, least of all the governors of Bengal, dissented; similarly when a historian of India like Sir H. M. Elliot planned his work, central to it was the notion of Indian barbarity.[7] An entire system of thought clustered around these conceptions. Climate and geography dictated certain character traits in the Indian; Orientals, according to Lord Cromer, one of their most redoubtable rulers, could not learn to walk on sidewalks, could not tell the truth, could not use logic; the Malaysian native was essentially lazy, the way the northern European was energetic and resourceful. V. G. Kiernan's book *The Lords of Human Kind* gives a remarkable picture of how widespread these views were.[8] Disciplines like colonial economics, anthropology, history and sociology were built out of these dicta, with the result that almost to a man and woman the Europeans who dealt with colonies such as India became insulated to the facts of change and nationalism. Even Karl Marx succumbed to thoughts of the changeless Asiatic village, or agriculture, or despotism. And as colonial work progressed in time it became specialized. A young Englishman sent to India would belong to a class whose national dominance over each and every Indian, no matter how aristocratic and poor, was absolute. He would have heard the same stories, read the same books, learned the same lessons, joined the same clubs as all the other young colonial officials. Ronnie Heaslop in E. M. Forster's *A Passage to India* is a well-known portrait of such an official.

All of this is absolutely relevant to *Kim*, whose main figure of worldly authority is Colonel Creighton. This ethnographer-scholar-soldier is no mere accidental creature of invention, sprung fully grown and ready from Kipling's imagination. He is almost certainly a figure drawn from Kipling's experiences in the Punjab, and he is most interestingly interpreted both as an evolution out of earlier figures of authority in colonial India as well as someone whose role answered to Kipling's own needs.

In the first place, although Creighton is seen infrequently and his character is not as fully drawn as either Mahbub Ali's or the Babu's, he is nevertheless very much there, a point of reference for the action, a discreet director of events, a man whose power is eminently worthy of respect. Yet he is no crude martinet. He takes over Kim's life by persuasion, not by imposition of his rank. He can be flexible when it seems reasonable – who could have wished for a better boss than Creighton during Kim's footloose holidays? – and stern when events require it.

In the second place, what makes Creighton especially interesting is Kipling's rendition of him as a colonial official and scholar. This union of power and knowledge is contemporary with Conan Doyle's invention of Sherlock Holmes (whose faithful scribe, Doctor Watson, is a veteran of the North-West Frontier), also a man whose approach to life includes a healthy respect for, and protection of, the law, allied with a superior, specialized intellect. In both instances, Kipling and Conan Doyle represent for their readers men whose unorthodox style of operation is rationalized by relatively new fields of experience turned into quasi-academic specialities. Colonial rule and crime detection appear now to have almost the respectability and order of the classics and chemistry. When Mahbub Ali turns Kim in for his education, Creighton, overhearing their conversation, thinks 'that the boy mustn't be wasted if he is as advertised'. Creighton sees the world from a totally systematic viewpoint. Everything about India interests him, because everything in it is significant for his rule. The interchange between ethnography and colonial work in Creighton is fluent; he can study the talented boy both as a future spy and as an anthropological curiosity. Thus when Father Victor wonders whether it might not be too much for Creighton to attend to a bureaucratic detail concerning Kim's education, the colonel dismisses the scruple. 'The transformation of a regimental badge like your Red Bull into a sort of fetish that the boy follows is very interesting.'

Two further points should be made about Creighton the anthropologist. Of all the modern social sciences, anthropology is the one historically most closely tied to colonialism, since it has often been the case that since the mid-nineteenth century anthropologists and ethnologists were also advisors to colonial rulers on the manners and mores of the native people to be ruled. Claude Lévi-Strauss's allusion to anthropological investigations in *The Scope of Anthropology* as 'sequels to colonialism' is a recognition of this fact;[9] the excellent collection of essays edited by Talal Asad, *Anthropology and the Colonial Encounter*, develops the connections still further.[10] And, finally, in Robert Stone's recent novel on United States imperialist involvement in Latin American affairs, *A Flag for Sunrise*[11] its central character is Holliwell, an anthropologist with ambiguous ties to the CIA. Kipling was simply one of the first novelists to portray a logical alliance between Western science and political power at work in the colonies.

[. . .]

Notes

1   For recent accounts see Christopher Hibbert, *The Great Mutiny* (Viking, 1978), and the shorter version contained in Percival Spear, *History of India*, vol. 2 (Penguin, 1985).
2   Edward Thompson, *The Other Side of the Medal* (Hogarth Press, 1925).
3   Francis G. Hutchins, *The Illusion of Permanence: British Imperialism in India* (Princeton University Press, 1967).
4   John M. McKenzie, *Propaganda and Empire* (Manchester University Press, 1984).
5   Angus Wilson, *The Strange Ride of Rudyard Kipling* (Penguin, 1977), p. 43.
6   Edward W. Said, *Orientalism* (Penguin, 1985).
7   Sir H. M. Eliot, Preface to *India's History As Told By Its Own Historians*, ed. J. Dowson (1867).
8   V. G. Kiernan, *The Lords of Human Kind* (Columbia University Press, 1986).
9   Claude Lévi-Strauss, *The Scope of Anthropology* (Cape, 1967).
10   Talal Asad, *Anthropology and the Colonial Encounter* (Ithaca Press, 1973).
11   Robert Stone, *A Flag for Sunrise* (Knopf, 1981).

39 Imperial Gothic

Atavism and the occult in the British adventure novel, 1880–1914

Patrick Brantlinger

[. . .]

In "The Little Brass God," a 1905 story by Bithia Croker, a statue of "Kali, Goddess of Destruction," brings misfortune to its unwitting Anglo-Indian possessors. First their pets kill each other or are killed in accidents; next the servants get sick or fall downstairs; then the family's lives are jeopardized. Finally the statue is stolen and dropped down a well, thus ending the curse.[1] This featherweight tale typifies many written between 1880 and 1914. Its central feature, the magic statue, suggests that Western rationality may be subverted by the very superstitions it rejects. The destructive magic of the Orient takes its revenge; Croker unwittingly expresses a social version of the return of the repressed characteristic of late Victorian and Edwardian fiction, including that blend of adventure story with Gothic elements—imperial Gothic, as I will call it—which flourished from H. Rider Haggard's *King Solomon's Mines* in 1885 down at least to John Buchan's *Greenmantle* in 1916. Imperial Gothic combines the seemingly scientific, progressive, often Darwinian ideology of imperialism with an antithetical interest in the occult. Although the connections between imperialism and other aspects of late Victorian and Edwardian culture are innumerable, the link with occultism is especially symptomatic of the anxieties that attended the climax of the British Empire. No form of cultural expression reveals more clearly the contradictions within that climax than imperial Gothic.

Impelled by scientific materialism, the search for new sources of faith led many late Victorians to telepathy, séances, and psychic research. It also led to the far reaches of the Empire, where strange gods and "unspeakable rites" still had their millions of devotees. Publication of Madame Blavatsky's *Isis Unveiled* in 1877 marks the beginning of this trend, and the stunning success of Edwin Arnold's *The Light of Asia* (1879) suggests the strength of the desire for alternatives to both religious orthodoxy and scientific skepticism.[2] For the same reason, A. P. Sinnett's *Esoteric Buddhism* (1883) was widely popular, as was his earlier *The Occult World* (1881).[3] The standard explanation for the flourishing of occultism in the second half of the nineteenth century is that "triumphant positivism sparked an international reaction against its restrictive world view." In illustrating this thesis, Janet Oppenheim lists some manifestations of that reaction: "In England, it was an age of . . . the Rosicrucian revival, of cabalists, Hermeticists, and reincarnationists. In the late 1880s, the Hermetic Order of the Golden Dawn first saw the light of day in London, and during its stormy history, the Order lured into its arcane activities not only W. B. Yeats, but also the self-proclaimed magus Aleister Crowley. . . . Palmists and astrologers abounded, while books on magic and the occult sold briskly."[4] Oppenheim's thesis that "much of the attraction of these and related subjects depended on the dominant role that science had assumed in modern culture" (160) is borne out by the testimony of those drawn to occultism, among them Arthur Conan Doyle,

Annie Besant, Arthur J. Balfour, and Oliver Lodge. At the same time an emphasis on the occult aspects of experience was often reconciled with "science" and even with Darwinism; such a reconciliation characterizes Andrew Lang's interests in both anthropology and psychic research, as well as the various neo-Hegelian justifications of Empire. Thus in *Origins and Destiny of Imperial Britain* (1900), J. A. Cramb argues that "empires are successive incarnations of the Divine ideas," but also that empires result from the struggle for survival of the fittest among nations and races. The British nation and Anglo-Saxon race, he contends, are the fittest to survive.[5]

Imperialism itself, as an ideology or political faith, functioned as a partial substitute for declining or fallen Christianity and for declining faith in Britain's future. The poet John Davidson, for instance, having rejected other creeds and causes, "committed himself to a cluster of ideas centering on heroes, hero worship, and heroic vitalism," according to his biographer, which led him to pen ardent celebrations of the Empire.[6] In "St. George's Day," Davidson writes:

> The Sphinx that watches by the Nile
> Has seen great empires pass away:
> The mightiest lasted but a while;
> Yet ours shall not decay—

a claim that by the 1890s obviously required extraordinary faith.[7] The religious quality of late Victorian imperialism is also evident in much of Rudyard Kipling's poetry, as in "Recessional":

> God of our fathers, known of old,
>   Lord of our far-flung battle-line,
> Beneath whose awful Hand we hold
>   Dominion over palm and pine—
> Lord God of Hosts, be with us yet,
> Lest we forget—lest we forget![8]

In his study of William Ernest Henley, who did much to encourage the expression of imperialism in fin-de-siècle literature, Jerome Buckley remarks that "by the last decade of the century, the concept of a national or racial absolute inspired a fervor comparable to that engendered by the older evangelical religion."[9]

Imperialism and occultism both functioned as ersatz religions, but their fusion in imperial Gothic represents something different from a search for new faiths. The patterns of atavism and going native described by imperialist romancers do not offer salvationist answers for seekers after religious truth; they offer instead insistent images of decline and fall or of civilization turning into its opposite just as the Englishman who desecrates a Hindu temple in Kipling's "Mark of the Beast" turns into a werewolf. Imperial Gothic expresses anxieties about the waning of religious orthodoxy, but even more clearly it expresses anxieties about the ease with which civilization can revert to barbarism or savagery and thus about the weakening of Britain's imperial hegemony. The atavistic descents into the primitive experienced by fictional characters seem often to be allegories of the larger regressive movement of civilization, British progress transformed into British backsliding. So the first section of Richard Jefferies's apocalyptic fantasy *After London* (1885) is entitled "The Relapse into Barbarism."

Similarly, the narrator of Erskine Childers's spy novel *Riddle of the Sands* (1903) starts his tale in this way: "I have read of men who, when forced by their calling to live for long periods in utter solitude—save for a few black faces—have made it a rule to dress regularly for dinner in order to . . . prevent a relapse into barbarism."[10] Much imperialist writing after about 1880 treats the Empire as a barricade against a new barbarian invasion; just as often it treats the Empire as a "dressing for dinner," a temporary means of preventing Britain itself from relapsing into barbarism.

After the mid-Victorian years the British found it increasingly difficult to think of themselves as inevitably progressive; they began worrying instead about the degeneration of their institutions, their culture, their racial "stock." In *Mark Rutherford's Deliverance* (1885), William Hale White writes that "our civilization is nothing but a thin film or crust lying over a volcanic pit," and in *Fabian Essays* (1889), George Bernard Shaw contends that Britain is "in an advanced state of rottenness."[11] Much of the literary culture of the period expresses similar views. The aesthetic and decadent movements offer sinister analogies to Roman imperial decline and fall, while realistic novelists—George Gissing and Thomas Hardy, for instance—paint gloomy pictures of contemporary society and "the ache of modernism" (some of Gissing's pictures are explicitly anti-imperialist). Apocalyptic themes and images are characteristic of imperial Gothic, in which, despite the consciously pro-Empire values of many authors, the feeling emerges that "we are those upon whom the ends of the world are come."[12]

The three principal themes of imperial Gothic are individual regression or going native; an invasion of civilization by the forces of barbarism or demonism; and the diminution of opportunities for adventure and heroism in the modern world. In the romances of Stevenson, Haggard, Kipling, Doyle, Bram Stoker, and John Buchan the supernatural or paranormal, usually symptomatic of individual regression, often manifests itself in imperial settings. Noting that Anglo-Indian fiction frequently deals with "inexplicable curses, demonic possession, and ghostly visitations," Lewis Wurgaft cites Kipling's "Phantom Rickshaw" as typical, and countless such tales were set in Burma, Egypt, Nigeria, and other parts of the Empire as well.[13] In Edgar Wallace's *Sanders of the River* (1909), for example, the commissioner of a West African territory out-savages the savages, partly through police brutality but partly also through his knowledge of witchcraft. Says the narrator: "You can no more explain many happenings which are the merest commonplace in [Africa] than you can explain the miracle of faith or the wonder of telepathy."[14]

In numerous late Victorian and Edwardian stories, moreover, occult phenomena follow characters from imperial settings home to Britain. In Doyle's "The Brown Hand" (1899), an Anglo-Indian doctor is haunted after his return to England by the ghost of an Afghan whose hand he had amputated. In "The Ring of Thoth" (1890) and "Lot No. 249" (1892), Egyptian mummies come to life in the Louvre and in the rooms of an Oxford student.[15] In all three stories, western science discovers or triggers supernatural effects associated with the "mysterious Orient." My favorite story of this type is H. G. Wells's "The Truth about Pyecraft," in which an obese Londoner takes an Indian recipe for "loss of weight" but instead of slimming down, begins levitating. The problem caused by oriental magic is then solved by western technology: lead underwear, which allows the balloonlike Mr. Pyecraft to live almost normally, feet on the ground.

The causes of the upsurge in romance writing toward the end of the century are numerous, complex, and often the same as those of the upsurge of occultism. Thus the new romanticism in fiction is frequently explained by its advocates—Stevenson, Haggard, Lang, and others—as a reaction against scientific materialism as embodied in "realistic" or "naturalistic" narratives. The most enthusiastic defender of the new fashion for romances was Andrew Lang, who thought the realism of George Eliot and Henry James intellectually superior but also that the romances of Stevenson and Haggard tapped universal, deep-rooted, "primitive" aspects of human nature which the realists could not approach. "Fiction is a shield with two sides, the silver and the golden: the study of manners and of character, on one hand; on the other, the description of adventure, the delight of romantic narrative."[16] Although he sees a place for both kinds of fiction, Lang has little patience with, for example, Dostoevsky's gloomy honesty: "I, for one, admire M. Dostoieffsky so much . . . that I pay him the supreme tribute of never reading him at all" (685). Lang prefers literature of a middle-brow sort, on a level with his own critical journalism, or, farther down the scale of cultural value, he prefers adventure stories written for boys: "'Treasure Island' and 'Kidnapped' are boys' books written by an author of whose genius, for narrative, for delineation of character, for style, I hardly care to speak, lest enthusiasm should seem to border on fanaticism" (690). Lang feels that Haggard is by no means so sophisticated a writer as Stevenson, but this is almost an advantage: the less sophisticated or the more boyish, the better.

All the same, Lang believes, realism in fiction should coexist with romanticism just as the rational, conscious side of human nature coexists with the unconscious. Lang can appreciate realistic novels intellectually, but "the natural man within me, the survival of some blue-painted Briton or of some gipsy," is "equally pleased with a *true* Zulu love story" (689). He therefore declares that "the advantage of our mixed condition, civilized at top with the old barbarian under our clothes, is just this, that we can enjoy all sorts of things" (690). Romances may be unsophisticated affairs, but because they appeal to the barbarian buried self of the reader, they are more fundamental, more honest, more natural than realism. In Lang's criticism, romances are "'savage survivals,' but so is the whole of the poetic way of regarding Nature" (690).

An anthropologist of sorts, Lang acquired his theory of savage survivals from his mentor Edward Burnett Tylor, who contends that occultism and spiritualism—indeed, all forms of superstition (and therefore, implicitly, of religion)—belong to "the philosophy of savages." Modern occultism, according to Tylor, is "a direct revival from the regions of savage philosophy and peasant folk-lore," a reversion to "primitive culture."[17] At the same time Tylor associates poetry with the mythology of primitive peoples: "The mental condition of the lower races is the key to poetry, nor is it a small portion of the poetic realm which these definitions cover" (2:533). Literary activity in general thus appears to be a throwback to prerational states of mind and society. Similarly, Arthur Machen, author of numerous Gothic horror stories from the 1890s onward, defines literature as "the endeavour of every age to return to the first age, to an age, if you like, of savages."[18]

Robert Louis Stevenson, who echoes Lang's defenses of romances as against novels, discovered sources of "primitive" poetic energy in his own psyche, most notably through the nightmare that yielded *Dr. Jekyll and Mr. Hyde*. Stevenson entertained ambivalent feelings toward the popularity of that "Gothic gnome" or "crawler," in part because *any* popular appeal seemed irrational or vaguely barbaric to him. Although not overtly about imperial matters, *Jekyll and Hyde*, perhaps even more than *Treasure Island* and *Kidnapped*, served as a model for later writers of imperial Gothic fantasies. Because "within the Gothic we can find a very intense, if displaced, engagement with political and social problems," it is possible, as David Punter argues, to read *Jekyll and Hyde* as itself an example of imperial Gothic: "It is strongly suggested [by Stevenson] that Hyde's behaviour is an urban version of 'going native.' The particular difficulties encountered by English imperialism in its decline were conditioned by the nature of the supremacy which had been asserted: not a simple racial supremacy, but one constantly seen as founded on moral superiority. If an empire based on a morality declines, what are the implications . . .? It is precisely Jekyll's 'high views' which produce morbidity in his *alter ego*."[19] Jekyll's alchemy releases the apelike barbarian—the savage or natural man—who lives beneath the civilized skin. Not only is this the general fantasy of going native in imperial Gothic, but Hyde—murderous, primitive, apelike—fits the Victorian stereotype of the Irish hooligan, and his dastardly murder of Sir Danvers Carew resembles some of the "Fenian outrages" of the early 1880s.[20]

Imperial Gothic is related to several other forms of romance writing which flourished between 1880 and 1914. Judith Wilt has argued for the existence of subterranean links between late Victorian imperialism, the resurrection of Gothic romance formulas, and the conversion of Gothic into science fiction. "In or around December, 1897," she writes, "Victorian gothic changed—into Victorian science fiction. The occasion was . . . Wells's *War of the Worlds*, which followed by only a few months Bram Stoker's . . . *Dracula*."[21] A similar connection is evident between imperial Gothic and the romance fictions of the decadent movement, as in Oscar Wilde's *Picture of Dorian Gray*, which traces an atavistic descent into criminal self-indulgence as mirrored by a changing portrait. Both Stoker's and Wells's romances can be read, moreover, as fanciful versions of yet another popular literary form, invasion-scare stories, in which the outward movement of imperialist adventure is reversed, a pattern fore-shadowed by the returned convict theme in Botany Bay eclogues. *Dracula* itself is an individual invasion or demonic possession fantasy with political implications. Not only is Stoker's bloodthirsty Count the "final aristocrat," he is also the last of a "conquering race," as Dracula explains to Jonathan Harker:

> We Szekelys have a right to be proud, for in our veins flows the blood of many brave races who fought as the lion fights, for lordship. Here, in the whirlpool of European races, the Ugric tribe bore down from Iceland the fighting spirit which Thor and Wodin gave them, which their Berserkers displayed to such fell intent on the seaboards of Europe, aye, and of Asia and Africa, too, till the peoples thought that the were-wolves themselves had come. Here, too, when they came, they found the Huns, whose warlike fury had swept the earth like a living flame, till the dying peoples held that in their veins ran the blood of those old witches, who, expelled from Scythia, had mated with the devils in the desert. Fool, fools! What devil or what witch was ever so great as Attila, whose blood is in these veins? . . . Is it a wonder that we were a conquering race?[22]

The whirlpool of the Count's own ideas, confounding racism with the mixing of races, pride in pure blood with blood-sucking cannibalism, and aristocratic descent with witchcraft and barbarism, reads like a grim parody of the "conquering race" rhetoric in much imperialist writing, a premonition of fascism. In common with several other Gothic invaders in late Victorian fiction, moreover, Dracula threatens to create a demonic empire of the dead from the living British Empire. "This was the being I was helping to transfer to London," says Jonathan Harker, "where, perhaps for centuries to come, he might, amongst its teeming millions, satiate his lust for blood, and create a new and ever widening circle of semi-demons to batten on the helpless" (67).

A similar demonic invasion is threatened in Haggard's *She*: Ayesha plans to usurp the British throne from Queen Victoria, though fortunately her second dousing in the flames of immortality kills her before she can leave the Caves of Kôr for London.[23] Horace Holly, the principal narrator of Haggard's romance, explains the situation: "Evidently the terrible *She* had determined to go to England, and it made me shudder to think what would be the result of her arrival. . . . In the end, I had little doubt, she would assume absolute rule over the British dominions, and probably over the whole earth, and, though I was sure that she would speedily make ours the most glorious and prosperous empire that the world has ever seen, it must be at the cost of a terrible sacrifice of life."[24] Though Haggard resurrects Ayesha in later romances, his archetype of feminine domination grows tamer and never travels to Britain. Several critics have seen in both *She* and *Dracula* the threat of the New Woman to Victorian patriarchy, and Queen Tera, the mummy who comes to life in Stoker's *Jewel of the Seven Stars* (1903), represents the same threat. Norman Etherington calls Ayesha "a Diana in jack-boots who preaches materialism in philosophy and fascism in politics" (47), while Nina Auerbach notes that Ayesha's dream of eternal love and immortality is fused with the nightmare of universal empire. In Ayesha's case, "love does not tranquilize womanhood into domestic confinement, but fuels her latent powers into political life."[25] Although the New Woman is one of the threats underlying the demonism of Ayesha and also of Dracula and his female victims, however, Haggard's and Stoker's apocalyptic fears are comprehensive: the demons who threaten to subvert the Empire and invade Britain are of both sexes and come in many guises.

Often Wells's translations of Gothic conventions into quasi-scientific ones also suggest demonic subversions of the Empire or—what amounts to the same thing in late Victorian and Edwardian writing—of civilization. "It occurred to me that instead of the usual interview with the devil or a magician, an ingenious use of scientific patter might with advantage be substituted," Wells writes of his "scientific romances." "I simply brought the fetish stuff up to date, and made it as near actual theory as possible."[26] *The War of the Worlds* is the classic science fiction, invasion-from-outer-space fantasy, though Wells wrote many related stories—"The Empire of the Ants," for example, in which superintelligent, poisonous ants from the Amazon Basin threaten to overwhelm first British Guiana and then the entire world, founding their insect empire upon the ruins of human ones.

Numerous invasion fantasies were written between 1880 and 1914 without Gothic overtones. The ur-text is Sir George Chesney's *The Battle of Dorking*, which first appeared in *Blackwood's Magazine* in 1871. In the bibliography to *Voices Prophesying War*, I. F. Clarke lists dozens of "imaginary war" novels published between 1871 and 1914, many of them following an invasion-of-Britain pattern. Among them are T. A. Guthrie's *The Seizure of the Channel Tunnel* (1882), H. F. Lester's *The Taking of Dover* (1888), and the anonymous *The Sack of London in the Great French War of* 1901 (1901). Several novels also appeared, both in Britain and elsewhere, with titles along the lines of *Decline and Fall of the British Empire*, as well as invasion-of-India stories.[27] Clearly this was not the fiction of a generation of writers confident about the future of Britain or its Empire. The essence of the genre is captured in P G. Wodehouse's 1909 parody *The Swoop . . . A Tale of the Great Invasion*, in which Britain is overwhelmed by simultaneous onslaughts of Germans, Russians, Chinese, Young Turks, the Swiss Navy, Moroccan brigands, cannibals in war canoes, the Prince of Monaco, and the Mad Mullah, until it is saved by a patriotic Boy Scout named Clarence Chugwater. The only question left to the reader's imagination is why these various forces of barbarism should want to invade so decrepit a country.[28]

Invasion-scare stories often intersect with spy stories. David Stafford gives 1893 as the date of "the birth of the British spy novel," with publication of William Le Queux's *The Great War in England in* 1897, and the subgenre includes many stories, among them Childers's *Riddle of the Sands*, that contain elements of imperial Gothic.[29] Spy stories can be as upbeat as Kipling's *Kim*, full of an evident delight in playing the Great Game in Asia, with little to fear from the bungling French and Russian agents whom Kim helps to foil, or as fear-ridden as Buchan's *Thirty-Nine Steps*, characterized by a breathless paranoia as the hero flees his would-be assassins through a British countryside where no one is to be trusted. Even *Kim*, however, fits Stafford's general description of spy fiction: "The world presented by these novels is a . . . treacherous one in which Britain is the target of the envy, hostility, and malevolence of the other European powers" (497–98).

[. . .]

Notes

1 Bithia M. Croker, *The Old Cantonment; with Other Stories of India and Elsewhere* (London: Methuen, 1905), 48–63.

2 See Brooks Wright, *Interpreter of Buddhism to the West: Sir Edwin Arnold* (New York: Bookman Associates, 1957).

3 A brief account of the development of late-Victorian romanticism in conjunction with occultism appears in Tom Gibbons, *Rooms in the Darwin Hotel: Studies in English Literary Criticism and Ideas, 1880–1920* (Nedlands: University of Western Australia Press, 1973), 1–24. See also Ruth Brandon, *The Spiritualists: The Passion for the Occult in the Nineteenth and Twentieth Centuries* (New York: Knopf, 1983); Janet Oppenheim, *The Other World: Spiritualism and Psychical Research in England, 1850–1914* (Cambridge: Cambridge University Press, 1985); and Frank M. Turner, *Between Science and Religion: The Reaction to Scientific Naturalism in Late Victorian England* (New Haven: Yale Univeristy Press, 1974).

4 Oppenheim, *Other World*, 160.

5 J. A. Cramb, *The Origins and Destiny of Imperial Britain* (New York: Dutton, 1900), 230.

6 Carroll V. Peterson, *John Davidson* (New York: Twayne, 1972), 82.

7 John Davidson, "St. George's Day," in *The Poems of John Davidson*, ed. Andrew Turnbull, 2 vols. (Edinburgh: Scottish Academic Press, 1973), 1:228.

8 Rudyard Kipling, "Recessional," in *Works*, 36 vols., Pocket Edition (London: Methuen, 1923), 34:186.

9 Jerome Hamilton Buckley, *William Ernest Henley: A Study in the "Counter-Decadence" of the 'Nineties* (Princeton: Princeton University Press, 1945), 134. See also John Lester, *Journey through Despair, 1880–1914: Transformations in British Literary Culture* (Princeton: Princeton University Press, 1968), 9: both the imperialism and the socialism of the turn of the century "became charged with an overplus of fervor which exalted each at times almost to religion."

10 Erskine Childers, *The Riddle of the Sands: A Record of Secret Service* (1903; New York: Dover, 1976), 15.

11 Both White and Shaw are quoted by Lester, *Journey through Despair*, 50n and 5.

12 Lester (*Journey through Despair*, 3) notes that this quotation from 1 Corinthians 10:11 "crops up recurrently in the literature of the time."

13 Lewis S. Wurgaft, *The Imperial Imagination: Magic and Myth in Kipling's India* (Middletown: Wesleyan University Press, 1983), 57.

14 Edgar Wallace, *Sanders of the River* (1909; Garden City, N.Y.: Doubleday, Doran, 1930), 277.

15 For these and other examples see *The Best Supernatural Tales of Arthur Conan Doyle*, ed. E. F. Bleiler (New York: Dover, 1979). An interesting variant is W. Somerset Maugham's *The Magician* (1908), based on the career of Aleister Crowley.

16 Andrew Lang, "Realism and Romance," *Contemporary Review* 52 (November 1887), 684. Page numbers are given parenthetically in the next two paragraphs of the text. See also Joseph Weintraub, "Andrew Lang: Critic of Romance," *English Literature in Transition* 18:1 (1975), 5–15.

17 Sir Edward Burnett Tylor, *Primitive Culture*, 2 vols. (1871; New York: Harper & Row, 1970), 1:155, 142.

18 Quoted by Wesley D. Sweetser, *Arthur Machen* (New York: Twayne, 1964), 116.

19 David Punter, *The Literature of Terror: A History of Gothic Fictions from 1765 to the Present Day* (London: Longman, 1980), 62, 241.

20 See Patrick Brantlinger and Richard Boyle, "The Education of Edward Hyde: Stevenson's 'Gothic Gnome' and the Mass Readership of Late-Victorian England," in *Jekyll and Hyde after 100 Years*, ed. William Veeder (Chicago: University of Chicago Press, 1987).

21 Judith Wilt, "The Imperial Mouth: Imperialism, the Gothic and Science Fiction," *Journal of Popular Culture* 14 (Spring 1981), 618–28.

22 Bram Stoker, *Dracula* (Harmondsworth: Penguin, 1979), 41. Punter (*Literature of Terror*, 257) calls Dracula "the final aristocrat."

23 See Norman Etherington, *Rider Haggard* (Boston: Twayne, 1984), 47.

24 H. Rider Haggard, *Three Adventure Novels: She, King Solomon's Mines, Allan Quatermain* (New York: Dover, 1951), 192–93.

25 Nina Auerbach, *Woman and the Demon: The Life of a Victorian Myth* (Cambridge: Harvard University Press, 1982), 37. See also Sandra M. Gilbert, "Rider Haggard's Heart of Darkness," *Partisan Review* 50 (1983), 444–53, and Carol A. Senf, "*Dracula:* Stoker's Response to the New Woman," *Victorian Studies* 26 (Autumn 1982), 33–49.

26 Quoted by Brian Aldiss, *Billion Year Spree: The True History of Science Fiction* (New York: Schocken, 1976), 8–9.

27 See I. F. Clarke, *Voices Prophesying War*, 1763–1984 (London: Oxford University Press, 1966), 227–39. See also Samuel Hynes, *The Edwardian Turn of Mind* (Princeton: Princeton University Press, 1968), 34–53.

28 P. G. Wodehouse, *The Swoop! and Other Stories*, ed. David A. Jasen (New York: Seabury, 1979).

29 See David A. T. Stafford, "Spies and Gentlemen: The Birth of the British Spy Novel, 1893–1914," *Victorian Studies* 24 (Summer 1981), 489–509.

40 Missionary men and Morant Bay 1859–1866

Catherine Hall

Anthony Trollope and Mr Secretary Underhill

In the metropole the figure of the African remained highly contested, and part of the work of the missionaries was to counter those representations which damaged their cause. They needed to maintain the support, both financial and otherwise, of missionary and abolitionist enthusiasts. The mid-nineteenth century saw a proliferation of ways of being English in relation to Africans. In 1857 Livingstone's immensely popular *Travels* was published, bringing the explorer and the African continent into the heart of the civilising vision.[1] There were intense debates and disagreements as to what place Africans under the tutelage of Englishmen should occupy, and what role Englishmen should take. But metropolitans were united by their distance from the backward time and archaic space of both Africa and the West Indies, their shared conviction that it was they who could bring the African or the West Indian negro into modern times.[2] The appearance in 1859 of Anthony Trollope's *The West Indies and the Spanish Main* was a damaging blow to the missionary cause, and the missionaries martialled their troops, in the figure of the secretary of the BMS, Edward Bean Underhill, to reply. These two books on the West Indies, by a popular novelist and a missionary stalwart, marked a new moment of discursive instability in representations of the negro.

Trollope was a very different kind of Englishman from the missionaries. In 1858 he was asked by his employers, the Post Office, to go and 'clean up' the Post Office system in the West Indies, for the colonial postal systems were mainly managed from 'home'.[3] Before he left, he arranged a contract with Chapman and Hall for a book about his journey, which he wrote while he was away. The book was published on his return and was an immediate success, going into a sixth edition by the following year, as well as being published in the USA. Trollope regarded it retrospectively 'as the best book that has come from my pen. It is short, and, I think I may venture to say, amusing, useful, and true.' This truth claim was important to Trollope, who wrote as he travelled, never making any notes or doing any preparation, aiming to reproduce 'that which the eye of the writer has seen and his ear heard', 'the exact truth as I saw it'.[4] Some readers in Britain may have believed what they read, but readers in the West Indies were less impressed by this claim to have truthfully represented their societies. 'Going a-Trolloping' passed into the Jamaican vernacular as a synonym for travelling commentators who knew not what they saw.[5]

[. . .]

In his mapping of particular parts of the empire, Trollope was always reflecting on the differences between 'them' and 'us'. 'I wish to write of men and their manners and welfare, rather than of rivers and boundaries,' he remarked.[6] His journey was to do with the mapping of peoples, his ethnographic mission to describe difference. The observations, supposedly based on an innocent eye, provided a basis from which to later generalise about race, nation and empire.[7] While Darwin painstakingly constructed his theory of evolution from his discoveries on the voyage of the *Beagle*, Trollope engaged in a different kind of cartography, one which filled the sites of empire with men and women whom he characterised as in different stages of development: stages of development which provided the justification for different forms of colonial rule. His curiosity, and his desire to pass on the information he acquired quickly, meant that he wrote down what he saw without reflecting deeply on the judgements which he made. His writing was a craft and a livelihood to him, and he set himself a daily number of words to complete.[8] His mapping of empire was presented as descriptive, with no pretence at intellectual or philosophical depth. His contemporary, Frederick Harrison, a man with more liberal sympathies, described Trollope retrospectively as the 'photographer' of mid-Victorian England.[9] But, like all photographers and reporters, whether in London, provincial Ireland or the West Indies, he framed his pictures and constructed his narratives, working with established discourses but hoping to reinflect meanings. By visiting new sites, he aimed for fresh insights, into England and its empire. In England his ethnographic eye rested little on the poor, for whom, unlike Dickens, he had little interest or sympathy. Class and gender differences were carefully delineated inside a community which tended to exclude absolute others, the rich Jewish financier the closest thing to 'a race apart'. In the colonies he was fascinated by race, by the 'natural' differences associated with different bodies, differences which he explained, as his friend Merivale did, in terms of a hierarchical discourse. Such a discourse, with its assumptions of the backwardness of other peoples and their distance from the heartlands of civilisation, underpinned the authority of Englishness. It was the space between Ireland and England, between the West Indies and England, between the domestic and the colonial, which confirmed the right of Anglo-Saxons to rule.

Trollope's first encounter with race as difference was in Ireland, where he trained himself in careful description, learning the imaginative capacity to engage with other societies and to capture something of that otherness for consumption 'at home'. Travel writing, as Gikandi argues, is a referential gesture that brings the unknown back to the known, the strange back to the familiar.[10] Trollope's Irish novels aimed to explain Ireland to the English.[11] His particular strength in his later travel writing was his ability to provide colonial knowledge in a new register, one which entertained as well as informed. His journey to the West Indies took place in 1858, the year after the 'Indian Mutiny'. Throughout 1857 and 1858 the daily press had been centrally preoccupied with reports from India. When *The West Indies* appeared in 1858, it both reflected and was constitutive of the hardening in racial thinking which characterised the times. Trollope's ironic, gossipy, anecdotal account of the relations between races made clear to his readers that black people needed 'civilising', but reminded them that violence and force were not always the order of the day. Its style of writing belied its harsh diet of black racial inequality. India provided one model of colonial relations, the West Indies another.

The book was speedily taken up by *The Times*, a fact which Trollope himself saw as crucial to its success.[12] Always a friend to the plantocracy, and managed at this time by the son of a West Indian planter,[13] the newspaper published two long pieces based on *The West Indies*, welcoming the book with open arms. For years the paper's editorial policy had been deeply hostile to the anti-slavery lobby. Trollope's book was a valuable addition to its armoury. The real value of Trollope, the paper argued, was that he was not afraid to recognise the differences between the races and to insist, therefore, on giving the planter a chance. 'Negroes, coolies and planters; what is the position of each', it asked, 'and what are the rights of each?'

Floods of pathetic eloquence and long years of Parliamentary struggling have taught us to imagine that the world was made for Sambo, and that the sole use of sugar is to sweeten Sambo's existence. The negro is, no doubt, a very amusing and a very amiable fellow, and we ought to wish him well; but he is also a lazy animal, without any foresight, and therefore requiring to be led and compelled. We must not judge him by ourselves.

Trollope's illustrations of negro character, the paper suggested, demonstrated that 'there is little self-sustaining power and no sense of the future in the negro – facts that are all important in determining the question of labour in the West Indies'.[14] New immigration was essential. On the same day, it published an editorial on the white colonies of settlement which argued that the public should be more aware of the potential of the new territories and the special connection between colonisation and the Anglo-Saxon race – sentiments with which Trollope would have heartily agreed.[15]

Trollope's account of the West Indies focused on Jamaica, and his imagined interlocutor was an abolitionist. His first shock in encountering the Caribbean islands was the fact of blackness. 'The negro population', he noted, 'is of course the most striking feature of the West Indies,' and it was the inadequacies of the negro which were largely responsible for the unfortunate state of the island.[16] 'Nothing was so melancholy' as Jamaica was to him, a country 'in its decadence', a truly melancholy sight.[17] The plentiful supplies of food in that particular habitat, combined with the interference of philanthropists who had protected the negroes from low wages, had meant that labour, the great civiliser, could not get to work on its subjects. It was the absence of the need to labour as he saw it – and in this he followed Carlyle – that had provoked disaster in Jamaica. Negroes 'have no care for tomorrow, but they delight in being gaudy for today . . . they laugh and sing and sleep through life', all of which was anathema to Trollope. 'He *is* a man,' he wrote, playing directly on anti-slavery rhetoric, 'and, if you will a brother; but he is the very idlest brother.' 'God has created men of inferior and superior race', and slavery had meant a forced encounter for black people with a superior race.

This inevitably meant progress. The emancipated creole Africans were, to him, 'a servile people in a foreign land'; they had 'no idea of country and no pride of race'. Idle, unambitious and sensual, the West Indian negro 'has made no approach to the civilisation of his white fellow creature, whom he imitates as a monkey does a man'. Their religion was ritualistic, not truly reaching their minds. Their love of the Bible he compared to a Roman Catholic girl who 'loves the doll of a Madonna which she dresses with muslin and ribbons'. Their familial attachments he compared with those of a dog. If left to themselves, West Indian negroes would slip back into barbarism. Emancipation for them had meant freedom from work, rather than the desire for progress and property.[18] The English had expected too much from emancipation. The only way to remedy this was to force black people to work, a familiar refrain of the plantocracy and its supporters.[19] Yet it was their separation from barbarism, and from Africa, which made progress possible: 'There is no race which has more strongly developed its own physical aptitudes and inaptitudes, its own habits, its own tastes, and its own faults.'[20] Here creolised Africans were granted cultural patterns: 'In their liminality, these subjects are close to white civilisation, but not close enough.'[21]

If the refusal of emancipated black people to work was one major problem in Jamaica, the other was the nature of the white population. The planters had borne emancipation with 'manly courage', but the ending of protection and the difficulties over immigration had defeated them. They had become 'sore, and vituperative and unconvinced'. The planter felt that he had been ill used by the mother country; he had become 'a bore and a nuisance', and 'in his heart of hearts there dwells a feeling that after all slavery was not so vile an institution'.[22] Jamaican planters had many of the characteristics of English gentlemen, and always talked about England as 'home'. They cared about their pedigrees, their country houses, their sport, their parishes and their local politics. Staying on a sugar estate on the west of the island, Trollope found that his host's occupations 'were exactly those of a country gentleman in England'. He fished and went shooting, looked after his estate, acted as a magistrate, cared a lot about his dinner and seemed to have no interest in sugar.[23] He found such men good company, yet they were poor mimics of real English gentlemen: their towns were dirty and dismal; their roads appalling and bridges broken; their coffee plantations had gone back to bush, and their sugar estates were sold for a song; they had no time for industry, no faith in their legislature, and would have preferred Jamaica to be entirely ruled from home. Nothing could be farther from Trollope's imagined ordered, deferential and paternalistic England, that England of the Barsetshire chronicles.

Trollope did not despair, however, of the future of the West Indian islands. The best days of Jamaica were over, and white people no longer wanted to go there; but Guiana, organised as a mild despotism, was doing relatively well. Immigration to Guiana had gone ahead, and the presence of 'coolies' and 'Chinamen', both groups of whom were prepared to work, made for a more prosperous picture. Philanthropic attempts to prevent immigration should be abandoned. The hope in Jamaica, as he saw it, lay with the coloured class, whom he thought were going to be the 'ascendant race'. This he knew would deeply offend his white friends in Jamaica, for 'both the white man and the black man dislike their coloured neighbours'. Jamaican whites were fearful of the ways in which they were being displaced, but there were 15,000 of them to 70,000 coloured people. 'The coloured men of Jamaica cannot be despised much longer,' he concluded.[24] The British should let Jamaica go; they had left their sign in blood. Englishmen, he argued, had needed the wild and savage energy of their vandal forefathers; similarly, the mix in the coloured race would allow them to combine negro strength with European intellect, and this mixed with the Asian willingness to work. 'The white man has been there, and has left his mark,' he argued. There was still a little more civilising to do in terms of the spreading of commerce and education, for coloured men still could not speak with 'natural English pronunciation'; but enough white blood had entered the national bloodstream to ensure survival. Coloured women, he argued, had not yet abandoned the legacy of concubinage and illegitimate sexuality, and this was a serious sign of decadence, but the men were leading the way. 'Providence has sent white men and black men to these regions in order that from them may spring a race fitted by intellect for civilization; and fitted also by physical organization for tropical labour.'[25] Trollope believed Jamaica had a future: one that was made possible by the mixing of races. This liberal view of 'miscegenation' may have been influenced by his brother Tom's marriage to a woman whose father was the son of an Indian officer and a high-caste Brahmin. She had Scottish, Jewish and Indian blood.[26] Racial purity might be a moral imperative for the likes of Knox, but in Jamaica Trollope could see that coloured men could not simply be classified as degenerate. They were shopkeepers, parliamentarians, public servants, lawyers and doctors. Jamaican white men were unnecessarily jealous of them: the future was in their keeping.[27]

To be independent was, for Trollope, the essence of white manhood, and the best kind of independence was that which was earned. Like Carlyle, he had a high regard for labour, and a workmanlike attitude to his own writing. 'Work with fair wages has done infinitely more to civilise, and even to christianise, the so-called savage races than has the energy of missionaries,' he argued.[28] In his colonial discourse, labour was one civiliser; family was the other. Like most middle-class men of the mid-Victorian period, he believed that familial and domestic order were at the heart of social order. A good society was one in which the classes, the races and the sexes knew their place and stayed in it. As Trollope travelled the white settler colonies in the years to come, he was to argue that if these colonies were to become well established, they needed a clear gender order with bread-winning husband and father and domesticated wife and mother. The character of frontier societies meant that aspects of North America and Australia fitted very well with this notion of the idealised family, secure in its homestead. Jamaica, on the other hand, with its troubling combination of white settlement and a black majority population, demonstrated through its sexual incontinence its fundamentally decadent character. It might have a future, but it could never regenerate the race in the way that he came to believe the white settler colonies could.

As a male writer of fiction, Trollope's manhood was constantly at risk on the feminised site of the novel, particularly since so much of his writing was focused on romance and domestic life. In his travel writing that interest in manners, in dress and in emotionality could be offset with a commentary on economic and political life – of a sort which women were not supposed, in his view, to be able to make. Women who ventured out of their sphere were troubling to Trollope, perhaps partly because of his own vulnerability as a writer, and partly because of his complicated and rivalrous relation with his writing mother. The split which Victoria Glendinning points to in her biography of him, between his desire for a dutiful and ever present wife and the excitement and challenge of the independent and resourceful mother who had abandoned him, was perhaps re-enacted in his hostile response to public forms of feminism.[29] He was excited by the prospect of independent women, but castigated them for not knowing their place. But his assertion of the necessity of the 'supremacy of man over woman' was disrupted by his fascination with feminism and his preoccupation in his novels of the 1860s with the newly public presence and claims of women.[30]

His encounter with a number of white, coloured and black West Indian women on his first long journey on his own was exciting. He enjoyed flirting, though he was shocked by the extent to which white creole women in the West Indies engaged in it, and the female creole characters in his fiction are characterised as rampant flirts.[31] The period before marriage, as he saw it, was a time when women could exercise their power – a period which he explored extensively in his novels about English women. But that power must be properly contained: by marriage and men. As the Jamaican beauty who comes to live in England puts it in *Ralph the Heir*, 'I do love the idea of an English home, where things are neat and nice.'[32] Any upsetting of this gender order was deeply troubling. Black women, who do not appear in his fiction, were both exciting and disturbing to him. His first encounter with a black West Indian woman was on the island of St Thomas.

> [A]s I put my foot on the tropical soil for the first time, a lady handed me a rose, saying, 'That's for love, dear'. I took it, and said that it should be for love. She was beautifully, nay, elegantly dressed. Her broad-brimmed hat was as graceful as are those of Ryde or Brighton. The well-starched skirts of her muslin dress gave to her upright figure that look of easily compressible bulk, which, let 'Punch' do what it will, has become so sightly to our eyes. Pink gloves were on her hands. . . . What was it to me that she was as black as my boot, or that she had come to look after the ship's washing?[33]

But her blackness was enticing, 'let "Punch" do what it will', and her hands, inside those gloves, a further sign of transgression. Her beautiful elegant dress disrupted the stereotype of the African woman and reminded the reader of the illicit sexuality on which that image of the large buttocks, the sign of physicality, rested.[34]

A vignette which *The Times* chose to reproduce in full in its feature caught much of the ambivalence of Trollope's representations of 'black beauties'. 'One Sunday evening', his story began,

> far away in the country, as I was riding with a gentleman, the proprietor of the estate around us, I saw a young girl walking home from church. She was arrayed from head to foot in virgin white. Her gloves were on, and her parasol was up. Her hat also was white, and so was the lace, and so were the bugles which adorned it. She walked with a stately dignity that was worthy of such a costume, and worthy also of higher grandeur; for behind her walked an attendant nymph, carrying the beauty's prayer-book on her head. . . . When we came up to her, she turned towards us and curtsied. She curtsied, for she recognized her 'massa'; but she curtsied with great dignity, for she recognized also her own finery. The girl behind with the prayer-book made the ordinary obeisance. . . . 'Who on earth is that princess?' said I. 'They are two sisters who both work at my mill', said my friend. 'Next Sunday they will change places. Polly will have the parasol and the hat, and Jenny will carry the prayer-book on her head behind her.'[35]

Readers were invited to chuckle over these young black women dressed up in borrowed finery, playing at princesses. These were mill girls, not the troubling Lancashire mill girls who dominated the streets of Northern towns with their clogs and their claims for independence, but black mill girls, dressed all in white and pretending to be ladies. 'This little incident is very characteristic of the negro', pontificated *The Times*, 'who is void of self-reliance and is the creature of circumstances . . . it is evident that he [*sic*] is scarcely fitted to take care of himself.'[36]

Trollope's ambivalence regarding the mimicry which he observed both among creolised Africans and planters, both aspiring and failing in their different ways to be English, marked the distance between the domestic and the colonial, that distance which legitimated colonial rule. Yet these mimics were attractive too: the planters genial and hospitable, the black women sexually provocative and inviting. But the confident masculinity he found among these colonial gentlemen, at home with the gun, the rod, the port and the beef, assuming that negroes were born to be servants, letting nothing disturb the even tenor of their lives, was appealing rather than admirable, for it was independence which Trollope admired in men. West Indian planters were part of a dying world. And the women were to be admired and caricatured at one and the same time: confined within their eroticised black bodies.

[. . .]

Notes

1 David Livingstone, *Missionary Travels and Researches in South Africa* (John Murray, London, 1857); see also Felix Driver, *Geography Militant. Cultures of Empire and Exploitation* (Blackwell, Oxford, 2001).

2 Johannes Fabian, *Time and the Other. How Anthropology Makes its Object* (Columbia University Press, New York, 1983).

3 Anthony Trollope, *Autobiography*, 2 vols (William Blackwood and Sons, London, 1883), vol. 1, p. 171.

4 Ibid., pp. 172–4.

5 [Sydney S.] Olivier, *Myth of Governor Eyre*, [(Leonard and Virginia Woolf, London, 1933)], pp. 41–4.

6 Anthony Trollope, *Australia and New Zealand*, 2 vols (Chapman and Hall, London, 1873), vol. 1, p. 29.

7 I have found [Simon] Gikandi's discussion of Trollope in *Maps of Englishness*[*: Writing Identity in the Culture of Colonialism* (Columbia University Press, New York, 1996], pp. 91–106 very helpful.

8 Trollope, *Autobiography*, vol. 2, pp. 103–4.

9 Frederick Harrison, *Studies in Early Victorian Literature* (Chapman and Hall, London, 1895), p. 208.

10 Gikandi, *Maps of Englishness*, esp. pp. 87–90.

11 *The Macdermots of Ballycloran*, for example, his first novel, attempted to understand the sources of violence in Irish society, particularly the Ribbonmen, and communicate that to an English audience.

12 Trollope, *Autobiography*, vol. 1, p. 175; ironically, Trollope was preoccupied in his early novels with the tyrannical power of the modern newspaper. See, e.g., Trollope, *The Warden*, 1st edn 1855 (Robert Hayes, London, 1925).

13 Richard Mullen, *Anthony Trollope. A Victorian in his World* (Duckworth, London, 1990), p. 341.

14 *The Times*, 6 Jan. 1860.

15 Ibid.

16 [Anthony] Trollope, *West Indies* [*and the Spanish Main* (Chapman and Hall, London, 1859)], p. 55.

17 Anthony Trollope, 'Miss Sarah Jack, of Spanish Town, Jamaica', 1st edn 1860, repr. in Trollope, *The Complete Short Stories in Five Volumes*, vol. 3: *Tourists and Colonials* (Trollope Society, London, n.d.), p. 1.

18 Trollope, *West Indies*, pp. 56, 58, 60, 62.

19 Ibid., pp. 59–60, 62, 65.

20 Ibid., p. 55.

21 Gikandi, *Maps of Englishness*, p. 107.

22 Trollope, *West Indies*, pp. 92–3.

23 Ibid., p. 40.

24 Ibid., pp. 74, 80.

25 Ibid., pp. 64, 75, 81, 84.

26 [Victoria] Glendinning, *Anthony Trollope* [(Hutchison, London, 1992)], p. 168.

27 Trollope, *West Indies*, p. 80.

28 [Anthony] Trollope, *Australia and New Zealand*, [2 vols. (Chapman and Hall, London, 1873)] vol. 1, pp. 118, 133.

29 Glendinning, *Anthony Trollope*, pp. 147–9.

30 See particularly Lady Laura in Anthony Trollope, *Phineas Finn. The Irish Member*, 1st edn 1867 (Oxford University Press, Oxford, 1992).

31 Anthony Trollope, *Ralph the Heir*, 1st edn 1871 (Penguin, Harmondsworth, 1993); *idem*, 'Miss Sarah Jack'.

32 Trollope, *Ralph the Heir*, p. 53.

33 Trollope, *West Indies*, p. 8.

34 Sander Gilman, 'Black Bodies, White Bodies. Towards an Iconography of Female Sexuality in Late Nineteenth Century Art, Medicine and Literature', in James Donald and Ali Rattansi (eds), *'Race', Culture and Difference* (Sage, London, 1992), pp. 171–97.

35 Trollope, *West Indies*, pp. 69–70.

36 *The Times*, 6 Jan. 1860.

41 Fantasy and ideology

John Kucich

[. . .]

Masochism is often regarded as a site of social and cultural intersections. But in late-nine-teenth-century British colonial fiction, it focused one particular conjunction more than any other: the relationship between imperial politics and social class. This relationship has lately been an unfashionable topic for scholarly analysis, despite the intense scrutiny being applied to nearly every other aspect of British colonialism and some noteworthy protests about the imbalance. David Cannadine, for example, recently claimed that the "British Empire has been extensively studied as a complex *racial* hierarchy (and also as a less complex *gender* hierarchy); but it has received far less attention as an equally complex *social* hierarchy or, indeed, as a social organism, or construct, of any kind."[1] Ann Stoler has registered a similar complaint, while emphasizing the interdependence of these categories: "We know more than ever about the legitimating rhetoric of European civility and its gendered construals, but less about the class tensions that competing notions of 'civility' engendered. We are just begin-ning to identify how bourgeois sensibilities have been coded by race and, in turn, how finer scales measuring cultural competency and 'suitability' often replaced explicit racial criteria to define access to privilege in imperial ventures."[2] Many cultural critics share Stoler's assump-tions about the mediated nature of colonial identities. In Anne McClintock's much quoted formulation from *Imperial Leather* (1995): "no social category exists in privileged isolation; each comes into being in social relation to other categories, if in uneven and contradictory ways."[3] But methodologically sophisticated imperial studies have persistently marginalized social class or have falsely stabilized it in relation to fluid hybridizations of gender, race, sexual orientation, and other forms of social classification. The former is evident in the subti-tle of McClintock's book, for example (*Race, Gender and Sexuality in the Colonial Contest*).

Analyzing representations of masochism can help to rectify this imbalance. Although mas-ochism is not usually associated with social class, images of colonial masochism tended to bear with special weight on problems of status hierarchy, no matter how much they were also articulated upon other forms of social identity. These strong correlations between masochism and social class are not the explanatory key to colonial experience, nor can they be studied in "privileged isolation." But they do provide a reminder that class was a more important and a more complicated aspect of colonial life than recent scholarship has recognized. They can also demonstrate that ideologies of social class were intertwined with imperial self-consciousness in immensely variable ways.

The principal contention of this book is that figurations of masochism in British colonial fiction constituted a psychosocial language, in which problems of social class were addressed through the politics of imperialism and vice versa. I am not arguing that masochism had an inherent class or imperial politics. Neither would I wish to claim that social or imperial identity can be understood through collective psychology, masochistic or otherwise. My argument is simply that elements of masochistic fantasy resonated powerfully with both imperial and class discourses in late-nineteenth-century Britain. This discursive resonance presented writers of fiction with an extraordinary opportunity to refashion both imperial and class subjectivities by manipulating the complex intersections between them that masochistic fantasy helped to forge. In this sense, I am arguing that masochism played a vital role in the shaping and reshaping of social identity at the imperial periphery, which had important consequences in domestic British culture as well. I am also arguing that imperial and class ideologies in nineteenth-century Britain exploited a common and very powerful form of affective organization.

[. . .]

Masochism in context

Although we are not used to scrutinizing instances of cherished pain in British imperial iconography very deeply, the glorification of suffering was an enormously important theme well before Victorian evangelicalism tried to Christianize every aspect of the imperial project. British imperialism may have fostered countless narratives of conquest, and it may have celebrated victorious heroes like Wellington, Clive, and Wolseley or great triumphs like Waterloo, Trafalgar, Plassey, and Red River. The arrogance of the British abroad was legendary, too, and often a source of perverse national pride. But British imperialism also generated a remarkable preoccupation with suffering, sacrifice, defeat, and melancholia. As Linda Colley has reminded us, one paradigm of British imperial narrative may well have been Crusoe. But another was Gulliver, a figure whose ordeals of enslavement and humiliation culminate in his subjection to an unquestionably superior race.[4] This subjection compels Gulliver to disavow the sense of legitimacy he had once vested in his nation and in himself, making melancholic abjection, in his case, a vehicle for self-transformation.

What is particularly striking about British imperial culture is how often it mythologized victimization and death as foundational events in the teleology of empire. There was, seemingly, a different crucifixion scene marking the historical gateway to each colonial theater: Captain Cook in the South Pacific, General Wolfe in Canada, General Gordon in the Sudan; or else there was mass martyrdom (the Black Hole massacre in India) or crucifixion averted (the popular tale of Captain John Smith and Pocahontas in America). When, in 1871, W.H.G. Kingston lionized Cook for "the founding of two nations of the Anglo-Saxon race," for example, he was echoing a long tradition of Cookiana that continued to sustain the cultural identities of Australia and New Zealand well into the twentieth century.[5] This foundational myth, like the others mentioned above, revolved around the sanctification implicit in the imperial martyr's suffering—a sanctification that allied imperial pain with redemption and with the beginning, rather than the end, of history. In short, sanctification transformed the pain and finality of death or defeat into pleasurable fantasies of ecstatic rebirth or resurrection. After Cook's death in 1779, poems by Helen Maria Williams, William Cowper, and Hannah More, along with a famous elegy by Anna Seward, all compared him to Christ and stressed his having been deified by the Hawaiians who killed him (an assertion later contested by British and American missionaries). One of the first important paintings of Cook's death, Philip James De Loutherbourg's *Apotheosis of Captain Cook* (1785), which was used as the backdrop for an immensely successful London pantomime and later published as an engraving, shows Cook being assumed into heaven by the figures of Britannia and Fame. Other influential paintings of the death scene by John Webber, John Cleveley, and Johann Zoffany represent Cook as an icon of emotional and spiritual transcendence—the only serene figure in a scene of chaotic violence.

Wolfe was similarly sanctified in the public imagination. A painting by Benjamin West, viewed by enthusiastic crowds when first exhibited in 1771, possesses, in Simon Schama's words, a "radiance illuminating the face of the martyr and bathing the grieving expressions of his brother officers in a reflection of impossible holiness."[6] The West painting is transparently modeled on Passion scenes, with an upraised British flag standing in for the cross. The Black Hole massacre, which took place in Calcutta in 1756 (helping in some measure to motivate Clive's successful campaign against the French at Plassey), was also transformed into a foundational myth in the second half of the nineteenth century by those who portrayed the victims as saintly martyrs. In 1902, ignoring warnings from the India Council in London against "parading our disaster," Lord Curzon lavishly restored the Black Hole monument in Calcutta and praised the "martyr band" in his dedicatory speech.[7] He defended his actions to the India Council on the grounds that "their death was practically the foundation stone of the British Empire in India."[8]

Many of these foundational scenes of martyrdom were military. The siege of Mafeking, the Mysore disaster, the catastrophic First Afghan War, Gordon's death at Khartoum—all figured in the national imagination as spectacles of military weakness or defeat that also inspired British resurgence. Many contemporary accounts of these military episodes, such as William Thomson's *Memoirs of the Late War in Asia* (1788) or Robert Sale's *A Journal of the Disasters in Afghanistan* (1843), are remarkable excursions into martyrology rather than documentary accounts. But the sanctification of the imperial sufferer was not simply a rallying point for military conquest. Imperial iconography is littered with nonmilitary martyrs as well: missionaries like John Williams and David Livingstone, for example, and explorers like Sir John Franklin, Mungo Park, and, of course, Cook. India was especially rich in civilian martyrs. These included Bishop Heber, whose death in 1826 was widely mourned in both India and Britain, as well as the many young scientists whose lives and work were tragically cut short by disease: William Griffith, Alexander Moon, William Kerr, John Champion, George Gardner, John Stocks, John Cathcart (to name only a few of the botanists).[9] These Keatsian deaths ensured that many a scientific text emerging from India was read as an implicit memorial to its prematurely deceased author. Celebrated instances of self-sacrifice such as these helped stiffen the ethos of martyrdom that underlay even the most ordinary colonial life. In Charlotte Bronte's *Jane Eyre* (1847), St. John Rivers sees in Jane "a soul that revelled in the flame and excitement of sacrifice," which he regards as the supreme qualification for a life—inevitably short—of unheralded colonial service.[10] With a more penitential spirit, Peter Jenkyns in Elizabeth Gaskell's *Cranford* (1853) expiates his youthful sins through the ennobling suffering of colonial service.

Of course, images of imperial martyrdom, self-sacrifice, or even self-abasement cannot be conflated with masochism. The images of cherished imperial suffering I am describing served a great many purposes. In part, they simply reflected the dangerous and often disastrous side of imperial enterprise. From the perspective of the empire at its height, narratives of conquest may have seemed like the most accurate descriptions of imperial history. But from the perspective of those who could not have anticipated future successes and who either knew of or had themselves experienced harrowing encounters with disease, captivity, enslavement, military defeat, dependence on nonwhites, or sadistic cruelties (whether at the hands of Europeans or non-Europeans), narratives of British suffering may have seemed more honest.

Mythologies of imperial suffering also have rather obvious propaganda value, as we know too well in our own time from the political exploitation of the events of 9/11. Indeed, most studies of British imperial pathos regard it simply as a means of legitimating aggression and inspiring vengeance. Mary Louise Pratt has also demonstrated how such images could serve a mythology of anticonquest, engendering the notion that British colonizers were beneficent innocents.[11] On a practical level, representations of imperial suffering were a means of raising money for the redemption of British captives held overseas or the funding of missionary organizations.

But among the many kinds of significance inhering in the iconography of imperial suffering (whatever the intentions of those who promoted it) was the inevitability of its being inhabited by masochistic fantasy. At the very least, the melancholic potentials of imperial suffering were widely indulged. David Arnold has pointed out, for instance, that nineteenth-century India was transformed into a morbid topography, dotted with immense marble funerary monuments commemorating victims of the high colonial mortality rate.[12] Travel writing about India by Emily Eden and James Dalhousie featured mournful, lengthy descriptions of these cemeteries and funeral monuments, a tradition sustained in some of Rudyard Kipling's early journalistic sketches. Similar monuments back home, which introduced exotic Indian place names to British churchyards, helped reinforce a melancholic view of colonial India that had a strong hold from at least the late eighteenth century onwards, as novels like *Jane Eyre*, *Cranford*, or Flora Annie Steel's popular success *On the Face of the Waters* (1896) make abundantly clear. More broadly, encounters with decaying cultures often produced melancholic reflections on the inevitability of British imperial demise. On first contact with Polynesian culture, Robert Louis Stevenson reflected: "I saw their case as ours, death coming in like a tide, and the day already numbered when there should be no more Beretani, and no more of any race whatever, and (what oddly touched me) no more literary works and no more readers."[13]

But imperial masochism took more overt forms than melancholia, as we will see in detail throughout this book. The notion that colonial spaces offered opportunities for glorious suicide was deeply conventionalized in British culture, so much so that in *Daniel Deronda* (1876), George Eliot could count on readers recognizing the triteness of Rex Gascoigne's wish to banish himself to the colonies in order to dramatize his having been jilted in love. The rhetoric of histrionic imperial self-destructiveness has entered quite casually into much contemporary analysis of the imperial mind. Thus, James Morris echoes a common theme in writing about Gordon by declaring that he was "trapped by his own death-wish."[14] The unconfirmed but much relished story that Wolfe read Thomas Gray's "Elegy in a Country Churchyard" (1750) to his troops as a way of inspiring them on the eve of battle has helped lionize him as a melancholic fatalist. This rhetoric of histrionic martyrdom is not simply a retrospective imposition. It was often recirculated quite deliberately by military figures and colonists themselves. Robert Baden-Powell's cavalierly desperate dispatches from Mafeking, for instance, were modeled self-consciously on Gordon's from Khartoum. They also titillated the British public with images of endangered women and children that were bound to evoke memories of the massacre at Cawnpore during the 1857 Sepoy Rebellion—itself the single most engrossing spectacle of the British imperialist as victim, with over fifty novels about the rebellion published before the end of the century.

In the late nineteenth century, the masochistic overtones of imperial suffering were amplified by public debates about the rapidly growing but increasingly precarious empire. During this period of "new imperialism," when many Victorian writers sought to bolster public support for expansion, images of the imperialist as willing victim or martyr proliferated. Kipling's "The White Man's Burden" (1899) is perhaps the most famous expression of masochistic jingoism. With its rapturous celebration of sacrifice, toil, and ingratitude, it promotes an apocalyptic vision of history, bestowing on the imperialist the mantle of the Israelites—a chosen people tried by suffering. In "Recessional" (1897), Kipling encouraged a national posture of submissive humility in exchange for divine blessing: "Thy mercy on Thy People, Lord!"[15] More vulgar affirmations of painful self-sacrifice and bravery in the face of death saturated the adventure fiction for boys that boomed in popularity during the last decades of the nineteenth century: novels by G. A. Henty, R. M. Ballantyne, H. Rider Haggard, Robert Louis Stevenson, W. H. G. Kingston, Gordon Stables, Arthur Conan Doyle, Henry Seton Merriman, and many others. This body of fiction helped foster a fundamentally masochistic ethos of British masculinity, in which the ability to absorb pain stoically—or even ecstatically—was greatly prized.

Late-nineteenth-century narratives of desired or self-inflicted imperial suffering fueled cautionary tales and anti-imperialist allegories as well. Haggard's *She* (1887) described the dangerous, seductive power an exotic dominatrix could exercise over willingly subservient British men. Bram Stoker's *Dracula* (1897) represented the threat of the native "other" in terms of its erotic power to compel the submission of both men and women. These novels portray imperial adventure as an initiation into perverse, willing victimage; symptomatically, Dracula cannot enter his victim's sanctuaries to attack them until he is invited to cross the threshold. Much of the late-century fiction Patrick Brantlinger has described as "Imperial Gothic" revolves around the unconsciously self-destructive impulses of Britons, who persistently and inexplicably seek out exotic forces that prove to be cruel, powerful, and pitiless: Doyle's "The Ring of Thoth" (1890) and "Lot No. 249" (1892), in which mummies removed to England come alive to torment their captors; Kipling's "The Mark of the Beast" (1891), in which an arrogant Englishman who provokingly insults a temple idol is possessed by a sadistic demon; or Stoker's *Jewel of the Seven Stars* (1903), which is also about a removed mummy who comes to life, turning vindictively on her reanimators.[16]

These multivalent images of desired, self-inflicted, or otherwise cherished imperial pain could not fail to intersect attitudes toward suffering maintained elsewhere in British culture. In particular, glorified suffering had a prominent history in nineteenth-century conceptions of social class, most of all among the middle classes. Of course, a variety of British class ideologies reserved a place for the moral exaltation and social authority that might be conferred by suffering. Chivalric ideals long held by the upper class, which were appropriated by gentrified and professionalized middle-class ranks in the second half of the nineteenth century, revolved around the honor conferred by both physical and emotional trials. The ideals of stoic masculinity exalted by late-century adventure fiction were already present, in one form or another, among all Victorian social classes, including working-class cultures, whether conservative, militaristic, or radical. The high ground of noble sacrifice was, in fact, an extremely important objective of ideological competition in nineteenth-century British culture. Harold Perkin once observed that the "struggle between the moralities was as much a part of the class conflict of the period as Parliamentary Reform or the campaign against the Corn Laws."[17] Perkin argued further (as have more recent historians, notably Dror Wahrman) that competition over moral authority was a central factor in the birth of class society itself.[18] Although cherished suffering played a role at many sites in this social transformation, it was particularly effective in helping to sustain the moral hegemony over Victorian culture that the middle classes had acquired by midcentury.

It is tempting to find the sources of this widespread valorization of suffering in British Protestantism. John Foxe's *Book of Martyrs* (1563) and John Bunyan's *Pilgrim's Progress* (1678), which, until the twentieth century, trailed only the Bible in circulation, are distinctively British texts in their emphasis on suffering and exposure to danger as signs of grace.[19] But nineteenth-century middle-class moralism far exceeded the rigors of English Puritanism in its exaltation of self-punishment. Thanks to middle-class moral despotism, Sunday in Victorian England was not simply a day of prayer but also a time for mortification. In addition, pleasurable amusements like the theater and popular sports came under increasing attack early in the nineteenth century. Middle-class self-abnegation even pervaded entrepreneurial ideals. The Congregationalist minister Robert Vaughan once declared: "In relation to the affairs of this world, no less than to the affairs of religion, the man who would be successful 'must take up his cross and deny himself.'"[20] Contemporary observers were sometimes appalled at the consequences for middle-class social power of this pervasive ethos of self-denial. In *The English Constitution* (1867), Walter Bagehot excoriated middle-class culture for what he saw as its compulsive tendency to abase itself before authority—a "hypothesis of an essentially masochistic cultural and political unconscious," as Christopher Herbert has described it.[21] While popular accounts of Victorian prudery and self-denial have often made them seem absurd or even freakish, we must not forget how powerful a role ideals of virtuous suffering played in the consolidation of middle-class culture.

Middle-class fiction, for example, drew on a theme placed at the heart of the British novel by Samuel Richardson: the notion that individuals are redeemed by suffering. Widely read works such as Emily Brontë's *Wuthering Heights* (1847) and Charles Dickens's *Great Expectations* (1861) defined the self-lacerating individual as the moral center of middle-class culture, an equation that inevitably gave rise to complex uncertainties and anxieties. In Brontë's novel, Heathcliff's apocalyptic wish to be annihilated follows on and parallels Cathy's enigmatic decision to frustrate her own passions by marrying a man she admits loving only superficially. These self-destructive choices, which are driven to some degree by the two characters' otherworldly idealism, are represented by Brontë as the darkest of threats to social stability—impulses that must be moderated in the more palatable forms of emotional restraint adopted by the novel's succeeding generation of lovers. Dickens, however, demonstrated how individuals could transform self-destructive tendencies directly into virtues. In the first third of *Great Expectations*, Pip's self-lacerating guilt is represented as the dangerous internalization of persecutions he suffers at the hands of hypocritical adults, a form of self-torture every reader can only hope he outgrows. But as the novel develops, it gives Pip reasons to embrace his guilt. His increasing remorse over his desire to rise out of the working classes and to enter the ranks of the gentry is precisely what defines Pip as a legitimately middle-class subject. Significantly, his moral and social purification is consummated in his penitential acceptance of colonial employment. In both novels, the struggle to define correctly the proportions, the means, and the social significance of willful self-martyrdom is represented as central to the emergence of middle-class culture.

At the fin de siècle, such struggles were aggravated by intraclass competition of several different kinds. Late-century bohemianism often posed the purity of its intellectual and fiscal askesis against the material complacency of the bourgeoisie. As Terry Eagleton has pointed out, too, late-century intellectuals who experimented with spiritualism, underworld sensationalism, or the reification of the aesthetic symbol were performing what he calls a "collective intellectual suicide" as they sought forms of experience outside of bourgeois self-interest and rationality.[22] Many of those intellectuals were performing their internal resistance to the class from which they had originated—a phenomenon we will see in more detail in Stevenson's career and to some extent in Olive Schreiner's. At the same time, the late-Victorian lower middle class developed its own commitments to ideals of self-denial and hard work, which it saw as a means to respectability. These and other intraclass struggles to exploit the intellectual, moral, and social authority conferred by suffering and self-denial will be pivotal to my discussion of Victorian social hierarchies throughout the following chapters.

Just as imperial suffering cannot be conflated with masochism, so, too, glorifications of suffering in the realm of class ideology were overdetermined and cannot be regarded as intrinsically masochistic. It may not even be clear in what sense the class-coded exaltations of suffering I have been describing might be considered a discrete set of phenomena. The grouping of these various social trends together can suggest as many differences among them as similarities. From the global cultural perspective of Max Weber's *The Protestant Ethic and the Spirit of Capitalism* (1905), the promotion of self-denial appeared to be a rationalized instrument of productivity in the nineteenth century, whereas Friedrich Nietzsche argued, in *The Genealogy of Morals* (1887), that it was a weapon wielded by priestly elites against secular authority. As I have suggested, glorified suffering took a variety of class-coded forms in nineteenth-century British society as well as taking part in a cultural climate unique to British Protestantism, which was intensified by mid-Victorian evangelicalism (rather than being wholly abstracted from religion, as Weber argued). Moreover, class-coded forms of suffering were mediated by other elements in late-Victorian culture, including the mythology of imperial suffering I have already sketched out. It would be reductive to derive from multifaceted British ideologies of glorified suffering a singular psychological or ideological determinant. Nevertheless, class-coded ideals of cherished suffering inevitably invited, encouraged, and sustained masochistic fantasy. In the chapters that follow, I contend that the potential of these class ideologies to trigger masochistic fantasy opened up crucial channels of symbolic exchange between discourses of class and empire in late-Victorian Britain. Masochistic fantasy should thus be considered a switching point between these two domains of discourse but not as their point of origin. That the intersection was complex and variable is precisely what made it such a contested ideological arena.

[. . .]

Notes

1 David Cannadine, *Ornamentalism: How the British Saw Their Empire* (Oxford: Oxford University Press, 2001), p. 9. Italics in original.

2 Ann Laura Stoler, *Race and the Education of Desire: Foucault's History of Sexuality and the Colonial Order of Things* (Durham: Duke University Press, 1995), p. 99.

3 Anne McClintock, *Imperial Leather: Race, Gender and Sexuality in the Colonial Contest* (New York: Routledge, 1995), p. 9.

4 Linda Colley, *Captives: Britain, Empire, and the World, 1600–1850* (2002; New York: Random House, 2004), pp. 1–4.

5 William H. G. Kingston, *Captain Cook, His Life, Voyages and Discoveries* (London: Religious Tract Society, 1871), p. 319.

6 Simon Schama, *Dead Certainties (Unwarranted Speculations)* (New York: Alfred A. Knopf, 1991), p. 21.

7 Quoted in Zetland, Lawrence John Lumley Dundas, Marquis of, *The Life of Lord Curzon: Being the Authorized Biography of George Nathaniel, Marquess Curzon of Kedleston, K.G.*, 3 vols. (London: Ernest Benn, 1928), 2:158.

8 Quoted in Zetland, 2:159.

9 I. H. Burkill, *Chapters on the History of Botany in India* (Delhi: Government of India Press, 1965), makes for chilling reading on these and other untimely deaths.

10 Charlotte Brontë, *Jane Eyre* (New York: Norton, 2001), p. 344.

11 Mary Louise Pratt, *Imperial Eyes: Travel Writing and Transculturation* (London: Routledge, 1992), p. 7.

12 For this point and for several other observations about India I am indebted to David Arnold, "Deathscapes: India in an Age of Romanticism and Empire, 1800–1856," *Nineteenth-Century Contexts* 26 (2004), 339–53.

13 Robert Louis Stevenson, *In the South Seas*, *The Works of Robert Louis Stevenson*, Skerryvore Edition, 30 vols. (London: Heinemann, 1924–1926), 18:26. "Beretani" was pidgin for Britain.

14 James Morris, *Farewell the Trumpets: An Imperial Retreat* (London: Faber & Faber, 1978), p. 33.

15 Rudyard Kipling, "Recessional," *The Five Nations* (New York: Doubleday, 1903), p. 215.

16 Patrick Brantlinger, *Rule of Darkness: British Literature and Imperialism, 1830–1914* (Ithaca: Cornell University Press, 1988), pp. 227–54.

17 Harold Perkin, *The Origins of Modern English Society, 1780–1880* (London: Routledge and Regan Paul, 1969), p. 279.

18 Perkin, p. 281. Dror Wahrman, *Imagining the Middle Class: The Political Representation of Class in Britain, c. 1780–1840* (Cambridge: Cambridge University Press, 1995), p. 395, argues that evangelical conceptions of separate sphere ideology were crucial to the formation of coherent middle-class political values.

19 Linda Colley, *Britons: Forging the Nation, 1707–1837* (New Haven: Yale University Press, 1992), pp. 27–28, makes this point.

20 Robert Vaughan, *The Age of Great Cities* (London: Jackson & Walford, 1843), p. 312.

21 Christopher Herbert, *Culture and Anomie: Ethnographic Imagination in the Nineteenth Century* (Chicago: University of Chicago Press, 1991), p. 137.

22 Terry Eagleton, "The Plight to the Real," *Cultural Polities at the Fin de Siècle*, ed. Sally Ledger and Scott McCracken (Cambridge: Cambridge University Press, 1995), p. 17.

42 Imperialism and literature in the age of colonialism

Muireann O'Cinneide

The empire over which Victorian Britain ruled recurs as a presence throughout the literature of the period, whether as a stage for exotic adventure, a destination for doomed or resurgent characters in prose and poetry, or the shadowy edges of seemingly localized, quintessentially "English" settings. What understanding this empire might entail is, however, a considerably more charged issue: empire itself was at the time (as it continues to be today) a matter of intensive critical and cultural debate. In addition to arguments about its purpose, morality, governance, and future, the nature, extent, and viability of imperial rule as a concept were subject to debate during the Victorian period. There was even some dissension on whether empire existed as a meaningful entity at all.

The extracts in this section are from four seminal critics of the twentieth and twenty-first centuries, addressing the presence of empire in nineteenth-century texts across a range of decades and genres, and centering upon regions which have varying claims to be characterized as "colonial"—that is, dependent territories under the often-exploitative rule of a stronger state power. Victorian writing about empire coalesced around common themes and rhetorical models, usually aimed at reinforcing hierarchies of race and culture that enabled salutary re-definitions of Englishness and of the supremacy and benefits of British global power. But such themes and models also spoke to profound anxieties at the heart of much Victorian thinking about progress and civilization, anxieties which emerged from the often-uncategorizable realities of imperial experience and the varied understandings—by British Victorians and by their subject people—of how imperial rule might operate across very different territories and races. For all the monolithic solidity of the term "the British Empire," the entity itself took strikingly variant forms across different regions, cultures, and time periods. The perceptions of empire suggested by these critical extracts highlight the extent of this variation: Edward Said's strategically Orientalized India; Patrick Brantlinger's Africa as a Gothic setting for late-century cultural anxieties; Catherine Hall's West Indies as a site of meditation upon Englishness; John Kucich's narratives of imperial anguish in and out of Victorian Britain itself.

The British Empire(s)

The summary in this section is not intended to cover all the territories, races, and modes of colonial control encompassed by the nineteenth-century British Empire—for a greater understanding of this, students are referred to some of the histories of empire and of imperial literature listed in the bibliography. It is intended, however, to give some sense of just how complex the exertion of imperial power proved to be, and how important it is for scholars of empire, even as we trace common patterns of colonial representation, to pay attention to the cultural and economic specificities of time and place.

The British Empire was about race as much as space, with theories of racial categorization and degeneration underpinning the dynamics of colonial expansion and domination. Race and empire were never simply aligned in imperial discourse, however: internal alliances and enmities often proved significant factors in conquests, while gender and social or economic status produced competing hierarchies of alignment or distinction. The dynamics of racial thought shifted during the nineteenth century. Victorians (at least as regards white male colonists) viewed cross-racial relationships with greater unease than their eighteenth-century colonial predecessors had, an attitude increasingly reflected in colonial administration. Post-Darwinian science placed more emphasis on biological rather than cultural models of civilization, constructing factitiously empirical anthropological and physiological frameworks of racial typography. Scientific race theory undoubtedly contributed to the concept of the Anglo-Saxon race as "natural" rulers, on the one hand, and, on the other, to psychological dehumanization that facilitated the conquest and sometimes the obliteration of large numbers of indigenous peoples. The savage (if sometimes noble) dark-skinned "native" of early Victorian racial stereotypes became the biologically doomed lesser species of late Victorian scientific typology. Yet conflicts with other European settlers (such as the Boer Wars of 1880–81 and 1899–1902, against the Dutch Boers in South Africa) raised troubling questions about the civilizing values of whiteness and colonial rule. Moreover, the imperial roles played by subjects of the United Kingdom such as the Irish and Scots further complicate any easy racial alignments. The ambiguous nature of Ireland's long-term colonial status continues to be a particular source of critical debate: a people who were predominantly white, but also predominantly Celtic and Catholic, who simultaneously rebelled against and helped to sustain the rule of an empire whose authority was rooted in traditions of Anglo-Saxon Protestantism.

The structure and nature of imperial control also varied considerably between different regions. The indigenous populations of Canada and Australia were small enough to be relatively powerless against the settlement of their lands by white colonists, leaving those countries with a long-term legacy of racial depopulation to the point of near-extermination. (Such regions were popular destinations for the characters of mid-Victorian novels, whether exiled by law or by circumstances.[1]) By contrast, India's many inhabitants and extensive history of previous ruling dynasties meant that the initial control of the British East India Company after 1600 was gradual and heavily dependent upon interactions with established rulers. The historian Thomas Babington Macaulay (1800–1859) propounded models of the civilizing forces of empire that underlined rule by the elite (British) few over the unruly (Indian) many; the intrinsic superiority of western culture over that of "the Orient"; and consequently the civilizing effects of British education, especially over select Indian subjects through whom imperial rule could be channeled. The Indian Uprising of 1857–58, however, begun by Indian soldiers in the British Army, sent drastic reverberations through such complacent conceptions. The implications of so dramatic a loss of imperial control haunted the Victorian imagination for decades to come.[2]

Capital and the effects of the Industrial Revolution also influenced Victorian colonial expansion, with free trade being seen by many as itself an instrument of civilization. (This was despite the "Opium Wars" with China (1839–42, 1856–60), fought to enforce British trading of Indian-grown opium.) Older mercantile models of economic control—such as that of the East India Company—gave way to more modern commercial concerns, with expanding trade routes facilitating greater access to areas such as East Asia. Substantial British investment in

Latin America opened up considerable scope for economic influence. Some areas of British control in the Pacific likewise operated under informal trade-centered colonial structures. The ugly realities of Caribbean plantation labor occasionally flared up before the Victorian public with controversies such as Governor John Eyre's brutal quashing of the 1865 Morant Bay rebellion in the colony of Jamaica. Having outlawed slavery from their colonies in 1834, most Victorians prided themselves on Britain's anti-slavery stance—especially in pointed contrast to their former colony, the United States. Yet the coercive forces of economic inequity, exploitative systems of trade and contract, and imperial capitalism underlay an empire hailed by its admirers as a global force of liberation and civilization.

The scope of European empires changed dramatically in the closing decades of the nineteenth century. Whereas the colonial expansion of the early Victorian period tended to be quasi-informal in nature, driven by the forces of trade and culture, the militaristic, state-oriented imperial expansion commonly associated with the concept of empire was more a feature of the later century. Africa had long been significant to British imaginations in relation to the late eighteenth- and early-nineteenth century debates over slavery, and mid-Victorian missionary and explorer accounts such as David Livingstone's *Missionary Travels and Researches in South Africa* (1857) and Henry Morton Stanley's *How I Found Livingstone* (1872) cemented popular interest. But the continent itself really came to the forefront of Victorian visions of empire towards the end of the century, when the "Scramble for Africa" between various European powers fed into a resurgence of the romance genre in the form of imperial adventure fiction.[3] The so-called "Dark Continent" became a repository for European dreams of wealth and expansion, even as Africans suffered exploitation, dispossession, and racially driven threats of extermination. Across time and place, therefore, the British Empire meant very different things to those who governed, worked for and were ruled by it.

Empire and literary studies

The 1970s saw a resurgence of academic critical interest in imperial literature and history. Victorian London became re-envisaged by scholars as the metropolitan center of a global empire, even as others challenged the language and mindset of western centers and eastern peripheries. Edward Said's *Orientalism* (1978) was radical because it positioned the canons of western literature (including many of the touchstones of English cultural identity) as deeply implicated in colonial control, patterning representations of "the East" as eroticized and other, in timeless perpetual contrast with a "civilized," progressive, naturalized set of western cultures and histories.[4] The concept of Orientalism has been intensively critiqued for offering an unduly monolithic vision of imperial power. But *Orientalism* remains a definitive moment in debates regarding the imperial nature of British Victorian literature—a text whose intellectual dominance has proved fruitful to challenge, but sometimes frustratingly difficult to transcend.

Postcolonial theorists, literary critics and historians continued to challenge, revise or seek to move beyond Said. Homi Bhabha's concepts of mimicry and hybridity furthered psychological understandings of the workings of imperialism and the imaginative possibilities for anti-colonial resistance (Bhabha 1984). Spivak's interrogation of unvoiced "subaltern" experiences produced eastern women as unspeaking, un-recoverable silences in works often celebrated for formulating modes of western feminist individuality—such as Charlotte Brontë's *Jane Eyre* (1847) (Spivak 1985; Spivak 1998).[5] Robert Young critiqued the universalizing effects of Eurocentricism, while Frederick Cooper and Ann Laura Stoler's collection

Tensions of Empire (1997) showed metropolis and colony alike as representational sites for the workings-out of concepts of bourgeois modernity. The evolution of postcolonial theory as a discipline was attacked by Aijaz Ahmad, who argued that it had abandoned Marxist class analysis. New understandings of the actual scope and operation of imperial control emerged from works such as Partha Chatterjee's *The Nation and its Fragments* (1993), which emphasized strategic patterns of *inclusion*. In more recent years, Nicholas Dirks's *Castes of the Mind* (2001) examined the role of British ethnography in creating "manageable" constructions of Indian social orders.

The historiographical debates over concepts such as informal empire or unfinished empire have helped to delineate multiple modes of colonial control and expansion.[6] If the "new imperial history" sees the experience of empire as endemic to Victorian culture and daily life, fueled by the forces of commerce, religion, and political activism, others argue that the British barely noticed or thought about their empire unless it was forced on their attention.[7] Interactions between imperial historians (especially those skeptical of empire as a significant cultural force) and postcolonial theorists have often tended towards the combative—the former claiming a disregard of empiricism in favor of hegemonic ideologies; the latter decrying an overly limited perception of the representational dynamics of cultural discourse. These contrasting viewpoints pose productive challenges to literary critics, accustomed to perusing imperial literature as much for its absences and elisions as its presences and inclusions. Our readings are naturally informed by our own contemporary ideologies regarding modernity, global power, and the politics of cultural representation; at the same time, such readings must still engage with the experiential realities of nineteenth-century life and literature. Yet what these realities were—what "the Victorian experience of empire" entailed—remains perpetually contested.

Critical extracts

Edward Said's 1987 introduction to Rudyard Kipling's *Kim* (1901) brings the key precepts of Orientalism to bear upon one of the great Victorian novels of empire—and on the most influential portrayer of British India to the late-Victorian reading public. Said establishes the central potential conflict in *Kim*—between Kim's affiliation with India and love of the gentle Buddhist lama, and Kim's duty to the "Great Game" of British imperial power struggles with Russia—while highlighting the narrative mechanisms through which Kipling reconciles (or rather, elides) this tension. For Kipling, Said argues, "it was India's best destiny to be ruled by England" (Said 1987: 308 [Chapter 38: 333]). Even alternative colonial models are dismissed in favor of the Orientalist approach of Indians ruled by those Englishmen who truly "know" India. Kipling, Said claims, was among the first novelists to depict "a logical alliance between Western science and political power at work in the colonies" (Said 1987: 318 [Chapter 38: 338]), which foregrounds the importance of sciences such as anthropology and ethnography to the construction of models of racial and cultural superiority. Readers can sometimes experience theoretical and ideological approaches to texts, such as postcolonialism, as implicitly opposed to more "pure" formal critiques or the narrative pleasures of the reading experience. The artificiality of such binary thinking is clear in Said's insistence upon the ironic artistic possibilities of *fiction* as a genre "as opposed to discursive prose" (Said 1987: 309 [Chapter 38: 333]). He points out that to read *Kim* simply as a boy's adventure story, disregarding or disclaiming the novel's careful political coding, is in fact to undervalue its literary worth: "*Kim* is a work of great aesthetic merit" (Said 1987: 315 [Chapter 38: 336]). But this aesthetic merit, he contends, cannot be achieved or acknowledged in a vacuum, without the ideological structural support of nineteenth-century European cultural and racial assumptions.

The extract in this volume from Patrick Brantlinger's *Rule of Darkness: British Literature and Imperialism, 1830–1914* (1988) examines the late Victorian adventure novel's mode of "imperial Gothic," which "combines the seemingly scientific, progressive, often Darwinian ideology of imperialism with an antithetical interest in the occult" (Brantlinger 1988: 227 [Chapter 39: 339]). Brantlinger argues that imperialism and occultism offered alternative quasi-religious faiths as bulwarks against fears of British civilization's cultural and racial degeneration, with imperialism serving as "as a partial substitute for declining or fallen Christianity" (Brantlinger 1988: 228 [Chapter 39: 340]). Imperial romance became a channel through which to enact—and at times even revel in—regressions to savagery and barbarism, even as its various subgenres uneasily explored the implications of such regression for concepts of British civilization. Brantlinger sees anxieties about mass culture and critiques of imperialism as closely aligned with concerns about the failure of progress. Adventure fiction, therefore, becomes a means through which to explore the psychological landscapes of the western mind, with colonized peoples and territories transformed into fantastical backdrops for authorial self-exploration and imperial desire. Scientific materialism seemed to place the late Victorian subject in a world tied to phenomenological realities; imperial gothic, he contends, offered a means for authors to re-conceive this subject as accessing literal and figurative other worlds.

As Brantlinger's investigation of the occult also underlines, the influences of early Victorian evangelicalism can be seen later in the century in different ideological and rhetorical forms. The "return" of religion to Victorian Studies in recent decades has furthered critical analysis of the role of Christian missionaries as instruments of empire, as well as potential channels for anti-colonial resistance.[8] Catherine Hall's *Civilising Subjects: Metropole and Colony in the English Imagination 1830–1867* (2002) traces associations between Baptists and the West Indies, foregrounding the legacy of slavery and the abolition movement. As ideologies of racial (rather than cultural) degeneration came to dominate stereotypes of African laborers, *Civilising Subjects* contends that "the mid-nineteenth-century saw a proliferation of ways of being English in relation to Africans" (Hall 2002: 209 [Chapter 40: 347]). The extract in this volume examines the responses of the prolific Victorian novelist and travel writer Anthony Trollope (1815–82) to the figure of "the African or the West Indian negro" (Hall 2002: 209 [Chapter 40: 347]). The "fact of blackness" was mediated by the West Indies as a sort of racial halfway house, where "creolised Africans were granted cultural patterns" (Hall 2002: 217 [Chapter 40: 349]). Trollope's writing, Hall posits, forges a model of imperial masculinity that is centered on earned economic capabilities and the need to preserve clear gender structures.[9] The travelogue's structures of epistemological authority enable Trollope to offset the supposedly feminized sphere of the mid-nineteenth-century novel, with its realist concerns and plethora of women authors (Hall 2002: 219 [Chapter 40: 351]).[10] Hall's approach allows us to make significant connections between the empire and the recent emphasis in Victorian Studies on liberalism as a literary and rhetorical mode.[11] Her work does not simply challenge the metropole-periphery binary of empire; rather, it exposes its profound inadequacy as a conceptual model or a framer of political language.

John Kucich's *Imperial Masochism: British Fiction, Fantasy, and Social Class* (2006) turns its attention to the psychological constructions of imperial thought, tracing its interrelationship with crucial formulations of sexuality and social status. The rise of imperial adventure fiction in the later nineteenth century allowed writers such as Kipling and Haggard to use colonial settings to claim fiction as newly re-masculinized domains. (This approach can be productively read alongside Hall's depiction of Trollope's turn to travel writing as an assertion of masculinity in *counterpoint* to mid-Victorian realist fiction.) Such fictions, therefore, grappled with the psychic vulnerabilities inherent to models of English masculinity based on class and mastery. The extract from Kucich in this volume should be read in the context of his theorizing of masochism (i.e., the taking of pleasure in one's own experience of pain) as a psychosocial structure of fantasy, which provides an organizational mode for the social structures of British colonialism. He traces the mythologization of "victimization and death as foundational events in the teleology of empire" (Kucich 2006: 4 [Chapter 41: 355]), whereby imperial pain becomes inextricably aligned with pleasurably redemptive colonial history. Anti-imperial allegories also offer cautions against the threat posed to imperial masculinity by the seductive erotics of submission (Kucich 2006: 9 [Chapter 41: 358]). Such visions of "cherished imperial pain," Kucich argues, are inseparable from the class dynamics of "glorified suffering," whereby class conflicts play out as a struggle for the moral authority granted by endurance of pain. Abasement and self-denial became psychological cornerstones of bourgeois Protestant identity, shaping the self-immolating decisions of fictional protagonists like those of Emily Brontë's *Wuthering Heights* (1847) or Charles Dickens's *Great Expectations* (1861). In addressing these canonical texts, Kucich reminds us of the interconnectedness of psychological and social formulations, and of the inextricability of imperial pain from the narrative dynamics of the middle-class British Victorian novel and the internal class unease modeled by its writers.

Conclusion

Said, Brantlinger, Hall, and Kucich all draw on interrelated genres—adventure fiction, travel writing, life writing, realist fiction—which appealed to wide Victorian readerships, and use them to explore the psychological and ideological work done by writing about empire. All four extracts share a common concern with the frameworks of literary representation through which identities are built. Such attention to the nuances of genre and rhetoric lies—or should lie—at the heart of literary studies, yet valuable incorporations of historical and cultural contexts can all too often occlude these aspects—even against theorists' stated intentions. While deeper understandings of socio-political contexts continue to inspire exciting new avenues of literary research, postcolonial literary critics cannot allow attention to form, genre, and rhetoric to become swamped by a wealth of historical contextualization. This issue is, of course, particularly pertinent to postcolonial discourse, with its crucial emphasis on the inseparability of text and context; but it goes to the heart of broader concerns about the future of literary studies within the academy. Literary studies risks painting itself into a corner of existence as a perpetual subordinate, or at best a complement, to history, politics, and associated disciplines. Part of Said's analysis of Kipling lies in the difference between fiction and discursive prose, and the ironies that emerge from using the former to represent "both the Empire and conscious legitimizations of it" (Said 1987: 308 [Chapter 38: 333]). The presence of imperial spaces—especially in the later nineteenth-century—enabled new formulations of traditional genres, such as narrative romances. Brantlinger's "imperial gothic" is both a literary and a political mode: a re-introduction of eighteenth-century literary tropes into the exoticized, heightened terrains of imperial adventure fiction. The extracts from Hall's *Civilising Subjects* and Kucich's *Imperial Masochism* signal the importance of bringing the well-worn historicist categories of race, class, and gender into productive dialogue with invocations of genre and cultural narratives, without seeing these categories as themselves fixed or inevitable.

Ultimately, future debates in Victorian Studies on empire are likely to move towards the re-shaping of older models of understanding Victorian imperial experiences, such as the re-visiting of critical models of psychological literary analysis in relation to more recent investigations of the dynamics of violence and desire. Victorian empire offers an access point for concepts of pan-nationalism, but also offers insights into modern dominance patterns—and the psychological implications of such patterns. Studies of empire—and its attendant vocabularies and ideologies—will continue to benefit from increased attention to the formal *and* informal dynamics of colonial governance: the interpersonal relationships and communications that underlay the imperial paraphernalia of bills and proclamations. Governance should not, however, be seen simply as a matter for the nation state, nor should the often-complex dynamics of relationships between missionaries and converts, merchants and traders, officials and clerks be reduced simply to that of masters and servants of a homogenous imperial project. Moreover, in both historical and literary studies, easy polarities of powerful colonizers and helpless indigenous inhabitants have been productively complicated by exploring the dynamics of relationships between (for example) explorers and African guides, British statesmen and Indian princes, travelers and interpreters, collectors and antiquarians.[12] Our understanding of class, that much-rehearsed critical category in Victorian Studies, requires a more fluid sense of social structures and identities, especially their psychological formulations and ramifications, and their contextual nuances in alternative cultural settings. Studies on religion and imperialism would still benefit from more intensive attention to the specific class implications of different religious affiliations in relation to British military and administrative forces; to the wider relationship between early Victorian colonialism and the uneasily matched Whig political traditions of religious tolerance and cultural superiority; and perhaps above all, to the biblical vocabularies associated with Protestant and Catholic interpretations of British selfhood and the Victorian nation state.

Allowing other nineteenth-century European empires greater prominence in our understanding of British Victorianism would help to avoid a still-prevailing Anglocentrism in critical studies, while incorporating the earlier imperial histories and imperial cultures of colonial terrains—such as the Mughal Empire in India—would further problematize ahistorical and/or Eurocentric concepts of colonization. In gender studies, the critical attention to masculinity discussed above has helped in "making strange" previously normalized gender categories, while the relationship between feminist theories of gender performativity and the performative gendered identities of colonial femininity still remains somewhat under-explored, especially in contexts such as material and book histories. As critics, we need to continue our attention to subaltern voices while acknowledging the absences of these voices—which is to acknowledge the biases and limitations of the archives—and avoiding fetishizing outliers. The nation state retains its fascination—and its convenience—as a framework for literary analysis, particularly given the power structures associated with it in nineteenth-century geopolitics, but Victorian writing on race and empire has benefited from more global understandings of literature. Questions of colonial identities and models of Englishness are profitably complicated by, for example, Transatlantic Studies—it is no technicality that Kipling's deservedly infamous (if often misread poem) "The White Man's Burden" (1899) is in effect addressed to the United States.[13] Ecocriticism's re-visiting of Victorian industrial landscapes in literature opens up intriguing possibilities for imperial spatial discourse, while Victorian Studies' enhanced focus on material histories allows a fusion of textual studies with object analysis.[14] Attention to economic forces in the light of modern debates about globality and capitalism are opening up more nuanced, fluid understandings that encompass trade routes, modes of transport, and patterns of exchange. Likewise, debates on multiculturalism and globalization permit a greater understanding of the complicating effects of social status and of cultural and biological hybridity upon racial identities.

In conclusion, modern parallels can come overly readily when considering Victorian debates on their empire. Concepts of the colonial and the postcolonial risk themselves becoming strait-jackets on national and social histories, imposing ongoing Eurocentric models across the globe. As the British Empire grows increasingly historically distant, we turn to models of cultural imperialism and globalization that do not always accord neatly with previous patterns of understanding.[15] Yet the changing nature of critical debates about British Victorians and their empire continues to be matters of crucial importance, both to our understanding of this area of literary studies, and to our understanding of representation and power in the modern world.

Notes

1 Notable examples include Elizabeth Gaskell, *Mary Barton* (1848); George Eliot, *Adam Bede* (1859); Charles Dickens, *David Copperfield* (1850) and *Great Expectations* (1861); and Mary Elizabeth Braddon, *Lady Audley's Secret* (1862).
2 See Charles Dickens and Wilkie Collins, "The Perils of Certain English Prisoners" (1857); Christina Rossetti, "In the Round Tower at Jhansi, June 8, 1857" (1862); Alfred Tennyson, "The Defence of Lucknow" (1880); Flora Annie Steel, *On the Face of the Waters* (1896); and (indirectly) Wilkie Collins, *The Moonstone* (1868).
3 See esp. Henry Rider Haggard, *King Solomon's Mines* (1885) and Joseph Conrad's bleaker *Heart of Darkness* (1899).
4 For Said's own theoretical role models, see McCarthy 2010 18, 35–40, 48–55, 103–7.
5 For further critiques, see Mohanty 1984 and Lewis 1996.
6 See esp. Gallagher and Robinson 1953 and for a wide-ranging study, Darwin 2013.
7 For the former, see Hall 2002 and also Antoinette Burton, esp. Burton 1998; for the latter, see Porter 2005.
8 See "Religion and Literature" in this volume, and also Porter 1999. Missionaries in Victorian fiction include *Jane Eyre*'s St John Rivers (India), and Norman May in Charlotte Yonge's *The Daisy Chain* (1856) (New Zealand).
9 For earlier work, see Bristow 1991, Hall 1992, and Mrinalini Sinha 1995.
10 See Pratt 1992.
11 See "Liberalism" in this volume. For earlier work on liberalism and empire, see Mehta 1997, esp. pp. 59–62; Metcalf 1997, esp. ix–x, 28–42.
12 See, for example, Leask 2002, Jasanoff 2005, Gilmour 2005, or Kennedy 2013.
13 See Giles 2006 or Flint 2009.
14 See esp. Freedgood 2006.
15 See, for example, Michael Hardt and Antonio Negri's conception of a universalizing modern imperialism as emerging from anti-colonial nationalism in Hardt and Negri 2000.

Bibliography

Ahmad, A. (1992) "Orientalism and After . . . ," *In Theory: Classes, Nations, Literatures*, London: Verso, 159–219.

Bhabha, H. (1984) "Of Mimicry and Man: The Ambivalence of Colonial Discourse," *October*, 28: 125–133.

Brantlinger, P. (1988) *Rule of Darkness: British Literature and Imperialism, 1830–1914*, Ithaca, NY, and London: Cornell University Press.

Bristow, J. (1991) *Empire Boys: Adventures in a Man's World*, London: Harper Collins.

Burton, A. (1998) *At the Heart of the Empire: Indians and the Colonial Encounter in Late Victorian Britain.* Ithaca, NY: University of California Press.

Cooper, F. and Stoler, A. L. (eds.) (1997) "Between Metropole and Colony," in F. Cooper and A. L. Stoler (eds.), *Tensions of Empire: Colonial Cultures in a Bourgeois World*, Berkeley: University of California Press, 1–37.

Darwin, J. (2013) *Unfinished Empire: The Global Expansion of Britain*, London: Bloomsbury Press.

Fanon, F. (1965) *The Wretched of the Earth*, intro. J-P. Sartre, trans. C. Farrington, London: Macgibbon & Kee.

Flint, K. (2009) *The Transatlantic Indian, 1776–1930*, Princeton: Princeton University Press.

Freedgood, E. (2006) *The Ideas in Things: Fugitive Meaning and the Victorian Novel*, Chicago and London: University of Chicago Press.

Gallagher, J. and Robinson, R. (1953) "The Imperialism of Free Trade," *Economic History Review*, 6.1: 1–15.

Giles, P. (2006) *Atlantic Republic: The American Tradition in English Literature*, Oxford: Oxford University Press.

Gilmour, D. (2005) *The Ruling Caste: Imperial Lives in the Victorian Raj*, London: John Murray.

Hall, C. (1992) *White, Male, and Middle Class: Explorations in Feminism and History*, Cambridge: Polity Press.

—— (2002) *Civilising Subjects: Metropole and Colony in the English Imagination 1830–1867*, Chicago and London: University of Chicago Press.

Hardt, M. and Negri, A. (2000) *Empire*, Cambridge, MA: Harvard University Press.

Jasanoff, M. (2005) *Edge of Empire: Lives, Culture & Conquest in the East 1750–1850*, New York: Alfred A. Knopf.

Kennedy, D. (2013) *The Last Blank Spaces*, Cambridge, MA: Harvard University Press.

Leask, N. (2002) *Curiosity and the Aesthetics of Travel Writing, 1770–1840*, Oxford: Oxford University Press.

Lewis, R. (1996) *Gendering Orientalism: Race, Femininity and Representation*, London and New York: Routledge.

Loomba, A. (2005) *Colonialism/Postcolonialism*, New Critical Idiom, 2nd edn., London and New York: Routledge.

McCarthy, C. (2010) *The Cambridge Introduction to Edward Said*, Cambridge: Cambridge University Press.

McClintock, A. (1995) *Imperial Leather: Race, Gender and Sexuality in the Colonial Context*, London & New York: Routledge.

Mehta, Uday S. (1997) "Liberal Strategies of Exclusion," in F. Cooper and A. L. Stoler (eds.), *Tensions of Empire: Colonial Cultures in a Bourgeois World*, Berkeley: University of California Press, 59–86.

Metcalf, T. (1997) *Ideologies of the Raj*, Cambridge: Cambridge University Press.

Mohanty, C. (1984) "Under Western Eyes: Feminist Scholarship and Colonial Discourses," *Boundary*, 2. 12(3)–13(1): 333–358.

Porter, A. (1999) "Religion, Missionary Enthusiasm and Empire," in B. Porter (ed.), *The Oxford History of the British Empire*, Volume 3, Oxford: Oxford University Press, 222–46.

Porter, B. (2005) *Absent-Minded Imperialists: Empire, Society, and Culture in Britain*, Oxford: Oxford University Press.

Pratt, M. L. (1992) *Imperial Eyes: Travel Writing and Transculturation*. London and New York: Routledge.

Sinha, M. (1995) *Colonial Masculinity: The "Manly Englishman" and the "Effeminate Bengali" in the Late Nineteenth Century*, Manchester: Manchester University Press.

Spivak, G. (1985) "Three Women's Texts and a Critique of Imperialism," *Critical Inquiry* 12.1: 243–61.

—— (1998) "Can the Subaltern Speak?," in C. Nelson and L. Grossberg (eds.), *Marxism and the Interpretation of Culture*, Basingstoke: Macmillan Education, 271–313.

Young, Robert (2008) *The Idea of English Ethnicity*, Malden: Blackwell.

—— (1990) *White Mythologies: Writing History and the West*, London and New York: Routledge.

Part XI

Economics, the market, and Victorian culture

Introduction

Money is everywhere in the Victorian novel. From the inheritances of Jane Eyre, Pip, and Dorothea Brooke and the sudden impoverishments of Miss Matty and Mr. Tulliver to Mr. Micawber's debts and the grand financial swindles of Messrs. Merdle and Melmotte, references to money abound, serving both as pivotal plot points and as tests of character and moral fortitude. But despite the frequency with which money appears in the core canon of Victorian literature, many scholars—with the important exception of Marxism-inflected critics, including Georg Lukács and the Frankfurt school—overlooked the relationship between economics and literature for the first half of the twentieth century. In many English departments, money and literature were regarded as mutually exclusive topics at the twentieth century's midpoint. This was due to a number of factors, including the success of neoclassical economics in reconfiguring the field as a mathematical science at the expense of its older associations with literary writing, the dominance of formalist approaches to literature, and a lingering academic suspicion of the marketplace (a legacy of the Romantics).

As the sway of the New Critics and Leavisites waned in the 1960s, however, a new breed of explicitly political critic emerged, determined to historicize and contextualize Victorian literature. Most significant amongst them was Raymond Williams. Following in the Marxist tradition, Williams's work situated the Victorian novel firmly within nineteenth-century economic history. Focusing largely on the social-problem novels of the 1840s and 1850s, Williams argued that Victorian fiction both reflected and shaped Victorian responses to industrial capitalism. As the seventies and eighties progressed, feminist critics, too, became interested in the relationship between Victorian literature and economics, especially the way in which women authors used the social problem novel to intervene in supposedly masculine debates about the effects of industrialization.

The rise of New Historicism in the late eighties and nineties saw the development of different ways of thinking about literature and money. Christened "The New Economic Criticism" by Mark Osteen and Martha Woodmansee in their highly influential volume of that name, this new approach was "predicated on the existence and disclosure of parallels and analogies between linguistic and economic systems" (Osteen and Woodmansee 1999: 14). Its influence is clear in two of this section's excerpts, Jeff Nunokawa's *The Afterlife of Property* (1994) and Catherine Gallagher's *The Body Economic* (2006), both of which identify formal and thematic correspondences between economic and literary writing. In doing so, each contests the assumptions of neoclassical economics by realigning writing about money with imaginative writing.

By the early twenty-first century, economics and literature had grown to become one of the most dynamic areas in Victorian studies, producing what Nancy Henry and Cannon Schmitt call a field of "intense interdisciplinarity" (Henry and Schmitt 2009: 3). But while the broad cultural scope of New Historicism continued to influence economic criticism, scholars such as Mary Poovey (excerpted here) now advocated alternative critical approaches to understanding the relationship of nineteenth-century economics and literature. Rejecting the assumption that "textual interpretation" can "provide evidence to support a historical argument," Poovey instead favors "historical description," an approach which attempts to recover "the historical conditions that made some uses of texts possible while rendering others nonsensical or obsolete" (Poovey 2008: 20–21). In this way, Poovey endeavors to identify not the ways in which economics resembles literature in the nineteenth century so much as the generic mechanisms that increasingly separated imaginative writing from economic texts in this period.

In the wake of the worldwide financial crash of 2008, economic matters (or what the Victorians called Political Economy) remain on all of our minds, as we continue to deal with its repercussions on academic institutions, their workers, and their students. In such a climate, economic criticism is thriving, as scholars seek to understand the nineteenth-century origins of the financial instruments and systems that have proven to be so fragile. But along with the burgeoning growth in empirical studies of Victorian financial capitalism, economic criticism also seems likely—as Jill Rappoport notes below—to move beyond discussion of "competitive individual producers, consumers, and owners" to consideration of "dynamic communities of circulation, possession, and exchange" (Chapter 46: 398), as cultural scholars continue to challenge neoclassical economics' persistent—and potentially risky—assumption that economics is an objective, mathematical science rather than socially situated discourse.

See also: *Gender, sexuality, domesticity*; *Print culture*

Bibliography

Henry, N. and Schmitt, C. (eds.) (2009) *Victorian Investments: New Perspectives on Finance and Culture*, Bloomington: Indiana University Press.

Osteen, M. and Woodmansee, M. (1999) "Taking Account of the New Economic Criticism: An Historical Introduction," in M. Woodmansee and M. Osteen (eds.), *The New Economic Criticism: Studies at the Intersection of Literature and Economics*, London: Routledge.

43 *Daniel Deronda* and the afterlife of ownership

Jeff Nunokawa

[. . .]

By the middle of the nineteenth century, the right to alienate has become the centerpiece of proprietorial prerogative; as John Stuart Mill indicates, "the power to bestow" has become the sine qua non of the right of ownership:

> The ownership of a thing cannot be looked upon as complete without the power of bestowing it, at death or during life, at the owner's pleasure: and all the reasons, which recommend that private property should exist, recommend *pro tanto* this extension of it.[1]

The conviction that the right to alienate is an inherent and characterizing constituent of proprietorial prerogative manifests itself in the escalating inability of nineteenth-century Anglo-American culture to imagine forms of possessive power that stop short of the "power to bestow." In her famous summary of laws pertaining to married women, Barbara Bodichon designates the husband's legal claim to his wife as just such a form of ownership:

> A married woman's body belongs to her husband; she is in his custody, and he can enforce his right by a writ of habeas corpus. But . . . the belief that a man can rid himself of his wife by going through the farce of a sale, and exhibiting his wife with a halter round her neck is a vulgar error. This disgusting exhibition, which has often been seen in our country, is a misdemeanor, and can be punished with fine and imprisonment. The author of a recent publication asserts that a man may lend his wife; a man may not lend, let out, or sell his wife; such transactions are considered as being against public decency, and are misdemeanors.[2]

But if the husband's possession of his wife does not include the right to "lend, let out, or sell" her, Bodichon's account here exhibits the widely held belief that it does. And this "disgusting exhibition" is an instance of a more general inability or refusal to recognize forms of ownership that do not include the right to sell. The widely manifested belief that proprietorial right per se, including, most acutely, the proprietorial right in persons, necessarily involves "the power to bestow" surpasses the bounds of "vulgar error"; it also appears in the inability of antebellum American jurisprudence to sustain a theoretical separation between the possession of slaves and the possession of commodities, as well as the inability of postbellum American jurisprudence to produce a coherent justification for its general refusal to endorse the assertion that people have an unrestricted right to sell their interest in themselves.[3]

In *Daniel Deronda*—and not only there—the centrality, for possession, of the "power to bestow" often asserts itself in the utter identification of proprietorial prerogative with this power; an owner's power over his or her property becomes, simply, an owner's power to alienate it: "If Sir Hugo Mallinger could have done as he liked with his estates, he would have left them to . . . Mr Deronda" (378). The testimony of our own consciousness may furnish the last word here: what does our now stripped sense of owning usually mean, other than the right to sell?

. . . . . .

An idea of proprietorial power reposited primarily, even exclusively, in the "power to bestow" may dwell in the happiest alliance with the market economy, but it does so by severely restricting the boundless ambitions for mastery that form a deep part of the ideological heritage of possession. We can begin to assess the infinitude of these ambitions by glancing at the Physiocrats, whose emphatic expressions of how much it means to own are regarded by some historians as the first thorough articulation of absolute property. "The property the physiocrats had in mind," Elizabeth Fox-Genovese and Eugene Genovese remark, "predated society." "Property was sacrosanct, natural, divine. . . . It constituted a presocial right." For the Physiocrats, ownership helps define the charmed circle of humanity's "immutable essence": "Material possession, unequal though it may be [is, according to the Physiocrats] inseparable from the essence of humanity."[4]

The power of ownership has no history. It is not just that the right to possess inhabits the magic place outside of history that Marxists call the sphere of ideology; absolute possession itself transcends the limits of temporality: the power of owning, according to the sense we are considering here, is supposed to last forever. In the Victorian novel, this great expectation makes its most memorable appearance in the severe shock or irritation that always comes when property fails to endure. This includes the various quotidian disappointments that afflict the property owner in Eliot's fiction who crosses the bar of marketplace possession, the inexorable temporal limit that constricts proprietorial prerogative when that prerogative is defined as the opportunity to alienate. The sense of "imperfect mastery" that "clings and gnaws within Grandcourt" (399) when he is compelled to petition his mistress to return the diamonds that he gave her refers by negation to the expectation of endless prerogative, an expectation inevitably disappointed by the temporal form cast upon possession when it is readied for the marketplace. Such possession will always upset the expectation of enduring proprietorial power, because it can be exercised only once: expenditure is an event rather than a condition; the alienation of property is an irreversible act, at once the realization and termination of ownership's potence.

Such "imperfect mastery" is signaled in *Middlemarch* by the dead hand of Peter Featherstone, who, despite cunning efforts to maintain control of what he owns, is finally compelled to relax his grip: "Peter Featherstone was dead, with his right hand clasping the keys, and his left hand lying on the heap of notes and gold."[5] But the lethal loosening of Featherstone's grasp began with the falling of his shocked hand the night before, when his servant refused to enable him to change his will:

> "Not do it? I tell you, you must," said the old man, his voice beginning to shake under the shock of this resistance. . . .
> He let his hand fall, and . . . beg[an] to cry childishly. (261)

Having given herself to Grandcourt, Gwendolen "could not go backward now" (*DD* 355); she is "irrevocably engaged" (356). "Her capability of rectitude told her again and again that she had no right to complain of her contract, or to withdraw from it" (665).[6] Solemnity greets her announcement that she has engaged herself to Grandcourt ("'My darling child!', said Mrs. Davilow, with a surprise that was rather solemn than glad"), a solemnity that reflects the first economic rule that a "spoiled child" must learn: what is given can't be taken back. Once performed, the power of owning falls into the irretrievable past. As if to dramatize this, the act of owning, once performed, is not merely cast into the sphere of anteriority, it works to construct it. Grandcourt, by giving his mistress his mother's diamonds, "had made a past for himself which was stronger than any he could impose. He must ask for the diamonds which he had promised to Gwendolen" (294).

Marketplace possession, accordingly, is throned in a reign of potentiality, prior to the actual exercise of the power that defines and ends it. This is the region where Featherstone seeks to linger; Grandcourt inhabits it while pondering his uncle's offer to buy one of his estates. Gwendolen enjoys the same ephemeral dominium more fleetingly when, presented with Grandcourt's offer of marriage, the marriage that the novel unflinchingly calls a "contract" where she "sells herself" (733), her waning sense of power is briefly reanimated by a taste of the pleasures of absolute ownership.

She invites Grandcourt's efforts to "to bribe [her] will," because

> Firmness hath its appetite and craves
> The stronger lure, more strongly to resist
> Would know the touch of gold to fling it off
> Scent wine to feel its lip the soberer;
> Behold soft byssus, ivory, and plumes
> To say "They're fair, but I will none of them,"
> And flout Enticement in the very face.   (332)

The evil hour of temptation forms a virtual allegory for the ephemeral Eden of proprietorial prerogative:

> "You will tell me now, I hope, that Mrs Davilow's loss of fortune will not trouble you further. You will trust me to prevent it from weighing upon her. You will give me the claim to provide against that."
> The little pauses and refined drawlings with which this speech was uttered, gave time for Gwendolen to go through the dream of a life. As the words penetrated her, they had the effect of a draught of wine, which suddenly makes all things easier, desirable things not so wrong, and people in general less disagreeable. She had a momentary phantasmal love for this man who chose his words so well, and who was a mere incarnation of delicate homage. Repugnance, dread, scruples—these were dim as remembered pains, while she was already tasting relief under the immediate pain of hopelessness. She imagined herself already springing to her mother, and being playful again. Yet when Grandcourt had ceased to speak, there was an instant in which she was conscious of being at the turning of the ways. (347)

The ambitions of mastery that inhere in the idea of absolute ownership can be sensed here in Gwendolen's feeling of the compliance of others; and if the images housed by this dream refract the power of possession, its anticipatory structure mimics the situation of absolute ownership. Just as the glow of power that warms possession is cast upon it by the potential exercise of mastery before which it is poised, Gwendolen's fantasy stages future possibilities as immediate pleasures of power.

The ominous sound of the knowledge that descends when Grandcourt is done with his proposal knells the limit of absolute possession: "When Grandcourt had ceased to speak, there was an instant in which she was conscious of being at the turning of the ways." Since its realization is its end, absolute ownership can be sustained only by deferring its ultimate exercise. Only by "eluding a direct appeal" can "Gwendolen recover . . . some of her self-possession" (346).

Eliot's novel registers and intensifies the capitalist construction of absolute ownership by casting the exercise of the prerogative that defines such ownership as the terminus of a trajectory, the inevitable end of an inexorable progression. In *Daniel Deronda*, economic mastery is everywhere coaxed to what we can call, in both senses of the term, its end. According to Eliot's account, possession lives in the space between a question and its answer, between the calling of a name and its recognition: "'You accept my devotion?' said Grandcourt. . . . 'Yes,' came as gravely from Gwendolen's lips as if she had been answering to her name in a court of justice." By "sell[ing] herself," Gwendolen Harleth merely acknowledges and completes an inexorable sentence.

As we have seen, *Daniel Deronda* dramatizes the trajectory of proprietorial prerogative by merging this movement with Eve's tragic steps. Gwendolen's self-possession rehearses the fate that it carefully echoes when it seeks to confront temptation and "flout Enticement in the very face." She sells herself to Grandcourt in a late emanation of Eve's trade, "not that she could still imagine herself plucking the fruits of life without suspicion of their core" (333).

And if it likens the exercise of proprietorial prerogative to the unfolding of a mythic doom, *Daniel Deronda* also affiliates the trajectory of proprietorial prerogative with the nonsectarian teleological undertow of narrative itself.[7] One of Eliot's most considered images nears the surface when she describes the form of Gwendolen Harleth's entrapment, the cage that draws her to the end of her self-possession, to the "contract" with Grandcourt, as a "net." This figure recalls the "web" that is Eliot's figure for the resolution of novelistic narrative. Here is Eliot's famous defense of her method in *Middlemarch*: "I at least have so much to do in unravelling certain human lots, and seeing how they were woven and unwoven, that all the light I can command must be concentrated on this particular web" (116). The resemblance between the plot of the novel and the net that draws Gwendolen forward to the end of her self-possession signals their deep collaboration. In *Daniel Deronda* the inexorable sentence that urges the proprietor to the terminus of possession joins the force that a reader feels in the urge to get to the end.

The intimacy between the telos of ownership and the telos of narrative surpasses their end rhyme when Deronda's mother calls fulfilling the dictates of proprietorial will a matter of finishing a story: "If I tell everything—if I deliver up everything—what else can be demanded of me?" (702). And this identification extends beyond the particular predicament of Deronda's mother. Narrative drive is merged most comprehensively with the trajectory of absolute ownership through the habits of Lapidoth, a character whom the novel makes into a screen upon which it projects its own teleological dynamic:

> By no distinct change of resolution, rather by a dominance of desire, like the thirst of the drunkard—it so happened that in passing the table his fingers fell noiselessly on the ring, and he found himself in the passage with the ring in his hand. It followed that he put on his hat and quitted the house. The possibility of again throwing himself on his children receded into the indefinite distance, and before he was out of the square his sense of haste had concentrated itself on selling the ring and getting on shipboard. (678)

Lapidoth's little narrative of ownership takes on the larger status of narrative generally: this is not only a story, it is also the figure of story itself. What some observers of the form call the bare elements of narrative work through the character of Lapidoth here,[8] a sequence of events that we recognize as the rhetorical elements of a story ("it so happened," "it followed"), that serve as prelude to a motivating conclusion. The elements of narrative emerge into view in this passage as determining entities, overwhelming the specific agency and affect of the character enmeshed in it.

This instance of what Neil Hertz describes as the "oddly generic" quality of the weird prose that surrounds Lapidoth is consonant with the labor of embodiment he is made to perform generally in *Daniel Deronda*:[9] to serve as the site upon which the impersonal, even invisible force of narrative and specifically the novel's own narrative can be apprehended. The disappearance of Lapidoth's consciousness is the disappearance of a text, the "widening margin where consciousness once was"; his habitual dissimulation, "reflecting every phase of . . . feeling with mimetic susceptibility" (810), likens him to the realist novel; most important for us, the "numbers and movements that seemed to make the very tissue of Lapidoth's consciousness" (849) identify him with the numbers and movements that mark the progress of that text.

And if the dominance of desire that works through Lapidoth is the teleological demand of novelistic narrative, it is at the same time the inevitable performance of proprietorial prerogative, the "sense of haste" that "concentrate[s] itself . . . on selling the ring." And this is not the only place in the novel where the fascination of owning takes on the form and force of the demand to complete a story. Who are the entranced gamblers crowding the first chapter of *Daniel Deronda*, if not the "attention bent" (36) readers of the sensational serial novel, unable to stop before they have reached its generic ending?

> While every single player differed markedly from every other, there was a certain uniform expression which had the effect of a mask—as if they had all eaten of some root that for the time compelled the brains of each to the same narrow monotony of action. (37)

The "moment hand" drama of fascinated ownership ("each time her stake was swept off she doubled it. . . . Such a drama takes no long while to play out; development and catastrophe can often be measured by nothing clumsier than the moment hand") is a spectacular enactment of the fate that always shadows possession. When the novel makes the "development and catastrophe" of ownership the "development and catastrophe" of narrative, it dramatizes their common character: possession, like narrative, is prologue to its own demise.

[. . .]

Notes

1 As cited in [Atiyah, *Rise and Fall*], 93.
2 Bodichon, "A Brief Summary of the Laws Concerning Women," 17.
3 For a general review of the remarkable philosophical contortions that American law performed in an effort to maintain this distinction, and its ultimate failure to do so, see Fox-Genovese and Genovese's "Jurisprudence and Property Relations," in *Fruits of Merchant Capital.* The sense that proprietorial prerogative necessarily included "the power to bestow" is conversely confirmed by the insistence frequently heard in the second half of the nineteenth century that people cannot be property precisely because they *cannot* be bestowed. Here, for example, is the religious socialist Thomas Hill Green addressing the Leicester Liberal Association in 1880: "We are all now agreed that men cannot rightly be the property of men. . . . A contract by which any one agreed for a certain consideration to become

the slave of another we should reckon a void contract. Here, then, is a limitation upon the freedom of contract which we all recognize as rightful" (Thomas Hill Green, "Liberal Legislation and Freedom of Contract," excerpted in Elizabeth Jay and Richard Jay, eds., *Critics of Capitalism* [New York: Cambridge University Press, 1986], 188).

4 Fox-Genovese and Genovese, "Physiocracy and Propertied Individualism," in *Fruits of Merchant Capital*, 277, 285.

5 George Eliot, *Middlemarch* (New York: Oxford University Press, 1988), 262. All subsequent references to this text (hereafter abbreviated as *MM*) refer to this edition.

6 This dilemma, according to which the exercise of the utmost power of possession is one with its end, is registered, in different terms, in the paradoxical character of the contract. On one hand, the contract, during the nineteenth century, was the record and ritual of absolute proprietorial prerogative. Claire Dalton notes that "contractual obligation was seen . . . into the latter part of the nineteenth century . . . to arise from the will of the individual" (Claire Dalton, "An Essay in the Deconstruction of Contract Doctrine," in Sanford Levinson, ed., *Interpreting Law and Literature* [Evanston, Ill.: Northwestern University Press, 1988], 285–318). On the other hand, this mirror and means of absolute proprietorial prerogative are also the means by which the owner contracts his will.

7 This is what D. A. Miller calls the "discontent" of "traditional" narrative: "In the last analysis, what discontents the traditional novel is its own condition of possibility. For the production of narrative— what we called the narratable—is possible only within a logic of insufficiency, disequilibrium, and deferral" (Miller, *Narrative and Its Discontents*, 265). See also Barthes, *S/Z*.

8 See, for example, Shlomith Rimmon-Kenan, *Narrative Fiction: Contemporary Poetics* (New York: Methuen, 1983), 1–5; Miller, *Narrative and Its Discontents;* Peter Brooks, *Reading for the Plot* (New York: Random House, 1984).

9 Neil Hertz, "Some Words in George Eliot: Nullify, Neutral, Numb, Number," in *Languages of the Unsayable: The Play of Negativity in Literature and Literary Theory*, ed. Sanford Budick and Wolfgang Iser (New York: Columbia University Press, 1989), 280–97. Hertz furnishes a very different account of Lapidoth's status as the site of a linguistic function, or dysfunction.

Works cited

Atiyah, P. S. *The Rise and Fall of Freedom of Contract*. New York: Oxford University Press, 1979.

Barthes, Roland. *S/Z*. Translated by Richard Miller. New York: Hill & Wang, 1974.

Bodichon, Barbara Leigh Smith. "A Brief Summary, in Plain Language, of the Most Important Laws of England Concerning Women." London, 1854.

Eliot, George. *Daniel Deronda*. 1876. New York: Penguin, 1988.

Fox-Genovese, Elizabeth, and Eugene Genovese. *Fruits of Merchant Capital*. New York: Oxford University Press, 1985.

Miller, D. A. *Narrative and Its Discontents*. Princeton: Princeton University Press, 1981.

44 The bioeconomics of *Our Mutual Friend*

Catherine Gallagher

Wealth and illth

Our Mutual Friend draws on an antithesis that John Ruskin had named in *Unto This Last* (1862) a few years before the novel appeared: that of wealth and illth. In developing this antithesis, Ruskin began with a question and an anecdote, both of which anticipated in striking detail the opening chapter of Dickens's novel. Ruskin's question was, "[I]f we may conclude generally that a dead body cannot possess property, what degree and period of animation in the body will render possession possible?"[1] In the first chapter of *Our Mutual Friend*, Gaffer Hexam also insists on the absurdity of the idea that a dead man can possess property. He raves, "Has a dead man any use for money? Is it possible for a dead man to have money? . . . How can money be a corpse's? Can a corpse own it, want it, spend it, claim it, miss it?"[2]

Gaffer seems to think that these questions automatically call for a negative reply: "No, a dead body cannot possess property." The novel, however, not only leaves this issue open but also goes on to ask Ruskin's more complicated question, the one that introduces the possibility of "illth": what degree of health, of life, of animation, is necessary before the body can no longer be properly said to possess something? Ruskin's question turns into an anecdote, like the one that opens *Our Mutual Friend* of drowning and dredging up. Ruskin writes,

> [L]ately in a wreck of a California ship, one of the passengers fastened a belt about him with two hundred pounds of gold in it, with which he was found afterwards at the bottom. Now, as he was sinking—had he the gold? or had the gold him?
>
> And if, instead of sinking him in the sea by its weight, the gold had struck him on the forehead, and thereby caused incurable disease—suppose palsy or insanity,—would the gold in that case have been more a "possession" than in the first? Without pressing the inquiry up through instances of gradually increasingly vital power over the gold . . . I presume that the reader will see that possession . . . is not an absolute, but a graduated power; and consists not only in the . . . thing possessed, but also . . . in the possessor's vital power to use it. (169–70)

Ruskin, then, begins his investigation into the nature of economic value with death in order, it seems, to root wealth in bodily well-being. Wealth, he concludes, is the possession of useful things by those who can use them. Useful things are those that nurture life, and those who can use them are those who are (at the very least) in a state of bodily animation. To the degree that possessions cause bodily harm, as in the story of the drowned man, to the degree that they incapacitate or make people ill, they are "illth."

The hero of *Our Mutual Friend*, John Harmon, is closely identified with, indeed, is identified as, the drowned body dredged up by Gaffer Hexam in chapter 1. As a possessor of gold, he has also been killed by the action of illth because he has been murdered for the sake of his money. We might say that his story is Ruskin's retold, although in Dickens's version both the man and the gold have surrogates. George Radfoot takes Harmon's place and, as Harmon later explains, is "murdered for the money" by "unknown hands," conceived merely as extensions of what Harmon calls "the fate that seemed to have fallen on my father's riches—the fate that they should lead to nothing but evil" (370). Thus, John Harmon is officially drowned and dredged up at the novel's outset, a victim of illth. After being proclaimed dead, he staggers dazed through the novel's opening episodes, as if, following the stages of Ruskin's inquiry, he had reached the state of merely being wounded in the head by his would-be riches. The question that drives the plot is the same as that asked by Ruskin: what degree of animation in the formerly dead man would be necessary to render possible his possession of (instead of by) his money? "Should John Harmon come to life again?" the hero keeps asking. If he were to reanimate himself, gradually working his way from dead to ill to well, could he change illth to wealth?

The point of remarking these parallels between *Unto This Last* and *Our Mutual Friend* is to direct our attention to a pervasive pattern of mid-Victorian thought, a widespread insistence that economic value can be determined only in close relationship to vital power. In several key texts on economics, sanitation, social theory, and authorship, this way of structuring economic investigations around life and death took the dead body as a starting place and tried to move toward reanimation. However, as I hope to show through an analysis of *Our Mutual Friend*, this operation often resulted in the reseparation of value (equated with Life) from any of its particular instantiations (or bodies). That is, the attempt to put the human body at the center of economic concerns, to rewrite economic discourse so that it constantly referred back to the body's well-being, paradoxically itself tended to do what it accused unreconstructed political economists of doing: separating value from flesh and blood and relocating it in a state of suspended animation or apparent death.

[. . .]

[Ruskin] break[s] with the political economists [. . .] in a disjunction between value and cost. Ruskin conceived of both in vitalist terms, but he notes that a commodity's life-expending "cost" may have little to do with its life-bearing "value." [. . .] Armaments are his favorite examples of purely morbid production, but he observes as well that anything accumulated rather than consumed would be a chunk of mortality. He consequently looks askance at the store of goods in a society, its "wealth," as an encumbrance, a dead weight. "*Munera Pulveris*," "Gifts of the Dust," a phrase he takes from one of Horace's Odes, seems to signify the deathliness of mere accumulation.

Ruskin chose the title *Munera Pulveris* in 1871, the year after Dickens died and six years after *Our Mutual Friend* was completed. Dickens's death was a "great loss" for Ruskin,[3] and, although he claimed not to have felt a political kinship with the novelist, we might nevertheless surmise that the "*Pulveris*" of his title pays at least unconscious homage to the dust heaps of Dickens's last completed work, as surely as those heaps owe something to Ruskin's essays:

> For every hour of labour, however enthusiastic or well intended, which he spends for that which is not bread, so much possibility of life is lost to him. . . . Of all that he has laboured for, the eternal law of heaven and earth measures out to him for reward, to the utmost atom, that part which he ought to have laboured for, and withdraws from him (or enforces on him, it may be) inexorably that part which he ought not to have laboured for. The dust and chaff are all, to the last speck, winnowed away, and on his summer threshing-floor stands his heap of corn; little or much, not according to his labour, but to his discretion. (*Essays*, 201–202)

The main plot of *Our Mutual Friend* uncannily adheres to the outline of this little fable. To avoid having his father's dust mounds enforced on him, John Harmon feigns death while the piles are sifted and shifted, "winnowed away," and a heap of life-giving substance stands revealed.

Our first introduction to this plot insistently equates perishing and amassing. The solicitor Mortimer Lightwood regales a dinner party with a short description of old Harmon's so-called life, describing the dust mounds old Harmon collected as the assembled debris of a vast number of defunct lives. They also become, in Mortimer's highly metaphoric (and Ruskinian) narration, the spewed-forth life of old Harmon himself: "On his own small estate the growling old vagabond threw up his own mountain range, like an old volcano, and its geological formation was Dust. Coal-dust, vegetable dust, bone dust, crockery dust, rough dust and sifted dust,—all manner of Dust" (13). This is an image of peculiar fixity, seemingly ill assorted with the characterization of old Harmon as a "vagabond." It deemphasizes the circulation of debris in the scavenger trade and transforms the enterprise into Harmon's simultaneous expending and hoarding of his own substance. The expense of his life is a self-burying; dust erupts from him and settles on him, so that accumulation and interment are the same thing. The last we hear of old John Harmon makes his death seem the merest extension of the activity of his life: "He directs himself to be buried with certain eccentric ceremonies and precautions against coming to life" (15).

Old Harmon's whole existence seems to have consisted in "precautions against coming to life." He is the prototypically illthy individual, causing, in Ruskin's phrase, "various devastation and trouble around [him] in all directions" (171). He oppresses and anathematizes his own living flesh and blood, his son and daughter, while he builds up his geological formations of dust. The contrast between flesh and blood, and rock, echoes Ruskin's distinction between the true veins of wealth (purple and in flesh) and the false veins (gold and in rock). The conflation of gold and rock in mountains of dust turns both to death; Mortimer Lightwood, in telling old Harmon's story, makes this transformation explicit. But, at the same time, he calls attention to the clichéd nature of these associations: "[Harmon] chose a husband for [his daughter], entirely to his own satisfaction and not in the least to hers, and proceeded to settle upon her, as her marriage portion, I don't know how much Dust, but something immense. At this stage of the affair the poor girl respectfully intimated that she was secretly engaged to that popular character whom the novelists and versifiers call Another, and that such a marriage would make Dust of her heart and Dust of her life—in short, would set her up, on a very extensive scale, in her father's business" (13–14). Old Harmon was a death-dealer, both in the sense that he traded in the remains of life and in the sense that he converted life into those remains. His daughter, of course, dies after she is disowned.

The associations made here between dust, hoarded wealth, and death are presented by the blasé Mortimer as sentimental commonplaces, prompting us to take a closer look at them. Dickens's imagery mimics Ruskin's, but does his narrative really follow Ruskin's logic? Or does it, rather, veer off into a celebration of the transformative potential in drying out and storing up life's remains? Harmon's business emphasizes that value, as such, is always life expended and accumulated, stored up, and it can be stored for the long term only in inorganic form. Hence, Old Harmon's conversion of life into death, his death-dealing, is not different in principle from any other process of realizing value. Despite the death versus life metaphors in the passages that introduce us to the dustmen, the transmission of life into inorganic matter and thence into money is not consistently presented as life destroying in the novel. On the contrary, it is portrayed as a sanitizing process and one in which a pure potential called "Life" is released. This elongated circuit between life expended and life augmented is one of increasing abstraction in which a life-transmitting power finds itself outside of human bodies for a long period of time. And the liberation of such a vital potential turns out to be the novel's very means of making Life seem valuable. The curiously death-centered bioeconomics of *Our Mutual Friend*, therefore, may begin by echoing Ruskin, but it follows Ruskin's metaphor of winnowing into a paradox. In *Unto This Last* and *Munera Pulveris*, Ruskin's stated aim was to separate the grain of life-maintaining commodities from the dross of the rest, but Dickens seems to take the idea of a "grain" of life to signify a vital essence, from which the body itself all too easily falls away as "dust."

We have already seen that death from illth and the possibility of reanimation are at the core of the novel's main plot. But the book's obsession with the place of human bodies inside systems of economic accumulation and exchange goes far beyond John Harmon's story, and that story can best be illuminated by a view of the novel's overall bioeconomics. To begin once again at the beginning, our introduction to the theme shows us the dead body as a nexus of two kinds of economic exchange. John Harmon is not the only person interested in turning "his" dead body back into life. As one of the many kinds of garbage that Gaffer and Lizzie Hexam fish out of the river, the corpse forms a part of their livelihood. It is from this fact that Lizzie is trying to avert her own attention in the opening scene, as she and her father tow the putrefying corpse, which will later be identified as John Harmon's, to shore. In Lizzie's reluctant conversation with her father, the corpse and the river merge in the impersonal pronoun "it": "I—I do not like it, father." "As if it wasn't your living!" replies Hexam. "As if it wasn't meat and drink to you!" (3). The shocking power of this metaphor, which immediately turns Lizzie "deadly faint," is its removal of all mediations between the girl's "living," her sustenance, and the corpse's moldering flesh, which becomes, in this oddly literalizing image, her food; corpse and river are meat and drink. Lizzie's physical reaction is another literalizing metaphor of denial: she would rather turn her own body into the dead white thing than keep it alive on such carrion. This first suggestion of how death might be exchanged for life is the most primitive and horrific of bioeconomic possibilities encountered in the novel.

Gratefully, we move immediately on to another. We are relieved to learn, as the passage continues, that although the river has yielded many things that have directly nurtured Lizzie ("the fire that warmed you," "the basket you slept in," "the rockers I put upon it to make a cradle of it"), the dead bodies have been only *indirect* sources of life. They have been sources of money, and hence can be seen by Lizzie and the reader not as food itself but as the wherewithal to purchase food. Gaffer robs the bodies before turning them over to the police and also collects inquest money for having found them. Hence the bodies are part of a seemingly thoroughly civilized, if a bit ghoulish, network of economic circulation. Lizzie is also disturbed by this exchange of the body for money; indeed, she claims that the sin of pilfering from the corpses is the root of her shame. However, coming to us as it does in the context of the primitive alternative presented in Gaffer's metaphor, the intervention of money has a double moral impact. On the one hand, it brings the Hexams' living inside the pale of civilization. But on the other hand, the intervention of money itself seems just a metaphor that would (but can't quite) cover over the reality of vulturism emphasized by Gaffer's and the narrator's insistent metaphorizing. The metaphors of the corpse as a living and of Gaffer as a bird of prey make the trope of economics—the mediation of money—seem to be a euphemism directing our attention from that which the explicit metaphors reveal: the real exchange *is* life for life.

We are, then, given two ways in which a corpse can be a "living" in this passage, but the distinction between them is collapsible. The more acceptable account (in which the human body is an item of exchange in a money network that fails to distinguish it from other items) is disturbing. But the source of the disturbance, when sought, seems to be the open secret that money is always ultimately taken out of flesh. That is, the horror is not that human flesh becomes money, but that money is just a metaphor for human flesh. In this respect, the exchange made through the corpse is really not different from any other economic exchange, since all value is produced at the expense of life. So far, the novel follows the logic of both Ruskin and the political economists. But the opening of *Our Mutual Friend*, while echoing *Unto This Last* and *Munera Pulveris*, also carries out the logic of the dream of a speedy transfer between life and death to a nightmarish extreme. If any commodity, qua commodity, is expended life, and the dead body merely emphasizes this universal truth, it also renders the typical humanitarian suggestion that it should immediately become nutrition revolting, a revival of Swift's modest proposal. The opening pages of the novel reveal that the humanitarian critique, wishing as it does for the shortest possible circuit between expended and augmented life, conjures up as a reductio ad absurdum of itself, a fantastic, worse than cannibalistic bioeconomy.

Little wonder, then, that the revaluation of old Harmon's legacy, in the other main plot of this densely designed novel, is accomplished not simply by its attachment to a worthy body (as Ruskin would have it) but by its sustained suspension through the apparent death of young John Harmon. Apparent death is the structural principle of the narrative.[4] Young Harmon, as we have seen, describes himself as being dead but having the potential for reanimation. He is, like riches themselves, the possibility of embodied life in a state of suspended animation. And it is only in this state, when he has not claimed his money but has instead, by sloughing off his supposed body, achieved a kind of ontological oneness with the money as pure vital potential, that he can change illth into wealth. He is dead as its inheritor, and yet he manages the fortune as Mr. Boffin's secretary. "The living-dead man," as the narrator calls him, resolves to remain in this state of suspended animation until he has effaced even his function as manager, until he is a mere "method" by which the money manages itself: "[T]he method I am establishing through all the affairs . . . will be, I may hope, a machine in such working order as that [anyone] can keep it going" (373).

Apparent death becomes the only direct access to the essence and value of life. Apparent death is the condition of storytelling and regenerative change. It reveals the value of young Harmon's own story: "Dead, I have found the true friends of my lifetime still as true, as tender, and as faithful as when I was alive, and making my memory an incentive to good actions done in my name" (372). As John Harmon becomes merely a name, a memory, and a fortune, the nugget of value that the story of his life contained is scattered and proliferates. From this vantage point, John Harmon, like an omniscient narrator, can see the complete pattern and know its worth. Even better, like an omnipotent narrator, he can change the story to create more value. This he does by remaining apparently dead as John Harmon to win (disguised as a poor man) the love of the mercenary girl who would otherwise have married him simply for his money. Hence, although the final aim of the dust plot is to prevent the heroine Bella's reduction of herself to a commodity, its machinations all depend on Harmon's merger with the fortune, his organic death into it.

John Harmon's plot, then, demonstrates that value, even the value of Life itself, is only discoverable from some vantage point outside the body. And the novel, moreover, repeatedly relocates value outside the body through processes that resemble the substitution of inorganic wealth for live bodies, even though the origin of wealth in bodies is never effaced. Hence the fascination of the novel with macabre commodities. If the organic "death" of young John Harmon and his merger with his fortune is one example of the connection between money and the release of vital power, the commodities of Mr. Venus, a preserver of animals and birds and an articulator of human skeletons, recapitulate the same point in a grotesquely comic form. While the consciousness of the living-dead John Harmon hovers around the Boffin residence as secretary, the mortal remains of the man whose death has enabled this suspended animation are themselves suspended, it would seem, in Venus's shop. "I took an interest in that discovery in the river," Venus tells Wegg. "I've got up there—never mind, though" (84). Venus buys and sells body parts and also labors on them to make them dry, stable, and hence valuable. Of course, he also has a few fleshy organisms (various preserved babies), but most of his trade is in turning bodies into inorganic representations of themselves. It is this activity that not only releases value from the body and makes it a "living" for Venus but also bizarrely restores a kind of life to the bodies themselves. As he hands a stuffed canary to a customer, Venus triumphantly remarks, "There's animation!" (81).

The same drawing out of value from the organic body and storing it up, suspending it in inorganic forms, characterizes Jenny Wren's doll-making trade. Jenny imagines that the great ladies, whose clothes she copies to make her dolls' dresses, are working for her as models. She imagines that her own effort of "scud[ding] about town at all hours" (435) to see these fashionable clothes is matched by their owners' pains in trying on the dolls' dresses: "I am making a perfect slave of her" (436), she says of one of her "models." And the result of all this sweat is the thing of value, the inorganic body: "That's Lady Belinda hanging up by the waist, much too near the gaslight for a wax one, with her toes turned in" (436).

All of this metaphoric and imagistic insistence on the bodily origins of the commodity and on its disembodiment, on its transcendence of its organic origins and simultaneous conversion into vital potential, finds its culmination in the explicit vitalism of a villain's, Rogue Riderhood's, revivification. In this episode, Life takes on its pure reality and absolute value only because it has been entirely disembodied. Rogue's body itself is merely a "dank carcase," and no one (besides Rogue's pathetic daughter) has any interest in the fate of the man himself. It is neither body nor spirit that is of concern in this scene, "but the spark of life within him is curiously separable from himself now, and they have a deep interest in it" (443). For the sake of this abstracted entity, "All the best means are at once in action, and everybody present lends a hand, and a heart and soul." But when that potential and hence essential Life begins to instantiate itself in the particular body of Rogue Riderhood, its value dissolves: "As he grows warm, the doctor and the four men cool. As his lineaments soften with life, their faces and their hearts harden to him" (446). "The spark of life," the narrator comments, "was deeply interesting while it was in abeyance" (446).

"Life in abeyance" characterizes not only the temporary condition of Rogue Riderhood but also the condition of John Harmon. As such, as we've seen, it is the condition underlying the narrative itself. Moreover, especially for those who insist most strenuously on the flesh and blood origins of economic value, "life in abeyance" is the definitive condition of commodities and the abstract representation of their value in money. As Rogue Riderhood's suspended animation shows clearly, the curious separation of Life from the body is the refinement and purification of vitality itself. Hence, the humanitarian attempt to place and hold the human body at the center of inquiries into the nature of value has a paradoxical result; it leaves the body suspended, apparently dead, while the newly valorized essence, Life, achieves ever more inorganic and even immaterial representations.[5]

This, then, was the destiny of the illth/wealth distinction and of the bioeconomy on which it relied in *Our Mutual Friend*: those transfers of vigor that were at the heart of a body-centered economy kept proving the dependence of vitality on the suspension of animation in the body, on its apparent death. In Dickens's novel, the illth/wealth duality cannot be said to collapse, but the two terms enter into a dynamic fluctuation that breaks their immediate, one-to-one pairing with their supposed physiological reference points, illness and health. The storytelling, value-creating consciousness, like the consciousness of love, like economic value and the vital force itself are all released from physical forms and exist only in their purity while they remain outside of bodies. In the name of Life itself, Dickens repeats the logical trajectory that Ruskin attributed to political economy and dislodges animate, flesh-and-blood people from the center of his discourse.

[. . .]

Notes

1 *"Unto This Last" and Other Essays on Art and Political Economy*, ed. Ernest Rhys (New York: E. P. Dutton, 1932), 169. All quotations from Ruskin are from this edition, and subsequent page numbers are given in the text.
2 *Our Mutual Friend* (London: Oxford University Press, 1974), 4. All subsequent quotations from the novel are from this Oxford University Press edition, and page numbers are given in the text.
3 See Tim Hilton, *John Ruskin: The Later Years* (New Haven: Yale University Press, 2000), 193.
4 Critics have noted that *Our Mutual Friend* has more death in it than other Dickens novels. Patrick McCarthy explores the novel's treatment of one of Dickens's mythic themes, "how beleaguered life may make its way in the face of and by the use of death." See "Designs in Disorder: The Language of Death in *Our Mutual Friend*," *Dickens Studies Annual* 17 (1988): 129–44. In "'Come Back and Be Alive': Living and Dying in *Our Mutual Friend*" (*The Dickensian* 74 [1978]: 131–43), Andrew Sanders argues that in this novel "death becomes thematic and it is balanced by a parallel stress on rebirth" (134). Most recently, George Levine in *Dying to Know: Scientific Epistemology and Narrative in Victorian England* (Chicago: University of Chicago Press, 2002) takes the state of suspended animation in the novel to be the sine qua non of knowledge (148–70). Dickens's concerns, Levine argues in response to the article version of the present chapter, are as much espistemological as economic.
5 For an overview and history of the concept of apparent death, or suspended animation, see Martin S. Pernick, "Back from the Grave: Recurring Controversies over Defining and Diagnosing Death in History," in *Death: Beyond Whole-Brain Criteria*, ed. Richard M. Zaner (Boston: Kluwer Academic Publishing, 1988), 17–74. For a longer look at Dickens's interest in the topic, see Catherine Gallagher and Stephen Greenblatt, *Practicing New Historicism* (Chicago: University of Chicago Press, 2000), 185–204.

45 Literary appropriations

Mary Poovey

In June 1855, while Dickens was mired in what he described as "a hideous state of mind" about [*Little Dorrit*], journalists disclosed that the directors of the reputable banking firm of Strahan, Paul, and Bates had absconded with the bank's money.[1] Later that summer, another financial crime made news: the embezzlement (by forgery) of £150,000 from the Irish Tipperary Bank. The culprit was John Sadlier, a member of Parliament and a junior lord of the Treasury. Unable to face the shame of a trial, Sadlier committed suicide on 17 February 1856. Even after Dickens had figured out what the focus of his novel should be, the revelations of these crimes were obviously provocative: he began composing the sixth number of *Little Dorrit*, in which he introduced the financier Merdle, two days after Sadlier's suicide.

The financial crimes revealed in the summer of 1855 constitute one of the occasions for *Little Dorrit* [. . .] While Dickens openly acknowledged this—declaring, in the 1857 edition, that Merdle "originated after the Railway-share epoch, in the times of a certain Irish bank"[2]—the completed novel does not encourage readers to think about those crimes or to speculate about the conditions that made financial crime so common in the 1850s. Instead, the way that Dickens presented Merdle and his transgression, like his depictions of other contemporary events, made this character a part of the fictional world that existed within the pages of his novel.[3] Dickens might well have wanted to capitalize on readers' interest in Sadlier to support sales of *Little Dorrit*, but he did not want curiosity about the real-life financier to interfere with the moral lesson about the redemptive capacity of love that his reconfigured novel was shaped to deliver. Because the resemblance between Merdle and Sadlier had the potential to undermine this moralizing function—because it might make readers *classify* the novel as a journalistic revelation about contemporary events—he took pains to limit the reader's engagement with Merdle. Thus, the Merdle plot figures only briefly, the details of the financier's crimes remain vague, and the effects of the speculation he inspires are registered in a moral vocabulary that obscures his actual crimes. Even though Merdle's criminal activities lead to the collapse of the partnership formed by Clennam and Doyce, moreover, it is Arthur Clennam's insistence that he publicly take responsibility for the firm's debt that causes his creditors to bring suit against him; this, in turn, leads to Clennam's incarceration in debtor's prison; and it is this imprisonment that paves the way for his reunion with Amy Dorrit. This reunion culminates in marriage, of course, but it also enables Clennam to be spiritually reborn; and, when a successful Doyce returns from the Continent, pays Clennam's debts, and frees him from the Marshalsea, the novel dispenses with the entire subject of financial speculation. Merdle's transgression thus functions within the narrative as a blocking agent: it momentarily impedes the romance plot that links Arthur Clennam to Amy Dorrit and decisively colors the *bildung* chronicle of Clennam's reform. Because Clennam never blames Merdle for the failure of the firm, and because Dickens presents Merdle's crimes only as abstractions ("Forgery and Robbery" [*LD*, 777]), the narrative renders any attempt to refer Merdle to the men whose crimes inspired Dickens irrelevant to the function the character performs in the text.

Dickens does make the speculative mania that Merdle's actions spawn serve an aesthetic role, for this theme enables him to link two plots that otherwise barely overlap: the highly mannered treatment of high society, which is populated by stereotypical characters like the Barnacles, and the more detailed treatment of the Bleeding-Heart Yard plot, where individuated characters like Mrs. Plornish and her father appear. Rumors of riches to be made from speculating in Merdle's ventures travel from the first plot, where the Barnacles could afford to—but do not explicitly—risk money, to the second, where the rent agent Pancks spreads the "contagion" to Clennam, even though both must borrow to speculate. In Dickens's characterization of Clennam, the desire to speculate becomes a psychological disorder, a monomania that must be cured before he can merit Little Dorrit. While the character's ethical reform is crucial to the resolution of the novel, the precise form of his moral affliction is less important than that it be amenable to cure—not by an explanation that might enable readers to discriminate between a sound investment and irrational speculation, but simply through the moral transformation that Amy inspires.

As the narrative focus is increasingly trained on Clennam, the character Merdle is relegated to ever more marginal positions. When Merdle meets Mr. Dorrit in book 2, chapter 16, his presence is momentarily magnified by an elaborate apostrophe that equates him with solar bodies ("Merdle! O ye sun, moon, and stars, the great man!" [*LD*, 673]); but the figure rapidly begins to deflate, reappearing only as an escort in Mr. Dorrit's "rapturous dream" (677), then an inarticulate and shadowy presence in his stepson's apartment (chap. 24), then an unidentified body (771), then a mere series of words that dwindle to an adjective already demoted to a cliché ("the Merdle lot" [869; see also 865, 873]). Even though Dickens mentions that "the public mind" and "talk" inflate rumors about Merdle's wealth into the "roar" that he is guilty of crimes (776), Merdle's influence in the narrative is over. Almost immediately on his disappearance, Clennam takes responsibility for his company's debts, in a substitution that suggests that being in debt is equivalent to Merdle's forgeries and theft—even though the fictional version of the former, unlike the latter, can be redeemed by the rehabilitation Clennam has already begun to undergo.

Dickens's gestures toward actual financial crimes typify the way that many other midcentury novelists capitalized on the financial revelations of these decades. *Hard Times* also invokes a bank crime (embezzlement) to test a character's moral worth; Margaret Oliphant's *Hester* uses securities fraud to expose the fatal flaw in Edward Vernon's character; in Eliot's *Middlemarch*, the banker Bulstrode falls both because he lied about the legacy his wife left her daughter and because he has secretly invested in a manufacturer of toxic dyes; and, in *The Way We Live Now*, Trollope gestures toward another shadowy financier, one who draws young men too foolish for their own good into a speculative web as ruinous—and almost as imprecisely detailed—as Merdle's speculative ventures. While these thematic appropriations reveal how rich the vein of finance was for novelists looking both to entice readers with provocative reminders of actual events and to entertain them with morally edifying tales of perfect justice, they also show how thoroughly the aesthetic agenda had triumphed by midcentury.

*****

Like *Little Dorrit*, George Eliot's *Silas Marner* was a popular (i.e., a commercial) success (although, by the standard that Dickens set, the success of nearly any midcentury novelist is only relative): during its first six months, the one-volume edition of *Silas Marner*, which was priced at 12s., sold eight thousand copies. As with *Little Dorrit* again, *Silas Marner* received mixed responses from the periodical reviewers. Most reviewers praised the novel for its life-like depictions of the poor: unlike the "ordinary tales of country life that are written in such abundance by ladies," observed the *Saturday Review*, Eliot's fictional poor "are like real poor people." Some reviewers, however, were puzzled by Eliot's decision to feature such depressing poor people. "We see the people amid all their groveling cares, with all their coarseness, ignorance, and prejudice—poor, paltry, stupid, wretched, well-nigh despicable," wrote E. S. Dallas in the *Times*.[4] *Silas Marner* also resembles *Little Dorrit* in another sense: in their final versions, both novels were products of their authors' change of mind. Just as Dickens initially thought that the novel tentatively entitled *Nobody's Fault* would be a social critique, so the story of the linen weaver initially came to Eliot as "a sort of legendary tale." Dickens, as we have seen, eventually focused his attention on a smaller scale, and Eliot shifted hers from legend to something that might also be construed as smaller. "As my mind dwelt on the subject," Eliot explained to John Blackwood, "I became inclined to a more realistic treatment."[5]

The similarities between these two novels reveal some significant facts about midcentury novelistic practice. First, the gulf between the commercial success of both novels and the mixed reception they received from reviewers reminds us that the debate about how to measure Literary value [. . .] dominated the middle decades of the century. The particular reservations expressed by Eliot's reviewers reflect obliquely on this debate, moreover, for the feature that reviewers praised in her work—her ability to create "real poor people"—was the same quality that led so many ordinary readers to appreciate (and buy) her works: her ability to create characters so real that they seemed like virtual friends. The shared appreciation for this quality in the nineteenth century means that the disciplinary sense of "realism," which modern Literary critics emphasize, had not yet been articulated as a term *expert* readers could use to differentiate their responses from those of ordinary readers. In other words, even though reviewers were trying to acquire the social authority to make their judgments more decisive than the crude measure of popularity or sales, they had yet to cultivate a *technical* vocabulary that would immediately distinguish between the way they evaluated novels and the way less expert readers did. We can also see the lack of a modern, *disciplinary* system of classification in the fact that cultural biases—in this case, class biases—informed the judgments of reviewers and ordinary, middle-class readers alike. Finally, the change of mind Eliot described, which led her to give "a more realistic treatment" to a topic that had once seemed "legendary," like Dickens's decision to subordinate social commentary to a tale of individual redemption, reminds us that, at midcentury, a narrower focus promised larger returns. Both readers and writers assumed, that is, that cultivating an imaginatively engaging relationship between readers and individuated characters was an essential component of even the most ambitious Literary art.

These complexities remind us once more how difficult it is to provide a historical description of these works. For, on the one hand, such a description aspires to recover the novels' "compositional technologies"—the historically specific material and generic conditions that occasioned them—and, to do so, we need to invoke the terms and categories that prevailed when the novels were written, published, and consumed. On the other hand, however, in order to count *as* a *disciplined* description—in order to be *disciplinary knowledge now*—this account has to be formulated in the technical terminology used by today's professional Literary critics. Throughout this book, I have tried to manage the tension between these two demands by stressing both the terms in which a work was initially understood and the way that a retrospective view alters what we see by altering the categories through which our now-disciplined analysis proceeds. In this brief engagement with *Silas Marner*, I do not make these two perspectives speak to each other [. . .] so much as I highlight the way the novel now appears, when viewed in relation to a fully aestheticized model of Literary writing. The "historical deployments" of this novel, to invoke [Ian] Hunter's term, obviously varied in the 1860s, as responses to it show, but its historical *function*, when viewed retrospectively and in relation to the discipline of Literary studies, was to help demarcate certain uses of language as specifically *Literary* and, as a consequence, as the appropriate object for disciplined (professional) Literary work.

To emphasize only Eliot's treatment of language, as I do here, is admittedly to overlook features that other readers have justifiably celebrated, but it does enable me to isolate a development that was essential to the aestheticization of novels; it was difficult for readers to classify a novel as an aesthetic object, as Henry James urged them to do, until novelistic language came to seem different in some important way from the other uses of prose that seemed superficially so similar to it. We have already seen how Austen and Dickens curtailed the referential capacity of fictional worlds—by elaborating the formal complexities of overlapping plots as crafted interventions rather than simple depictions of everyday life and by flattening out characters that had real-life referents so that the situations that had inspired them would not distract readers from the function a character played within the novel itself. What this brief engagement with Eliot adds to my argument is some sense of how one novelist tried to alter her readers' understanding of language itself so that they would value the way a Literary novelist could augment the referential capacity of words with the mode of connotation Wordsworth had attributed to poetry.

In *Silas Marner*, Eliot uses the figure of gold to shift her reader's attention from the denotative capacity of language to its ability to conjure more than words can say. As the embodiment of a particular kind of value, of course, and the referent of all paper money, gold, even when invoked in a tale set in the not-too-distant past (i.e., a fiction), would have made most nineteenth-century readers think first of money. Lest her readers think that *Silas Marner* is simply a story about money, however, Eliot pushes such a denotative understanding aside. By presenting the weaver's relationship to gold as affective rather than instrumental, she begins to redefine how the word *gold* means as well as what it can be seen to signify. Having been driven out of the narrow religious community in which he was raised, Marner has settled at the outskirts of the obscure village of Raveloe, where he begins to hoard the gold he is paid for weaving. Marner hoards not in order to amass more money but because, in his eyes, the gold has become a quasi-sentient companion. Thus, the narrative informs us that the weaver loves the "bright faces" of the coins, that he imagines they are "conscious of him," and that he considers them "his familiars."[6] It is not immediately clear what, if anything, the gold represents, either to Marner or in the narrative. Instead of treating it as a symbol, the narrative depicts the weaver's obsession with it as a parody of a human relationship, one in which an arid simulacrum of love barely sustains, but emphatically is not, the genuine article: "His life had reduced itself to the functions of weaving and hoarding, without any contemplation of an end towards which the functions tended. . . . He loved the guineas best. . . . He spread them out in heaps and bathed his hands in them; then he counted them and set them up in regular piles, and felt their rounded outline between his thumb and fingers, and thought fondly of the guineas that were only half earned by the work in his loom, as if they had been unborn children" (*SM*, 20–21). Given how much life Marner has invested in the coins, it comes as no surprise that, when the gold is stolen, he falls into a state of near catatonia. In the thematic system Eliot has thus far established, he has attributed life to his gold so that it can sustain his life. Having given the gold a meaning it has for no one else in order to confer on himself what little meaning he can bear, Marner can barely survive its loss.

In the episode that awakens Marner from this state of suspended animation, the narrative extends the logic enacted in this transaction. Whereas Marner had substituted for an instrumental understanding of gold a meager set of meanings that just kept his heart alive, the narrative now begins to infuse the word *gold* with a new set of meanings that expand its animating capacity. This episode also signals Eliot's shift from a merely mimetic form of "realism"—the kind of writing that could convey information about "real poor people" to an audience curious to learn—to a mode of aesthetic representation that infuses even pictures of poor people with a "poetic" dimension. This dimension—the aura or excess that Literary writers consistently associated with poetry—was what novelists like Eliot wanted to produce in novelistic prose. The episode in which this double shift occurs, which appears in part 1, chapter 12, describes Marner's first encounter with a child who, having sought refuge in the weaver's cottage, has fallen asleep on his floor. The narrative relates this encounter through a version of the indirect discourse Austen refined, with the result that the reader's perspective is simultaneously aligned with that of the weaver and trained on him. When we read that Marner has "contracted the habit of opening his door and looking out from time to time, as if he thought that his money might be coming back to him" (*SM*, 109), for example, the phrase that begins with *as if* allows the reader to look at the weaver instead of looking with him, with the result that we interpret the weaver's action in a way that might or might not coincide with his understanding. When Marner reenters his cottage, this double perspective persists:

> He thought he had been too long standing at the door and looking out. Turning towards the hearth, where the two logs had fallen apart, and sent forth only a red uncertain glimmer, he seated himself on his fireside chair, and was stooping to push his logs together, when, to his blurred vision, it seemed as if there were gold on the floor in front of the hearth. Gold!—his own gold—brought back to him as mysteriously as it had been taken away! He felt his heart begin to beat violently, and for a few moments he was unable to stretch out his hand and grasp the restored treasure. The heap of gold seemed to glow and get larger beneath his agitated gaze. He leaned forward at last, and stretched forth his hand; but instead of the hard coin with the familiar resisting outline, his fingers encountered soft warm curls. In utter amazement, Silas fell on his knees and bent his head low to examine the marvel: it was a sleeping child. . . . How and when had the child come in without his knowledge? . . . But along with that question, and almost thrusting it away, there was a vision of the old home and the old streets leading to Lantern Yard—and within that vision another, of the thoughts which had been present with him in those far-off scenes. The thoughts were strange to him now, like old friendships impossible to revive; and yet he had a dreamy feeling that this child was somehow a message come to him from that far-off life. (110–11)

Parts of this passage clearly reproduce Marner's thoughts: "Gold!—his own gold—brought back to him as mysteriously as it had been taken away! . . . How and when had the child come in?" Insofar as these sentences align the reader's perspective with the weaver's "agitated gaze," we, too, see gold in the body of the child, then wonder at the girl's arrival. Insofar as Eliot allows the reader a point of view that does not coincide with Marner's, however, we know that the weaver is mistaken both in believing that his gold has returned and in imagining that the child is a message from his previous life. But the double perspective created by free indirect discourse does not simply correct Marner's literalism; nor does it provide only a clinically accurate depiction of a recluse's delusion. Instead, this passage paves the way for the child to *become* gold in a manner that differs from the literal sense Marner initially imagines. For, as the story unfolds, the value that most people would attribute to literal gold, and that the word *gold* would ordinarily denote, migrates to the child, where it is transformed into an altogether different kind of value. Thus, Marner is right in imagining that the child is gold, but only because he gradually learns that *gold* is not necessarily literal or limited to the coins the word usually denotes.

The plot of *Silas Marner* enacts another version of this displacement of literal meaning by connotation, for, as love for Eppie replaces the love he had once lavished on the gold, Marner ceases to miss his hoard and to view the money he now earns in quite a different way. At first, the weaver dismisses the monetary function of gold as incidental—not because the gold seems too alive to spend, as it once had seemed, but because gold no longer seems to matter at all. Soon, however, he restores the monetary function to gold because his interest is fixed on something other than himself: "The disposition to hoard had been utterly crushed at the very first by the loss of his long-stored gold: the coins he earned afterwards seemed as irrelevant as stones brought to complete a house suddenly buried by an earthquake. . . . And now something had come to replace his hoard which gave a growing purpose to the earnings, drawing his hope and joy continually onward beyond the money" (*SM*, 131). That which "replace[s]" the weaver's hoard, of course, is something literal gold could never buy; and, as his hopes are directed forward, "beyond the money," the monetary function can return, for the values the novel promotes are no longer jeopardized by the values associated with money.

Substituting the child for gold in the episode I have quoted enables Eliot to transform the weaver's initial nonmonetary relation to gold into a human relationship that puts money in its proper place: it becomes the mere "function" that sustains the "end" of a genuinely meaningful life. Such a life, of course, is what De Quincey's "literature of power" was also said to sustain by enlarging the reader's sympathies; by analogy, then, the "literature of knowledge" De Quincey described could do no more than provide the conditions in which such a life could be lived, as literal gold purchased the necessities of life. This expansion of sympathy is what Eliot depicts in the remainder of the narrative, for she shows Eppie so engaging Marner's sympathies that, when her real father appears and offers to make her rich, the weaver can allow her to make the choice for herself. When Eppie elects to remain in her humble surroundings, the narrator makes explicit what everything in the story has implied: the metaphoric "treasure" Eppie incarnates has brought Marner more than money can buy; in the process, it has "exalted" these humble characters beyond the ordinariness of prose to the heights associated with "poetry": "Perfect love has a breath of poetry which can exalt the relations of the least-instructed human beings" (*SM*, 146). Even her disappointed father, the landowner Godfrey Cass, ultimately has to accept that the rules associated with literal money have been rendered obsolete by the love whose value Marner and Eppie have demonstrated. "'There's debts we can't pay like money debts, by paying extra for the years that have slipped by,'" Cass admits as he relinquishes his claims to Eppie (174).

Silas Marner provides a particularly clear example of the way that mid-century novelists subjected economic matters—in this case, the monetary value of gold—to the alchemy of a moral lesson by emphasizing the connotative capacity of language—that is, the elevation of figuration and suggestion over denotation and reference. Marner initially mistakes Eppie for actual gold because he thinks that her blonde hair is literal "gold on the floor" (*SM*, 110), but, when the young girl is called a "treasure" (137, 172), metaphor trumps such literalness.

When Eppie chooses her adopted "father," Marner, over her actual father, she repeats this logic: what a linguistic figure can be made to mean, through imaginative elaboration and the power of connotation, is more valuable than what reference, denotation, or quantification can convey. Eliot's emphasis on language's ability to transfigure and ennoble also helps explain why the historical inaccuracies of this tale and the textual contradictions it contains do not matter to the ethical lesson it confers: in the first decades of the nineteenth century, when the events of *Silas Marner* are explicitly set, a weaver would have been far more likely to be paid in some kind of paper money than in gold; and, in the novel itself, Eppie's "auburn" hair (138) inexplicably metaphorizes into "gold" again at the end of the novel (181).

Eliot's attempt to make readers appreciate the connotative capacities of Literary language by troping terms associated with the market model of value is echoed in numerous Victorian novels. When, at the end of Dickens's *Our Mutual Friend*, Bella Wilfer becomes "the true golden gold" of feminine virtue, for example, Dickens also implies that metaphor can trump reference because the moral value a writer can cultivate in a novel is more powerful than the mere monetary value of literal gold in the merely actual world. Even if novels did circulate in the marketplace as commodities, such tropes suggest, they were able to create for readers experiences money could not buy and modes of imaginative engagement merely informational writing could never inspire.

[. . .]

Notes

1 Schlicke, *"Little Dorrit,"* 335.
2 Dickens, *Little Dorrit* (hereafter *LD*), 35 ("Preface to the 1857 Edition"). Page numbers for subsequent citations are given in the text.
3 Russell offers the following observation about Dickens's treatment of mercantile firms, an observation that also applies to his treatment of financial topics more generally: "Dickens creates four mercantile firms in his major works. They are all initially depicted with some fidelity to reality, and then shaped into an imaginative mould to conform with Dickens's preoccupation with theme or character" ("Money and Finance," 381). The best scholarly treatment of Dickens's moralizing is Klaver, *A/Moral Economics*, chap. 4.
4 Both reviews are reprinted in Carroll, ed., *George Eliot*, 171–72, 179.
5 Eliot quoted in Carroll, introduction to *Silas Marner*, viii,
6 Eliot, *Silas Marner* (hereafter *SM*), 17, 19. Page numbers for subsequent citations are given in the text.

Bibliography

Carroll, David, ed. *George Eliot: The Critical Heritage*. New York: Barnes & Noble, 1971.
——. Introduction to *Silas Marner*, ed. David Carroll, vii–xxv. London: Penguin Books, 1996.
Dickens, Charles. *Little Dorrit*. Edited by John Holloway. London: Penguin, 1967.
Eliot, George. *Silas Marner*. Edited by David Carroll. London: Penguin Books, 1996.
Klaver, Claudia C. *A/Moral Economics: Classical Political Economy and Cultural Authority in Nineteenth-Century England*. Columbus: Ohio State University Press, 2003.
Russell, Norman. "Money and Finance." In Schlicke, ed. *Oxford Reader's Companion to Charles Dickens*. 378–81.
Schlicke, Paul. *"Little Dorrit."* In Schlicke, ed. *Oxford Reader's Companion to Charles Dickens*. 335–41.
Schlicke, Paul, ed. *The Oxford Reader's Companion to Charles Dickens*. Oxford: Oxford University Press, 1999.

46 Economics, the market, and Victorian culture

Jill Rappoport

Both the economics of everyday life and economic theory changed dramatically during the nineteenth century. The vast inequalities of the Industrial Revolution produced class-consciousness and slum reforms as well as a retail and rail infrastructure designed to support the unprecedented consumerism of the expanding middle classes. Everything from soap to movements for workers' and women's suffrage connected the Victorians to an expanding, global marketplace and—depending on the perspective of the commentator—to its taints or triumphs. Critics bemoaned the worship of the cash nexus or celebrated Britain's industry and innovation; theorists shifted their focus from political economy's labor theory of value to neoclassical economics' consumption-based approach; and ordinary men and women bought, sold, gifted, stole, toiled, invested, speculated, faced or fashioned exploitative practices, fought for property rights, and sought forms of stable value. "Economics, the market, and Victorian culture" is thus fertile but extremely wide-ranging ground. This brief essay explores the intersection of Victorian economics and literature by narrowing its focus to three of the most prevalent topics of critical debate: how literature *makes* money, how literature is *about* money, and how literature is (or is not) *like* money.[1]

In the first category—how literature *makes* money—books are, at least in part, a matter of business, objects of labor, not just love. Here, Romantic ideals of inspired authorship collide with Anthony Trollope's late-century discussion of "literary labourers" who should be able to produce 250 words of a novel every fifteen minutes (1883: 236, 237). When Charles Dickens's Oliver Twist reflects that "it would be a much better thing to be a bookseller" than a book-writer, his comment prompts the laughing promise that "We won't make an author of you, while there's an honest trade to be learnt, or brick-making to turn to" (1836–37: 103), but the humorous exchange also makes a serious point by defining literature as a valuable material product, one that employed a range of publishers, printers, book-sellers, distributors, and readers, rather than simply manifesting an individual, writerly vision.[2]

Looking at this larger literary market, publication histories detail the monetary significance of publication format for booksellers, writers, editors, and audiences. Whether a work appeared in monthly numbers, in weekly periodicals, or in volumes better suited for distribution in circulating libraries shaped its composition and competition, its sales and advertising revenue. The study of authors' contracts and correspondence reveals who benefited, and to what degree, from these decisions. They show, for example, that certain canonical authors received astonishing figures for highly anticipated works: £6,000 for Charles Dickens's initial sale of *Our Mutual Friend*, £7,000 for George Eliot's *Romola*. They also provide details about then-popular women—including Felicia Hemans and Charlotte Riddell—who supported not only themselves but their families with income from their literary work (Feldman

1999: *passim*; Henry 2013: 194n4). Some of this work, then, is recovery, with important implications for studies of gender and class. Some of it springs from more recent critical interest in the overlap of law and literature, which has shown how Dickens fought literary piracy by advocating for expanded copyright protections while Eliot combatted fraudulent claims of authorship and unauthorized sequels to her books.

As critics such as Andrew H. Miller (1995) and Lorraine Janzen Kooistra (2011) have suggested, Victorian authors' awareness of their books as commodities shaped those books in many ways. Along these lines, scholars have been interested in the many ways that literature is *about* money or markets. Economics appears in literature's interests in visibility and display, circulation, and exchange; as an explicit theme or plot point (people making, losing, spending, or marrying money); or in the language used for purposes of characterization. In Anthony Trollope's *The Eustace Diamonds*, for instance, descriptions of one heroine as a "treasure" and of the other as "metal [that] did not ring true," one as "real stone" and one as "paste," draw analogies between the women and wealth circulating within the novel, revealing some of the many ways that the nineteenth-century marriage plot depends upon money, not just love (Trollope 1873: I: 23; I: 21; II: 230; Michie 2011).

More than simply excavating how literature documents its period's financial circumstances, the scholarly approach that Mark Osteen and Martha Woodmansee have dubbed "new" economic criticism "recognize[s] the reciprocity between social systems and individuals" (Osteen and Woodmansee 1999: 20). Such scholarship—still invested in determining how literature is *about* money—has pushed on how literature both shaped and was shaped by discourses of economic change: reports on the conditions of industrial laborers and urban slums, workers' movements, factory acts; debates over "surplus" women, divorce, and married women's property; the advent of department stores and modern consumerism; stock bubbles, bank failures, the emergence of limited liability; and literary-specific economics, such as changes in copyright law. New economic criticism's historical bent has also encouraged us to conceive of markets and exchange in broader ways: Victorianists have recently explored economies of information as well as money, markets that traded in flesh (slavery, prostitution, marriage) as well as objects, and the way that gift practices operated alongside the capitalist mechanisms of buying and selling.

Two of this section's extracts, from Jeff Nunokawa's *The Afterlife of Property* (1994) and Catherine Gallagher's *The Body Economic* (2006), model just such historically engaged approaches to the question of how literature is about economics. Nunokawa's showcases one way in which traditional and alternative economic systems shed light on each other, by showing how the Victorian novel responded to the "vicissitudes" of the market in its rendering of gender. Though he grounds his chapter in theoretical and historical understandings of property acquisition, display, and ownership, his project's energy gathers less around specific nineteenth-century capitalist activity than in the loss such activity entails and the efforts literature makes to deny that loss. In Nunokawa's longer work, property becomes figuratively embodied in Dickensian women, such as *Little Dorrit*'s eponymous heroine and *Dombey and Son*'s Florence, whose feminized value seems more secure than the financial fortunes that fluctuate so wildly in those novels. Despite real women's increasing economic rights during the period, these female characters seem to offer husbands their only lasting estate, putting a serious spin on Jane Austen's observation "that a single man in possession of a good fortune, must be in want of a wife" (1813: 3). For Nunokawa, "a Victorian construction of femininity is enlisted . . . as the site for the exercise of proprietorial prerogative" (Nunokawa 1994: 98). In his chapter on Eliot's *Daniel Deronda*, excerpted in this volume, a villain's "ongoing psychological mastery" over a guilt-ridden wife and an intimidated mistress makes up for his "limited prerogative of ownership" (Nunokawa 1994: 92). In other words, men thwarted in their desire to own absolutely—men for whom possession is limited, temporary, and terminated—exert power over women instead.

By exploring the psychological and gendered displacement of monetary relationships into forms of value that are at least ideologically more fixed, Nunokawa suggests one way to historicize the interconnections between literature and economics. In the second extract, Gallagher offers another by exploring how both nineteenth-century political economists and their literary counterpoints negotiated the meaning of value itself. Distinguishing between the Malthusian "bioeconomics" of "populations, the food supply, modes of production and exchange, and their impact on life forms generally" and what she describes as "Benthamite somaeconomics" or "the emotional and sensual feelings that are both causes and consequences of economic exertions," Gallagher understands Victorian political economy as organicist, as "concentrating on Man in nature, and on natural, corporeal Man" (Gallagher 2006: 3, 4, 3, 4). Showing how the definitions of wealth articulated by Dickens's *Our Mutual Friend* and political economists are rooted in "bodily well-being," she argues that, for the novel, this value can only be accessed "from some vantage point outside the body," making male characters' "apparent death" or "the possibility of embodied life in a state of suspended animation" key to "the essence and value of life" (Gallagher 2006: 87, 95 [Chapter 44: 383]).

In her longer chapter on *Our Mutual Friend*, Gallagher, like Nunokawa, turns to gender as an important lens for understanding both nineteenth-century economics and male economic subjectivity. If Nunokawa sees domestic ideology as a way to combat anxieties over masculine property ownership, however, Gallagher shows the reverse, as men's activity becomes the solution to threatened femininity: "Men are knocked out, drowned, dried out, stored up, and finally reanimated . . . so that women need not undergo any such self-alienation" (Gallagher 2006: 116). Thus in Gallagher's reading of Dickens's novel, John Harmon creates value by "prevent[ing] the heroine Bella's reduction of herself to a commodity" (Gallagher 2006: 95 [Chapter 44: 383]). The alchemy that transforms this mercenary woman into "the true golden gold" of the novel accords with Nunokawa's sense of stable value as always gendered, but for Gallagher this figurative gold is the novelist's alternative to a very real danger that women can be owned and exchanged.

The value of *Our Mutual Friend*'s Bella Wilfer is as much a question of genre as of gender, according to the third extract.[3] In *Genres of the Credit Economy*, Mary Poovey argues that as fiction and financial prose separated from each other and competed for authority in the nineteenth century, metaphor allows literary authors to "put . . . money in its proper place" (Poovey 2008: 382, also 383 [Chapter 45: 391]). Literature transmits and perpetuates its own sense of value in part by ensuring that its engagement with the world of contemporary finance supersedes straight reference to "serve an aesthetic role" (Poovey 2008: 376 [Chapter 45: 387]). Unlike Gallagher and Nunokawa, who focus on ways in which literature resembles money, finding analogies between "storytelling [. . . and] economic value" or between "ownership and . . . narrative," Poovey's commitment is to the distinction between economic and literary forms (Gallagher 2006: 97 [Chapter 44: 385]; Nunokawa 1994: 87 [Chapter 43: 376]). Poovey's book thus shows, in a historicized, literary, and economically nuanced way, how literature is (but really and increasingly is *not*) like money or the writing that developed to describe and explain it.

Poovey situates her argument about genre against the kind of new historicism practiced by Gallagher and Nunokawa, attacking the claim that literary interpretation "can generate *historical evidence*" (Poovey 2008: 344). Instead, she advocates a form of "historical description" which will focus on a text's historical "function" rather than its "meaning," arguing that this strategy "might enable modern scholars to see that projecting ourselves into the past—or subsuming the past into our present—as we do every time we extrapolate a universal subject from our own reading experience, does not yield or amount to evidence for an argument about the past" (Poovey 2008: 351–52).[4]

Despite the strong case she makes for the recovery of "the material and generic conditions that made composition of particular texts possible, and on . . . the function to which texts were put by past readers" (Poovey 2008: 345), I am not convinced that the best, and most responsible literary historicism, new or otherwise, is mere projection, nor have I found that this version of historical description necessarily eliminates the blinders imposed by our present critical stance. For instance, in attempting to locate the "situations or events that were *occasions* for writing and that *encouraged* publications *of a certain kind*," Poovey acknowledges that this "admittedly involves . . . speculation on my part" (Poovey 2008: 357). Or, to take a different example, in this excerpt's argument about Eliot's *Silas Marner*, Poovey extrapolates that "the feature that reviewers praised in her work—her ability to create 'real poor people'—was the same quality that led so many ordinary readers to appreciate (and buy) her works: her ability to create characters so real that they seemed like virtual friends" (Poovey 2008: 378 [Chapter 45: 388]). Yet it doesn't follow that either the educated, middle-class reviewers or ordinary readers she describes would have known much about "real poor people" (described by one of the reviews she quotes as "poor, paltry, stupid, wretched, well-nigh despicable") or that the realism of poverty itself would make a reader feel any form of "virtual friend[ship]" with the poor, however accurately depicted (Poovey 2008: 377 [Chapter 45: 388]). What variants of new historicism might add to historical description, then, beyond the recognition of "class biases" at the back of these judgments (Poovey 2008: 378 [Chapter 45: 388]) is a more thorough investigation of such comments—an effort to understand the specific assumptions that lead to a reviewer's equation of being poor with being "despicable," or the stakes of presenting poverty as entailing "stupid[ity]."

Without giving up on the analysis of meaning, that is, we can work to understand the history that "hide[s] interpretively as a reality effect," as Elaine Freedgood puts it (Freedgood 2006: 35). "Thing" theory, which pushes background objects to the front in order to read their social histories, is one strategy for doing so (Freedgood 2006: 51). In this vein, Freedgood demonstrates how the mahogany furniture in Charlotte Brontë's 1847 *Jane Eyre* "symbolizes, naturalizes, domesticates, and internalizes the violent histories of deforestation, slavery, and the ecologically and socially devastating cultivation of cash crops in Madeira and Jamaica" (Freedgood 2006: 35). Without recourse to the modern reader—indeed, delivering information the modern reader is unlikely to know, but that was "still all *too* present" for the period—Freedgood insists on "a moment of forestalling allegory, and of taking things literally," a project that is in certain respects opposed to Poovey's focus on the development of literary aesthetics, but one that allows us to see a text's historical *engagements*, rather than making causal arguments about the text's creation, reception, or function (Freedgood 2006: 35, 36).

Together, the works by Poovey, Gallagher, and Nunokawa excerpted in this volume contribute to the field of economic literary criticism by weighing in on value and the terms of its possession. They also leave room for expanding those categories. Along these lines, Freedgood is useful to me here for two additional reasons: she takes a female character's economic subjectivity seriously but also describes that character's selfhood as "permeable, able to open up to exchange with others" (Freedgood 2006: 46). Both emphases—on women's economic agency and on intersubjective exchange—are important to one of the turns that

I see economic criticism taking, and that I'd like to gesture toward now with my own brief reading of *Our Mutual Friend*.

Notoriously "willed away, like a horse, or a dog, or a bird" or "a dozen of spoons," Bella Wilfer epitomizes the economic dispossession and objectification of middle-class women that has concerned Victorianists, in various ways, for decades (Dickens 1864–65: 377, 37). Born to a clerk who can barely make ends meet, she will not inherit wealth, but with few options for earning money respectably, she must marry into it. Prior to her engagement, both Harmons and their friends make her an object to toy with and then traffic in and, once married, she loses any economic agency she might have possessed as a single woman under the common law doctrine of coverture (Shanley 1989: 8–9; *cf.* Rutterford 2013: 133–41). Characterized by plump elbows, curls, and cheeks, Bella embodies her value visibly and materially, rather than suspending her vital energy in the manner that, according to Gallagher, profits the author and his male heroes. When she becomes the "true golden gold," it is less as a result of her own worth than her husband's "triumph" (759; Schor 1999: 184–85; Shuman 1995: 159).

Such gendered dispossession was ideologically important to a culture alarmed both by its own acquisitiveness and by market instabilities (Michie 2011: 7–9; Poovey 1995: 160–61). Property is far from secure in the novel; Dickens rails against the speculation and ungrounded social power that lead to financial fluctuations. Unlike Harmon's dust mounds, which can be scavenged or dispersed, Bella's value is—at least in theory, for Nunokawa—long lasting, offering men the fiction of "safe estate" (Nunokawa 1994: 10, 13, 7), allowing Rokesmith to confidently claim Bella as "mine" (606). Yet this gendered dispossession was something of a fiction itself. The uncertainty of commercial instruments may present the most explicit threat to male possession in *Our Mutual Friend*, but the novel also demonstrates an awareness that women could have more than symbolic relations to gold; most of its female characters find remunerative occupations (at factories, dust mounds, needlework, pawn shops, public houses, and schools). The novel was published a decade after the first attempted Parliamentary petition for married women's property rights but several years before the legislation that finally began to grant them (Shanley 1989: 32–34). It appeared at a time when women's increasing demands for property rights were seen as threatening men's claims to ownership, making gender a key category for stoking fantasies about stable or enduring possession. The fiction that a woman can be willed away to become a man's most reliable treasure thus compensated both for the precariousness of other property rights, as Nunokawa suggests, *and* for the cultural reality that women were increasingly exerting their own economic will. Though women feature primarily as objects of value within the excerpted works of Nunokawa, Gallagher, and Poovey, other scholarship has begun to show the many forms that women's economic practices took, both in life and in literature, detailing their activities in traditional and alternative markets, and exploring not only the legal restrictions on their economic roles but the creative ways in which they maneuvered around them (Psomiades 1999; E. Rappaport 2000; Michie 2011; J. Rappoport 2012; Dalley and Rappoport 2013).

If most critics of *Our Mutual Friend*, stressing women's dispossession, have seen the elder John Harmon's will as problematic for its attempt to traffic in women, it strikes me as also important to read it as a failure of willed property: it doesn't actually express Harmon's final desires. His second will leaves almost everything to the Crown (493), while his third (and last) leaves everything to a former servant (787), who generously but also rebelliously defies those last wishes even when they are publicly known. Despite the significance of texts to discussions of literature and economics, the will has remained largely absent *as* a document from the cluster of ideas about writing and value. Gallagher suggests that Harmon's legacy is revalued both "by its attachment to a worthy body" and "by its sustained suspension" (Gallagher 2006: 94 [Chapter 44: 383]). Yet the old miser's words repeatedly fail him. In this sense, the novel's testamentary vision fits Poovey's account of how financial instruments and literary writing diverge in Victorian fiction. Harmon's will doesn't work. Unlike the literary texts that (for Gallagher) appear to function as repositories of vital power for authors such as Dickens (Gallagher 2006: 115), or (for Nunokawa) to provide a safer arena for ownership, this text gets away from its author.

Among the many reasons for this testamentary failure is the novel's repeated questioning of whether a deceased man has any right to direct his estate. Waterman Gaffer Hexam, defending his own corpse-robbing practices, raises this question early: "Has a dead man any use for money? . . . How can money be a corpse's? Can a corpse own it, want it, spend it . . . ?" (4). While Gallagher uses this passage as her point of departure for understanding nineteenth-century definitions of value (Gallagher 2006: 86 [Chapter 44: 379]), I find it a useful place for considering the conditions under which the novel *does* allow a corpse to own, want, and spend money. To a certain extent, that is, definitions of possession and value depend upon the circumstances of ownership and exchange. Even though a "dead man" may fail to "own [. . . or] spend" money in *Our Mutual Friend*, a dead woman proves better able to do so.

But not on her own. In addition to revisiting gender in the novel, then, this is a place where we might revisit the individualist logic that characterizes most economic criticism. Recent scholarship has begun to consider not merely the competitive individual producers, consumers, and owners that neoclassical economics described, but also larger, dynamic communities of circulation, possession, and exchange that include collaboration and more intersubjective economic activity (Bigelow 2013). In Nunokawa's rendering of a capitalist marketplace, sharing property necessitates its loss (Nunokawa 1994: 44–49), but my own work suggests that some Victorians understood ownership differently; in Elizabeth Gaskell's *Cranford*, for instance, I argue that "the only way to 'have' something is to share it" (Rappoport 2012: 80). Along these lines, *Our Mutual Friend* ultimately offers, in place of old Harmon's solitary, secretive, and finally futile attempts to direct money after his death, a testamentary team that works more successfully.

Betty Higden's story thus offers a useful counterpoint to that of Harmon and Bella Wilfer.[5] The great-grandmother of an orphan who dies before he can be adopted as a surrogate John Harmon, this deserving, working-class woman is the mouthpiece for Dickens's decades-old bitterness against the New Poor Law of 1834. She lives in fear of the workhouse and finally dies trying to earn a living rather than succumb to pauperism or patronage. Before departing with her basket of wares, however, she agrees to carry a note from her well-to-do, would-be benefactors (389), and her last words guide Lizzie Hexam to read it and learn her final wishes: to contact her friends and to use the money sewn into her clothing to pay for her burial (511). Unlike Old Harmon's directives, these wishes are "fulfilled" (515).

What allows Betty's will, but not Harmon's, to be fulfilled is partly a function of character and poetic justice, of course, but in a novel so driven by testamentary trouble, I think that there's something more at stake in the way that the material decisions of Betty, but not Harmon, are permitted to matter after death. Despite the novel's earlier refusal to allow a single, secretive "corpse" to claim or direct the use of money, it offers here a model for collaborative directives that will do just that. Rokesmith and the Boffins anticipate the setting which might require documentation of Betty's desires, while an oral exchange between women— Betty's deathbed message to Lizzie—directs attention to the document she carries and allows Lizzie to confirm "solemnly" and "[f]aithfully" (513) that she will fulfill Betty's wishes.

To some degree, this is the novelist's fantasy of a single reader-recipient—a unified audience—who is intent on carrying out an author's wishes and who does so both by attending to the written word and by reading its larger spirit. Lizzie's execution of Betty's will requires her newly acquired literacy, which allows her to read the document and write to Betty's friends, but it also requires the longstanding, sympathetic vision that allows her to engage with and understand Betty, who by that point can barely speak. Although Gallagher has suggested that Dickens's ideal reader will blindly "wait and trust . . . very much like the reformed Bella Wilfer at the novel's end" (Gallagher 2006: 114, 115),[6] Lizzie's interaction with Betty suggests another, more active model for receptive readership than that of wifely submission. "[E]arnest" intent on "understand[ing]" (512), and sympathetic to the meaning it will strive to learn, this is an audience who will also *act*, quickly and bravely, to ensure that a "last request [is] religiously observed" (516).

From another standpoint, this episode highlights some remarkably collaborative economic action, by women as well as men, protecting Betty's monetary decisions through the solemn and faithful description and then execution of her will.[7] Betty and Lizzie together suggest that Victorian novelists such as Dickens were imagining women as more than merely objects of men's will; nineteenth-century women's economic agency is not simply our twentieth- or twenty-first-century discovery. It is telling, though, that Betty and Lizzie, rather than Bella, demonstrate this point. Betty and Lizzie are working-class characters who possess little money and—as a widow and an orphaned single woman, respectively—earn their own livings without needing "a penny" (515) of additional support. Posing no private threat to husbands or fathers, their small-scale economic agency seems just as unlikely to disturb larger economic operations: Betty's insistence on her own grave will not shut down the workhouse, and Lizzie's execution of Betty's desires doesn't even make her late to her job at the mill (517). When the first Married Women's Property Act was passed in 1870, it focused similarly on working-class women, protecting their earnings and small inheritances from disreputable husbands, but doing little to protect women of Bella Wilfer's rank (Shanley 1989: 74; Ablow "One Flesh"). When we look exclusively at the middle-class women threatened by commodification or the fiction of being someone's "safe estate" in the novel, we miss the characters whose plot lines offer a different story about gender, class, and economics.

Yet this story develops that earlier plot, too. Lizzie Hexam is the daughter of Gaffer, the corpse-robbing waterman who first raised the question of whether or not a dead man could own, want, or spend money. After his death, she strives to make "Any compensation—restitution" for his thefts (227). In her ability to help another poor woman direct her own burial, she offers a model distinct from her father's in every way. The money found on Betty's body is used as she intended; Lizzie's aid to her quietly rebuts Gaffer's assertion that "money [cannot] be a corpse's" (4). This economic action, which thus bears significantly on the novel's larger discourses, comes into focus when we expand our understanding of ownership beyond the bounds of competitive individualism and when we grant to nineteenth-century fiction some of the interest in gender and class that we take up ourselves as economic critics of literature.

Notes

1 See also Osteen and Woodmansee 1999, 3–50 and Poovey 2008, 10–14.
2 See "Print Culture" in this volume.
3 In *Making a Social Body*, Mary Poovey argues that *Our Mutual Friend* aligns women with representation itself (Poovey 1995: 170).

4　Poovey credits Ian Hunter's formulation of "historical description" as a starting point for her method, but distinguishes between their emphases and methods (Poovey 2008: 344–5).
5　For another approach to Betty Higden and economics, see Schaffer 2011.
6　Rachel Ablow (2007: 19) reverses the gender but also suggests a marital model for novel-reading.
7　Though women did serve as executors of wills, Mr. Boffin would have been unusual in appointing his wife as "sole executrix" (93). See Green 2009: 140–45.

Bibliography

Ablow, R. (2007) *Reading Sympathy in the Victorian Marriage Plot*, Stanford: Stanford University Press.
—— "'One Flesh,' One Person, and the 1870 Married Women's Property Act," *BRANCH: Britain, Representation and Nineteenth-Century History*, ed. Dino Franco Felluga, Extension of Romanticism and Victorianism on the Net. Available at www.branchcollective.org/?ps_articles=rachel-ablow-one-flesh-one-person-and-the-1870-married-womens-property-act (accessed 28 April 2014).
Austen, J. (1813; 2001), *Pride and Prejudice*, D. Gray (ed.), New York and London: W. W. Norton & Company.
Bigelow, G. (2013) "The Cost of Everything in *Middlemarch*," in L. L. Dalley and J. Rappoport (eds.), *Economic Women: Essays on Desire and Dispossession in Nineteenth-Century British Culture*, Columbus: The Ohio State University Press, 97–109.
Dalley, L. L. and Rappoport, J. (eds.) (2013) *Economic Women: Essays on Desire and Dispossession in Nineteenth-Century British Culture*, Columbus: The Ohio State University Press.
Dickens, C. (1836–37; 1966) *Oliver Twist*, Oxford: Oxford University Press.
Dickens, C. (1864–65; 2008) *Our Mutual Friend*, Oxford: Oxford University Press.
Feldman, P. R. (1999) "The Poet and the Profits: Felicia Hemans and the Literary Marketplace," in I. Armstrong and V. Blain (eds.), *Women's Poetry, Late Romantic to Late Victorian: Gender and Genre, 1830–1900*, New York: St. Martin's Press, 71–101.
Freedgood, E. (2006) *The Ideas in Things: Fugitive Meaning in the Victorian Novel*, Chicago: The University of Chicago Press.
Gallagher, C. (2006) *The Body Economic: Life, Death, and Sensation in Political Economy and the Victorian Novel*, Princeton: Princeton University Press.
Green, D. R. (2009) "To Do the Right Thing: Gender, Wealth, Inheritance and the London Middle Class," in A. Laurence, J. Maltby, and J. Rutterford (eds.), *Women and their Money 1700–1950: Essays on Women and Finance*, London and New York: Routledge, 133–50.
Henry, N. (2013) "Charlotte Riddell: Novelist of 'The City,'" in L. L. Dalley and J. Rappoport (eds.), *Economic Women: Essays on Desire and Dispossession in Nineteenth-Century British Culture*, Columbus: The Ohio State University Press, 193–205.
Kooistra, L. J. (2011) *Poetry, Pictures, and Popular Publishing: The Illustrated Gift Book and Victorian Visual Culture 1855–1875*, Athens: Ohio University Press.
Michie, E. B. (2011) *The Vulgar Question of Money: Heiresses, Materialism, and the Novel of Manners from Jane Austen to Henry James*, Baltimore: The Johns Hopkins University Press.
Miller, A. H. (1995) *Novels Behind Glass: Commodity Culture and Victorian Narrative*, Cambridge: Cambridge University Press.
Nunokawa, J. (1994) *The Afterlife of Property: Domestic Security and the Victorian Novel*, Princeton: Princeton University Press.
Osteen, M. and Woodmansee, M. (1999) "Taking Account of the New Economic Criticism: An Historical Introduction," in M. Woodmansee and M. Osteen (eds.), *The New Economic Criticism: Studies at the Intersection of Literature and Economics*, London: Routledge.
Poovey, M. (1995) *Making a Social Body: British Cultural Formation, 1830–1864*, Chicago: The University of Chicago Press.
—— (2008) *Genres of the Credit Economy: Mediating Value in Eighteenth- and Nineteenth-Century Britain*, Chicago: The University of Chicago Press.

Psomiades, K. (1999) "Heterosexual Exchange and Other Victorian Fictions: *The Eustace Diamonds* and Victorian Anthropology," *NOVEL: A Forum on Fiction*, 33.1: 93–118

Rappaport, E. D. (2000) *Shopping for Pleasure: Women in the Making of London's West End*, Princeton: Princeton University Press.

Rappoport, J. (2012) *Giving Women: Alliance and Exchange in Victorian Culture*, Oxford: Oxford University Press.

Rutterford, J. (2013) "'A pauper every wife is': Lady Westmeath, Money, Marriage, and Divorce in Early Nineteenth-Century England," in L. L. Dalley and J. Rappoport (eds.), *Economic Women: Essays on Desire and Dispossession in Nineteenth-Century British Culture*. Columbus: The Ohio State University Press. 127–42.

Schaffer, T. (2011) *Novel Craft: Victorian Domestic Handicraft and Nineteenth-Century Fiction*, Oxford: Oxford University Press.

Schor, H. M. (1999) *Dickens and the Daughter of the House*, Cambridge: Cambridge University Press.

Shanley, M. L. (1989) *Feminism, Marriage, and the Law in Victorian England*, Princeton: Princeton University Press.

Shuman, C. (1995) "Invigilating *Our Mutual Friend*: Gender and the Legitimation of Professional Authority," *NOVEL* 28.2: 154–72.

Trollope, Anthony (1883; 1905), *Autobiography of Anthony Trollope*, New York: Dodd, Mead, and Company.

—— (1873; 2008), *The Eustace Diamonds*, Oxford: Oxford University Press.

Part XII

Print culture

Introduction

> *The prejudice that cheap literature cannot be good has now completely worn away, the differ-*
> *ence between the cheap and the dear consisting merely in the alternatives whether profit shall*
> *be sought in a very large or a very limited circulation . . . At all events . . .* [we] *have no doubt*
> *of being able to establish a journal which may be deemed a truly national specimen of the best*
> *possible literature at the lowest possible price.*
>
> *Those who may purchase this journal are earnestly requested, should they approve of it, to*
> *recommend it to their friends, and introduce it amongst the circle of their acquaintance. . . . This*
> *journal shall be a sign of the times—a proof of the elevated condition of the public taste and*
> *intellect!*
>
> —From "Notice to Correspondents," in *The London Journal and Weekly Record of*
> *Literature, Science, and Art*, March, 1845, Vol. 1, num. 1, p. 16

Seen from a great distance and with a Whiggish squint of the eye, the definitive liberalization projects of the Victorian period are easy to make out: they include the steady expansion of the franchise to include male property holders, reforms of child and adult labor laws, and changes in divorce law and married women's property rights. But there was a less well-known phenomenon that had a similarly profound impact on Victorian politics and culture. This was the gradual removal of what were called the "taxes on knowledge." These included the taxes on advertising, newspapers, and paper that had begun during the time of Queen Anne and that had been manipulated by the state in the early nineteenth century to restrict the radical political press. The recession of these taxes began in 1836 with a cut in the newspaper stamp tax from 4d to 1d, advanced further with the elimination of that tax in 1851 and the repeal of the duty on paper in 1861, and culminated in 1869 with the removal of the registration and securities requirements on newspapers.[1]

What resulted was that quintessential modern phenomenon, a mass media explosion, the impact of which was registered early on by ambitious editors like George W. M. Reynolds, whose *London Journal* became one of the most popular penny fiction weeklies of the Victorian period.[2] In the first issue in 1845 (quoted above), Reynolds announces several promotional strategies that would become important in this period of publication history. These include the implementation of a low-cost pricing plan that the early tax repeals had made possible; an attack on the "prejudice that cheap literature cannot be good," which was in effect a challenge not only to the existing publishing conventions but also to notions of fixed class divisions among readers; a related conceptualization of a mass reading public whose democratic tastes could coalesce around popular fiction like Mary Braddon's *Lady Audley's Secret* (later serialized in the *London Journal* in 1863); and finally, an embrace of the fact that, once available, reading matter would inevitably be distributed informally by readers who would "introduce it amongst the circle of their acquaintance."

As Reynolds suggests, changes in standards of taste, in the nature and size of the reading public, and in the scale of marketing and distribution were indeed "signs of the times" in the wake of the repeal of the taxes on information. But what was the response to this explosion in print matter on readers themselves? Many of them registered a mixture of disorientation and helpless excitement, something like an encounter with Kant's mathematical sublime. Indeed, both that affective experience and the phenomenon that produced it seem strikingly familiar to students and scholars now adapting to our own rapidly expanding nineteenth-century online archive (along with archives of funny cat videos and much else). What qualitative impact this quantitative expansion will have on our scholarship is very much a live question in the field of print culture.

Matthew Rubery captures the methodological diversity of current print culture studies in defining it as "a field comprising book history, periodical research, and media studies" (Rubery 2009: 11 [Chapter 48: 415]) and both Jennifer Phegley's capstone essay and the dynamic critical range of all three selections below attest to it. These selections include Laurel Brake's market-focused explanation of how the novel helped to bolster the growth of the periodical press; Matthew Rubery's genre-focused reading of how specific types of newspaper writing were translated into the Victorian novel; and Leah Price's playful evocation of the purposes to which print media was put in the nineteenth century. Brake demonstrates the ways in which religious tracts could work both as the novel's *bete noir* and secret sharer; she also reminds us that people did all sorts of other things with printed matter other than just *read* it, like stuffing those tracts into bottles and dropping them into the sea. The paper spread everywhere.

See also: *Genre fiction and sensation*; *Disinterestedness and liberalism*; *Economics, the market, and Victorian culture*

Notes

1 For a recent account of this history, see Martin Hewitt, *The Dawn of the Cheap Press in Victorian Britain: The End of the 'Taxes on Knowledge', 1849–1869* (London: Bloomsbury, 2013).
2 On the history of this remarkable publication, see Andrew King, *The London Journal, 1845–83: Periodicals, Production, and Gender* (Aldershot: Ashgate, 2004).

47 The advantage of fiction

The novel and the 'success' of the Victorian periodical

Laurel Brake

The English Common Reader and the field of print culture

Fifty years ago, when Richard Altick published *The English Common Reader*, he shaped a critical map of a vast field that had been recognized by few scholars in English. The notion of the 'common' reader signalled an apparent distinction between the consumers of literature – the object of study in departments of English – and 'common' readers of the 'popular' press, a working class readership associated with cheap and sensationalist literature huddled at one end of the spectrum, reading papers that insulted the intellect and left ink on one's hands. If that distinction is slowly collapsing, its demise was fuelled by Altick's remarkable achievement.

The text alone is prodigious, but the rich back matter – the 'Chronology of the Mass Reading Public', the list of best sellers with cumulative sales figures, circulation figures for periodicals and newspapers, an extensive bibliography, and a detailed index including topics such as 'pocket-sized books' as well as 'reading', which he was putting on the map – made Altick's volume unique in its breadth of achievement to date. All of those accustomed to working on the press know how difficult it is to manage the profligacy of serial publications, to extricate oneself from the number, and to step back to interpret and map meaning. *The English Common Reader* is that rare thing, a combination of vast and visibly detailed knowledge and shaped argument. Since 1957 few such books on nineteenth-century publishing by a single author have appeared, and scholars understandably favour studies of single titles or categories of print, or multi-authored books with their range of expertise to 'cover' a broad subject such as New Journalism, for example.

Most recently, William St Clair's *The Reading Nation in the Romantic Period* (2004) is one of the exceptions with respect to its scope, its ambitiousness, and its detailed appendices and a bibliography for our time, and he begins by presenting his study as a necessary supplement to Altick.[1] But the context in which *The Reading Nation* is published is a measure of our distance from the scholarly community and discourse of the mid-1950s, which was before Victorian (and Romantic) interdisciplinary 'area' studies, before *Victorian Studies* and *Victorian Periodical Studies*, before the linguistic turn and its passport to popular culture with its nomenclature of 'text' and 'discourse' to supplement 'literature' and the novel, and before the new perspectives on publishing history and bibliography that D.F. McKenzie and the History of the Book offer. Most of these have turned to *The English Common Reader*, seeking information (a privileged term now), the map, and interpretation, and remarkably still do, as a reference point for further work. There is nothing else like it, or to replace it. Its reprint history supports this reading.

The 50th anniversary of its publication and the appearance of St Clair's book, with its list of desiderata, specifically in respect to archive work, in themselves justify study of Altick's legacy. Moreover, the field Altick's book fuelled, that of nineteenth-century print culture, is on the verge of a significant transformation of access to archival materials that sharply distinguishes the present from the mid-1950s. For the last half-century, to augment geographically specific access we have relied on historically determined forms of media, reference works, transport, and funding. These include: microfilm, that enabling but frustrating portable medium; pioneering search mechanisms produced in the period such as the *Wellesley Index*, Alvin Sullivan's *English Literary Magazines*, and the prodigious and still growing *Waterloo Directory*; and transport, such as air travel ('cheap'/affordable with respect to cash but also to time), which has enabled researchers physically to reach their objects of study. And in the last decade we have gained electronic access to fragments of the nineteenth-century press through projects such as *ILEJ* (*Internet Library of Early Journals*), the British Library Pilot Periodicals Project, the electronic edition of the *Times*, the Modernist Journals Project at Brown University, Jerome McGann's NINES, *Harper's*, the Library of Congress's Making of America, *PAO* (*Periodicals Archive Online*), formerly *Periodicals Contents Index*, and SciPer. 'Research', as an activity associated with the professionalization of the academy, has also proliferated in this half century, along with enhanced funding opportunities associated with it. More scholars have had more access to the archive by these varied means in the last 50 years.

However, I think that we are in the last moments before changes in access and searchability affect our methodology in this field profoundly. In the near future, the fruition of a number of ongoing electronic projects dedicated to the publication of nineteenth-century newspaper and periodical titles will potentially multiply access to runs of titles prodigiously. In 2008–2010 alone, a clutch of digital materials has become available. These include the British Library's publication of some 70 titles in British newspapers 1800–1900, ProQuest's British Periodicals, the Thomson Gale/British Library partnership in the periodical tranche of 'Nineteenth-Century Collections Online', and smaller projects, such as ncse (an edition of a cluster of six nineteenth-century serials) and the *Dictionary of Nineteenth-Century Journalism*. The origins of these expensive projects are various – some are research council or foundation funded (the Arts and Humanities Research Council (AHRC), Joint Information Systems Committee (JISC), Mellon, or Leverhulme), some emanate from great national libraries (the British Library and the Library of Congress), and some from the commercial sector. Many of them involve partnerships among these groups, but the significance of this cross-sector cooperation is that access to this immensely enhanced historical resource may be restricted by price. Clearly, this needs to be addressed. Nevertheless, while such issues of dissemination and variable distribution will mean that scholars and students may still have to travel to resource-rich centres, the likelihood is that more of them will have access to more, and searchable, titles. Computer software has some way to go to accommodate the nuanced theorizing of text by scholars of print culture, but once stable and sustainable electronic texts of periodical and newspaper runs, in facsimile, and with accessible optical character recognition (ocr) are created and disseminated, they are there for scholars to work on.

'The convergence of the twain': fiction and the press

In a critical history of nineteenth-century literature published in 1896, George Saintsbury identified the 'rise' of the novel and that of the periodical as the salient developments of the century. Altick puts it slightly differently, but his comparison of the expansion of book production more generally with that of the periodical press is analogous and the judgment similar: the growth of the periodical press emerges from both accounts as the greater, and it becomes the privileged term. However, Altick gingerly entertains the notion of overlap between book/novel and press production on one count only, viewing the miscellany and the individual novel part as 'blood brothers' ('It is almost hopeless to draw a firm line between the penny part-issue of an individual novel and the cheap miscellany; they were both serials').[2] Saintsbury goes further by positively deploying the efflorescence, popularity, and visibility of the 'triumph' of the novel rhetorically to enhance his claim for the superior status of periodicals. Rather than perpetuate Saintsbury's notion of a contrast, a binary, and contestation between the novel and the periodical, or Altick's notion of limited overlap between them, I want to explore a model in which they are inextricably coupled.

Particularly after 1850 I see their relation as symbiotic, productively mutual, and interdependent. Rather than claiming credit for the greater importance of periodicals on the basis that they 'carried' literature, as Saintsbury and other scholars do (and of course the periodicals carried much else), I want to suggest that the widespread incorporation of the novel into mainstream periodicals in the 1850s and after helped assure the proliferation and economic viability of the periodical press. Consumers of popular culture, attracted to fiction, supplemented those arguably graver readers of the miscellany of articles on history, philosophy, and science to make journals viable and sustainable; the greater inclusion of fiction, its appropriation, crucially broadened readership, and arguably advertising as well. Basically, I am arguing that the novel 'made' the periodical press in these 50 years, as much as the press fostered and 'carried' the novel (as well as other literature), legitimizing it in the admixture of a 'miscellany' context.

From the onset of the three-volume novel as the publication format of choice for first editions of new novels in the early nineteenth century, fiction had a problem. Its modes of publication and distribution were at considerable odds with its large and ever-increasing, even popular audience. The arrangements for the format and distribution of new fiction favoured the few wealthy individuals who could afford to purchase new titles at one and a half guineas, the circulating libraries who comprised the principal destination of the expensive and multiple volumes, and readers who could afford to belong to libraries. If publishers were content to sell primarily to circulating libraries, some authors, such as Dickens, who had his eye on a wider market, were not. Dickens deployed two formats in the 1830s, neither of which were new in themselves, to circumvent the high price of three volumes and to get his new fiction to readers directly, at prices (from 2s 6d, to 6d) that the middle classes could afford. One was part issue, in which fiction was issued in standalone serial parts at regular intervals (weekly or monthly), often with frontispiece illustrations, normally for 6d or a shilling. The second was serialization in miscellanies or serials, similarly weekly or monthly and also relatively cheap; at 2s 6d initially, magazines *were* more expensive than part issues, befitting their breadth of contents, but by 1860 they were similarly priced, and the shilling monthlies were a great bargain for new serial writing.[3] Moreover, instead of hazarding the market as a standalone title, dependent on author or illustrator recognition by the purchaser, magazine fiction was guaranteed by the 'brand' of the journal and accompanied by other copy, verbal and possibly visual. There was less risk all round for the reader/consumer, the author, and the publisher. Thus, I am arguing that magazine serialization was an excellent 'fit' for the contents of new fiction with its potentially wide appeal.

For the periodicals' part, as the power of fiction to attract readers demonstrably grew in the nineteenth century, so desire for news and information of all sorts fuelled the growth of the press. The inclusion of fiction in commodity forms of journalism (magazines, reviews, and eventually newspapers) is similar to other strategies in the industry of the period to expand readership. The appropriation of fiction into the wide maw of the press is comparable to claims to cover as wide a geographic area as possible for news contents as well as distribution, or publishing at multiple intervals to reach different consumer groups (early and late editions), or including closing prices, law reports, racing news, and/or theatre reviews to attract different niche audiences. This is not to mention the advertising revenue, again increasingly important and increasingly linked to circulation. On balance, not only are the advantages to the press of including fiction many, and basic to journalism, but also its inclusion may be seen as typical of the operation of the industry of the day.

Evidence of the power of fiction for the press by the end of the century, the advantage of fiction for drawing readers, may be seen in W.T. Stead's practice as an editor. In 1893–1894, and again in 1904, Stead, who nurtured throughout his life, personally and as a journalist and editor, a longstanding prejudice against the novel (and the theatre), was simply unable to resist the lure of serialized fiction as a necessary ingredient of his two 'daily paper' projects of cheap newspapers for the people. It is a measure of the popularity of the novel that Stead's resistance was overcome. Claiming in November 1893 that in England 'no first-class newspaper demeans its columns by the publication of a novel in instalments', Stead is critically eloquent and revelatory in his reasoning in reaching a contrary conclusion:

> There are millions of human beings, especially among the young and among women, who will never read anything unless it is served up to them in the form of fiction. As a newspaper only deals with fictions of another sort and religiously abstains from publishing fiction that is honestly labelled as such, it fails to secure as readers those whose only literary diet is romance.[4]

What we hear in Stead's anguished explanation for the inclusion of fiction in his newspaper is a late example of the deep reluctance of Nonconformists to give readers what they want, noted by Altick in *The English Common Reader*. But make no mistake, this is not only an antipathy based on the inappropriateness of fiction in a *newspaper*, but a suspicion of the nature of the novel as a genre – its capacity for dubious moral content and for fancy, and its dearth of practicality. Stead preferred to admit serialized fiction to his publications in a new, self-styled form, which he dubbed 'journalistic' fiction, which was to be based (daily, weekly, or monthly) on breaking news.[5] But this reluctant embrace of the novel, late in the nineteenth century, is also reflected in Altick, in the attitudes of public librarians in 1897 to readers and borrowers of novels, whom they termed 'fiction vampires', novels being a genre which, by the 1890s, to their dismay, accounted for between 65 and 90 per cent of borrowing.[6]

From 1884, the year of Walter Besant's lecture to the Royal Institution asserting the *art* of fiction and the subsequent debate that provoked Henry James's famous article,[7] through the symposia of the early 1890s in the *New Review* on 'Candour in English Fiction' (January 1890), 'The Science of Fiction' (April 1891), and 'The Science of Criticism' (May 1891), the status of fiction and the constraints upon it in Britain were interrogated by novelists and critics including Moore, Besant, Lynn Linton, Hardy, James, Lang, and Gosse. Besant, a vehement defender of the novel, laments its status ('Fiction is not an art of the first rank'), while Moore and Hardy think its quality in England suffered from censorship.[8] That is, there is ample evidence to show that despite the overwhelming popularity of the English novel among readers in the latter half of the nineteenth century, and indeed perhaps because of it, refusal to recognize it as literature, or worthy of the time and attention of serious readers, remained among many of the older and established educated as late as the 1890s, and among some of the powerful publishers and distributors. James found a chapter missing from his novel when it appeared in *Harper's*, Moore had difficulty publishing his fiction because of its alleged immorality, and Mr Mudie and W.H. Smith continued to 'select' the fiction they distributed in their respective circulating library and shops.[9]

One indication of this in the journals is that while fiction proliferates in periodicals between 1850 and 1900, often in unexpected environments, reviews of fiction in the same periodicals are not normally commensurate in number, length, or prominence either with the fiction that is carried or that which is advertised. Nor do some of the most well-known critics of the day, such as Carlyle, Matthew Arnold, and Pater, bother much, if at all, with reviewing English novels. Renowned reviewers of novels who championed the genre were relatively few, and those who signed their reviews even fewer. Geraldine Jewsbury, George Henry Lewes, E.S. Dallas, R.H. Hutton, and Margaret Oliphant stand out retrospectively as critics engaged with the novel over time, although most of their reviews appeared without signature. The profile of fiction in the periodicals, then, is not univocal. There are eloquent absences as well as a kind of racy presence, as fiction elbows its unruly way into the columns of *Chambers's Edinburgh Journal*, for example, renamed in the 1854 new series *Chambers's Journal of Popular Literature*, signalling its capitulation to the regular publication of serial fiction; or into a new and weighty review in 1865, the *Fortnightly*, whose first decade included the serialization of Trollope's *The Belton Estate* from the outset, and two other titles; and novels by Meredith, T.A. Trollope, and Frances Trollope.

A similar mixture of resistance and embrace of the novel is true of Oxbridge in the nineteenth century. If English literature gradually made its way into the syllabuses and degrees of Oxford and Cambridge toward the end of the century, it was a slow coach and late comer, not least because of the status of the popular and contemporary novel, written in the vernacular language, and the association of its consumption with two specific groups – women and students with no education in classics. With the model of classics so firmly established in academic study of the day, medieval and early modern authors and texts were favoured in the new syllabuses in English, and contemporary or even modem literature was normally excluded. In our own period, when the novel sits comfortably at the table of English studies, it is important to recall that its generic respectability (which was doubtful and uneven) throughout the nineteenth century, for many of those in authority, was not unlike that of journalism. Is it possible that Saintsbury plumped for periodicals in his history of English literature because the mainstream press was more defendable than the novel?

Despite resistance to recognition of the literary status of the English novel among some critics, editors, Utilitarians, Evangelicals, Anglicans, and Nonconformists after 1850, the novel became a necessary ingredient of a large number of periodicals in the second half of the century. This was the result of a gradual gathering of momentum of fiction from the preceding decades. The growth of popular fiction in the 1840s, the impact of the first railway novels and bookstalls from around 1848, and the cluster of quality writing by Dickens, Thackeray, the Brontës, and Gaskell all contributed to the increased claims of the novel for recognition. Sally Ledger has recently argued that the prominent place of serial fiction in *Household Words* in the 1850s was pioneering in the middle-class weekly press, while Lorna Huett's work on the format of *Household Words* suggests its similarities to the penny press, which in the weekly *London Journal* had been featuring serial fiction throughout the forties.

Earlier still, the impact of fiction on the press in the first half of the century is also notable. The absence of novels in the 'great' quarterlies (a necessary absence given their infrequency) – the

Edinburgh Review, the *Quarterly Review*, and the *Westminster Review* – helped define them as 'weighty', while the presence of fiction in *Blackwood's* helped establish its comparatively 'lighter' note and distinctive character in its early years, as a monthly *magazine* (not a review) that published original fiction anonymously and serially. Other monthlies, such as the *New Monthly Magazine* and later *Tait's*, reviewed literature and published original essays and articles, but not novels. *Fraser's* (founded in 1830 and a scion of *Blackwood's*) followed *Maga's* example to an extent, with an emphasis on wit, satire, and the comic, but it decried the poor quality of fiction of the day in spoof, and cutting occasional reviews of Colburn's and Bentley's new novels, accompanied by virulent denunciation of the puffing practices of those two publishers. Serial fiction only began to appear with some regularity in *Fraser's* in 1837, including Thackeray's early novel *Catherine* in 1839–1840 and two novels by Kingsley in 1848 and 1852. *Bentley's Miscellany*, founded in 1837 to compete in the same market niche as *Blackwood's* and *Fraser's* with its congregated wits, featured serial fiction more than the others (for example, *Oliver Twist*). Initially dominating the contents of *Bentley's*, serialized instalments, often of short fiction, were only gradually balanced by other kinds of literary contents in the 1840s. By July 1856, four serial fiction instalments appeared in a single number of 100 pages. This tension between the novel and other forms of prose in the typically miscellaneous nineteenth-century magazine (even more pronounced in the newspaper) indicates to me a persistent aspiration for a general rather than specialized press, and an attempt to bring different reading constituencies together in single titles – including women and men, political economists and novel readers, men of science and poetry. While there was increasing specialization in the nineteenth-century periodical press, the contents of many of the journals echoed the eclecticism of their adverts.

There is one aspect of the circulation of fiction that the nineteenth-century press before 1850 managed differently than most publishers of novels in volume form, and that is signature. For 60 years *Blackwood's* imposed anonymity (or pseudonymity) on all contributors to *Maga* to foster coherence under the brand name of the journal itself. This also prevented celebrity authors of novels from outshining the nameless contributors of the other contents of the monthly. But both *Fraser's* and *Bentley's* deployed pseudonyms, initials, and outright signature in fiction, as well as other articles and encouraged readers to piece together attributions to identifiable author-figures.

[. . .]

The advantage of fiction

I want to discuss the 'advantage[s]' of fiction for the periodical press after 1850 from three perspectives – content and its relation to readership, publishers, and authors. Advantages for readers of magazine fiction appear in all three categories.

The benefits for the periodicals themselves, the first perspective that I adumbrate here, are largely extrapolated from the material culture of serial parts over time. The incorporation of fiction helped both specialized and 'general' periodicals survive by broadening their appeal to include readers outside of their original remit of coverage and mode of address, such as expository articles on politics or religion, or by enhancing the breadth of a wider, miscellany title. In this way, the political front and middle of the *Spectator* were supplemented by its serious reviews of fiction, the original fiction in *Good Words* might reflect its religious remit and entertain as well, while the evaluative reviews of new fiction in the *Athenaeum* and serial fiction in *Chambers's* spiced up the fare of these general weeklies. Then too, in the nineteenth century, fiction mapped onto a new audience of great potential for monthlies, weeklies, and dailies: Women were a relatively untapped and increasingly literate consumer group, whom editors and publishers alike were keen to cultivate. A preponderance of women readers might influence the nature of the entire contents of a journal, as well as expand its advertising base to include female desire. Moreover, the publication of fiction or reviews of fiction within journals attracted advertisements from publishers of novels in other formats (such as three-volume or cheap editions); the address of the advertisers to readers of these journals as *readers and consumers of fiction* reinforced the association of the papers with fiction and the readers' interest in it. Thus the publishers' advertised lists of new novels took their place for the readers alongside of literary gossip and lists of new publications in the letterpress as welcome information.

[. . .]

Reviews of fiction in the periodicals served the interests of periodicals and their editors, and publishers alike. Whatever their verdicts on the titles noticed, reviews of fiction attracted curious readers to the journals, thus enhancing circulation, and circulated the names of new fiction to potential borrowers or purchasers, benefiting authors, publishers, and the commercial libraries. Moreover, publishers often excerpted reviews from the magazines and reinserted them into the magazines in their adverts of their new lists to boost a title, thus enhancing the authority of the magazine cited and circulating its name, thereby covertly rewarding the magazine for reviewing its new titles.

What about the advantages of serial fiction from the perspective of the publishers? A number of publishers of novels and books more generally invested in periodical titles after 1850. *Macmillan's Magazine* and *Cornhill* were house journals of Macmillan and Smith Elder, respectively; the additional window for publication of fiction served a variety of functions. It helped publishers recruit authors, both unknown and famous, by attracting them initially to good terms and conditions of periodical publication, which was then used as a platform to sign authors up to further book and periodical contracts. The link between serial publication in the house journal and in volume form by the publisher is common, and the process could also go in both directions. Having published one novel successfully in either or both formats, the publisher is better positioned to claim and benefit from publication of the next title. Thus because in 1857 the publisher of *Macmillan's Magazine* (1959ff) had issued and reprinted *Tom Brown's Schooldays*, Macmillan was able to initiate the first number of the *Magazine* in 1859 with Hughes's sequel, *Tom Brown in Oxford*.

Magazine serialization also helped longer-term sales by covertly advertising the serialized text, through exposing and trailing it repeatedly before its later appearance in successive volume formats. It also opened the novel parts to pre-volume publication reviews, which may have brought the title for the first time to the attention of certain readers, who might then seek out the journal or simply remember it for future reference. Reviews and instalments created title recognition, familiarity with characters and text, and even engagement with plot events, all of which might foster sales of the first edition to readers and the circulating libraries and reader demand for the title in the libraries.

Publication of novel instalments as part of journal contents was also less of an economic risk for the publisher than standalone publication in part-issue or volume form, especially for new, unknown, or anonymous authors. Such embedded publication of fiction is carried by other articles, even other fiction, as well as the brand name of the journal, and helps overcome these disadvantages in the marketplace. Embedded serialization also protects the publisher against unpopular work, which may be more obtrusively withdrawn, curtailed, or improved.

This dilution of risk had a particular advantage for women writers of fiction. The anonymity and security of serial publication in some journals helped publishers employ women novelists, some of whom were at least initially reluctant to enter the public sphere in their own person and preferred to appear in a mediated environment in which both their names and their association with regular, paid work could be obscured. George Eliot is only one example of such a writer. In her book, *First Person Anonymous* (2004), Alexis Easley has argued that nineteenth-century women novelists moved in and out of anonymity, selecting it for their more controversial material, and Jennifer Phegley's *Educating the Proper Woman Reader* (2004) convincingly shows the potential danger of exposure to the public for women fiction writers and editors of the period, in the case of Mary Elizabeth Braddon.

Another manner in which publishers of periodicals after 1860 benefited from the popularity of fiction was to employ famous novelists – notably Thackeray, Trollope, and Braddon – to edit their journals. Thackeray's name as editor of George Smith's new journal was advertised far in advance of the appearance of the journal, and before a name had been decided upon. The novelist was the known brand, and Smith used Thackeray's writing to fill the early numbers of *Cornhill*, in which the novelist editor published not only a serialized novel but also his 'Roundabout Papers'. Trollope edited *Saint Paul's* for James Virtue, and Braddon *Belgravia* for John Maxwell. House journals such as *Macmillan's* and *Cornhill* served as regular, free advertising vehicles for their publishers, appearing monthly in tandem with the monthly issue of the new titles in the publishers' lists. So, the serialized fiction by which readers were lured to the house journals provided publishers with increasing access to consumers' exposure to the adverts for their general lists as well as their fiction, carried for free in the 'Advertisers' of the shilling monthlies.

Authors of new fiction had a significantly larger market for their novels, with less risk than initial volume publication, and if they were publishing anonymously, they were able to contribute other pieces – fiction or non-fiction – to the same or other serials. Weaker instalments or whole serials might be 'carried' by the brand name of the periodical, or later more well-known, named contributors, and new writers, such as Thackeray in the 1830s and '40s, or George Eliot in the 1850s, or Walter Pater in the 1860s could learn their craft anonymously, and in the cases of Thackeray and Eliot, earn their living and enter the profession. Authors were also paid at least twice for their novels, for serial as well as volume publication. Indirectly, they benefited from the pre-volume publication publicity afforded by magazine or miscellany serialization, insofar as it boosted subsequent sales on which royalties might depend.

The proliferation of the periodical press in this period was deeply implicated in the larger book trade, but it especially benefited from the explosion of the nineteenth-century novel in a particular set of social, industrial, and technological circumstances – the consumer demand across the classes, increase in the variety of formats of its publication, and the high price of new fiction, as Altick documents, as well as the removal of the tax on paper, changes in press technology, and the capacity to make and print images quickly, relatively cheaply, and easily, illustration being another of the significant sustaining features of periodicals in the period. Once the three-volume model of novel publication faltered in the mid-1890s, and cheap, shorter, single-volume formats for new fiction gradually encroached, the demise of serial publication of novels in magazines was inevitable. Already, from 1891, the *Strand* made a speciality of publishing short stories and, as serialized novels in the magazines waned, one-off fiction was to take its place more decorously among the article-length units of periodical publications. The transformation in the 1890s of the publishing arrangements for new fiction prevailing since Scott and Dickens, arrangements on which a system of mutual benefit to magazines, publishers, authors, and distributors had rested, resulted in nothing less than the transformation of the English novel itself, now to become slimmer, more tightly plotted, and compact. Serials, too, had to find new lures for the public, and the intensification of celebrity stories, investigative campaigns, sensation, illustration, and other elements of new journalism were brought to fruition in the mass market media, typified in 1896 by the admixture of Harmsworth's *Daily Mail.* Although the link between the press and the novel remained – in reviewing, adverts, interviews, and celebrity feature articles – the new journalism magazines and newspapers moved to other kinds of popular copy (including short fiction) to appeal to an even larger reading public, while new English novels were first read in single-volume form through direct purchase or from free public libraries, and eventually even the likes of Braddon, Moore, D.H. Lawrence, and Virginia Woolf were studied in schools and universities.

Notes

1 William St Clair, *The Reading Nation in the Romantic Period* (Cambridge: Cambridge University Press, 2004).
2 Richard Altick, *The English Common Reader: A Social History of the Mass Reading Public* (Chicago: University of Chicago Press, 1957), p. 291.
3 See Laurel Brake, *Print in Transition* (Houndmills: Palgrave, 2001), pp. 47–51 for a detailed comparison of part issue and magazine serialization.
4 Quoted in Frederic Whyte, *The Life of W. T. Stead*, 2 vols (London: Cape, 1925), II, p. 332.
5 Stead himself wrote at least two novellas of journalistic fiction, which comprised his early *Review of Review Annuals* (London, 1892 and 1893). These were entitled *From the Old World to the New* and *Two and Two Makes Four.*
6 Altick, pp. 239, 231.
7 See Mark Spilka, 'Henry James and Walter Besant: "The Art of Fiction" Controversy', *Novel* 6.2 (1973), pp. 101–19.
8 See their comments in George Moore, *Literature at Nurse: or, Circulating Morals* London: Vizetelly, 1885), and Thomas Hardy, 'Candour in English Fiction', *Review of Reviews* (January 1, 1890), pp. 15–21, respectively.
9 See Laurel Brake, *Subjugated Knowledges: Journalism, Gender and Literature in the Nineteenth Century* (Basingstoke: Macmillan, 1994), pp. 109–10 for Harper's letter to James on this occasion. See Moore's own indignant account in *Literature at Nurse.*

48 The age of newspapers

Matthew Rubery

[. . .]

A nation of news readers

Great Britain's transformation into a "reading nation" in which virtually everyone read books, magazines, and newspapers to some extent profoundly altered the individual citizen's relation to public life.[1] The term "journalism" first entered the English language through an article written by Gibbons Merle for the *Westminster Review* in 1833. It was a sorely needed replacement for the inadequate phrase "newspaper-writing," which gave little sense of how influential commercial print had come to be in forming national consciousness.[2] As Benedict Anderson has shown, the press brought individuals together through concurrent acts of reading that enabled them to conceive of themselves as a national body. The novel was a formal prerequisite for imagining the nation, according to Anderson's argument, which in turn emphasizes how closely the newspaper resembled the novel in its reliance on the literary conventions of time and space.[3] Nor were these print communities strictly virtual since readers communicated with one another through advertisements, correspondence, and, after coming up for air, conversations about news-worthy events. Advised by her father to read the newspapers constantly, Maria Edgeworth described their value to authors for this very reason: "How much the circulation of newspapers as well as books contribute to give subjects of conversation in common to people in the most distant parts of different countries."[4] Reading the news was already for Edgeworth an act of virtual participation in an expanding public sphere to which most men and women had only limited access.[5] The conversations taking place in the columns of the newspaper made it feel for many readers "as if the penny post sent letters open that all might be read by all," in the words of Joseph Cowen, editor of the Newcastle *Chronicle*.[6] The rapid expansion of the commercial press from the 1830s onward, far from eliminating communal bonds as many feared, instead provided a forum in which citizens compensated for the disappearance of face-to-face contact by forging deep attachments to one another through print. Instead of replacing *vivâ voce* discussion, newspapers dramatically expanded its scale.[7]

A number of writers responded to the growing influence of journalism by attacking its commercial or subliterary qualities. The commercial success of the newspaper industry invited skeptical accounts from Matthew Arnold, F. R. Leavis, Theodor Adorno, Raymond Williams, and others proposing the decline of a privileged sphere of high seriousness, general intellectuals, and public involvement. Jürgen Habermas notably identified the newspaper press as essential to the formation of a public sphere in which a self-conscious public was able to exchange ideas. Yet Habermas perceived a slow decline during the nineteenth century from a disinterested press discussing civic issues toward a commercial enterprise interested only in profits.[8] Hence the founding of Alfred Harmsworth's *Daily Mail* in 1896 has repeatedly been blamed for encouraging a style closer to "skimming," as Q. D. Leavis and others have charged, than to the sustained attention necessary for substantive deliberation.[9] Not only were newspaper audiences not reading between the lines, they were not reading the lines at all. The earliest dismissals of the press anticipate the outright hostility toward journalism that would become an explicit motif of modernist authors such as T. S. Eliot, Ford Madox Ford, James Joyce, Stéphane Mallarmé, and Ezra Pound at the turn of the century. Ironically, the most intense attacks on the press were made during the very decades in which its influence was increasingly diminished by competition from other media including radio, film, and television. The assumption that material produced for a large market is inevitably of inferior quality, however, overlooks compensatory gains in readership that have become the focus of recent cultural studies interested in how people make sense of news media as part of their everyday lives. Narratives of press decline rely too heavily on the projection of an undifferentiated public that would be better understood in terms of competing readerships or counterpublics.[10]

Resentment against the commercial success of the press has obscured how valuable newspapers were as a source of thematic and formal innovation for Victorian novelists. The devaluation of periodical writing by twentieth-century measures has tended to reinforce, rather than to scrutinize and call into question, the division between journalism and literature arising at the close of the nineteenth century.[11] Studies showing affinities between the two forms have done so largely in terms of subject matter alone by revealing how novelists exploited *causes célèbres* in thinly disguised retellings of adultery, divorce, and other scandals found in the press. Insofar as links have been made, scholarship has considered the most obvious or conventional connections: serial publication of novels within periodicals, newspaper items as historical background, or biographical details of authors *qua* journalists. Christian Johnstone's complaint that periodical writing was regarded as the "*et-cetera*" of literature in 1833 may be said to persist to this day in the minds of many literary critics influenced by modernist ideas of what qualifies as literature.[12] However, recent work on Victorian print culture (a field comprising book history, periodical research, and media studies) has renewed interest in the relation of ephemeral texts to other literary genres.[13] Work in this interdisciplinary field approaches journalism as a subject worthy of examination in its own right rather than as mere source material. Its findings offer a reminder that the anachronistic divide between journalism and literature would have made little sense at a time when much of the prose written by Victorian novelists bore some relationship to the periodical press in terms of style, subject, or source. "The journalism of one day becomes the classic literature of the next," as a contributor to *Macmillan's* insisted at the turn of the century.[14] What has not been sufficiently examined is the extent to which the novel emerged out of this highly competitive literary economy pitting the two forms against each other for attention and profit. While the commercial press was displacing forums for political discussion, it was at the same time creating new ways of communicating that did not go unnoticed by the period's novelists.

The narrative conventions inherited from Victorian journalism have become such standard features of realism to this day that it is easy to forget how controversial many of them once were for readers of a different era. We need look no further for evidence of this transformation in the period's print culture than its literary imprint left to us by novelists who struggled to read and be read amid the surge of newsprint. The novel had long rivaled the newspaper's ability to absorb disparate materials into a single narrative, and mimicking the competition was one of the primary tactics by which novelists sought to keep their work from becoming yesterday's news. Novelists used newspapers in a variety of ways: retelling events reported by the press; reproducing journalistic voices, styles, and features; the pastiche of news items through headlines and quotations; recording the process of news production; and, most dramatically, portraying the individual reader's reaction to the news. Paratextual markings such as headlines were just one of the many ways in which novelists played upon audience expectations by introducing competing layers of verisimilitude into the fictional narrative. The perceived need from within the literary sphere to distinguish between factual and fictional writing arose in part from the mutual dependence on narrative in its most fundamental sense as a way of telling a story. Journalists sound suspiciously like fiction writers when using the word "story" to describe their own craft of assembling *facta bruta* into intelligible narrative, a point emphasized by nineteenth-century novelists who display the methods of news production as one way of calling into question its uncritical reception by audiences. Journalistic wisdom holds that there is always a story behind the story, but novelists are the ones who bear out this claim.

The very distinction between "journalist" and "novelist" would have made little sense to a generation of writers who had always moved seamlessly between these different categories. The entire body of work of a crossover author such as Dickens might be classified as journalism according to one recent study.[15] *Hard Times* in particular combines the functions of novel and newspaper by encouraging its audience to read the fictional narrative in dialogue with the nonfictional contents of *Household Words*, the weekly magazine in which it first appeared in serial instalments.[16] This dual understanding of the novel's generic status urges audiences to restore the novel to its original journalistic milieu in order to understand the extratextual implications of narrative events. Yet the relationship between the news and the novel is even more complex than parallel reading allows since the news is not merely supplemental in many Victorian novels but rather a constitutive element of the narrative itself. Competition with other media affected the form of the novel at a number of intertextual levels, from the inclusion of topical material to the imitation of news formats. Jay Bolter and Richard Grusin have argued that such acts of "remediation," the representation of one medium in another—here, the representation of the newspaper in the novel—always critique and refashion competing media.[17] In this sense, the news was integral to the novel's development in its provision of narrative elements that were ultimately transformed into an altogether different enterprise. Victorian novelists drew upon the news both as a means of formal innovation and as a countertext against which to define their own fictional discourse in a way familiar to us from twentieth-century fiction. The influence of the news is pronounced over fictional narrative of all lengths (short stories, novellas, triple-deckers), although it is the self-conscious genre of the novel whose identity was most at stake once the two media came into direct competition.

The influence of the commercial press over the Victorian novel is dramatically apparent in fictional scenes of newspaper reading that bring British residents into contact with distant events, from a terrible shipwreck amid the East Indian seas to a trading company's conduct along the banks of the Congo River. These scenes indicate the close relationship between Victorian journalism, on the one hand, and literary representation of the news reader, on the other. Attention to the newspaper reader on the part of novelists was one way of tapping into the reader's changing relationship with the outside world. The presumed discrepancy between factual and fictional realms is evident in a letter Thackeray once wrote to Trollope regarding the first issue of the *Cornhill*: "One of our chief objects in this magazine is the getting out of novel spinning, and back into the world."[18] The scenes of reading marshaled together by this book, not to mention Thackeray's own novels, confirm that the two spheres were not as distinct as Thackeray's letter might lead us to believe. As we will see, reading the news is less about interiority in these scenes than about interaction with the outside world, a key factor in making the Victorian novel a genuinely cosmopolitan form.

We might encounter in the pages of a Victorian novel a verbatim news report, a narrator's paraphrase of this report, or even a dramatized scene of reading in which a character apprehends the report before our eyes. Each of these scenarios entails an appropriate orientation from the novel's own reader. At one pole, a facsimile of the news story bids the audience's familiarity with newspaper conventions to supply a character's reaction in the absence of authorial commentary; at the other pole, we are bystanders before a spectacle in which access to a newspaper's content emerges solely from the theatrical response of its imagined reader. No matter where one stands along this spectrum, the newspaper's significance arises in each instance from its reception. What all novelistic representations recorded by this book share is an interest in capturing how the supposedly impersonal news can directly affect the emotional lives of its readers. Such scenes emphasize the markedly individual ways in which readers proceed through the newspaper according to self-interest rather than sensible layout. The personalization of news distinguished by this book takes place along two trajectories. First, private becomes public when newspaper publicity brings personal matters to the attention of a large audience (e.g., an indiscretion, an affair, a hidden past). Such is the mortifying case when Mr. Harding finds his supervision of a Barchester almshouse denounced by the *Jupiter* in Trollope's *The Warden* (1855). Second, public becomes private when information available to everyone has special relevance for an isolated reader (e.g., politics, crime, accidents). We see a dramatic instance of this when Richard Phillotson discovers the headline "Strange suicide of a stone-mason's children" concerning his estranged wife in Thomas Hardy's *Jude the Obscure* (1895).[19] The pastiche of news sheds its initial resemblance to epistolary form in the latter instance since we are not privy to a private communication made public but rather to a public communication made private. The emphasis in both examples is on the reader's response to personal information discovered in the pages of the supposedly impersonal press.

Consider for a moment what a departure the newspaper reader is from the Romantic tradition of the novel reader, typically an impressionable child such as David Copperfield or Jane Eyre whose state of absorption is noteworthy for its inattentiveness to the surrounding environment. As Garrett Stewart has noted, the metatextual scene imparts credibility to the imagined world of the novel at the very moment in which a character is absent from that world through the introspective act of reading.[20] More so than any other textual device, the newspaper effectively brings into contact ordinarily separate spheres. This is grotesquely evident in the case of one elderly newspaper reader who consulted a physician because "for several mornings past, she had not been able *to relish her murders*."[21] There was no more plausible way for novelists to bring British residents into contact with distant events—say, a husband learning of his wife's death in a trainwreck at Cammère—while adhering to the strictures of realism. The newspaper departs from the venerable tradition of literary solitude by bringing readers into contact with the most documentary of narrative forms. Richard Altick recognized as much in suggesting that Victorian authors used topical references drawn from the pages of the press to create an effect of contemporaneity shared among the novel's audience.[22] Scenes of reading thus generate empathy not only for the novel's characters but also toward its other readers. If possession of a novel implies an unbridgeable aesthetic experience varying in intensity from one reader to the next, a newspaper in hand suggests a reassuring affiliation among fellow recipients who may have digested the identical contents that very morning. The novel has never been as successful in becoming reading for the breakfast table.

This is not to say that novelists overlook how reading the news could at the same time set individuals apart from other members of the print community. On the contrary, novelists grasp the unique intimacy potentially available through the press, not to mention—and this is where novels and newspapers come together in their representation of the reading event— how novelistic the newspaper could be in eliciting a cathartic response. The diversity of news readers was no longer adequately represented by the patriarchal bore hidden behind a copy of *The Times* in his favorite armchair who had by this point become a stock figure of domestic fiction. The episodes of reading gathered together by this book instead capture the unexpect- edly personal responses evoked by the supposedly impersonal newspaper among a wide range of readers: from the trauma caused by a lover's reported suicide to the vicarious gratification felt during a celebrity interview; from the distress at finding one's behavior the subject of unflattering editorial commentary to the apprehension of distant cultures through the foreign correspondence. The exhilarating range of reactions to information first encountered in the newspaper will be taken up by the remainder of this book. The chapters to follow identify the ways in which Victorian novelists made use of the methods of the press, in the words of one newspaper editor, to strike the reader right between the eyes.

[. . .]

Notes

1 William St. Clair, *The Reading Nation in the Romantic Period* (Cambridge: Cambridge University Press, 2004), 13.
2 Gibbons Merle (unsigned), "Journalism," *Westminster Review* 18 (1833): 195.
3 Benedict Anderson, *Imagined Communities: Reflections on the Origins and Spread of Nationalism*, rev. ed. (London: Verso, 1991), 33. See also Jonathan Culler on the distinction between imagining and legitimating the nation by way of the novel ("Anderson and the Novel," *Diacritics* 29 [1999]: 20–39). This and other essays from a special issue of *Diacritics* devoted to Anderson's work have been gathered in Pheng Cheah and Jonathan Culler, eds., *Grounds of Comparison: Around the Work of Benedict Anderson* (New York: Routledge, 2003).
4 Maria Edgeworth to C. Sneyd Edgeworth, 1 May 1813, in *Letters from England 1813–1844* (Oxford: Clarendon, 1971), 41.
5 See the discussions of gendered reading practices in Kate Flint, *The Woman Reader* (Oxford: Oxford University Press, 1993); Margaret Beetham, *A Magazine of Her Own?* (London: Routledge, 1996); and Hilary Fraser, Stephanie Green, and Judith Johnston, *Gender and the Victorian Periodical* (Cambridge: Cambridge University Press, 2003). The influence of the press in Edgeworth's time is discussed in Hannah Barker and Simon Burrows, eds., *Press, Politics, and the Public Sphere in Europe and North America, 1760–1820* (Cambridge: Cambridge University Press, 2002).
6 Quoted in [Aled] Jones, *Powers of the Press[: Newspapers, Powers, and the Public in Nineteenth- Century England* (Aldershot: Ashgate, 1996)], 49.
7 For more on the relationship between the press and the British Empire, see Simon J. Potter, *News and the British World: The Emergence of an Imperial Press System, 1876–1922* (Oxford: Clarendon, 2003); and Potter, ed., *Newspapers and Empire in Ireland and Britain: Reporting the British Empire, c. 1857–1921* (Dublin: Four Courts Press, 2004).
8 See Habermas's *The Structural Transformation of the Public Sphere: An Inquiry into a Category of Bourgeois Society*, trans. Thomas Burger (Cambridge, Mass.: MIT Press, 1991). Responses to Habermas's concept of the public sphere can be found in Craig Calhoun, ed., *Habermas and the Public Sphere* (Cambridge, Mass.: MIT Press, 1992); and Bruce Robbins, ed., *The Phantom Public Sphere* (Minneapolis: University of Minnesota Press, 1993). Harold Mah provides a detailed bibli- ography of the secondary literature in "Phantasies of the Public Sphere: Rethinking the Habermas of the Historians," *The Journal of Modern History* 72 (2000): 153–82.

9   Q. D. Leavis, *Fiction and the Reading Public* (London: Chatto & Windus, 1932), 226. For more on the Victorian preoccupation with readerly comprehension, see Nicholas Dames's *The Physiology of the Novel: Reading, Neural Science, and the Form of Victorian Fiction* (Oxford: Oxford University Press, 2007), 16–22.

10   Michael Warner discusses the rhetorical use of the term "public" in *Publics and Counterpublics* (New York: Zone Books; London: MIT Press, 2002).

11   See Laurel Brake's account of the hostile reception given to periodical literature by twentieth-century writers, in *Subjugated Knowledges: Journalism, Gender and Literature in the Nineteenth Century* (Basingstoke: Macmillan, 1994), xi–xv; and *Print in Transition, 1850–1910: Studies in Media and Book History* (Basingstoke: Palgrave, 2001), 7–26.

12   Christian Johnstone (unsigned), "On Periodical Literature," *Tait's Edinburgh Magazine* (1833): 495.

13   For an introduction to recent work on Victorian print culture, see the essays collected in *Nineteenth-Century Media and the Construction of Identities*, ed. Laurel Brake, Bill Bell, and David Finkelstein (Basingstoke: Palgrave, 2000). This collection is indebted to pioneering research into the periodical press by Richard Altick, *The English Common Reader: A Social History of the Mass Reading Public, 1800–1900* (Chicago: University of Chicago Press, 1957); Joanne Shattock and Michael Wolff, eds., *The Victorian Periodical Press: Samplings and Soundings* (Leicester: Leicester University Press, 1982); and Laurel Brake, Aled Jones, and Lionel Madden, eds., *Investigating Victorian Journalism* (Basingstoke: Macmillan, 1990).

14   J. G. L. (pseud.), "The Newspaper," *Macmillan's Magazine* 87 (1902–3): 434.

15   John M. L. Drew makes this claim in *Dickens the Journalist* (Basingstoke: Palgrave, 2003), 2.

16   Joseph Butwin documents the journalistic aspects of Dickens's novel in *"Hard Times:* The News and the Novel," *Nineteenth-Century Fiction* 32 (1977): 167.

17   Jay David Bolter and Richard Grusin, *Remediation* (Cambridge: MIT Press, 2000), 45.

18   Letter to Trollope, 28 October 1859, in *Letters and Private Papers of William Makepeace Thackeray*, ed. Gordon N. Ray (Cambridge, Mass.: Harvard University Press, 1945), 158. On Thackeray's relationship to the periodical press, see Richard Pearson's *W. M. Thackeray and the Mediated Text: Writing for the Periodicals in the Mid-Nineteenth Century* (Aldershot: Ashgate, 2000).

19   Thomas Hardy, *Jude the Obscure* (New York: Bantam, 1996), 375.

20   Garrett Stewart, *Dear Reader: The Conscripted Audience in Nineteenth-Century British Fiction* (Baltimore: Johns Hopkins University Press, 1996), 18.

21   "Newspaper Readers," *The Mirror of Literature, Amusement and Instruction* 34 (1839): 360.

22   Richard Altick, *The Presence of the Present* (Columbus: Ohio State University Press, 1991),

49 The book as go-between

Domestic service and forced reading

Leah Price

[. . .]

The tract and *The Moonstone*

[. . .]

[B]y mocking tract-distributors for harassing a captive audience, secular novels and magazines congratulated themselves on being freely chosen and paid for. Although the R[eligious] T[ract] S[ociety] entitled its internal history *The Romance of Tract Distribution*—as if the wanderings of books, like foundlings, led providentially toward a happy ending—the secular press more often chose a satiric mode. In 1843, for example, Thackeray reprinted in *Punch* a note from the *Times*:

> 'The Agents of the Tract Societies have lately had recourse to a new method of introducing their tracts into Cadiz. The tracts were put into glass bottles, *securely corked*; and, taking advantage of the tide flowing into the harbour, they were committed to the waves, on whose surface they floated towards the town, where the inhabitants eagerly took them up on their arriving on the shore. The bottles were then uncorked, and the tracts they contain are *supposed to have been* read with much interest.'

Thus far verbatim; but Thackeray goes on to reply in the persona of the "Regent of Spain . . . and of the Regent's Park," calling the "manoeuvres of the Dissenting-Tract Smuggler (*Tractistero dissentero contrabandistero*)" worse than any Jesuit arts.

> Let *Punch*, let Lord Aberdeen, let Great Britain at large, put itself in the position of the poor mariner of Cadiz, and then answer. Tired with the day's labour, thirsty as the seaman naturally is, he lies perchance, and watches at eve the tide of ocean swelling into the bay. What does he see cresting the wave that rolls towards him? A bottle. Regardless of the wet, he rushes eagerly towards the advancing flask. 'Sherry, perhaps,' is his first thought (for 'tis the wine of his country). 'Rum, I hope,' he adds, while with beating heart and wringing pantaloons, he puts his bottle-screw into the cork. But, ah! Englishmen! fancy his agonising feelings on withdrawing from the flask a Spanish translation of 'The Cowboy of Kennington Common,' or 'The Little Blind Dustman of Pentonville.' ([W. Thackeray], "Singular Letter from the Regent of Spain")

The joke doesn't require much exaggeration. "The Cowboy of Kennington Common" is hardly more alliterative than real RTS titles like *Lucy the Light-Bearer* (1871), *Claude the*

Colporteur (1880), or *The Bookstall boy of Batherton* (1872). And RTS reports did in fact associate temperance with thirst for the Word:

> Eight men went in a punt to convey goods to a ship in the river; while they were on board, the captain asked them whether they would have a glass of rum each, or a book; they all chose a book, and said they did not drink rum. Tracts were given, which were gratefully received. (Jones 599)

The tract society that devised the message in a bottle was punning on the same confusion of word with drink that allowed the magazine to publish miscellanies like *A Bowl of Punch* (1848)—or Lady Southdown, in *Vanity Fair*, to "pitilessly dose [Miss Crawley's household] with her tracts and her medicine" (Thackeray, *Vanity Fair* 351). Even secular reformers could borrow the analogy: although Rowland Hill acknowledged grudgingly that "the wish to correspond with their friends may not be so strong, or so general, as the desire for fermented liquors," he persisted in predicting the effects on the revenue of the proposed penny post system by extrapolating from taxes on beer and wine (93).

[. . .]

Whether middle-class triple-deckers or penny serials, novels characteristically represent tracts as filler—a poor substitute either for a different genre of book (usually a novel), or for nonbookish objects like food, drink, or paper money. Thus when a canting character in Rymer's radical *The White Slave* leaves a piece of paper on the heroine's father's snowy grave: "Is it a bank note?" "No, this is a religious tract." Later, an Evangelical lady who has just denied the starving heroine food exclaims: "You would have been supplied with tracts, provided you kept them clean, and returned them" (34).

In invoking *Crusoe*, the Religious Tract Society's message in a bottle takes us back to a paper scarcity and a readerly solitude as far as possible from the modern overabundance of both literature and fellow readers. If the RTS's hawkers and chapmen mimicked the way that romances *were* distributed, its publicity stunt in Cadiz mimicked the way that romances *represent* the distribution of texts. Reciprocally, and obsessively, the Victorian novel represented the distribution of tracts. The two genres provided one another with mirror images: when characters in tracts read novels or characters in novels reject tracts, the stakes are intellectual-historical (Evangelical fiction opposite the epic of a world without God) as much as formal (both torn between narrative and didactic modes). But also affective: if the novel was the competitor that the tract was trying to beat at its own game, the novel returned the compliment by making the dullness of tracts a foil to its own pleasures.[1] And finally, economic: both widely distributed, neither much respected, tract and novel achieved their common ubiquity via opposite routes—one anonymously or even surreptitiously bought and rented, the other forced on readers through face-to-face relationships.

Like Trollope's or Thackeray's embedded newspapers and novels, embedded tracts perform an antiquixotic function: everywhere present in the hands of characters, but nowhere read.[2] Mrs. Jellyby and Mrs. Pardiggle emblematize the imbalance between supply and demand. In fact, when the latter "pull[s] out a good book as if it were a constable's staff," it's not enough for every character in *Bleak House* to refuse to read the tract. Adding insult to injury, characters are dragged in from another novel to second that refusal: "Mr. Jarndyce said he doubted if Robinson Crusoe could have read [the book], though he had had no other on his desolate island" (133). The mounting absurdity of those counterfactuals—if a nineteenth-century genre had already existed, if a copy had made its way to Crusoe's island—drives home the contrast between two models of transmission: one, viral, that organically diffuses an old romance across economic lines; another, top-down, in which middle-class adults bribe or bully others into owning (if not reading) demographically tailored fictions.[3]

Bleak House is one of three mid-Victorian novels that couple Robinson Crusoe's name with an imaginary tract. *Hard Times* contrasts Coke-town workers' eagerness to "[take] De Foe to their bosoms" with their reluctance—echoing the bricklayer's in *Bleak House*—to read "leaden little books [written] for them, showing how the good grown-up baby invariably got to the Savings-bank, and the bad grown-up baby invariably got transported" (Dickens, *Hard Times* 65). Not until *Crusoe* reappears for a third time in *The Moonstone* (1868), however, does a nineteenth-century novel stage an all-out battle between an earlier romance and the modern tract. As every reader will remember, the First Period of Collins's novel takes *Robinson Crusoe* as its intertext, the Second a tract-distributor as its narrator. Armed with a "little library of works . . . (say a dozen only)," its narrator, Miss Clack, throws tracts in windows, slips them under sofa cushions, stuffs them into flower boxes, sneaks them into the pockets of dressing gowns, and thrusts them into the hands of a cabdriver. "If I had presented a pistol at his head, this abandoned wretch could hardly have exhibited greater consternation" (W. Collins, *The Moonstone* 214): Miss Clack at once echoes Thackeray's mock-epic description of Lady Southdown "before she bore down personally upon any individual whom she proposed to subjugate, fir[ing] in a quantity of tracts upon the menaced party (as a charge of the French was always preceded by a furious cannonade)," and anticipates the logic of the journalist who remarks in 1899 that "the gratulations of a successful tract-writer may be only on a par with the boasts of a soldier who knows he has killed 150 of the enemy because he has fired 150 rounds," and adds: "it may be doubted if as high a proportion of tracts as of Mauser bullets reach their billets" (Thackeray, *Vanity Fair* 335; Ogden). Even Rowland Hill refers to advertisements for books as "random shots"—a metaphor that survives today in our term "mailshot" but was literalized more directly in the 1944 German experiment firing postcards in rifle grenades over France (89; Rickards and Twyman 11). The tone in which Miss Clack's struggles are chronicled is hardly more comic than a biographer's description of Canon Christopher: "On one occasion the younger members of his family thought they had prevented such untimely and embarrassing activity—as they conceived it—at a Governor's garden party in the Isle of Man. All his pockets had been quietly emptied, and those in the secret set out with a light heart. They were presently disillusioned by the sight of Christopher offering tracts. More alert than they had supposed, he had taken the precaution of stuffing a few packets into his elastic-sided boots" (Reynolds and Thomas 233).

The tract, then, is to the Second Period what *Robinson Crusoe* was to the First. As if to recapitulate the historical shift from chapbook to tract, a romance treated as if it were a bible gives way to a tract that feebly imitates the conventions of fiction. The bibliomancy that allows Betteredge to "[wear] out six stout copies" through the "wholesome application of a bit of ROBINSON CRUSOE" paves the way for Miss Clack's equally instrumental and equally discontinuous reading habits. Like Betteredge, she understands reading as both aleatory and combinatory, prefacing her quotations with the claim to have "chanced on the following passage" and wresting out of context snippets that "proved to be quite *providentially* applicable to" the recipient.

Miss Clack herself sees Bruff's reading not as identical to hers, however, but its competitor: when she describes Bruff as "equally capable of reading a novel and of tearing up a tract," she imagines the two genres fighting over a limited pool of readers' attention (W. Collins, *The Moonstone* 9, 193, 215). William Wilberforce's famous declaration that "I would rather go render up my account at the last day, carrying up with me The Shepherd of Salisbury Plain than bearing the load of [the Waverley novels], full as they are of genius," reminds us that one virtue of tracts is negative: they fill the time that might otherwise be spent reading novels (Rosman 188).

Novel and tract fight to occupy the same space twice over. In the editorial frame, Franklin Blake rejects the "copious Extracts from precious publications in her possession" that Miss Clack tries to insert into her "Narrative," forbidding her to slip quotations from tracts into the novel that we are reading: "I am not permitted to improve—I am condemned to narrate." The converse is more literal: within the "Narrative" Miss Clack tries to slip novels inside tracts. "On the library table I noticed two of the 'amusing books' which the infidel doctor had recommended. I instantly covered them from sight with two of my own precious publications" (W. Collins, *The Moonstone* 237, 24).

The image of a tract covering up a novel figures the uncomfortable proximity of the two genres. On the one hand, tracts represent novels competing with devotional texts. The narrator of the *Adventures of a Bible* reports, "I am sorry to say that Jane, was by no means pleased with the good woman's gift; but pouted, and said she would much rather, had it been left to her own choice, have a story book to amuse her" (12). And *Gilbert Guestling, or, the Story of a Hymn-Book* (published by the Wesleyan Conference Office in 1881) features a character moved to buy the hymnbook after reading Brontë's parody of a Dissenting Sunday school in *Shirley* (Yeames). Here as so often, More's Cheap Repository Tracts set the tone for their successors. In "Mr Bragwell and his Two Daughters," the title characters

> spent the morning in bed, the noon in dressing, and the evening at the Spinnet, and the night in reading Novels . . . Jack, the plow-boy, on whom they had now put a livery jacket, was employed half his time in trotting backwards and forwards with the most wretched trash the little neighborhood book-shop could furnish. The choice was often left to Jack, who could not read, but who had general orders to bring *all the new things, and a great many of them.*

The quantitative language in which More's tract describes novels anticipates the quantitative language in which Frances Trollope's novel evokes tracts. Just as reductively, "Mr Bragwell" lumps novels together with other, humbler, consumer goods: the title character complains that "our Jack the Plowboy, spends half his time in going to a shop in our Market town, where they let out books to read with marble covers. And they sell paper with all manner of colours on the edges, and gim-cracks, and powder-puffs, and wash-balls." One daughter rejects a good match because "he scorned to talk that palavering stuff which she had been used to in the marble covered books I told you of" (More, *Works* 133, 31, 41). Not for nothing did Bishop Porteus speak of More's "spiritual quixotism" (quoted in Pedersen 87): the tract's representation of novel renting and novel buying at once repeats the eighteenth-century novel's embedding of romance reading and prefigures the nineteenth-century novel's satire on tract distributing.

On the other hand, middle-class novels are themselves haunted by the fear of turning into tracts—as when Herbert Pocket refuses even to call Pip by a name that "sounds like a moral boy out of the spelling-book, who was so lazy that he fell into a pond, or so fat that he couldn't see out of his eyes, or so determined to go a-bird's-nesting that he got himself eaten by bears who lived handy in the neighborhood" (Dickens, *Great Expectations* 165). The tracts represented in *The Moonstone* share the pseudo-orality of the frame narrative ("There was a precious publication to meet her eye, or to meet her hand, and to say with silent eloquence, in either case, 'Come, try me! try me!'") as well as its strategy of mixing the domestic with the sensational (W. Collins, *The Moonstone* 223). Titles like "Satan in the Hair Brush" and "THE SERPENT AT HOME" parody the sensation novel's own obsession with "those most mysterious of mysteries, the mysteries which are at our own doors" (H. James, "Miss Braddon" 593).

Like tracts, too, sensation novels not only represent the home, but pervade it. Compare Trollope's assertion (also in 1868) that novels are in "our library, our drawing-rooms, our bed-rooms, our kitchens,—and in our nurseries," with Miss Clack's campaign to "judiciously distribute [tracts] in the various rooms [Rachel] would be likely to occupy" (Anthony Trollope, "On English Prose Fiction" 108; W. Collins, *The Moonstone* 224). Earlier, Miss Clack attempted to ensure that a tract lies in wait "in every room that [Lady Verinder] enters," an ambition that requires her to imagine—like the author of some domestic novel—what activities her victim will engage in over the course of an ordinary day:

> I slipped [one] under the sofa cushions, half in, and half out, close by her handkerchief, and her smelling-bottle. Every time her hand searched for either of these, it would touch the book; and, sooner or later (who knows?) the book might touch HER . . . In the drawing-room I found more cheering opportunities of emptying my bag. I disposed of another in the back drawing-room, under some unfinished embroidery, which I knew to be of Lady Verinder's working . . . I put a book near the matches on one side, and a book under the box of chocolate drops on the other . . . But one apartment was still unexplored—the bathroom, which opened out of the bed-room. I peeped in; and the holy inner voice that never deceives, whispered to me, "You have met her, Drusilla, everywhere else; meet her at the bath, and the work is done." (223–25)

Miss Clack's strategy recalls the *Quarterly's* observation that novels "come to us when we are off our guard, and gain their place and position before we have fairly begun to discuss them" ("Recent Novels"). Both reach their readers by stealth, in the places of daily life rather than in the dedicated space of classroom, church, or library. Yet no classroom teacher who spends her life "assigning" works of literature—including, in my case, *The Moonstone*—can escape recognizing herself in Miss Clack.

The tract doesn't just resemble *The Moonstone*; in the opposite direction, it resembles the moonstone. The Evangelical spinster who sneaks into bedrooms to deposit books mirrors the Evangelical suitor who sneaks into bedrooms to remove jewels. Miss Clack's reverse shoplifting anticipates the Religious Tract Society's invocation of Fagin—or another RTS anecdote in which an atheist flees a coach to escape the exhortations of an Evangelical passenger, but "as he got down, the pocket of his coat gaped open, and, unperceived, his fellow-traveller quickly and quietly dropped into it Mr. Blackwood's little book, *Eternal Life*" (N. Watts 7).

What would it mean to model book distribution after pickpocketing? The parallel between Miss Clack and Mr. Ablewhite makes tracts look as anomalous as the eponymous diamond: it's in people's interest to acquire books and jewels, but to get rid of tracts and moonstones.[4] Just as Sir John's bequest of the diamond turns out to be motivated by malice masquerading as kindness, so Miss Clack's and Lady Verinder's attempts to force tracts onto one another reflect aggression misrepresented as generosity. The niece disguises printed matter as personal letters, copying out extracts by hand to elude Lady Verinder's suspicions; the aunt, in turn, sends back the tracts disguised as a "legacy." Once tract and moonstone exemplify a circulation driven by push rather than pull, then Christian charity becomes hard to distinguish from Hindu curse. And when printed matter is imagined as burden rather than boon, it becomes more appropriate for mistresses to give their young maids than for a poor relation to thrust upon her aunt.

The two objects that *The Moonstone* places in parallel—printed matter so worthless, and exotic talismans so potent, that both need to be unloaded onto someone else—would eventually converge in the magic book that forms the subject of M. R. James's 1911 short story "Casting the Runes." To the extent that such a convoluted story can be summarized, its plot involves a scholar who gets into another researcher's "bad books" by returning his conference proposal and finds himself on the receiving end of papers containing an ancient curse. Those papers pursue both indoors and out: a billboard on the tram, "a handful of leaflets such as are distributed to passers-by by agents of enterprising firms . . . thrust" into his hand on the street, "a calendar, such as tradesmen often send," received by post, a paper that he never dropped returned to him in the British Library reading room. As the rarest of manuscripts becomes interchangeable with mass-produced junk mail, the claustrophobic intimacy of the library (where a scholar can penetrate the secrets of the anonymous reviewer at the next desk) becomes indistinguishable from the home whose door is now breached by a letter slot that any tradesman can penetrate, and the street where every passerby is exposed to billboards and leaflets (M. R. James 131, 42).[5] As the plot that begins with an unwanted scholarly paper ends with unwanted paper of a more literal and dangerous kind, free print becomes reenchanted—as if a tract could bear a Hindu curse [. . .].

The more tracts look like the moonstone, however, the less they look like *The Moonstone.* Even if, as I suggested a moment ago, the two genres share their osmotic distribution mode and their formal strategy of mixing the domestic with the wild and the oral with the printed, they stand opposite each other in one crucial way. Those who love a novel want to hold onto it (even, like Betteredge, wearing out multiple copies); those who love a tract want to give it away. Miss Clack unloads books as surreptitiously as *The Moonstone*'s own readers acquired them: according to one observer, "even the porters and boys were interested in the story and read the new numbers in sly corners, with packs on their backs" (W. Collins, *The Moonstone* xxxviii). The force-feeding of tracts throws into relief the hunger for sensation fiction.

Such hostility to religious tracts is hardly peculiar to the novel: Thackeray could vent his hatred just as easily through the medium of the sketch. But the representation of tract reading, or more precisely of the refusal to read tracts, took on a particular charge in this context, because the novel slotted the tract into the position traditionally occupied by a different embedded genre, the romance. Once fictional characters stop reading romances and start handling tracts, two things change. First, the novel can no longer define its own seriousness in contradistinction to the frivolity of the genre embedded within it. Second, embedded romance and embedded tract imply diametrically opposed models of how books reach their users. Framed by mass-distributed novels, embedded romances harked back to an earlier age of serendipitous individual finds: new novels rented out by circulating libraries represent dusty manuscripts whose price can be measured only in eyestrain. What distinguished frame narrative from framed genres in *Don Quixote* was that the latter never represented buying and selling; but what distinguishes embedded genres in the gothic is that they're never bought or sold themselves [. . .] [F]ound manuscripts obey an economics of scarcity: the candle gutters before the roll is finished, or the page is torn midsentence. In contrast, the tracts represented in mid-Victorian novels embody an economics of surplus: everywhere distributed and nowhere read, they substitute painful duties for guilty pleasures. That shift helps explain the novel's particular animus toward nonmarket forms of distribution, whether tract societies, missionary baskets, or bazaars—all competitors to the secular, commercial networks on which its own dissemination depends.

[. . .]

Notes

1 Thus Samuel F. Pickering, Jr., "The Old Curiosity Shop—a Religious Tract?" *Illinois Quarterly* 36.1 (1973), compares the plots of *The Old Curiosity Shop* and *The Dairyman's Daughter.* Tracts may, however, overstate the appeal of novels to readers like Caroline Cox: Jan Fergus and Carolyn Steedman both argue that, in the eighteenth century at least, verse was more accessible to them. Jan S. Fergus, "Provincial Servants' Reading in the Late 18th Century," *The Practice and Representation of Reading in England*, ed. James Raven, Helen Small, and Naomi Tadmor (Cambridge: Cambridge University Press, 1996); Steedman, *Labours Lost: Domestic Service and the Making of Modern England* [(Cambridge: Cambridge University Press, 2009)].
2 The one exception marks Becky Sharp's nadir: when reduced to living off pious ladies, "she not only took tracts, but she read them." Thackeray, *Vanity Fair* [(Ed. Peter L. Shillingsburg. New York: Norton, 1994)], 642.
3 On the difficulty of getting the poor to buy tracts, see [Robert K.] Webb, *The British Working Class Reader, 1790–1848: Literacy and Social Tension* [(London: Allen & Unwin, 1955)], 56.
4 If, as John Plotz argues, the moonstone exemplifies "reverse portability" (from imperial periphery to center), it also shares with the religious tract a kind of reverse desirability. John Plotz, *Portable Property: Victorian Culture on the Move* (Princeton, N.J.: Princeton University Press, 2008), 40–44.
5 Penny Fielding argues that "the distinctions between private collection and lending library are broken down" in "The Tractate Middoth" and "Casting the Runes": Penny Fielding, "Reading Rooms: M. R. James and the Library of Modernity," *Modern Fiction Studies* 46.3 (2000): 764. One might add that the library is dangerous precisely because it puts one reader into relation with others: speculating about the reviewer's confidentiality, the secretary concludes that "the only danger is that Karswell might find out, if he was to ask the British Museum people who was in the habit of consulting alchemical manuscripts" (132). In that sense, the relation among scholarly colleagues looks less cozy than the cross-class collaboration of the passenger and conductor examining a streetcar ad together.

Works cited

Adventures of a Bible; Or, the Advantages of Early Piety. London: Dean and Munday, 1825.

Collins, Wilkie. *The Moonstone*. Ed. John Sutherland. Oxford: Oxford University Press, 1999.

Dickens, Charles. *Bleak House*. Ed. Nicola Bradbury. New York: Penguin, 1996.

——. *Great Expectations*. New York: Bantam Books, 1981.

——. *Hard Times*. Ed. Paul Schlicke. Oxford: Oxford University Press, 1998.

Hill, Sir Rowland. *Post Office Reform, Its Importance and Practicability*. London: C. Knight and Co., 1837.

James, Henry. "Miss Braddon." *Nation*, 1865, 593–94.

James, M. R. *Collected Ghost Stories*. Ware: Wordsworth's Classics, 1992.

Jones, William. *The Jubilee Memorial of the Religious Tract Society: Containing a Record of Its Origin, Proceedings, and Results, A.D. 1799 to A.D. 1849*. London: Religious Tract Society, 1850.

More, Hannah. *Cheap Repository Tracts; Entertaining, Moral and Religious, vol. 1*. London: F. and C. Rivington, 1798.

——. *Works*. Vol. 1. New York: Harper & Brothers, 1846.

Ogden, R. "A Hundred Years of Tracts." *The Nation* 68.1769 (1899): 390.

Pedersen, Susan. "Hannah More Meets Simple Simon: Tracts, Chapbooks, and Popular Culture in Late Eighteenth-Century England." *The Journal of British Studies* 25 (1986): 84–113.

"Recent Novels: Their Moral and Religious Teaching." *London Quarterly Review* 27 (1866).

Reynolds, John Stewart, and W. H. Griffith Thomas. *Canon Christopher of St. Aldate's, Oxford*. Abingdon (Berks.): Abbey Press, 1967.

Rickards, Maurice, and Michael Twyman. *The Encyclopedia of Ephemera: A Guide to the Fragmentary Documents of Everyday Life for the Collector, Curator, and Historian*. New York: Routledge, 2000.

Rosman, Doreen M. *Evangelicals and Culture*. London: Croom Helm, 1984.

Rymer, James Malcolm. *The White Slave. A Romance for the Nineteenth Century. By the author of "Ada."* London, 1844.

[Thackeray, William Makepeace]. "Singular Letters from the Regent of Spain." *Punch*, 16 December 1843.

Thackeray, William Makepeace. *Vanity Fair*. Ed. Peter L. Shillingsburg. New York: Norton, 1994.

Trollope, Anthony. "On English Prose Fiction as a Rational Amusement." *Four Lectures*. Ed. Morris L. Parrish. London: Constable and Co., 1938.

Watts, Newman. *The Romance of Tract Distribution*. London: Religious Tract Society, 1934.

Yeames, James. *Gilbert Guestling, or, the Story of a Hymn-Book*. London: Wesleyan Conference Office, 1881.

50 Print culture

Jennifer Phegley

What is the study of Victorian print culture and why is it such an important topic at the present time? Critical approaches in this field are diverse, but they are all linked by a single goal: to determine how the market for print impacted its creation, dissemination, reception, and after-life. Thus, print culture studies revolves around research on books, periodicals, readers, writers, and publishers. The study of print culture has become particularly relevant in our digital age. Far from being a harbinger of the death of print, digital culture has spawned a rebirth in studies of otherwise obscure print sources. With the advent of Google Books, which has made thousands of nineteenth-century books and periodicals freely available to the public, and the corporate production of periodical and early printed material databases sold primarily to academic libraries, many more people are now able to study previously rare and difficult-to-access material.[1] One possible result of the vast quantity of printed material presented by all of these resources is paralysis in the face of so many newly available and unexamined texts. This sense of overwhelming abundance was, likewise, a hallmark of Victorian society that led many to describe their own print culture as a terrifying mass of uncontrollable text. With more than 50,000 magazines—and an equally vast number of books—published during Queen Victoria's reign, the job of sorting through these volumes to determine what was worthy of attention was staggering (North 1978: 4). Critics and book reviewers thus served an important purpose in filtering print material for readers.

Just as the Victorians struggled to manage their own information overload, so have recent scholars. Patrick Leary notes in his essay "Googling the Victorians" that the rapidity of the shift to digital scholarship "has been alternately exhilarating and bewildering, its long-term permutations and consequences difficult to gauge . . . The extraordinary power, speed, and ubiquity of online searching has brought with it a serendipity of unexpected connections to both information and people that is becoming increasingly central to the progress of Victorian research, and to our working lives as students of the nineteenth century" (Leary 2005: 2–3). While the digitization of primary sources has in some cases created a divide between those with access to expensive institutional subscriptions and those without, it is likely that most of us will have increasing exposure to Victorian print culture without traveling great distances as online resources improve and expand. These dramatic changes make print culture studies more important to Victorianists than ever before. Not only do we have the opportunity to study previously difficult-to-obtain resources and to dip into them via specific topics or themes that interest us, but students and scholars alike also have the chance to examine an immense body of work that has been neglected for 150 years or more. We can thus gain new insights into the ways in which Victorian readers, writers, and publishers interacted with and produced the first truly mass literary culture. Indeed, the digital revolution holds the key to the future of print culture studies as a field. What is digitized will, to a large degree, determine how we study the history of nineteenth-century print. And, right now, that history will largely be determined by the study of periodical literature, the form that dominates database development.

Prior to the current digital revolution it was perhaps Richard Altick who did the most to advance the study of Victorian print culture. The publication of his landmark book *The English Common Reader* in 1957 essentially set the parameters for a field of study examining the social, cultural, and economic history of print. As Altick notes, "From the very beginnings of publishing as a profit-making enterprise, the publisher's estimate of the size of a book's potential audience, its willingness to pay the price he will ask, and above all its current tastes, has been a major consideration in his decision whether or not to send the manuscript to the typesetter. The whole history of literature in the past few centuries is, in a sense, the aggregate history of such decisions" (Altick 1998: x). Altick briefly surveys the history of printing from Caxton to its maturity in the early 1800s, then turns his attention to the expansion of education and literacy, the development of public libraries, and advances in the publishing industry throughout the nineteenth century. His appendices on key events in the expansion of the mass reading public, the best-selling books of the century, and the circulation rates of newspapers and magazines pointed not only to a revolution in printed material and its modes of distribution and consumption, but also to the lack of knowledge of many of the essential details about the literary marketplace that was so central to nineteenth-century culture. In short, Altick's work invited other scholars to begin new scholarly adventures into print culture studies.[2]

In the past few decades, scholars have traced many aspects of Victorian print culture, especially the intersections among readers, serial fiction, and periodicals. Kate Flint and Patrick Brantlinger are among those who have focused on the pathologization of readers by literary critics who worried that so much free-flowing print would change society by influencing the attitudes, behavior, and expectations of readers. In *The Woman Reader* (1993), Flint examines paintings of women reading novels to demonstrate that this act was often depicted as a private, self-indulgent, and even dangerous experience. She argues that the voyeuristic painter is positioned to sneak a peek at the intimate, sexualized experience of a woman reading, usually in a prostrate position on a sofa, chair, or bed. Focusing on a wide range of fiction and non-fiction texts, Flint emphasizes how much the culture at large worried about the ways in which women's reading practices might disrupt their household duties, decrease their desire or eligibility for marriage, or even stimulate demands for further education and employment. Likewise, in *The Reading Lesson* (1998), Brantlinger explores how this kind of critical commentary on readers was incorporated into novels themselves and extended to working-class readers of both sexes in addition to middle-class women. He argues that it was not only critics but also authors who worried about "the spectre of distracted or deluded mass readers" (2). The predominant forms of print culture—periodicals and novels—thus betrayed anxieties about their own impact on society.[3]

Another important precedent for the critical works excerpted in this section, Graham Law's *Serializing Fiction in the Victorian Press* (2000) provides a detailed overview of the Victorian novel from the perspective of publishers rather than readers. Law discusses single-part issue novels, novels serialized in weekly or monthly parts in newspapers and magazines, and finally, the syndication of fiction in an international network of periodicals by agencies developed to ensure that writers would see a profit from their work if published in another country. Law asserts that the trend in publishing practices moved from stand-alone serial parts that included several chapters of a novel alongside illustrations and advertisements in the 1830s and 1840s, to monthly installments in magazines in the 1850s and 1860s, to weekly installments in newspapers in the 1870s and 1880s. Law admits that this evolutionary model is an overgeneralization, but maintains its usefulness for our understanding of the development of the novel-publishing industry. For much of the century, though, each of these forms peacefully coexisted until shorter fiction and single-volume novels took over the literary marketplace.[4]

While Law focuses on structural and economic aspects of the Victorian publishing industry, in another important earlier work, *The Victorian Serial* (1991), Linda Hughes and Michael Lund delve into the larger cultural significance of the serial form. Instead of looking solely at the business side of literary production, they examine how novel serialization coincided with other Victorian values. For example, they argue that the serial form embodies historicism, the belief in the inevitable progress of the individual and society over time, as well as uniformitarianism, a similarly gradualist philosophy derived from developments in biology and geology and spurred on by Charles Darwin's theory of evolution. In addition to these supporting philosophical and scientific perspectives, Hughes and Lund argue that communities of readers anticipated installments, shared reactions to them, and read aloud to one another. They ultimately maintain that while the serial form was discredited in the early twentieth century as both "fragmentary," and "loose and undisciplined," Victorian readers viewed it as a unifying form (Hughes and Lund 1991: 13).

Past works in print culture studies have defined the parameters of the field, mapped the ways in which Victorian publishing operated, and explored the impact of readers upon culture and culture upon readers. Recent studies have become increasingly specialized in their approaches to the same general subjects and have refined our views of subsets of printed materials. The three excerpts on print culture that precede this essay push beyond the boundaries of previous work to explore new issues such as the physicality of the book, while expanding our understanding of readers' interactions with print at all levels of culture, including elite journals and quarterly reviews, middle-brow magazines, mainstream daily newspapers, and cheap religious tracts. Tracing the trajectory of the approaches provided by Laurel Brake, Matthew Rubery, and Leah Price, we can see a common interest in mass and material culture that focuses on the magazine and the newspaper as genres and culminates in the study of books as "things" to be handled and manipulated.[5] As these scholars repeatedly remind us, whether Victorians were reflecting on higher journalism, reading fiction, scouring the daily newspapers, or doing other things with books, they were seemingly always engaged with the pervasive print culture around them.

Laurel Brake's "The Advantage of Fiction: The Novel and the 'Success' of the Victorian Periodical" (printed in a volume reassessing Altick's place in print culture studies, edited by Beth Palmer and Adelene Buckland) asserts that Altick's work is largely responsible for dismantling the division between "consumers of literature—the object of study in departments of English—and 'common' readers of the 'popular' press," whose reading material "insulted the intellect and left ink on one's hands" (Brake 2011: 9 [Chapter 47: 405]). Brake acknowledges Altick's important contribution to collapsing these divisions while simultaneously revising his conception of the "rise" of the novel as something that occurred alongside or even as a result of the expansion of the periodical press. Brake shifts the perspective, subtly but compellingly, by arguing that the process of novel serialization actually made the periodical industry the dominant print cultural form of the century. Indeed, "rather than claiming credit for the greater importance of periodicals on the basis that they 'carried' literature" she suggests that "the widespread incorporation of the novel into mainstream periodicals in the 1850s and after helped assure the proliferation and economic viability of the periodical press" (Brake 2011: 11 [Chapter 47: 407]). This argument complements her earlier work, in which she took a strong stand on the interconnectedness of literature and journalism and objected to the condescending attitude towards Victorian periodicals that pervaded an earlier phase of scholarship (an attitude that is, unfortunately, still alive in some quarters of Victorian studies today). In *Subjugated Knowledge*s (1994) Brake noted that the construction of literature as a field of study, both in the nineteenth and the twentieth centuries, was "predicated on" the "defeat, devaluation, and invisibility" of journalism, the erasure of the modes of production of literary forms, and a focus on aesthetics to the exclusion of cultural and historical context (Brake 1994: xi). As she pointed out, the attempts to "create a clear-cut dichotomy between literature and journalism belied the involvement of almost all Victorian writers with the periodical press, as contributors, editors and/or proprietors" (Brake 1994: xii).

In the excerpt, Brake argues that editors and publishers used fiction strategically to attract many readers who would not otherwise have read magazines. This appeal to new readers increased the circulation of periodicals and diminished the popularity of single-part issues of novels, which failed to provide a diverse array of additional reading material but cost roughly the same price. Despite many reviewers' complaints about the potentially negative effects of fiction, Brake claims the novel was crucial to the success of the periodical form. Even journals that did not publish serials relied upon book reviews to fulfill the seemingly insatiable desire for fiction. Since reviewers often quoted significant passages from the fiction, reviews served as an enticing advertisement to readers and even provided a kind of condensed form of novel reading. Brake shows how the increasing demand for serial fiction allowed publishers to sell magazines at lower prices and how growing audiences sparked the creation of new kinds of magazines, particularly the shilling monthlies of the 1860s, which incorporated increasingly lavish illustrations to accompany the fiction. Brake references an entire range of weekly, monthly, and quarterly magazines in order to bolster her case that the publication of fiction in magazines shifted audiences away from borrowing books from circulating libraries and toward perusing the pages of periodicals. As a result, both the novel and the periodical thrived. Journalism and literature were thus interdependent forms that, as Brake contends, should be studied together as key components of Victorian print culture.

Matthew Rubery's 2009 book *The Novelty of Newspapers: Victorian Fiction After the Invention of the News* shifts us away from Brake's focus on how fiction shaped monthly, weekly, and quarterly middlebrow magazines and highbrow journals to examine the connections between daily newspapers and realist novels. According to Rubery, "the newspaper went in a remarkably short time from being an item few could afford to an item few could afford to live without" (4). He examines how the daily rhythms of the news transformed reading and focuses on the ways in which the various sections of the newspaper—the shipping news, personal advertisements, leading articles, personal interviews, and foreign correspondence—influenced the writing and reception of novels. Like Brake, Rubery collapses the distinction between literature and journalism in order to see both forms in a new light. Following Benedict Anderson's conception of an imagined nation of readers, Rubery argues that the newspaper "provided a forum in which citizens compensated for the disappearance of face-to-face contact by forging deep attachments to one another through print" (10). Contrary to the notion that the increase in the quantity of newspapers drove readers into distinct niche audiences, Rubery contends that access to the daily news brought the reading public together through standard features that they could anticipate and rely upon. These were sometimes interactive, as in the case of personal advertisements, but they typically invited readers to participate in a virtual public exchange of ideas. Rubery claims that the news served as a more communal form of "reading for the breakfast table" than novels, which continued to provide a more individualized, private reading experience. However, he sees the novel and the newspaper coming "together in their representation of the reading event" by "eliciting a cathartic response," whether through the report of a train accident, a divorce trial, or an adventure in a foreign country (Rubery 2009: 14 [Chapter 48: 418]). According to Rubery, both forms narrate stories in interrelated ways, with the news borrowing from fiction to generate excitement and fiction borrowing from the news to gain verisimilitude.

Of course, many Victorian novels ripped events from newspaper headlines to drive their plots and shape their characters. But Rubery's individual chapters explore how the entire paper, rather than just the front page, influenced novel-writing. Moving from the front to the back of the paper, he illustrates the interdependence of the two forms thematically as well as chronologically. For example, he explores how writers incorporated the front-page news of shipwrecks and personal advertisements to bring lovers together in novels or to generate the plots of sensation fiction, channeled contempt for investigative journalists and interviewers into characters who were the subject of investigation themselves, and used foreign correspondence as a model for adventure narratives. Rubery concludes that "Victorian novelists moved back and forth in their attitudes toward journalism as both scourge and source" (Rubery 2009: 164), yet, once again, the newspaper and the novel are cast as interdependent rather than oppositional forms.

In *How to Do Things with Books in Victorian Britain*, Leah Price approaches the analysis of print through the lens of material culture. She asks how people physically interacted with books rather than how they interpreted them. By changing the questions we ask about books, Price significantly alters the critical conversation that has been developing over the past few decades. Moving from reception history to what she calls "rejection history," Price reconfigures the fear of books as a visceral one that, for instance, includes the specter of passing diseases through the pages of library books. Likewise, instead of thinking about printed materials solely as items to be read, she also sees them as objects to be displayed, props to be used, pages to be put to alternative uses. Price explores everything from decorating with books to hiding behind them, from using book pages for toilet paper to using them as food wrappers. As she notes, "books function both as trophies and tools," they engage "bodies as well as minds . . . in an age where more volumes entered into circulation (or gathered dust on more shelves) than ever before" (Price 2012: 2).

In the section excerpted here, Price is concerned with the circulation of free religious tracts, a genre she suggests may not have been read very often. She focuses on Wilkie Collins's *The Moonstone* to examine how popular fiction "established its own entertainment value . . . by mocking tract-distributors for harassing a captive audience." Her reading of this novel illustrates that novelists and magazines were "freely chosen and paid for," while tracts were often forced upon unsuspecting victims (Price 2012: 204). Exploring the ways in which tracts and novels were distributed (one as charity, the other as serial entertainment), the ways in which they may or may not have been used (one to resell for gin or bread, the other to feed fantasies), and the ways in which tracts were depicted in novels, Price claims that religious texts served as a foil for serial fiction and that fiction writers and magazine editors boosted the reputation of a previously suspicious form through this jarring juxtaposition. While Collins's Miss Clack assaults people with unwanted tracts at every turn, a work of fiction (*Robinson Crusoe*) becomes a bible for Betteredge. However, Price also points out that fiction threatens to turn into a kind of tract itself. Specifically, she argues that sensation fiction, of the kind Collins himself wrote, was seen by critics as invading the home in equally insidious ways. Just as Miss Clack's tracts are found stashed under sofa cushions and hidden among the unfinished embroidery, sensation novels were feared to be invading the middle-class household. However, one crucial difference remained between these forms: their means of distribution. As Price puts it, "Those who love the novel want to hold onto it" and "those who love the tract want to give it away." As a result, "the force-feeding of tracts throws into relief the hunger for sensation fiction" (212). Tracts are despised in fiction not only for their staid and condescending moral instruction, but also for their abundance and lack of commercial value. Fiction, on the other hand, represents the liveliness of a competitive marketplace. Here, then, is the key to Price's approach. She simultaneously reads the metaphorical and the material aspects of print culture and reveals how they reinforce each other, just as Brake and Rubery examine how the popular press and the literary text are mutually constructed and determined.

While Brake opens her essay with a brief discussion of the digitization of print media, Rubery and Price surprisingly neglect this important development that, as Patrick Leary has indicated, will certainly determine the future of print culture studies. The possible roles played by quantification and computation in this field of study are only just beginning to be explored in studies like Susan David Bernstein and Catherine Derose's "Reading Numbers by Numbers: Digital Studies and the Victorian Serial Novel," which merges digital humanities and print culture studies to examine Charles Dickens's and George Eliot's serial novels with a computer program called DocuScope. Bernstein and Derose use DocuScope "to detect the signal of seriality" in Victorian fiction (Bernstein and Derose 2012: 45). They searched for specific categories of words and phrases to determine what, if any, differences exist between weekly and monthly serials. They also compare serialized novels to those that were not serialized. Their data suggests, among other things, that weekly serials are more temporally and spatially oriented in their language use while monthly serials are driven more by words indicating the importance of character and dialogue. Non-serials, they found, have a greater incidence of self-reflective narration. Thus, computer analysis has allowed them to pinpoint specific language functions in a way that invites us to think differently about how print forms function. Such quantification will become easier and more pervasive as more and more texts are digitized and new modes of analysis developed. Yet, while such studies will certainly lead to new forms of research and new ways of seeing, there are risks involved if we rely too heavily on these approaches. As Bernstein and Derose note, "digital analysis provides a way to both defamiliarize and refamiliarize ourselves with literature," but it does not definitively answer questions about texts. Instead, it invites us to pose new questions and to open up new interpretative possibilities (63). The future of Victorian print culture scholarship will challenge us to use digital forms in productive ways that expand our understanding of the relationships among readers, writers, and publishers and their interactions with printed forms.

Notes

1 Thousands of pages of Victorian magazines and newspapers are available in digitized form in ProQuest's *British Periodicals I & II* and Gale's *Nineteenth-Century UK Periodicals, Nineteenth-Century British Newspapers*, and *Nineteenth-Century British Library Newspapers*. Likewise, pamphlets, broadsides, advertisements, ballads, and other forms of mass media can be accessed via Adam Matthew's *Victorian Popular Culture* database, covering visual and print materials on entertaining topics such as sensationalism, mesmerism, the circus, the music hall, and the early cinema. *The Dictionary of Nineteenth-Century Journalism*, housed online in *C19: The Nineteenth-Century Index*, a massive reference source for periodical literature, provides an interconnected compendium of facts and arguments about journalists, publishers, editors, novelists, poets, readers, magazines, and newspapers spanning the entire realm of Victorian society. Of course, accessing most of these databases requires being affiliated with an institution that has subscribed to them at considerable cost.

2 Altick's previous book, *The Scholar Adventurers* (1950), explored literary research as a kind of detective work involving the interpretation of clues and the discovery of new evidence in the historical record that were embodied in the *English Common Reader*. The founding of the *Victorian Periodicals Newsletter* in 1968 and the accompanying Research Society for Victorian Periodicals in 1969 were, at least in part, responses to Altick's call to action, echoed by hundreds of other periodical researchers who were surveyed. For more information see Van Arsdel 2003 and Wolff 1992. As Jonathan Rose

points out in his foreword to the 1998 reissue of *The English Common Reader*, Altick's call to arms was also a key inspiration behind the establishment of the Society for the History of Authorship, Reading, and Publishing in 1991 (Altick 1998: xii).
3 For a counter-argument exploring the ways in which periodicals promoted reading, particularly women's reading, see Phegley 2004.
4 Troy Bassett's *At the Circulating Library: A Database of Victorian Fiction, 1837–1901* (http://www.victorianresearch.org/atcl/), raises questions about how pervasive the serial form really was. According to the statistics provided by Bassett, of the 9,586 titles he has surveyed, 5,275 were published in three volumes. Of these three-volume novels, only 1,132 of them were serialized prior to publication as a book. Of the 4,311 remaining titles he has surveyed in one-, two-, and four-volume formats, an additional 554 novels were previously serialized. While the numbers in this incomplete survey may be lower than expected, it is nevertheless clear that the serial form was a central part of Victorian publishing.
5 For more on Victorian "thing" theory see Briggs 1988 and Freedgood 2006.

Bibliography

Altick, R. (1950) *The Scholar Adventurers*, New York: Macmillan.
—— (1957; 1998) *The English Common Reader*, Chicago: University of Chicago Press; Foreword by J. Rose.
Bernstein, S. D. and Derose, C. (2012) "Reading Numbers by Numbers: Digital Studies and the Victorian Serial Novel," *Victorian Review*, 38.2: 43–68.
Brake, L. (1994) *Subjugated Knowledges: Journalism, Gender, and Literature in the Nineteenth Century*, New York: New York University Press.
—— (2011) "The Advantage of Fiction: The Novel and the 'Success' of the Victorian Periodical," in B. Palmer and A. Buckland, ed., *A Return to the Common Reader: Print Culture and the Novel, 1850–1900*, London: Ashgate, 9–21.
Brantlinger, P. (1998) *The Reading Lesson: The Threat of Mass Literacy in Nineteenth-Century British Fiction*, Bloomington: Indiana University Press.
Briggs, A. (1988) *Victorian Things*, Chicago: University of Chicago.
Freedgood, E. (2006) *The Ideas in Things: Fugitive Meaning in the Victorian Novel*, Chicago: University of Chicago.
Flint, K. (1993; 1995) *The Woman Reader, 1837–1914*, Oxford: Clarendon Press.
Hughes, L. and Lund, M. (1991) *The Victorian Serial*, Charlottesville: University Press of Virginia.
Law, G. (2000) *Serializing Fiction in the Victorian Press*, Basingstoke: Palgrave.
Leary, P. (2005) "Googling the Victorians," *Journal of Victorian Culture*, 10.1: 72–86.
North, J. S. (1978) "The Rationale: Why Read Victorian Periodicals?," in J. D. Vann and R. T. Van Arsdel (eds.), *Victorian Periodicals: A Guide to Research*, New York: MLA: 3–20.
Palmer, B. and Buckland, A. (eds.) (2011) *A Return to the Common Reader: Print Culture and the Novel, 1850–1900*, Farnham: Ashgate Publishing, 1–6.
Phegley, J. (2004) *Educating the Proper Woman Reader: Victorian Family Literary Magazines and the Cultural Health of the Nation*, Columbus: The Ohio State University Press.
Price, L. (2012) *How To Do Things with Books in Victorian Britain*, Princeton: Princeton University Press.
Rubery, M. (2009) *The Novelty of Newspapers: Victorian Fiction after the Invention of the News*, Oxford: Oxford University Press.
Van Arsdel, R. (2003) "John North, the Waterloo Directory, and a RSVP History Lesson," *Victorian Periodicals Review*, 36.2: 100–108.
Wolff, M. (1992) "The Prehistory of RSVP and Me with a Few Words About Our Futures," *Victorian Periodicals Review*, 25.2: 88–90.

Index